The Data Model Resource Book
Revised Edition
Volume 2

A Library of Universal Data Models by Industry Types

Len Silverston

Wiley Computer Publishing

John Wiley & Sons, Inc.

NEW YORK · CHICHESTER · WEINHEIM · BRISBANE · SINGAPORE · TORONTO

Publisher: Robert Ipsen
Editor: Robert M. Elliott
Assistant Editor: Emilie Herman
Managing Editor: John Atkins
Associate New Media Editor: Brian Snapp
Text Design & Composition: Publishers' Design and Production Services, Inc.

Designations used by companies to distinguish their products are often claimed as trademarks. In all instances where John Wiley & Sons, Inc., is aware of a claim, the product names appear in initial capital or ALL CAPITAL LETTERS. Readers, however, should contact the appropriate companies for more complete information regarding trademarks and registration.

This book is printed on acid-free paper. ⊗

Published by John Wiley & Sons, Inc.

Published simultaneously in Canada.

This publication is designed to provide accurate and authoritative information in regard to the subject matter covered. It is sold with the understanding that the publisher is not engaged in professional services. If professional advice or other expert assistance is required, the services of a competent professional person should be sought.

Library of Congress Cataloging-in-Publication Data is available from Publisher.

ISBN-13: 978-0-471-35348-5
ISBN-10: 0-471-35348-5

Printed in the United States of America.

SKY10027773_062221

Advance Praise for The Data Model Resource Book, Revised Edition, Volume 2

"In addition to being an excellent resource for data modelers, this book will help managers, business analysts, and architects gain a high-level understanding of various industries and integration challenges facing IT professionals. Len's concepts, insights, and models provide a valuable contribution to data architecture."

Regina Pieper
Enterprise Architect, Sun Microsystems

"Len Silverston has produced an enormously useful two-volume compendium of generic (but not too generic) data models for an extensive set of typical enterprise subject areas, and for various industries that any data modeler will likely encounter at some point in his or her career. The material is clearly written, well organized, and goes below the obvious to some of the more perverse and difficult information requirements in an enterprise. This is an invaluable resource for doing one's homework before diving into any modeling session; if you can't find it here, there is certainly a very similar template that you can use for just about any situation with which you might be faced."

William G. Smith
President, William G. Smith & Associates

"In today's fast-paced e-oriented world, it is no longer acceptable to bury business constraints in hard-to-change data structures. Data architects must comprehend complex requirements and recast them into data architecture with vision for unforeseen futures. Len's models provide an outstanding starting point for novice and advanced data architects for delivering flexible data models. These models position an organization for the business rule age. Their proper implementation and customization allows the organization to externalize and manage business policies and rules so that the business can proactively change itself. In this way, the data architecture, based on Len's models and procedures for customizing them, becomes by design the foundation for business change."

Barbara von Halle
Founder, Knowledge Partners, Inc.
Co-author of Handbook of Relational Database Design

Contents

Foreword

Len Silverston has been a proponent of universal data models (also called generic data models, or data model patterns) for as long as I have known him. I have other friends that argue the case for "specific models" as opposed to "generic models." I am sure that there are trade-offs on both sides of the argument, as you would find trade-offs with any complex engineering solution.

However, when it comes to Len's most recent book, The Data Model Resource Book, Revised Edition, Volume 2, this generic model argument is not even an issue! It doesn't make any difference how you come down on the argument, and it doesn't make any difference if you consider Len's models to be generic or specific in nature. Any way you look at it, it is a lot easier and faster to start with something somebody else has already put down on paper than to have to start with a blank sheet of paper and create something from scratch yourself!

Len has made a major contribution to us in publishing the set of industry models in this book. It is clear that he has done a lot of research in preparing to write the book, and it is also clear that he has capitalized on his vast experience in implementing the universal models. He has created enterprise-wide models for eight different industries, which in various combinations and permutations may well satisfy the bulk of what is needed by any specific Enterprise in virtually any industry!

Now, let's get pragmatic. Starting with a universal data model does not absolve anyone of the responsibility of knowing his or her own enterprise intimately, at even an excruciating level of detail! Nor does it absolve anyone from the responsibility of learning how to build data models!! What you have to do is start with the universal model and then, understanding data modeling and understanding your own enterprise, make the necessary modifications to make the universal model your own.

By starting with an enterprise-wide universal model, you will save yourself one heck of a lot of work—that is, time and money—trying to create the model yourself. What's more, you're more likely to produce a higher quality model than if you started from scratch, since you can be assured that you won't overlook key components of the model. Even if you are implementing a single application—that is, you are not attempting to build an Enterprise-wide model—you are still way ahead of the game using one of Len's models. Because his models are enterprise-wide in nature, he has already anticipated other applications' semantic requirements for the entities you are embarking on implementing. If you use his more broadly defined, enterprise-wide structures, you will save yourself the time and cost of having to scrap and rebuild your application later or the untold frustrations that arise in management when the data in your application is not consistent with the data in ensuing applications.

This is a very helpful book, whether you are building Enterprise Architectures or whether you are just implementing applications . . . whether you like generic models or whether you like more specific models. If you have any idea of the profound enterprise significance of data models and the challenges of creating them from scratch, this is a book for you!

John A. Zachman
Glendale, California
2001

Acknowledgments

I wrote this book because I deeply feel that universal data models can provide effective solutions to many important data management and integration issues. However, this book would not have been possible without the insights and knowledge gained through my rewarding interactions and relationships with clients over the past 20 years. I am extraordinarily grateful to these clients who allowed me to provide service for them, while expanding my knowledge of business and information management. Their use, implementation of, and modifications to universal data model constructs have greatly contributed to the content of this book. From among the many people that have contributed, I want to thank Regina Pieper, Howard Jenkins, Rob Jakoby, Chris Nickerson, Jay Edson, Dean Boyer, Joe Misiaszek, Paul Zulauf, Steve Seay, Ken Haley, Ted Kowalski, Mike Brightwell, Dan Adler, Linda Abt, Joe Lakitsky, Trent Hampton, Kevin Morris, Karen Vitone, Tracy Muesing, Steve Lark, and Chuck Dana. I also want to thank the many client organizations that have added to and supported the universal data model paradigm.

I am very thankful to the people who added to the content of this current edition of the book. A person that made a significant contribution is Bob Conway, who took time to review these models out of a very busy consulting schedule and who scrupulously reviewed the models, making insightful suggestions as only Bob could have done. I greatly appreciate the work that Burt Holmes has done in implementing these universal data models with numerous clients and in providing valuable feedback regarding changes required for practical implementation of these models. I am very grateful to Natalie Arsenault, who provided ongoing ideas about the Universal Data Models based upon her extensive data modeling background and who also drafted the financial services and insurance chapters. I want to thank Mike Rampson, who drafted the Web chapter and provided invaluable insight into data structures to capture Internet information. I thank David Templeton, Gail Barrier, and Scott Bavis, who reviewed the financial services and insurance chapters, and Victor Korea for his review of the telecommunications models.

There were mentors that helped guide me and helped me see this work through completion. I am grateful to Richard Flint for his inspiration, guidance, and encouragement to follow my visions. I am very thankful to John DeMartini for helping me to view my life more holistically and for inspiring me to continually learn and write about holistic, integrated systems.

I feel honored to have been able to work on this book with Bob Elliott, the finest editor I know, at John Wiley & Sons, and I appreciate his excellent vision, management, editing, and support for this book as well as his ongoing encouragement to me. I want to thank Emilie Herman from John Wiley & Sons for taking care of a great number of tasks at Wiley in publishing this book.

I am thankful to my mom, Dede Silverston, a writer herself, who inspired and supported me in my writing; my dad, Nat Silverston, who has been a great father; my brother and great friend, Steve Silverston, who has lifted my spirits and been there for me; and my sister, Betty Silverston, who has such a big heart. Most of all, I am blessed to have had the support, patience, and love of my beautiful wife, Annette, and daughters, Danielle and Michaela, throughout the trial and tribulations of writing this book.

About the Author

Len Silverston is an author, lecturer, consultant, and pioneer in the field of data management. He has devoted the last 20 years to helping organizations build and integrate information systems, using his unique approaches to develop information architectures, design databases, and solve data management issues.

Mr. Silverston has been an invited speaker at numerous national and international conferences and has written many articles on database design and data warehousing in publications such as Data Management Review and Data Warehouse Institute's Journal of Data Warehousing.

Len Silverston is the founder and owner of Universal Data Models, LLC (www.universaldatamodels.com), a Colorado-based firm providing consulting and training to help enterprises customize and implement universal data models and develop holistic, integrated systems. Universal Data Models, LLC, has helped many diverse organizations develop data architectures and designs in a fraction of the typical time through its extensive repository of reusable data models and data warehouse designs. The company offers several seminars that provide tools to deliver higher quality databases and information systems in less time.

Mr. Silverston lives in Castle Rock, Colorado, with his wife Annette and his daughters, Danielle and Michaela. He holds a master's degree in Computer Science from Renssellear Polytechnic Institute with a specialization in database management systems.

He can be reached at lsilverston@univdata.com.

About the Contributors

Natalie Arsenault has worked for major Fortune 100 companies in database administration, design, and modeling for most of her 20-year career. Her current work supports an enterprise data framework that is consistently leveraged throughout the company. She is involved with data standards, meta data planning, and is a member of the enterprise technical architecture team.

Ms. Arsenault has been a conference speaker at several international conferences on data modeling, and her colleagues seek her expertise.

Mike Rampson (mrampson@paravance.com) is the CIO of Par Avance, Inc., a firm specializing in providing software and service solutions for e-commerce, product support, and other online business challenges. Mike has extensive cross-industry experience with designing integrated applications and operating environments that enable businesses to move online.

CHAPTER

1

Introduction

Why Is There a Need for This Book?

When organizations develop custom information systems or strive to integrate their existing systems, they spend a significant amount of time and effort developing data models. Most of the time, organizations start from scratch when developing these data models because there are not many available sources for common data models that can be reused.

A tremendous amount of time and money could be saved by using "templates" or, to coin a phrase, "Universal Data Models" providing common data structures that are applicable across many business applications and industries.

The first book, *The Data Model Resource Book: Volume 1*, provided some Universal Data Model templates for common subject data areas that *apply generally to most businesses*. The book offered data structures to model people, organizations, products, orders, shipments, invoicing, work effort management, accounting, budgeting, and human resources. This represents a significant tool for developers to use to save time and money.

Many people have asked, why not extend the concept of the first edition of *The Data Model Resource Book* to provide models for specific industries? While most people find the first book very useful, there is still more work in modifying the models to work for specific industries. Organizations want to have reusable data models for their own industry, such as for financial services firms, manufacturers, travel-related enterprises, health care organizations, telecommunications companies, and insurance providers.

This book can save readers even more time and money when developing data models as they can reuse concepts and specific data structures for the industry or application that applies to them. Data modeling professionals can use the data structures as a method for quality assuring their own models and determining if there is a better way to model these structures.

Each chapter will provide an overview of an industry and the type of information that is critical to running that type of business. Then the book will provide graphical data models, along with narrative text describing how to best model the information needs for the industry. Finally, chapters will also include some star schema designs to assist in developing data analysis solutions for each type of industry.

Both Volumes 1 and 2 of *The Data Model Resource Book, Revised Edition*, have companion electronic products (sold separately) containing the SQL code necessary to implement the models described in the books: a CD-ROM for the generic models in Volume 1; downloadable software products for each of the eight industries covered in Volume 2. Each of the industry models for the Volume 2 electronic products contains the new and modified models that are unique to that industry. These products include the SQL code, in several formats, to implement the generic and industry models from this volume. Note that the Volume 1 and Volume 2 products are sold separately; the CD-ROM provided with this book provides several free sample models for your review and evaluation. See the section "How to Use the Volume 2 Industry Electronic Products," at the end of this book to learn how to purchase and use one or more of the industry downloadable products.

To Integrate or Disintegrate? That Is the Question

A key benefit of this book is the ability to reuse its industry models, saving tremendous amounts of time by not reinventing the wheel doing analysis that has been done before. However, perhaps there is even a more substantial benefit to this book: *The models in this book are designed to facilitate the building of holistic, integrated systems.*

How often have you worked with non-integrated systems? Have you ever gone to the emergency room of a hospital and been asked to fill out a form with your information when you had, just recently, given that information to another ward of the hospital? Have you ever been called by a sales representative who was completely unaware of the issue for which you had just alerted the customer service department? Have you ever called up a travel organization about the travel bonus points that you had earned and then tried to find out the status of your reservation, only to find out that you need to call a separate phone number for that information? Have you ever dealt with a procurement department in an organization that does not realize (or care) that you are also customer of that organization and perhaps deserve a little more attention?

If you have experienced difficulties such as these when dealing with an organization, there is good likelihood that their systems are set up separately, with systems built for separate departments, without the benefit of weaving each system into the whole in order to facilitate a shared information systems environment across the enterprise. Of course, the enterprise often drives and compensates each department or project to be successful without looking at the whole.

The consequences of not building integrated, holistic systems are huge. If an enterprise (the term *enterprise* will be used for the organization for which the systems are to be designed and built) does not focus on integration, the enterprise will move toward *disintegration*. If the enterprise builds their systems without regard to their overall system, redundant and inaccurate information is bound to occur. Without a holistic approach, each system will most likely define and maintain the same types of data using different formats with different names and with different meanings, leading to confusion and difficulty obtaining information.

With the advent of the Internet and many other technological advances, information is becoming much more available and widespread. This information is valuable, and enterprises that know how to take care of this information and manage it will have a key competitive edge. Can you image the power of being able to see complete profiles of individuals, organizations, products, and their related transactions across the entire enterprise? Enterprises can improve their communications if information is defined and maintained consistently across the enterprise. Integrated systems can lead to more effective service, sales, and strategic analysis for any enterprise.

The data models in Volume 2, as well as the models from Volume 1, are designed to be used to help clarify and see the entire picture of an enterprise's data and how data is related across the enterprise. If the enterprise uses these models as a road map for building integrated data structures, and if the enterprise has the attitude and culture of building integrated, holistic systems, then they can yield tremendous benefits for the enterprise and the people and organizations that the enterprise affects.

Approach of This Book

The approach of this book is quite different from that of most data modeling books. This is not a how-to book on data modeling. Data modeling has been around long enough that most systems professionals know how to model data. This book goes a step beyond and offers practical, reusable data models that can save the reader many thousands of hours in systems development efforts. Industries share many of the same data structures, so why should they reinvent the wheel each time they develop an application?

This book builds on the models and data structures in *The Data Resource Book, Revised Edition, Volume 1*. Volume 1 provided a series of industry Universal Data Models for each phase of an enterprise's business life cycle:

- People and organizations interact and form various relationships.
- Products (services or physical goods) are defined, supplied, priced, costed, and possibly inventoried.
- Commitments to buy products are established between people and/or organizations (may be referred to as orders, agreements, contracts, financial transactions, and so on).
- Shipments transport physical items to their destinations.
- Work efforts are conducted and tracked such as repairs, manufacturing, projects, and services.
- Invoices establish moneys due.
- Budgeting and accounting assist in managing finances.
- Human resources are managed and tracked.

The data models in the first book apply to most enterprise because the preceding processes form the essential aspects of how most business is conducted. The data models represented in the first book identify basic information needs that are applicable across industries. This book shows how the models in the first book can be applied to many industries' unique information requirements.

Rather than repeat the common models found in Volume 1 for each industry, this book provides a table at the beginning of each chapter showing the major changes and additions required to transform the generic data models from Volume 1 into industry-oriented data constructs. Most industries use a very high percentage of the models in Volume 1 and thus the second volume would be quite voluminous if they were repeated for each industry. (The companion Industry Download products for each industry includes the SQL code for the industry-specific data models and data warehouse star schema designs).

Each chapter is roughly organized by the preceding eight major subject data areas (i.e., parties, products, orders, shipments, work efforts, invoices, accounting, and human resources) as well as additional subject data areas that are unique for that industry. Some of the subject data areas are combined into a single section if not much customization is needed. (For instance, accounting and human resources usually do not need much customization for a particular industry.) This book shows the reader how to customize each of the subject data areas for each industry. The combination of the first book's models with the suggested customizations provides industry-specific Universal Data Models that give the user an even greater jump-start to data modeling efforts.

Who Is the Intended Audience for This Book?

This book is written for data modelers, data warehouse designers, data analysts, data administrators, database designers, database administrators, database consultants, and any other information systems professionals who need to be involved in data warehouse designs, data models, database designs, and data integration issues.

Aside from being an invaluable toolkit for systems professionals who focus on this area, this book could also be used as a text for universities teaching data modeling.

Many people prefer to learn by example so this book is both a tremendous toolkit for the experienced practitioner as well as a guide for the novice by showing many well-thought-out examples

General Industry Models versus More Specific Industry Models

A question that came up when formulating the contents of this book was this: Should this book show very specific industry models or more generalized industry models? Should there be separate models for each very specific industry, or should the book have models that can be used across a broader scope of applications and related industries? For example, should there be a separate model for auto insurance, for property and casualty, and for life insurance, or should the book provide generic insurance data models? Similarly, should there be separate models for the airlines business, bus companies, and cruise ship carriers, or should there just be a more general model that provides models for travel enterprises?

There are pros and cons to having more general industry models versus very specific industry models.

Specific industry models provide the following advantages:

- If a company is in that specific line of business and over time continues within only that specific line of business, then more specific constructs can provide more meaningful terminology for that specific industry and perhaps some additional relevant constructs specific to that line of business.

- In some cases, it is easier to develop and implement the models because the models are more specific to the enterprise, provided that the enterprise has no plans for expanding its scope into other similar businesses within that industry.

General industry models provide the following advantages:

- More and more organizations are set up to provide products and services across many aspects of the industry. If they are not already involved in multiple aspects within that industry, they may have a broader vision of the future products and services that they will offer. If a company is in a specific line of business, such as a bus transportation enterprise or an airline, there are many benefits to branching out into other similar lines of business. This is becoming a trend in today's business world.

- If organizations have broader visions or need broader data structures, it is important to provide integrated data structures across the information areas of the enterprise.

- The model is much more stable and can withstand changes to processes if the data structures accommodate broader perspectives. Having a solid, stable database design that is capable of accommodating changing business rules is a key competitive advantage because the database forms the underlying foundation on which applications are built.

- Looking at a model from a general industry perspective (versus a more narrowly defined industry perspective) provides much more flexible data structures that are less likely to need modifications in the future.

- If an enterprise decides that its scope is a very specific industry (for example it is simply interested in airlines as opposed to travel), the models are easy enough to customize.

- Most of the constructs within a very specific line of business generally apply to the whole industry. For instance, most travel enterprises deal with carriers, passengers, reservations, tickets, and many of the same types of entities and attributes.

For these reasons and in order to provide the most value to both very specific organizations as well as more diversified organizations, this book is based on the concept of providing more generic, flexible data models for each industry. These generic data models may include data constructs applicable to the overall industry as well as providing entities, attributes, and relationships applicable to specific segments within that industry. For instance, the insurance chapter provides overall insurance data models as well as some entities, attributes, and relationships that are specific to health care insurance, property insurance, and casualty insurance. The chapters in this book provide models that roughly correspond to the left-most digit of the SIC (standard industry category) code. While the SIC code for airlines is 48xx, the travel models in the travel chapter can apply to most organizations with an SIC code beginning with 4xxx.

Industry Data Models versus Data Model Applications

Many of the data models that are presented in this book may be used for many industries, even though they may appear in a chapter designed for an industry. For instance, the professional service firm's time and expense entry models apply to any organization that tracks time and expenses. There are product deployment and usage models to track each installation of a product and how often the product is used, in the telecommunications industry as well as the manufacturing industry. There are models in this book to track the specific needs of the financial services customer in Chapter 6, as well as how needs are captured over the Web for retail e-commerce in Chapter 9.

There are many other examples of being able to use the models in this book for the industries covered in this book *plus examples of being able to use these models for industries not covered in this book*. In Chapter 10, a table is provided to show which models are applicable in which industries.

Why is this book subtitled *A Library of Universal Data Models for Industry Types* and not *A Library of Universal Data Models for Various Applications*? The models in the book can certainly be used as a reference for effective data structures for various applications. These models have been incorporated into each industry chapter to help readers understand the application of the models in specific contexts. However, *the reader should note that these models can and should be used freely to help design solid data structures for many different applications and are not just limited to the industries listed in this book.*

The Volume 2 Models: Customized and New Models for Each Industry

Table 1.1 provides a breakdown of the most significant changes to the Volume 1 models as well as additions of new models for each industry.

Conventions and Standards Used in This Book

The following section describes the naming standards and diagramming conventions used for presenting the models within this book. Details are provided for entities, subtypes, attributes, relationships, foreign keys, physical models, and illustration tables.

Entities

An *entity* is something of significance about which the enterprise wishes to store information. Whenever entities are referenced throughout the book, they are shown in capital letters. For example, ORDER represents an entity that stores information about a commitment between parties to purchase something. When the name of an entity is used in a sentence to illustrate concepts and business rules, it may be shown without capitalization—for example, the word "order" is not capitalized in the sentence: "Many enterprises have mechanisms such as a sales order form to record sales order information."

The naming conventions for an entity include using a singular noun that is as meaningful as possible to reflect the information it is maintaining. Additionally, the suffix TYPE is added to the entity name if the entity represents a classification of information such as an ORDER TYPE (i.e., sales versus purchase order) rather than a specific instance of a real thing such as an ORDER ("order #23987").

The data models in this book include TYPE entities on the diagrams, even though they usually have only an **ID** and a **description.** These entities are included for completeness and to show where allowable values or look-ups are stored.

Entities are included in the data model if it is a requirement of the enterprise to maintain the information included in the entity. For example, if an enterprise doesn't really care about tracking the tasks associated with a shipment, then even though this information exists in the real world, the data model should not incorporate this information since it may not be important enough information for the enterprise to maintain.

Table 1.1 Key Changes and Additions to Volume 1 Data Models for Each Industry Covered in Volume 2

	MANUFACTURING	TELECOMMUNI-CATIONS	HEALTH CARE	INSURANCE	FINANCIAL SERVICES	PROFESSIONAL SERVICES	TRAVEL	WEB-BASED MODELS
People and organizations (need to add party roles and party relationship subtypes only; addition of party roles are shown)	Add subtypes (i.e., distribution channel, end user customer)	Add subtypes (i.e., telecommunications carriers, billing agents, residential customers, organization customers)	Add subtypes (i.e., insured individual, insured contract holder, insured dependent, individual health care practitioner, patient, health care provider organization, group, network, third-party administrator, insurer, payor, health care facilities, patient and provider profile information)	Add subtypes (i.e., insured party, insurance support staff, insurance agent, claims adjuster, insurance provider, insurance agency, insurance administrator, insurance partner, insurance association)	Add subtypes (i.e., controlling syndicator, participating syndicator, add models for party financial plans, objectives and needs)	Add subtypes (i.e., professional, contractor, bill-to client, delivery client, professional services provider)	Add subtypes (i.e., traveler, travel account member, travel staff, operations crew, travel provider, carrier, hotel provider, car rental provider, travel port authority, travel agency, travel association, travel partner)	Add subtypes (i.e., Webmaster, consumer, visitor, subscriber, referrer, ISP, hosting server)

(continues)

Table 1.1 *(continued)*

	MANUFACTURING	TELECOMMUNICATIONS	HEALTH CARE	INSURANCE	FINANCIAL SERVICES	PROFESSIONAL SERVICES	TRAVEL	WEB-BASED MODELS
Product	Add products and parts model. Add design engineering models including product specification and engineering change models. Add bill of materials and product substitute models. Add inventory item configuration model	Modify products and features model to incorporate telecommunications products and features subtypes. Add product deployment model. Add models to show network components, circuits, and product deployments. Add telephone inventory and communication ID and appearance models	Modify product structures to accommodate health care service and good offerings in various health care discipline subtypes of hospital, physician, dental, vision, alternative medicine	Add insurance product categories and product structures for property, casualty, health, life disability, and other forms of insurance. Add coverage type, coverage level, insurance feature and insurance product rules models, add insurance underwriting and customize generic pricing models to insurance rate models	Add financial service products, features and functional settings models. Add product regulation models	Modify product models to cover deliverables, Skill requirements for products	Modify product models to accommodate travel enterprises by adding scheduled transportation offerings, hotel and rental car offerings, accommodation classes, accommodation maps, transportation vehicles, rental vehicles, hotels	Add objects model to be able to relate to product and product category images, text, and other electronic objects

Orders	Customize order to provide man-ufacturing orders	Customize order models to service order models	Provide for setting up appointments through scheduled health care visits	Add insurance application models, modify quotes models for insurance	Add Financial transaction instead of order	Expand requirements, request and quotes models for profes-sional service, customize order model to engage-ments model	Add reserva-tion and ticketing models with coupons, ticket com-ponents, sales, and payments	Extend party need model as it applies to discovered needs from Web visits. Add subscrip-tion requests for ongoing information such as news-letters and user group subscriptions. Add visit and server hit models along with user agent and Web address relationship information
Agreements			Modify agreements structures to handle health care agree-ments such as patient provider agreements, insurance policies, and provider network agreements	Modify agreement models to add subtypes of insurance policies to cover property, casualty, life, disability, and health plans. Add premium schedule models	Modify agreement models to cover finan-cial agree-ments such as loan agreements, investment agreements, and leasing agreements	Modify agreements model to cover profes-sional services agreements	Modify agreements structures to handle cor-porate travel agreement, distribution channel agreement, travel ticket agreement	

(continues)

Table 1.1 (continued)

	MANUFACTURING	TELECOMMUNICATIONS	HEALTH CARE	INSURANCE	FINANCIAL SERVICES	PROFESSIONAL SERVICES	TRAVEL	WEB-BASED MODELS
Delivery	Add deployment and usage tracking models	Add telecommunications deployment usage models	Add structures to handle health care incidents, episodes, symptoms, visits, and health care delivery at various health care facilities	Claims processing and payments		Extend time entry models to include professional service entry models to cover time, expenses, materials, and deliverable turnover	Travel experience and events including baggage handling, seat assignment, boarding, amenities, rental car checkouts, customer service events, travel surveys, travel feedback	
Work Efforts	Customize work effort models to provide process plan and production run models					Extend work effort models to cover projects that integrate with engagements or service entries of time, expenses, materials, and deliverable turnover		

Invoicing	Add invoicing models to cover usage of telecommunications services	Modify invoice structures for claims processing. Modify payment models to handle claims payment settlement	Premium notice, Renewal billing	Add incidents and claims submission and settlement models	Extend invoice models to cover billings of professional service entries
Accounts		Add financial accounts of deposit accounts, financial card accounts, loan accounts, and line of credit accounts, along with the media (cards) for the account and the account transaction models. Add account notification model			Set up Travel Accounts with activities and travel points

(continues)

Table 1.1 *(continued)*

	MANUFACTURING	TELECOMMUNI-CATIONS	HEALTH CARE	INSURANCE	FINANCIAL SERVICES	PROFESSIONAL SERVICES	TRAVEL	WEB-BASED MODELS
Accounting and budgeting	Use models from Volume 1	Use models from Volume 1	Use models from Volume 1	Use models from Volume 1	Use models from Volume 1	Use models from Volume 1	Use models from Volume 1	Use models from Volume 1
Human resources	Use models from Volume 1	Use models from Volume 1	Use models from Volume 1	Use models from Volume 1	Use models from Volume 1	Use models from Volume 1	Use models from Volume 1	Use models from Volume 1
Star Schema Designs	Production-run star schema	Deployment usage star schema	Health care episode outcome analysis star schema	Claims star schema	Account star schema and account transaction star schema	Service entry (resource utilization) star schema	Passenger transportation star schema. Non-transportation travel product star schema	Hits star schema. Visits star schema
Other additions			Add health care referral model			Add risk analysis and marketing target model		

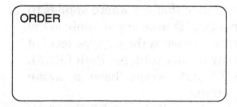

Figure 1.1   An entity.

Entities are represented by rounded boxes. Figure 1.1 shows an example of the entity ORDER.

Subtypes and Supertypes

A *subtype*, sometimes referred to as a subentity, is a classification of an entity that has characteristics such as attributes or relationships in common with the more general entity. LEGAL ORGANIZATION and INFORMAL ORGANIZA-TION are, for example, subtypes of ORGANIZATION.

Subtypes are represented in the data modeling diagrams by entities inside other entities. The common attributes and relationships between subtypes are shown in the outside entity, which is known as the *supertype*. The attributes and relationships of the supertype are therefore inherited by the subtype. Figure 1.2 shows the supertype ORGANIZATION and its subtypes LEGAL ORGA-

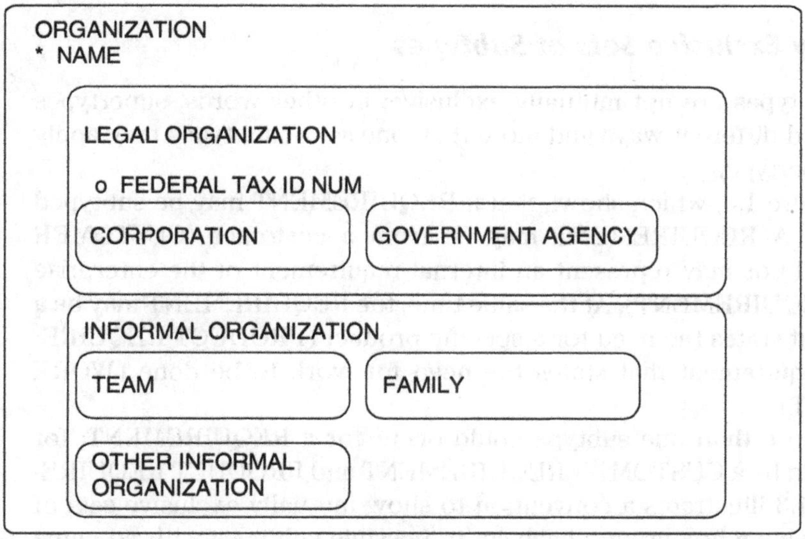

```
ORGANIZATION
* NAME

    LEGAL ORGANIZATION

      o FEDERAL TAX ID NUM

      CORPORATION          GOVERNMENT AGENCY


    INFORMAL ORGANIZATION

      TEAM                 FAMILY

      OTHER INFORMAL
      ORGANIZATION
```

Figure 1.2   Subtypes and supertypes.

NIZATION and INFORMAL ORGANIZATION. Notice that the **name** applies to the supertype ORGANIZATION and the **federal tax ID num** applies only to the LEGAL ORGANIZATION subtype and is therefore shown at the subtype level of LEGAL ORGANIZATION because it applies only to that subtype. Both LEGAL ORGANIZATION and INFORMAL ORGANIZATION would have a **name** because they will inherit the values of the supertype.

Supertypes may have many levels. Figure 1.2 shows that a CORPORATION and GOVERNMENT AGENCY are subtypes of LEGAL ORGANIZATION, which is also a subtype of ORGANIZATION. Thus boxes may be in boxes down to any level to illustrate which subtypes inherit the attributes and relationships of the parent supertype (its outer box).

The subtypes within an entity should represent a complete set of classifications (meaning that the sum of the subtypes covers the supertype in its entirety) and at the same time be mutually exclusive of each other (an exception of handling separate sets of non-mutually exclusive subtypes will be covered in the next section). Many times the data model includes an OTHER...subtype to provide for other possible classifications of the entity that may be defined by the enterprise using the model. For example, each INFORMATION ORGANIZATION may be a TEAM, FAMILY, or OTHER INFORMAL ORGANIZATION.

While the subtypes represent a complete set of possible classifications, there may be more detailed subtypes that are not included in the data model; instead, they may be included in a TYPE entity. In this case, subtypes are shown in two places on a model: as a subtype and in a TYPE entity that shows the domain of allowed types for the entity.

Non-Mutually Exclusive Sets of Subtypes

Sometimes, subtypes are not mutually exclusive; in other words, supertypes may be subtyped different ways and more than one set of subtypes may apply to the same supertype.

Consider Figure 1.3, which shows that a REQUIREMENT may be subtyped different ways. A REQUIREMENT may be from a customer (CUSTOMER REQUIREMENT) or may represent an internal requirement of the enterprise (INTERNAL REQUIREMENT). At the same time, the REQUIREMENT may be a requirement that states the need for a specific product (PRODUCT REQUIRE-MENT) or a requirement that states the need for work to be done (WORK REQUIREMENT).

Therefore, more than one subtype could occur for a REQUIREMENT; for instance, it could be a CUSTOMER REQUIREMENT and PRODUCT REQUIRE-MENT. Figure 1.3 illustrates a convention to show mutually exclusive sets of subtypes by having a box around each set of possible subtypes with no name

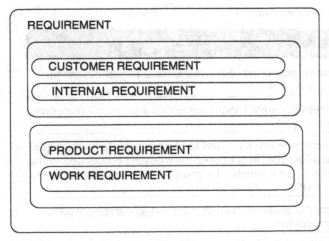

Figure 1.3 Non-mutually exclusive subtypes and supertypes.

for the box. The boxes merely serve to establish when there is more than one set of subtypes for a supertype.

Attributes

An *attribute* holds a particular piece of information about an entity, such as the **order date** on an order. Attributes are identified in the text of the book by boldface, lowercase letters such as the previous **order date** example.

Attributes may be either part of the unique identifier of an entity (also referred to as a primary key), mandatory, or optional. The primary key attribute(s) is identified by a "#" sign preceding the attribute name on the diagram. Mandatory attributes are signified by a "*" before the attribute name. Optional attributes have an "o" before the attribute. Figure 1.4 shows that the ORDER entity has **order ID** as a primary key attribute, **order date** as a mandatory attribute, and **entry date** as an optional attribute.

```
 ORDER
 #  ORDER ID
 *  ORDER DATE
 o  ENTRY DATE
```

Figure 1.4 Attributes.

Table 1.2 Conventions Used in Attribute Naming

STRING WITHIN ATTRIBUTE NAME	MEANING
ID	System-generated sequential unique numeric identifier (i.e., 1, 2, 3, 4, ...)
Seq id	System-generated sequence within a parent ID (e.g., order item seq id)
Code	Unique pneumonic—used to identify user-defined unique identifiers that may have some meaning embedded in the key (i.e., an example of a geo code to store Colorado may be "CO")
Name	A proper pronoun such as a person, geographical area, organization
Description	The descriptive value for a unique code or identifier
Flag or Ind (indicator)	A binary choice for values (i.e., yes/no or male/female)
from date	Attribute that specifies the beginning date of a date range and is inclusive of the date specified
thru date	Attribute that specifies the end date of a date range and is inclusive of the date specified (**to date** is not used since **thru date** more clearly represents an inclusive end of date range)

Certain strings included in an attribute's name have meanings based on the conventions shown in Table 1.2.

Relationships

Relationships define how two entities are associated with each other. When relationships are used in the text, they are usually shown in lowercase as a normal part of the text. In some situations, where they are specifically highlighted, they are identified by boldface lowercase letters. For example, **manufactured by** could be the way a relationship may appear in the text of this book.

Relationship Optionality

Relationships may be either optional or mandatory. A dotted relationship line next to an entity means that the relationship from that entity is optional, and a continuous line means that the relationship is mandatory (the relationship has to exist for all occurrences of each entity). Figure 1.5 shows a relationship that "each SHIPMENT *must be* **shipped from** one and only one POSTAL

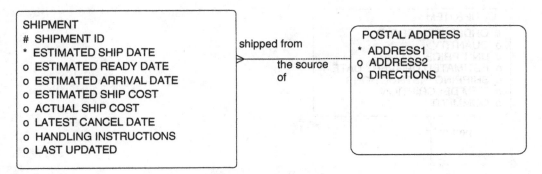

Figure 1.5   Mandatory versus optional relationships.

ADDRESS." This means that the postal address for each shipment must be specified in order to create a shipment instance. The same relationship has an optional aspect when read in the other direction: "Each POSTAL ADDRESS *may be* **the source of** one or more SHIPMENTs." Hence, there could be a postal address that has not been used for a shipment yet.

Relationship Cardinality

Relationships may be one-to-one, one-to-many, or many-to-many. This is generally known as the cardinality of the relationship. The presence of a *crowsfoot* (a three-pronged line that looks like a crow's foot) defines whether an entity points to more than one occurrence of another entity. Figure 1.6 shows that "each ORDER must be **composed of** *one or more* ORDER ITEMs" since the crowsfoot is at the ORDER ITEM side. The other relationship side states that "each ORDER ITEM must be **part of** *one and only one* ORDER." A one-to-one relationship doesn't have any crowsfeet on the relationship, and a many-to-many relationship has crowsfeet at both ends of the relationship. Sometimes, one-to-many relationships are referred to as parent-child relationships.

Sometimes the term "over time" needs to be added to the relationship sentence to verify whether the relationship is one-to-many. For instance, an ORDER may appear to have only one ORDER STATUS; however, if status history is required, then each ORDER may be in the state of one or more ORDER STATUSes, *over time*.

The data models in the book have very few one-to-one relationships because most of the time one-to-one relationships can be grouped together into a single entity when normalized. The data model diagrams do not show many-to-many relationships because many-to-many-relationships are broken out into *intersection* entities.

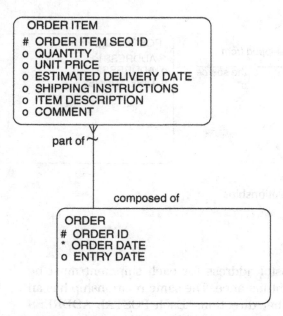

Figure 1.6   One-to-many relationship.

Foreign Key Relationships

A *foreign key* is defined as the presence of another entity's (or table's) primary key in an entity (or table). For example, in Figure 1.6 the **order ID** from the ORDER entity is part of the ORDER ITEM entity even though it is not specifically shown. The relationship indicates that it is a foreign key. Any one-to-many relationship indicates that the primary key of the entity on the *one* side of the relationship is brought into the entity on the *many* side of the relationship. Some data modelers show this foreign key as an attribute of the entity (this is sometimes known as key migration). *The data models in this book do not show the foreign keys of entities as attributes because this is redundant.* Instead, the relationship itself identifies the foreign key. In Figure 1.6, the **order ID** is not shown as an attribute in the ORDER ITEM entity because the one-to-many nature of the relationship reveals that it is a foreign key.

Foreign Key Inheritance

A diagramming convention in this book is to use a tilde ("~") relationship line to indicate that the inherited foreign key is part of the primary key of the child entity. The tilde ("~") line across the relationship in Figure 1.6 indicates that the **order ID** is part of the ORDER ITEM entity primary key. This convention allows a shorthand notation, providing for the primary key to be identified as a combination of the primary key attributes (identified with a "#") as well as the primary keys of the entity to which the relationship with a tilde is pointing.

Therefore the primary key to the ORDER ITEM is the **order item seq id** plus the primary key of the ORDER entity, the **order id**.

This convention allows a shorthand notation to document the primary keys of each entity without taking up a great deal of space by repeated foreign keys that form part of another entity's primary key. This notation also shows the semantics of the primary key by clearly specifying the relationships that are part of the primary key as well as any attributes with a "#" symbol next to them.

Intersection or Association Entities to Handle Many-to-Many Relationships

Intersection entities are also known as associative entities or cross-reference entities. They are used to resolve many-to-many relationships by cross-referencing one entity to another. Often they include additional attributes that may further delineate the relationship. Figure 1.7 shows a many-to-many relationship between a PARTY and a CONTACT MECHANISM that is resolved in this way. The diagram indicates that a PARTY may be **contacted via** *more than one* CONTACT MECHANISM such as a POSTAL ADDRESS, TELECOMMUNI-

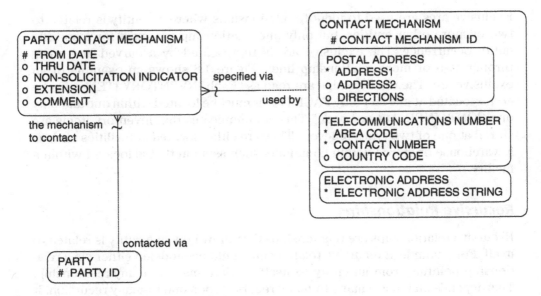

Figure 1.7 Many-to-many relationships.

CATIONS NUMBER, or ELECTRONIC ADDRESS because a party may have many ways to be contacted. Conversely, a CONTACT MECHANISM may be **used by** *more than one* PARTY. For instance, many people may have the same work address or work phone number. This many-to-many relationship is resolved by the intersection entity PARTY CONTACT MECHANISM.

Each associative entity inherits the key to each of the entities it intersects. Therefore the tilde ("~") is always used in the reference relationships of an associative entity to show that the associative entity inherits the key of each of the referenced entities (see "foreign key inheritance"). For example, the **party id** and the **contact mechanism id** are parts of the primary key to PARTY CONTACT MECHANISM, along with the **from date**.

Notice that in all the examples given, each relationship has two relationship names associated with it that describe the relationship in both directions. The relationship names should be combined so that they read as a complete sentence, as shown in the following format: "Each ENTITY {must be/may be} relationship name {one and only one/one or more} ENTITY, over time," where the appropriate choices are filled in.

In the models presented, the crowsfeet on the relationships generally point up and to the left in order to provide a consistent mechanism for reading the diagrams. This tends to organize the data models in a more understandable format.

Exclusive Arcs

Exclusive arcs are used to identify relationships where an entity is related to two or more other entities, but only one relationship can exist for a specific entity occurrence. The exclusive arc is represented by a curved line going through two or more relationship lines. Figure 1.8 shows an example of an exclusive arc. The relationships are read as "Each INVENTORY ITEM must be *either* located at one and only FACILITY or must be located within one and only one CONTAINER, *but not both*." This communicates that inventory items are stored at one of two types of levels: They are either located at facilities such as a warehouse or stored within containers such as a bin that is located within a facility.

Recursive Relationships

Recursive relationships are relationships that show how one entity is related to itself. For example, a recursive relationship could be modeled either via a relationship pointing from an entity to itself or via a many-to-many-relationship. This depends on if it is a many-to-many recursion or a one-to-many recursion. It is possible for an entity to have many recursive relationships.

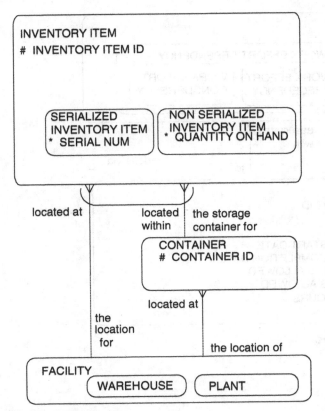

Figure 1.8 Exclusive arcs.

Figure 1.9 shows an example of a one-to-many recursion around the WORK EFFORT entity to show that each WORK EFFORT may be redone via one or more WORK EFFORTs. It also shows a many-to-many recursion that is resolved by the intersection entity WORK EFFORT ASSOCIATION to show that work efforts may be either dependent on other work efforts (WORK EFFORT DEPENDENCY subtype) or broken down into several lower-level work efforts (WORK EFFORT BREAKDOWN subtype).

Physical Models

The data warehouse models and diagrams used in the star schema designs at the end of each chapter represent physical database designs. The same notations can be used as previously stated with the exception that because these models represent physical database designs, each box represents a table, and the field names are columns.

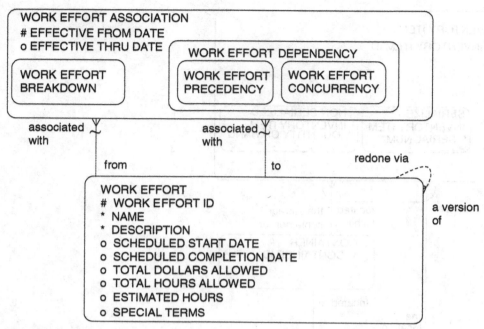

Figure 1.9   Recursive relationships.

The star schema design at the end of each chapter will show the dimension tables in the plural in order to distinguish them from the logical data model entities. The dimension tables may represent a denormalized view of the entity. For instance, a PRODUCT entity has a relationship to PRODUCT CATEGORY, however, a PRODUCTS dimension may include the product category as a level in the dimension.

Conventions Used for Illustration Tables

Many parts of the data models are illustrated via tables that contain possible values for attributes. Each illustration table is normally defined to show a specific entity and the relevant information from related entities. For instance, there may be a table illustrating the ORDER ITEM entity, as shown in Table 1.3. In order to illustrate the details, the table may show information from directly related entries. For example, Table 1.3 brings in some attribute information from the ORDER entity. Whenever data from each illustration table is referenced in the text of this book, it is surrounded by double quotes. For instance,

Table 1.3   Order Item

ORDER ID	ORDER DATE	ORDER ITEM SEQ ID	COMMENT
12930	April 30, 2000	1	Need this item urgently
		2	There's no time pressure at all on this item

the text may refer to specific order "12930", order item seq id "1", which has a comment of "Need this item urgently."

Conventions Used to Reference Figures

Because there are two volumes for the *Data Model Resource Book*, figures are referenced by the following notation:

Vx:Figure x.x

Where   Vx signifies a reference to either Volume 1 or Volume 2
and   Figure x.x references a specific figure in that volume.

For example, V1:2.1 references Figure 2.1 in Volume 1, the Organization data model. V2:2.2 references Figure 2.2 (Parts and products) in the second volume. If there is no Vx in front of the reference, then the reader may assume that the figure is in the current volume.

The Data Model Resource Book, Volume 2, Industry Download Products

This book and its appendices provide very detailed descriptions of the industry models. The diagrams lay out the entities, relationships, primary keys, foreign keys, and the mandatory and optional attributes. With this information, it would be possible for a data modeler or database designer to recreate these models in the tool of his or her choice or write the SQL code to build them in a database.

This, however, would take a substantial amount of time and opens the possibility of data entry errors. To assist those interested in quickly implementing the models, a companion *Data Model Resource Industry Downloads* are available for sale separately. The download products provide access to a series of SQL scripts for each industry, derived directly from the models in the book. All the entities, attributes, tables, and columns discussed are implemented with this code. Scripts are provided for Oracle, Microsoft SQL Server, and ODBC scripts for use with other databases. Because these are standard SQL scripts, they should work with not only the current versions of these database management systems but also future versions. This includes object-relational databases that should continue to support relational designs. The constructs in the book are, of course, also generally applicable to any relational or object-relational database.

The downloadable electronic products for each industry also contain that industry's data model diagrams in electronic format (Visio 2000 and jpeg formats) and a series of reports that list and cross reference the subject data areas, diagrams, entities, attributes, tables, and columns of the data model.

The CD-ROM in the back of this book provides a sample of an industry model for your review. If you wish to purchase one or more of the complete industry models, you can link directly from the accompanying CD-ROM to the companion Web site at silverston.wiley.com, where you can purchase and download the models. Refer to the "How to Use the Volume 2 Industry Electronic Products" section in the back of this book for instructions.

In summary, using the SQL scripts will allow an enterprise to more rapidly deploy the models presented in this book. In addition to the time savings, there is obviously a cost savings as well. These scripts may be used to reverse-engineer the models into your favorite CASE tool (most popular CASE tools provide a reverse-engineering feature). Once the models have been brought into a repository, they are easily accessible and may be customized for a specific enterprise's needs. Additionally, they can be used to jump-start the development of corporate data models, database designs, or data warehouse designs.

CHAPTER 2

Manufacturing

Since many other firms and industries are dependent on the products that are created by manufacturing organizations, an explanation of manufacturing models is a logical place to start a discussion of industry models. Distributors and retailers depend on selling products that are manufactured, usually by other organizations. And businesses and people depend on using manufactured goods.

There are two types of manufacturers: discrete manufacturers and process manufacturers. Discrete manufacturers assemble tangible parts into components. Examples of discrete manufacturers include manufacturers of computers, appliances, all types of machines, and anything that has tangible parts. Examples of process manufacturers include chemical companies, paint manufacturers, soft drink manufacturers, and any company that mixes liquids to create products. This chapter will focus mainly on discrete manufacturing although many of the constructs will also apply to process manufacturers.

Manufacturers are principally concerned with issues such as the following:

- How can we engineer and manufacture high-quality products?

- How can we control our costs?

- How can we maximize our sales and profitability?

To answer these questions, manufacturing enterprises need to track information about the following:

- The people and organizations they deal with, namely customers, suppliers, distributors, and internal staff.
- Tracking of parts required in manufacturing process.
- Design engineering information such as recording the specifications of parts and products that are to be designed and manufactured.
- Product and parts configurations and bill of materials information to record the components within products.
- Inventory control information to manage raw materials, work in process, and finished goods inventories.
- Order, shipping, and invoicing information for both customers and vendors.
- Material requirements planning (MRP) information, which allows manufacturers to forecast how much raw materials and finished goods they will need.
- Fixed assets management to track purchase, depreciation, and major equipment and other significant assets of the enterprise. This is usually more important in manufacturing because the manufacturer's fixed assets often represent a significant portion of the enterprise's worth.
- Process plan information to track how products will be manufactured.
- Manufacturing operations information to track usage of materials, labor, and overhead in producing products.
- Cost accounting information to allocate costs of manufacturing products.
- Financial management such as budgeting and accounting for the internal organizations within the enterprise.
- Human resources information to record and track employee information.

The *Data Model Resource Book, Volume 1,* addresses many of the information needs of manufacturing enterprises. For instance:

- Chapter 2, "People and Organizations," in Volume 1 provides generic data structures useful for handling many of the needs of people and organizations within manufacturing enterprises.
- Chapter 3, "Products," in Volume 1 discusses inventory control.
- Chapter 4, "Ordering Products," in Volume 1 covers order processing.
- Chapter 5, "Shipments," in Volume 1 discusses shipping models for deliveries as well as receipts and issuances of inventory.
- Chapter 6, "Work Effort," in Volume 1 covers manufacturing operations to manage production runs and fixed asset management models.
- Chapter 7, "Invoicing," in Volume 1 discusses invoicing data models that may be used for manufacturing companies.

- Chapter 8, "Accounting and Budgeting," in Volume 1 addresses financial management models.

- Chapter 9, "Human Resources," in Volume 1 covers human resources and employee tracking.

The key changes and additions to the Universal Data Models that are needed to support manufacturing enterprises are the following:

- Extending the people and organization data models, adding entities that are applicable to manufacturing organizations

- Managing parts as a distinct entity from product because it is such a key item in manufacturing

- Adding design engineering data models to record how products are engineered and modified

- Adding engineering change data models to maintain change history.

- Extending the bill of material and item configuration data models

- Extending the substitutability models allowing for part substitutions

- Adding product deployments and usage models.

- Extending the work effort data models to incorporate process planning and production runs of manufactured items

Table 2.1 shows which models can be used for manufacturing directly from Volume 1, which models need to be modified, which models not to use, and which new models are required. This chapter describes the generic models from Volume 1 that have significant modifications, plus the new industry models. (Minor modifications are explained within the text of the chapter.)

Table 2.1 Volume 1 and Volume 2 Data Models for Manufacturing

SUBJECT DATA AREA	USE THESE VOLUME 1 MODELS DIRECTLY	MODIFY THESE VOLUME 1 MODELS (AS DESCRIBED IN VOLUME 2)	DO NOT USE THESE VOLUME 1 MODELS	ADD THESE VOLUME 2 MODELS
Parties, people, and organizations	All models, V1:2.1–V1:2.14 except for subtyping party roles and relationships, V1:2.5 and V1:2.6	Party roles and relationships, V1:2.5 and V1:2.6 to include manufacturing roles and relationships as shown in V2:2.1		

(continues)

Table 2.1   (*continued*)

SUBJECT DATA AREA	USE THESE VOLUME 1 MODELS DIRECTLY	MODIFY THESE VOLUME 1 MODELS (AS DESCRIBED IN VOLUME 2)	DO NOT USE THESE VOLUME 1 MODELS	ADD THESE VOLUME 2 MODELS
Product	V1:3.1–V1:3.11			Parts and products, V2:2.2; parts specifications and documentation, V2:2.3; part specifications roles and status, V2:2.4; engineering changes, V2:2.5; bill of materials, V2:2.6; part substitutions, V2:2.7; Inventory item configurations, V2:2.8
Order	All models V1:4.1–4.17 except for V1:4.2	Slight modifications as shown in manufacturing order model of V2:2.9		
Delivery	All models V1:5.1–5.8			Product deployment and usage, V2:2.10
Work Effort	All models V1:6.1–6.13 except for slight modifications shown in next column	Work Effort, V1:6.1–6.13 (incorporate process plans and specialized production run requirements into work efforts as shown in in V2:2.11; add production run subtypes as shown in V2:2.12)		
Invoicing	All models V1:7.1–7.10			
Accounting	All models, V1:8.1–8.12			
Human Resources	All models, V1:9.1–9.14			
Star Schema				Production run star schema, V2:2.13

People and Organizations in Manufacturing

Manufacturers, just like any other organizations, need to track various people and organizations. The most critical needs are usually to track their suppliers and customers. Many times they need to track information about organizations and people who distribute their products, such as wholesalers, distributors, or agents. They also need to track information about the people working within their organization, such as employees and contractors. Manufacturers need to track information about their internal organizations such as their various companies, subsidiaries, divisions, departments, plants, and locations.

Figure 2.1 shows a data model for PARTY, PARTY ROLEs, and PARTY RELATIONSHIPs within manufacturing enterprises. This model represents a manufacturing-oriented, customized version of the models in V1:2.5 and V1:2.6a, which portray common party roles and relationships. Many of the generic PARTY ROLEs from Volume 1 are included here in Figure 2.1, such as EMPLOYEE, CONTACT, CONTRACTOR, FAMILY MEMBER, SHAREHOLDER, CUSTOMER, PROSPECT, DISTRIBUTION CHANNEL, AGENT, DISTRIBUTOR, PARTNER, COMPETITOR, HOUSEHOLD, REGULATORY AGENCY, SUPPLIER, ASSOCIATION, ORGANIZATIONAL UNIT, SUBSIDIARY, DEPARTMENT, DIVISION, PARENT ORGANIZATION, and INTERNAL ORGANIZATION.

Many of the generic PARTY RELATIONSHIPs are also included, such as CUSTOMER RELATIONSHIP, DISTRIBUTION CHANNEL RELATIONSHIP, PARTNERSHIP, ORGANIZATION ROLLUP, ORGANIZATION CONTACT RELATIONSHIP, and EMPLOYMENT. Many other relationships could occur in manufacturing organizations, hence the relationship to PARTY RELATIONSHIP TYPE; however, the subtypes shown represent some of the key relationships that are important to track.

For the most part, the roles and relationships within manufacturing are very similar to the generic party roles from Volume 1 that can be used within most organizations. The difference may be in the emphasis or importance of some of the roles as they apply to manufacturing. The key roles that are most important for manufacturers are the DISTRIBUTION CHANNEL, CUSTOMER, SUPPLIER, CONTRACTOR, and EMPLOYEE. It is most important to track the method of getting out their products through the DISTRIBUTION CHANNEL and then track the CUSTOMER, defined as the party that ends up using, paying for, or being shipped the product. The CUSTOMER entity is further subtyped into BILL TO CUSTOMER, SHIP TO CUSTOMER, and END USER CUSTOMER to distinguish between parties responsible for paying, parties that receive the product(s), and parties that use the manufacturer's products. The SUPPLIER is critical—in order to manufacture quality products, the manufacturer is dependent on good relationships with its suppliers. Of course, the EMPLOYEE and CONTRACTOR roles are important to do the work to actually manufacture the products.

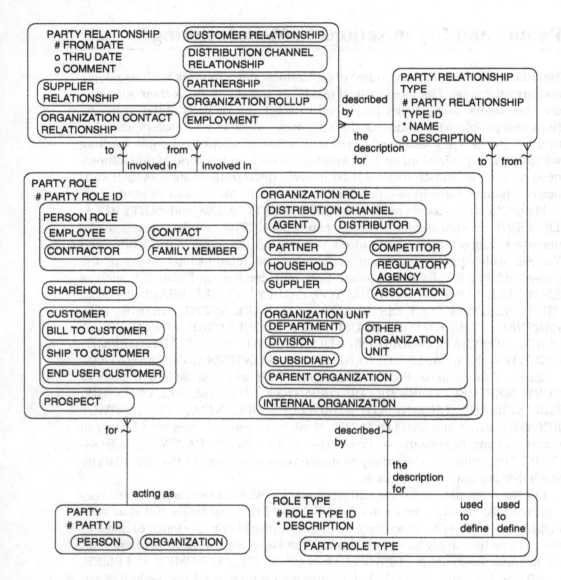

Figure 2.1   Manufacturing party roles and relationships.

Who is the customer of the manufacturing enterprise? Is it the distributor of the manufacturer's product or the party that ends up using, paying for, or being shipped the product? The model distinguishes the DISTRIBUTOR party role from the CUSTOMER party role. DISTRIBUTORS are organizations that sell the manufacturers' products and while they may be considered customers in some contexts, they will not be referred to as "customers" since they play a more extensive role. The CUSTOMER represents the parties that pay for, get shipped to, or end up using the manufacturer's product, and this does not include the parties that serve as distributors.

One of the most important roles to track is the DISTRIBUTION CHANNEL and the associated DISTRIBUTION CHANNEL RELATIONSHIP, which is between the DISTRIBUTION CHANNEL and an INTERNAL ORGANIZATION. A manufacturer is often dependent on distributors, wholesalers, or agents to sell their products because the enterprise is focused on manufacturing the products, and they often rely on other parties to distribute their products. The DISTRIBUTION CHANNEL subtype stores information on relationships that are established to market and sell the manufacturer's products. A DISTRIBUTOR is a relationship that is established to buy and sell the manufacturer's products. For example, a PC manufacturer probably has numerous computer stores and/or chains where their products are sold. An AGENT is a role played by a party that represents the manufacturer in selling its products. An independent agent or manufacturer's representative may sell products—blinds and draperies, for example—from various manufacturers.

This section has shown how to use the PARTY, PARTY ROLE, and PARTY RELATIONSHIP models from Volume 1 (refer to models V1:2.1–V1:2.7) within manufacturing. The rest of the data models in Chapter 2 of Volume 1, such as models for contact mechanisms, facility information, and communications events (refer to models V1:2.8–V1:2.13), also apply very readily to manufacturers.

Product Models in Manufacturing

The following section will cover some additional areas needed in the product data models for manufacturing enterprises: part maintenance, design engineering, bill of materials structures, part substitutes, and inventory item configurations.

Products and Parts

Volume 1 illustrated that the data structures for modeling PRODUCT may be similar for the enterprise's products as well as its competitors' and its suppliers' products. Products have prices, features, categories, identifiers, substitutes, and many other common information items, whether they are our products, supplier products, or competitor products.

Are the parts that manufacturers buy really products? Are they not products of the organizations selling them? Do they not have the same characteristics of other products? Why not use the models from Chapter 3, "Products," of Volume 1? For many types of firms this makes sense, especially when firms are buying the products from a supplier (or competitor) and reselling the same products to its customers.

On the other hand, at the very core of the manufacturing business (and especially in discrete manufacturing) there is the need to manage and track parts. Because manufacturers are responsible for building products and assembling the parts that go into a product, the data models in this chapter will more directly handle the management of parts as an entity distinct from PRODUCT, but closely related to PRODUCT and within the product subject data area.

The Product Part data model in Volume 1, V1:2.10b, addresses the need to manage parts separately from the PRODUCT entity in some circumstances, such as when the aspect of managing parts is a key aspect for an enterprise.

Figure 2.2 shows the relationship from PRODUCT to PART when parts are treated as a separate entity from products. (For ease of reference, key definitions from Volume 1 for V1:2.10b will be reexplained in this paragraph—please read the end of the product chapter in Volume 1 for more information on this

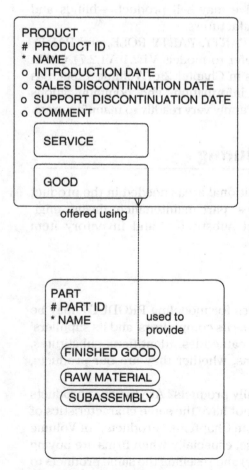

Figure 2.2   Parts and products.

subject.) A PART represents the type of physical items that go into the product; the PRODUCT represents the type of thing that is marketed or offered for sale. Note that both products and parts represent types of things. Instance of real, physical items tracked is handled by the INVENTORY ITEM entity, as explained in Chapter 3 of Volume 1.

A PART may be subtyped into a FINISHED GOOD, a RAW MATERIAL, or a SUBASSEMBLY. A FINISHED GOOD is a part that is ready to be shipped as a product; some work was probably performed to get the item to its current state. A RAW MATERIAL is a component used in making a product; no work has been performed by the enterprise, and it is the lowest level component that makes up a product. A SUBASSEMBLY is a part that is in a state of partial completion and is not generally sold to a customer or purchased from a supplier.

What is the difference between a FINISHED GOOD and a PRODUCT, and why is there a one-to-many relationship between them? Because a FINISHED GOOD is a subtype of a part, it represents the type of physical good that exists. A PRODUCT represents the offering of the good and hence can have a marketing spin on it as well. For instance, the exact same part may be sold as more than one marketing offering (with a different product name), depending on where and to whom it is sold. The telephone line sold by a telecommunications company may be the same finished good, but there may be two different products, one for residential and one for business use. A FINISHED GOOD may have several products associated with it if the same good is marketed in different countries as separate product offerings. This explains why there is a one-to-many relationship from FINISHED GOOD to PRODUCT.

Table 2.2 provides examples of products and parts for our fictitious manufacturing company, which we will call Super Extreme PC Manufacturing. The Extreme 5 PC is a FINISHED GOOD that is produced by the company. There are two associated products, the Super Extreme 5 PC, which is sold to individuals, and the Business Classic 5 PC, which is sold to businesses. There are different marketing strategies, support plans, and pricing structures for each of the products. Even though both of these products correspond to the same physical type of item (an Extreme 5 PC part), the marketing and support needs are projected to be different and thus two separate product offerings are needed.

Table 2.2 Examples of Parts and Products

PART NAME	PART SUBTYPE	PRODUCT NAME
Extreme 5 PC	Finished good	Super Extreme 5 PC Business Classic 5 PC
Extreme motherboard	Subassembly	
Extreme Main Memory 128 MB SIM stick	Raw material	

Different product features (variations for the product) may be available for each product.

The Extreme motherboard is an example of a SUBASSEMBLY because Super Extreme Manufacturing does some work to assemble the parts within the motherboard. The Extreme Main Memory 128 MB SIM stick is a RAW MATER-IAL because Super Extreme Manufacturing always deals with this as the lowest-level part and buys this as a whole from other companies (other enterprises may view this as a subassembly or a finished good—for instance, the manufacturer of this part may consider this a finished good).

Design Engineering

One unique aspect of a manufacturer is that it designs and builds products. Design engineering is the starting point for most product manufacturers. It represents the process of engineering and designing the specifications required to introduce and build the parts that make up products. Typically, engineers will use tools for drafting, documenting, and modeling to engineer their products.

At a high level, design engineers need three types of information about their parts and products: specifications, documentation, and engineering changes. Specifications define the details of the way the item works, dimensions of the item, characteristics of the item, and anything that technically defines it. Documentation tracks the documents that support parts and products and may include engineering models, marketing materials, and drawings. Engineering changes record information about changes to the design of products.

The following models will relate these specifications and engineering changes to the parts that make up the products rather than to the products directly. The thing that needs specifications is really the type of physical item, namely the PART, not the PRODUCT, which represents the marketing offering. Of course, the PRODUCT can inherit the specifications for any PART because there is, at most, only one finished good for a product. The specifications may be about a RAW MATERIAL, a SUBASSEMBLY, or a FINISHED GOOD because any of these may have specification details. Each FINISHED GOOD represents something that is ready to be sold; however, it is possible that the same finished good is sold many different ways and thus may be related to many PRODUCT instances.

Documentation may be about parts, products, or many other entities throughout the models. Documentation is particularly important within design engineering because this process is about defining and documenting the design and specification of a product.

Part Specifications and Documentation

Figure 2.3 illustrates a data model to record part specification and documentation information. The entity PART SPECIFICATION is used to record all the

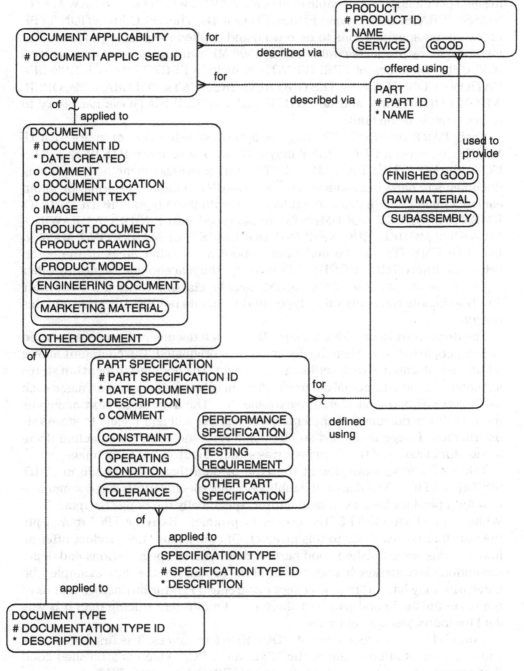

Figure 2.3   Part specifications and documentation.

design specifications applicable to specific PARTs, which include RAW MATE-RIALS, SUBASSEMBLYs, and FINISHED GOODs. The SPECIFICATION TYPE entity allows specifications to be reused and applied to specific products. For instance, many products could have a "1500 MH processing" specification or a "686 CPU." Subtypes of SPECIFICATION include PERFORMANCE SPECIFI-CATIONs, CONSTRAINTs, TESTING REQUIREMENTs, TOLERANCEs, OPER-ATION CONDITIONS and all OTHER PART SPECIFICATIONs necessary to define what is being built.

Each PART or PRODUCT may be described using one or more DOCU-MENTs. Because a DOCUMENT may refer to one or more PARTs or PROD-UCTs, the DOCUMENT APPLICABILITY entity provides the method for linking documents to parts or products. The DOCUMENT maintains information about each document that in this context has to do with the subtype PRODUCT DOC-UMENT. PRODUCT DOCUMENTs are subtyped into PRODUCT DRAWING, PRODUCT MODEL, ENGINEERING DOCUMENT, or MARKETING MATER-IAL. DOCUMENTs may be maintained about many other areas of the enter-prise, and thus OTHER DOCUMENT provides the placeholder for storing other types of documents. Each DOCUMENT may be classified with a DOCUMENT TYPE to handle the many other types of documents not directly shown in this diagram.

The **document id** provides a unique ID for each document. The **date created** allows people to know when the document was originated. The **comment** allows additional information to describe the document. The **document location** stores a pointer to locate the actual document. This may be a server and path name such as "ServerA@C:\product literature\extreme PC." The **document text** maintains the text of the document if the enterprise has the will and means to store this information. **Image** maintains an electronic representation of the actual docu-ment—for instance, if the document was scanned and stored as an image.

Table 2.3 shows examples of the type of data that could reside in PART SPECIFICATION. The data in the table provides specifications and documenta-tion for a product for a PC manufacturer, specifically the Super Extreme 5 PC. While "Super Extreme 5 PC" represents the product, "Extreme 5 PC" represents the part that corresponds to this product. Of course, another product offering may use this same finished good part (and associated specifications and docu-mentation) but market it under a different product name. For example, the enterprise may have a "Business Super Extreme 5 PC" for businesses that have the same finished good part, but there may be different pricing than if it was sold for individual consumer use.

Table 2.4 provides examples of DOCUMENT instances. The first three rows show documents that relate to the "Extreme 5 PC," which is a finished good that corresponds to the product offering of "Super Extreme 5 PC."

The fourth row shows that the "extreme processor" has an engineering draw-ing that diagrams the details of the processor. The last two rows show that the

Table 2.3 Part Specifications

PRODUCT NAME	PART NAME	SPECIFICATION ID	DATE DOCUMENTED	SPECIFICATION TYPE DESCRIPTION	SPECIFICATION TYPE
Super Extreme 5 PC	Extreme 5 PC	1	9/9/2000	Not designed for Macintosh	Constraint
Super Extreme 5 PC	Extreme processor	2	9/10/2000	1000 GigaHz processing	Performance metric
Super Extreme 5 PC	Extreme Main Memory	3	9/10/2000	Expandable to 4GB	Size
Super Extreme 5 PC	Extreme 5 PC	4	9/11/2000	Capable of withstanding up to 120 degrees	Tolerance
Super Extreme 5 PC	Extreme 5 PC	5	9/12/2000	Must be compatible with Windows 2000	Operating condition
Super Extreme 5 PC	Extreme 5 PC	6	9/11/2000	Must pass checksum diagnostics	Testing requirement

Table 2.4 Product and Part Documentation

PRODUCT NAME	PART NAME	DOCUMENT ID	DATE DOCUMENTED	DOCUMENT TYPE DESCRIPTION	DOCUMENT TYPE
Super Extreme 5 PC	Extreme 5 PC	1293893	9/13/2000	CAD machine drawing	Product drawing
Super Extreme 5 PC	Extreme 5 PC	2394790	9/14/2000	Simulated prototype model	Product model
Super Extreme 5 PC	Extreme 5 PC	3242134	9/15/2000	Tool information documentation	Engineering document
	Extreme processor	3084098	6/19/2000	Processor engineering drawing	Engineering drawing
Super Extreme 5 PC		3433324	9/11/2000	Super Extreme PC brochure	Marketing document
Super Extreme 5 PC		3485858	10/21/2000	Extreme PC product line brochure	Marketing document

same product may have more than one document associated with it. The "Super Extreme PC brochure" provides marketing information about this product. The "Extreme PC product line brochure" maintains information about the "Super Extreme PC brochure" as well as other related products that are part of the same product line. This document would be related to those products as well in order to maintain the appropriate documentation available for each product.

Part Specification Roles and Status

Figure 2.4 further defines the part specifications showing the various statuses and stages of part specifications within the product evolution. The diagram also portrays the various parties that may be associated with the part specification.

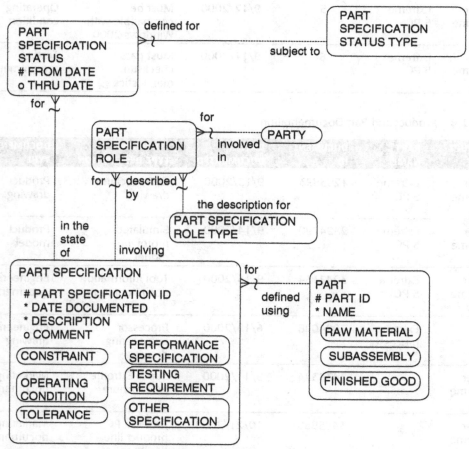

Figure 2.4 Part specifications roles and status.

Table 2.5 Part Specification Status

PART NAME	PART SPECIFICATION	FROM DATE	THRU DATE	PART SPECIFICATION STATUS TYPE
Super Extreme 5 PC	Windows 2000 compatible	10/12/2000	10/14/2000	Requirement specified
		10/14/2000	11/15/2000	Designed
		11/15/2000	11/30/2000	Tested
		12/5/2000	12/6/2000	Approved

Figure 2.4 shows that each PART SPECIFICATION may be in the state of one or more PART SPEFICATION STATUSes, over time, each of which must be defined for a particular PART SPECIFICATION STATUS TYPE. Table 2.5 illustrates the type of data that may be contained within this entity. The table shows that there is a specification for Windows 2000 compatibility. The requirement occurred on October 12. The specification was then accounted for in the design process from October 14 through November 15. The specification was tested during the latter part of November and was approved as passing this part requirement on December 6.

Table 2.6 shows the responsibilities or roles that various parties could play in the specification process. John Smith is responsible for the inclusion of the specification in the design; Larry Jones is responsible for testing to make sure that this specification works properly. The design approval board (an internal organization) is responsible for approving this specification.

Engineering Change

After part specifications are approved, they are subject to change. Engineering changes are normally classified into engineering change requests, engineering change notices, and engineering change releases. Although the engineering community views these as separate events, in reality they represent the statuses or stages that the engineering change goes through. An engineering change is

Table 2.6 Part Specification Party Role

PART NAME	PART SPECIFICATION	SPECIFICATION ROLE	PARTY NAME
Super Extreme 5 PC	Windows 2000 Compatible	Designer	John Smith
		Tester	Larry Jones
		Approver	Design Approval Board

initially requested that results in an engineering change request. Then the enterprise decides to implement the change and issues an engineering change notice, giving all parties involved a heads-up that the change will occur. Finally, the engineering change release is issued, which shows that the engineering change is in effect.

Figure 2.5 shows the data model for engineering changes. An ENGINEERING CHANGE may affect more than one PART SPECIFICATION or PART BOM (bill of materials), and a PART SPECIFICATION or PART BOM may be affected by more than one ENGINEERING CHANGE. The ENGINEERING CHANGE IMPACT entity allows these many-to-many relationships. Each ENGINEERING CHANGE may pass through several ENGINEERING CHANGE STATUSes over

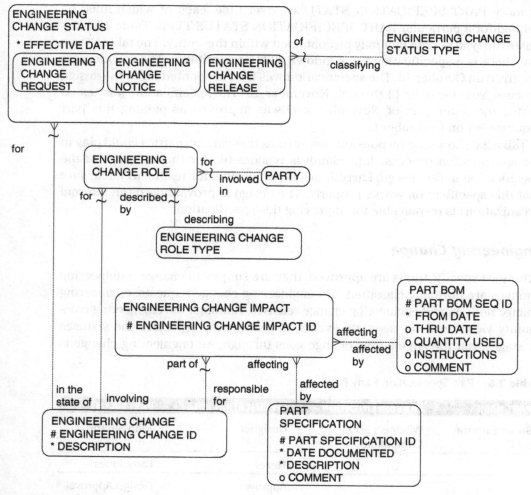

Figure 2.5 Product engineering change.

time. This allows an ENGINEERING CHANGE to evolve from an ENGINEERING CHANGE REQUEST to an ENGINEERING CHANGE NOTICE to an ENGINEERING CHANGE RELEASE. Each ENGINEERING CHANGE may involve one or more PARTYs; therefore, the ENGINEERING CHANGE PARTY ROLE entity is the associative entity between PARTY and ENGINEERING CHANGE.

The enterprise may need to capture the impact that the engineering change has on one or more parts as well as one or more bill of materials structures. For instance, the engineering change may affect the speed of a component and/or it may affect how components fit together. Therefore, the ENGINEERING CHANGE may be responsible for many ENGINEERING CHANGE IMPACTs, each of which may have an effect on a PART SPECIFICATION or a PART BOM (this stands for bill of materials, which will be discussed in the next section). If the enterprise decided to track engineering changes and their effect on product composition, this relationship would show which engineering changes affected which product bill of materials structures.

Table 2.7 provides an example of the type of information that may be recorded for an engineering change. Engineering may have received a request from marketing to include two parallel ports on all the Super Extreme models. This change affects the specifications for the corresponding parts.

Similarly to part specifications, parties play various roles in the engineering changes such as "requestor," "analyst," and "approver." Additionally, the engineering change goes through various stages starting with an ENGINEERING CHANGE REQUEST, which if approved becomes an ENGINEERING CHANGE NOTICE and then when engineered and implemented becomes an ENGINEERING CHANGE RELEASE.

Product Bill of Material, Substitutes, and Inventory Configurations

Manufacturers need to track product bill of materials structures, allowable substitutions, and sometimes the actual configurations of installed items. A product's bill of materials structure represents the prescribed configuration of each product's components and provides a hierarchical breakdown of the product

Table 2.7 Engineering Change

ENGINEERING CHANGE ID	ENGINEERING CHANGE DESCRIPTION	PART SPECIFICATION (AFFECTED)
1098	Two parallel ports must be included on Super Extreme models	Back panel
		Super Extreme motherboard
		Parallel port wire

structure. For instance, a certain product may be made up of assemblies that, in turn, are made up of subassemblies that, in turn, are made up of certain parts. Manufacturers often have the leverage to substitute one part for another, and we therefore need to model the substitution of parts. Aside from modeling the product structure we also need to model the configurations of items that have been manufactured because the item configuration that was actually manufactured may vary from the standard product bill of materials structure (for instance, if a substitute part was used or if a part was switched for another part during a repair effort).

Product Bill of Materials

Products can actually have several structures depending on the view that is being considered. One area of complexity is that different areas of the enterprise may have different views and needs regarding the breakdown of products or parts. For the same product ID or part ID, there may be a different product or part breakdown structure for engineering, manufacturing, sales, and service functions.

The engineering division creates a bill of materials structure to define the part components and subcomponents from an engineering view with precise specifications. This bill of materials structure is used to define the blueprints and engineering specifications for finished goods that are sold as products.

Then the manufacturing division may define the bill of materials differently than engineering. They will reference the engineering bill of materials because they need to manufacture the finished good according to the engineering specifications; however, they may use specific parts in the manufacturing process that best meet their own objectives. For example, they may base their part selection within a bill of materials structure on the cost, quality, and maintainability of the various components. Thus, manufacturing may have their own bill of materials structure for the purpose of building quality and cost-efficient products.

Marketing departments will generally use their gift of creativity to create ingenious ways of grouping together products in the interest of making more sales. They may include incentives and promotional items within their product component structures. For instance, a T-shirt or mouse pad may be one of the components included with certain PCs as part of a marketing package.

Finally, the service department of the enterprise may need a bill of materials to identify the components that are actually installed in a particular deployment of a product. It would be fairly inefficient for service people to maintain or repair the product without knowing the configuration and part component breakdown of the installed product. As a product is used and serviced, the components may change, and it is usually worthwhile for the service technicians to maintain the configurations of the installed product. Service technicians, though, may just want to solve the problem and not worry about maintaining the parts configuration. Often they focus on the immediate solution and are not motivated to track parts usage or substitutions in order to help the next service call. Therefore, the service department generally needs to know and record the breakdown of the part components as the product evolves through usage and maintenance. This is another form of bill of materials structure needed to service components properly.

Other areas of the company, aside from service technicians, can also benefit from knowing the actual configurations of parts and products. For instance, as a finished good changes and undergoes part substitutions even while it is still at the manufacturer's facilities, it is worthwhile to maintain the actual part component breakdown in order to trace the cause of part failures later.

Figure 2.6 shows a data model that handles engineering, manufacturing, and marketing breakdowns of parts and products. The tracking of actual part com-

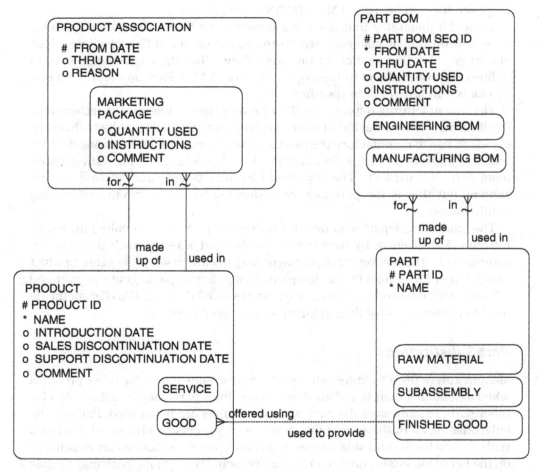

Figure 2.6 Bill of materials.

ponent breakdowns as parts change in the field will be handled later in this chapter in the section, "Inventory Item Configurations."

Figure 2.6 shows a recursive PART BOM (bill of material) entity that provides for PARTs to be made up of other PARTs. These structures allow the enterprise to maintain different part breakdowns to handle both an ENGINEERING BOM and a MANUFACTURING BOM for the same part.

PRODUCTs may also be made up of other PRODUCTs in a many-to-many fashion. The MARKETING PACKAGE entity maintains this information. Note that MARKETING PACKAGE is a subtype of PRODUCT ASSOCIATION since it represents a type of association from one product to another.

Some of the bill of materials structures may be named differently than the model in Figure 2.6 if the enterprise uses specific terminology for various bill of materials structures. The ENGINEERING BOM may be named ENGINEERING CONFIGURATION. The data model shows a MARKETING PACKAGE subtype; however, it could be named MARKETING OFFERING.

Table 2.8 illustrates that the same product, the Super Extreme 5 PC, may have several bill of materials structures based on the different views of an enterprise. The first section of the table shows that the engineering division defines the components in the Super Extreme 5 PC based on certain generic products that have certain specifications.

The manufacturing department then follows the engineering specifications, but it further defines the bill of materials based on the exact products that they decide to use to manufacture the product. For example, manufacturing decides that the "Superfast CPU" is the exact product they will use to meet the requirement of a 1500 MH CPU. The Superfast CPU may be supplied by many organizations, but that is the part they have decided to use in the manufacturing configuration.

The marketing department decides to create a new product called the Super Extreme 5 PC Deluxe by packaging a printer and a T-shirt with the product. Alternatively, the marketing department may decide to keep the same product name, Super Extreme 5 PC, and implement a policy of packaging a printer and a T-shirt with the product. Either way, the MARKETING PACKAGE structure is used to determine what the customer will ultimately receive.

Part Substitutions

Manufacturers need to know what parts may be substituted for other products when assembling their bill of materials. Sometimes parts may be substituted for other parts regardless of the context in which they are being used. Perhaps the enterprise has a business rule that Jones' side panels can always be used as a replacement for Smith's side panels. Sometimes part substitutions are dependent on the bill of materials context. For instance, some types of memory may be able to be replaced only with certain other types of memory within certain PCs.

Table 2.8 Engineering BOM

TYPE OF PART BOM	PART NAME (PARENT)	PART NAME (COMPONENT)	QUANTITY USED
Engineering	Super Extreme 5 PC	1500 MH CPU	1
		100 GB hard drive	2
		101 keyboard	1
		128 MB memory	1
		24"*10"*26" tower case	1
	24"*10"*26" tower case	Side panels	2
		Tower case	1
		½" screws	12
Manufacturing	Super Extreme 5 PC	Superfast CPU	1
		Jones 100 GB hard drive	2
		Flexible 2 keyboard	1
		King's 128 MB memory	1
		24"*10"*26" tower case	1
	24"*10"*26" tower case	Smith's side panels	2
		Perfect tower case shell	1
		Billings ½" screws	12
		24"*10"*26" tower case	1
Marketing	Super Extreme 5 PC Deluxe	Super Extreme 5 PC	1
		Super Extreme printer	1
		Super Extreme T-shirt	1

Part substitutions may occur for engineering or manufacturing needs. Engineering may specify that certain products may be substituted by other products based on an analysis of whether the product will still function the same way. Manufacturing may determine their allowable substitutions based on the costs, quality, and availability of substitute products. Marketing may also deem that some products may be substituted for other products.

Marketing will determine substitutes based on *products* as opposed to parts. They will evaluate whether the substitute products will yield the same customer satisfaction. Product substitutions are not unique to manufacturing and are therefore covered in Volume 1, V1:2.9a and V1:2.9b, via a recursive relationship from PRODUCT to PRODUCT SUBSTITUTE (which is a subtype of PRODUCT ASSOCIATION in Figure 2.9b) as a generic construct.

Figure 2.7 illustrates the data model for part substitutions. There are two types of part substitutions: Part substitutions may be completely independent of the bill of materials structure (PART SUBSTITUTE), or they may vary based on the bill of materials structure context (PART BOM SUBSTITUTE).

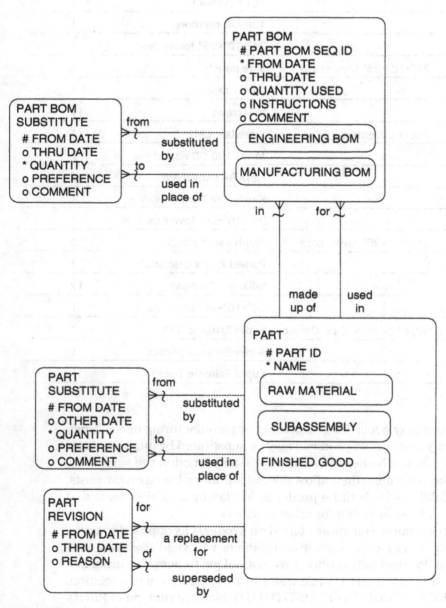

Figure 2.7 Part substitutions.

The PART SUBSTITUTE allows each PART to be substituted by one or more PARTs and conversely for each PART to be used in place of one or more PARTs. The PART SUBSTITUTE is a recursive entity that maintains parts that are substitutes for other parts independent of the context of its usage.

The PART BOM SUBSTITUTE allows each PART BOM to be substituted by one or more different PART BOMs. This records which part components may be substituted for other part components but *only within the context of that specific assembly*. The substitutability of the part may be different within a different bill of materials context.

The data model also includes the PART REVISION recursive entity to show that a substitution is not the same thing as a revision. A PART REVISION identifies which parts have become obsolete and for that reason have been superceded with the newer replacement part.

The primary key to the PART BOM are two part IDs as well as a **part bom seq id**. This shows that the same two parts can be related in more that one subtype. In other words, the ENGINEERING BOM may need to show how the two parts are included in their view, and the MANUFACTURING BOM may need to show how these same two parts are included in their bill of materials structure. Some of the attribute values that are filled in may be different; for example, there may be different **instructions** (used to explain how parts fit together) or **comments**.

The **part bom seq id** is also needed as an extra part of the primary key because it is possible that over the life of the bill of materials structure, the same part combinations may be valid, then invalid, then valid again. To account for the same part combination appearing more than once in different time periods, the **part bom seq id** makes the primary key unique.

Table 2.9 shows that "Smith's side panels" can be substituted for "Jones' side panels" or "Jerry's side panels." The preference is to first try and use "Jones' side panels" before "Jerry's side panels" because the preference of 1 indicates preferred status. The third entry in the table shows that it is OK to substitute two 6' power cords for a 12' power cord.

Table 2.9 Part Substitutions

FROM PART NAME	TO PART NAME	FROM DATE	THRU DATE	QUANTITY	PREFERENCE
Smith's side panels	Jones' side panels	12/9/2000		1	1
Smith's side panels	Jerry's side panels	1/4/2001		1	2
12' power cord	6' power cord	12/30/2000		2	1

Table 2.10 Part BOM Substitutions

FROM PART NAME	FROM PART NAME (PARENT)	TO PART NAME	TO PART NAME (PARENT)	FROM DATE	THRU DATE	QUANTITY
King's 128 MB memory	Super Extreme 3 PC	King's 64 MB memory	Super Extreme 3 PC	12/9/2000		2

Table 2.10 shows an example of a part substitution that is dependent on the bill of materials context. The data shows that a King's 128 MB memory can be replaced with a quantity of two King's 64 MB memory. This replacement is valid only within the Super Extreme 3 PC configuration according to the data in the table.

Note that since there are several recursive entities around PART that share some of the same information, an alternative data model could be to include a PART ASSOCIATION supertype with subtypes of PART BOM, PART SUBSTITUTE, and PART REVISION. This would be similar in concept to the PRODUCT ASSOCIATION entity.

Inventory Item Configurations

Figure 2.6 provided a way to maintain the part breakdown structures for engineering, manufacturing, and marketing purposes. But what about maintaining the part configurations once it has been deployed and serviced over time?

This information may be useful to many areas of the enterprise but, in particular, will be helpful to the service or maintenance function of the enterprise. The service organization in the enterprise is interested in the individual parts and their configurations of the deployed products, in case they need to maintain or replace a part. While the manufacturing BOM is useful to them to determine the standard bill of materials structure for the part they are servicing, certain roles within the enterprise, such as service technicians, need to know more: They need to know the actual parts, or in other words, the inventory items and how they are assembled in the installed part and deployed product that may exist in the field. Therefore, there is another bill of materials structure that is based on the INVENTORY ITEM. Alternatively, some enterprises may decide to use the manufacturing BOM for their service technicians if they decide that this is good enough and they do not want to capture the ongoing detailed breakdowns of the products and its components as changes occur in the field.

The way that actual part configurations will be maintained is by linking INVENTORY ITEMs to other INVENTORY ITEMs. Remember that a good or part defines the *type* of item and an inventory item defines the *physical instantiation* of that item. Aside from knowing how parts are supposed to be configured, the

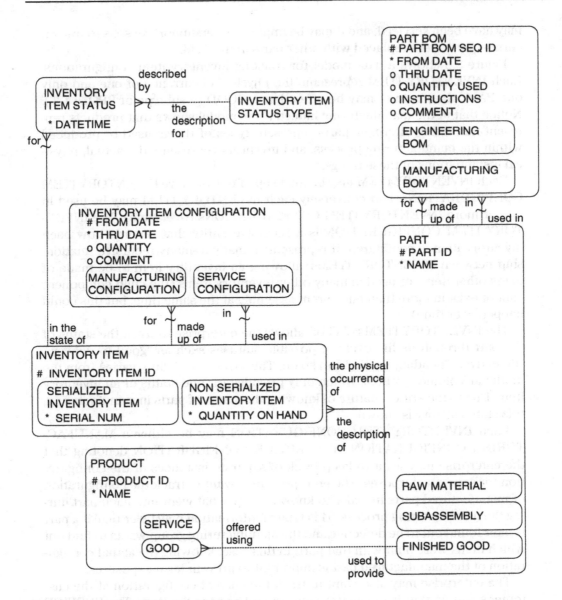

Figure 2.8 Inventory item configurations.

upcoming data model will maintain how the parts are configured within a product as time progresses and changes are made to the parts configurations.

Inventory item configurations may vary from the standard configurations during the manufacturing process or anytime during the life of the part. For instance, the configuration may have changed for a part based on decisions in the manufacturing process, such as using an alternate part. The inventory item may have been serviced, and it may be important for support reasons to track if certain parts were replaced with other parts in the field.

Figure 2.8 shows a data model for tracking inventory item configurations. Each INVENTORY ITEM represents the physical occurrence of one and only one PART that, in turn, may be offered as a GOOD (a subtype of PRODUCT). Notice that in the manufacturing industry, the model shows that products represent marketing offerings, parts represent types of things used or produced within the manufacturing process, and inventory represents the actual, physical instantiations of these things.

Each INVENTORY ITEM may be made up of one or more INVENTORY ITEM CONFIGURATIONs, and conversely each INVENTORY ITEM may be used in one or more INVENTORY ITEM CONFIGURATIONs (over time). The INVENTORY ITEM CONFIGURATION is a recursive entity that records how each inventory item is configured. It represents a many-to-many recursive relationship between INVENTORY ITEMs, allowing an inventory item to be made of many other items or used in many other inventory items (the child component cannot exist in more than one parent assembly at the same time, but this could happen over time).

The INVENTORY ITEM STATUS allows the enterprise to track the status of the part through its life cycle of possible statuses such as "good to deliver," "defective," "pending repair," and so on. This structure slightly varies from the model in Volume 1, V1:3.6, which only provides for one status of an inventory item. Due to the critical nature of knowing the status of parts in manufacturing, this status history is shown.

Each INVENTORY ITEM CONFIGURATION may be either a MANUFACTURING CONFIGURATION or a SERVICE CONFIGURATION denoting that the enterprise may want to keep track of separate instances of the configuration for separate purposes. The enterprise may want to track the configuration of manufactured parts in order to know exactly what went into each part during the manufacturing process. This type of information may be critical if a part is later found out to be defective and the manufacturing group wants to find out which items were built with that part. In this case, knowing the actual configuration of the manufactured part is important to prevent legal exposures.

The enterprise may also want to track the current configuration at the customer's site so that it can better support and service the item. The SERVICE CONFIGURATION would maintain this information. As upgrades and service are performed on a part that is installed at a customer site, the service technician could update the configuration of that inventory item. This would allow future service technicians to know exactly how that item was configured. Notice that the **from date** and **thru date** fields provide a history of configuration changes that could help service technicians diagnose problems.

Table 2.11 provides examples of inventory item configurations. Each inventory item, as identified by its **inventory item id**, is broken down into the com-

Table 2.11   Inventory Item Configurations

INVENTORY ID (PARENT)	PART NAME (PARENT)	INVENTORY ITEM ID (CHILD)	PART NAME (CHILD)	QUANTITY	FROM DATE	THRU DATE
8239894	Super Extreme 5 PC	3874897	Superfast CPU	1	12/23/2000	
		3549775	Jones 100 GB hard drive	2	12/23/2000	
		3489785	Flexible 2 keyboard	1	12/23/2000	
		3486576	King's 128 MB memory	1	12/23/2000	
		4875987	24"*10"*26" tower case	1	12/23/2000	
3978497	24"*10"*26" tower case	3897498	Smith's side panels	2	12/23/2000	3/13/2001
		7438975	Jones' side panels		3/14/2000	
		9380549	Perfect tower case shell	1	12/23/2000	
		4985980	Billings ½" screws	12	12/23/2000	

ponents (also identified by the **inventory item id**) within it. The inventory id 8239894 (a "Super Extreme 5 PC") has specific components that are included within it, namely inventory id 3874897 ("a Superfast CPU"), 3549775 ("Jones 100 GB hard drive"), 3489785 ("Flexible 2 keyboard"), 3486576 ("King's 128MB memory"), and 4875987 ("24"*10"*26" tower case"). The bill of materials for the tower case is shown in the last four rows.

The actual configuration for a product may change over time. The example in Table 2.11 shows that on Mar 14, 2000, Jones' side panels were substituted for Smith's side panels within the tower case. This change of components may have occurred during a service call where the Jones' side panels replaced the Smith's side panels.

Other Product Models

This product section has covered numerous additions to the product data models for manufacturers including parts maintenance, design engineering, bill of materials, substitutions, and inventory item configurations. Many of the other data models in the product chapter may be used for manufacturers such as the product definition, product supplier, inventory item storage, product costs, and product pricing models (refer to Volume 1 product models, V1:3.1–V1:3.11)

Orders

Like most organizations, manufacturing enterprises will have sales and purchase orders. These orders can be modeled using the generic order models from Volume 1, V1:4.1–4.11 and the agreement models V1:4.12–4.16. The general nature of these data models is well suited to manufacturers and represents a solid basis as a starting point. Of course, these models may be customized for the specific enterprise that is being modeled.

There are some unique aspects of the manufacturing enterprise. One difference is in minor modifications in the manufacturing order information needs to accommodate the ordering of parts for its manufacturing operations. Another even more major difference is in the great need for planning for required parts. This is called materials requirements planning or MRP. The first part of this section will discuss changes to order model for manufacturers and the second part of this section will describe how the MRP information requirement need is met.

Usage of the Order Models for Manufacturers

Two of the key needs of the manufacturer are to purchase parts for use in manufacturing their products and then record customer orders that may be custom manufacturing orders ("job shop manufacture" is a term used for organizations that take custom orders) or orders for standard products.

In purchasing parts, the standard PURCHASE ORDER (see V1:4.2) entities can be used; these are subtypes of the ORDER entity. A minor difference is that because it was established that manufacturers will track PARTs as a separate entity from PRODUCT, the PURCHASE ORDER ITEM will now be related to PARTs or PRODUCTs. PURCHASE ORDER ITEMs may be related to PRODUCTs instead of PARTs since there may be other products from suppliers that are not used in the manufacturing process and are not considered parts.

Therefore, Figure 2.9 illustrates that PURCHASE ORDER ITEMs may be for a PART (or PRODUCT) and SALES ORDER ITEMs are for a PRODUCT. For PURCHASE ORDER ITEMs, the manufacturer may be involved in purchasing RAW MATERIALs, SUBASSEMBLYs, or FINISHED GOODs.

Since SALES ORDER ITEM will be for a PRODUCT, the enterprise may elect to define PRODUCTs as including only their own offerings as opposed to including other offerings of competitors and suppliers. With this strategy, the manufacturing enterprise may use the PART entity to define offerings from sup-

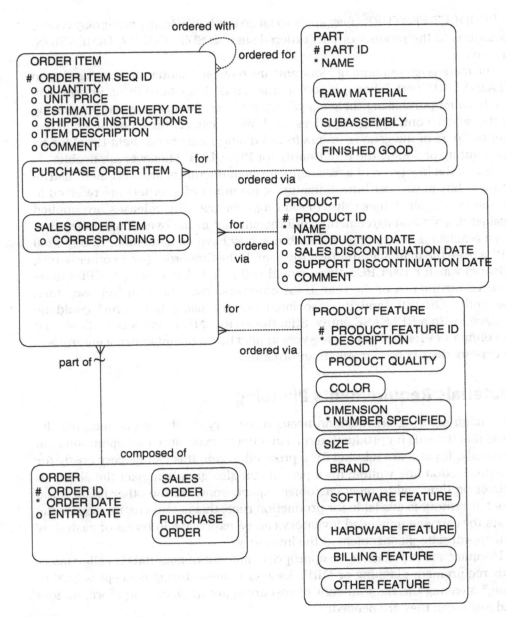

Figure 2.9 Manufacturing orders.

pliers and competitors. Note that this varies from the Volume 1 Product chapter, which defines a PRODUCT as being an offering from the enterprise, supplier, or competitor.

PRODUCT FEATUREs may apply to all orders because any order may record variations to the product or part ordered such as SIZE, COLOR, DIMENSION, and so on.

The models encompassing requirements, requests, quotes, and agreements in V1:4.9–V1:4.16 certainly apply to manufacturers. They have these information needs when purchasing their machinery for manufacturing, when purchasing parts, when contracting suppliers, and when establishing customer agreements. Some of the generic orders from Volume 1 may need slight tweaking by substituting or adding the PART entity for PRODUCT whenever applicable.

One of the key types of agreements for manufacturers are with their distributors to buy parts over time. Sometimes, manufacturing orders are referred to as releases against these distribution agreements. The releases are applied against distribution agreements until the amount in the overall agreement has been reached. For example, a distributor may have an agreement to buy 1200 CPUs from the manufacturer over the year. If the first order (or, in other words, release) was for 100 CPUs, there would still be a balance of 1100 CPUs to be ordered for the rest of the year. If the enterprise uses the term "release," then the entity ORDER (and its associated entities using that term) could be replaced with a RELEASE entity. Still, the AGREEMENT models as illustrated in Volume 1 (V1:4.12–V1:4.16) are very applicable to manufacturing enterprises to capture distributor agreement information.

Materials Requirements Planning

The manufacturing organization needs to be very careful in planning out the parts that it needs for production runs in order to make sure that operations run smoothly. If parts are missing for a production run, this can be very costly for the production line waiting for a part. It can also greatly impact the ability to deliver on time and to meet customer expectations. On the other hand, if too much inventory is available for production runs, this is also costly because the costs for carrying unneeded inventory can be expensive in terms of cash flow and appropriate management of the inventory.

Planning and purchasing the appropriate amount of materials is called materials requirement planning or MRP. Another manufacturing concept is "just in time," meaning the right amount of resources are in place—no more, no less and just when they are needed.

The models already shown in Volume 1 and in this chapter provide most of the information necessary to perform materials requirements planning, and they can facilitate just-in-time operations. Along with the data models, sophisticated algorithms are needed to appropriately determine when and where these resources are needed. The specific algorithms are beyond the scope of this book, however; the following bullet points describe the main data models that need to be used in the MRP process. MRP will primarily determine what parts are needed based on these factors:

- MRP requires forecasting demand in order to determine how much to produce. This can be estimated based on known customer requirements, sales orders, and customer sales agreements. The REQUIREMENT entities (V1:4.9) represents possible orders stemming from these needs, SALES ORDER ITEM (V1.4.2) entities represent commitments for various products, and SALES AGREEMENTs (a subtype of AGREEMENTs) (V1:4.12) represent longer-term commitments to buy from the manufacturer.

- MRP needs to access the existing purchase orders and create new purchase orders based on anticipated needs. Thus, the PURCHASE ORDER ITEMs (V1:4.2) will be reviewed, and new instances of purchase order items will be added. Also, the PURCHASE AGREEMENTs (a subtype of AGREEMENT) (V1:4.12) should be accessed to assess long-term purchasing commitments.

- MRP needs to analyze sales order product commitments and forecasts in order to establish the required manufacturing of parts that are needed cover their product demand. Thus the MANUFACTURING BOM models (V2:2.6) and PART SUBSITITUTION (V2:2.7) models can be used to explode the customer needs down to the needed parts.

- MRP needs to know what parts exist in what locations, and thus the inventory item storage data models (V1:3.6) will most probably be accessed to determine the current level of INVENTORY ITEMS and the FACILITIES in which they are located.

Other models may be used, depending on the MRP algorithms used. For instance, the SHIPMENT entities (V1:5.1–5.8) may be used to determine what parts are expected at what facilities and when they are expected. Many of the PRODUCT ASSOCIATIONs may be used such as PRODUCT COMPLEMENTs and PRODUCT SUBSTITUTEs to better forecast demand.

Thus, most of the data requirements for MRP have already been captured in the data models in these volumes.

Delivery

Similar to many other enterprises, manufacturers need to ship and deliver their products. Therefore, the generic shipment models in Volume 1 (V1:5.1–5.8) are very applicable to manufacturers. Because manufacturers are ultimately responsible for the product, an additional delivery need for some manufacturers is the need to track the deployment and use of their products in the field.

Deployment and Use of Products

Many manufacturing organizations need to track the inventory item and resulting product through its life cycle of customer deployments and use of the product. There are many reasons for this. For instance, billing is sometimes based on use of the product. Additionally, there may be legal exposure reasons for tracking the deployment of parts because the manufacturer may be held liable for things that go wrong with the product. In order to service the product or to determine if the manufacturer's warranties apply, the manufacturer may want to know the history of deployments of that product as well as information about its usage.

Not all manufacturers track the deployment and usage of their products; however, it is common for numerous types of manufacturers. Examples of manufacturers that need to track the deployment and use of their products include manufacturers of meters (postage, gas, oil), hazardous materials, military weapons, and computer-based systems. It is beneficial for most manufacturers to track the deployment and usage of their products; however, it is often difficult for the manufacturer to get this information. The following data structures can be used when the manufacturer has access to deployment information. For some enterprises that are required to capture this information, these data structures may be essential.

Figure 2.10 provides a data model that maintains information about deployment and usage of the product and its associated inventory items as it goes from the warehouse to deployments at various customer locations. This model represents an expansion from the generic model in Volume 1 on inventory item storage, V1:3.6, to handle tracking deployments and use of products. Each INVENTORY ITEM may be deployed as one or more DEPLOYMENTs, which may be of a PRODUCT. Each DEPLOYMENT may be tracked via several DEPLOYMENT USAGEs. DEPLOYMENT USAGEs may be based by recording information for each transaction (ACTIVITY USAGE), recording volumetric usage (VOLUME USAGE, which may be measured in various UNITS OF MEASURE), or TIME PERIOD USAGE. Each of these DEPLOYMENT USAGEs may have specific time periods associated with it, which are recorded via the **start datetime** and **end datetime** attributes or by using the STANDARD TIME PERIOD entity to relate the usage to standard periods of time. For example, a standard time period may be from Jan 15, 2001 to Feb 14, 2001 which represents a period that the enterprise has defined for tracking the usage of their manufactured meters.

Deployments

The model in Figure 2.10 uses some of the generic structures found in Volume 1, V1:3.6, which shows that INVENTORY ITEMs may be located within either a CONTAINER or a FACILITY. This model expands the tracking of items via the

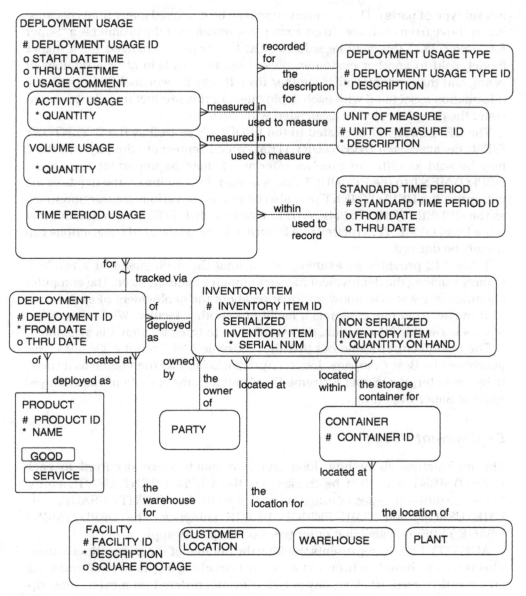

Figure 2.10 Product deployment and usage.

relationship from INVENTORY ITEM to DEPLOYMENT. A DEPLOYMENT represents the event of setting up a product at a customer site with the associated inventory items. The INVENTORY ITEM will usually represent a SERIALIZED INVENTORY ITEM that is indirectly associated with a finished good (this is not shown in this figure, but inventory items are related to parts, and finished good is a subtype of parts). The inventory item may be deployed many times because it may move from customer to customer. For instance, if the product is a "Super Extreme 5 PC," this may be sold to ABC Company, exchanged for a higher model, sold to another customer, picked up as a trade-in after a number of years, and then redeployed at another firm. It may be worthwhile to track the information associated with each deployment of this product in order to understand the complete picture associated with the item.

The DEPLOYMENT is related to the PRODUCT as well as the INVENTORY ITEM. Because each INVENTORY ITEM, which represents the physical item, may be sold as different product offerings, it may be important to link the DEPLOYMENT to the PRODUCT that was sold. Depending on the needs of the enterprise the DEPLOYMENT may also be related to various transactions such as the ORDER ITEM, SHIPMENT ITEM, or INVOICE ITEM. Keep in mind that if the DEPLOYMENT is related to a PRODUCT, the associated transactions can usually be derived.

Table 2.12 provides an example of tracking the deployment of a product, namely tracking the deployment for our computer manufacturer. The computer manufacturer wants to know information about the deployment of each server as it moves from one customer's facility to another facility. While they won't always know this information, they would like to track it when it is available.

The manufacturer found out that the "Extreme 5 PC" serial # 3984d98e was purchased by Best Company, Inc. on April 23, 2000, was then taken as a trade-in by the enterprise, Super Extreme PC Manufacturing, and then was deployed again at Super Duper, Inc.

Deployment Usage

The information about how long and how much usage occurred in each DEPLOYMENT may then be tracked via the DEPLOYMENT USAGE entity. There are different types of usage, as portrayed by the ACTIVITY USAGE, VOLUME USAGE, and TIME PERIOD USAGE subtypes. The DEPLOYMENT USAGE TYPE indicates that other types of usage may apply

ACTIVITY USAGE represents tracking the number of times a product is used. This is usually based on transactions such as tracking the number of times that an aircraft is used, tracking pay-per-view events ordered on a cable subscription, or call detail activity for telecommunications products (in the telecommunications chapter this will be subtyped CALL DETAIL). The **quantity** maintains the amount of times an activity occurred and the relationship to UNIT OF MEASURE determines what measurement to use. For instance, for a security alarm product, the **quantity** may be 5 and the UNIT OF MEASURE may be "number of tripped calls" to establish how many times the customer's security alarm was tripped within a certain time frame. Depending on the business rules of the enterprise, this may result in additional charges.

Table 2.12 Deployment Example

INVENTORY ID	SERIAL #	PART NAME	PRODUCT NAME	OWNED BY	DEPLOYMENT	FACILITY	FROM DATE	THRU DATE
8239894	3984d98e	Extreme 5 PC	Super Extreme 5 PC	Best Company, Inc.	1	124 Main Street	4/23/2000	5/23/2002
			Super Extreme 5 PC	Super Extreme PC Manufacturing		100 Main Street	5/24/2000	5/28/2000
			Refurbished Extreme PC	Super Duper, Inc.	2	3490 Smith Street	5/29/2002	

VOLUME USAGE tracks volumetric amounts for the product being used. For instance, this may be used to track the amount of space used by a customer on a Web hosting company's server. (Customers are often charged by the amount of megabytes they use for their Web sites.) It may be used to track the number of software users who have been accessing a system. It may track the amount of bandwidth being used for a provider of telecommunications connectivity. (Again, the customer may be charged by the amount of bandwidth used.) Other examples are tracking energy consumption or postage meter consumption.

For VOLUME USAGE, the quantity attribute records how much was used or consumed, and the UNIT OF MEASURE relationship defines how the amount is measured. For example, a web hosting company may define the **quantity** as 140 and the UNIT OF MEASURE **description** of megabytes, indicating that there were 140 megabytes used on their server for the indicated time period (using the **start datetime** and **thru datetime** attributes in DEPLOYMENT USAGE).

TIME PERIOD USAGE tracks the time periods for which products are used. Examples of this type of usage include tracking the time periods when a telephone line is active, tracking periods when a postage machine is being used, or tracking periods of time when heavy equipment is being used. The **start datetime** and **thru datetime** attributes of the DEPLOYMENT USAGE may be used to record the time frame of the usage. Alternatively, if there are standard time periods which apply to many TIME PERIOD USAGEs, the relationship to STANDARD TIME PERIOD may be used.

Different enterprises may need to track different types of usage based on their business models. These models may be used by manufacturers that want to track deployments and usage of their products, whenever possible, to gain valuable information and to protect themselves. These models may also be applicable to other industries, such as telecommunications, subscription-based services, gas and oil enterprises, energy companies, or any organization that tracks utilization of their products.

Inventory Ownership

The relationship that an INVENTORY ITEM may be owned by one and only one PARTY, accounts for tracking inventory ownership even when it is not owned by the enterprise. A manufacturer may store inventory that is not theirs (it is on consignment from another party) or may track inventory at a distributor's location that is still owned by the manufacturer (it is on consignment to another party and being warehoused by that party until it is sold). Therefore, it is necessary to record who owns the inventory.

In some cases, inventory ownership may be derivable from associated transactions such as INVOICE ITEMs, which may be related to the INVENTORY ITEM (see V1:7.1a), and which record the sale of specific inventory items to a particular party. Another means of determining ownership is to review the PAY-

MENT transactions, which record payments for INVOICE ITEMs that are related to INVENTORY ITEMs. There may be cases where there are not associated transactions, and hence it may be necessary to explicitly state the ownership of the inventory. For example, there may not have been a sale of the inventory when a supplier has the manufacturer maintain their inventory at the manufacturer's site on consignment. Additionally, depending on the business rules of the enterprise, an INVOICE ITEM for an INVENTORY ITEM may not indicate ownership of the item. For instance, one party may pay for an inventory item even though it is owned by another party.

It is therefore necessary to use the **owned by** relationship from INVENTORY to PARTY in Figure 2.10 to record the party that owns the inventory since it is most probably not derivable information.

Work Effort

Two main areas within the work effort data models that are needed for manufacturing enterprises are these:

- Capturing the process plans that represent how manufacturing runs are supposed to be performed
- Capturing information on the actual work efforts, specifically the production runs, which are how the manufacturing processes actually worked

Of course, the second item is a key aspect of the manufacturing organization. The generic models in Chapter 6 of Volume 1 provide examples of work efforts to manufacture goods, which are usually called production runs (see V1:6.1–6.13). These models from Volume 1 may be used to track the production runs work efforts, generally referred to as shop floor control in manufacturing terms.

The first item in the manufacturing process is to maintain process plans that maintain the standards associated with various types of production runs. The next section provides a model for modeling this information requirement. The model is based on the Volume 1 model for work effort type standards (V1.6.11).

Process Plan

The manufacturer needs a way to define the precise steps that will take place to manufacture their various products. The manufacturer refers to this as their process plans. Many of the models in the work effort section of Volume 1 can be used to record the process plan.

Figure 2.11 shows a slightly modified structure of the generic model in Volume 1 (V1.6.11). The generic model shows the standards used for any work effort, and the model in Figure 2.11 uses basically the same structure with a few

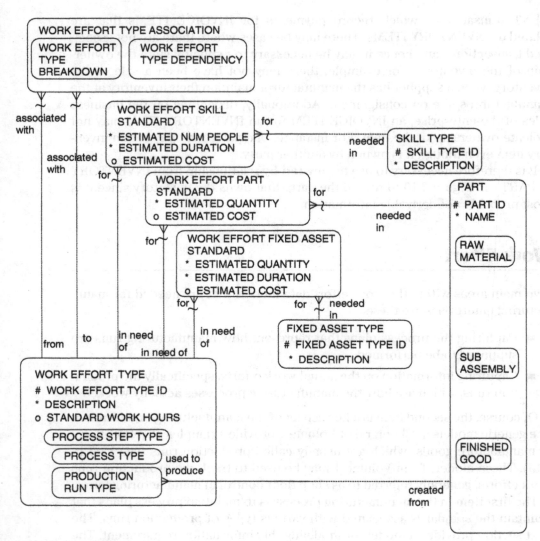

Figure 2.11 Process plan.

additional subtypes and a relationship to PART instead of GOOD in order to use the model for manufacturing process plans.

A process plan really is another WORK EFFORT TYPE that is used to capture the steps and resource requirements for producing or manufacturing various finished goods or subassemblies. The data model shows that each WORK EFFORT TYPE may be subtyped into a PRODUCTION RUN TYPE (a complete cycle of producing a type of item), PROCESS TYPE (describing a type of process involved in the production of an item), and PROCESS STEP TYPE (a lower-level task within a process). Each WORK EFFORT TYPE may be made up of, as well as dependent on several other WORK EFFORT TYPEs, hence the WORK EFFORT TYPE ASSOCIATION entity.

PRODUCTION RUN TYPE, PROCESS TYPEs, and PROCESS STEP TYPEs are subtypes of WORK EFFORT TYPE and so require various types of resources. Within each of these types and levels of work efforts, there are standard needs and metrics for types of skills, parts, and fixed assets. The figure shows associative entities for each of these required resources (WORK EFFORT SKILL STANDARD, WORK EFFORT PART STANDARD, WORK EFFORT FIXED ASSET STANDARD) as it relates to each type of work effort.

The resulting data model maintains information on standard expectations for different types of processes and production runs. This can be used to measure productivity against actual production run/manufacturing standards.

Production Runs

While the previous "process plan" data model (Figure 2.11) maintained standards for manufacturing processes, Figure 2.12 maintains the key information requirements for actual manufacturing production runs. This model uses many of the data constructs from Chapter 6 in Volume 1 (V1:6.1, V1:6.3–6.5, V1:6.8–6.9).

There may be many subtypes of WORK EFFORTs; however, the two most applicable to manufacturing are the PRODUCTION RUN, which tracks the efforts involved in producing products, and MAINTENANCE, which the manufacturing enterprise may track to maintain efforts of fixed machines used in the manufacturing process.

Each WORK EFFORT may be the result of one or more WORK REQUIRE-MENTs; for instance, a requirement to product 1000 widgets on January 15 and then another requirement to product 500 widgets may lead to a WORK EFFORT to produce 1,500 widgets. One WORK REQUIREMENT may lead to several WORK EFFORTs. For instance, a requirement to product 3,000 widgets may result in two production runs of 1,500 each in order to better manage the process—hence the WORK REQUIREMENT FULFILLMENT associative entity to resolve the many-to-many relationship from WORK EFFORT to WORK REQUIREMENT.

The enterprise may track several WORK EFFORT STATUSes, for instance, the **datetime** the production run started, stopped, resumed again, and finished. Each WORK EFFORT may be performed at a FACILITY, such as a plant or a warehouse.

WORK EFFORTs may be associated with other WORK EFFORTs through the WORK EFFORT ASSOCIATION entity. WORK EFFORTs may be broken down

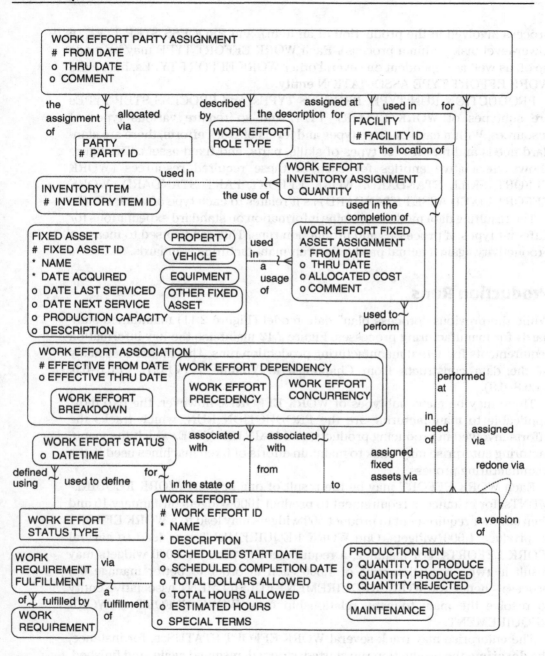

Figure 2.12 Production runs.

into several lower-level WORK EFFORTs, such as processes, or production line tasks via the WORK EFFORT BREAKDOWN. In the production run, some efforts may need to be done before or at the same time as other work efforts, hence the WORK EFFORT DEPENDENCY with subtypes of WORK EFFORT PRECEDENCY and WORK EFFORT CONCURRENCY. WORK EFFORTs may need to be redone with another WORK EFFORT, perhaps if the production run did not produce sufficiently high-quality products. The one-to-many recursion around WORK EFFORT documents this requirement.

WORK EFFORTs require the assignment of PARTYs to do or manage the work, INVENTORY ITEMs, which are the components that may be used in the production run, and FIXED ASSETs, which are the PROPERTY, VEHICLEs or EQUIPMENT or other FIXED ASSETs necessary for the production run. The WORK EFFORT PARTY ASSIGNMENT, WORK EFFORT INVENTORY ASSIGNMENT, and WORK EFFORT FIXED ASSET ASSIGNMENT maintain this information.

Table 2.13 provides an example of using the data structures in Figure 2.12 to maintain information about a production run and its lower-level efforts, in order to produce 100 engraved mechanical pencils.

The work effort chapter has other models that may also be used in manufacturing that are not shown in this chapter, such as time entry tracking, rates charged, costs association with work efforts, and the details of the requirements for a work effort. Rather than repeat these models from Volume 1, the reader is encouraged to review the work effort models from Volume 1.

Invoicing, Accounting, Budgeting, and Human Resources Models

Manufacturing organizations have similar budgeting, ordering, invoicing, payments, accounting, and human resource management processes because these are relatively universal information needs. Many of the other generic data models from Volume 1, including the invoicing (V1:7.1–7.10), accounting/budgeting (V1:8.1–8.12), and human resource models (V1:9.1–9.14), can be used for most manufacturing organizations.

Table 2.13 Production Run Example

WORK EFFORT ID (JOB)	WORK EFFORT SUBTYPE	WORK EFFORT DESCRIPTION	ASSOCIATED WORK EFFORT(S) ID AND DESCRIPTION	WORK EFFORT PARTY ASSIGNMENT	WORK EFFORT INVENTORY ASSIGNMENT	WORK EFFORT FIXED ASSET ASSIGNMENT
28045	Production run	Production run #1 to produce 100 engraved mechanical pencils		John Jones, shop floor manager	100 lead cartridges, 100 erasers, 100 mechanical pencil holders	Mechanical pencil assembly machine, Pencil engraver #125
120001	Activity	Set up production line	28045 Production run #1 51245 Production run #2	Jerry Right, worker, Larry Mooney, worker		
120002	Activity	Operate machinery	28045 Production Run #1	Jerry Right, worker, Larry Mooney, worker		
120003	Activity	Clean up machinery	28045 Production run #1	Harry Cleeney, worker		
120004	Activity	Quality assure goods produced	28045 Production run #1	Joe Quelter, quality assurance manager		
3454587	Task	Move pencil manufacturing machinery in place	120001 Set up production line	Jerry Right, worker		

Star Schema for Manufacturing

The most common needs for data analysis for manufactures are the following:

- Sales analysis
- Financial analysis
- Human resources analysis
- Shipment analysis
- Purchase order analysis
- Inventory management analysis
- Operations analysis, specifically production run metrics

Volume 1 shows standard data mart designs that may be used for manufacturing enterprises such as data analysis models for sales, financial, human resources, shipment, purchase order, and inventory management. The last item, operations analysis, is a unique data analysis need for manufacturers that is concerned with tracking the efficiency of production runs (or work efforts). Manufacturers are generally interested in monitoring production of goods as compared with costs and quality. Some of the questions that manufacturing managers need to answer are these:

- How efficient are my production runs during various time periods?
- Which plants are running most cost-effectively and time-efficiently?
- What are the costs of manufacturing various types of parts?
- What are the average durations for producing various types of parts?
- Which production run managers and supervisors are most effective?

Figure 2.13 shows a data mart design that can be used to answer these questions and track work effort and production run efficiency. The design allows for analysis by MANUFACTURED_PARTS, PLANT_LOCATIONS, TIME_BY_DAY (the time dimension down to a day level), RESPONSIBLE_PARTYS, and PRODUCTION_RUN_TYPEs. Operations managers can use this design to measure their people, work efforts and production run types in terms of **cost**, **cost_variance_from_standard**, **duration**, **duration_variance_from_standard**, **quantity_produced**, and **quantity_rejected** (an indication of quality).

Note that within the figure, the dimensions represent tables and thereby they are named in the plural to distinguish them from entities in the logical data models.

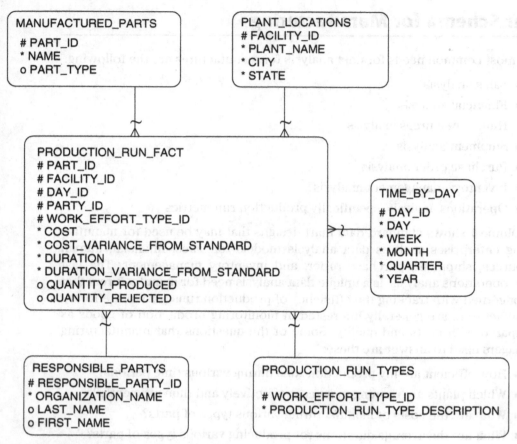

Figure 2.13 Production run star schema.

Production Run Fact

The fact table, PRODUCTION_RUN_FACT, stores various measures for selected work efforts that have to do with production runs. The **cost** maintains how money was spent for the production runs that met the criteria. The **cost_variance_from_standard** measures how much difference there was between the actual cost and the standard cost for the production runs (this may be extracted from the **estimated cost** attributes in the process plan—Figure 2.11). The **duration** provides an average duration for work efforts and is based on the total time between the start and finish times of the work effort. This can be derived from the production run model (Figure 2.12). These start times and finish times are stored in the WORK EFFORT STATUS **datetime** for WORK EFFORT STATUS TYPEs of "start" and "finished." The **duration variance_ from_standard** again measures the difference between the estimated duration from the process plan model (Figure 2.11) and the actual duration (the previously described measure). The **quantity produced** comes directly from the quantity produced attribute in the PRODUCTION RUN, and the **quantity rejected** comes from the PRODUCTION RUN quantity rejected attribute, which is shown in Figure 2.12, **quantity rejected** attribute, which is shown in Figure 2.12.

Dimensions

Most of the data in this data mart design is sourced from information within the work efforts data models and specifically the subtype of WORK EFFORT named PRODUCTION_RUN. This PRODUCTION_RUN information is summarized into the dimensions MANUFACTURED_PARTS, PLANT_LOCATIONS, TIME_BY_DAY, PRODUCTION_RUN_TYPES, and RESPONSIBLE_PARTYS.

The MANUFACTURED_PARTS information represents the part being manufactured and can be found by tracing the relationship from the WORK EFFORT to the corresponding PART being produced. The **part_type** is either "finished good" or "subassembly." If the enterprise needs it, parts can be further categorized.

The PLANT_LOCATIONS dimension is sourced from the WORK EFFORT (PRODUCTION RUN) in this case, which is performed at a FACILITY (more specifically a PLANT), which in turn is located within a city and state using GEOGRAPHIC BOUNDARY. The **facility_id** will be sourced from the manufacturing facility information (FACILITY entity) where the product is produced, most likely a plant. This dimension allows operations managers to compare various plants and analyze which ones are most productive.

The time dimension (TIME_BY_DAY) is granularized to the day and is selected based on the **scheduled end date** within the WORK EFFORT entity for subtype of PRODUCTION RUN. This could also be pulled from the **scheduled start date** of the WORK EFFORT entity (which is a supertype of PRODUCTION RUN). This dimension allows analysis of when the production runs are performed, indicating if there are any trends of productivity during various times of the year.

The information is summarized to group together the statistics for PRODUCTION RUN TYPEs (as opposed to showing individual production runs) because it is designed to analyze the efficiency of various types of production runs.

The RESPONSIBLE_PARTYS entity shows which person or organization was responsible for the production run. This can be extracted from the WORK

EFFORT PARTY ASSIGNMENT, WORK EFFORT ROLE TYPE, and PARTY entities in Figure 2.12. The party that is identified as "supervisor" for the production run could be selected to analyze how effective the party was in achieving the efficiency. If analyzing the effectiveness of each laborer is important, another dimension could be created to record the party that did the work and hence evaluate the efficiencies of each laborer.

This production run star schema therefore gives the operations manager some key information to measure the efficiency and output of different production runs by part, by plant, over time, by responsible party, and by the type of production run. It allows business analysts to measure the productivity and costs of production runs, thus providing a very useful design.

This design captures data summarized by types of production runs. If the specifics on the actual production runs are needed, the design could provide a mechanism to drill back to the source data and see information on each production run.

Variations of Production Run Data Mart

There are several different design variations on the preceding production run data mart that could be used instead of previous star schema, depending on the needs of the enterprise. The following paragraphs describe these options.

The selection criteria could be expanded to include more types of work efforts other than production runs to be able to analyze the efficiency of other types of work efforts. For instance, maintenance efforts on machinery could also be included. If this design is desired, the dimension PRODUCTION_RUN_TYPES could be changed to WORK_EFFORT_TYPES in order to include other types of work efforts. The fact table could be renamed to WORK_EFFORT_FACT.

The granularity of the work effort could be expanded to analyze lower levels of the work in order to better pinpoint where there may be productivity issues. For instance the PROCESS and PROCESS STEP subtypes could be included to analyze bottlenecks in the process. Again, PRODUCTION_RUN_TYPES could be changed to WORK_EFFORT_TYPES and the fact table changed to WORK_EFFORT_FACT.

What if the granularity needed to be at the transaction level, which in this case would be recording the specific production runs? The dimension PRODUCTION_RUN_TYPES could be changed to PRODUCTION_RUNS, and analysis could be drilled down to specific production runs. If there are a great number of production runs, a data warehouse that holds this atomic data may be a better-suited place for this level of information. As mentioned previously, the design could accommodate drilling back to the data warehouse to see this transaction-oriented information. If there are relatively few production runs, the designer may decide to include this detail in the star schema for easier access.

Manufacturing Summary

Some key aspects of changing universal data models for manufacturing organizations are the following:

- Modifying the types and names of party roles and relationships associated with manufacturing
- Distinguishing parts from products and maintaining information about parts
- Adding design engineering data models for specifying parts and products
- Adding models to accommodate engineering changes
- Adding bill of materials structures for various views of the organization, which may include engineering, manufacturing, and marketing
- Providing more comprehensive models for product (and parts) substitutions
- Adding inventory item configuration data models to record changes to the actual parts
- Tracking deployments and usage of products and parts over time
- Changing the names of the work effort and work effort standards models to focus on production runs

Manufacturers can use many of the data warehouse and data mart designs from Volume 1, such as the sales analysis, financial analysis, and human resource analysis designs. Manufacturers usually have a strong need to monitor and analyze their operations in order to improve productivity and reduce costs. One example of a data mart design was provided that can be used to help operations managers analyze their production run efficiency.

Figure 2.14 provides a high-level summary of the manufacturing models.

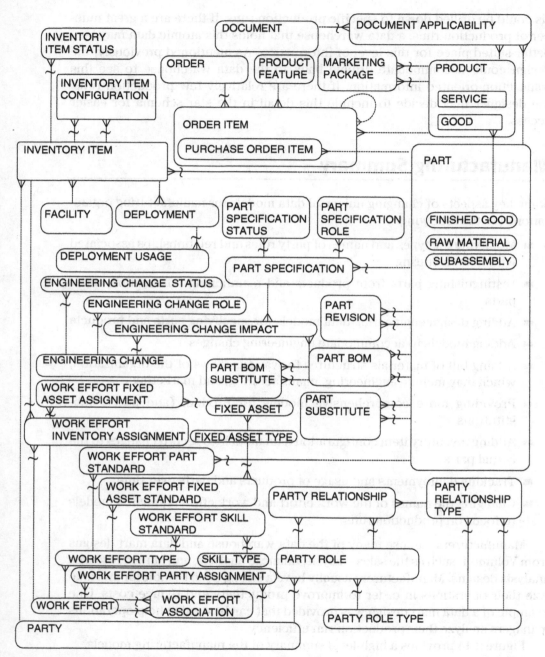

Figure 2.14   Overall manufacturing model.

CHAPTER

3

Telecommunications

Telecommunications companies provide an important service: They allow us to better communicate with each other. Telecommunications companies include local exchange carriers (LECs), regional Bell operating company (RBOC or BOC), competitive local exchange carriers (CLECs), wireless communications providers, digital local exchange carriers (DLECs), interexchange carriers (IEC) (a synonym for long distance carriers), cable companies, resellers of telecommunications goods and services, and organizations involved in a combination of these functions. This chapter will focus principally on the needs of enterprises that provide communications connectivity; although many of the data structures in this chapter may apply to other industries as well. For instance, enterprises with information needs to manage their infrastructures, such as utility organizations, may use similar types of data constructs (even though the entities may have different names).

Telecommunications companies are concerned with issues such as the following:

- How can we build and support high-quality telecommunications networks?

- How can we build innovative products and services to enhance communications?

- How can we improve customer service and satisfaction with our offerings?

- How can we maximize revenues and minimize costs?

- How can we ensure that our systems accommodate the fast technological pace within telecommunications?

To answer these types of questions, telecommunications enterprises need to track information about the following:

- The people and organizations they are concerned with, namely, telecommunications carriers, billing agents, distribution channels, customers, suppliers, employees, and internal organizations.

- Their network infrastructure including network components, assemblies, circuits (logical configurations providing communications channels), issues regarding the network, and availability of the network. This is sometimes referred to as service provisioning, which includes network engineering, construction, and turn-up.

- Service orders and repair orders. There is a need to be able to order telecommunications services and items, easily activate service, and track repair orders to fix problems.

- Invoice and billing data.

- Products, product deployments, and deployment usage.

- Work effort management to monitor projects to construct and repair network facilities.

- Budgeting and accounting information.

- Human resources management.

Volume 1 addresses many of the needs of a telecommunications company. For instance, it addresses the following:

- People and organization structures that can be used within telecommunications.

- Product structures that a telecommunications company can build on. These product structures need to be capable of not only handling today's products, but anticipating future telecommunications product information requirements, taking into consideration the fast pace of change within this industry.

- Customer and prospect needs and demographics.

- Order data models that can be used for ordering items, activating service, or responding to repair orders.

- Shipment models used to track shipments of products or parts sent out to customers.

- Invoice models that can be used to store telecommunications invoice information.

- Work effort models that can be used to track network installation and repair efforts.

- Accounting, budgeting, and human resource models to manage finances and people.

Key aspects of telecommunications that are not addressed in Volume 1 include these:

- The information needed to maintain one of a telecommunications enterprise's most important assets: their network facilities

- Data structures set up specifically for telecommunications products, deployments of products, and product usage

- Data structures that tie networks (the physical components) to circuits (logical configurations) to products (marketing offerings)

- Information showing product and network availability when ordering telecommunications services

- Specific data structures to handle invoicing within telecommunications

Table 3.1 shows which models can be used directly from Volume 1, which models need to be modified, which models are not used, and which new models are required. For the people and organizations area, most of the models from Volume 1 apply; however, there is a need to add PARTY ROLEs and PARTY RELATIONSHIPs suitable to telecommunications enterprises. Many of the product models can be used with appropriate modifications and product subtyping. For instance, a DEPLOYMENT entity will be added to identify the instance of a telecommunications product currently in use by customers. The most significant data modeling requirement for telecommunications is adding new data structures to accommodate information associated with the network infrastructure. This includes adding data models to handle network assemblies, network components, circuits, products, product deployments, and deployment usage. The order models from Volume 1 generally apply with some minor modifications such as tracking the deployment of the product ordered as well as having the capabilities to track network availability. The order also needs to accommodate new products or upgrades and maintenance, depending on whether the service order is for a new product or a telecommunications product that is already deployed at a customer site. The invoice models need some changes, for example, including relationships to the billing agent and the ability to bill for deployment usage and deployed products.

Table 3.1 Volume 1 and Volume 2 Data Model for Telecommunications

SUBJECT DATA AREA	USE THESE VOLUME 1 MODELS DIRECTLY	MODIFY THESE VOLUME 1 MODELS (AS DESCRIBED IN VOLUME 2)	DO NOT USE THESE VOLUME 1 MODELS	ADD THESE VOLUME 2 MODELS
People and organizations	Models V1:2.1–V1:2.14 except V1:2.5 and V1:2.6	Party roles and relationship, V1:2.5, and V12.6 modify with Telecommunications party roles and relationships V2:3.1		
Product		Product models V1:3.1–3.11		Telecommunications products and features, V2:3.2, Product deployments, V2:3.3, Telecommunications product associations, V2:3.4, Network components V2:3.5, Network assembly, V2:3.6, Products, circuits, and network assemblies, V2:3.7, Products, circuits, and network assembly capabilities, V2:3.8, Communication IDs and contact mechanisms, V2:3.9
Order	Requisition, request, quote, V1:4.9–4.11 Agreement models, V1:4.12–4.16 (subtype agreements) with slight modifications	Generic order models, V1:4.1–4.8, Service order model as a customized version of orders, V2:3.10		

Delivery	Shipment models, V1:5.1–5.8 with slight modifications	Product deployment usage, V2:3.11
Work effort	Work effort, V1:6.1–6.11 for internal projects with slight modifications	
Invoicing	Invoice models, V1:7.17.9 with slight modifications	Telecommunications billing, V2:3.12
Accounting	All models, V1:8.1–8.11	
Human resources	All models, V1:9.1–9.13	
Telecommunications deployment usage star schema		Deployment usage star schema, V2:3.13

People and Organizations in Telecommunications

Telecommunications companies generally have similar needs for tracking people and organizations as other enterprises. They need to track information about their customers, suppliers, employees, distribution channels, and organization structures.

Generic Person and Organization Roles from Volume 1

Figure 3.1 shows a customized version of the generic party roles and relationships model (V1:2.6a) for telecommunications enterprises. Many of the generic roles are included. There are generic person roles such as EMPLOYEE, CONTACT, CONTRACTOR, and FAMILY MEMBER. There are generic ORGANIZATION ROLEs of COMPETITOR, DISTRIBUTION CHANNEL, REGULATORY AGENCY (in telecommunications this may be more significant), PARTNER, ASSOCIATION, HOUSEHOLD, SUPPLIER, INTERNAL ORGANIZATION and ORGANIZATION UNITs of PARENT ORGANIZATION, SUBSIDIARY, DEPARTMENT, DIVISION, and OTHER ORGANIZATION UNIT. Common subtypes that apply to either a PERSON or ORGANIZATION include SHAREHOLDER and PROSPECT.

Party Roles and Relationships for Telecommunications

Figure 3.1 customizes the generic party roles and relationship model by adding the subtypes of BILLING AGENT and TELECOMMUNICATIONS CARRIER. Also, CUSTOMER is shown as two separate party role subtypes: RESIDENTIAL CUSTOMER and ORGANIZATION CUSTOMER in order to accommodate servicing individuals and organizations.

A unique aspect of the data model is the TELECOMMUNICATIONS CARRIER subtype allowing the enterprise to track telecommunications carriers, for example, long distance carriers, competitive local exchange carriers (CLECs), interexchange carrier (IEC), and data local exchange carriers (DLECs). Interexchange carriers (also referred to as long distance carriers), CLECs, and DLECs could be subtypes of TELECOMMUNICATIONS CARRIER if more

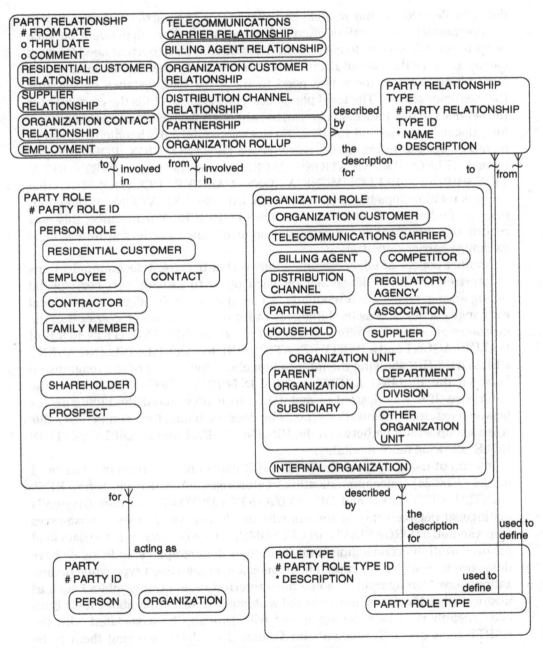

Figure 3.1 Telecommunications party roles and relationships.

detail is desired on the model. The reason for the carrier subtype is that telecommunications carriers often work together and are dependent on each other to provide service to customers. Thus there is an important need for each carrier to store data about each other. For instance, when a customer orders local phone service, there is a need to track the long distance carrier that the customer selects. The local phone company typically bills the customer for the services of this long distance carrier, although the customer could have the long distance carrier bill for their services separately. To handle the need to maintain carrier information, there is an ORGANIZATION ROLE subtype named TELECOMMUNICATIONS CARRIER, and there is a PARTY RELATIONSHIP of TELECOMMUNICATIONS CARRIER RELATIONSHIP that records relationships between the INTERNAL ORGANIZATIONS of the enterprise and other TELECOMMUNICATIONS CARRIERs. For instance, this may record the relationships of approved long distance carriers within a local exchange carrier organization.

Another aspect of telecommunications is that because telecommunications enterprises are often dependent on each other to provide services, special billing arrangements are often made. A common example occurs when a local exchange carrier acts as the billing agent for the long distance carrier that the customer chooses. Therefore, the model shows an ORGANIZATION ROLE of BILLING AGENT and a PARTY RELATIONSHIP to record the BILLING AGENT RELATIONSHIP showing the information about the nature of the relationship between the BILLING AGENT and the INTERNAL ORGANIZATION of the enterprise. If it was desired to maintain information about the billing agents between external organizations (i.e., who does the billing for a competitor), this relationship would be between the BILLING AGENT and an ORGANIZATION ROLE, allowing more flexibility.

Instead of using the generic CUSTOMER data construct from our Volume 1 model (V1:2.6a), telecommunications enterprises often use the terms RESIDENTIAL CUSTOMER and ORGANIZATION CUSTOMER as they frequently distinguish between the customers who are in residences versus businesses (represented as ORGANIZATION CUSTOMER). One difference in the data kept for organizations versus individuals is in their demographics. Individuals have demographics such as occupation, income, and employment type while organizations have demographics (sometimes referred to as firmographics) such as business classifications and financial statement information about their business customers. These demographics will generally be associated with the PARTY (and occur throughout the Volume 1 models), allowing them to be maintained independently of their customer role.

Example of Party Roles and Relationships for Telecommunications

Our case example for this chapter is a local telephone provider named Transparent Communications. Table 3.2 provides examples of roles within this enterprise.

According to Table 3.2, "Transparent Communications," "Transparent Networks," and "Transparent Digital Services" are all internal organizations of the enterprise being modeled, with Transparent Communications as the parent organization. "ABC Manufacturing" is an organization customer, "John Smith" is a customer contact, "Len Goldstein" is a residential customer, and "ABC Manufacturing" also happens to be a supplier of "Transparent Communications." "Jerry Right" is a supplier contact. Table 3.2 show that "Bill Jones" is an employee and "Hal Sellers" is an agent. The table shows two examples of telecommunications carriers, namely, "ABCD Long Distance" and "WXYZ Long Distance." Finally, "ABCD Long Distance" provides billing for some services and is therefore a billing agent.

Table 3.2 Telecommunications Party Roles

PARTY ROLE	PARTY NAME
Internal organization (and parent organization)	Transparent Communications
Internal organization (and subsidiary)	Transparent Networks
Internal organization (and subsidiary)	Transparent Digital Services
Organization customer	ABC Manufacturing
Contact (customer contact)	John Smith
Residential customer	Len Goldstein
Supplier	ABC Manufacturing
Contact (supplier contact)	Jerry Right
Employee	Bill Jones
Distribution channel (agent)	Hal Sellers
Telecommunications Carrier	ABCD Long Distance
Telecommunications Carrier	WXYZ Long Distance
Billing agent	ABCD Long Distance

Table 3.3 provides additional information about which roles are involved within which relationships. It is not enough to simply show the role; it is important to show the various relationships that the same role may play. For example, "Transparent Network Subsidiary" is a subsidiary of "Transparent Communications." The next two rows show that "ABC Manufacturing" is an organization customer of both of the two internal organizations within the enterprise, "Transparent Networks" and "Transparent Communications." Therefore there are two relationships for "ABC Manufacturing" that may have different information associated with them, such as different priorities, statuses, and so on. "John Smith" is a contact within the manufacturing firm. "Len Goldstein" is a residential customer of "Transparent Communications." "ABC Manufacturing" is a supplier of "Transparent Communications" (yes, they are a customer also). One of its supplier contacts is "Jerry Right." The table shows that "Bill Jones" is an employee of "Transparent Communications." Hal Sellers is an agent who distributes products and services for "Transparent Communications." The next two rows show that "ABCD Long Distance" and "WXYZ Long Distance" are long distance carriers that can offer these services through "Transparent Communications." The last row shows that "Transparent Communications" is a billing agent for "ABCD Long Distance." This party relationship instance shows that "Transparent Communications" serves to provide bills for "ABCD Long Distance" in order to make things easier for the customer.

Telecommunications Products

The majority of the data model changes for the telecommunications industry are within the product subject data area. Many of the Volume 1 product data models need to be modified for telecommunications environments, and there is a need for many new product models that can capture the information requirements for the network infrastructure. The modifications needed to the generic data models from Volume 1 will be addressed first, and the section that follows will provide data structures to accommodate the telecommunications network as well as how products relate to the network infrastructure models.

Telecommunications Modifications to the Generic Product Data Models

This section will discuss the changes and additions to the generic product data model constructs needed for telecommunications. This section will address the types of products and features within telecommunications, provide an additional product deployment model, and show various ways that products can relate to each other.

Table 3.3 Telecommunications Party Relationships

PARTY ROLE 1	PARTY 1	PARTY ROLE 2	PARTY 2	PARTY RELATIONSHIP TYPE
Organization unit (parent)	Transparent Network subsidiary	Organization unit (subsidiary)	Transparent Communications	Organization roll-up (subsidiary)
Organization customer	ABC Manufacturing	Internal organization	Transparent Communications	Organization customer relationship
Organization customer	ABC Manufacturing	Internal organization	Transparent Networks	Organization customer relationship
Contact (customer contact)	John Smith	Organization customer	ABC Manufacturing	Organization contact relationship (customer contact relationship)
Residential customer	Len Goldstein	Internal organization	Transparent Communications	Residential customer relationship
Supplier	ABC Manufacturing	Internal organization	Transparent Communications	Supplier relationship
Contact (supplier contact)	Jerry Right	Internal organization	ABC Manufacturing	Organization contact relationship (supplier contact relationship)
Employee	Bill Jones	Internal organization	Transparent Communications	Employee relationship
Distribution channel (agent)	Hal Sellers	Internal organization	Transparent Communications	Distribution channel (agent) relationship
Long distance carrier	ABCD Long Distance	Internal organization	Transparent Communications	Telecommunications Carrier relationship
Long distance carrier	WXYZ Long Distance	Internal organization	Transparent Communications	Telecommunications Carrier relationship
Billing agent	Transparent Communications	Telecommunications Carrier	ABCD Long Distance	Billing agent relationship

Most of the product data models from Volume 1 can be used within a telecommunications environment. Telecommunications products may have features (V1:3.4), identifiers (V1:3.3), categorizations (V1:3.2), suppliers (V1:3.5), manufacturers (V1:3.5), prices (V1:3.7), costs (V1:3.8), components, substitutes, replacements (V1:3.9a and V1:3.9b), and some products may be inventoried (V1:3.6). While many of the product data model structures remains similar, the subtypes and instances within telecommunications are quite different.

Figure 3.2 provides a data model that shows subtypes of PRODUCT and PRODUCT FEATURE that are relevant within telecommunications enterprises. It is primarily based on the generic product feature model shown in V1:3.4.

Figure 3.2 shows that telecommunications products, like most industries, are subtyped into SERVICE and GOOD to show how to provide maintenance of tangible, hard products as well as service-oriented products. Services are further subtyped into CONNECTIVITY SERVICE, CONNECTIVITY FEATURE, LISTING OFFERING, CHANNEL SUBSCRIPTION, INSTALLATION AND REPAIR SERVICE, SERVICE AGREEMENT OFFERING, CREDIT CARD OFFERING, and OTHER TELECOMMUNICATIONS SERVICE to cover other services not shown here. GOODs include subtypes of TELECOMMUNICATIONS SYSTEM, TELECOMMUNICATIONS DEVICE, and TELECOMMUNICATIONS ACCESSORY.

Similar to the generic product feature data model in Volume 1 (V1:3.4), each PRODUCT may be available with many PRODUCT FEATUREs and each PRODUCT FEATURE may be used within many PRODUCTs, hence the associative entity PRODUCT FEATURE APPLICABILITY. This entity shows what PRODUCT FEATUREs may be used within which PRODUCTs. The PRODUCT FEATURE INTERACTION entity shows which PRODUCT FEATUREs are incompatible with (FEATURE INTERACTION INCOMPATIBILITY), or dependent on (FEATURE INTERACTION DEPENDENCY), other PRODUCT FEATURES within the context of a PRODUCT.

Telecommunications Services

CONNECTIVITY SERVICEs include LOCAL CONNECTIVITY for basic telephone service, LONG DISTANCE CONNECTIVITY for capability to provide service across LATAs (Local Access and Transport Area—defines geographic service area regions identified by a three-character code, which implies long distance if going from one LATA to the next), WIRELESS CONNECTIVITY for having a service on which to make cell phone calls, DEDICATED LINE for buying exclusive usage of a circuit from one location to another location, and INTERNET ACCESS for signing up for dial-up access to the Internet via an Internet service provider. These are only examples of some of the subtypes of CONNECTIVITY SERVICE that are possible.

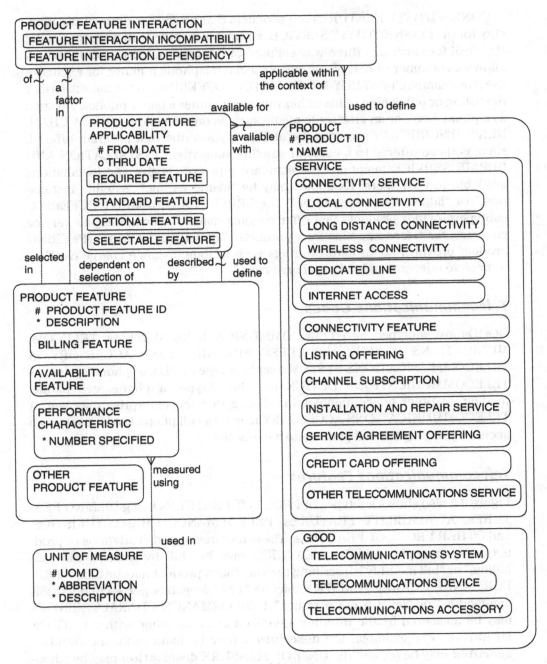

Figure 3.2 Telecommunications products and features.

CONNECTIVITY FEATUREs are products that provide additional functionality for the CONNECTIVITY SERVICE. Examples include "call waiting," "caller ID," "call forwarding," "three-way calling," or a "phone number option," which allows a customer to reserve or buy a special telephone number for exclusive use (for example, 1-800-BUY-MINE). LISTING OFFERINGs offer the subscriber the listing or publishing of his or her number in either a paper publication such as a phone book or an electronic media such as online yellow pages. A CHANNEL SUBSCRIPTION provides the ability to subscribe to a program offered, such as those offered to a cable or satellite subscriber. INSTALLATION AND REPAIR SERVICE maintains the standard types of repairs and installations available to customers. Examples may be "inside wiring," "satellite installation," or "adjust satellite receiver." The SERVICE AGREEMENT OFFERING subtype provides products that offer ongoing maintenance and repair service coverage for telecommunications products. The CREDIT CARD OFFERING product provides credit card offerings such a "long distance charge card" or "complete telecommunications charge card."

Telecommunications Goods

GOODs are subtyped into TELECOMMUNICATIONS SYSTEMs, TELECOMMUNICATIONS DEVICE, and TELECOMMUNICATIONS ACCESSORY. A TELECOMMUNICATIONS SYSTEM may be a type of PBX or phone system. A TELECOMMUNICATIONS DEVICE may be a type of phone, cell phone, modem, or other telecommunication device that the enterprise may sell. A TELECOMMUNICATIONS ACCESSORY may be a cell phone holder case or an accessory to plug the cell phone into a car outlet.

Telecommunications Features

Figure 3.2 also shows subtypes of PRODUCT FEATUREs being BILLING FEATUREs, AVAILABILITY FEATUREs, PERFORMANCE CHARACTERISTICS, and OTHER PRODUCT FEATUREs. These features provide variations of products. For example, BILLING FEATUREs may be "bill by usage," "flat rate billing," or "bill monthly" describing the way that a product may be billed. PERFORMANCE CHARACTERISTICs may be "1.544 Megabits per second," "128K bandwidth," or "level 5 noise rating." PERFORMANCE CHARACTERISTICs may be measured by the **number specified** attribute along with a UNIT OF MEASURE. For example, the **description** may be bandwidth, the **number specified** may be 56, and the UNIT OF MEASURE **description** may be "thousand characters per second." AVAILABILITY FEATURE provides a means to offer different types of availability on a product. For example, a certain CONNECTIVITY SERVICE may be available all the time or at various times during the week, such as during business hours only. INSTALLATION AND REPAIR SERVICE may have AVAILABILITY FEATUREs to distinguish different times that it may be available.

The subtypes of REQUIRED FEATURE, STANDARD FEATURE, OPTIONAL FEATURE, and SELECTABLE FEATURE are taken from the generic product feature data model (V1:3.4) to indicate if the feature as used with the products is required to be in the product, the default (standard) for the product, an optional choice available by the customer, or that the customer must select from one or more features.

Product Feature Interaction

Another generic data structure from the product feature data model (V1:2.4) is the PRODUCT FEATURE INTERACTION recursive relationship that stores which features are incompatible with other features within a product (FEATURE INTERACTION INCOMPATIBILITY) or what features are dependent on other features. For example, perhaps a fax queuing feature on a specific fax connectivity service is dependent on operating from a line having a 256K bandwidth. (Other bandwidths could be stored as incompatible features with the fax queuing feature).

Telecommunications Product and Product Feature Example

Table 3.4 provides examples of various telecommunications products. The first two rows show two different products within the LOCAL CONNECTIVITY subtype. Even though these may be similar in capabilities and functionality, there may be differences in pricing or features available for these different services. For instance, the second row shows that for residential services the customer has an option to sign up for either a usage-based service where the customer would pay for each local call, or unlimited usage where there would be the same rate, regardless of the number of local calls. The next two rows show examples of the subtype DEDICATED LINE. These dedicated line services have features regarding the bandwidth of 1.544 megabits per second or 44.763 megabits per second. Some enterprises will choose to create different products for each of these bandwidths instead of using the PRODUCT FEATURE instances. However, the product feature allows flexibility to define products and features according to the business rules of the enterprise, which need to be defined. Connectivity features include "call waiting," "call forwarding," and the ability to have a "personalized telephone number," such as 1-800-TRY-USGUYS because these are products added to basic connectivity services. The next few rows show listings available. Although these are products, they may or may not

Table 3.4 Telecommunications Products and Features

PRODUCT TYPE	PRODUCT NAME	PRODUCT FEATURES
Connectivity service—local connectivity	Business Line	
Connectivity service—local connectivity	Residential Line	Billing feature—usage based Billing feature—unlimited usage
Connectivity service—dedicated line	High Grade Dedicated Office Line	Performance characteristic, 512K, 1.544 megabits per second or 44.763 megabits per second
Connectivity service—dedicated line	High Grade Dedicated Residential Line	Performance characteristic, 128K, 512K, 1.544 megabits per second, 44.763 megabits per second, 512 KB bandwidth
Connectivity feature	Call Waiting	
Connectivity feature	Call Forwarding	
Connectivity feature	Personalized Telephone Number	
Listing Offering	Yellow Pages Listing	
Listing Offering	White Pages Listing	
Listing Offering	Internet Yellow Pages Listing	
Good—telecommunications system	PBX Spectacular 1000	
Good—telecommunications device	Cellular Phone 1000	
Good—telecommunications device	Princess Phone 2300	
Service agreement offering	One-year maintenance agreement	Availability feature—24*7 or business hours only

have prices associated with them. Then goods are shown that a telecommunications enterprise may offer. Finally, an example of a service agreement plan is shown with various variations on availability of service such as 24 hours a day, 7 days a week (24*7) or just during business hours. There could be many more variations for this availability feature for the product.

Product Deployment

Now that examples of types of products have been illustrated, the next step is to define the instantiations of those products. In other words, when a customer buys a product, the telecommunications enterprise needs to track the deployment of each product.

One of the key differences is that while some products may be inventoried, telecommunication enterprises principally sell usage of their network facilities (or someone else's network facilities). Therefore, there is a need to track the product after it is sold and while it is being used instead of just accounting for the sale of an inventory item out of stock (although we need to allow that also). Telecommunications companies need to track what items are deployed and where they are deployed in order to properly service them.

Figure 3.3 shows a data model that maintains deployments and instantiations of products. The DEPLOYMENT entity stores instances of all products or inventory items that have been bought by particular customers. The DEPLOYMENT entity is created for products that need to be tracked after the installation. The DEPLOYMENT may represent the installation of a PRODUCT or of an INVENTORY ITEM (for GOODs that are being sold). The DEPLOYMENT may be of a product when the customer is not buying an inventoried item, such as when a customer buys the use of a residential line. Because it is important to keep track of where these products are deployed, each DEPLOYMENT is deployed at one or more FACILITY DEPLOYMENTs. The FACILITY may be a CENTRAL OFFICE (the location for the switches and other network equipment that handles a specific geographical area) or may be tracked by CUSTOMER LOCATION if more specific information is desired. This allows the enterprise to know at which facilities the product is deployed.

Each DEPLOYMENT may be deployed with one or more DEPLOYMENT FEATUREs, allowing the enterprise to track what features were selected and installed for the customer. While the PRODUCT to PRODUCT FEATURE relationship maintains what features are available, the DEPLOYMENT to PRODUCT FEATURE relationship maintains the features that were selected and deployed.

Some types of products are instantiated and tracked by using relationships to other entities instead of DEPLOYMENT. The diagram shows that the instantiation of SERVICE AGREEMENT OFFERINGs is via a relationship to AGREEMENT, which would be set up with a particular customer(s). A LISTING OFFERING is implemented via a LISTING, which would track information such as the text and formatting of the listing in a phone book or electronic media.

Each PRODUCT may have many PRICE COMPONENTs that allow for ONE TIME CHARGEs, RECURRING CHARGEs, or charges base on UTILIZATION

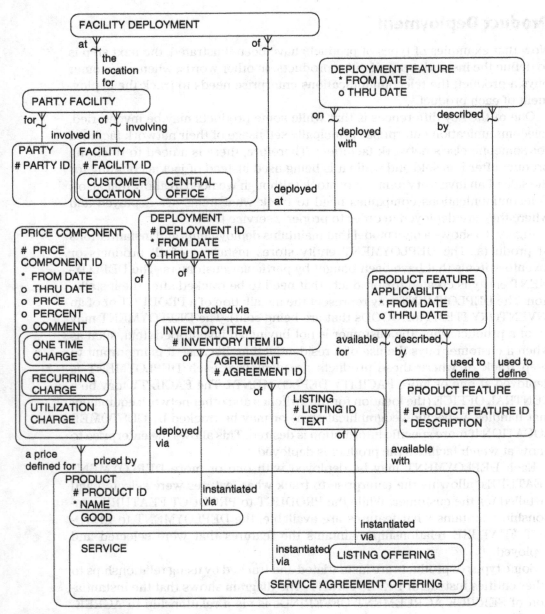

Figure 3.3 Product deployments.

CHARGEs (see the product pricing model, V1:3.7, for more details on the generic pricing model). Only part of the pricing model is shown; however, the generic model in Volume 1 (V1:3.7) is highly applicable for telecommunications enterprises.

Table 3.5 gives some examples of the types of data that may reside in the DEPLOYMENT entity. As the table shows instantiations of products, each of the products may have relationships with DEPLOYMENTs, INVENTORY ITEMS (for goods that are deployed and need to be tracked), AGREEMENTS with customers, or LISTINGs. It is critical to track deployments of connectivity services, and the table shows product deployment IDs to track the instances of both local connectivity service and dedicated lines. The first row shows local connectivity service at Len Goldstein's house at 234 Main Street. Also the billing feature of usage-based service (as opposed to flat-rate billing) was selected, and thus the UTILIZATION CHARGE subtype of PRICE COMPONENT will apply. (The feature of usage-based service is a different piece of information than the UTILIZATION CHARGE price component, which signifies the price). The second and third rows indicate that a dedicated line connectivity service may be deployed between two locations. One of these dedicated lines has selected a "44.763 megabits per second" bandwidth feature, and the other line has selected the "1.544 megabits per second" feature (again, some enterprises may consider that different transmission speeds indicate different products).

The next rows show that call waiting, call forwarding, and personalized telephone numbers can have product deployment IDs in order to track instantiations of these products.

The listing offerings will not have deployment IDs because they will be related to an entity called LISTING, which is where the instantiation of the listings are tracked. The table shows features listed such as "bold print," "number of lines," "multiple company listing," and "multicolor listing."

The next rows show the PBX Spectacular 1000 with an inventory item ID of 9784758 and two product deployments of this item (there are also attributes showing different product deployment dates, which are not shown in the table). The Cellular Phone 1000 has an inventory item ID and a deployment ID, indicating that this item will be tracked over time. The Princess Phone 2300 has only an inventory item ID, indicating that this item is tracked only while in inventory; after it is sold, it is not tracked by the telecommunications enterprise.

Finally, the last two rows show instances of service agreement offerings that correspond to customer agreements with agreement IDs of 38978979 and 38749837. Each of these agreements has a different feature in effect (DEPLOYED FEATURE); one is 24*7, and one is for business hours only.

Telecommunications Product Associations

Telecommunications products can be quite complex, and therefore there are many relationships between different products. Some product offerings complement other product offerings, such as call waiting on a connectivity service. Other product offerings may or may not be compatible with other product offerings. The product associations may depend on how the deployed product

Table 3.5 Telecommunications Product Deployments

PRODUCT TYPE	PRODUCT NAME	PRODUCT DEPLOYMENT ID	DEPLOYMENT FEATURE	AGREEMENT ID	INVENTORY ITEM ID	DEPLOYMENT FACILITY(S)
Connectivity service—local connectivity	Residential Line	398498	Billing feature—usage based			Len Goldstein's house at 234 Main Street
Connectivity service—dedicated line	High Grade Dedicated Office Line	459879	44.763 Megabits per second			ABC's Dallas office, ABC's NY office
Connectivity service—dedicated line	High Grade Dedicated Residential Line	504385	1.544 Megabits per second			Len Goldstein's house at 234 Main Street, Len Goldstein's summer home in Vail
Connectivity feature	Call Waiting	6940984				
Connectivity feature	Call Forwarding	780749				
Connectivity feature	Personalized Telephone Number	87890				
Listing Offering	Yellow Pages Listing		Bold, five lines			
Listing Offering	White Pages Listing		Multiple company			

Listing Offering	Internet Yellow Pages Listing				
Good—telecommunications system	PBX Spectacular 1000	3948989		9784758	Bold, Multicolor
Good—telecommunications system	PBX Spectacular 1000	3434566		9784758	
Good—telecommunications device	Cellular Phone 1000	34544454		58747684	
Good—telecommunications device	Princess Phone 2300			29019333	
Service agreement offering	One-year Maintenance Agreement	38978979	24*7		
Service agreement offering	One-year Maintenance Agreement	38749837	Business hours only		

was implemented within the network and the type of network components on which the product is implemented. For instance, voice messaging may not be available on some types of switches.

Figure 3.4 offers a model to handle the various product associations that may be important to capture. The TELECOM PRODUCT ASSOCIATION is similar to the model in Volume 1 (V1:3.9b); however, there are some additional relationships to the NETWORK COMPONENT TYPE and NETWORK ASSEMBLY COMPONENT TYPE. There is also an additional subtype of PRODUCT DEPENDENCY because sometimes products must exist in order to have other products. For instance, one must have a local connectivity service in order to add call waiting. In addition to PRODUCT DEPENDENCY, the generic PRODUCT ASSOCIATION subtypes from Volume 1 are included in the TELECOM PRODUCT ASSOCIATION and include PRODUCT COMPLEMENT, PRODUCT INCOMPATIBILITY, PRODUCT SUBSTITUTE, PRODUCT OBSOLESCENCE, and PRODUCT COMPONENT. A PRODUCT COMPLEMENT records the products that are recommended to be sold with other products. For example, call waiting and call forwarding may be complementary products to CONNECTIVITY SERVICE products. The PRODUCT INCOMPATABILITY maintains products that cannot exist together; for example, certain connectivity features may not be able to reside on residential local connectivity services. PRODUCT SUBSTITUTE captures products that may serve the same purposes as other products and can therefore sometimes be used as a substitute. PRODUCT OBSOLESCENCE shows products that have been superceded by other offerings, and MARKETING PACKAGE shows products that may be packaged together to form other products (this could also be called PRODUCT COMPONENT).

The TELECOM PRODUCT ASSOCIATION instance in this model may be dependent on what types of components were used to deploy the product, and it is therefore optionally related to the NETWORK COMPONENT TYPE or NETWORK COMPONENT ASSEMBLY entity. This entity will be discussed in more detail later in this chapter. For example, the type of switch (which is a network component) involved may affect the possibilities. In other words, whether a product is complementary (as depicted in the subtype PRODUCT COMPLEMENT) or incompatible (PRODUCT INCOMPATABILITY) with another product may also depend on the type of switch being used or other network components used in the implementation.

Table 3.6 gives some examples of product associations. It shows that call waiting and call forwarding are natural complements to a residential line. This implies that perhaps the service representative may suggest the use of these features when ordering a residential line. An example of a product incompatibility instance could be that a fax queuing product that enables faxes to be queued and stored until the printer is ready to accept them is not compatible with residential lines.

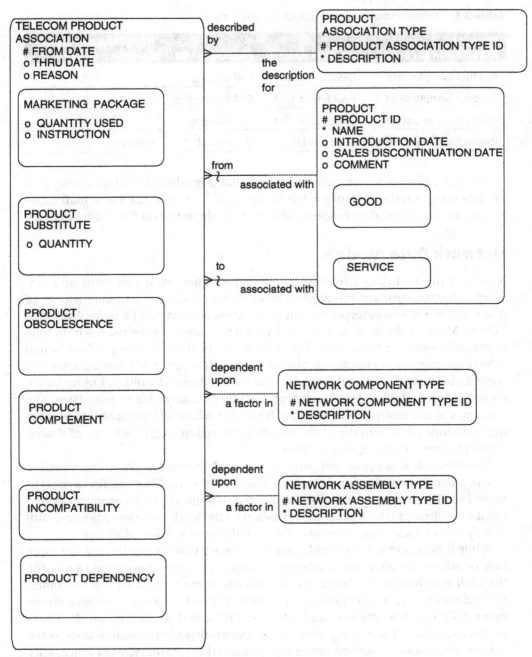

Figure 3.4 Telecommunications product associations.

Table 3.6 Telecommunications Product Associations

PRODUCT ASSOCIATION TYPE	PRODUCT NAME	PRODUCT NAME	NETWORK COMPONENT TYPE (SWITCH TYPE)
Product complement	Residential Line	Call waiting	
Product complement	Residential Line	Call forwarding	
Product incompatibility	Residential Line	Fax queuing	
Product incompatibility	Business Line	Voice mail	Erickson

The last example in the table illustrates that a product association may also be dependent on the type of switch being used. It shows that voice mail capabilities are not allowed on business lines that are deployed on Erickson switches.

Network Data Models

Now that product data structure has been provided, what platforms and network infrastructure are required to offer these products? A unique aspect of telecommunications enterprises is in their extensive network facilities and capabilities. Many of the generic Volume 1 product models can be used within telecommunication organizations. The difference is that, in many cases, when telecommunications customers buy products, they are really buying usage of the capabilities offered by the product via their network facilities. For instance, a customer may buy access to a telephone line outside of his or her office. The customer is not really buying the line; he or she is buying the capability of making telephone calls from the office, which is offered through the usage of shared network lines, switches, and devices.

Therefore, this section will provide a model for one of the most valuable assets a telecommunications company has: its network. There is also a need to show how these network data structures relate to products, to product deployments, to circuits (the logical instantiation of network components), and ultimately to orders in order to check the availability of service offerings.

While it is important to provide product models that handle buying the capabilities offered by telecommunications products, it is also important to provide the ability to handle products that are simply items bought by the customer. One example of this is maintaining products that are customer premise equipment (CPE) such as phones, multiplexers, PBXs, and so on. The product data models mentioned in the previous "Telecommunications Modifications to the generic data models" section can accommodate these latter types of items without the need for the subsequent models. The majority of telecommunications offerings, though, are based on having a network infrastructure; the following section will provide template models for maintaining network infrastructure information.

Network Components

The primary components in the network are the network servers (such as switches), connection components (such as telephone lines), and devices (to alter the signal within the network configurations). Network servers are powerful computers or intelligent devices used by telecommunications companies to control network operations. Communication components represent physical connections carrying telecommunications signals from one location to another location. These may be implemented using cables, fiber, or some other medium for telecommunications. Devices are additional pieces of equipment such as amplifiers, multiplexers/demultiplexers, testing gears, main distribution frames, cross connects, load coils, alarms, and so on. There may be network support structures such as towers, poles, or other structures to physically support the network infrastructure. It is important to model information about specific components as well as information about types or categories of network components.

Figure 3.5 shows a data model for these network components. NETWORK COMPONENT is broken down into the subtypes NETWORK SUPPORT STRUCTURE, NETWORK SERVER, DEVICE, and CONNECTION COMPONENT. These represent instances of actual network components that may be serialized. An instance of this entity may be a specific DMS100 switch identified by serial number 390784. Each network component may already be installed on the network or available within an inventory location.

The NETWORK SUPPORT STRUCTURE represents components used to put other network components physically in place—for example, telephone poles, manholes, or towers. NETWORK SERVERs represent physical intelligent components that direct signal traffic as well as control network operations. Subtypes of NETWORK SERVERs are SWITCHes, ROUTERs, and COMMUNICATION APPEARANCEs. A SWITCH is a specialized computer for telecommunications that directs telecommunications traffic. A ROUTER provides the capability to send, manage, and control signals and information across various networks. A COMMUNICATIONS APPEARANCE is the physical input slot or port allowing connection into the network. Switches have a limited number of communications appearances, and each telephone number, fax number, and cell number corresponds to a certain communication appearance (see Figure 3.9, Communication IDs and contact mechanisms for more information on this relationship).

A DEVICE maintains physical components that modify communication signals—for example, AMPLIFIER, FILTER, LOADING COIL, and FREQUENCY SHIFTER. An AMPLIFIER is a device that strengthens the communication signal as it travels along the network. A FILTER is a device that filters out part of the signal, usually attempting to filter out noise to make the transmission more clear. A LOADING COIL is a device specifically used to improve voice

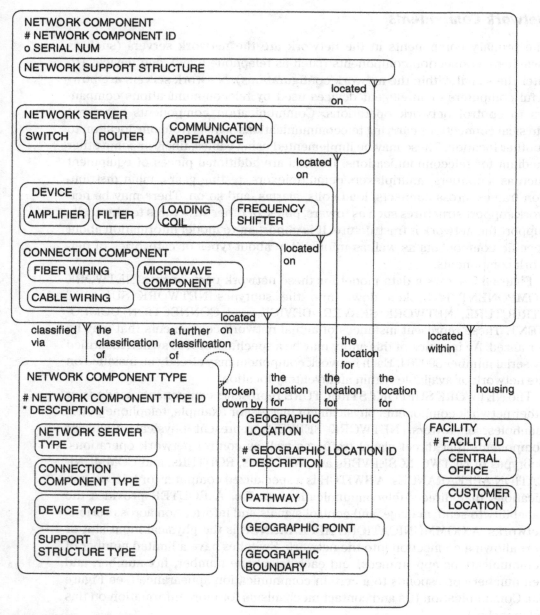

Figure 3.5 Network components.

transmission. A FREQUENCY SHIFTER is a device that modulates the frequency or speed of the transmission. These devices (and other devices because this list is only a sample of devices) in some way modify the communication signals by boosting the signal, filtering out noise, or making the signal more reliable.

The NETWORK COMPONENT TYPE entity records information about the type of network component. This entity provides an instance of every type of network component that can be used. Note the recursion around NETWORK COMPONENT TYPE. This allows certain types of components to be made up of other types of components. A "switch" type of component can be further classified into "5ESS switch" or a "DMS100 switch." A "5ESS switch" may be further classified into a "5ESS series 1" switch and a "5ESS series 2" switch.

The GEOGRAPHIC LOCATION may be subtyped into PATHWAY (a line between two points), GEOGRAPHIC POINT (a specific geographic spot), or GEOGRAPHIC BOUNDARY (a geographic area) on which the NETWORK COMPONENT is located. NETWORK SUPPORT STRUCTUREs, NETWORK SERVERs, and DEVICEs are located at one specific GEOGRAPHIC POINT. The location for a CONNECTION COMPONENT is on a PATHWAY because it represents the path of the telecommunications connection such as a telephone line. This structure is an expansion of the Volume 1 postal address model (V1:2.8) because it incorporates more types of geographic structures other than just GEOGRAPHIC BOUNDARY. This geographic location part of the model is widely applicable to many types of enterprises such as gas and oil enterprises, utility enterprises and any enterprise needing to maintain detailed geographic location information.

Each NETWORK COMPONENT may be within a FACILITY, such as a CENTRAL OFFICE or CUSTOMER LOCATION that houses the network. While not shown in this model, FACILITYs are indirectly related to GEOGRAPHIC LOCATIONs. (Figure V1:2.11 shows that each FACILITY will have one or more contact mechanisms, including POSTAL ADDRESSes and V1:2.8 shows that POSTAL ADDRESSes have a many-to-many relationship to GEOGRAPHIC BOUNDARYs).

Table 3.7 describes instances of the NETWORK COMPONENT entity. It is important to distinguish what data belongs with the "type" entity, NETWORK COMPONENT TYPE, and what belongs with the "instance" entity, NETWORK COMPONENT. The NETWORK COMPONENT TYPE stores standard descriptions and categorizations of these network components. Examples of types of network components in the table include "DMS100" switches and "5ESS" switches (for the SWITCH subtype within NETWORK SERVER TYPE). There may be many instances of this same switch, each having a different **serial num**. Each NETWORK COMPONENT instance may or may not have a serial number. For instance, the table shows examples of switches and devices that have serial numbers, whereas the connectivity services have only identifiers.

Network Assemblies

A network assembly is a combination of network components that can be used to deliver telecommunications service to a potential customer. A particular

Table 3.7 Network Component

NETWORK COMPONENT TYPE ID	NETWORK COMPONENT TYPE DESCRIPTION (PARENT)	NETWORK COMPONENT TYPE DESCRIPTION (CHILD)	NETWORK COMPONENT ID	NETWORK COMPONENT SERIAL #
14857	Network server type—switch	DMS100 switch	476555	390784
14857	Network server type—switch	DMS100 switch	645444	374788
14857	Network server type—switch	DMS100 switch	476786	374847
16445	Network server type—switch	5ESS switch	645444	37489797
16445	Network server type—switch	5ESS switch	839748	83974893
16445	Network server type—switch	5ESS switch	874784	39874987
16445	Network server type—switch	5ESS switch	479889	47547878
89574	Connection component	Cable line	987383	
48495	Connection component	Fiber line	394894	
43906	Device	Hub	478497558	7384798748
85945	Device	Line amplifier	934854	A39849933

network assembly may be made up of many support structure components, network server components, devices, and/or connection components.

Figure 3.6 shows the data model for network assemblies. A NETWORK ASSEMBLY must be made up of one or more NETWORK COMPONENTs, and a NETWORK COMPONENT may be within one or more NETWORK ASSEMBLYs (for example, the same switch may be used within many assemblies). The associative entity NETWORK COMPONENT ASSEMBLY resolves the many-to-many relationship. The from and thru date fields provide historical tracking of which components were used in which assemblies and when. This could be critical information for diagnosing network issues.

Network assemblies could be made up of other network assemblies. A particular network circuit may include components of cables, loading coils, ports, main distribution frame slots, and so on. A number of network assemblies may be combined to form a larger network assembly. The NETWORK ASSEMBLY STRUCTURE entity provides the ability to combine NETWORK ASSEMBLYs very flexibly.

An alternative data model could be to define NETWORK COMPONENTS as either individual parts and/or assemblies, thereby consolidating the NETWORK COMPONENT and NETWORK ASSEMBLY entities together. If we use this broad definition, then there could be a many-to-many recursive entity, NETWORK COMPONENT STRUCTURE, which could be used to group together NETWORK COMPONENTS. This data structure would be in lieu of any of the

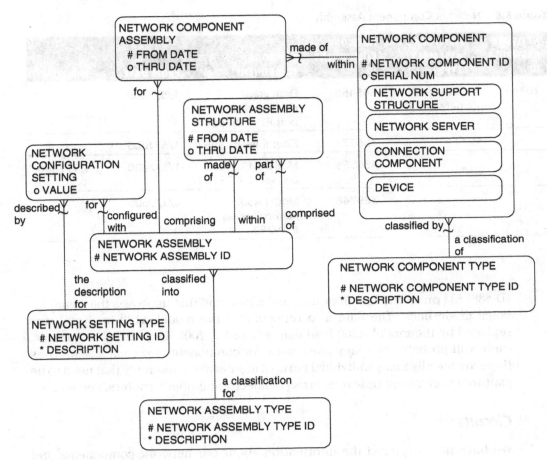

Figure 3.6   Network assembly.

NETWORK ASSEMBLY entities. This data structure is similar to the PRODUCT ASSOCIATION recursive data structures in the product association models in V1:3.9a or V1:3.9b.

Additionally, each NETWORK ASSEMBLY may be configured either via hardware (for example, dip-switches) or software settings. For example, a switch or router may have many software parameter settings that control how they function. Thus each NETWORK ASSEMBLY may have many NETWORK CONFIGURATION SETTINGs of NETWORK SETTING TYPEs, each setting having its own **value**, allowing the recording of the configuration of the assembly.

Table 3.8 shows data instances for these structures. Network assembly 10345 is a data grade circuit switch, and some of the network components are shown in the first few rows of the table. The assembly's components include the port

Table 3.8   Network Component Assembly

NETWORK ASSEMBLY ID	NETWORK ASSEMBLY TYPE	NETWORK COMPONENT ID	NETWORK COMPONENT	FROM DATE	THRU DATE
10345	Data grade network 32	345455	Data grade circuit switch— port ID # 387434	1/5/2000	
		465675	Fiber line—ID 3987	1/5/2000	
		456565	Model A120 load coil serial # 39489	1/5/2000	4/7/2000
		389748	Model A500 load coil serial # 19289	4/7/2000	

ID #387434 on a switch, a fiber line, and a load coil that improves the signal for voice grade lines. The data also reflects that the model A120 load coil was replaced by the model A500 load coil on April 7, 2000. In actual data records, there will probably be many more network components for each assembly as there are usually many individual parts of any network assembly that need to be captured such as multiplexers, cross connects, amplifiers, routers, and so on.

Circuits

We have now captured the information about our network components and how they are assembled. What makes telecommunications industry interesting is that telecommunications companies do not primarily sell their inventory items like many other companies. They sell the functionality or capabilities of their network. Even when a customer buys a dedicated line, the customer is not really buying the network assembly; the customer is buying the right to use the functionality provided by that line. This may or may not be shared with other customers who may also be using some of the same network components and/or assemblies. These capabilities are encompassed in the ability to use a portion of the network, and this could be referred to as a circuit. A circuit is defined as a set of capabilities that use portions of network assemblies to provide telecommunications connectivity. It is a functional package that may be offered in a product. For example, a circuit may be the functionality offered for the line from 100 Main Street in Denver to 240 Smith Street in Dallas. The network components within the circuit may change over time and the way that the product is marketed may change, but the functionality of the circuit stays the same.

What is the difference between the product, network component, and circuit? The product defines what is marketed as an offering—for example, a residential line. The network components define the physical parts that are used to provide the line. The circuit defines the functionality of the line. Many products may have the same functionality but are marketed under different product names. For example, a residential line and business line may have the same type of circuit but may be different products with different pricing, features, and terms associated with them. The circuit therefore provides the basis for what is available to be sold (what circuits are currently available to be used), and the type of circuit defines what various types of functionality exist.

Figure 3.7 provides a data model that shows the relationships between PRODUCTs, DEPLOYMENTs, CIRCUITs, and NETWORK ASSEMBLYs. The CIRCUIT may be residing on one or more NETWORK ASSEMBLYs, and the same NETWORK ASSEMBLY may be used in creating one or more CIRCUITs, thereby establishing the CIRCUIT PRESENCE associative entity. This provides

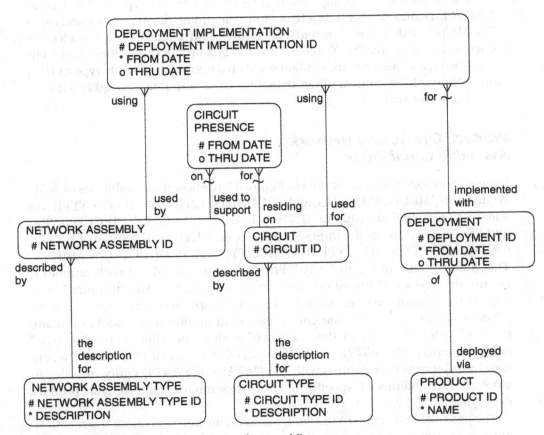

Figure 3.7 Products, circuits, and network assemblies.

a mechanism for setting up functional packages (or sets of capabilities) that use the network assemblies and that can be used for implementing DEPLOY-MENTs. The DEPLOYMENT IMPLEMENTATION entity stores the combination of CIRCUITs and/or NETWORK ASSEMBLYs that are used to implement the deployment of a product.

Table 3.9 provides examples of possible associations between DEPLOY-MENT, CIRCUIT, and NETWORK ASSEMBLY. The first row shows that the "High grade dedicated office line, deployment ID 459879" was implemented using a "DS 3 Line 1000" (DS 3, Digital Service 1, is a telecommunications transmission standard of 44.763 Mbits/s) circuit type on the specific circuit ID 8939849. That type of circuit has certain capabilities, namely a 44.763 Megabits per second bandwidth, a certain noise rating, and a certain dual redundancy as well as other possible specifications. This circuit resides on the "Data Grade Network 32" network assembly type and more specifically on network assembly ID 878574.

The second product deployment, a "High grade dedicated residential line, Deployment ID 504385" is implemented by using a circuit type of "DS 1 Line" 1000 (DS 1, Digital Service 1, is a telecommunications transmission standard of 1.544 Mbits/s) that has different capabilities and resides on a Data Grade Network 30 assembly. The Triple Max Value is a product that offers three circuits—two data lines that are implemented on a network assembly type of Data Grade Network 34 and another data line of a different assembly type of Data Grade Network 45.

Product, Circuit, and Network Assembly Capabilities

Figure 3.8 expands the data model in Figure 3.7 to show the capabilities of NET-WORK ASSEMBLYs, CIRCUITs, and PRODUCTs. Each CAPABILITY TYPE has a many-to-many relationship to NETWORK ASSEMBLY TYPE, CIRCUIT TYPE, and PRODUCT through the intersection entities, NETWORK ASSEMBLY TYPE CAPABILITY, CIRCUIT TYPE CAPABILITY, and PRODUCT CAPABILITY. This allows determining the capabilities of each type of network assembly, circuit, or product. If the enterprise's capabilities vary at the "instance" level (i.e., if the capabilities can vary for each network assembly, circuit, and/or product deployment) then the enterprise could modify this model and relate the CAPABILITY TYPE to the "instance" entities in addition to the "type" entities; namely, NETWORK ASSEMBLY, CIRCUIT, and DEPLOYMENT would also have intersection entities with the CAPABILITY TYPE entity in order to store the capabilities of specific network assemblies, circuits and, product deployments.

The capabilities related to product, maintain information about the functionality from a marketing perspective, and these capabilities may be listed on

Table 3.9 Product Deployments, Circuits, and Network Assemblies

DEPLOYMENT	CIRCUIT TYPE	CIRCUIT ID	CAPABILITY	NETWORK ASSEMBLY TYPE	NETWORK ASSEMBLY
High grade dedicated office line, Deployment ID 459879	DS 3 Line 1000	8939849	44.736 Megabits per second	Data grade network 32	878574
			A3 noise rating		
			B2 dual redundancy		
High grade dedicated residential line, Deployment ID 504385	DS 1 Line 1000	7878549	1.544 Megabits per second	Data grade network 30	089896
			A3 noise rating		
			B2 dual redundancy		
Triple max value, deployment ID 3984984	DS 1 Line—2000	3989846	Two data lines	Data grade network 34	439859
	DS 1 Line—2000	5089678			540985
	DS 1 Line—3000	5086989	One data grade line	Data grade network 45	409095
			1.544 Megabits per second		
			A5 noise rating		
			Voice, even if data fails		

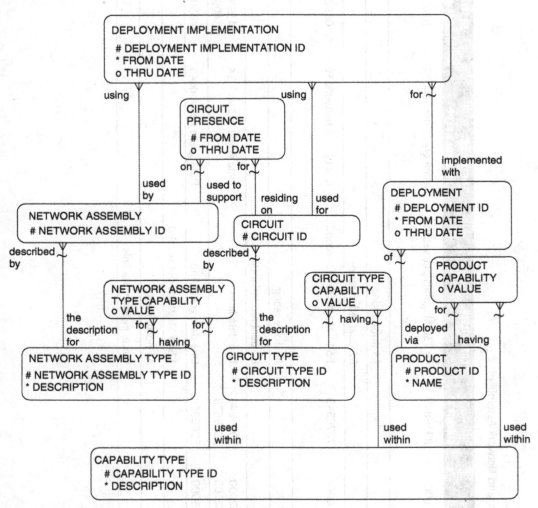

Figure 3.8   Product, circuit, and network capabilities.

product marketing literature. The speed, general reliability, and functional capabilities of the PRODUCT may also be included in marketing literature. The capabilities related to CIRCUIT and NETWORK ASSEMBLY would be more technical in nature and can be used to define more precise functional capability specifications for the circuits and network assemblies. For instance, a network assembly may have certain maximum bandwidth capabilities, reliability ratings, and so on.

Communication IDs and Contact Mechanisms

Some of the most important items to manage in telecommunications are the various telephone numbers, fax numbers, cellular numbers, pager numbers, e-mail addresses, and other contact mechanisms that are used for communications purposes. Volume 1 (V1:2.10) discussed the importance of storing contact mechanisms as an entity, rather than embedding them at attributes within entities. Similar to other industries, telecommunications enterprises need to track these numbers in order to maintain how to get in touch with parties, and these numbers are stored in the CONTACT MECHANISM entity.

Many telecommunications enterprises have an additional requirement: They need to maintain the inventory of available telecommunication numbers (i.e. phone numbers, fax numbers, cell numbers, and so on), and assign available contact mechanisms to the parties using their services. These contact numbers are much more critical in telecommunications because this is where the source of these numbers lie and telecommunications enterprises are responsible for adding, changing, assigning, and managing the pool of available contact numbers. Telecommunications companies will often inventory these numbers, and they need to track which telephone numbers are assigned to which product deployments as well as who has reserved certain numbers.

Because telecommunications enterprises inventory these contact mechanisms, the telecommunications models will make a distinction between COMMUNICATION IDENTIFIERs and CONTACT MECHANISMs. Telecommunications companies can use the same data structures in Volume 1 (V1:2.10) and use the CONTACT MECHANISMs entity for storing basic contact information because telecommunication enterprises have the same need as any other organization to store ways to contact important parties. COMMUNICATION IDENTIFIER will be used to store the various telephone numbers, pager numbers, cell numbers, e-mail addresses, and other identifiers that are part of the telecommunications inventory and assignment process.

Figure 3.9 shows a data model to track COMMUNICATION IDENTIFIERs and associated entities. Each COMMUNICATION IDENTIFIER may be related to one or more COMMUNICATION APPEARANCEs (i.e., ports) and vice versa. The COMMUNICATION ID ASSIGNMENT provides a mechanism for storing which logical number (COMMUNICATION IDENTIFIER) is attached to which physical appearance (COMMUNICATION APPEARANCE). A DEPLOYMENT IMPLEMENTATION may use this COMMUNICATION ID ASSIGNMENT because part of the implementation of the product could involve certain phone numbers and the physical appearance, or port, on which they are located. The COMMUNICATION IDENTIFIER may be reserved via a SERVICE ORDER ITEM (discussed in the next section), as in the case of a connectivity service being ordered and being assigned a certain telephone number (or other

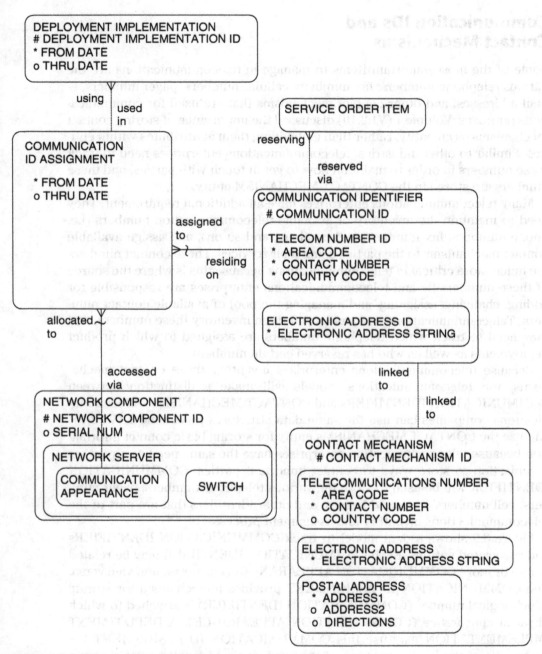

Figure 3.9 Communication IDs and contact mechanisms.

communication identifier). This allows the company to make sure that phone numbers, cell numbers, beeper numbers, and so on are appropriately reserved and that the same number is not given out more than once at the same time.

Why not use the same entity to store both communication identifiers and contact mechanisms? After all, they represent the same thing: the record of the identification string used to communicate. One answer is that these represent two completely different aspects of their organization. CONTACT MECHANISMs are maintaining information about how to contact parties. COMMUNICATION IDENTIFIERs are maintaining information about the inventory of identification strings that are used within the telecommunications network for communication connections. If a single entity was used to maintain this information, it may imply that one needs to access the details within the telecommunications network to reach an important shareholder.

The next question is, Should these entities be related? One can make the point that this information can help link the inventory of telecommunications numbers with a contact management system in order to ensure better integrity of information and to find out more about the information associated with a number. Therefore, a relationship from CONTACT MECHANISM to COMMUNICATION IDENTIFIER is shown. As a practical matter, though, many enterprises will not have the will or means to maintain this relationship, and if this is the case for the enterprise in question, then merely do not include this one-to-one optional relationship.

Orders

Most of the order data models in Volume 1 can be used for telecommunications organizations. This section will point out a few customizations to these models for telecommunications enterprises.

Service Orders

Figure 3.10 shows a derivation from the order data model in Volume 1 (V1:4.2), with a few changes. While the same structures can be used for ORDER and ORDER ITEMs, telecommunications companies often call these SERVICE ORDERs and SERVICE ORDER ITEMs instead of SALES ORDER ITEM. This allows them to record both new sales and upgrades to existing deployments. As in Volume 1, the SERVICE ORDER ITEM is for a PRODUCT or a PRODUCT FEATURE; however, an additional relationship is needed. The fulfillment of this order is tracked via a relationship to a DEPLOYMENT entity. This allows the enterprise to record the product ordered and the deployed product installed, providing an audit trail from ordering the product through installation.

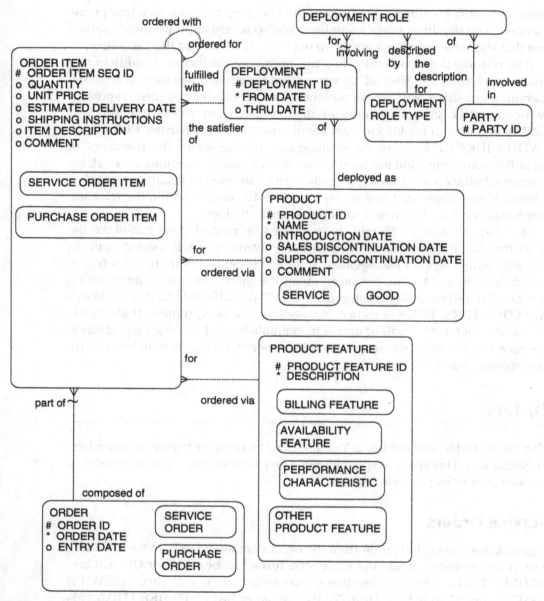

Figure 3.10 Service orders.

This model also allows for service orders to be placed directly against existing deployed products.

Another added relationship maintains the PARTYs that are involved in the DEPLOYMENT. This relationship provides the ongoing tracking, over time, of the users, administrators, contact people, and any other role within the product deployment over the life of the deployed product.

The relationships from Volume 1 of SHIPMENT ITEM to ORDER ITEM may still exist in the case of shipment of goods; however, the previously mentioned additional relationships provide for additional tracking needs of deployed products needed within telecommunications.

Product Availability

One of the most important processes that takes place when ordering service from a telecommunications company is the checking of availability for the products the customer is requesting as well as checking the availability of the required network infrastructure to support the product. Product availability can have many different meanings depending on its context. It could mean the following:

- Is the product available for the central office (with the needed network components/assemblies) that is associated with the customer's geographic area?
- Is the product available based on policies that the company or an outside regulatory agency establishes?
- Is the product available based on the existing network facilities and the current load?

The service order process will need to answer these questions of availability. The previous data models can provide information to answer these questions. To answer the first question of central office availability, the data structures are provided in the products, circuits, and network assemblies model of Figure V2:3.7, the product deployment model of Figure V2:3.3, and the product associations model of Figure V2:3.4. The products, circuits, and network assemblies model of Figure V2:3.7 shows the network assemblies that exist as well as the circuits and products that are deployed. The product deployment model of Figure V2:3.3 will help determine where the deployments are in terms of the facilities on which they are deployed. It will also provide information on what features are currently deployed and where they are. By using the PRODUCT INCOMPATABILITY subtype in Figure V2:3.4, it can be determined if any incompatibilities exist with current products. Given this information, one has a great deal of information to determine if the requested product is available to be sold at the customer's location and for the associated central office.

The second question about the availability of the product based upon company policies, can be answered based on the business rules of the enterprise. It may be possible to create a data structure to store these business rules; however, this data structure may be highly unique to the enterprise in question, and therefore we will not make an attempt to create a universal data model for this information in this chapter (although the V2:5.5, V2:5.16, and V2:6.4 provide examples of data models that store rules).

The third question about whether the capacity exists to support the proposed product can be answered using many of the network data models that have been shown in this chapter along with the appropriate business rules and algorithms to analyze network capacity. The capabilities model of Figure V2:3.8 provides some information on the capabilities and capacities of the network infrastructure. The **value** attribute in the CIRCUIT TYPE CAPABILITY and the **value** attribute of the NETWORK ASSEMBLY TYPE CAPABILITY will give information about the capacity of the network. This can be compared to the current load, to see if the additional products or features can be supported. An example of this is that a certain type of switch within a central office may support only certain capabilities and configurations and have capacities for a certain number of ports coming into it.

To address the third question to a greater extent, information about the current load would be useful in order to forecast the expected load and plan for how many products to add to the circuits and network assemblies. In order to find out the current load, the usage for the deployments needs to be tracked. Models for this information will be discussed in the next models "Product Deployment Usage." The sample star schema designs at the end of this chapter can also be used to help forecast usage and expected loads.

Delivery

While many of the delivery models using the SHIPMENTs models from Volume 1 apply to shipments of goods, the most common form of delivering telecommunications services occurs in an ongoing fashion and is measured based on the usage of the customer's products. Thus, the next section will address the unique needs within telecommunications to track product deployment usage.

Deployment Usage

Products and their associated deployments may fall into one or more of the following three general categories.

- One time delivery. These products are generally goods that are delivered to the customer, and there is no need to track usage of the product. An example of this is selling a phone to a customer. Depending on the nature of the product, the telecommunications enterprise may or may not track deployments of the product but will generally not track the customer's product usage. The models in Chapter 5 of Volume 1 (V1:5.1–5.8) may be used to manage the shipments of goods to customers.

- Subscription-based product. These products are tracked over time because the customer is billed for the time periods for which they have access to the product. An example of this is local connectivity service, where the customers are charged every month for access to phone service.

- Usage-based product. These products require the enterprise to track each use of the product after it is deployed. The usage may be by the activity such as call detail or by the volume used. An example of a usage-based product is a local connectivity service where it is important to track each call that takes place over the line for billing as well as regulatory reasons.

There is a need to track the activity details for usage-based products. Therefore, Figure 3.11 shows the data necessary to record the usage of each product deployment. Each DEPLOYMENT may be tracked via one or more DEPLOYMENT USAGE entities. The subtypes of CALL DETAIL, VOLUME USAGE, and TIME PERIOD USAGE provide tracking of three types of usage. CALL DETAIL represents logging each telecommunications call, for example, phone calls, cell calls, fax communications, and beeper communications. This information may be required for several purposes, such as for regulatory purposes (telecommunications companies are required to maintain this information to help with future investigations), analysis purposes (to analyze network traffic), or for billing purposes. VOLUME USAGE maintains information on product deployments that track a certain volume or activity such as the amount of disk space that is being used for a web hosting service or the number of hits that are being received against a system. Web hosting services typically charge different amounts based on the amount of space being used or the volume of hit activity. The UNIT OF MEASURE entity records what unit of measure is being used to track the VOLUME USAGE—for example, megabytes, gigabytes, and so on. TIME PERIOD USAGE tracks instances of usages for subscription-based services that are tracked and billed for certain periods of time.

Each DEPLOYMENT USAGE may be calculated either at regular intervals (such as weekly, monthly, or quarterly), as in the case of volume usage and time period usage, or may be calculated for each specific usage, as in a call detail record. Because usage is frequently tracked through preset time intervals, the STANDARD TIME PERIOD entity is set up to maintain standard time periods and is used to store the from and thru dates only once instead of storing them in each DEPLOYMENT USAGE instance. The DEPLOYMENT USAGE data structure provides the capability to maintain **start datetime** and **thru datetime** for tracking deployment usages where the dates and times are not within standard time periods.

This model is very similar to the Manufacturing Product Deployment and Usage model (V2:2.10) because manufacturers may also have to track usage of their product deployments. One main difference is that in telecommunication enterprises, the network infrastructure that is related to the deployment is quite different. The manufacturing model showed that the DEPLOYMENT was for an INVENTORY ITEM. As shown in V2:3.7, the telecommunications model shows

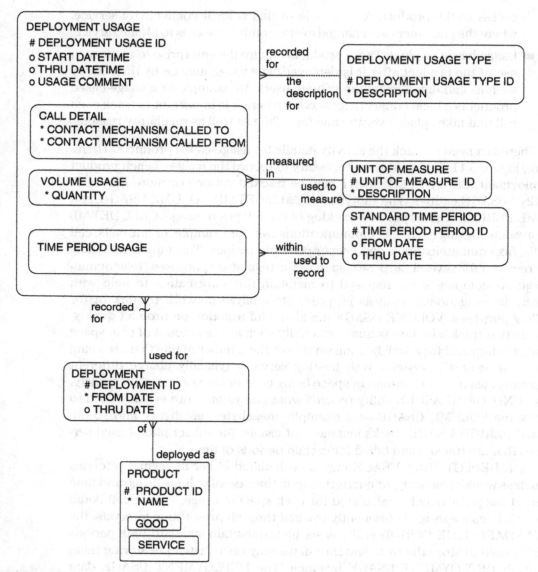

Figure 3.11 Product deployment usage.

DEPLOYMENTs related to DEPLOYMENT IMPLEMENTATIONs that specify the associated NETWORK ASSEMBLYs, which are related to NETWORK COMPONENTs (these are similar to INVENTORY ITEMs but are used specifically for the telecommunications industry). In either event, both industries have a need to track the deployments and usage of products.

Table 3.10 provides examples of data instances for the DEPLOYMENT USAGE entity. The first two rows show two call detail records for the product

Table 3.10 Product Deployment Usage

PRODUCT DEPLOYMENT	PRODUCT DEPLOYMENT USAGE TYPE DESCRIPTION	PRODUCT DEPLOYMENT USAGE, START DATETIME, THRU DATETIME, CONTACT MECHANISM CALLED FROM, CONTACT MECHANISM CALLED TO	STANDARD TIME PERIOD
Connectivity service—local connectivity, Deployment ID 858979	Call detail	From datetime: Jan 12, 2000 3:30 p.m. Thru Jan 12, 2000 4:15 p.m. Called from 333-984-9450 Called to 333-390-5909	
		From datetime: Jan 20, 2000 1:40 p.m. Thru Jan 20, 2000 1:45 p.m. Called from 333-984-9450 Called to 333-898-4985	
Connectivity service—local connectivity, Deployment ID 858979	Time period usage		Period 49 From date: Jan 1, 2000 Thru date: Jan 31, 2000
			Period 50 From date: Feb 1, 2000 Thru date: Feb 28, 2000
Web hosting service, Deployment ID 767675	Volume usage	Qty: 1345 Unit of measure: hits	Period 49 From date: Jan 1, 2000 Thru date: Jan 31,2000
	Volume usage	Qty: 27 Unit of measure: Megabytes	Period 49 From date: Jan 1, 2000 Thru date: Jan 31, 2000

deployment of local connectivity service. The first call started on January 12 at 3:30 p.m. and ended at 4:15 p.m. and was made from 333-984-9490 to 333-390-5909. The second call was made on January 20 at 1:40 p.m. and ended at 1:45 p.m. One may think that the "called-from" number is not needed because it can be derived from the phone number associated with the deployed product. (See Figure V2:3.9—there is a COMMUNICATION ID associated with the DEPLOYMENT IMPLEMENTATION.) This may be derived only for half of the call detail—either the outgoing called-from number or the incoming called-to number. Therefore, it is more practical and less confusing to store both numbers in the call detail.

The third and fourth rows show time period usage instances, recording usage each month for the deployed product, local connectivity service. Instead of entering the same dates for many instances within the same standard period from January 1, 2000 to January 31, 2000 the table shows using the standard periods of "49" and "50," thus providing a means to enter these dates only once and ensuring more data integrity.

The fifth and sixth rows show product deployment usage based on volumes of usage. In this case, the deployed product is a Web hosting service and the charges are based on the number of hits on the Web site as well as the number of megabytes taken up by the site's pages. These records allow the enterprise to track the volume of usage for the Web site and bill appropriately for the usage. These instances are also tracked using standard time periods.

Invoicing

Many of the invoicing models from Volume 1 apply to telecommunications enterprises. Two unique aspects of invoicing that are common in telecommunications are these:

- Invoicing is often based on product deployment usage.
- Invoicing is often administered by BILLING AGENTs that may be external to the enterprise that provides the service. For instance, long distance carrier charges may be billed by the local phone organization, and not by the long distance carrier that actually provides these capabilities.

Figure 3.12 provides an expansion of the invoice model from Volume 1 (V1:7.1a). Similar to most types of enterprises the INVOICE is made up of INVOICE ITEMs that may be charges related to PRODUCTs (such as a dedicated line), PRODUCT FEATUREs (such as 1.544 megabit per second bandwidth), or specific INVENTORY ITEMs (a specific PBX system).

The data model also shows some of the entities and relationships within billing that are unique to telecommunications. The entity BILLING AGENT ASSIGNMENT provides the capability of designating a BILLING AGENT to a

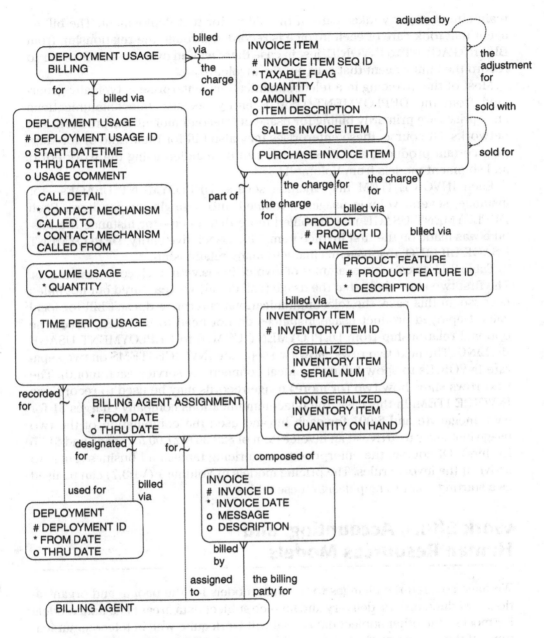

Figure 3.12   Telecommunications billing.

DEPLOYMENT. The **from date** and **thru date** within the BILLING AGENT
ASSIGNMENT allow the billing agent to be changed during the life of the product deployment. This relationship is used to drive the invoicing process and

maintain what party takes care of the billing for that deployment. The billing agent that took care of each invoice is recorded through the relationship from BILLING AGENT to INVOICE, just in case there was an override and in order to record the billing agent that sent out the invoice.

Most of the invoicing in a telecommunications enterprise is typically generated from the DEPLOYMENT USAGE entity because telecommunications enterprises are primarily billing for usage of telecommunications products and networks. Of course, these enterprises may also bill for their time or for shipping certain products, and these needs can be handled using the work effort and shipment models from Volume 1.

Each INVOICE ITEM may include several DEPLOYMENT USAGEs—for instance, several volume usages combined into a single invoice item. Each DEPLOYMENT USAGE may be billed more than once—for instance if a mistake was made on the first invoice item. The associative entity, DEPLOYMENT USAGE BILLING, resolves this many-to-many relationship.

Table 3.11 gives a few examples of invoice items within telecommunications. The first two rows show that the usage (call detail) was captured but not billed because, in this case, the telecommunications enterprise doesn't bill for local calls. Deployed product usage instances do not need to be billed, hence the optional relationship from DEPLOYMENT USAGE to DEPLOYMENT USAGE BILLING. The next two rows show two separate INVOICE ITEMS on two separate INVOICEs to show billing for local connectivity service each month. The next rows show how two (or more) usage records may be used to record one INVOICE ITEM. In this case, the telecommunications company charges $1 for each megabyte and $.001 for each hit and used the combination of the two usage instances to arrive at an invoice item of $28.35 ($27.00 for space and $1.35 for hits). Of course, the enterprise needs pricing tables and business rules to arrive at the invoice rules. The pricing models in Volume 1 (V1:3.7) can be used as a starting point to help design these tables.

Work Effort, Accounting, and Human Resources Models

We have covered the changes to the data models for the people and organizations, product, orders, delivery and invoice subject data areas. The data models for most of the other subject data areas will work quite well in telecommunications. If the enterprise ships out tangible items, the shipment models will work. The work effort and work order models can be used for repair projects as well as for network development projects. The accounting and budgeting data models will probably be usable with very few changes. The human resources models should apply as well.

Table 3.11 Telecommunications Invoice Items

PRODUCT DEPLOYMENT	PRODUCT DEPLOYMENT USAGE TYPE DESCRIPTION	PRODUCT DEPLOYMENT USAGE	INVOICE ITEM
Connectivity service—local connectivity, Deployment ID 858979	Call detail	From datetime: Jan 12, 2000 3:30 p.m. Thru Jan 12, 2000 4:15 p.m. Called from 333-984-9450 Called to 333-390-5909	
		From datetime: Jan 20, 2000 1:40 p.m. Thru Jan 20, 2000 1:45 p.m. Called from 333-984-9450 Called to 333-898-4985	
Connectivity service—local connectivity, Deployment ID 858979	Time period usage	Standard time period 49 From date: Jan 1, 2000 Thru date: Jan 31, 2000	Invoice # 48989 Item seq ID 1 Amount $30.00
		Standard time period 50 From date: Feb 1, 2000 Thru date: Feb 28, 2000	Invoice # 39849 Item seq ID 1 Amount $30.00
Web hosting service, Deployment ID 767675	Volume usage	Standard time period 49 From date: Jan 1, 2000 Thru date: Jan 31, 2000 Qty: 1345 Unit of measure: hits	Invoice # 59789 Item seq ID 1 Amount $28.35
	Volume usage	Standard time period 49 From date: Jan 1, 2000 Thru date: Jan 31, 2000 Qty: 27 Unit of measure: megabytes	

Star Schema for Telecommunications

Telecommunications enterprises have a need to measure product deployment usage in order to forecast network demand, forecast business demand, and analyze what customers are using which products and how much. A key star schema design that is very relevant within telecommunications is the product usage star schema, for which an example is found in Figure 3.13.

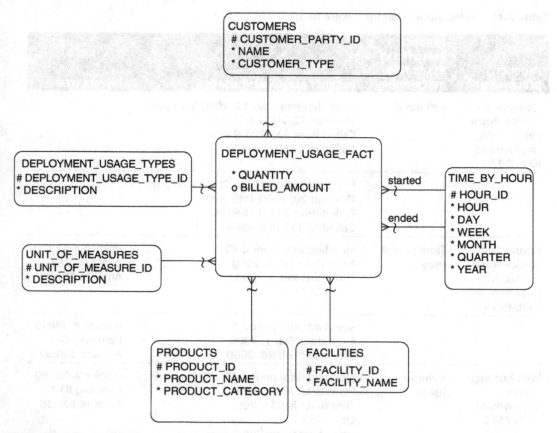

Figure 3.13   Deployment usage star schema.

The manufacturing star schema in Chapter 2 showed the primary keys of the star schema as "#" attributes. Because the primary key of the star schemas in this book is evident as is always a combination of the primary keys of the dimensions, the star schema in this chapter and the remaining chapters will just show the measures in the fact table and will not show the primary key explicitly.

Product Deployment Usage Fact

The DEPLOYMENT_USAGE_FACT table stores the **quantity** field, which can be used to store the amount of usage. The DEPLOYMENT_USAGE_TYPES and the UNIT OF MEASURES dimensions will determine the meaning behind the quantity. For instance, for types of "call detail," the **quantity** may be in units of measures of "minutes" (or fractions thereof). For types of Web hosting disk space, the **quantity** may be in units of measures of "megabytes" or in "hits." The **billing_amount** is a measure that may be extracted from the INVOICE ITEM **amount** attribute for the related DEPLOYMENT USAGE.

Customers

This dimension provides a mechanism to measure which customers and types of customers had how much usage. This can help determine usage profiles for residential or business customers to better know each customer; if the enterprise can find out what they are using, this data can provide insight into what they need. The **customer_type** could store categories such as "residential" and "organization," or it could store the various industry categorizations of customers such as "manufacturing" or "retail." This can be very helpful to target certain market segments. If more than one industry categorization is used for each customer or if analysis for more than one customer categorization is needed, then a separate dimension should be added, for example, INDUSTRY CATEGORYS.

Deployment Usage Types and Unit of Measures Dimensions

The DEPLOYMENT_USAGE_TYPES dimension maintains the type of usage record that is recorded. Examples include "call detail," "space usage," "hits usage," or any other form of product usage.

The UNIT_OF_MEASURES defines the measurement used for the DEPLOYMENT_USAGE_TYPES dimension. "Call detail" records may be measured in minutes or seconds depending on the analysis needs. "Volume usage" types may be measured in megabytes.

Products

The PRODUCTS dimension allows analysis of which types of products are being used and how much. The **product_category** level allows analysis by product classifications to determine which product categories are being used more or less. For instance, a telecommunications company may want to compare fiber optic usage versus wireless communications usage.

Facilities

It may be useful for load-balancing purposes to determine which FACILITIES are handling DEPLOYMENT USAGE of types "call detail." The **quantity** in units of measure (for example, how many minutes) may be recorded for the FACILITIES that are sending or receiving the call details. The facility may be a central office (the location for the switches and other network equipment that handles a specific geographical area) or may be tracked by customer location if more specific information is desired. DEPLOYMENT USAGEs of "volume usage" may be recorded by FACILITY in order to measure the activity of various FACILITIES. If it is important to distinguish the DEPLOYMENT_USAGE_TYPES quantities that are *sent* by a FACILITY versus *received* at a FACILITY, then these could be set up as separate measures in the fact table.

Time by Hour

The time dimension (TIME_BY_HOUR) allows analysis over time to determine trends of product usage and at what times of the day and times of the year the greatest usage occurs. This can be extremely beneficial to determine what types of pricing specials to offer, aiming to balance the telecommunications workload in peak and off-peak times and days. The level of granularity is at the hour; however, a telecommunications company may even want to store this at the level of minutes or seconds to determine more detail behind the trends. Also note that there are two relationships for the TIME_BY_HOUR dimension, allowing analysis of the starting and ending times of the product usage in order to provide reporting on either criteria.

Telecommunications Summary

While many of the data models from Volume 1 apply to telecommunications, the data models within this chapter focused on the unique data model constructs needed within telecommunications. Perhaps the most important additional data models needed are those that capture the information requirements for the network facilities of a telecommunications firm. These data models included network components, network assemblies, circuits, capabilities, telecommunications products, and communication identifiers such as inventories of contact mechanism numbers.

Some data model modifications were provided to show how to modify some of the constructs from Volume 1 to suit telecommunications companies. Appropriate party relationships were subtyped, product data structures were tailored, order data structures were renamed to service orders, and invoices were

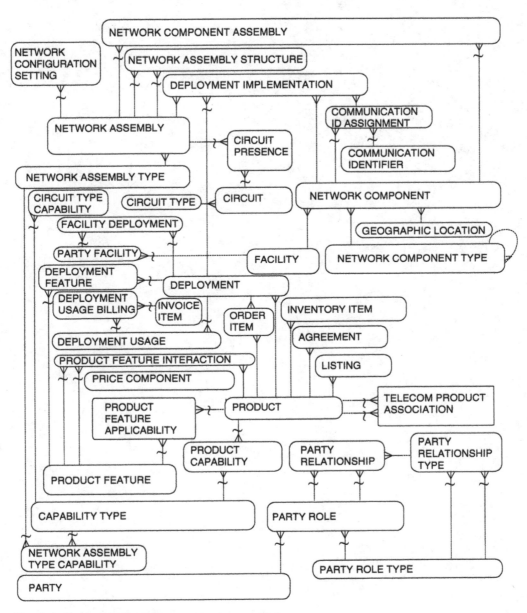

Figure 3.14   Overall telecommunications model.

expanded to allow billing for deployment usage. Models for product deployments and usages such as call detail and volume and time-based usages were added and a star schema was provided to analyze this information.

Figure 3.14 provides a high-level summary of the telecommunications models within this chapter.

Health Care

To provide a more global view of health care, this chapter addresses enterprises that provide treatment for any types of illnesses and/or injuries, non-preventative treatments, and all types of health care categories including hospitals, institutions, medical offices, ambulatory surgery facilities, alternative medicine providers, vision specialists, dentists, and any enterprise treating patients for health care.

Health care organizations are concerned with such issues as these:

- How can we treat people most effectively?
- How can we ensure that we will get reimbursed for most of our health care treatments?
- How can we reduce administrative costs such as claims processing?
- How can we effectively record and track patients' medical history?
- How can we best manage health care delivery schedules for practitioners as well as patients?

To answer these types of questions, health care enterprises need to track information about the following:

- The people and organizations they are concerned with, namely, patients, health care provider organizations, individual practitioners, insurance companies

- Relationships between parties such as patient relationships with their practitioners, with which health care networks the provider is associated, and which practitioners are associated with which health care provider organizations

- The types of services and goods available from the health care providers

- The types of agreements that exist between various parties such as patient practitioner agreements, provider network agreements, and supplier agreements to purchase health care supplies and drugs

- Records of health care services performed as they relate to various health care incidents, visits, and episodes

- Claims submitted and the status of the claims

- Amounts directly owed from patients as well as payments made by patients

- Other supporting information such as accounting information to create financial statements and human resource information to track personnel

Volume 1 provides a starting point to model the needs of health care organizations. For instance, it addresses the following:

- Data models for parties, roles, and party relationships.

- Product data model constructs that can be used as a starting point for modeling health care services and goods.

- Agreement data model constructs that are the basis for various health care-related agreements

- Delivery (shipment) and invoice data model structures for delivering and billing of health care services. Health care "deliveries" are usually referred to as performing certain services such as procedures and diagnoses or dispensing certain items such as pharmaceuticals or medical supplies. Then they are usually paid for via insurance claims submission; although it may not be readily apparent, the data structures are very similar to the shipment and invoice data structure in Volume 1.

- Accounting, budgeting and human resource models to manage finances and people.

Key aspects of health care that are not addressed in volume 1 include the following:

- The specific roles and relationships that are important to track within health care

- Patient information such as medical conditions and physical characteristics

- Individual health care practitioner information such as skills and qualifications

- Data structures set up specifically for health care services, goods, and health care offerings
- The specific types of health care agreements needed within the health care industry
- Information about health care visits, delivery, episodes, symptoms, and incidents
- Diagnosis and delivery outcome information
- Claims submission
- Payment settlement information
- Health care referral information

Table 4.1 shows which models can be used directly from Volume 1, which models need to be modified, which models not to use, and which new models are required. This chapter describes the generic models from Volume 1 that have significant modifications, plus the new industry models. (Minor modifications are explained in the text.)

People and Organizations in Health Care

Just like other enterprises, health care organizations need to track information about the people and organizations with which they interact. They need to record information about the people involved in health care such as patients, insured individuals, individual health care practitioners, administrators, provider support staff, and contact people such as those within insurance companies and pharmaceutical companies.

They also need to track information about the organizations involved in health care. This includes information about health care providers, employers (and their associated groups), insurance companies, health care networks, and health care associations.

Figure 4.1 illustrates examples of person roles, organization roles, and party relationships within health care. The generic data models, as shown in Volume 1, are used as the basis for identifying PERSON ROLEs, ORGANIZATION ROLEs, and PARTY RELATIONSHIPs within the health care industry.

Person Roles

There are some generic roles and relationships, as identified in Volume 1, that can be reused in health care. Standard person roles include CONTACT and EMPLOYEE. A health care organization may need to record various contacts within pharmaceutical companies, third-party administrator organizations, or

Table 4.1 Volume 1 and Volume 2 Data Models for Health Care

SUBJECT DATA AREA	USE THESE VOLUME 1 MODELS DIRECTLY	MODIFY THESE VOLUME 1 MODELS (AS DESCRIBED IN VOLUME 2)	DO NOT USE THESE VOLUME 1 MODELS	ADD THESE VOLUME 2 MODELS
People and organizations	Models V1:2.1–V1:2.14 except V1:2.5 and V1:2.6	Party relationship, V1:2.6 and V1:2.5, need to add health care PARTY ROLES and PARTY RELATIONSHIP subtypes as in V2:4.1, V1:2.11 modified by health care facilities and contact mechanism model, V2:4.2		Patient and provider information, V2:4.3
Product		Product models V1:3.1–3.11 modified with health care offering model, V2:4.4		
Order		Standard order models, V1:4.1–4.8 for supply side processing. Requirement, request, quote, V1:4.9–4.11, Agreement models, V1:4.12–4.16 (health care agreement subtypes are included in V2:4.5)		
Delivery	Shipment models, V1:5.1–5.8 for supply deliveries			Health care, delivery, V2:4.7
Work effort	Work effort, V1:6.1–6.13			
Invoicing		Invoice models, V1:7.1–7.10		Health care claims, V2:4.8b, Claims submission, V2:4.9, Payment settlement, V2:4.10
Accounting	All models, V1:8.1–8.12			
Human resources	All models, V1:9.1–9.14			
Additional health care models				Health care referrals, V2:4.11
Health care star schema design—episode outcome analysis				Star schema for health care—episode analysis, V2:4.12

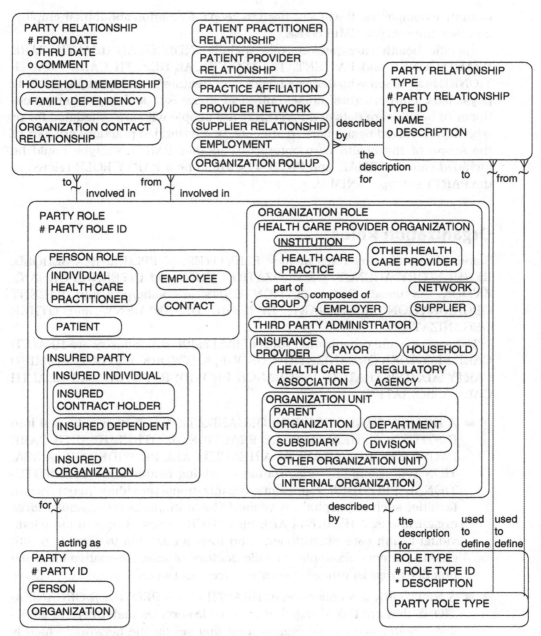

Figure 4.1   Health care party roles and relationships.

insurance companies. It will also need to keep information about their employees, thus the subtype EMPLOYEE.

Specific health care person roles include INDIVIDUAL HEALTH CARE PRACTITIONER and PATIENT. The INDIVIDUAL HEALTH CARE PRACTITIONER is a person who delivers health care treatment, and examples include physicians, chiropractors, nurses, physical therapists, and any other practitioner of health care delivery. PATIENTs are people who are scheduled for or who have received health care treatments. If veterinarian practices are part of the scope of the health care enterprise, another PARTY subtype could be included called ANIMAL, and PATIENTs would be a PARTY ROLE related to the PARTY subtype, ANIMAL.

Organization Roles

Standard organization roles include EMPLOYER, SUPPLIER, HOUSEHOLD, REGULATORY AGENCY, ORGANIZATION UNIT, and INTERNAL ORGANIZATION. As usual, ORGANIZATION UNITs are subtyped into PARENT ORGANIZATION, SUBSIDIARY, DIVISION, DEPARTMENT, and OTHER ORGANIZATION.

Industry-specific organization roles of the health care industry are HEALTH CARE PROVIDER ORGANIZATION, GROUP, NETWORK, EMPLOYER, THIRD PARTY ADMINISTRATOR, INSURANCE PROVIDER, PAYOR, and HEALTH CARE ASSOCIATION.

- A HEALTH CARE PROVIDER ORGANIZATION is further subtyped into INSTITUTION, HEALTH CARE PRACTICE, or OTHER HEALTH CARE PROVIDER ORGANIZATION. A HEALTH CARE PROVIDER ORGANIZATION represents any organization providing health care. An INSTITUTIONAL PROVIDER represents organizations providing major health facilities such as hospitals, psychiatric institutions, or other similar large organizations. A HEALTH CARE PRACTICE represents one or more individual health care practitioners who form a coalition to provide health care to patients. Examples include doctors' offices, alternative medicine practices, dentist offices, eye care offices, and so on.

- A NETWORK is a collection of HEALTH CARE PROVIDER ORGANIZATIONS that are linked together to provide services under certain guidelines established by the organization that set up the network, which is usually an insurance company.

- A GROUP is a collection of individuals who are classified within an organization to receive coverage through that organization. The most common type of GROUP is for an EMPLOYER (as opposed to a group for an association or union); groups within groups (or subgroups) could represent different geographic areas, business lines, or other group classification criteria of the employer to distinguish between different areas of the business for insurance coverage. Therefore, the recursive relationship around GROUP provides for these subgroups.

- An EMPLOYER is an organization that has employees, who may be covered for insurance as part of their employment.

- A THIRD PARTY ADMINISTRATOR is an organization that handles the administration of a health care policy and is usually hired in cases where an organization self-insures and hires an organization to administer the insurance enrollments, claims, and other paperwork. This role may be important to the health care provider organization because it may be responsible for processing health care claims.

- The INSURANCE PROVIDER is the organization that is ultimately taking the risk of the health care insurance and is typically the insurance company; however, it could be another organization if the organization decides to self-insure.

- The PAYOR is the organization that pays for the claims. This could be a different organization than the one that is taking the risk (the insurance provider)—for example, if an employer self-insures and takes the risk and a third-party administrator actually pays the claims.

- A HEALTH CARE ASSOCIATION is an organization that supports or provides guidelines within the health care industry such as the American Medical Association (AMA).

Insured Party Roles

Insurance plays a large role in health care because a great deal of the revenues from health care comes from insurance companies. As either an organization or a person may be insured for health care, the INSURED PARTY role captures information about people or organizations that have insurance.

The INSURED ORGANIZATION is the organization that is insured and covers individuals for health care. The INSURED ORGANIZATION may also play the role of an EMPLOYER; however other organizations such as associations or unions may also be INSURED ORGANIZATIONs.

INSURED INDIVIDUALs are important to track for proper insurance reimbursement because a great deal of health care treatments are paid by insurance, and therefore it is important to track who is insured. The INSURED CONTRACT HOLDER is the main party that is covered for the insurance—for instance, the person who holds the insurance through their workplace or is the principal person being covered under an individual policy. The INSURED DEPENDENT is the person being covered for a policy in addition to the insured contract holder (usually spouses, children, or domestic partners).

An alternative model could be to include the INSURED ORGANIZATION as a subtype of the ORGANIZATION ROLE and the INSURED PERSON as a subtype of PERSON ROLE. Because there is probably more common information about the insurance information surrounding these parties, the decision to sub-type based on INSURED PARTY was selected. Unfortunately, there is no way to show multiple inheritance principles (where a subtype has two parents) in this data modeling notation.

Party Relationships

ORGANIZATION CONTACT RELATIONSHIP, SUPPLIER RELATIONSHIP, EMPLOYMENT, and ORGANIZATION ROLLUP are some standard party relationships. While it could be a common type of entity, the FAMILY DEPENDENCY subtype of HOUSEHOLD MEMBERSHIP is particularly important in health care in order to identify possible candidates for health insurance because dependents of the insurance contract holders could possibly be covered for insurance.

PATIENT PRACTITIONER RELATIONSHIP, PATIENT PROVIDER RELATIONSHIP, PRACTICE AFFILIATION, and PROVIDER NETWORK are important PARTY RELATIONSHIP subtypes within health care. The PATIENT PRACTITIONER RELATIONSHIP entity maintains which PATIENTs have relationships with which INDIVIDUAL HEATLHCARE PRACTITIONERs. For instance, a patient may have selected a doctor as a primary care provider (PCP), and this would represent an occurrence of this entity. The PATIENT PROVIDER RELATIONSHIP identifies which patients are with which HEALTH CARE PROVIDER ORGANIZATIONS. Patients may have relationships with either the practitioner and/or the health care provider organization, and therefore both of the previous relationships are needed. The PRACTICE AFFILIATION subtype identifies which INDIVIDUAL HEALTH CARE PRACTITIONERS are associated with which HEALTH CARE PROVIDER ORGANIZATIONs. Examples include a physician employed by a medical practice, a chiropractor who plays the role of backup within a chiropractic office, or a doctor who plays the role of visiting physician within a hospital. The PROVIDER NETWORK RELATIONSHIP shows which providers are associated with which health care networks.

Party Roles Example

Our case example for this chapter is an integrated health care organization called "Utterly Complete Health Care" that performs a great variety of both in-patient and out-patient services.

Tables 4.2, 4.3, and 4.4 provide examples of person roles, organization roles, and party relationships within this health care organization.

Table 4.2 shows that Johnny Wreck is a patient and also an insured individual, namely the insured contract holder. A patient is a person who receives health care; an insured individual is a person who has or has had a health care policy. Sammy Wreck is a dependent, Dr. Jim Right is a physician, Jill Helpful works as a benefits coordinator, Harry Motives is the contact representative for a pharmaceutical company, and Larry Lookey is the contact representative for a third-party administrator.

Some of the roles could have subtypes within those roles. For example, Dr. Jim Right is an individual health care provider and specifically a physician. The role "individual health care provider" may encompass physicians, chiropractors, nurses, and anyone administering treatments to patients. While the data model in Figure 4.1 does not show these as subtypes, if one wanted to be more specific, these also could be identified as subtype entities within INDIVIDUAL HEALTH CARE PRACTITIONER.

Table 4.3 illustrates possible roles for organizations. "Utterly Complete Health Care" is the overall provider. It happens to own a physician's office called "Utterly Complete Physicians," a hospital called "Utterly Complete Hospital," and a chiropractic office that is incredibly called "Utterly Complete Chiropractic." Utterly Complete Hospital has many internal organizations such as admissions, surgery, and emergency room. It has many insurance organizations for which it tracks information, such as Always Paying Insurance, Inc. and Premium Insurance, Inc. Health Administrators is a third-party administrator

Table 4.2 Health Care Person Roles

PARTY	PERSON ROLE	INSURED PARTY ROLE	ATTRIBUTES OR RELATIONSHIPS
Johnny Wreck	Patient	Insured individual, Insured contract holder	Medical history
Sammy Wreck	Dependent—son		
Dr. Jim Right	Individual health care provider—physician		Medical degrees, certifications
Jill Helpful	Employee—benefits administrator		
Harry Motives	Contact—pharmaceutical company		
Larry Lookey	Contact—third-party administrator		

Table 4.3 Health Care Organization Roles

PARTY	ORGANIZATION ROLE
Utterly Complete Health Care	Provider
Utterly Complete Physicians	Provider—doctor's office
Utterly Complete Hospital	Provider—hospital
Utterly Complete Chiropractic	Provider—chiropractic
Admissions	Internal organization
Surgery	Internal organization
Emergency Room	Internal organization
Always Paying Insurance, Inc.	Insurance provider
Premium Insurance, Inc.	Insurance provider
Health Administrators, Inc	Third-party administrator
Feel Better Drugs	Pharmaceutical company
Always HMO	Network
Physicians of America	Health care association
Wreck household	Household

responsible for paying claims for some of their patients who are employed by companies that use this third-party administrator. When they need to order pharmaceuticals, one of their key suppliers is "Feel Better Drugs." "Always HMO" is an HMO network that was set up through "Always Paying Insurance, Inc." "Physicians of America" is a health care organization to which many of their physicians belong. Finally, households may be organizations also, and the Wreck Household is an example of a specific household for Mr. and Mrs. Wreck, who are married with three children. The household would have a **party id** to identify the unique instance of this Wreck household because there may be other households whose last name is Wreck.

The PARTY ROLES entity stores only the fact that these parties may be involved in these roles. The PARTY RELATIONSHIP entity shown in Figure 4.1 will link roles to relationships that exist between parties. Table 4.4 depicts how roles work together to define relationships. The first row shows that Johnny Wreck is a patient of the individual health care provider, Dr. Jim Right, who is actually the primary care provider for Johnny. Johnny Wreck has a relationship with "Utterly Complete Health Care," the health care provider. The next row shows that Dr. Jim Right is affiliated with "Utterly Complete Health Care" as a practicing physician. Johnny and Sammy Wreck are both members of the "Wreck household." Sammy Wreck is also an insured dependent of the insured contract holder, Johnny Wreck. "Utterly Complete Health Care" and "Knee

Table 4.4 Health Care Party Relationships

PARTY ROLE 1	PARTY 1	PARTY ROLE 2	PARTY 2	PARTY RELATIONSHIP TYPE
Patient	Johnny Wreck	Individual health care practitioner	Dr. Jim Right	Patient practitioner relationship—primary care provider
Patient	Johnny Wreck	Health care provider organization	Utterly Complete Health Care	Patient provider relationship
Individual health care practitioner	Dr. Jim Right	Health care provider organization	Utterly Complete Health Care	Practice affiliation
Person	Johnny Wreck	Household	Wreck household	Household member
Person	Sammy Wreck	Household	Wreck household	Household member
Insured contract holder	Johnny Wreck	Insured dependent	Sammy Wreck	Family dependency
Health care Provider Organization	Utterly Complete Health Care	Network	Always HMO	Provider network member
Health care Provider Organization	Knee Specialists, Inc.	Network	Always HMO	Provider network member
Contact—pharmaceutical company	John Roberts	Pharmaceutical company	Feel Better Drugs	Organization contact
Subsidiary	Finest Treatment Health	Parent organization	Utterly Complete Health Care	Organization roll-up

Specialists" are both HEALTH CARE PROVIDER ORGANIZATIONs in the "Always HMO" network. Therefore "Utterly Complete Health Care" knows that they are in this network, and they also know that people within the Always HMO network are covered if they send them to "Knee Specialists, Inc." John Roberts is a contact at "Feel Better Drugs." "Finest Treatment Health" is a subsidiary of "Utterly Complete Health Care."

With the data structures in Figure 4.1, health care organizations can track information about the people and organizations that are important within their enterprise. The previous examples illustrated only some examples and a starting point for the data modeling effort. Your enterprise may include other types of people, organizations, and relationships that need to be further subtyped within the party, party roles, and party relationship structures that have been provided.

Health Care Facilities and Contact Mechanisms

Because most health care services and goods are delivered using the provider's health care facilities such as their offices, hospital, clinic, rooms, and so on, the health care facility is a significant entity to track. These facilities need to be scheduled and accounted for in order to render appropriate levels of health care. The delivery section later in this chapter will allow patients to book both visits and the facility. This section identifies the types of facilities that are typical in health care.

Figure 4.2 modifies the generic contact mechanism and facility data model, V1:2.11, and customizes the subtypes of FACILITY for health care. All of the generic contact mechanism data constructs, as modeled in Volume 1, apply in health care because health care parties still have the same types of contact mechanism needs. The subtypes for FACILITY include HOSPITAL, MEDICAL OFFICE, MEDICAL BUILDING, AMBULATORY SURGERY CENTER, CLINIC, ROOM, and FLOOR. These subtypes may need to be modified further for the enterprise's needs. For instance, an institution such as a hospital may also want to track and schedule BEDs, which would be related to ROOMs, which are related to FLOORs, which are related to BUILDING. The data structure in Figure 4.2 is left in a generic fashion, and it allows data modelers to build on it with their own requirements, depending on the type of health care provider organization being modeled.

Patient, Practitioner, and Provider Information

While many of the previous PARTY ROLE subtypes have information associated with them, patients, individual health care practitioners, and health care

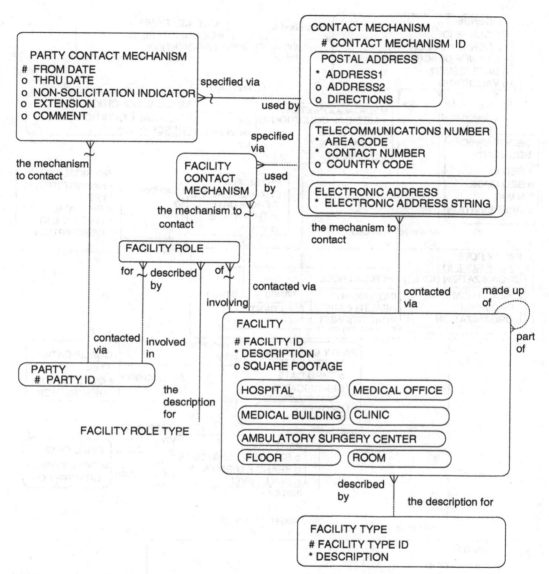

Figure 4.2   Health care facilities and contact mechanisms.

providers represent some of the key roles in health care, and therefore this sec-tion will identify some of the important information associated with these roles.

Figure 4.3 provides a data model to illustrate information about PARTY ROLES of PATIENT, INDIVIDUAL HEALTH CARE PRACTITIONER, and HEALTH CARE PROVIDER ORGANIZATION as well as some information associated with other PARTYs.

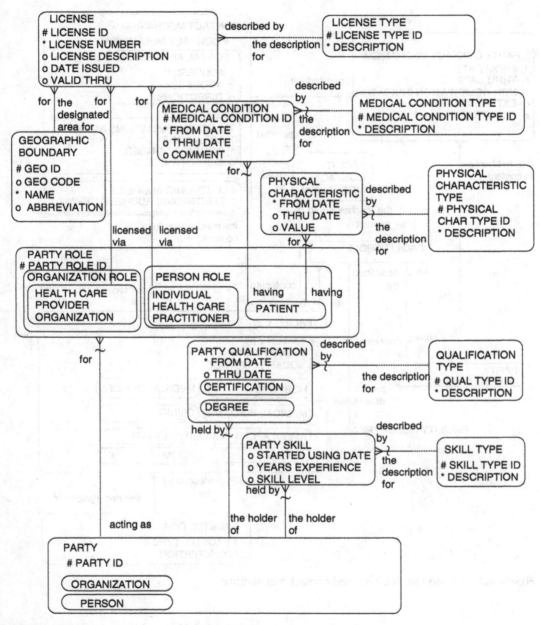

Figure 4.3 Patient and provider information.

The PARTY QUALIFICATION and PARTY SKILL entities are associative entities that maintain the competencies and background expertise for PARTYs. This information is important not only for individual health care practitioners and health care providers, but also for other roles such as for employees and suppliers. Because this information can apply to many roles, the relationships are maintained for the PARTY entity. If there was a desire to be more specific, the data modeler could portray these relationships for each role that applies to SKILL TYPE and QUALIFICATION TYPE.

It is important to store license information for HEALTH CARE PROVIDER ORGANIZATIONs as well as for INDIVIDUAL HEALTH CARE PRACTITION-ERs in order to maintain LICENSE information and the states, provinces, countries, or other GEOGRAPHIC BOUNDARYs for which the license may apply. MEDICAL CONDITIONs and PHYSICAL CHARACTERISTICs are very important information for PATIENTs. There may be information regarding MEDICAL CONDITIONs of PATIENTs that may be needed in order to properly provide health care services. This medical condition information may be used in conjunction with subsequent models in this chapter, which deal with health care visits, service delivery, diagnosis, and outcomes. For example, some medical conditions that a patient may communicate on his initial visit may be an allergy to certain drugs, a particular disease that he or she has had, or a particular phobia. PHYSICAL CHARACTERISTICs maintain information about the PATIENT such as height, weight, cholesterol level, blood pressure, and other characteristics that may change over time.

Health Care Products

Health care organizations don't generally think of themselves as being product-oriented. They are service providers, and they perform procedures, offer diagnoses, and help patients through their time and expertise. What about the pharmaceuticals, supplies, and medical equipment that they may offer? Therefore they offer both goods and services according to our Volume 1 data model structures. We will refer to these "products" as HEATH CARE OFFERINGS because that term more accurately reflects the nature of health care.

In this section, the product definition model will be modified to show the subtypes associated with health care offerings. The generic models, such as supplier product, inventory item storage, price components, cost components, and price components, from Volume 1 may be used with minor modifications to accommodate different terminology for health care. New or significantly modified models will be discussed in the following sections.

Health Care Offering Definition

Figure 4.4 identifies the major types of offerings available in health care. The HEALTH CARE OFFERING entity defines services or items that a health care provider may deliver to its patients. The HEALTH CARE SERVICE OFFER-ING entity records possible services that may be performed by health care

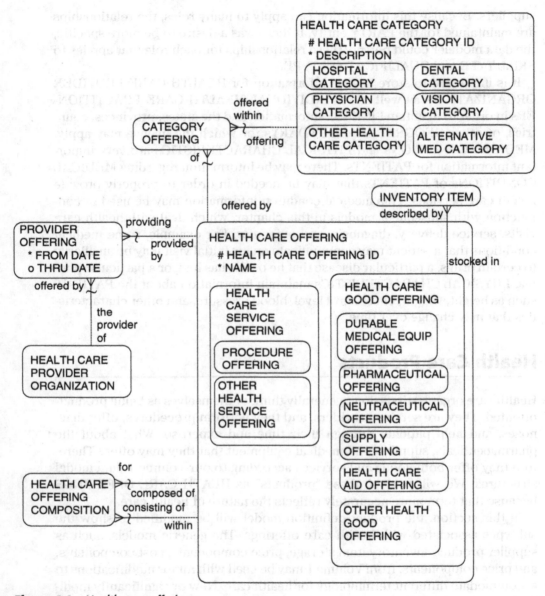

Figure 4.4   Health care offerings.

practitioners. The PROCEDURE OFFERING entity stores types of standard health care treatments that practitioners can offer to patients. OTHER HEALTH SERVICE OFFERINGs maintain all other treatments that are not typically categorized as procedures—for instance, if a practitioner offers a health care plan to see a patient for several visits over an extended period of time. The HEALTH CARE GOOD OFFERING stores tangible items that may be delivered to patients that are subtyped into DURABLE MEDICAL EQUIP OFFERING, PHARMACEUTICAL OFFERING, NEUTRACEUTICAL OFFERING, SUPPLY OFFERING, HEALTH CARE AID OFFERING, and OTHER HEALTH GOOD OFFERING. Different providers may have different health care offerings.

The PROVIDER OFFERING entity records which HEALTH CARE PROVIDER ORGANIZATION delivers which HEALTH CARE OFFERINGs. This is important for enterprises that are tracking many providers—for instance, where there are many health care subsidiaries that each provides different types of health care services.

HEALTH CARE CATEGORY OFFERING records which types of HEALTH CARE OFFERING may be offered within which types of HEALTH CARE CATEGORYs. Subtypes of HEALTH CARE CATEGORYS include HOSPITAL CATEGORY, PHYSICIAN CATEGORY, DENTAL CATEGORY, VISION CATEGORY, and ALTERNATIVE MED CATEGORY. This would allow the provider to show that a PROCEDURAL OFFERING such as an "emergency room exam" may be offered only within a HOSPITAL CATEGORY.

Some of the HEALTH CARE GOOD OFFERINGs may be inventoried in supply closets or other containers and/or locations, and therefore the INVENTORY ITEM entity is related to HEALTH CARE GOOD OFFERING to accommodate physical storage and tracking of items. Refer to V1:3.6, inventory item storage, for a more comprehensive inventory storage model. Also note an alternative to the model shown would be a relationship between INVENTORY ITEM and PARTs (which may make up GOODs) instead of directly to goods, depending on whether individual parts and assemblies are required. Refer to Chapter 2 of this book for a discussion of PARTs.

Claims sometime request payment based upon a diagnosis. With this in mind, should health care service offerings include diagnoses as well as procedures? A health care service offering represents types of services that health care professionals can deliver. Procedures represent the rendering of specific health care-related tasks. Diagnoses are the rendering of a medical opinion about the patient's condition. Is a diagnosis really a health care offering, or is it related to a procedure? If a patient sees a doctor for a medical opinion about certain symptoms, and the doctor renders a diagnosis after examining the patient, what services just occurred? One can argue that the service was an examination and that the diagnosis was related to the exam. The patient doesn't get charged for the diagnosis; he or she is charged for the related exam, which is a procedure. Because diagnoses are not generally chargeable items, we will not include diagnosis as a subtype of health care offering. We will discuss diagnoses later in the health care delivery section. Diagnoses are based on the ability and experience of the health care practitioner to evaluate the tests, physical exams, and overall presentation of the patient.

Table 4.5 lists a few examples of health care offerings available within "Utterly Complete Health Care." Some offerings are provided within only certain

Table 4.5 Health Care Offerings

* PROVIDER OFFERING	HEALTH CARE OFFERING NAME	HEALTH CARE OFFERING TYPE	HEALTH CARE CATEGORY
Utterly Complete Physicians	General examination	Procedure offering	Physician
	X-ray	Procedure offering	Physician
	Blood test	Procedure offering	Physician
Utterly Complete Hospitals	Emergency room exam	Procedure offering	Hospital
	X-ray	Procedure offering	Hospital
	Chemotherapy	Procedure offering	Hospital
	Blood test	Procedure offering	Hospital
	Prozac	Pharmaceutical offering	Hospital
Utterly Complete Chiropractic	Initial consultation	Procedure offering	Chiropractic
	Adjustment	Procedure offering	Chiropractic
	Car seat cushion	Health care aid offering	Chiropractic

categories of health care. For example, "emergency room exam" is a procedure offered only by hospitals. Some offerings are available within many categories. "General examination" is a procedure that may be offered within physician's offices or hospitals. "Prozac" is an example of a health care good offering, namely a pharmaceutical. "Car seat cushion" is an example of a health care aid offering. These represent only a small sampling of possible health care offerings.

Health Care "Orders"

An order is a commitment to buy particular products or services. Health care organizations don't typically record orders for their services, as it is often difficult to predetermine services needed for a patient until the patient comes in for a visit. The closest thing to a health care order is an appointment to see an individual health care practitioner. This is unlike an order in that it does not specify what products or offerings are being committed (unless one considers the commitment of the health care practitioner to that time slot). The appointment will be handled within the health care delivery section as a possible status of "scheduled" for a health care delivery.

While it is possible for patients to order health care goods, the individual practitioner generally recommend the types of health care goods needed, such as medical equipment, pharmaceuticals, and health care aids. The order models can be used, however, to record purchase orders for these types of goods within health care organizations.

All the order and agreement models from Volume 1 may be used as is with the exception of the need to specify subtypes of agreements that are specific to health care. The order models V1:4.1–4.8 are generally used to track orders for the purchase of health care items by providers, and they are not generally used to maintain orders from patients (because in health care, practitioners generally give the orders).

Models V1:4.9–4.11, which store requirements, request, and quote information, may be used to track purchasing information needed by health care provider organizations. Health care organizations may want to record requirements for supplies. Requests such as RFI and RFPs may be used by health care providers to research possible options they have regarding purchases. The providers may want to record quotes for both services they offer as well as quotes they receive from their suppliers.

Agreements are understandings between parties over extended time periods. An important agreement that exists within health care is the patient/provider agreement. This type of agreement specifies the terms of the health care relationship between the patient and the provider.

The generic Volume 1 agreement models (V1:4.12–4.16) maintain agreement information that may be used to track patient/practitioner relationships or supplier agreements. The following section will show the agreement model with applicable health care agreement subtypes and examples.

Agreement Definition

Figure 4.5 shows a customized version of the V1:4.12 agreement model. The only difference is that the AGREEMENT includes the subtypes of PATIENT PROVIDER AGREEMENT, INSURANCE POLICY (see Chapter 5, "Insurance," for more details on this type of agreement), and PROVIDER NETWORK AGREEMENT in addition to some of the standard agreement subtypes of EMPLOYMENT AGREEMENT and PURCHASE AGREEMENT.

Table 4.6 provides examples of the type of information that may be recorded in a patient/practitioner agreement. Agreement 12983 is a patient/provider agreement that specifies the terms of Johnny Wreck seeking treatment at Utterly Complete Chiropractic. This is a six-month agreement whereby Johnny may receive as many adjustments as needed within the limits specified by the terms.

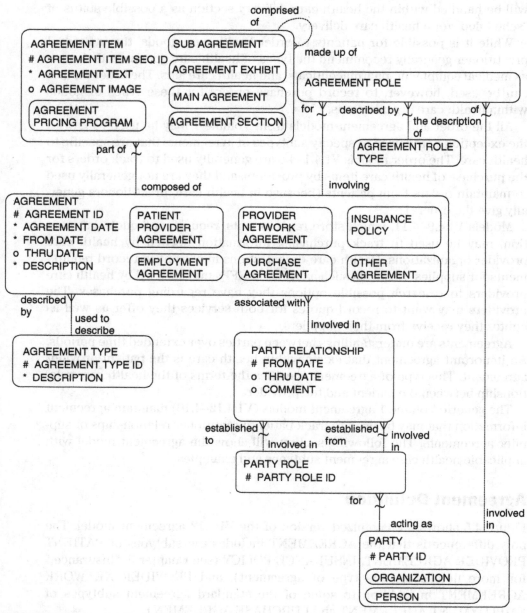

Figure 4.5 Health care agreements.

Johnny Wreck also has an agreement with Utterly Complete Health Care to provide therapy and massage. The provider network agreement 38049 represents the agreement that "Utterly Complete Health Care" signed to be in the "Always HMO network."

Table 4.6 Health Care Agreements

AGREEMENT	PARTY RELATIONSHIP	AGREEMENT DESCRIPTION	AGREEMENT FROM DATE	AGREEMENT THRU DATE	AGREEMENT ITEM	AGREEMENT ITEM TERMS	AGREEMENT ITEM PRICE COMPONENT
12983 Patient/ provider agreement	Johnny Wreck, Utterly Complete Chiropractic	Chiropractic treatment agreement	Jan 1, 2000	Jun 30, 2000	Chiropractic adjustments	Patient may receive as many adjustments as needed within agreement time frame, Patient may not receive more than one adjustment per day or more than three per week	$3,000 00
237487 Patient/ provider agreement	Johnny Wreck, Utterly Complete Health Care	Therapy treatment agreement	June 3, 2000	Sept 3, 2000	Physical therapy sessions	Patient receives a fixed price for therapy for next three months	$100
					Massage		$50
390849 Provider network agreement	Utterly Complete Health Care, Always HMO Network	Provider network agreement	Jan 1, 2001	Dec 31, 2001	Provider network sign-up		

Health Care Shipments and Delivery

Health care organizations deliver services as well as goods. The following section will cover data models to maintain information about health care incidents, episodes, visits, health care delivery, diagnosis, outcomes, and information related to these entities.

The shipment models from Volume 1 (V1:5.1–5.8) may be needed because health care providers may sell and ship health care good offerings such as pharmaceuticals, supplies, or equipment as well as receiving shipments of these goods. Because shipments are not the primary information focus of health care organizations, this section will focus on the information requirements for delivering health care services.

Health Care Episodes, Incidents and Visits

Health care delivery usually begins with the reasons that people need health care, whether it is for preventative treatments or whether it is related to health care issues that arise. People unfortunately have health care incidents and episodes for which they need treatment. They will then set up appointments with health care providers and receive treatments. The following section will illustrate the information requirements for patients' incidents, episodes, visits, health care deliveries, and diagnoses.

Figure 4.6 provides a data model for health care incidents, episodes, and visits. There may be INCIDENTs, such as a car accident, epidemic, or other event, that may have led to HEALTH CARE EPISODEs, such as injuries or illnesses. An INCIDENT describes a particular event, such as a car accident, that may require health care. The **empl related ind** indicates whether the health care incident occurred during the hours of the patient's employment. An EPISODE captures information about a particular health care injury, disease, or ailment and allows the ongoing tracking of a particular health care case. The relationship from INCIDENT to HEALTH CARE EPISODE shows that one INCIDENT may lead to multiple EPISODES; for example, a car crash incident could lead to a concussion episode as well as a psychological episode. The INCIDENT TYPE and EPISODE TYPE entities describe the possible types of episodes and incidents that could occur.

PATIENTS will then set up HEALTH CARE VISITs. A HEALTH CARE VISIT may have been scheduled for several VISIT REASONs such as because of a HEALTH CARE EPISODE, because of various SYMPTOMs or for another reason that may be recorded in the **description** for VISIT REASON. Each SYMPTOM may subsequently be determined that it is related to a HEALTH CARE

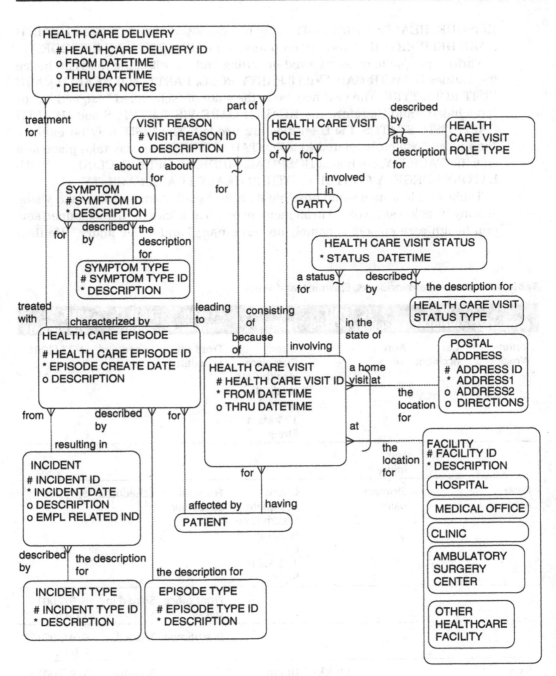

Figure 4.6 Health care incidents, episodes, and visits.

EPISODE. HEALTH CARE VISITS may be composed of one or more HEALTH CARE DELIVERYs that may be treatments for a HEALTH CARE EPISODE.

Various people may be involved in setting and coordinating the visit, hence the entities HEALTH CARE VISIT PARTY ROLE, PARTY, and HEALTH CARE VISIT ROLE TYPE. The visit may be in the state of "scheduled," "signed in," or "concluded," and therefore the HEALTH CARE VISIT STATUS and HEALTH CARE VISIT STATUS TYPE entities are needed. The VISIT may be either a "home call," which is related to a POSTAL ADDRESS, or may take place at a specific FACILITY, such as a HOSPITAL, MEDICAL OFFICE, CLINIC, AMBULATORY SURGERY CENTER or OTHER HEALTH CARE FACILITY.

Table 4.7 illustrates some possible data for health care episodes and visits. Johnny Wreck was involved in an incident of a "car accident." He sustained several health care episodes, namely an "arm injury" and a "leg injury." He then

Table 4.7 Health Care Incidents, Episodes, and Visits

PATIENT	INCIDENT	EPISODE	VISIT REASON	FACILITY	PERSON VISIT ROLE	VISIT STATUS	VISIT STATUS DATE
Johnny Wreck	Car accident	Arm injury		Utterly Complete Health Care medical office, 123 Main Street	Front office scheduler	Scheduled	2/23/2001
		Leg injury					
Peter Acher		Stomach pains		Utterly Complete Health Care medical office, 123 Main Street	Front office scheduler	Scheduled	5/7/2001
					Front office sign-in	Signed in	5/9/2001 11 a.m.
					Practitioner	Treated	9/9/2001 2 p.m.
Sam Healthright			Check-up	Utterly Complete Health Care, 123 Main Street		Scheduled	7/9/2001 3 p.m.

scheduled a visit with the 123 Main Street address of "Utterly Complete Health Care." Peter Acher needed health care based on stomach pains. In this case, there was no incident, only a health care visit. Sam Healthright had no incident or episode, but he did have a visit reason; he scheduled a preventative maintenance check-up.

Health Care Delivery

Figure 4.7 identifies the types of information used for delivering health care. Within each HEALTH CARE VISIT there may be several HEALTH CARE DELIVERYs, such as an EXAMINATION, PROCEDURE DELIVERY, DRUG ADMINISTRATION, SUPPLY ADMINISTRATION, or DME (DURABLE MEDICAL EQUIPMENT) DELIVERY. Each HEALTH CARE DELIVERY may be tied back to the specific HEALTH CARE EPISODE it is treating. Each HEALTH CARE DELIVERY must be associated with a HEALTH CARE OFFERING, which identifies the list of possible HEALTH CARE SERVICEs and HEALTH CARE GOODs that may be delivered. HEALTH CARE DELIVERY may be related to one or more other HEALTH CARE DELIVERYs and hence the recursive relationship to HEALTH CARE DELIVERY ASSOCIATION. For example, a PROCEDURE DELIVERY may need to be applied with a SUPPLY ADMINISTRATION or a DRUG ADMINISTRATION.

Each HEALTH CARE OFFERING may also need to have a CERTIFICATION REQUIREMENT before being delivered, such as requiring a "specialist prescription" before administering certain pharmaceuticals. Many different PARTYs may be involved in HEALTH CARE DELIVERYs through the associative entity HEALTH CARE DELIVERY ROLE.

The DIAGNOSIS TREATMENT allows the practitioner to associate the HEALTH CARE DELIVERYs that were administered for each DIAGNOSIS. The DIAGNOSIS could be from more than one INDIVIDUAL HEALTH CARE PRACTITIONER, hence the PRACTITIONER DIAGNOSIS entity. Finally the outcomes of treatment are recorded in the DELIVERY OUTCOME and EPISODE OUTCOME, which matches possible OUTCOME TYPEs against each HEALTH CARE DELIVERY and each HEALTH CARE EPISODE.

Some HEALTH CARE DELIVERYs require certifications from the insurance company that the delivery is reasonable and necessary. The CERTIFICATION REQUIREMENT entity stores which HEALTH CARE OFFERINGs need to be approved by CERTIFICATION REQUIREMENTS of a CERTIFICATION TYPE. For instance, a heart transplant operation may need to be approved and "certified" by the medical management department of an insurance company before it is conducted in order to ensure payment. Each HEALTH CARE DELIVERY has a CERTIFICATION STATUS indicating the status of HEALTH CARE DELIVERYs that may be scheduled but not yet "certified." Possible statuses include "certification requested," "pending," and "certified."

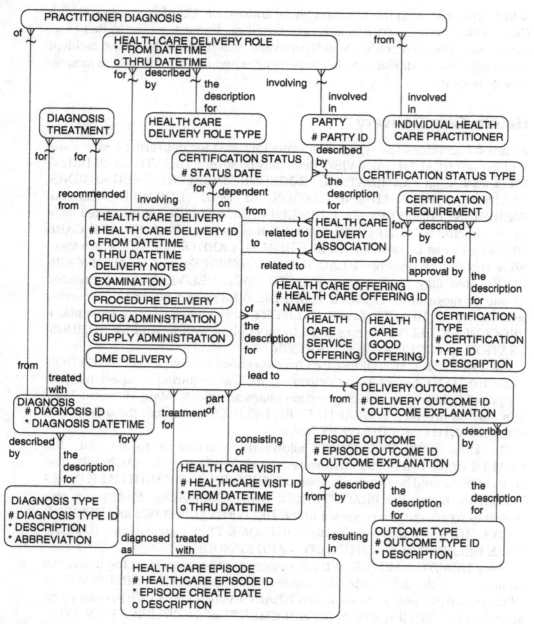

Figure 4.7 Health care delivery.

Table 4.8 identifies a sample episode of health care that may be contained within these data structures. Johnny Wreck came in for a visit on Feb 23, 2001 for an episode of a broken leg. During that visit and for that episode, he received five health care deliveries, namely, an "X-ray," (a PROCEDURE

Table 4.8 Health Care Delivery

PATIENT	EPISODE	VISIT DATE	HEALTH CARE DELIVERY	PRACTITIONER DELIVERY ROLE	PRACTITIONER DIAGNOSIS	DELIVERY OUTCOME	EPISODE OUTCOME
Johnny Wreck	Broken leg	2/23/2001	X-ray	Joe Exery, X-ray technician, Dr. Jones, radiologist	Simple fracture of the fibula, Dr. Jones, radiologist		Patient's fractured fibula healed
			Examination	Dr. Jim Right, physician			
			Set bone	Dr. Jim Right, physician		Bone correctly set in place	
			Application of cast	Dr. Ripley, intern			
			Drug administration of pain reliever	Dr. Jim Right, physician		Reduced pain, Side effect of sleepiness	
		3/1/2001	X-ray	Joe Exery, X-ray technician, Dr. Jones, radiologist		Bone healing well	
			Follow-up examination	Dr. Jim Right, physician			
		5/1/2000	Follow-up examination	Dr. Jim Right, physician		Bone healed	
			X-ray	Joe Exery, X-ray technician, Dr. Jones, radiologist			
			Removal of cast	Dr. Ripley, intern			

DELIVERY), an examination (another PROCEDURE DELIVERY), setting of the bone (another PROCEDURE), an application of a cast to keep the setting of the bone in place (a SUPPLY ADMINISTRATION), and the administration of pain medication (a DRUG ADMINISTRATION). The information in the "Health Care Delivery" column of the table may be maintained either in a relationship to the HEALTH CARE OFFERING or stored in the **delivery notes** attribute if more specific information is needed to describe the delivery. Dr. Jones, the radiologist, diagnosed this as a simple fracture of the fibula. This was followed up with two additional visits, each consisting of multiple health care deliveries. Through the course of the health care episode there are several delivery outcomes and a health care EPISODE OUTCOME of "Patient's fractured fibula healed."

Health Care Claims

Many would argue that claims processing is a unique information requirement for businesses involved in any type of insurance reimbursements. While claims processing is a unique process with unique information requirements, it shares some similarities with invoice processing. A health care insurance claim is a request for reimbursement for health care deliveries. Isn't an invoice also a request for reimbursement? Each of these transactions' purposes is to track amounts owed, and they both have items, status, payments applied against them (with an associative entity between the item and a payment), and some similar attributes for each item such as the quantity and amount owed. The quantity in health care may describe the number of days of care or the amount administered of a particular drug. The amount corresponds to the charges for the health care delivery.

Invoice Data Models versus Claims Data Models

Figures 4.8a and 4.8b illustrate the invoice model as compared to a claims model. The point of these models is to illustrate that the invoice model from Volume 1 can be a starting point for understanding the structure of a claim and what a claim represents. These models also serve to identify required pieces of information by cross-referencing the claims and invoicing models because the function of a claim and an invoice is the same, namely a request for payment.

Figure 4.8a shows some of the key entities from a combination of the invoice models from Volume 1, Chapter 7. Each INVOICE has an INVOICE RESUBMISSION entity to allow for tracking the resending of an invoice due to errors or changes. Each INVOICE also may have several INVOICE STATUSes because it is critical to track the status of moneys owed. Each invoice has several

INVOICE ITEMs that track the pieces of the invoice with the key attributes of **amount** and **quantity** to identify how much is owed and the UNIT OF MEASURE describing the measurement of the **quantity** for the INVOICE ITEM. Each INVOICE ITEM has a many-to-many relationship with SHIPMENT ITEM and is resolved through the associative entity SHIPMENT ITEM BILLING. The INVOICE ITEM also has a many-to-many relationship to PAYMENT resolved by the associative entity PAYMENT APPLICATION to track which invoices have been paid by which PAYMENTs.

The structure of Figure 4.8b is almost identical to represent CLAIM information. Each CLAIM could be resubmitted due to errors or changes and tracked via a CLAIM RESUBMISSION entity. CLAIMs, like invoices, need to be carefully tracked, and therefore the CLAIM STATUSes are very important. CLAIM STATUSes may be "submitted," "pending," "denied," "sent back for correction," and "settled." Similar to invoices, each CLAIM has a CLAIM ITEM representing the various items that are being claimed. Most of these items will correspond to a particular claim code such as a CPT (Current Procedural Terminology) or REV CODE, which will be shown in the next data model. These claim items have attributes of **claim amount** and **quantity** with a UNIT OF MEASURE to help identify the meaning of the quantity. UNIT OF MEASUREs may be "days" for a hospital stay, "milligrams" for an administration of a drug, or "units" for a health care aid or health care supply.

Just as INVOICEs are often related to some type of delivery or shipment item, CLAIM ITEMs have a many-to-many relationship to the HEALTH CARE DELIVERYs that were performed. A CLAIM ITEM may be related to many HEALTH CARE DELIVERYs because one may elect to group together two deliveries on a single claim item—for example, two administrations of the same drug. Conversely, a HEALTH CARE DELIVERY may be related to more than one CLAIM ITEM because the same delivery may be covered by more than one policy. Note that coordination of benefits (COB) rules would need to be accounted for in the business rules of the organization and not in the data model. Another case of more than one CLAIM ITEM for the same HEALTH CARE DELIVERY is if the HEALTH CARE DELIVERY had a CLAIM ITEM submitted and then a subsequent CLAIM ITEM submitted if the first settlement was not satisfactory.

The payments of CLAIM ITEMs are similar to INVOICE ITEMs. They differ in one respect, however: CLAIM ITEMs go through a CLAIM SETTLEMENT process whereby the insurance provider decides what will be paid. Therefore, each CLAIM ITEM may be settled via a CLAIM SETTLEMENT that has a many-to-many relationship to PAYMENT. Similar to INVOICE ITEMs, one PAYMENT could pay for many CLAIM SETTLEMENTs (i.e., a combined reimbursement for two claim settlements of DRUG ADMINISTRATION), and more than one PAYMENT may relate to the same CLAIM SETTLEMENT (i.e., a partial payment of a CLAIM SETTLEMENT and later on more of a payment toward the same CLAIM ITEM).

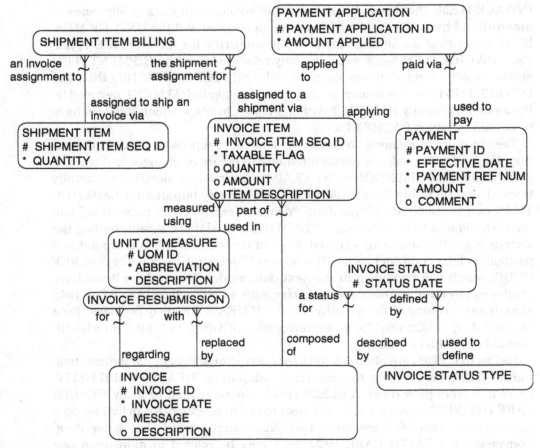

Figure 4.8a Invoices versus claims.

This section illustrates that it is often useful to use other similar Universal Data Model structures when developing a data model because it can help to identify correct data structures as well as possible data needs by offering another perspective.

Health Care Claims Submission

Now that there is a basic claims data model, the next section describes the claims information requirements for health care industries in more detail. Figure 4.9 provides a more detailed claims model and includes information that is needed to submit a health care claim.

Figure 4.9 adds data constructs to the previous claims data models: The model adds information about subtypes of CLAIMs, CLAIM STATUSes, CLAIM ROLEs, CLAIM ITEMs, CLAIM ITEM DIAGNOSIS CODEs, CLAIM SERVICE

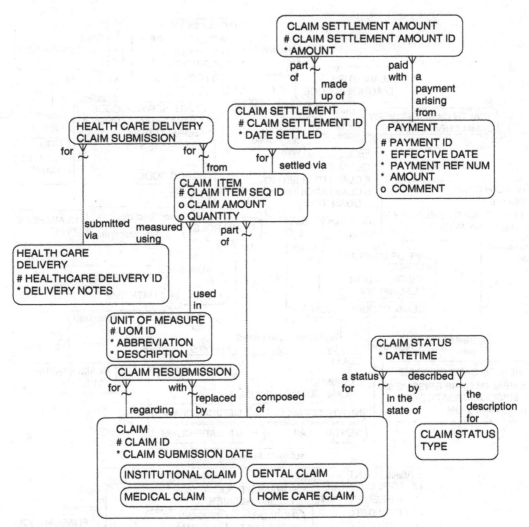

Figure 4.8b   Health care claims as it compares to invoicing.

CODEs, HEALTH CARE DELIVERY CLAIM SUBMISSIONs, and INSURANCE POLICYs related to the claim..

Claim Header Information

Figure 4.9 shows that CLAIMS are subtyped into INSTITUTIONAL CLAIMs, MEDICAL CLAIMs, DENTAL CLAIMs, and HOME CARE CLAIMs because the health care industry tends to have separate claim forms and processes for these categories. The health care industry has developed universal claim forms for institutional (hospital) claims, which are called UB-92 forms, as well as medical

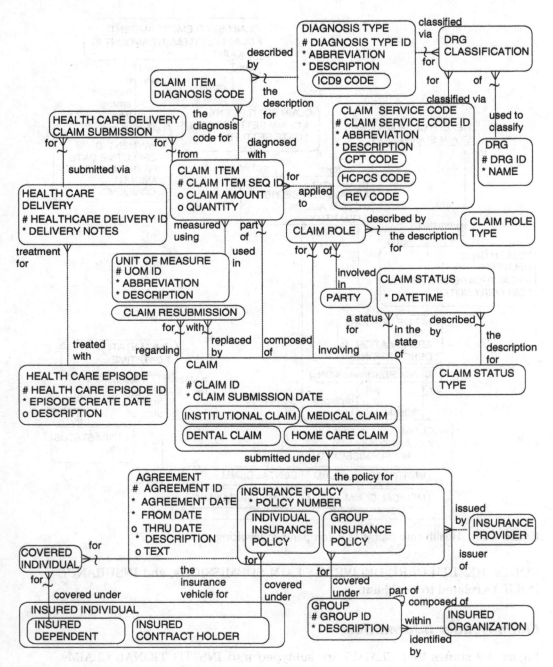

Figure 4.9   Claims submission.

claims, called HCFA 1500 (this is the standard claims form set by the Health Care Financing Administration), dental claims, called ADA-94 Dental Forms, and standard home care forms. These claims contain similar information; personal information about the patient, information about the insurance, and information about the health care deliveries that are requested to be reimbursed. Regardless of which type of claim is being submitted, each CLAIM will have CLAIM ITEMs with information.

Figure 4.9 also shows that there are many CLAIM ROLEs associated with a CLAIM, each with a CLAIM ROLE TYPE and an associated PARTY. Examples of claim roles could be to record the person filling out the claim form "claim enterer," the person "submitting the claim form," the person responsible for following up the claim's "claim manager," and so on. The patient is not necessarily maintained as a claim role because it can be derived; the CLAIM ITEM is tied to a HEALTH CARE DELIVERY, which is part of a HEALTH CARE VISIT, which is for a PATIENT. However, in the physical implementation, it is probably practical to include the "patient" as a CLAIM ROLE instance.

As already discussed previously, each CLAIM also has one or more CLAIM STATUSes, each CLAIM may be resubmitted and tracked through the CLAIM RESUBMISSION entity, and HEALTH CARE DELIVERYs have a many-to-many relationship to CLAIM ITEM through the intersection entity HEALTH CARE DELIVERY CLAIM SUBMISSION.

Claim Codes

Figure 4.9 shows information about various CLAIM SERVICE CODEs and CLAIM ITEM DIAGNOSIS CODEs that may be applied to CLAIM ITEMs. Each claim (and claim form) will maintain claim header information and claim detail information that records information on each procedure, service, supply, or other item being claimed. One of the key pieces of information stored on each CLAIM ITEM is the CLAIM SERVICE CODE and the CLAIM ITEM DIAGNOSIS CODE. Different types of CLAIM SERVICE CODEs are used in different settings, and this term, the claim service code, was made up for the purpose of supertyping different claim codes.

For instance, one subtype of CLAIM SERVICE CODE used in medical claim forms is the CPT (Current Procedure Terminology) code, which corresponds to various procedures. The HCPCS (HCFA Common Procedure Coding System) code is used for other types of health care deliveries. REV codes are used on hospital claim forms to indicate the procedures performed.

The DIAGNOSIS TYPE stores the possible types of diagnosis under different circumstances. A subtype of possible diagnosis types include the ICD9 CODE.

Medical claims use the ICD9 (International Classification of Diseases) code (soon to be updated by the medical industry to the ICD10 code) to identify one or more CLAIM ITEM DIAGNOSIS CODEs for a CLAIM ITEM. The CLAIM ITEM DIAGNOSIS CODE entity shows there is a many-to-many relationship between DIAGNOSIS TYPE and CLAIM ITEM. For instance, a CLAIM ITEM relating to a physical therapy service may be related to two diagnoses of a fractured arm and a fractured wrist.

DRG (diagnostic related groups) represent another health care code developed by the health care industry to allow the classification of procedures and diagnoses in order to facilitate payments. The entity DRG CLASSIFICATION allows DIAGNOSTIC TYPEs in conjunction with SERVICE CLAIM CODEs to be categorized into DRGs.

While codes such as the CPT and ICD9 codes represent standards in the health care industry, the data models use the terms DIAGNOSIS TYPE and CLAIM SERVICE CODE in order to stay neutral to health care industry standards decisions, in case they change over time. This is not to underemphasize the importance of establishing data standards, especially these critical health care coding standards. This is why the DIAGNOSIS TYPE and CLAIM SERVICE CODE include specific subtypes containing health industry standard codes.

The models in this book are not meant to be a precise data interchange health care standard, but they serve to represent the nature of the true information requirements needed in health care in a logical fashion. They are designed to more easily present the information requirements for the health care industry. The Health Insurance Portability and Accountability Act of 1996 (HIPAA) is an important act that requires health care enterprises to follow data and security standards. There are both data interchange and security data standards in the health care industry for each type of data element and within each health care transaction. In order to properly follow health care data interchange standards in designing physical databases, readers of this book are urged to not only use the models in this chapter, but to also refer to HIPAA, Health Level 7 (HL7 is another excellent source for health care standards) and other medical resources that are beyond the scope of this book.

Insurance Policy Information

Figure 4.9 adds to the health care models by providing insurance policy information. It is important for the health care provider to track health insurance information to facilitate claims and to get paid. Each CLAIM must be submitted under one and only one INSURANCE POLICY. This does not mean that the same health care delivery could not be submitted for two or more insurance policies because coordination of benefits rules may allow health care deliveries to be partially paid by more than one insurer. It simply means that a claim item is only for one policy. This example further illustrates the need to capture health care delivery information distinctively from claim item information.

An INSURANCE POLICY is shown as a subtype of AGREEMENT as it represents a type of agreement between insured parties and the insurance company. Although this is technically correct for a data model, the database designer may elect to store insurance policy information in a separate table as it is a very specific type of agreement for the purposes of helping the health care provider collect payment for services. One may conclude that because an INSURANCE POLICY is a subtype of AGREEMENT, the insured and insuring parties are maintained in the AGREEMENT ROLE entity; however, in order to show the specific information requirements for INSURANCE POLICYs, the specific relationships to various PARTY ROLEs are shown.

There are two types of INSURANCE POLICYs, a GROUP INSURANCE POLICY and an INDIVIDUAL INSURANCE POLICY. A GROUP INSURANCE POLICY is an insurance policy that is covering an INSURED ORGANIZATION such as an employer, union, or association. An INDIVIDUAL INSURANCE POLICY is an insurance policy that is directly contracted for by an individual. Both of these types of INSURANCE POLICY CONTRACTs cover INSURED INDIVIDUAL(s) through the associative entity COVERED INDIVIDUAL. An INSURED INDIVIDUAL may be either an INSURED CONTRACT HOLDER, which is the person who has contracted for the insurance, or an INSURED DEPENDENT, which is the person associated with the contract holder who is entitled to insurance under the policy. Examples of INSURED DEPENDENTs include the spouse, child, or domestic partner of the contract holder. GROUP INSURANCE POLICYs have GROUPs associated with them that represent a collection of individuals with a certain coverage within an INSURED ORGANIZATION. It is possible for the INSURED ORGANIZATIONs to have several GROUPs (and subgroups, which is why there is a recursive relationship) that have different coverage even though it is within the same organization.

One may think that it would be important to relate the PATIENT to his or her INSURANCE POLICY because that is the party about whom the health care provider is concerned. This model only shows information about the insured parties to the policy and the patient for the health care delivery. The health care provider will be able to find out if the PATIENT is also an INSURED INDIVIDUAL through the PARTY to PARTY ROLE relationship and thus find out if the patient is covered. This model could be extended to record the levels of coverage and benefits for the insured individuals; however, the health care provider may not have the will and means to store this information and will probably call the insurer to determine benefits and levels of coverage. Chapter 5 will cover these additional insurance data constructs.

Payment Settlement

Near and dear to health care providers (and to most of us) is the tracking of being paid for the health care deliveries. Figure 4.10 provides a template model for health care payments.

In Figure 4.10, the entity PAYMENT has three main subtypes: INSURANCE RECEIPT, PATIENT RECEIPT, and SUPPLIER DISBURSEMENT. The data model shows that PAYMENTs are from and to a PARTY. If a more specific data model is desired, the modeler could add the specific PARTY ROLEs and relate them to each subtype of PAYMENT instead of relating the supertype of PAYMENT to PARTY. For example, INSURANCE RECEIPT could be related to the PARTY ROLEs of PAYOR and HEALTH CARE PROVIDER ORGANIZATION. SUPPLIER PAYMENTS are payments that the enterprise makes to suppliers that provide goods or parts that it needs, such as supplies or health care equipment to run the health care organization. The PAYMENT TYPE entity provides a list of other types of payments, such as returns of payments to patients or to payors. The PAYMENT METHOD TYPE records the means of payment, such as "cash," "credit card," or "check."

The two primary means by which a health care provider gets paid are through insurance receipts or receipts directly from the patient. An INSURANCE RECEIPT represents payments from the payor of the claims. Note that the payor is not always the insurance company because the payor of the claim could be other types of organizations—for instance, a self-insured employer or a third-party administrator. A PATIENT RECEIPT is a receipt from a PATIENT that covers co-payments and health care deliveries that are not eligible for insurance.

The INSURANCE RECEIPT comes from a CLAIM SETTLEMENT, which is made up of many CLAIM SETTLEMENT AMOUNTs, each of which records the details behind how the claim item was settled by the claims adjudication rules of the party that processes the claim (most likely the insurance provider).

The CLAIM SETTLEMENT AMOUNT is subtyped to include several subtypes. The DEDUCTABLE AMOUNT subtype is the amount applied to the insured's deductible. The USUAL AND CUSTOMARY AMOUNT subtype is the amount that is determined to be a standard amount assigned for that type of service and may be based on other criteria, such as the geographic boundary. This usual and customary amount may be used as the basis to determine the CLAIM PAYMENT AMOUNT, or it may be the same as the CLAIM PAYMENT AMOUNT. There may be several DISALLOWED AMOUNTs, which are amounts that are not paid by the payor for various reasons, usually explained by the associated EXPLANATION OF BENEFIT TYPE. The CLAIM PAYMENT AMOUNT represents amounts that are actually paid by the payor. These amount subtypes could alternately be represented as attributes in the CLAIM

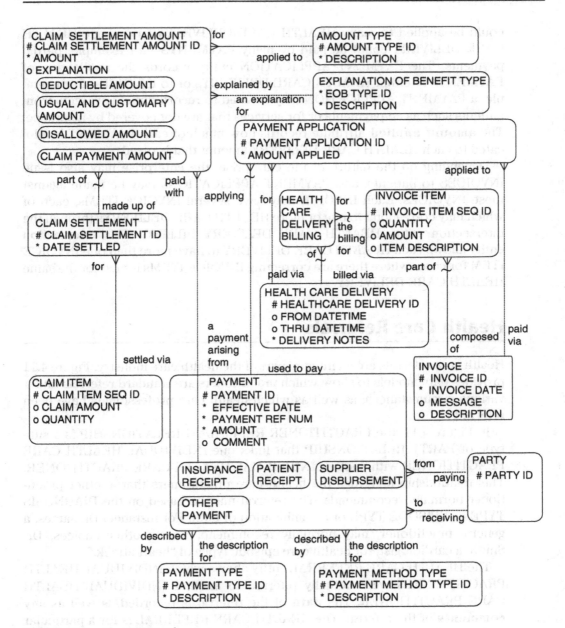

Figure 4.10 Payment settlement.

SETTLEMENT AMOUNT entity. The relationship to AMOUNT TYPE adds the flexibility of being able to add other types of amounts.

Another way that a health care provider receives monies is through direct payments from patients or from someone paying for the patient's care. Similar to the standard payments model from Volume 1 (V1:7.8a), a single PAYMENT could be applied to many HEALTH CARE DELIVERYs, or a single HEALTH CARE DELIVERY could be paid by many PAYMENTS—for example, partial payments. The PAYMENT APPLICATION entity records the application of PAYMENTs to either HEALTH CARE DELIVERYs or to INVOICEs. For example, a PAYMENT APPLICATION may be used to record direct payments from patients such as co-payments or for services that are not covered by insurance. The **amount applied** attribute records how much of each PAYMENT is allocated to each HEALTH CARE DELIVERY amount that is owed.

Depending on the nature of the enterprise, the enterprise may also issue INVOICES to patients, and PAYMENT APPLICATIONs may be made against these INVOICEs. Each INVOICE may have several INVOICE ITEMs, each of which may correspond to one or more HEALTH CARE DELIVERYs through the intersection entity HEALTH CARE DELIVERY BILLING. This intersection entity allows each HEALTH CARE DELIVERY to have more than one INVOICE ITEM for cases where there are correcting INVOICE ITEMs issued for the same HEALTH CARE DELIVERY.

Health Care Referrals

Health care referrals are an integral part of the health care industry. Figure 4.11 provides data models to show which practitioners are standard referrals under various circumstances, as well as which health care professionals have been referred.

In Figure 4.11, the PRACTITIONER REFFERING RELATIONSHIP is a subtype of PARTY RELATIONSHIP that links one INDIVIDUAL HEALTH CARE PRACTITIONER with another INDIVIDUAL HEALTH CARE PRACTITIONER. This relationship identifies the health care practitioners that another practitioner normally recommends. The referral may be based on the DIAGNOSIS TYPE or EPISODE TYPE or a combination of both. For instance, Dr. James, a general practitioner, may normally recommend, among other choices, Dr. Smith, a cardiologist, for health care episode types of "heart attack."

The HEALTH CARE REFERRAL entity shows which INDIVIDUAL HEALTH PRACTITIONERs were actually referred to another INDIVIDUAL HEALTH CARE PRACTITIONER. The **date** of the referral is recorded as well as any **comments** of the referral. The HEALTH CARE REFERRAL is for a particular patient and may be regarding a certain HEALTH CARE EPISODE or related to a specific DIAGNOSIS. For instance, Dr. James may have referred a patient to Dr. Smith, a cardiologist, based on a diagnosis of a heart beat irregularity or due to the health care episode of "heart attack."

The enterprise may have a business rule that the referral must come from a PCP (primary care provider). The data model supports this requirement through the PATIENT PRACTITIONER RELATIONSHIP that identifies whether the INDIVIDUAL HEALTH CARE PRACITIONER is a PCP for the PATIENT.

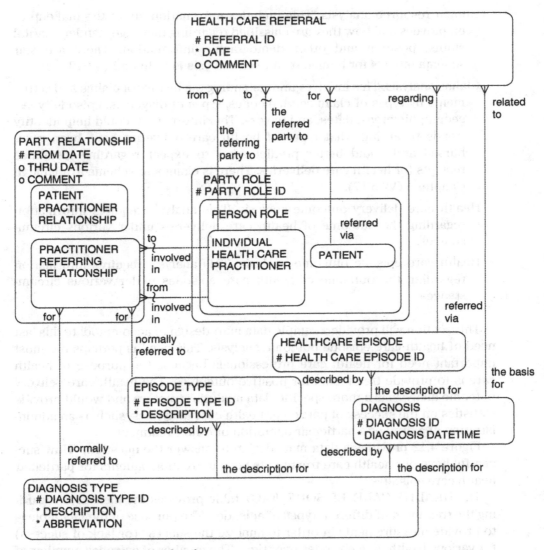

Figure 4.11 Health care referrals.

Star Schema for Health Care

How successful has the enterprise's health care been in treating patients?
Some health care data analysis needs include the following:

Financial analysis. Balance sheet and income statement trends can determine trends on the net worth of the organization and their profitability
over time. Data mart designs from Volume 1 may be used for this purpose.

Human resource analysis. This includes information about the makeup of employees and how they are classified regarding race, age, gender, marital status, position and other demographic information. There are star schema models for human resources analysis in Volume 1 (V1:13.1–13.2).

Claims analysis. This involves understanding the history of claims and settlements by types of claim service codes, types of diagnosis, episode types, geographic areas, dates, and payors. This information could help identify trends regarding what types of health care deliveries have been reimbursed and could better predict what to expect regarding insurance receipts for health care deliveries. There is claim star schema available in Chapter 5 (V2:5.17).

Health care delivery outcome analysis. This analysis requires information regarding the outcome of health care deliveries under various circumstances.

Health care episode outcome analysis. This analysis requires information regarding the outcome of health care episodes under various circumstances.

This section will provide a sample data mart design to accommodate this last need of health care episode outcome analysis. This need is perhaps the most important need for health care professionals because the purpose of health care is to provide treatments for positive outcomes. The health care delivery outcome analysis is a more specific data analysis structure and would provide statistics on the success of particular health care deliveries, such as an administration of a drug or a particular operation or other treatment.

Figure 4.12 provides a data mart design to answer the question, "How successful have our health care treatments been in treating patients for particular health care episodes?"

The HEALTH_CARE_EPISODE_FACT table provides the measures regarding the treatment of different types of episodes. The purpose of the fact table is to provide measurements in order to analyze the success (or lack of success) for various health care episodes over time. The number of episodes, number of health care visits within those episodes, number of health care deliveries, average length of the episode, and the total charges associated with the episodes are all measures.

The dimension OUTCOME_TYPES is the most significant dimension in this data mart design because the purpose of the data analysis is to view the various outcomes for different health care episode types under different circumstances, as differentiated by the other dimensions. The dimensions, EPISODE_TYPES, DIAGNOSIS_TYPES, INCIDENT_TYPES, TIME_BY_WEEK, INDIVIDUAL_ HEALTH_CARE_PRACTITIONERS, HEALTH_CARE_PROVIDER_ORGANIZA- TIONS, and PATIENT_TYPES, allow the analysis of health care episodes to be

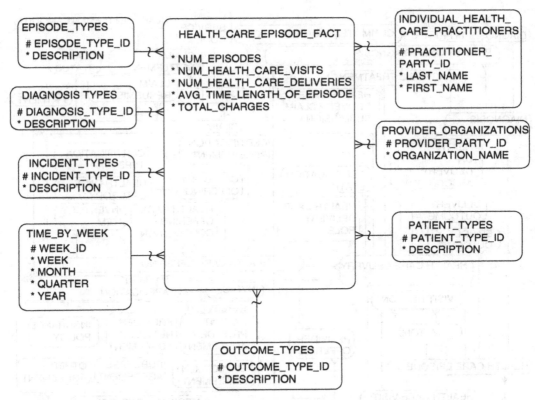

Figure 4.12 Star schema for health care—episode outcome analysis.

viewed under different conditions. This allows measurement of the outcomes by any of these factors. For instance, each individual health care practitioner's performance could be measured according to the outcomes for different types of episodes. Similarly, the performance of health care providers could be measured.

The PATIENT TYPES allows the classification of these results for categories of patients. These categories may be set up differently depending on the needs of the analysis. Some example patient types could include EEOC categorization of patients to see if the race of the individual is significant to the outcome. Another possible type of patient type could be by age classification.

Health Care Summary

While many of the data models from Volume 1 apply to health care, the data models within this chapter focused on the unique data model constructs needed for health care organizations. Perhaps the most important additional

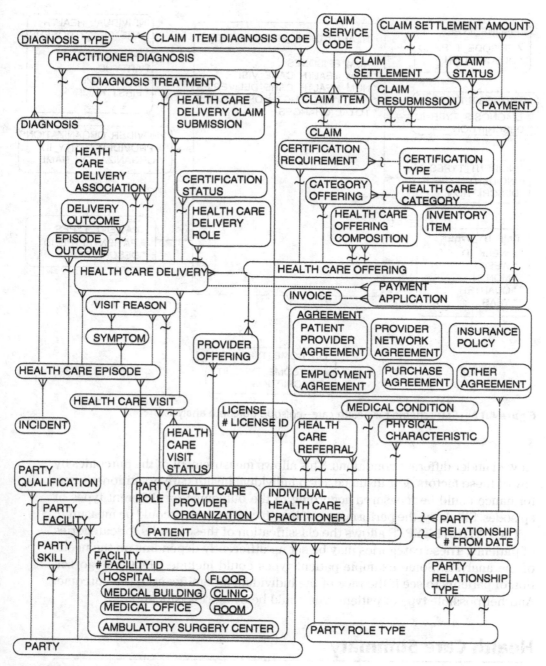

Figure 4.13 Overall health care model.

data models needed are those that capture the information requirements for incidents, health care episodes, health care visits, health care delivery, claims processing, payments, and health care referrals.

Some data model modifications were provided to show how to modify some of the constructs from Volume 1 to suit health care companies. Appropriate party relationships were subtyped, health care facility subtypes were added and product data structures were tailored. While some of the ideas from the Volume 1 data constructs were used, new models were presented to better handle health care scenarios. Specifically, the order and invoice data structures from Volume 1 were replaced with health care visit, health care delivery, and claims processing models.

Figure 4.13 provides an overview of the models in this chapter for health care.

CHAPTER

5

Insurance

An insurance enterprise is a specialized form of financial services company that provides services to protect assets from loss. This chapter focuses on the needs of an enterprise providing insurance services, including insurance providers (those who underwrite the policy and take the risk), insurance agencies, insurance brokers, third party administrators, and any other organization that provides insurance-based services.

Insurance companies are concerned with such issues as the following:

- How can we support the insurance coverage needs of our customers?
- How can we best sell products and services to meet those needs while maintaining proper risk levels?
- How can we improve customer service and maintain our customer relationships?
- How can we maximize revenues, minimize costs, and still maintain excellent service levels?
- How can we ensure that our systems are flexible enough to allow us to change our business models quickly and easily?

To answer these types of questions, insurance enterprises need to track information about the following:

- The people and organizations they are concerned with—namely, insured parties, insurance providers, insurance agents, prospects, affiliates, suppliers, employees, and internal organizations
- The product and service offerings that provide insurance coverage at various levels with different features and rules
- Servicing of and assistance for the customers, with the ability to support their ever-changing needs by tracking the specific agreements the company makes with the insured
- Providing access to those services through the policies issued to the insured; accurately tracking all activity on that policy and quickly handling any claims that arise
- Managing proper use of the insured party's information in order to assess risk for the company; assisting the insured in gaining the services required
- Managing insurance rate and underwriting information
- Providing the insured with accurate premium and billing information
- Budgeting and accounting information
- Human resources management

Volume 1 addresses many of the needs of an insurance services enterprise. For instance, it addresses the following:

- People and organization structures that can be extended for use in insurance
- Product models with product features to allow the variations that certainly occur for insurance products
- Quote models to form the basis for insurance quotes
- Agreement data structures that can provide a basis for insurance policy agreements
- Work effort models that can be used to perform service tasks and prepare needed information
- Invoice, payment, accounting, budgeting, and human resource models to manage finances and people

Key aspects of insurance companies that are not addressed in Volume 1 include these:

- Data structures set up specifically for insurance products that address flexible coverage types, coverage levels, and features
- Specific information about regulatory requirements, including internal and external regulations and their impact on products, services, and insured parties

- Specific structures for insurance policies and other agreements and their impacts on the products and services
- Specific structures for applications and quotes for services
- Rating and pricing models for insurance premium calculations
- The information needed for processing incidents and claims for the insured
- Work efforts that are specific to the insurance industry around analysis and management of risk
- Premium schedules stating what premiums are owed when and by whom
- Claims submission and settlement
- Analysis of claims history

Table 5.1 shows which models can be used directly from Volume 1, which models need to be modified, which models are not used, and which new models are required. For the people and organizations area, most of the models from Volume 1 apply; however, we need to add PARTY ROLEs and PARTY RELATIONSHIPs suitable to insurance enterprises. The existing agreement models can be used in insurance. A significant addition to the AGREEMENT is the specific subtypes of agreements for insurance policies found within the insurance industry. The most significant data modeling requirements for insurance are a revised product model, premium schedule models, insurance rate and underwriting models, and claims processing models. These models allow insurance enterprises to provide flexible insurance products, rate and underwrite insurance policies, collect premiums, and track claims.

People and Organizations in Insurance

Insurance companies generally have similar needs for tracking people and organizations as other enterprises. They need to track information about their agents, insured parties, prospects, and staff. Insured parties within the insurance industry are important, as they represent the people or organizations that must be protected from loss. In some cases, their lives, health, and ability to earn an income are the assets to be protected. It is also important to understand the relationships between the parties and the potential roles they may play. Should the loss involve a family member, it is necessary to know who is related to the insured and what their relationship is.

In the same instance, it is important to understand the relationships between organizations and persons who either are insured through them or use their services to gain insurance. These particular roles are critical in understanding the nature of the relationships between provider, agent, and insured, as well as between multiple insured parties.

Table 5.1 Volume 1 and Volume 2 Data Models for Financial Services

SUBJECT DATA AREA	USE THESE VOLUME 1 MODELS DIRECTLY	MODIFY THESE VOLUME 1 MODELS (AS DESCRIBED IN VOLUME 2)	DO NOT USE THESE VOLUME 1 MODELS	ADD THESE VOLUME 2 MODELS
People and organizations	All models, V1:2.1–2.14 except for subtyping party roles and relationships, V1:2.5 and V1:2.6	Party role and relationships, V1:2.5 and V1:2.6 replace with V2:5.1		Insurance coverage, V2:5.3, Insurance product rules, V2:5.5, Insurance underwriting, V2:5.6, Insurance rate tables, V2:5.7
Product	Product costing, V1:3.8,	Product category V1:3.2 modify with Insurance products and categories, V2:5.4, Product features V1:3.4 modify with Insurance product features V2:5.4, Product pricing, V1:3.7 modify with Insurance rate tables, V2:5.7	Product definition, V1:3.1, Product Identification, V1:3.3, Suppliers and manufacturers of products, V1:3.5, Inventory item storage, V1:3.6, Product to product associations, V1:3.9a and V1:3.9b, Products and parts, V1:3.10a and V13.10b	
Order	Standard order models, V1:4.1–4.8 for purchasing purposes, Requirements, V1:4.9 for purchasing, Request V1:4.10 for purchasing functions	Quote, V1:4.11 modified with V2:5.9, Agreement models, V1:4.12-4.16, modified with V2:5.10-5.12		Insurance application V2:5.8, Insurance quotes, V2:5.9, Insurance policy roles, V2:5.10, Insurance policies V2:5.11, Health care policy, V2:5.12

	Premium schedule, V2:5.13, Insurance claim incidents, V2:5.14, Insurance claim submission, V2:5.15, Insurance payment settlement, V2:5.16
	Claims star schema V2:5.17
Delivery	Shipment models, V1:5.1-5.8, used to track incoming purchases
Work effort	Work effort, V1:6.1-6.12
Invoicing	Invoice models, V1:7.1-7.10
Accounting	All models, V1:8.1-8.12
Human resources	All models, V1:9.1-9.14
Insurance data analysis design	

Figure 5.1 shows a data model for PARTY, PARTY ROLEs, and PARTY RELA-TIONSHIPs within insurance enterprises. Many of the generic ORGANIZATION ROLEs are included, such as SUPPLIER, ORGANIZATION UNIT, DEPART-MENT, DIVISION, SUBSIDIARY ORGANIZATION, PARENT ORGANIZATION and INTERNAL ORGANIZATION. Generic PERSON ROLEs include CONTACT, EMPLOYEE, PROSPECT, and SUSPECT and many more of the generic PARTY ROLE subtypes from Volume 1.

As in other industries, both PERSONs and ORGANIZATIONs are involved as PARTYs. There are unique PARTY ROLEs within the insurance industry. Many apply to both PERSONs and ORGANIZATIONs, while others apply only to one particular kind of PARTY. These roles are dependent on the function the PARTY is filling within the relationship.

Like other industries, PARTYs in their PARTY ROLEs have many PARTY RELATIONSHIPs that need to be identified. These include INSURED PARTY TO AGENT RELATIONSHIP, ORGANIZATION CONTACT RELATIONSHIP, and PARTNERSHIP relationships.

Person Roles

Specialized roles for persons exist within the insurance industry. The primary roles that are unique are the DEPENDENT, CLAIMS ADJUSTER, and INSUR-ANCE AGENT roles. The DEPENDENT is one where a person is related to the primary INSURED PARTY. This relationship exists for the extension of insurance coverage to that PERSON in the DEPENDENT role. For example, for a health insurance policy, "Jane Doe" is in the role of the INSURED PARTY, as she gets her health insurance through her employer. She has added to her policy her family members "John Doe" and "JR Doe" as additional insured dependents, and therefore they need to be dependents of Jane Doe in order to qualify. The DEPENDENT party role signifies a party that is a dependent of another party even if the they are not a dependent on an insurance policy.

In the CLAIMS ADJUSTER role, one individual assesses damage from a particular incident. The major focus of this role is to determine the current state of the item and to assist in valuing the item and determining the cost of restoration. The main function of the role is to supply the insured with the restoration of the loss at a fair and reasonable price.

Of key interest to an insurance provider is the INSURANCE AGENT, whose role is to sell and service INSURANCE PRODUCTs for the INSURED PARTYs. The INSURANCE AGENT may be related to the INSURANCE AGENCY if an agent is an independent agent for the agency, if they work within an agency, or if they work directly for the insurance provider. In either case, some of the functions filled by this role are to provide quotes to the insured prospect, establish and deliver policies, collect payments and fees, handle any questions or needs of the insured, and assist in the event of a claim. The involvement of the

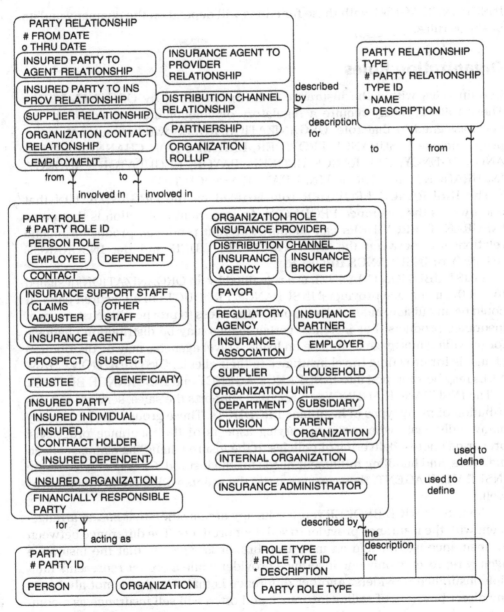

Figure 5.1 Insurance party roles and relationships.

INSURANCE AGENT with these functions will depend on the company and its business rules.

Organization Roles

Certain roles within the insurance industry are filled by ORGANIZATIONs. These roles typically require a regulatory or conglomerate to complete the tasks assigned to that role. ORGANIZATION ROLES within insurance enterprises include INSURANCE PROVIDER, DISTRIBUTION CHANNEL, INSURANCE AGENCY, INSURANCE BROKER, PAYOR, REGULATORY AGENCY, INSURANCE PARTNER, and INSURANCE ASSOCIATION.

The INSURANCE PROVIDER role is filled by the ORGANIZATION that underwrites the insurance PRODUCTs. An important distinction is that many INSURANCE PROVIDERs can support different products, producing unique relationships between the INSURANCE PROVIDER and the INSURANCE AGENCY or INSURANCE BROKER.

A DISTRIBUTION CHANNEL is a role filled by an ORGANIZATION designed to sell the insurance providers' INSURANCE PRODUCTs to an insured party. It could be an outside, independent group with access to prospective customers of insurance products. For instance, certain banks may be distribution channels for providing mortgage insurance on loans. Travel agencies may be distribution channels for providing travel insurance to their clients. DISTRIBUTION CHANNELs may be subtyped into INSURANCE AGENCY and INSURANCE BROKER.

The INSURANCE AGENCY is a role that supports the sales, service, and distribution of many types of insurance PRODUCTs. These groups tend to employ many individuals who assist in varying aspects of the insurance processes: preparing quotes, delivering of policies to the insured, handling claims, collecting funds, and handling fulfillment needs for the insured. Closely aligned to the INSURANCE AGENT, these groups assist the agents with clerical functions as well.

The INSURANCE BROKER represents any organization that has an arrangement with the insurance provider to sell their products. The difference between an insurance agency and an insurance broker is typically that the insurance agency represents only one insurance provider while a broker represents multiple insurance providers. Another difference is that a broker is not always in the direct business of selling insurance and often will sell insurance as a complement to their products. For example, a travel agency may have a brokerage agreement to sell travel insurance and a bank may sell mortgage insurance as a complement to their loan-based services.

A PAYOR is the role that is responsible for paying claims. This is usually the insurance provider, but may be a responsibility of an employer, as in the case of a self-insured organization.

A unique and important aspect of the insurance party data model is the REGULATORY AGENCY role subtype, which allows the enterprise to track those groups that enforce and communicate either internal or external requirements to the insurance enterprise. Within the insurance industry, many regulations govern the operations and processes used. These regulations, both internal and external, are strictly enforced and monitored for compliance. Insurance companies must report critical information to these agencies at frequent intervals. Often these agencies are governmental groups, but they could also be an auditing company.

An INSURANCE PARTNER role is filled by an ORGANIZATION involved in joint ventures, mutually beneficial marketing arrangements, or where companies combine equity to support higher levels of risk. These ORGANIZATIONs work with other groups in order to spread the risk of certain types of asset loss in order to keep costs and prices reasonable. Other examples of partnerships include arrangements where organizations distribute information about the provider's products or refer clients to the insurance provider in exchange for a fee. There could be many members within the partnerships formed between organizations.

An INSURANCE ASSOCIATION role is filled by an ORGANIZATION that standardizes various aspects of insurance operation. These include risk analysis, language, practices, policy contracts and other critical items required by the insurance industry. These groups offer these standards as a starting point to insurance companies. Smaller startup companies can leverage these standards to get a basic underwriting, policy contract, and set of rates in order to manage an insurance business without having to maintain a large staff to support it. Larger corporations typically have all of these areas covered, but they can use the association standards to validate and test their own standards.

Person or Organization Roles

Either a PERSON or an ORGANIZATION can fill certain roles within the insurance industry. These roles include PROSPECT, SUSPECT, TRUSTEE, BENEFICIARY, INSURED PARTY, and INSURANCE ADMINISTRATOR.

A PROSPECT is a role filled by a PARTY who is interested in services offered by the insurance service enterprise. These parties may either seek out the insurance enterprise or may be contacted by them.

A SUSPECT is a role filled by those PARTYs who are chosen for a marketing campaign but have not shown any interest in the solicitations made to them. Often within the insurance industry, marketing will purchase lists of names to offer services to and will send information to those parties.

A TRUSTEE is the role whose duty is to protect specific funds from a policy. The insurance provider may be a trustee in that it administers the funds of the policy and serves as a trustee for the insured. The party may be paid a monetary fee in filling this role as it is compensated for its administrative work.

A BENEFICIARY is the recipient of the claims settlement amounts from the policy in the event that the INSURED PARTY loses either life or health. The INSURED PARTY identifies the PARTY filling this role when the policy is established.

An INSURED PARTY is the person or organization that is covered for insurance. The INSURED ORGANIZATION is the organization that is insured and the INSURED INDIVIDUAL maintains individuals that are insured. The INSURED CONTRACT HOLDER is the main party that is covered for the insurance—for instance, the person who holds the insurance through their workplace or is the principal person being covered under an individual policy. The INSURED DEPENDENT is the person being covered for a policy in addition to the insured contract holder (usually spouses, children, or domestic partners).

A FINANCIALLY RESPONSIBLE PARTY is the person or organization that is financially responsible for the insurance or insured asset. For example, the party that is responsible for the property that is covered by the property/casualty policy. This role may include the financial responsibility for the payment of premiums and fees incurred. They are also responsible in the event of an incident or claim.

An INSURANCE ADMINISTRATOR is a role that is often filled by an outside PARTY to handle the administrative functions concerning the servicing of the INSURANCE PRODUCT. This would be the ORGANIZATION or PERSON who takes the information and handles changes, claims, and other work efforts in order to provide the insured party with the support required. Often this is another insurance enterprise that does not underwrite the policy but simply handles all the administrative functions for the underwriting company (the INSURANCE PROVIDER). Sometimes this role is referred to as a "third party administrator." It is named an INSURANCE ADMINISTRATOR in order to record the party that plays this role even when the party administering the insurance is not a third party.

Our case example for this chapter is an insurance provider, "XYZ Insurance." Table 5.2 provides examples of roles within this enterprise.

According to Table 5.2, "XYZ Life," and "XYZ Indemnity" are both insurance providers and internal organizations of the enterprise being modeled, namely, "XYZ Insurance," which is also an insurance provider and an internal organization. "Bill Smith" is an insurance agent for "XYZ Insurance," while "ABC Insurance Agency" is an insurance agency. "JJJ Insurance Company" is an insurance provider, as it is the company responsible for underwriting the policy. "Mary Doe" is considered a prospect because a quote was prepared for her by "ABC Insurance Agency." "Len Jones" is the insured for a life policy from "XYZ Insurance" and "Jean Jones" is his beneficiary. "Joe Jones" is considered a suspect because his name has been added to a list of potential insured parties, but he has not responded to any marketing campaign. "Bob Smith" works as a claims adjuster for "XYZ Insurance" and "Bill Jones" works in the actuarial department. "IEE Insurance" is considered a trustee because it handles the funds for many policies. "BBC Insurance" is considered the payor for certain claims and also is functioning as an insurance administrator for "XYZ Insurance" policies at local companies. "XYZ Marketing" is a distribution channel, as it supplies some insurance products to their customers. "A State Insurance Commission"

Table 5.2 Insurance Party Roles

PARTY ROLE	PARTY NAME
Internal organization (parent organization)	XYZ Insurance
Insurance provider	XYZ Insurance
Internal organization (subsidiary)	XYZ Life
Insurance provider	XYZ Life
Internal organization (subsidiary)	XYZ Indemnity
Insurance agent	Bill Smith
Insurance agency	ABC Insurance Agency
Insurance provider	JJJ Insurance Company
Prospect	Mary Doe
Insured party	Len Jones
Beneficiary	Jean Jones
Suspect	Joe Jones
Claims adjuster	Bob Smith
Employee	Bill Jones
Trustee	IEE Insurance
Payor	BBC Insurance
Insurance administrator	BBC Insurance
Distribution channel	XYZ Marketing
Regulatory agency	A State Insurance Commission
Insurance association	Insurance Standards Group
Insurance partner	Big Insurance Company

works closely with "XYZ Insurance" to ensure that all regulations are maintained and supported. "Insurance Standards Group" is a centralized group supplying all the standards for underwriting and policies for many insurance companies. "Big Insurance Company" is an insurance partner for many insurance companies, as it has sufficient claim reserves and specializes in varying risk efforts.

Insurance Party Relationships

Specific relationships are identified within the insurance industry. These relationships help fill the needs of the INSURED PARTY and how they work with the insurance enterprise. Relationships between ORGANIZATIONs within the insurance industry are critical to the functioning of the company, as many of the services insurance companies offer are to other ORGANIZATIONs from the insurance industry and outside of it.

Many of the relationships are between companies within the insurance industry. The related PARTYs may make agreements to fulfill part of the insurance business in order for other companies to save money and maintain costs. This provides the insured with better premiums and assists in minimizing risks that could threaten the smaller insurance company. Often, the service functions of underwriting, servicing, and processing are outsourced to a larger company that has more capacity. The smaller company pays fees for these services and is able to offer their insured parties more services at a reasonable rate.

The INSURED PARTY TO AGENT RELATIONSHIP maintains information about a central relationship in insurance—how the INSURANCE AGENT is treating and representing the INSURED PARTY.

The INSURANCE AGENT TO PROVIDER RELATIONSHIP relates an INSURANCE AGENT to the INSURANCE PROVIDER that it is representing. The agent may be within an INSURANCE AGENCY or they may work directly for the provider.

An INSURED PARTY TO INS PROV RELATIONSHIP is the primary relationship between the INSURANCE PROVIDER and an INSURED PARTY. This relationship is where an INSURED PARTY will receive insurance coverage from the INSURANCE PROVIDER in the event of loss. This relationship will most likely be linked to the AGREEMENT made by the policy statement. A person or organization may have the role of the INSURED PARTY, and an organization must be the INSURANCE PROVIDER. For example, "Len Jones" is the insured, with "XYZ Life" the insurance provider for his life insurance needs. He has a current policy for which his wife "Jean Jones" is the beneficiary. "XYZ Life" is the underwriting company for the policy and therefore the insurance provider. There may be several other policies associated with this relationship.

A DISTRIBUTION CHANNEL RELATIONSHIP is between an INTERNAL ORGANIZATION and the DISTRIBUTION CHANNEL responsible for selling insurance, such as the travel agency that sells insurance for the insurance enterprise through its channels. For example, another organization may sell insurance to "Joe Jones" and offer him certain services to meet his life insurance needs. "XYZ Life" uses this organization to further expand their marketing capabilities.

A PARTNERSHIP is a critical party relationship between an INSURANCE PARTNER and the INTERNAL ORGANIZATION. A partnership relationship is made between parties in order to meet common goals and objectives. In many instances, two insurance companies will work together to provide superior services at lower costs in order to spread risk and distribute costs. For example, "AAA Little Insurance" is a small company without sophisticated departments. Its product offerings are limited because of its small capacity to process policies and claims. In order to grow the business, the company makes an agreement with "XYZ Insurance" to take on its policy rating, claims processing, and underwriting functions. With the arrangement, "AAA Little Insurance" no longer has to pay any staff to perform these functions and can offer a wider variety of products to its policyholders.

Table 5.3 provides additional information about which roles are involved within which relationships. It is not enough to simply show the role; it is important to show the various relationships that the same role may play. For example, "XYZ Indemnity" will report to "XYZ Insurance" as a subsidiary company. "ABC Company" maintains its employee insurance plans with "XYZ Insurance," thus maintaining an insured party to insurance provider relationship. "Len Jones" also has an insured party to insurance provider relationship in which he has a property insurance policy for his home and vehicles with "XYZ Insurance." "K & K Supply Company" has a supplier relationship with "XYZ Insurance" because it delivers office products and forms to "XYZ Insurance." "Jane Doe" is the organization contact for "K & K Supply Company." "Bill Jones" works for "XYZ Insurance" in the actuarial department as a direct employee. "Mary Smith" also works for "XYZ Insurance" as a contractor in the underwriting department. "XYZ Marketing" is a distribution channel for "XYZ Insurance." "BBC Insurance" is in a partnership with "XYZ Insurance" in order to offset some high-risk policies.

Table 5.3 Insurance Party Relationships

PARTY RELATIONSHIP TYPE	FROM PARTY NAME	TO PARTY NAME
Organization rollup (subsidiary)	XYZ Indemnity	XYZ Insurance
Insured Party to Ins Prov relationship (Organization)	ABC Company	XYZ Insurance
Insured Party to Ins Prov relationship (Person)	Len Jones	XYZ Insurance
Supplier relationship	K& K Supply Company	XYZ Insurance
Organization Contact relationship (supplier contact relationship)	Jane Doe	K & K Supply company
Employment relationship (employee)	Bill Jones	XYZ Insurance
Employment relationship (contractor)	Mary Smith	XYZ Insurance
Distribution channel relationship	XYZ Marketing	XYZ Insurance
Partnership relationship	BBC Insurance	XYZ Insurance

Insurance Product

The main difference between an insurance product and other industries is that the product is not a manufactured, tangible good but a service offered to protect against a loss. The insurance product is defined in terms of what combinations of coverage types, coverage levels, and features are available under different insurance plans (products). The product that is sold to the insured party will be based on these available combinations and then will be further defined in an insurance policy agreement in which the insured will select from these available variations of the product. The agreement data models that will cover policies and the selection from the product's available coverage types, coverage, and features will be discussed later in this chapter.

It is important to understand the nature of assessing risk of loss to understand the insurance product. Regardless of what is insured—whether a person's life, health, ability to earn income, or a valuable asset like a house or car—risk is associated with its loss. The insurance provider must assess that risk; assuming that the asset may be lost, the insurance provider will decide how to protect that risk for a reasonable price. The products address the risk by focusing on what must be protected and by providing insurance coverage types with certain coverage levels and features that offer compensation if loss occurs.

Standardization within the insurance product may be found for groups under similar circumstances, with similar assets to protect, and facing similar risks. Many cases demand a customized product to protect against small group risks and potential losses. Also, there must be sufficient flexibility in the larger group risk in order to meet the customer's expectations. Regulatory requirements, such as those from the government or within the industry, will limit what is available and usable within the insurance product.

The model that will be presented takes into consideration the need for very flexible insurance product models that can be easily customized or changed over time.

Insurance products are understood by what is insured, what types of insurance coverage apply, how much is covered, and what other options or features can be applied as well as the rules that dictate how the product will operate.

Regarding what is insured, each type of insurance protects different types of things. Property insurance protects tangible assets such as a home, vehicle, vessel, special valuables, and other items against damage or loss. Casualty insurance protects income or property against an unforeseen event, such as an accident or a natural disaster. Life insurance protects the loss of income against the death of the insured. Disability insurance protects the loss of income of the insured in the event of illness. Health insurance protects the loss of income against the illness of the insured and covers the cost of treatment of that illness. Other insurance coverage exists for many other potential loss situations.

The following sections along with figures 5.2 through 5.5 will define the models necessary to define insurance products.

Insurance Products and Categories

With the above explanations, what constitutes an instance of an insurance product and what constitutes an insurance product category? This is dependent on the insurance enterprise and how it structures its products. A product may be as simple as "health care insurance" or more likely, the enterprise has designed specific insurance plans that all fall into the health care insurance category such as "PPO Plan A" or "HMO Plan A." These products are usually designed to be very flexible and each product may specify different combinations of coverage types, coverage levels, and features that are possible within the product. The coverage types, coverage levels, and features that are available will be discussed in the section after this one and the coverages that are picked will be discussed later in the "Order" section of the chapter when the policy (which is a type of agreement) is created.

Figure 5.2 shows the entity INSURANCE PRODUCT that stores a record for each basic product offering that an insurance provider offers. Each INSURANCE PRODUCT may be categorized into many types of PRODUCT CATEGORYs via the associative entity PRODUCT CATEGORY CLASSIFICATION. Types of PRODUCT CATEGORYs include an INSURANCE TYPE CATEGORIZATION, INDIVIDUAL or GROUP, or INDUSTRY TARGET CATEGORIZATION that identifies which industry(ies) may be interested in the insurance product.

The INSURANCE TYPE CATEGORIZATION includes subtypes of PROPERTY INSURANCE, CASUALTY INSURANCE, LIFE INSURANCE, DISABILITY INSURANCE, HEALTH INSURANCE, and OTHER INSURANCE to allow for other types of insurance not covered. Each of these is further subtyped and within each subtype there may be different types of product offerings or plans that may be available by the insurance provider. These subtypes show some main classifications of insurance; however, there may be other INSURANCE PRODUCT subtypes such as key employee insurance, workman's compensation, general liability insurance, errors and omissions, and so on.

In Figure 5.2, the data model shows that each PRODUCT CATEGORY may be further classified into several other PRODUCT CATEGORYs using the associative entity PRODUCT CATEGORY ROLLUP. Each PRODUCT CATEGORY can be composed of other PRODUCT CATEGORYs using the recursive relationship. This provides the capability to roll-up categories for use in reporting.

Table 5.4 provides examples of INSURANCE PRODUCTs and INSURANCE PRODUCT CATEGORYs. For example, "Home Owners Plan A" and "Home Owners Plan B" are examples of INSURANCE PRODUCTs. They can be categorized into several product categories—for example by the type of insurance

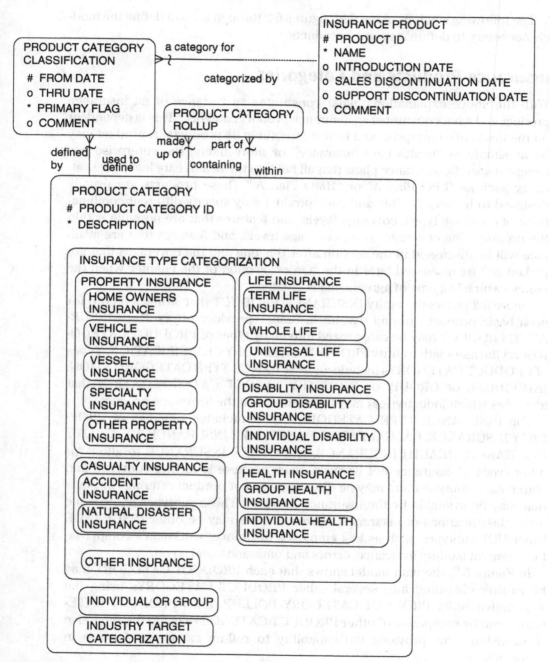

Figure 5.2   Insurance products and categories.

(home owners insurance versus property insurance) or by whether they are designed for individuals or organizations or both.

Not only can products be slotted into several categories, categories can also be rolled up into other categories. For example, "Home Owners Insurance," "Vehicle Insurance," "Vessel Insurance," "Specialty Insurance," and "Other Property Insurance" would roll into the "Property Insurance" products. "Accident Insurance" and "Natural Disaster Insurance" would roll into the "Casualty Insurance" products. "Term Life Insurance," "Whole Life," and "Universal Life Insurance" would roll into the "Life Insurance" products. "Group Disability Insurance" and "Individual Disability Insurance" would roll into the "Disability Insurance" category while "Group Health Insurance" and "Individual Health Insurance" would roll into the "Health Insurance" category. These rollups are illustrated in Table 5.4.

Table 5.4 Insurance Products and Categories

PRODUCT CATEGORY	PRODUCT CATEGORY	PRODUCT CATEGORY	PRODUCT NAME
Property insurance	Home owners insurance	Individual insurance	Home owners Plan A
		Individual insurance	Home owners Plan B
	Vehicle insurance	Individual/organizational insurance	Premium auto coverage
	Vessel insurance	Individual/organizational insurance	Premium insurance plan
		Individual/organizational insurance	Standard insurance plan
	Specialty insurance	Individual/organizational insurance	Plan A1 specialty
		Individual/organizational insurance	Plan A2 specialty
	Other property insurance	Individual/organizational insurance	Jewelry insurance plan extraordinary
Casualty insurance	Accident insurance	Individual/organizational insurance	Trip accidence policy
		Individual/organizational insurance	Common accident plan
	Natural disaster insurance	Individual/organization insurance	Natural diaster plus

(*continues*)

Table 5.4 (*continued*)

PRODUCT CATEGORY	PRODUCT CATEGORY	PRODUCT CATEGORY	PRODUCT NAME
Life insurance	Term life insurance	Individual insurance	Low cost term
		Individual insurance	Full feature term
		Individual insurance	Non-smoker Simple term life
	Whole life insurance	Individual insurance	Whole life 65
		Individual insurance	Whole life 75
	Universal life insurance	Individual insurance	Universal life premium
Disability insurance	Group disability insurance	Organization insurance	Disability plus
		Organization insurance	Disability protection A
	Individual disability insurance	Individual insurance	Individual Disability Plan A
			Individual Disability Plan B
Health insurance	Group health insurance	Organization insurance	PPO plan deluxe
		Organization insurance	HMO plan A
		Organization insurance	PMO plan superior
	Individual health insurance	Individual insurance	Maximum Individual Health A
		Individual Insurance	Low cost individual health coverage B

Insurance Product Coverage

Each type of insurance product needs to specify the available coverage types, what level of coverages are available, and what types of features can be applied. For instance, property insurance can have various coverage types such as structural coverage and personal property coverage in various amounts with different options. Vehicle coverage types can be for bodily injury, collision, and/or comprehensive in different coverage amounts with different options available under each. Health insurance could include major medical, hospital-ization, and dental coverage types, again with different coverage amounts and various optional or required features.

Figure 5.3 shows a data model for the INSURANCE PRODUCT to capture these needs for insurance enterprises. This model is an extended model of the principles described in the Volume 1 Product Feature data model (V1:3.4).

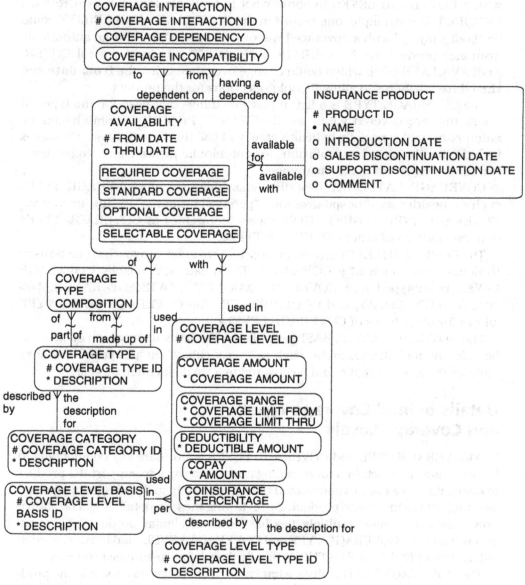

Figure 5.3 Insurance coverage.

The basic offering of an INSURANCE PRODUCT provides for many types of coverage variations as provided by the COVERAGE AVAILABILITY entity. Each COVERAGE AVAILABILITY is a compilation of possible COVERAGE TYPEs available at various COVERAGE LEVELs for the INSURANCE PRODUCT. Figure 5.3 addresses the COVERAGE TYPEs and COVERAGE LEVELs available for an INSURANCE PRODUCT.

The COVERAGE AVAILABILITY defines each COVERAGE TYPE together with a COVERAGE LEVEL to show what is available for each INSURANCE PRODUCT. For example, one record in the COVERAGE AVAILABILITY could be "bodily injury" with a coverage level of "100,000/300,000" for an automobile insurance product. Each INSURANCE PRODUCT may have several COVERAGE AVAILABILITYs, which could change over time using the **from date** and **thru date** attributes to allow flexible selections for the product.

The COVERAGE TYPE is a list of possible things that describe the types of things that are covered within an INSURANCE PRODUCT. Some insurance enterprises, and especially in health care, will call this benefit types. Examples include "bodily injury" or "collision" for automobile insurance or "major medical" and "dental" for health insurance.

COVERAGE CATEGORY describes classifications of COVERAGE TYPEs such as "health care ,""hospitalization," "personal property," or "life insurance." COVERAGE TYPE COMPOSITION allows hierarchies of COVERAGE TYPEs that are made up of other COVERAGE TYPEs.

The COVERAGE LEVEL stores the possible coverage ranges that can be used to define how much of a COVERAGE TYPE can be available. COVERAGE LEVEL is subtyped into COVERAGE AMOUNT, COVERAGE RANGE, DEDUCTIBILITY, COPAY, and COINSURANCE. The COVERAGE LEVEL TYPE allows for other types of COVERAGE LEVELs.

The COVERAGE LEVEL BASIS establishes the basis upon which claims will be paid and includes examples such as "per incident" or "per year." This may indicate the amount that could be covered in a single incident or year.

Details behind Coverage Types and Coverage Levels

The COVERAGE TYPE and COVERAGE LEVEL entities are key components to the insurance product. In understanding how these work to support the product makeup, it is necessary to understand their relationship in defining the scope and workings of the insurance product. By reviewing these in detail, it will be shown how they can support multiple flexible views of similar products. This section will address COVERAGE TYPE and COVERAGE LEVELs and the next section will address PRODUCT FEATUREs that further define insurance products.

The COVERAGE TYPE defines what types of coverages can exist in the product. Does the product support major medical, hospitalization, and dental? Does the product offer bodily injury coverage, comprehensive, or collision? These are examples of types of coverage.

The COVERAGE LEVEL describes possible amounts of risk protections that can be available to be used to further describe the insurance being offered in an insurance product. COVERAGE LEVEL subtypes include COVERAGE AMOUNT, COVERAGE RANGE, DEDUCTIBILITY, COINSURANCE, and CO-PAY as well as numerous other possibilities that could be described in COVERAGE LEVEL TYPE. COVERAGE AMOUNT defines a single amount of insurance coverage that may be available for products such as a standard amount of $100,000 for a life insurance policy. COVERAGE RANGE describes numerous values for insurance coverage such as "100,000" and "300,000" for bodily injury on a car insurance policy. DEDUCTIBILITY is another way of describing the level of coverage because it describes how much the insured party has to pay before the payor will pay insurance claims. COINSURANCE states what percentage of the amount the payor pays as opposed to the amount that the insured party pays. COPAY defines how much the insured party pays for a healthcare practitioner's visit for in-network services.

The COVERAGE AVAILABILITY describes what is or can be included in the product in terms of the combinations of COVERAGE TYPEs and COVERAGE LEVELs just described. This entity is subtyped into the REQUIRED COVERAGEs, which are a mandatory part of the insurance offering; STANDARD COVERAGE, which includes default features of the product that can be customized; OPTIONAL COVERAGE, which allows the insured party the ability to select or not select these features; or SELECTABLE COVERAGEs, which require a selection from among several available options. An example of REQUIRED COVERAGE for car insurance is when the law requires a certain level of bodily insurance. A STANDARD COVERAGE example may be a certain level of major medical insurance that is standard but may be excluded in a health plan—for example, if someone just wants the hospitalization coverage. An OPTIONAL COVERAGE could be "towing coverage" for up to $200 coverage level on a car insurance product. A SELECTABLE FEATURE could be one in which the insured party needs to select among three options such as pharmaceutical coverage, nutraceutical coverage, or both pharmaceutical coverage and nutraceutical coverage (each for a certain level of coverage), assuming that one of these options needs to be picked.

COVERAGE INTERACTION describes what coverages are either dependent or incompatible with other coverages with a certain product. COVERAGE DEPENDENCY describes what coverages are needed if another combination is selected. For instance, maintaining a collision deductibility record in COVERAGE AVAILABILITY is dependent on having a record of a certain level of collision insurance that was selected. COVERAGE INCOMPATIBILITY shows which COVERAGE TYPE coverages cannot exist with other COVERAGE TYPE coverages within a product. For example, if a comprehensive vacation plan

COVERAGE TYPE was selected, perhaps airplane insurance COVERAGE TYPE would not be compatible because it was already included.

The COVERAGE TYPE COMPOSITION maintains hierarchies of COVERAGE TYPEs that include other lower level COVERAGE TYPEs. For example, hospitalization insurance may by definition consist of emergency room visits, hospital stays, and psychiatric institution stays, among other COVERAGE TYPEs. These may be further broken down into more detailed descriptions of what COVERAGE TYPEs are included, such as X-rays, initial exams, setting bones, and so on. This allows one COVERAGE TYPE to be included in a product and to be described through this COVERAGE TYPE COMPOSITION entity to indicate the COVERAGE TYPE that is ultimately included.

The COVERAGE LEVEL BASIS describes the basis upon which the COVERAGE LEVELs apply. For example, how is the coverage level of $1,000,000 of bodily injury insurance calculated? Is it per incident? If there are several people that are injured, will it cover $1,000,000 per person? The COVERAGE LEVEL BASIS further defines the COVERAGE LEVEL by specifying the basis for the coverage. Instances of the COVERAGE LEVEL BASIS could include multiple specifications in a single row; for example, bodily injury may be specified on a per person, per incident basis .

Table 5.5 provides examples of COVERAGE TYPEs and COVERAGE LEVELs for two INSURANCE PRODUCTs, namely "Premium Auto Coverage" and "HMO Plan A," which represent an auto insurance offering of an insurance provider and a health care offering from an insurance provider. For the automobile coverage, "Bodily Injury" is a SELECTABLE COVERAGE, meaning that some selection of coverage for this COVERAGE TYPE is required. The table shows that there are two selections possible for this product, either "100,000" or "300,000," or "250,000" or "500,000." These coverages are available for the "Vehicle Insurance" type of product. "Collision Coverage" is an optional coverage, meaning that it does not have to be selected when the product is offered. If collision is selected, then the collision deductible coverage level would need to be selected; hence, it is another selectable coverage type. This is also an example of where the COVERAGE INTERACTION entity would be used to show that if the "Collision Coverage" is selected, then the Collision Deductible must also be selected as a related instance of the COVERAGE AVAILABILITY.

Another example is given for the health care insurance product, "HMO Plan A," where a number of coverage levels are available for the various coverage types, "major medical," "hospitalization," "dental," and "vision." Multiple levels of coverage are available for major medical and hospitalization; hence, these are selectable coverages (one of these coverage levels must be selected). A required part of the product is to have coinsurance of 80 percent, meaning that the insurance provider will pay 80 percent of the COVERAGE TYPEs for out-of-network coverage. This is an example of product rules that are applicable to the coverage, which will be defined in the product rule section. Another required

Table 5.5 Insurance Coverage Types and Coverage Levels Available

INSURANCE PRODUCT	COVERAGE TYPE DESCRIPTION	COVERAGE LEVEL SUB-TYPE	COVERAGE AMOUNT	COVERAGE LIMIT FROM	COVERAGE LIMIT THROUGH	COVERAGE LEVEL BASIS	COVERAGE AVAILABILITY TYPE
Premium auto coverage	Bodily injury	Coverage range		100,000	300,000	Apply per person, per occurrence	Selectable coverage
	Bodily injury	Coverage range		250,000	500,000	Apply per person, per occurrence	Selectable coverage
	Comprehensive	Deductible	500			Apply per incident	Optional coverage
	Collision	Coverage amount			10,000	Apply per incident	Optional coverage
	Collision	Deductible	500			Apply per incident	Selectable coverage
	Collision	Deductible	250			Apply per incident	Selectable coverage
HMO Plan A (health insurance)	Major medical	Coverage		100,000	500,000	Apply per incident, per year	Selectable coverage
		Coverage		200,000	750,000	Apply per incident, per year	Selectable coverage
		Coinsurance	80 percent			Apply per incident	Required coverage
		Co-pay	10			Apply per incident	Required coverage
	Hospitalization	Coverage		300,000	1,000,000	Apply per incident	Selectable coverage
		Coverage		500,000	2,000,000	Apply per incident	Selectable coverage
	Dental	Coverage		30,000	50,000	Apply per incident	Optional coverage
	Vision	Coverage		20,000	40,000	Apply per incident	Optional coverage

coverage is to have a $10 co-pay, which means that the insured can pay just $10 at the healthcare practitioner's office to take care of their part of the payment and the insurance provider will cover the rest. Dental and vision are optional coverages because they may or may not be selected as part of this product offering.

Insurance Product Features

A good deal of the insurance product offering has been covered with coverage types and coverage levels. Many aspects of what is in an insurance product have not yet been covered. For instance, what about the information requirements of maintaining other insurance product features such as an automatic loan provision for a life insurance product or a stipulation that it is necessary to use in-network health care providers if a co-pay is to be used?

Figure 5.4 describes how PRODUCT FEATUREs add to the definition of what is available in an insurance product. This figure builds on Figure 5.3, adding possible features that may apply to products and/or coverage types. The PRODUCT FEATURE describes additional things that can further define the product, and it provides more definition to how the product works. Product features may define the additional options that may be available for the product, such as "Excludes flood damage" or that there is a "multi-car discount." These features may be applicable for an INSURANCE PRODUCT via the associative entity PRODUCT FEATURE COVERAGE, which records the many-to-many relationship from PRODUCT FEATUREs to INSURANCE PRODUCTs. It also may be qualified by a specific COVERAGE TYPE via the relationship from PRODUCT FEATURE to COVERAGE TYPE.

Although not shown in the data model, these features could be defined as required, standard, optional, or selectable, similar to the COVERAGE AVAILABILITY subtypes. The PRODUCT FEATURE CATEGORY maintains classifications of features such as "billing feature" or "exclusion feature."

Table 5.6 provides examples of features for insurance products or COVERAGE TYPEs, which gives an overall understanding of how the INSURANCE PRODUCT can work. In the example given, the PRODUCT FEATURE of "Apply under 21 discount" is a nice feature for the "whole life 65" INSURANCE PRODUCT. The next row shows that the "whole life 65" product also offers a loan option feature that allows borrowing against the cash value of the policy. In the PRODUCT FEATURE CATEGORY of "loan options," the feature of an 8 percent loan is also available (there could be other features in this category such as a 10 percent loan option and other stipulations). A renewal feature that could be applied to the "whole life 65" product is "Issue renewal every 120 days." In a "Property insurance" policy for automobile coverage, the feature may be "Apply multi-car discount when more than 2 vehicles."

The next type of feature describing what is or isn't a "covered loss" is available not at the product level but at the COVERAGE TYPE level, and it states

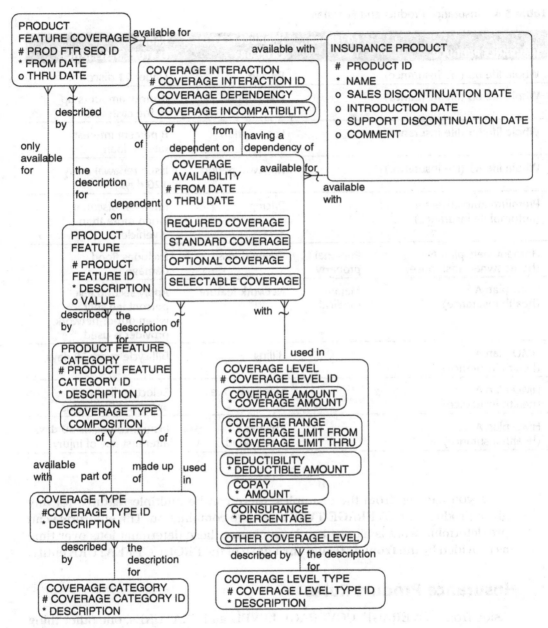

Figure 5.4 Insurance product features.

that it "excludes flood damage" for "personal property loss." For a "health insurance" product, "apply second level percentage split when out-of-network provider is used" is an important feature. This functionality allows the insurance provider to customize its products to meet important requirements of the insured parties.

Table 5.6   Insurance Product and Features

INSURANCE PRODUCT	COVERAGE TYPE	PRODUCT FEATURE CATEGORY	PRODUCT FEATURE DESCRIPTION
Whole life 65 (life insurance)		Pricing	Under 21 discount
Whole life 65 (life insurance)		Loan option	Borrow amounts up to the cash value
Whole life 65 (life insurance)		Loan option	8 percent interest rate on loan
Whole life 65 (life insurance)		Renewal period	Issue renewal every 120 days
Premium auto coverage (automobile insurance)		Pricing	Multi-car discount when more than 2 vehicles
Homeowners plan A (homeowners insurance)	Personal property	Covered loss	Excludes flood damage
HMO plan A (health insurance)	Major medical	Network feature	Apply second level percentage split when out-of-network provider is used
HMO plan A (health insurance)		Billing	Bill cycle every 30 days
HMO plan A (health insurance)		Managed care	Selection limited to approved Physicians
HMO plan A (health insurance)		Coverage type period	Insurance begins 30 days after first day of injury

As you can see from the examples, there can be multiple features for any given product or COVERAGE TYPE coverage combination. The enterprise can pre-determine what is allowed and can change these determinations over time as provided by the **from date** and **thru date** of the PRODUCT FEATURE entity.

Insurance Product Rules

Aside from COVERAGE, COVERAGE LEVEL, and FEATUREs, one other thing can define how the product operates. In the insurance business, many rules govern the way that products work.

Figure 5.5 provides a data model to maintain PRODUCT RULEs. A PRODUCT RULE governs the way that products work and therefore may be a condition that is applicable to an INSURANCE PRODUCT, PRODUCT FEATURE, COVERAGE LEVEL, COVERAGE TYPE, INSURED ASSET TYPE, or any combination of these entities. The rule may be set by an INTERNAL ORGANIZA-

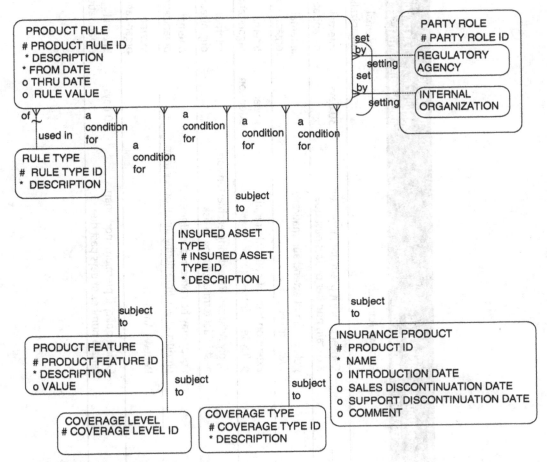

Figure 5.5   Insurance product rules.

TION within the enterprise or may be mandated by a REGULATORY AGENCY. The **from date** and **thru date** provide for when the rule is valid and the **rule value** provides the flexibility to stipulate a value to better describe the rule.

Table 5.7 provides examples of some of these rules. The rules shown are examples of rules for combinations of INSURANCE PRODUCT, COVERAGE TYPE, COVERAGE LEVEL, or PRODUCT FEATUREs. The first number of product rules is for the INSURANCE PRODUCT "Non-smoker simple term life." The "Universal life" product has a few rules as well as a rule for the loan feature within it. The health insurance product illustrates rules that are based on coverage types and coverage levels within the product. Most of the rules are originated from the internal organization; however, there are a couple that are dictated by an insurance board, namely about the re-investment of dividends for the universal life product as well as setting a limit for the interest rate for the loan feature.

Table 5.7 Insurance Product Rules

INSURANCE PRODUCT DESCRIPTION	COVERAGE TYPE	COVERAGE LEVEL	PRODUCT FEATURE	INSURANCE PRODUCT RULE	INSURANCE PRODUCT RULE VALUE	PARTY ROLE THAT SET RULE
Non-smoker simple term life				Renews Annually		Internal organization
Non-smoker simple term life				Cancel policy if premium more than a certain number of days past due	30 days	Internal organization
Non-smoker simple term life				Policy will not extend automatically past term end		Internal organization
Non-smoker simple term life				Extension term of policy after initial policy term is past	1 year extension	Internal organization
Non-smoker simple term life				Apply Adjusted Rate during each extension past initial term according to risk		Internal organization
Non-smoker simple term life				Policy may be converted to Universal product at any time during initial policy term		Internal organization
Universal life				Renews Annually		Internal organization
Universal life				Cancel policy if premium more than a certain number of days past due	30 days	Internal organization

Plan	Type	Benefit	Condition	Oversight
Universal life			Reinvested dividends must be used to offset premium, increase coverage types or be paid to insured	Regulatory agency—insurance board
Universal life	Loan	Prime interest rate + 3	Loan interest rate cannot be more than	Regulatory agency—insurance board
HMO plan A (health insurance)	Major medical	100,000 (per incident) 500,000 (total per year)	Incidents must be managed and approved by case management	Internal organization
HMO plan A (health insurance)	Major medical	80 percent coinsurance	Insured is responsible for 20 percent for care outside healthcare network	Internal organization
HMO plan A (health insurance)	Major medical	$10 co-pay	Only available for in-network healthcare practitioners	Internal organization
HMO plan A (health insurance)	Dental		Dentists must be within network for any compensation	Internal organization

Insurance Pricing

Now that we have an understanding of an insurance product, we can focus on the methods of calculating the price or premiums charged for these services. The function of rating a policy varies, depending on the insurance product. It is important to understand the basis for the product pricing and how it impacts the policy. Premium setting is accomplished through the actuarial tables listed for the potential losses.

There are two primary categories of rating: community-based rating and experienced-based rating. If the risk is shared by a wide group of insured parties with similar risk, it is convenient to standardize the premiums through rates for a wide group of parties; this is generally referred to as community-based rating. If the risk is for a specialized insured or there are too many unknown factors, the individual risk will need to be evaluated and the premium set for each risk. This is generally known as experienced-based rating. In the latter case of experienced-based rating, premiums may be evaluated on the basis of past claims history, appropriate demographics data, and numerous other factors, depending on the type of insurance. In either case, the base premium set for the risk must be calculated for any type of loss. This is the nature of pricing in the insurance industry.

First, we will focus on the underwriting information required to establish the community-based rates, then move to the information required for experienced-based rates. Later in this chapter, we will apply the community-based rates to a specific policy for premium calculation (see Figure 5.13).

Community-Based Rating

Figure 5.6 shows a data model that describes the information needed to accomplish the underwriting for the calculation of rates.

The main focus of insurance underwriting is the assessment of risk. Therefore, the model begins with a WORK EFFORT subtype of RISK ANALYSIS. This analysis is specifically about the risk associated with the potential for loss within a group or individual situation. Each RISK ANALYSIS will have several parts to it that are called ACTUARIAL ANALYSIS. The ACTUARIAL ANALYSIS may be for an INSURANCE PRODUCT, PRODUCT FEATURE, COVERAGE TYPE, COVERAGE LEVEL, or any combination of these. The purpose of the ACTUARIAL ANALYSIS is to understand and assess factors and parameters, taking into account the potential for loss. To determine the probability of that loss, the ANALYSIS PARAMETERs—the set of factors to be considered in the event of loss—are determined and understood. Often, these are weighted in light of the coverage required and the expected loss. In the case of property and casualty insurance, the ACTUARIAL ANALYSIS may also be assessing the risk of one or more INSURED ASSET TYPE—hence, the associative relationship INSURED TARGET.

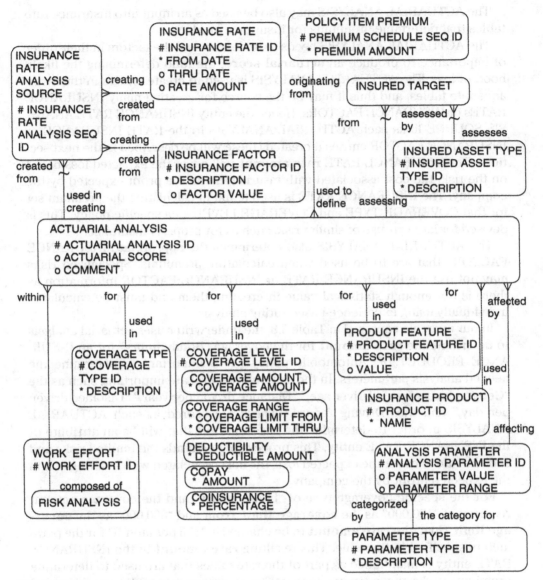

Figure 5.6 Insurance underwriting.

The ACTUARIAL ANALYSIS entity may be used for two purposes: either to determine premiums for a specific policy or to determine the basis for the insurance rate tables. In experienced-based underwriting, the ACTUARIAL ANALYSIS is conducted for an individual policy and the POLICY ITEM PREMIUM may be determined from this underwriting effort.

The ACTUARIAL ANALYSIS may also be used as an input into insurance rate tables that determine premiums for insurance products.

The ACTUARIAL ANALYSIS needs to understand all the factors in their order of importance to produce an **actuarial score**, the ratio determining the likelihood of loss. The ACTUARIAL ANALYSIS is used to create entries in the insurance rate tables, and thus it may be the source for creating many INSURANCE RATEs or INSURANCE FACTORs. Hence the entity INSURANCE RATE ANALYSIS SOURCE links each ACTUARIAL ANALYSIS to the RATE INSURANCE or INSURANCE FACTOR entries it created (these will be described in the next section). The INSURANCE RATE **rate amount** will cover the expected loss based on the risk, the cost associated with insuring it, and the profit expected by the company. The INSURANCE RATE is used to aid in calculating the premium set for that COVERAGE TYPE and COVERAGE LEVEL on a specific policy. This is devised for large groups of similar risk, such as for property insurance.

The ACTUARIAL ANALYSIS also determines the appropriate INSURANCE FACTORs that are to be used when calculating premiums. Specialized risks may not use the INSURANCE RATE or INSURANCE FACTOR information as there is not enough statistical value in creating them and must be calculated individually using experience-based rating analysis.

In our example captured in Table 5.8, the underwriter uses actuarial analysis to determine the **rate amount** for the coverage "Bodily Injury" for an INSURANCE PRODUCT of "Automobile policy." It is important to determine the needed analysis parameters. In the example, several are important, such as the "Geographic region," "Driver age," "Distance driven per year," "Distance driven per day," and the "Driving record." These are scored in each ACTUARIAL ANALYSIS in order to determine the **rate amount** that will be an attribute of the INSURANCE RATE entity. This process understands the implied risks and sets the rate to cover the expected loss, the cost associated with insuring it, and the expected profit by the company.

For the specific coverage type of "bodily injury" and the coverage amount required of "100,000" as the **coverage limit from** and "300,000" as the **coverage limit thru**, the **rate amount** to be charged is "$75 per month" for the parameters specified in the table. This resulting **rate amount** in the INSURANCE RATE entity is maintained as part of the rate tables that are used to determine premiums under these circumstances. The insurance rate tables are discussed in more detail in the next section.

Proper risk analysis and premium setting is an important task. Without doing a thorough job, the risk to the insurance company is great. Should the losses not be properly assessed, they could cause the company to exhaust their claim reserves and not be able to pay for the expected losses. Underwriting is a critical task. It may take many hours to properly assess each risk. Where there are large groups of similar risk, the insurance provider uses a standard method that is proven to determine the rates for all members of the same risk class. These

Table 5.8   Risk Analysis Work Effort—Rate Setting

RISK ANALYSIS DESCRIPTION	COVERAGE TYPE	COVERAGE LIMIT FROM	COVERAGE LIMIT THRU	ANALYSIS PARAMETER DESCRIPTION AND (PARAMETER VALUE)	ACTUARIAL ANALYSIS ACTUARIAL SCORE	RATE AMOUNT
Determine premium	Bodily injury	100,000	300,000	Geographic region (New York)	60	$75 per month
				Driver age (21–24)	80	
				Distance driven per year (15,000–25,000 miles)	75	
				Distance driven per day (50 miles)	85	
				Driving record (fair)	65	

rates can be successfully used to rate specific policies by using an automated system to apply these rates, thus allowing agents or other personnel to use the output of the underwriting process.

Flexible models are needed in insurance premium rate calculations, because there may be a tremendous number of factors and parameters that will change frequently over time. The models can then be modified as the parameters change to increase rates in order to handle the changing risk factors.

Insurance Rate Tables

The next model provides the details about how rates assist in calculating premiums for a policy. The rate entities in this section are largely a result of the actuarial process from the last section, which created the rate information based on various parameters and factors.

The model shown in Figure 5.7 shows the application of insurance rates to the large risk groups. Typically, this is used in various types of large group insurance, such as automobile, homeowner, life, or health insurance. The INSURANCE RATE may be specified for an INSURANCE PRODUCT, COVERAGE TYPE, COVERAGE LEVEL, PRODUCT FEATURE, INSURED ASSET TYPE, or a combination of these.

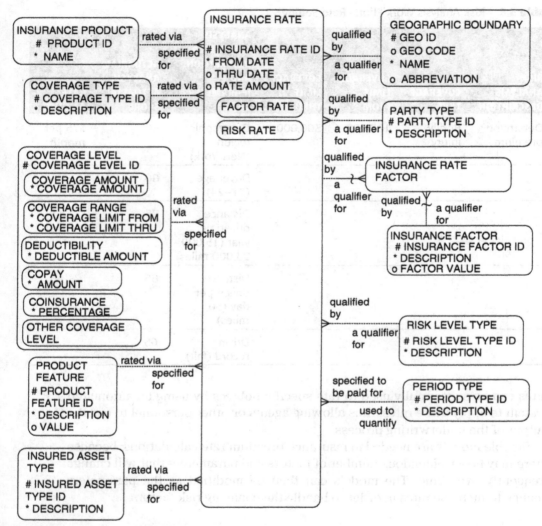

Figure 5.7 Insurance rate tables.

Once these are identified, there are questions that must be answered in order to determine which rate to use and how to apply it. The GEOGRAPHIC BOUNDARY, PARTY TYPE, RISK LEVEL TYPE, and INSURANCE FACTORs further determine the rate. Based on all these criteria, the **rate amount** is calculated for each PERIOD TYPE, such as a monthly rate, quarterly rate, or yearly rate.

An example of this can be seen in the Table 5.9. Here, an "Automobile" INSURANCE PRODUCT is being rated for an insured asset of a "2000 new sports car" that requires several COVERAGE TYPEs, such as "Bodily Injury," "Property Damage," "Uninsured Motorists," "Medical Payments," "Comprehensive" and

Table 5.9 Applied Insurance Rates

INSURANCE PRODUCT NAME	PERIOD TYPE–DESCRIPTION	GEOGRAPHIC BOUNDARY–NAME	INSURANCE ASSET TYPE–DESCRIPTION	COVERAGE TYPE–DESCRIPTION	COVERAGE LEVEL	INSURANCE RATE–RATE AMOUNT	INSURANCE FACTOR–FACTOR DESCRIPTION	RISK LEVEL TYPE–DESCRIPTION
Auto	Six month renewal	Denver, CO	2000 new sports car	Bodily Injury	100,000–300,000	$220	Young Driver	High
				Property Damage	100,000	$400	Driving Record	
				Uninsured motorists	100,000–300,000	$100	10+ miles to work	
				Medical payments	1000	$50	1 Speeding ticket	
				Comprehensive	$250 deductible	$200	Warm car	
				Collision	$500 deductible	$300	Exceeds 15,000 miles per year	

"Collision." Based on the COVERAGE LEVELs chosen by an insured, the area in which he lives, key INSURANCE FACTORs, and his RISK LEVEL TYPE, a premium amount is calculated for each type of automobile coverage. The period involved is a "six-month" PERIOD TYPE with a "high" RISK LEVEL TYPE.

Experienced-Based Insurance Rating

The previously described community-based insurance rates are applicable to insurance products that may be obtained by many parties. Experienced-based insurance addresses the rating needs of a particular risk for a particular insured party. When the risk factors cannot be looked at in a typical manner, the underwriting group needs to factor and calculate the insurance rates on a case-by-case basis. This process is complex, requiring significant expertise and time to understand the risks and factors needed to support the proper loss potential.

The set of information needed to do experienced-based rating is very similar to the insurance underwriting information discussed previously and therefore is addressed by the entities in Figure 5.6. The WORK EFFORT of RISK ANALYSIS for the particular risk is assessed by one or more ACTUARIAL ANALYSIS efforts. Each ACTUARIAL ANALYSIS is for a COVERAGE TYPE at specific COVERAGE LEVELs for various INSURANCE PRODUCTs and/or PRODUCT FEATUREs. Each ACTUARIAL ANALYSIS needs to consider various ANALYSIS PARAMETERs as well as information about any INSURED TARGETs. Many ACTUARIAL ANALYSIS **actuarial score**s may be used to define a POLICY ITEM PREMIUM that corresponds to a particular insurance coverage. This specialized rating method is focused on creating the needed premiums for the unusual or non-standard risk.

Insurance Policies (Orders for Insurance)

Now that party roles and relationships have been established and there are products with rates to offer, the data model can address how to model the information requirements associated with ordering insurance or, in other words, putting insurance into effect. Similar to most industries, the order section will address how a commitment is made to establish a commitment to provide insurance to and from parties. Insurance enterprises would think of this commitment process as applying for an insurance policy, quoting rates, and issuing insurance policies.

Insurance Application

Usually, after relationships have been formed between the insurance agent and the insured party and there is an understanding of what is needed, an insurance application is filled out requesting the type of insurance required.

Figure 5.8 provides a data model for the information requirements of an application. The application stores who has applied for what types of insurance including the COVERAGE TYPEs, COVERAGE LEVELs, and PRODUCT FEATUREs needed. Each APPLICATION may have several APPLICATION STATUSes over

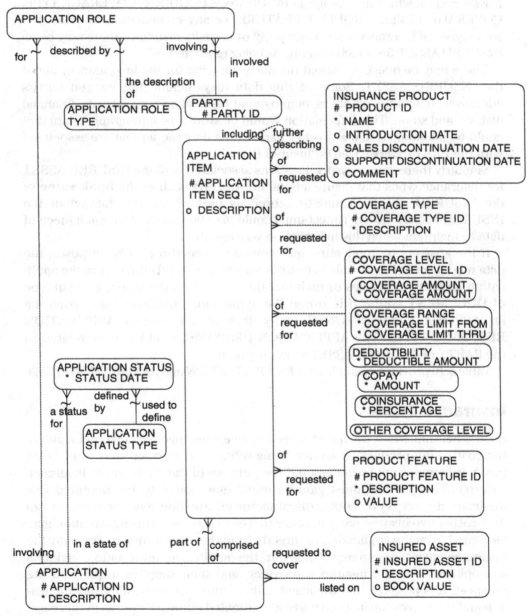

Figure 5.8   Insurance application.

time with STATUS TYPEs such as "Submitted," "Being Reviewed," "Sent back for more information," "Rejected," and so on. There may be many APPLICATION ROLEs associated with the application with APPLICATION ROLE TYPEs such as "Insured Party" (there may be many), "Beneficiary," "Insurance Agent," and "Insurance Provider." An APPLICATION ITEM may be for several APPLICATION ITEMs each of which may be for an INSURANCE PRODUCT, COVERAGE TYPE, COVERAGE LEVEL, PRODUCT FEATURE, or any combination of these. For some types of insurance such as property or casualty insurance there may be an INSURED ASSET for which coverage is being requested.

There may be questions about the party applying for the insurance or about the INSURED ASSET. Some of this data may include the insured party's addresses, telephone numbers, employment history, driver's records, financial history, and so on. This information would be stored as demographic data that could be maintained in many other parts of the data model that are associated with the PARTY whose role is "Insured Party."

Similarly there may be many questions associated with the INSURED ASSET for insurance types that insure assets. Information such as the **book value** of the INSURED ASSET would be stored as part of the information of the INSURED ASSET entity. Timestamps could also be recorded for each piece of data to maintain when this information was updated.

If the answers to application questions are needed for audit purposes, the data model could handle this in one of two ways: It could either store the application answers in entities or maintain the application document as a subtype of DOCUMENT entity. If it stored the application questions, there could be an APPLICATION RESPONSE entity that stored various APPLICATION RESPONSE TYPEs. The APPLICATION RESPONSE could also be related to the PARTY or INSURED ASSET as appropriate.

Table 5.10 provides example data for APPLICATION and APPLICATION ITEMs.

Insurance Quote

As in other industries, the quote is used to give a prospective customer a potential cost of the product or service being offered prior to an agreement being made. It is important to understand the purpose of the quote in the insurance industry. This process must gain an initial assessment of the potential risk the insured asset represents. Critical factor information must be gained from the prospective insured party in order to assess this risk. This information may be gained from the application or directly from the quote process. Typically the insurance agent or agency finds out the applicable information, submits an application to the insurance provider, and then supplies a quote to the prospect. It is possible that the agent gathers information without the application and then gives the insured party an estimated quote. Of course in this case, the final premiums have not been determined yet, as all the risk factors have

Table 5.10 Insurance Application

APPLICATION ID AND DESCRIPTION	INSURED ASSET	APPLICATION ITEM	INSURANCE PRODUCT	COVERAGE TYPE	COVERAGE LEVEL AND BASIS	FEATURE
2909 application for automobile insurance	1999 Ford Escort	1	Premium auto coverage	Bodily injury	$100,000 per person, $300,000 per incident	
		2	Premium auto coverage	Comprehensive	$120 deductible	
		3	Premium auto coverage	Collision	$240 deductible	
3909 universal life application		1	Death benefit	Coverage amount	$400,000	
		2				8 percent loan feature

not been completely understood. The final underwriting process will determine the risks involved and the proper premiums to be charged.

Figure 5.9 is a modified version of the generic quote model in Volume 1, V1:4.11. In this context, QUOTEs are statements of the potential cost of the ser-

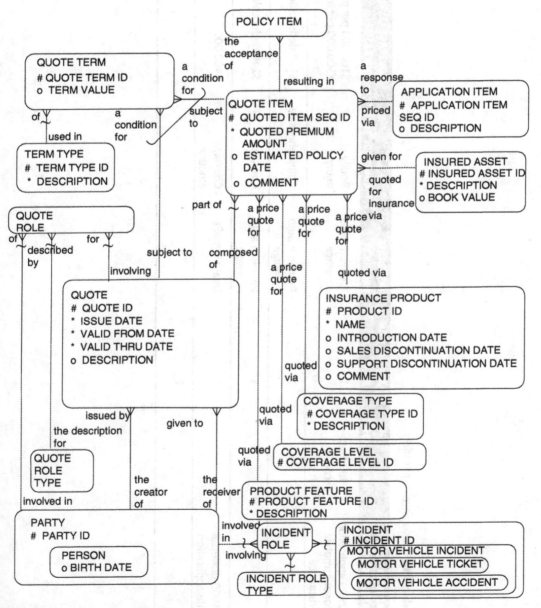

Figure 5.9   Insurance quotes.

vice to protect the insured asset, and must be given to the potential INSURED PARTY. The function of the quote is for the insurance agency and/or insurance provider to get the business from the insured parties. Insured parties, insurance agents, and insurance providers all represent instances of QUOTE ROLE that are of a QUOTE ROLE TYPE and related to PARTYs. Each QUOTE may have terms associated with it that are of TERM TYPEs that maintain the conditions associated with the QUOTE—for example, "quote valid for certain number of days" with "30" as the **term value**.

QUOTEs may be composed of one or more QUOTE ITEMs that also may have QUOTE TERMS associated with them. Instead of relating QUOTE ITEMs to PRODUCT and/or a WORK EFFORT as in the generic quote model in V1:4.11, the model in Figure 5.9 shows that QUOTE ITEMs may be related to INSURANCE PRODUCT, COVERAGE TYPE, COVERAGE LEVEL, or PRODUCT FEATUREs, and they may be for a particular INSURED ASSET. The APPLICATION ITEM may be priced via one or more QUOTE ITEMs; for instance if collision coverage of $250 was applied for and the quote was too high, then another quote for a $500 deductible may be given as well. Each QUOTE ITEM may be from an APPLICATION ITEM or there may not be an application as was discussed in the previous paragraph, making this relationship optional. Each QUOTE ITEM, if accepted, may result in a POLICY ITEM, which is part of the INSURANCE POLICY and will be discussed in the next section.

The QUOTE has an **issue date** maintaining the date the quote was given, a **valid from date** (the beginning date from when the quote can be acted on), a **valid thru date** (the last date that the quote can be acted upon), and a **description**, which may describe the nature of the quote. The QUOTE ITEM, which may be for an INSURED ASSET, has a **quoted premium amount** telling the prospective insured party how much it may cost for the insurance. The **estimated policy date** states when the insurance is expected to go into effect.

Each QUOTE may use information about the PARTY, such as INCIDENTs in which the party was PARTY involved in various INCIDENT ROLE TYPEs. Incidents will be covered later in this chapter in Figure 5.14. The subtype of INCIDENT shown in Figure 5.9 illustrates how incidents may affect quotes. The diagram shows that MOTOR VEHICLE INCIDENTs may affect the quoted premiums. MOTOR VEHICLE INCIDENTs include MOTOR VEHICLE TICKETs and MOTOR VEHICLE ACCIDENTs. This example applies to automobile insurance quotes. Other INCIDENT subtypes may also affect quotes such as the applicant's previous history of property loss, property theft, or illnesses (see Figure 5.14).

An example is given in Table 5.11 where "JR Doe" is shopping for automobile insurance for his "2000 New Sports Car." He contacts "ABC Insurance Agency" to discuss potential companies. Mary Smith, who is an agent for "ABC Insurance Agency," recommends several providers to "JR Doe." Certain factors need to be gathered for proper rating: his age, driving record, desired coverage,

Table 5.11 Insurance Quotes

QUOTE	QUOTE ROLES	INFO AFFECTING QUOTE (OTHER INFORMATION SUCH AS PARTY INFORMATION)	QUOTE ITEM	INSURED ASSET DESCRIPTION	COVERAGE TYPE	COVERAGE LEVEL	QUOTED PREMIUM AMOUNT
8738	JR Doe, prospective insured party	1 Speeding ticket in last 6 months, Young driver, Exceeds 15,000 driving miles per year	1	2000 New sports car	Bodily injury	100,000–300,000	$220
	ABC Insurance Agency, insurance agency						
	Mary Smith, insurance agent						
	XYZ Insurance, insurance provider		2		Property damage	100,000	$400
			3		Uninsured motorists	100,000–300,000	$100
			4		Medical payments	1000	$50
			5		Comprehensive	$250 deductible	$200
			6		Collision	$500 deductible	$300

automobile, and how far he drives each year and to work. "JR Doe" supplies the information with the list of desired coverages for his car. "Mary Smith" then identifies the important information to properly evaluate the risk for "JR Doe" and prepares a statement of insurance coverage costs for each provider. "ABC Insurance Agency" determines that "XYZ Insurance" provides the best rates for "JR Doe," as he has some challenges to overcome: "One speeding ticket" and "Under 25 years of age." Once given the estimate of cost, "JR Doe" then decides to accept the quote, which will lead to an insurance policy agreement. Typically the insurance agent will try to find the best coverage for the least cost, depending on the risk level presented by the insured party. The quote allows the prospective insured party to evaluate his or her needs and to determine if a proposed agreement is acceptable.

The Insurance Agreement or Insurance Policy

The insurance policy represents agreed-on coverages and features that will be available for the insured confirmed within a policy. This agreement states what will occur, when, and how. The INSURANCE PRODUCT maintains what coverages could be available, the INSURANCE APPLICATION represents the requesting of coverages within an insurance policy, the insurance QUOTE represents a statement of what the coverages would cost if acted on, and the INSURANCE POLICY represents the agreement of what will be covered, what features are included, and how much it costs.

When an insured makes the agreement with the insurance provider, a policy is established and any required activity is recorded and monitored. For instance, if "Mary Smith" purchases a new automobile, she has the option of choosing from a variety of coverages to protect her new car from potential damage, as has been illustrated in the INSURANCE PRODUCT models. She meets with agency "ABC Insurance Agency," a representative of "XYZ Insurance." After discussing her needs, "ABC Insurance Agency" produces for her a quote. If Mary accepts the quote, "ABC Insurance Agency" gives her a policy with the coverage she requires. She already knows how much it will cost and is given an overall agreement that she can read. When her finalized policy arrives from "XYZ Insurance," she will receive the policy declarations and overall statement of what will be protected. This example is for a large group product that covers many people like "Mary Smith."

From this example, it can be seen that the insurance policy has direct links to the insurance product and to the regulations that govern them. Unlike a manufactured product, the insurance products, coverage types, coverage levels, and features within the policy may be modified over time to reflect the insured's changing needs and demands. In this scenario, "Mary Smith" finds that she needs to alter her coverage for collision, as she feels the cost for the coverage is too high. She contacts "ABC Insurance Agency" and requests an increase in her collision deductible. Because "Mary Smith" is a good driver and has not had an accident in 25 years of driving, she feels the likelihood of having an accident is very small. Because the overall cost savings is significant, she decides to increase her deductible amount to $500 to save some money. This change can be at the discretion of the insured party and may be changed at any time. This fluid, changing structure requires the insurance enterprise to track its agreements with the ability to change them easily over time.

Insurance Policy Roles

Figure 5.10 is a modified version of the generic agreement roles data model from volume 1, V1:4.12. The model illustrates how the generic agreement model applies to insurance enterprises. Similar to other types of enterprises, there are many subtypes of AGREEMENT that are applicable within insurance enterprises. Examples include SUPPLIER AGREEMENTs, PARTNERSHIP AGREEMENTs, EMPLOYMENT AGREEMENTs, and HEALTH CARE NETWORK AGREEMENTs (that define which healthcare providers have contractually agreed to be in which health care networks), as well as numerous OTHER AGREEMENTs that can exist. For insurance enterprises, however, the most significant type of AGREEMENT is the INSURANCE POLICY, which is also a subtype of AGREEMENT.

There may be many types of INSURANCE POLICYs, hence the subtypes HEALTH CARE POLICY, LIFE INSURANCE POLICY, CASUALTY INSURANCE POLICY, PROPERTY INSURANCE POLICY, DISABILITY INSURANCE POLICY, and OTHER INSURANCE POLICY. These roughly correspond to the PRODUCT CATEGORYs mentioned before because different insurance policies are applicable to different products.

The INSURANCE POLICY is also subtyped into INDIVIDUAL INSURANCE POLICY and GROUP INSURANCE POLICY. An INDIVIDUAL INSURANCE POLICY is a policy that is set up for a particular person. There may be more than one person covered on an individual insurance policy, for example, the policy may cover dependents of the insured contract holder. A GROUP INSURANCE POLICY is a policy that is set up for a group. A group is a collection of people within an organization for whom insurance is issued.

Like any AGREEMENT, each AGREEMENT may be associated within a PARTY RELATIONSHIP that formed the basis of the agreement. In the case of INSURANCE POLICY AGREEMENTs, the relationship may have stemmed from the INSURED PARTY TO AGENT RELATIONSHIP that involves the party roles of INSURANCE AGENCY and INSURED PARTY.

Each AGREEMENT may have many AGREEMENT ROLEs that state what AGREEMENT ROLE TYPE each PARTY plays. For example, in an INSURANCE POLICY, there is usually one or more AGREEMENT ROLEs of "insured party,"

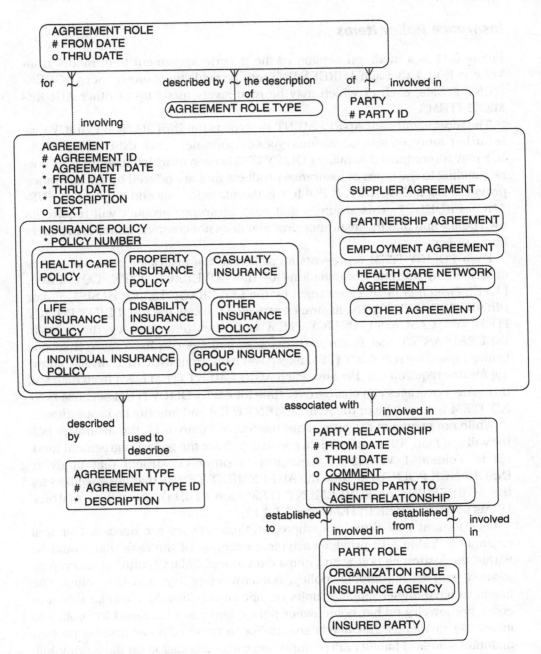

Figure 5.10 Insurance policy roles.

a role of "insurance agent," a role of "insurance provider," possibly one or more roles of "beneficiary," and perhaps roles of "party that approved policy," "recording party" (party recording the policy into the system), and so on.

Insurance Policy Items

Figure 5.11 is a modified version of the generic agreement item model from Volume 1, V1:4.13. Each AGREEMENT may be made up of one or more AGREEMENT ITEMs, each of which may be recursively made up of other AGREEMENT ITEMS.

The most significant AGREEMENT subtype is the INSURANCE POLICY that is further subtyped into the various types of insurance. Each INSURANCE POLICY may be composed of many POLICY ITEMs each of which has subtypes corresponding to the types of insurance products that are offered by the insurance provider. Each INSURANCE POLICY is therefore for one and only one INSURANCE PRODUCT. This assumes that each insurance product will require its own policy and that the insurance provider does not combine multiple products into a policy.

Each POLICY ITEM represents an aspect of the insurance coverage that is described by various combinations of the COVERAGE TYPE, COVERAGE LEVEL (which is further described by the COVERAGE LEVEL BASIS), and/or PRODUCT FEATURE. The insurance provided through the PROPERTY POLICY ITEM and CASUALTY POLICY ITEM is further described by the specific INSURED ASSET that is covered. Because policies can have more than one insured asset, each POLICY ITEM may cover a different INSURED ASSET allowing for this requirement. Because each AGREEMENT ITEM has a from date and thru date, coverages can change over time for each POLICY ITEM because POLICY ITEM is a subtype of the AGREEMENT ITEM and inherits its properties.

While not shown in the agreement models of Figure 5.11, the insurance policy will use many of the other data constructs from the generic agreement models in Volume 1 V1:4.12-16. Examples of other constructs that apply to INSURANCE POLICYs include the AGREEMENT TERMs that are specified for the AGREEMENT or AGREEMENT ITEM (see V1:4.14), as well as ADDENDUMs to AGREEMENT ITEMs (see V1:4.13).

Let's look at two situations where multiple policies are needed. Our first example in Table 5.12 provides a typical example of the data that would be within the insurance policy and items data model. "Mary Smith" is an average insured with an automobile policy, homeowner policy, and life policy. She needs to have higher liability limits on her auto policy, has special riders to cover her jewelry on her homeowner policy, and has a universal life policy to invest her dividends. Her needs are similar to those of other insured parties: maintain standard liability and comprehensive and collision on the automobile policy, keep the standard full-replacement on her homeowners, and establish a life policy to protect her family. Her product suite might look like those of many other insured parties, as shown in Table 5.12. As can be seen by the example, the data structures provide the ability to easily accommodate different types and levels of coverage with different features.

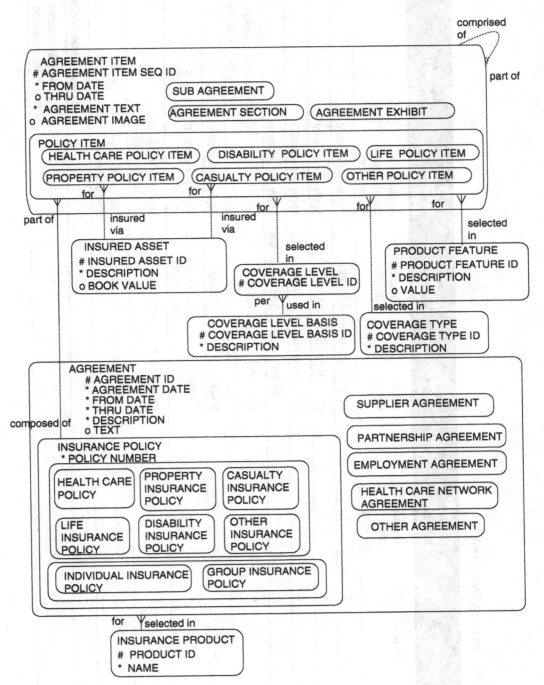

Figure 5.11   Insurance policies.

Table 5.12 Insurance Policy Example 1

INSURED PARTY	POLICY ID	POLICY ITEM	INSURANCE PRODUCT DESCRIPTION	INSURED ASSET	COVERAGE TYPE	COVERAGE LEVEL	COVERAGE LEVEL BASIS	PRODUCT FEATURE
Mary Smith	JJK1234	1	Premium auto coverage		Bodily injury	100,000/ 300,000	Apply per person, per occurrence	
		2			Property damage	100,000	Apply per incident	
		3			Medical payment	2500	Apply per incident	
		4			Comprehensive	250 deductible	Apply per incident	
		5			Collision	500 deductible	Apply per incident	
		6			Car rental endorsement	$25/day	Apply per incident	Protect on collision only Cover for max 30 days
	KLK3455	1	Homeowner		Building	250,000	Apply per incident	
		2			Content	Full Replacement value	Apply per incident	
		3			Jewelry rider	10,000	Apply per incident to scheduled items	
	LLL3456	1	Universal life		Death coverage type	250,000	Pay beneficiary at time of loss	
		2						8 percent loan option
		3						Reinvest dividends to buy more insurance

An alternative look at an insurance policy coverage situation is shown in Table 5.13. This insurance policy coverage is based on the needs of a small business, "XYZ Company," and the related parties to that business, "Mr. Jones" and "Mr. Smith." As you can see, there is a greater need to customize the products for this insured party, as the requirements are quite different from those of the previous example. "XYZ Company" needs to have a group insurance plan for "Mr. Jones" and "Mr. Smith," a fleet policy for the company vehicles, driven by "Mr. Jones" and "Mr. Smith," and a property/casualty policy for the business property. "Mr. Jones" and "Mr. Smith" each have their own private automobile and life policies. "Mr. Jones" went with a "Non-smoker term-life" policy that offers a feature that gives a "30 percent" discount for "insured has never smoked," as he has been a non-smoker. "Mr. Smith," on the other hand, smokes a minimal amount. He has chosen the "Smoker term-life" policy that has a feature of charging a "10 percent" surcharge if "the insured smokes one to two packs per day."

As you can see from these two examples, the structure within the INSURANCE PRODUCT and INSURANCE POLICY models can accommodate complex scenarios and is quite flexible. Each of these situations requires a specific set of INSURANCE PRODUCTs with various COVERAGE TYPEs, COVERAGE LEVELs, and PRODUCT FEATUREs.

While there are substantial similarities between various insurance policies, each type of insurance has some differences that will be discussed in the following sections.

Health Care Insurance Agreement

Health care insurance agreements are probably the most complex within the insurance industry. Because there may be health care agreements at a group level and also at an individual health care enrollment level, these policies may involve many parties.

There are many types of agreements in health care. Insurance agreements may exist between the insurance provider and the health care practitioners, such as in HMO network plans. A group insurance policy agreement may exist between the insurance provider and the organization offering the plan to their employees. Within this group insurance policy, there are also enrollments of individuals within the plan.

In administering group policy agreements, multiple insurance organizations could be involved, such as the organization that underwrites the insurance and the organization that administers the insurance. Many larger companies may be "self-insured" meaning they have enough resources to fund their own health insurance. Typically, they will use an insurance administrator to administer their private plan.

Group insurance policies may exist for different types of insurance such as health care, disability, or life insurance policies. Enrollments within these

Table 5.13 Insurance Policy Example 2

INSURED NAME	POLICY NUMBER	INSURANCE PRODUCT NAME	COVERAGE TYPE	COVERAGE LEVEL	COVERAGE LEVEL BASIS	FEATURE DESCRIPTION AND VALUE
XYZ Company	67890	PPO plan deluxe group health insurance	Approved doctor	100 percent up to $1,000,000	In network coverage payment	
			Co-pay	$15	Payment per office visit	
			Drug coverage	$8	Generic prescription	
				$15	Brand name prescription	
	99002	Fleet policy	Bodily injury	250,000/500,000	Apply per person, per incident	
			Property damage	250,000	Apply per incident	
			Uninsured motorists	250,000/500,000	Apply per person, per incident	
			Medical payment	10,000	Apply per incident	
			Comprehensive	1000 deductible	Apply per incident	
			Collision	1000 deductible	Apply per incident	
	88990	Property and casualty policy (insured asset of the XYZ office building)	Wind damage	Actual Cash Value up to $500,000	Apply per incident per structure	
			Sewer backup	Actual Cash Value up to $25,000	Apply per incident per structure	
			Theft	Actual Cash Value up to $300,000	Apply per incident	

Insured	Policy #	Policy Type	Coverage	Amount	Application
Mr. Jones	898980	Automobile (insured asset of a 2000 sports car)	Bodily injury	100,000/300,000	Apply per person per incident
			Property damage	100,000	Apply per incident
			Uninsured motorists	100,000/300,000	Apply per person per incident
			Medical payment	5,000	Apply per incident
			Comprehensive	250 deductible	Apply per incident
			Collision	500 deductible	Apply per incident
	009890	Non-smoker term-life	Death benefit	500,000	Pay to beneficiary at time of loss
					Non-smoker discount 30 percent (Apply discount if insured never smokes)
Mr. Smith	990932	Automobile	Bodily injury	100,000/300,000	Apply per incident
			Property damage	100,000	Apply per incident
			Uninsured motorists	100,000/300,000	Apply per incident
			Medical payment	5,000	Apply per incident
			Comprehensive	250 deductible	Apply per incident
			Collision	500 deductible	Apply per incident
	23467	Smoker term-life	Death benefit	250,000	Pay to beneficiary at time of loss
					Minimum smoker surcharge 10 percent (Apply surcharge if insured smokes one to two packs per day)

policies allow individuals to sign up for insurance within the group plan. The insured enrolling often needs to specify the specific enrollment elections that he or she needs to select and the rules regarding the policies. Health care policies allow for multiple election options within their policies and the ability to enroll multiple people within a single enrollment.

Figure 5.12 builds upon the model in Chapter 4 (V2:4.9, claims data model). Health care organizations generally record less information about the insur-

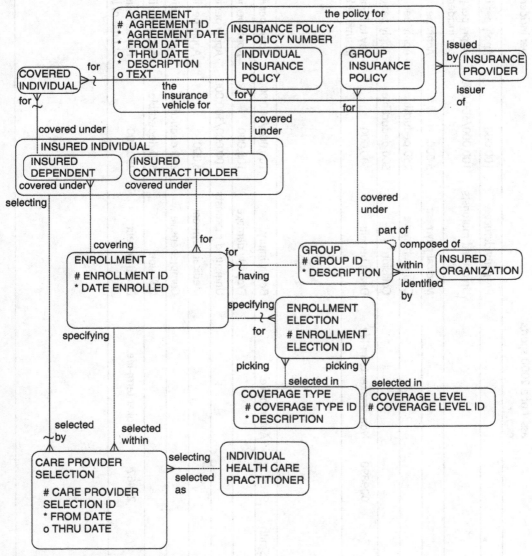

Figure 5.12   Health care policy.

ance policy than insurance enterprises. For instance, insurance enterprises need to track more detailed information about enrollments and enrollment elections of a group's participants.

In a health care agreement, the INSURANCE POLICY subtypes of INDIVIDUAL INSURANCE POLICY and GROUP INSURANCE POLICY are very applicable. In the INDIVIDUAL HEALTH CARE POLICY, there is an INSURED CONTRACT HOLDER that is the principal person being insured and there may also be other INSURED DEPENDENTs that are covered under the plan. The INSURANCE PRODUCT, COVERAGE TYPEs, COVERAGE LEVELs, and PRODUCT FEATUREs are maintained in the POLICY ITEMs (see Figure 5.11) as in the previous models.

The ENROLLMENT involves more detailed information, as there are two levels at which the policy is in force. The first level is the GROUP level that defines a set of individuals that can be covered within an INSURED ORGANIZATION. Each GROUP may be having several ENROLLMENTs that allow people within the GROUP (generally an employer) to be signed up under the plan.

There is a great deal of information about each ENROLLMENT, some of which is shown in Figure 5.12. For example, there is a single INSURED CONTRACT HOLDER and numerous COVERED INDIVIDUALs of INSURED DEPENDENTs for an ENROLLMENT that signifies additional people that are covered within the enrollment.

There may be various ENROLLMENT ELECTIONs, allowing the person enrolling in the plan to choose desired COVERAGE TYPEs at desired COVERAGE LEVELs. The available elections for a group participant can be maintained using the relationships in Figure 5.11 from COVERAGE TYPE and COVERAGE LEVEL to the POLICY ITEMs of the INSURANCE POLICY.

As part of the enrollment process, some group insurance polices require the participant to select an INDIVIDUAL HEALTH CARE PRACTITIONER, perhaps as their primary care provider. Therefore each INSURED INDIVIDUAL may be selecting a CARE PROVIDER SELECTION that may be selected within an ENROLLMENT.

For example, "ABC Company" is offering its "2001 enrollment" for the health care plan for the next calendar year. "Jane Smith," an insured contract holder to the plan, is an employee of "ABC Company," the organization that is offering the plan. "Jane Smith" is including several "insured dependents," her husband "Jim Smith," her daughter, "Susie Smith," and her son "Jeff Smith." All of the members of the Smith family are considered part of the enrollment. From the available enrollment elections, the Smiths have their choice of "dental," "medical," "accident," and "life" policies. "Jane Smith" decides to elect the "life" policy, and does not elect the "accident" policy. She decides to cover herself and all her dependents regarding the "dental" and "medical" elections. These choices are recorded in the ENROLLMENT ELECTION entity.

The final choice, that of the "Individual Health Care Practitioner," is made for each party in the enrollment. Each member of the family may choose a health care practitioner that will act as his or her "primary care provider" to manage their overall care. While "Jane and Jim Smith" select "Dr. Watson" as their primary care provider, "Susie and Jeff Smith" select "Dr. Jones." "Jane Smith" may also elect a "secondary care provider" for special circumstances. She chooses "Dr. Nickels" as her gynecologist. Once all the enrollment elections are made, they are submitted to the insurance provider.

Once everything is confirmed for the Smith family, appropriate documentation is sent to them describing the arrangements of the agreement. Based on changes or additional needs, the insured individuals may update their elections during the year. Often, certain circumstances will demand a change in the elections. An example of a change is the birth of another child or a desired change to a primary care provider. Another example could be the removal of an enrollment for example if "Jane Smith" decided to change jobs.

Casualty Insurance Agreement

Another type of agreement within the insurance industry is a casualty insurance policy, shown in Figure 5.10 and Figure 5.11. This protects against a loss caused by unforeseen events, such as a flood or accident. It is important to understand that these are typically risks that are not necessarily covered by other types of agreements. Their nature is that they are specialized, such as flood insurance or accident insurance, and for specific purposes, such as airline hazards. The risks they support tend to be higher and require more specialized insurance protection.

It is also important to realize that these specialized risks tend to require additional premiums and do not always apply to everyone. For example, flood insurance is not required of every homeowner, just those whose chances of being in a flood are greater. Accident insurance is not required for those that do not travel extensively. These policies are needed for special instances, when the standard insurance does not accommodate the requested risk levels.

In casualty insurance, the insured party needs to identify the item to be protected and how it will be protected. The agreement is usually very specific and has a limit as to what it will cover. This is due to the greater risk involved in protecting the loss. For example, if a homeowner requires flood insurance, the chance of loss is much greater because the home is in a flood plain.

The key information requirement for casualty policies is the CASUALTY POLICY ITEM (a subtype of POLICY ITEM) and the relationship to INSURED ASSET. There may be many CASUALTY POLICY ITEMs, each with different INSURED ASSETs with different COVERAGE TYPEs, COVERAGE LEVELs, or PRODUCT FEATUREs. The insurance policy and items model in Figure 5.11 provides for the information requirements to handle casualty policies.

The following example illustrates how the model in Figure 5.11 captures the required information for casualty policies. "Jim Smith" needs to insure his home on "123 Main Street" against flooding, as he lives near a creek that sometimes overflows. He tends to have water in his backyard from time to time, and in the spring or fall the levels may rise significantly. His casualty COVERAGE TYPE may state that the "house is protected from water damage" up to a certain COVERAGE LEVEL of "the actual cash value or $100,000." It may also protect his property within the home against water damage to a certain limit of "$80,000" (another COVERAGE LEVEL). Should his home become flooded and he cannot live in it, it may "provide living expenses for a temporary residence" (a PRODUCT FEATURE or AGREEMENT ITEM TERM). Another potential CASUALTY POLICY ITEM would be that the home be "rebuilt in the event of a total loss" (a COVERAGE TYPE) up to a limit of "$150,000" (a COVERAGE LEVEL). The risks to be excluded would also be stated, such as "no outside plants, trees, bushes, or shrubs would be covered" (an AGREEMENT TERM) or "no damage done to automobiles on the property would be covered" (an AGREEMENT TERM). Each POLICY ITEM would link to the specific property to be covered, such as the "building structure" (an INSURED ASSET) or the "building contents" (an INSURED ASSET).

Property Insurance Agreement

The property insurance agreement protects an INSURED ASSET such as a vehicle or house from potential loss in the event of damage, fire, or theft. These agreements are unique in that they provide specific coverage for different loss potentials and allow for varying levels of protection. Because loss is not always certain, the chance of loss is the risk that must be identified for these agreements. Similar to the casualty insurance agreement, these are usually in a broader risk group. Usually the INSURED ASSET is either a vehicle or home, but the agreement also may cover vessels, special assets such as fine art, collectibles, jewelry, and any type of equipment and the contents of a home or office. All of these have common aspects such as a market value, replacement value, and the potential to be destroyed, stolen, or lost.

PROPERTY INSURANCE POLICYs have POLICY ITEMs for the specific INSURED ASSET as shown in the general data model in Figure 5.11. They also carry exclusions, especially around damage or loss due to normal use. For example, an automobile policy will cover the vehicle damage in the event of an accident or theft, but will not cover repairs due to mechanical failure. In a similar way, a homeowner's policy will protect against fire or theft of the home's contents, but will not cover a loss that is from living in it, such as worn carpet or replacement of worn appliances or furniture. These exclusions are clearly stated within the terms of the agreement (AGREEMENT TERM) and are usually articulated clearly. The agreements may exclude other types of damage that is considered too high of a risk, such as flooding or other "acts of God."

As with the other agreements, they may be terminated at any time by either party. Special termination may occur with property insurance that may not exist with other kinds of agreements. Should the insured party have too many losses within a period of time, the insurance provider may decide to terminate the agreement. The basis for this is that the cost of providing the service is far too expensive than the profits gained. In some areas, local laws prohibit this from happening for certain types of agreements, but often the insurance provider has the right to end the agreement for these reasons. Where the company has no choice and they must provide coverage, they will elevate the insured party into a proper risk category and charge for their services accordingly.

The insurance policy and items model in Figure 5.11 together with the generic agreement data model from Volume 1 (V1:4.14) handle the information requirements for property insurance. Continuing the previous example, "Jim Smith" requires an automobile insurance agreement (a PROPERTY INSURANCE POLICY) and each PROPERTY POLICY ITEM may have specific AGREEMENT TERMs. He needs the standard protection package including PROPERTY POLICY ITEMs of "Liability coverage," "Comprehensive," and "Collision" for his three automobiles. Certain exclusions would be listed as well—for example, "Normal use damage will not be covered" (an AGREEMENT TERM). Included in each PROPERTY POLICY ITEM is the COVERAGE TYPEs, COVERAGE LEVELs, or PRODUCT FEATURE within the property policy. Each property item shows how it will protect the insured asset from loss for the INSURED ASSET.

Life Insurance Agreement

The life insurance agreement is unique in that it covers loss of life. Other kinds of insurance policies will have potential losses, but life insurance involves an inevitable loss, as long as the policy is held during that loss. The key issue for life insurance agreements is when the loss will occur. This is particularly important, as certain factors influence the risk level. If the insured party is older or critically ill, the risk of the loss happening is much greater than for a healthy or younger person. The LIFE POLICY ITEM will reflect the information given to the company with regard to the risk of loss. Should the insured misrepresent his or her age or health information, the company would have the right to terminate the agreement. Usually the company will require a health assessment of the individual insured in order to protect its interests against potential fraud. These assessments require a certified medical examination usually performed by the physician employed by the insurance provider. These illustrate some of the information associated with the LIFE POLICY ITEMs that would be included within a life insurance policy.

Another important facet of life insurance agreements is the identification of the beneficiary role. In other types of insurance, typically the insured party would be the recipient of the proceeds in the event of loss. With life insurance, the insured party is the covered asset, therefore in the event of loss, the beneficiary will receive the proceeds of the agreement. This is an important section in the list of AGREEMENT TERMs for each LIFE POLICY ITEM. The beneficiary role is maintained as an AGREEMENT ROLE in Figure 5.10 insurance policy roles. Typically the beneficiary is a family member: a spouse, parent, or sibling. In the event that the insured party has no surviving family members, he or she may elect anyone to the role of beneficiary, including an organization, such as a charity or other group. Some regulatory bodies do have restrictions on this, especially where a spouse is involved. These restrictions would have to be articulated within the agreement for those conditions.

Again, the models in Figure 5.10 and 5.11 (in conjunction with the generic models from V1:4.14) would cover the main information requirements for life insurance policies.

An example would be that "Jim Smith" has a life insurance agreement with "XYZ Insurance" through his employer "ABC Company." He has designated his wife "Jane Smith" as his "primary beneficiary" and his children "Susie Smith" and "Jeff Smith" as his "secondary, joint beneficiaries." These would be considered AGREEMENT ROLEs as shown in Figure 5.10. In the agreement terms (from the generic agreement model V1:4.14), it is specifically stated that if the "primary beneficiary" does not survive him, the "secondary beneficiary" would receive the proceeds of the policy. In addition to his employee policy, he also maintains a separate agreement with "ABC Insurance Agency" for another policy with higher coverage. Similar to his work policy, the private policy will pay a death COVERAGE TYPE of a certain COVERAGE LEVEL to the surviving beneficiary. For this agreement, "ABC Insurance Agency" had required a physical to be performed by their designated physician in order to verify "Jim Smith" as a healthy person. Once accepted, "Jim Smith" also had to verify that he had been "smoke free for two years" in order to get the preferred rate, as he had previously smoked.

Premium Schedule

Within the insurance policy agreement, the schedule for premium payments is an important facet of how the policy will work. Unlike other industries, payment for the insurance services is important to continuous coverage against loss. Should the insured party fail to pay the policy premiums, the coverage would lapse and the policy would not be enforced if a loss occurred. Therefore, proper scheduling of the premiums is a critical task for the insurance provider. The premium schedule will drive the invoicing process that will notify the insured parties of their responsibility to make the payments.

If the insurance provider fails to properly bill the insured, the agreement would be violated. Under these circumstances a loss could trigger litigation toward the insurance provider. It is important for these processes to be executed within the times required.

The model in Figure 5.13 shows the information associated with premium scheduling.

Based on the INSURANCE POLICY, the PREMIUM SCHEDULE is created and established for the policy in order to ensure proper billing. The PERIOD TYPE identifies the duration between billing cycles in order to secure payment of the required premiums—for example, whether the premium is due monthly, quarterly, or semiannually. Each PREMIUM SCHEDULE may be broken down into many POLICY ITEM PREMIUMs that state the premium that is associated with each aspect of the coverage as stated in the POLICY ITEM. As incidents such as tickets, accidents, bad health, or other analysis factors come into play, they may be underwritten via ACTUARIAL ANALYSIS (see Figure 5.6), which could in turn lead to POLICY PREMIUM ADJUSTMENTs that maintain to what **percentage** either the PREMIUM SCHEDULE or POLICY ITEM PREMIUMs are adjusted.

The PREMIUM SCHEDULE may be originating from the INSURANCE RATE entity in Figure 5.7. The INSURANCE RATE determines the standard rates that will be applied under various conditions and the POLICY ITEM PREMIUM states the **premium amount** that was applied to the POLICY ITEM, based on the applicable circumstances that determined the INSURANCE RATE.

The PREMIUM SCHEDULE and POLICY ITEM PREMIUM have attributes that define what is due and when it is due. The **valid from date** and **valid thru date** maintain when these premium schedules are valid for the INSURANCE POLICY. The **insured from date** and **insured thru date** state the period of time for which the premiums payments are providing coverage. The **due date** shows when the premium is due and payable. According to the terms of the agreement, the insured party may have a period of time after the due date to make the payment. The **premium amount** is the designated amount required at the due date.

For the POLICY ITEM PREMIUM entity, the **premium amount** shows the amount for a certain POLICY ITEM that would be for a particular coverage type, coverage level, or product feature. From and thru dates are not needed in the POLICY ITEM PREMIUM because the POLICY ITEM PREMIUM is part of the PREMIUM SCHEDULE that maintains date information.

Table 5.14 shows examples of premium amounts that are charged on a policy for automobile insurance. The premium amounts came from the INSURANCE RATE (see Figure 5.7) and then, when a speeding ticket occurred, there was a POLICY PREMIUM ADJUSTMENT to each POLICY ITEM, increasing the rate by 20 percent.

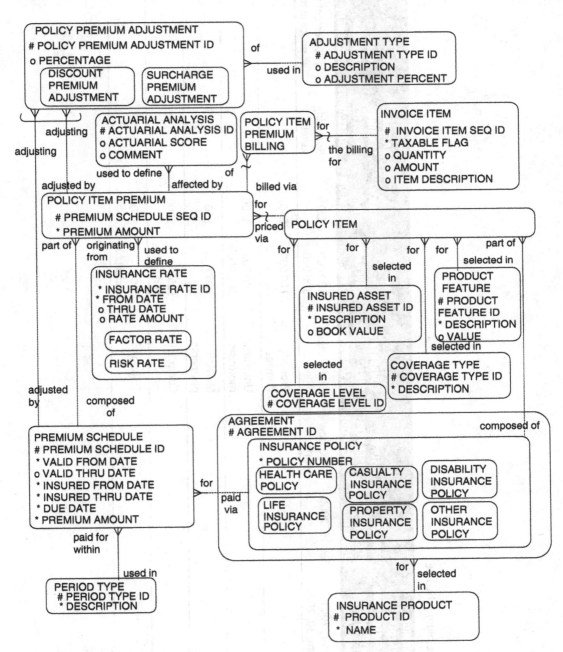

Figure 5.13   Premium schedule.

Table 5.14 Premium Schedule

POLICY ID	PREMIUM SCHEDULE INSURED FROM DATE INSURED THRU DATE	PREMIUM SCHEDULE DUE DATE	INSURED ASSET TYPE- DESCRIPTION	COVERAGE TYPE- DESCRIPTION	COVERAGE LEVEL	POLICY ITEM PREMIUM	FACTORS LEADING TO POLICY ADJUSTMENTS	POLICY PREMIUM ADJUSTMENT
JJK1234	Jan 1, 2001 June 30, 2001	Dec 15, 2000	2000 new sports car	Bodily injury	100,000–300,000	$220	Speeding ticket	+20 percent to all policy items
				Property damage	100,000	$400		
				Uninsured motorists	100,000–300,000	$100		
				Medical payments	1000	$50		
				Comprehensive	$250 deductible	$200		
				Collision	$500 deductible	$300		

Premium Invoicing and Payments

The task of supplying an invoice to the insured for payment is similar to other industries. The POLICY ITEM PREMIUM entity in Figure 5.13 may be billed via the intersection entity POLICY ITEM PREMIUM BILLING to the INVOICE ITEM. The POLICY ITEM PREMIUM only represents a record of what should be billed; the POLICY ITEM PREMIUM BILLING serves as the mechanism to record what was actually invoiced for insurance premiums. The PREMIUM SCHEDULE is usually set up in advance and may be used to generate POLICY ITEM PREMIUMs, POLICY ITEM PREMIUM BILLINGs and finally INVOICE ITEMs over a period of time. The INVOICE ITEMs may be incorporated into an INVOICE that may be sent to the FINANCIALLY RESPONSIBLE PARTY for payment. The FINANCIALLY RESPONSIBLE PARTY may be a direct relationship to the INVOICE or it may be maintained in an INVOICE ROLE, if a more flexible data model is desired.

Because the invoicing information requirements are very similar to the generic data models in Volume 1 (see V1:7.1–7.10), the generic invoice and payment models will apply (V1:7-8a and 7-8b). The PREMIUM SCHEDULE from the previous model is included to show how it generates the appropriate POLICY ITEM PREMIUM, POLICY ITEM PREMIUM BILLING, and INVOICE ITEM for the INVOICE.

To conclude this example, "Jim Smith" will receive the invoice "21345" on "12/01/2000" in order for him to make his payment of "$1270" by the due date of "12/15/2000." The invoice shows what has been paid, what is currently due, the yearly premium balance, and any messages that the company wishes to send to him, such as "Call now for a free quote on your homeowners insurance to see how you can save." The company will track the status of the invoice and any terms attached to it, such as "payable upon receipt."

Policy Claims

Insurance has been termed by some a "gamble." The inference is that the insured party is taking a chance that there will be a loss. This is a misconception because the possibility of a loss is always there. It might not happen often or even at all, but when it does, the results may be a financial disaster for the uninsured. The insured party is protecting all of the valuable assets he or she owns. It is important to the insured to do so, because the prudent person understands the nature of loss and the risks involved in not protecting assets from those certain times.

When those times arise, the insurance services enterprise has a responsibility to adequately compensate the insured party according to the agreement made. It is important for the insurance provider to keep an adequate reserve of resources available to cover any potential losses for any of its insured parties. Should the number of losses exceed the reserve for claims, the company could become insolvent and cause undue hardship to the insured parties it is set to protect.

This process of protection is based on the risk levels of the insured parties. The focus of this section is to be able to adequately manage loss in order to be able to settle and pay for any loss through the claim process.

The insured party makes a claim when a loss occurs. Typically claims begin as reported incidents that then are assessed for loss. Once the value of the loss is identified, the claim is settled according to the rules found within the agreement.

Insurance Claim Incidents

Incidents are events that occur to cause damage or loss to an insured asset. Depending on the circumstances and the extent of damage, they may result in a claim being filed. Regardless of their claim status, the insurance provider often wants to track specific incidents, as they paint a picture that can affect the risk level of the insured party.

Reporting of incidents is left up to the insured party for the majority of incidents. Governmental groups, such as the Division of Motor Vehicles, may report some incidents to the insurance provider. It is also important to track the incident's relationship to claims. This relationship gives the insurance provider important information to assist in assigning and understanding the risk involved with the insured party.

In the model shown in Figure 5.14, the INCIDENT, an event where loss or damage occurs or a related event occurs, involves a group of PARTYs through the INCIDENT ROLE entity. Those PARTYs may be the cause or result of the INCIDENT. The INCIDENT TYPE is a kind of loss or damage or related event. This assists the insurance provider in assessing the potential damage or rules of loss. It is important to understand that the INCIDENT TYPE is critical to the overall handling of any potential claim resulting from the INCIDENT. In the case of property casualty insurance, the INCIDENT PROPERTY DAMAGE is the specific loss resulting from the INCIDENT involving the INSURED ASSET. Insurance claims may have CLAIM ITEMs, each of which may be associated with an INCIDENT. It is important to recognize that not all INCIDENTs result in a CLAIM ITEM. Each INCIDENT may result in one or more INCIDENT PROPERTY DAMAGEs of DAMAGE TYPEs involving an INSURED ASSET.

The following example illustrates the nature of incidents. Jim Smith has sustained damage to his "1997 SUV" (INSURED ASSET) that is insured with "XYZ Insurance." "Peggy Warrent" is sent to review the damage sustained to the "1997 SUV" and to discuss the nature of the claim. On investigation, she finds that the vehicle was damaged when "a tree limb fell on the car during a recent wind storm" (the INCIDENT **description**). The INCIDENT TYPE in this case is PROPERTY DAMAGE and the specific INCIDENT PROPERTY DAMAGE val-

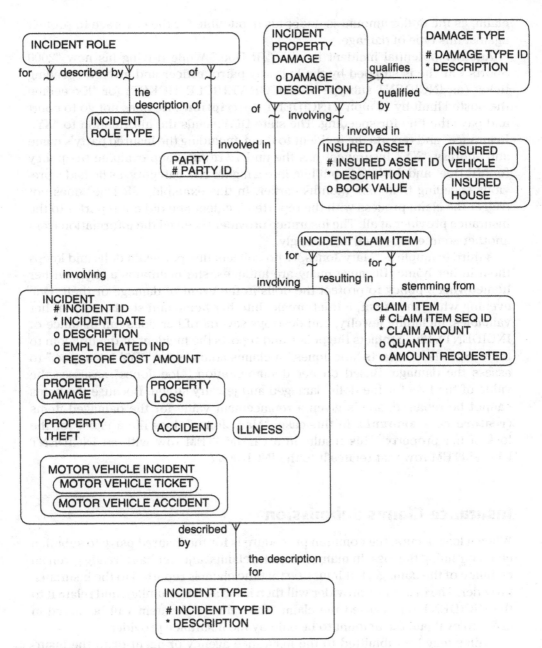

Figure 5.14   Insurance claim incidents.

ues for **damage description** are "Broken Windshield" and "Dent on car hood." The initial assessment of the repair cost is "$450" (**restore cost amount**). Based on the discussion with "Jim Smith," "Peggy Warrent" does not file a claim, as the dollar amount is under his deductible for the coverage to protect against this type of damage.

Another potential incident is with "JR Doe." While driving his new "2000 Sports Car" he is stopped by the highway patrol officer and given a speeding ticket (an INCIDENT subtype of MOTOR VEHICLE TICKET) for "Exceeding the posted limit by 18 mph" (INCIDENT **description**). He does not go to court and pays the fine for speeding. The state DMV sends the information to "XYZ Insurance" and reports the incident to them, including the insured party's name and address. "XYZ Insurance" has the underwriting group evaluate the policy for "JR Doe" and decides to put him into a higher risk category, as he had a previous speeding ticket six months earlier. In this example, "JR Doe" does not trigger the claim process with the reported incident and did not report it to the insurance provider at all. The insurance provider received the information from another source and acted accordingly.

A third example is "Mary Jones," who collects fine porcelain dolls and keeps them in her home. Because many are antiques, she maintains a rider on her homeowner's policy to protect the dolls in the event of damage or theft. One evening while she is out, a thief breaks into her home and steals many of her valuables, including jewelry, and destroys several of her dolls (an instance of INCIDENT). She contacts the police and reports the incident of the break-in to them. She also contacts "Joe Jones," a claims adjuster for "XYZ Insurance," to assess the damage. Based on her documentation, "Joe Jones" assesses the value of the loss for the dolls damaged and jewelry stolen. Because the items cannot be repaired, she is given a replacement value for the damaged items (**restore cost amount**). In this case, "Mary Jones" does file a claim for the loss of her property. This results in a CLAIM ITEM row with an INCIDENT CLAIM ITEM row that relates it to the INCIDENT.

Insurance Claims Submission

When a loss occurs, the common procedure is for the insured party to submit a claim outlining the loss. In many cases, the claims adjuster has already given an estimate of the damage, but it may be that the claim is reported to the insurance provider. The insurance provider will then issue a claim number, and relate it to the INCIDENT that caused the claim. The value of the item will be stated in order to evaluate the amount to be paid by the insurance provider.

Claims may be submitted to the insurance agency or agent or to the insurance provider directly. Larger organizations have a centralized group to handle claims, as they typically can handle more information in a more timely fashion.

Figure 5.15 shows the information requirements for claims submissions and shows a similar data model to the health care data model (please refer to V2:4.9 for more details), however, it is expanded to cover not only health care claims

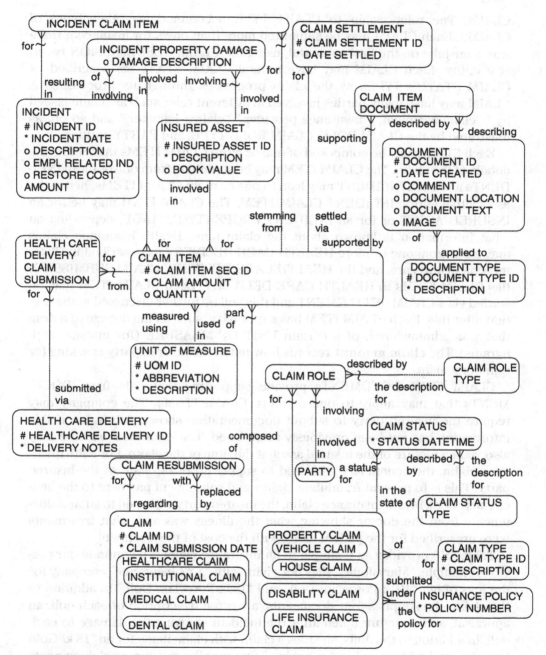

Figure 5.15 Insurance claims submission.

but also any insurance claim. A CLAIM is an event where the report of a loss is submitted under an INSURANCE POLICY. CLAIMs have subtypes of HEALTH CARE CLAIM, PROPERTY CLAIM, DISABILITY CLAIM, and LIFE INSURANCE

CLAIM. The relationship to CLAIM TYPE accommodates other types of CLAIMS. Each CLAIM may be submitted more than once, for instance if there was a mistake on the first submittal, using the CLAIM RESUBMISSION recursive entity. Each CLAIM may have several CLAIM STATUSes described by CLAIM STATUS TYPEs as the claim progresses through its processing. A CLAIM may have many parties involved in different roles such as "claim issued by," "claim recipient," "insurance provider," "claims adjuster," and so on, as illustrated by the CLAIM ROLE, CLAIM ROLE TYPE, and PARTY entities.

Each CLAIM may be composed of one or more CLAIM ITEMs that define the details of the claim. The CLAIM ITEM may be stemming from one or more INCIDENTs and each INCIDENT may lead to one or more CLAIM ITEMs, hence the associative entity, INCIDENT CLAIM ITEM. The CLAIM ITEM may be for an INSURED ASSET or for an INCIDENT PROPERTY DAMAGE, depending on what information is known about the claim item. Health insurance claims may stem from one or more HEALTH CARE DELIVERY as described in Chapter 4 on health care, and the HEALTH CARE DELIVERY CLAIM SUBMISSION ties CLAIM ITEMs to HEALTH CARE DELIVERY. Each CLAIM ITEM may be settled via a CLAIM SETTLEMENT and this will be further discussed in the section after this. Each CLAIM ITEM has a **quantity**, such as the dosage of a drug that was administered, of a certain UNIT OF MEASURE (for instance milligrams). The **claim amount** records how much the insured party is asking for reimbursement.

CLAIM ITEM DOCUMENTs provide supporting materials from DOCUMENTs that may apply to one or more CLAIM ITEMs. The company may require the insured party to submit documentation showing its value if this information has not been previously established. The insurance provider may also want a picture of the insured asset at the time of the claim. For a life insurance claim, the beneficiary will need to supply proof of death of the insured party. This is to prevent fraudulent claims and subsequent payment to the beneficiary. For a health insurance claim, the insured party will need to submit documents from the doctor showing what the illness was and what treatments were prescribed for the patient along with the cost of the treatment.

Table 5.15 provides an example of an insurance claim. To continue our previous example, "Mary Jones" files her claim with "XYZ Insurance" company for the loss of her "1912 Porcelain Doll" and "1922 Porcelain Doll." In addition to the claim, she supplies four documents: a written description of each doll, an appraisal, and a picture taken after the incident showing the damage to each doll. In addition to the dolls, she files a claim with claim items for an "18 kt Gold bracelet" and a "diamond and ruby ring." She supplies the appraisal documents outlining a description of each piece and a picture she had prior to them being taken. The claims adjuster gathers the information, lists all the claim items, assigns her claim ID "78901" and a CLAIM STATUS of "adjusted" on the **status**

Table 5.15 Claim Submission

CLAIM INCIDENT NUMBER	CLAIM STATUS DATE	CLAIM ID	CLAIM ITEM INSURED ASSET	CLAIM ITEM CLAIM AMOUNT	CLAIM DOCUMENT DESCRIPTION
9017892	2/15/2000 (status date that claim was adjusted)	78901	1912 porcelain doll	$500	Antique porcelain doll appraisal
					Picture taken of doll after incident
			1922 porcelain doll	$850	Antique porcelain doll appraisal
					Picture taken of doll after incident
			18 kt gold bracelet	$1500	18 kt gold bracelet appraisal
					Picture taken of bracelet
			Diamond and ruby ring	$2800	Diamond and ruby ring appraisal
					Picture taken before incident

date of "2/15/2000." "Joe Jones" then links the claim items to the incident and notes that it was reported to the police.

Claims Settlement

The insurance provider assumes the responsibility for determining what compensation will be paid for the loss after the claim has been submitted. This settlement process reviews the insurance policy agreement made with the insured party, the type of loss sustained, and the settlement adjudication rules. After reviewing this information, the claim settlement group will make a decision on what compensation is to be paid and to whom. The remittance is sent to the appropriate party along with some explanation of what is paid and why. Each claim item within a claim must be handled separately, as each item tends to have its claims processing requirements.

   In some instances where large groups are associated with the type of claim, such as in an automobile claim, the evaluation process will use standardized calculation methods in order to determine what is to be paid. This saves time and money and expedites a quick turn-around on the claim. Other claims will be handled on a more individual basis due to the specialized nature of the asset.

In the case of life insurance, a death benefit will be paid to the beneficiary. Some life insurance policies will either pay additional money or less money to the beneficiary, depending on the product features that were included in the life insurance product. For instance, if the product includes a loan, any outstanding balance will be subtracted from the death benefit prior to payment.

For health insurance policies, the scheduled fees to be paid are determined ahead of time with the health care practitioners within a provider network. If the health care practitioner is outside of the network, reduced benefits may be paid according to the agreement made. If the provider disputes the amount that was paid by the provider, the provider must file a request with the insurance provider in order to alter the amount paid. The insured party is responsible for a co-pay, as determined by the insurance provider. If a more traditional health insurance policy is used, the providers are still paid only what is considered "reasonable and customary," in other words, the amount the insurance provider has determined to be adequate for the services provided. In this case, the insured party is responsible for the remainder of the payment to the provider.

The model in Figure 5.16 shows the details of the claims settlement information requirements. Once the CLAIM has been submitted to the insurance provider (a CLAIM ROLE), the CLAIM INCIDENT and the loss of the INSURED ASSET are evaluated. The CLAIMS ADJUSTER may perform an APPRAISAL, which is defined as the valuation of the INSURED ASSET. The CLAIM SETTLEMENT occurs for each CLAIM ITEM, and ADJUDICATION RULEs may be applied to determine the settlement. These are ELIGIBILITY RULEs (identifying if the loss is covered under the policy), AUDIT RULEs (identifying if all the proper codes and information were correctly stated in the claim), and PRICING RULEs (determining how much of the loss will be covered). These rules will be based on many ADJUDICATION FACTORs, such as the circumstances of the incidents or claims and whether the product rules and coverages are allowed considering those factors. Once decided, the CLAIM PAYMENT AMOUNTs that are owed to the INSURED PARTY are determined. The CLAIM SETTLEMENT AMOUNT entity also maintains other amounts that were calculated through the settlement process such as the DEDUCTIBLE AMOUNT, USUAL AND CUSTOMARY AMOUNT, and DISALLOWED AMOUNT. Based on the rules of the policy, a subsequent PAYMENT of a PAYMENT TYPE and PAYMENT METHOD TYPE (see V1:7.8a and 7.8b for more information on payments) will be paid to the appropriate PARTY designated to receive the payment, such as the beneficiary or the health care provider.

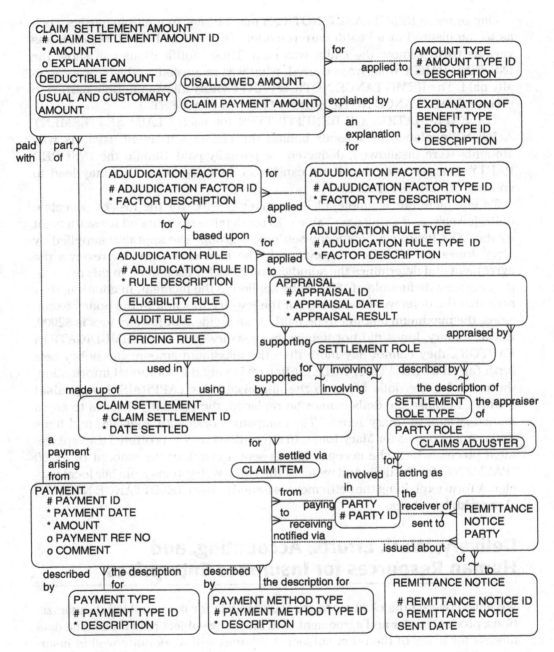

Figure 5.16   Insurance payment settlement.

One or more REMITTANCE NOTICEs may be sent to multiple parties, such as to the insured or a health care provider. This REMITTANCE NOTICE lets various parties know the claim was paid. These notifications can show the INSURED PARTY what was covered, what was requested, and what was actually paid. The REMITTANCE NOTICE PARTY entity allows multiple parties to receive REMITTANCE NOTICEs issued about a PAYMENT.

The EXPLANATION OF BENEFIT TYPE for each CLAIM SETTLEMENT AMOUNT explains the reasons behind the claims settlement, such as why amounts were disallowed, deducted, or partially paid. Should the INSURED PARTY disagree with this, there can be an appeal process that may lead to another CLAIM SETTLEMENT.

To complete our example, claim number "78901" for the loss of porcelain dolls, jewelry, and a ring (see Table 5.15 for details) is evaluated for settlement by the "XYZ Insurance" company settlement group. The appraisal supplied by Mary Jones for each item is reviewed. The insurance provider reviews the agreement and determines the adjudication rules for each item. In this process, they notice a deductible of "$50" to be applied to the incident. In addition, they note that the dolls were itemized, but the jewelry was not. In the policy exclusions, the maximum amount to be paid for an incident of jewelry loss is $2000. Because Mary Jones did not itemize her jewelry (this is an ADJUDICATION FACTOR), they cannot pay more than the maximum amount the policy sets forth (an ADJUDICATION RULE). After reviewing the additional information, the price for the dolls is set to the appraisal price (APPRAISAL **appraisal result**). Because the dolls cannot be replaced, the company decides to pay a monetary sum to "Mary Jones." The company works with a jeweler and finds replacement pieces for Mary Jones. In the settlement, she is offered the replacement pieces, which she accepts. She is sent a check in the amount of $2000 (PAYMENT) for the dolls and receives the two jewelry items from her local jeweler. A form explaining the settlement is issued to her (REMITTANCE NOTICE) along with her check.

Delivery, Work Efforts, Accounting, and Human Resources for Insurance Enterprises

We have covered the changes to the data models for the people and organizations, product, order and agreement, and invoicing subject data areas. The data models for many of the other subject data areas will work quite well in insurance. The order and shipment models may be used for incoming shipments on the supply side of the business. The work effort models can be used for a variety of service tasks that need to be accomplished. The accounting and budgeting data models will probably be usable with very few changes. The human resources models should apply as well.

Star Schemas for Insurance

In the insurance industry, the number of analytical models to support analysis could be numerous. The intention of this discussion is to highlight the most widely used, effective, and important analysis functions within the insurance industry. It is important to recognize that these are templates, and the enterprise needs to evaluate their own data analysis requirements.

It is the intention to share this template to assist the reader in understanding some possible considerations in an insurance star schema design. This work is not intended to be exhaustive, nor will it span all possibilities.

Analysis Information

It is well understood that all information within the scope of this chapter has been at an atomic level. In developing a solid star schema, it is necessary to understand what is to be analyzed, its significance, and why it must be analyzed. In insurance, the basic function that requires constant analysis is claims information. It is important to analyze this because this gives the insurance provider insight into the circumstances behind losses, the results of the losses, and how to assist in preventing excessive losses in the future.

The main focus for the majority of analysis is on claims submissions and their settlement. Important insight to understanding the settlement is also gained from analyzing the loss and its understood risk.

Claim Star Schema

The claim star schema within the insurance industry helps the enterprise determine how it is performing their risk analysis. As stated throughout this chapter, the insurance provider must master the balance between the premiums charged and the risk of loss. Should the number of losses be too high or the settlements paid too much, the company will not be able to maintain the proper claim reserve to continue in a profitable business. Proper risk analysis is critical to maintaining this business balance. The claim star schema is a good tool to determine if the current risk models in use are beneficial or if they need adjusting.

Typically, the information given within the claim star schema can help provide feedback to the rating and underwriting functions. Based upon analysis of the claims information, the rating model information may be adjusted in order to charge premiums that are in excess of their expected claims payouts. In analyzing the claims information, insurance policies may be reevaluated to provide the best level of service for the insured party while limiting risks to the insurance provider.

An important benefit to this model is the understanding of what factors should be tracked in order to manage risk. Claims analysis may indicate factors that cause losses—for example, what types of coverages lead to the highest payouts.

Fact Table

Figure 5.17 provides a star schema to analyze claims information. The CLAIM FACT table of this star schema maintains information about settled CLAIMs in order to determine the effectiveness of the enterprise in managing losses. The measures for the claims star schema are the **claim_item_requested_amount** (the amount requested for the loss), the **claim_payment_amount** (the amount paid to the INSURED PARTY for the settlement of a CLAIM ITEM within a CLAIM), and the **estimated_cost** (the amount that it costs to process the claim). It is important to be able to analyze these measures in relationship to the many dimensions shown next, in order to determine the effectiveness of the enterprise's risk models.

Dimensions

The claim star schema common dimensions are based on the information in the previously discussed logical data models within this chapter. The logical data models provide the necessary understanding of the measures and dimensions in this star schema.

TIME_BY_DAY is an important dimension within the claim star schema. This provides a picture of what was paid within various time frames. Trend analysis can be used to determine if there are any time-based patterns for claims payments. For instance, there may be more accidents that occur during certain times of the year, and this could influence underwriting considerations.

The type of insured party (PARTY_TYPES) can be a key aspect of analyzing claims. For instance, it is useful to analyze the claims history for various types of parties—for example, to analyze claims payments to insured parties that are in the construction business or similarly risky businesses.

Another key dimension is GEOGRAPHIC_BOUNDARYS. Because most claims occur within a particular geographic region, it is important to know what areas are generating the most losses and how much is paid in claims. This has a very important bearing on the premium rating models because it can help determine if the rate charged for a geographic boundary is in line with actual generated losses.

The RISK_LEVEL_TYPES dimension is used to reevaluate the categorization of risk level types. Remember that risk level types could be high, medium, and low and are used in the insurance rate table. This dimension allows analysis to determine whether the risk level assigned to rate tables needs adjusting. If the

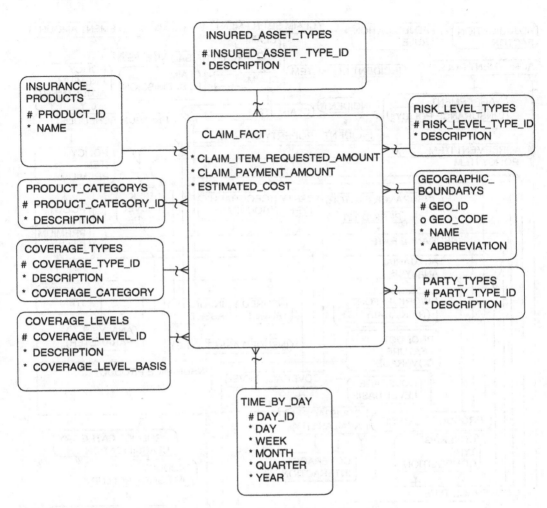

Figure 5.17 Claim star schema.

dollars paid exceed the dollars gained within a claims category type, the risk level and rates may need to be increased in the rate table for that claims category.

The type of asset insured (INSURED_ASSET_TYPES) may help analyze claims. Certain assets have a higher incidence of claims. When assigning risk, it is important to understand what should be excluded in order to avoid costly claims or excessive losses. If there are substantial losses for a particular type of insured asset, the enterprise may decide to add insurance policy exclusions for these assets in order to avoid costly, frequent losses. For instance, an insured asset type of "speed boat" may require additional exclusions to restrict any claims payments that occur during any type of racing activity.

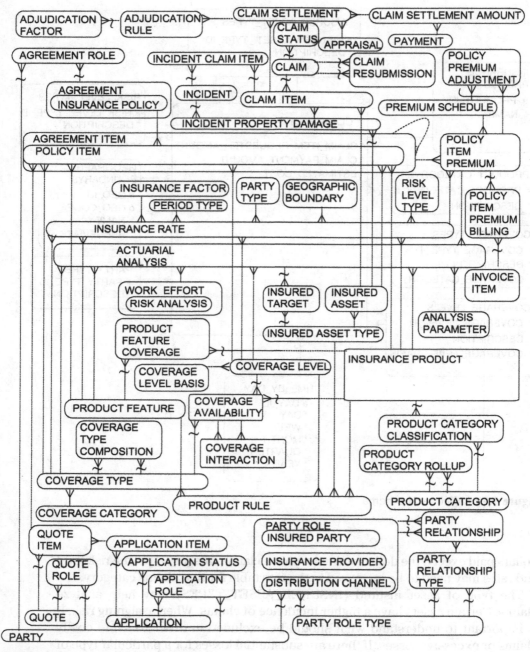

Figure 5.18 Overall insurance model.

The type of insurance (by INSURANCE_PRODUCTS or PRODUCT_CATE-GORYS) is another important dimension. Certain lines of business tend to generate more claims. Typically, property and casualty insurance lines are high-claim businesses and must be more closely managed. If there is a sudden surge of claim payments within the life insurance line, more analysis may be needed to determine the reason for the increase of payments. This dimension could also provide comparisons between individual policies and group policies.

The insurance enterprise may need to evaluate requested amounts and settlement amounts for various COVERAGE_TYPES at various COVERAGE_LEVELS. This information can help the enterprise understand which types of coverage tend to result in more claims payments. The payments made at various levels of coverage may provide further insight into what an insurance provider should offer. For instance, the provider may decide that a $50 deductible level of coverage may not be cost effective on collision insurance.

Insurance Summary

Even though many of the data models from Volume 1 apply to insurance, the data models within this chapter focused on the unique data model constructs needed within insurance. Perhaps the most important additional data models needed are those defining the information requirements for insurance products, coverage types, coverage levels, product features, insurance rates, underwriting, insurance policies, premiums, incidents, and claims.

This chapter illustrated data model modifications to the generic data constructs in Volume 1 to meet the needs of most insurance enterprises. Appropriate party roles and relationships subtypes were added, product data structures were tailored, the pricing models were modified to maintain information in insurance rate tables, the quotes model was expanded to handle insurance quotes, and the agreement data models were extended to include insurance policy information requirements.

Figure 5.18 provides an overall model for the insurance industry.

CHAPTER 6

Financial Services

Financial services companies provide services for managing money; they include banks, credit unions, brokerage services, securities firms, and insurance companies. This chapter focuses on the needs of an enterprise providing banking, brokerage, and securities services. Financial service companies are concerned with such issues as the following:

- How can we identify and support the financial needs of our customers?

- How can we provide supporting products and services to meet those needs?

- How can we improve customer service and maintain our customer relationships?

- How can we maximize revenues, minimize costs, and still maintain excellent service levels?

- How can we ensure that our systems are flexible enough to allow us to change our business models quickly and easily?

To answer these types of questions, financial service enterprises need to track information about the following:

- The people and organizations they are concerned with, namely, customers, prospects, affiliates, suppliers, employees, and internal organizations
- Their product and service offerings that support required customer needs, compliance with regulatory requirements, and the continual improvement of those services
- The proper delivery mechanisms to get the information about the product to the customer
- Servicing and assistance for the customers, with the ability to support their ever-changing needs by tracking the specific agreements the company makes with the customer
- Providing access to those services through the customer's account and accurately tracking all activity for that account and reporting it back to the customer
- Managing proper use of the customer's information in order to assess risk for the company, assisting the customer in gaining the services required, and providing the customer with accurate invoicing information
- Budgeting and accounting information
- Human resources management

Volume 1 addresses many of the needs of a financial services enterprise (financial services company). For instance, it addresses the following:

- People and organizations structures that can be used within financial services
- Generic product models that can form the basis for financial service products
- Work effort models that can be used to perform service tasks and prepare needed information
- Accounting, budgeting, and human resource models to manage finances and people

Key aspects of financial services that are not addressed in Volume 1 include these:

- The information needed for financial planning, needs assessment, and identification of key customer objectives
- Data structures set up specifically for financial services products

- Specific information about regulatory requirements, including internal and external regulations and their impact on products, services, and customers
- Specific structures for financial product delivery to the customers
- Specific structures for agreements and their impacts on the products and services
- Detailed data models for account and account transaction activity
- Work tasks that are specific to the financial services industry about analysis and management of risk

Table 6.1 shows which models can be used directly from Volume 1, which models need to be modified, which models are not used, and which new models are required. For the people and organizations area, most of the models from Volume 1 apply; however, we need to add PARTY ROLE and PARTY RELATIONSHIP subtypes suitable to financial services enterprises. The existing agreement model can be used in financial services, with modifications, to add FINANCIAL AGREEMENT subtypes. The most significant data modeling additions for financial services enterprises include data structures for product maintenance, financial objectives, financial regulations, agreement set up, account maintenance, account transaction models, risk analysis, and account analysis.

People and Organizations in Financial Services

Financial services companies generally have similar needs for tracking people and organizations as do other enterprises, and the very nature of financial services is to support people and the business in which they work. Financial enterprises need to track information about their customers, prospects, suppliers, employees, shareholders, and organization structures. The critical relationships between these parties must be captured and managed for customer service, sales, supply, and human resource management functions. Financial service enterprises have a critical need to maintain this information accurately as it helps facilitate close relationships with their customers. In financial service enterprises, customer service is a key component of the business.

Figure 6.1 shows a data model for PARTY, PARTY ROLEs, and PARTY RELATIONSHIPs within financial services enterprises, which is a customized version of the generic party roles and relationships model (V1:2.6). The two subtypes of PARTYs, a PERSON or ORGANIZATION, can fulfill multiple PARTY ROLEs, a function that must be supported for the relationship. These PARTY ROLEs are

Table 6.1 Volume 1 and Volume 2 Data Models for Financial Services

SUBJECT DATA AREA	USE THESE VOLUME 1 MODELS DIRECTLY	MODIFY THESE VOLUME 1 MODELS (AS DESCRIBED IN VOLUME 2)	DO NOT USE THESE VOLUME 1 MODELS	ADD THESE VOLUME 2 MODELS
People and organizations	Person, V1:2.1-2.14 except for V1:2.5-2.6	Party relationship, V1:2.5 and V1:2.6, revised with Financial services party roles and relationships, V2:6.1		Financial objectives, needs, and plans, V2:6.2
Product		Product categories, V1:3.2, Product features, V1:3.4, Product pricing, V1:3.7, Estimated cost component, V1:3.8	Product definition, V1:3.1, Product identification, V1:3.3, Suppliers and manufacturers of products, V1:3.5, Inventory item storage, V1:3.6 Products and parts, V1:3.9a and V1:3.9b, Product components, V1:3.10a and V1:3.10b	Financial services product definition, V2:6.3, Financial product regulations and rules, V2:6.4
Order		Standard order models, V1:4.1-4.8 for supply-side processing. Requirement, request, quote, V1:4.9-4.11 on the supply side, Agreement models, V1:4.12-4.16 (need to subtype agreements)		Financial agreement, V2:6.5

Delivery	Shipment models, V1:5.1–5.8 for supply deliveries		Financial account, V2:6.6, Financial account transaction V2:6.7
Work effort	Work effort, V1:6.1–6.13	Work effort generations, V1:6.3a (need to add subtypes for financial services tasks)	Account notification, V2:6.8 Analysis task, V2:6.9
Invoicing	Invoice models, V1:7.1–7.10		
Accounting	All models, V1:8.1–8.12		
Human resources	All models, V1:9.1–9.14		
Financial services star schema designs			Financial account star schema, V2:6.10 Account transaction star schema, V2:6.11

linked to the appropriate PARTY RELATIONSHIPs, a statement of how two or more PARTY ROLEs interact with each other.

Generic Party Role Subtypes

Many of the generic PARTY ROLES from Volume 1 are included in Figure 6.1. Generic ORGANIZATION ROLEs include SUPPLIER, COMPETITOR, HOUSE-HOLD, PARTNER, ORGANIZATION UNIT, PARENT ORGANIZATION, SUB-SIDIARY, DIVISION, DEPARTMENT, OTHER ORGANIZATION UNIT, and INTERNAL ORGANIZATION.

Standard PERSON ROLEs include EMPLOYEE, CONTRACTOR, and CON-TACT. EMPLOYEE and CONTRACTOR have been supertyped into a WORKER. The WORKER supertype simplifies the data model in certain circumstances, for example when work efforts need to be related to either the employee or a contractor.

SHAREHOLDER, PROSPECT, and CUSTOMER are generic PARTY ROLE subtypes that may be for either a PERSON or an ORGANIZATION.

Financial Service Party Roles

The role FINANCIAL INSTITUTION is used to describe banks, lending organizations, credit unions, brokerage services, securities firms, insurance companies, or any other organization that is involved in providing financial service. The modeler may choose to subtype this entity with the examples just given for more clarity within the model diagram. This role of FINANCIAL INSTITUTION may be played by an internal organization or an external organization in order to identify which parties are involved in these services.

A key role within financial services companies is the role of REGULATORY AGENCY, those groups that establish guidelines and that enforce and communicate internal or external requirements to the financial services company. Within the financial services industry, many regulations govern the operations and processes used. These regulations are strictly enforced and monitored for compliance. Financial services companies must report to these agencies at frequent intervals and make their operations available for auditing.

The CUSTOMER role is subtyped into INVESTOR or LOAN CUSTOMER, signifying whether the customer is providing money to be invested or is borrowing money from the financial institution. Because a PARTY may play many PARTY ROLEs, each party could be identified with both of these roles or simply to the CUSTOMER role to establish this fact.

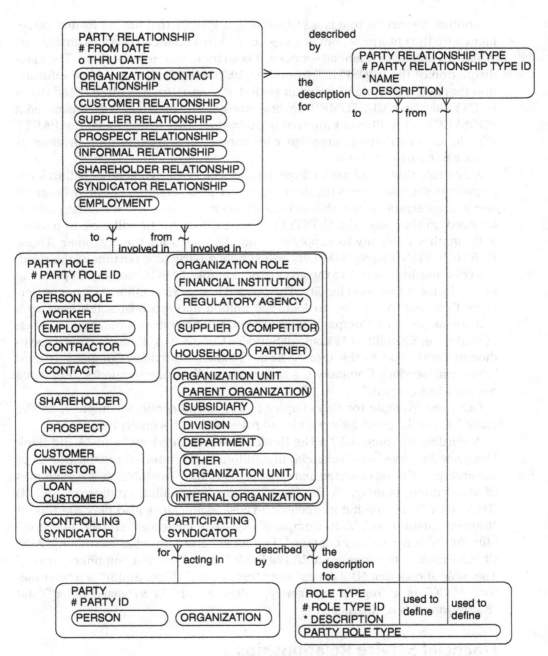

Figure 6.1   Financial services party roles and relationships.

Another important role is a PROSPECT, a PARTY that has no formal agreement with the enterprise, but is a key interest to a financial services enterprise. While not unique to financial services, it is an important role for them. The main distinction of the PROSPECT from the CUSTOMER is the amount of information that may be kept and for what period of time. Also, it is often noted that a PARTY may be a CUSTOMER for one internal organization, but considered a PROSPECT for a different internal organization. This would make the PARTY eligible for a marketing campaign with another organization for a product or service not currently used.

A key role that is unique to financial services is the syndicator. Within large organizations, many times the financial needs are so great that a single financial services enterprise is not able to bear all the risk associated with that particular need. In that case, the CONTROLLING SYNDICATOR will look to partner with another company to supply the complete need for the customer. Those PARTICIPATING SYNDICATORs will supply a particular portion of the need, thus distributing the risk to the group; for example, "ABC Company" is planning to build a manufacturing facility. The needed loan is $60 million. "Financial Services Company A" is able to loan $20 million and syndicates the loan with "Financial Services Company B" and "Financial Services Company C," each contributing $20 million. "Financial Services Company A" then controls the syndication and collects the money from "Financial Services Company B" and "Financial Services Company C," generating additional revenue for "Financial Services Company A."

Our case example for this chapter is a financial services company, "A Big Bank." Table 6.2 provides examples of roles within this enterprise.

According to Table 6.2, "A Big Bank Brokerage Services," and "A Big Bank Mortgage Services" are "financial institutions" and "internal organizations" of the enterprise being modeled, namely, "A Big Bank." The table shows examples of syndication, namely, "A Big Bank" as the "controlling syndicator" and "B Bank" as a "participating syndicator." These syndicators also play the role of "financial institution." "ABC Company" is a "loan customer" and an "investor." "Jim Smith" is a customer contact," "Len Jones" is an "investor customer." "ABC Check Printing" is a supplier of "A Big Bank." "Jane Doe" is a "supplier contact." The table shows that "Bill Jones" is an "employee," "Mary Smith" is a "contractor," "OCC" is a "regulatory agency," "Jane Smith" is a "shareholder," and "Kathy Jones" is a "prospect.

Financial Service Relationships

Table 6.3 provides additional information about which party roles are involved within which relationships. For example, "A Big Bank Mortgage Services" is a subsidiary of "A Big Bank." The next two rows show that "ABC Company" is a

Table 6.2   Financial Services Party Roles

PARTY ROLE NAME	PARTY NAME
Financial institution, internal organization (parent organization)	A Big Bank
Financial institution, internal organization (subsidiary)	A Big Bank Brokerage Services
Financial institution, internal organization (subsidiary)	A Big Bank Mortgage Services
Financial institution, controlling syndicator	A Big Bank
Financial institution, participating syndicator	B Bank
Loan customer, Investor	ABC Company
Contact (customer contact)	Jim Smith
Investor customer	Len Jones
Supplier	ABC Check Printing
Contact (supplier contact)	Jane Doe
Employee	Bill Jones
Contractor	Mary Smith
Regulatory agency	OCC
Shareholder	Jane Smith
Prospect	Kathy Jones

customer of two internal organizations within the enterprise, "A Big Bank Brokerage Services" and "A Big Bank Mortgage Services." Therefore, there are two relationships that may have different information associated with them, such as priorities, statuses, and so on. "Jim Smith" is a contact within the "ABC Company." "Len Jones" is a person customer of "A Big Bank." "ABC Check Printing" is a supplier of "A Big Bank." One of its supplier contacts is "Jane Doe." "B Bank" maintains a syndicator relationship with "A Big Bank," which is the controlling syndicator. There is an employment relationship with "Bill Jones" who is an employee of "A Big Bank." "Mary Smith" has a contractor relationship with "A Big Bank."

"Jane Smith" has a shareholder relationship with "A Big Bank" but also has an informal relationship with Mary Smith. The nature of their informal relationship is that Mary Smith works with Jane Smith in their law practice, "Smith & Smith." "Mary Smith" currently is not a customer of "A Big Bank" but is tied in a critical relationship with a significant person "Jane Smith." Both persons are important to "A Big Bank" due to the informal relationship. Notice that the

Table 6.3 Financial Services Party Relationships

FROM PARTY NAME	FROM PARTY ROLE	TO PARTY NAME	TO PARTY ROLE	PARTY RELATIONSHIP TYPE NAME
A Big Bank Mortgage Services	Subsidiary	A Big Bank	Parent organization	Organization roll-up (subsidiary)
ABC Company	Customer	A Big Bank Brokerage Services	Internal organization	Customer relationship
ABC Company	Customer	A Big Bank Mortgage Services	Internal organization	Customer relationship
Jim Smith	Contact	ABC Company	Customer	Organization contact relationship
Len Jones	Customer	A Big Bank	Internal organization	Customer relationship (person)
ABC Check Printing	Supplier	A Big Bank	Internal organization	Supplier relationship
Jane Doe	Contact	ABC Check Printing	Supplier	Organization contact relationship (supplier contact relationship)
B Bank	Participating Syndicator	A Big Bank	Controlling syndicator	Syndicator relationship
Bill Jones	Employee	A Big Bank	Internal organization	Employment relationship (employee)
Mary Smith	Contractor	A Big Bank	Internal organization	Contractor relationship (contractor)
Jane Smith	Shareholder	A Big Bank	Organization role	Shareholder relationship
Jane Smith	Person role	Mary Smith	Person role	Informal relationship (partnering together)
Kathy Jones	Prospect	A Big Bank	Internal organization	Prospect relationship

relationship is maintained at a higher level of roles, from one person role to another, to allow for any informal connections between parties. The PARTY RELATIONSHIP TYPE for this relationship could be more specifically defined as "informal partnership." Finally, "Kathy Jones" has a prospect relationship with "A Big Bank," as she is currently part of a marketing campaign.

Financial Objectives, Needs, and Plans

This section provides a model to capture the objectives, financial plans, and needs that are critical within the financial services industry. Most industries will record customer needs, and sometimes customer objectives, but they will usually not record information about customer plans.

The generic model captured CUSTOMER REQUIREMENTs in Chapter 4 of Volume 1 (V1:4.9); however, this model provides a much more in-depth version of the model for financial services, and the term "need" is used instead of REQUIREMENT. Furthermore, the REQUIREMENT entity was used to capture PRODUCT REQUIREMENTs or WORK EFFORT REQUIREMENTs, while the "need" entity captures a broader range of possible things that may be of interest to the financial service customer.

Financial service enterprises often outline customers' objectives, create and maintain financial plans, and maintain customer needs to accomplish their objectives and plans. Financial services providers identify specific products to meet these financial objectives, plans, and needs. The objectives, plans, and needs can also become the basis for future investments and strategies as the customer's portfolio of products grows and they can be periodically reviewed with the customer for refinement and alteration.

Figure 6.2 shows the relationships between the PARTY, PARTY OBJECTIVE, PLAN, and PARTY NEED, and their link to the FINANCIAL PRODUCT and PRODUCT CATEGORY.

Each PARTY has several PARTY NEEDs that are described by NEED TYPE. These are governed by many factors, such as market considerations and available products, such as specific funds, bonds, or stocks available for investing. Therefore, each PARTY NEED may be qualified by the PARTY TYPE (interested in investing in manufacturing firms), by the FINANCIAL PRODUCT (interested in the "C Bond Fund" product), or by the PRODUCT CATEGORY (interested in bond funds). The need may also be described more specifically via the **description** attribute of PARTY NEED.

Based on the input from the PARTY, there are specific PARTY OBJECTIVEs, the clear and focused direction the party wishes to take, stated as required for a specific **from date**, **thru date**, and **goal date**. PARTY OBJECTIVES fall into two subtypes: an INVESTMENT OBJECTIVE (those directions specifically focused on investment vehicles) or a LENDING OBJECTIVE (those directions

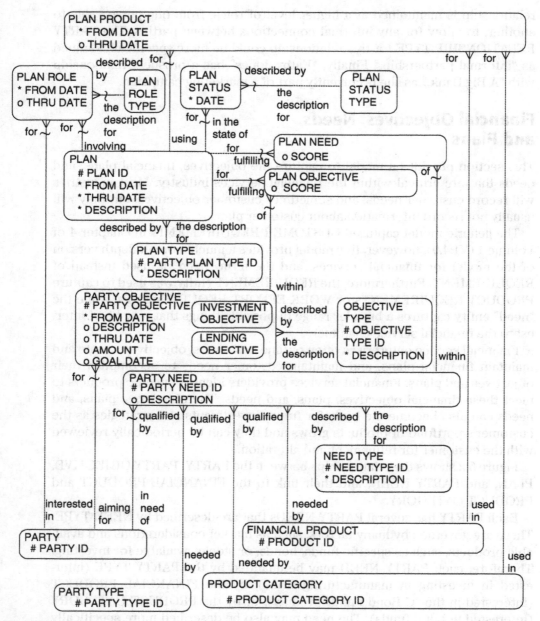

Figure 6.2　Financial objectives, needs, and plans.

specifically focused on loan vehicles). They may be further classified by the OBJECTIVE TYPE.

　　These PARTY OBJECTIVEs and PARTY NEEDs are considered when developing the PLAN. The PLAN is a financial course of action and has certain statuses such as "created,," "approved,," and "shown to customer." This PLAN is based upon and relates to PARTY OBJECTIVEs and PARTY NEEDs, thus showing what objectives and needs the plan satisfies. The **score** attribute allows each need or objective to maintain the relative importance of the need or objective, with a "1" as the highest priority, "2" as the next highest priority, and so on.

Is there a strong enough will by the enterprise to map objectives to financial plans? Most plans should generally match most of the objectives and needs stated by the customer. A full understanding of all objectives assists with the most appropriate plan for the customer. Each person or organization involved in a plan is encouraged to state its objectives in terms of risk. Some investors are willing to take greater risks; other investors are conservative. The plan is usually based on certain objectives and needs, and each customer may have several plans that are designed to meet different objectives and needs. Once all of the needs and objectives of the plan are determined, the PLAN will determine which FINANCIAL PRODUCTs are most appropriate for the plan; thus, the PLAN PRODUCTs will articulate those chosen to meet the PLAN.

The PLAN ROLE shows the number of PARTYs involved with the PLAN and the role of each party in the plan. Each PARTY will assume a PLAN ROLE TYPE, such as "financial planner," "investor," or "beneficiary." Each PARTY may be engaged within the PLAN ROLE for a specified period of time, thus requiring a **from date** and a **thru date** on the PLAN ROLE.

Table 6.4 shows the needs and objectives for multiple investors. "John Doe," a potential small business owner, wishes to begin his own consulting company. His specific objectives of establishing this company with an increased net worth have generated two needs: One is for a money management advisor in the stock market; the other is a low-interest loan to start his business. In scoring the order of importance for his objectives, his number one priority is "Increase Net Worth," while the second is "Establish New Company." "Jane Doe" is looking to save for her retirement. Her needs are in low-risk investments to support her retirement objective. "Mary Jones" wishes to create a trust fund for her minor children. Her needs are to build a multi-risk investment portfolio to give a steady interest return allowing the fund to sufficiently grow in the next 10–20 years. "ABC Company" is looking to eliminate short-term debts to increase its cash flow. Its desire is to leverage existing capital within the company to pay off debts and improve the company's financial position.

Once the objectives and needs are identified, the financial services representative will devise a plan to support these needs with specific products. At this point, the financial services company may change the representative working with the customer, as different representatives work with different levels of risk. "John Doe" may change to a financial planner who works with higher-risk customers because he is willing to take a greater risk than "Jane Doe."

Based on the products available, the financial services representative will create a PLAN, a scenario based on the decided needs and objectives. Each

Table 6.4 Party Needs and Objectives

PARTY NAME	PARTY OBJECTIVE DESCRIPTION	PARTY NEED DESCRIPTION	SCORE
John Doe	Increase net worth	Invest in high-return stock	1
	Establish new company	Find low-interest loan	2
Jane Doe	Save for retirement	Invest in low-risk fund	1
Mary Jones	Establish trust fund	Invest in mixed-risk funds to build trust fund for children	1
ABC Company	Eliminate short-term debts	Leverage capital to pay off specific short-term debts	1

plan is identified with a specific **plan ID,** as shown in the table, and each plan also is associated with a PLAN TYPE, also shown. Often several plans will be created, giving the customer multiple choices of investments and options. These PLANs will include a series of FINANCIAL PRODUCTs or PRODUCT CATEGORYs in the PLAN PRODUCT in order to meet the objectives and needs of the customer(s) of that plan. The FINANCIAL PRODUCTs are chosen from a wide array of available products and managed by the financial services representative.

Table 6.5 gives examples of this. For "John Doe" a plan, "123563," with a type of "Income" is described as "Build net worth" and will include several products: "A Stock," "B High return mutual fund," "A Bond fund," and "C Stock." The financial planner, "Bill Jones," selects these products due to specific characteristics that align with the objectives for this plan. A second plan, "958456," for the same customer, of plan type "Venture" described as "Establish new business," has a product, "A Bank low-interest loan." Due to the different nature of the type of plan, "John Jones" is the associated "Financial Planner." "Jane Doe" has a plan type of "Long term" described as "Retirement plan" with two products: "C Bond fund" and "D Mixed-risk mutual fund." "ABC Company" has a **plan id** of "958454," with a PLAN TYPE **description** of "Capital" and a PLAN OBJECTIVE **description** of "Payoff short-term Debts" and that uses a product of "A Margin loan." "Mary Jones" has plan "498589" with a plan type of "Long term" described as "Build trust fund" with products "D Mixed-risk mutual fund," "A Stock," and "A Bond fund." The financial planners pick the plan's products based on previous history product performance, return characteristics, and the customer objectives and needs.

Multiple financial services representatives may work the plan based on specialized skills in various risk areas. For example, "Bill Jones" specializes in "Income" type plans and knows specific products to assist in this, while "John Jones" is certified in "Venture" type plans that require larger capital for start-up companies.

Table 6.5 Party Plans and Products

PLAN ID	PARTY NAME AND PLAN ROLE	PLAN TYPE DESCRIPTION	PLAN OBJECTIVE DESCRIPTION	PLAN PRODUCT NAME
123563	John Doe, investor, Bill Jones, financial planner	Income	Build net worth	A Stock
				B High-return mutual fund
				A Bond Fund
				C Stock
958456	John Doe, investor, John Jones, financial planner	Venture	Establish new business	A Bank low-interest loan
456756	Jane Doe, investor, Joe Jones, financial planner	Long term	Retirement plan	C Bond fund
				D Mixed-risk mutual fund
958454	ABC Company, loan customer, John Jones, financial planner	Capital	Pay off short-term debts	A Margin Loan
498589	Mary Jones, investor, Joe Jones, financial planner	Long term	Build trust fund	D Mixed-risk mutual fund
				A Stock
				A Bond fund

Financial Services Products

Financial services products require a highly customizable set of features and functional settings that may be applied to meet the needs of a customer. In any service industry the main focus of business is to determine the customer needs and to fulfill them. In financial services, the focus is on money management. Financial service products assist the customer in growing his or her financial assets and protecting them for future use. It is critical to any financial services company's success to supply these services at the lowest cost in order to remain competitive.

A key difference between a financial services product and products in other industries is that the "products" are really services with particular arrangements around them. Unlike manufacturing, there are usually no tangible products that are engineered or cataloged in advance of the sale. The financial services product is often supplied to the customer through the agreement process that will be covered later in this chapter.

The virtual nature of the financial service product leads to the need for extreme flexibility. While the goal is to offer flexible products, there are factors limiting this flexibility, for instance regulations imposed by governing bodies. Standardization within the financial services product may be found; however, most cases allow the standards to be modified for various reasons: VIP customers, customer needs, and customer expectations.

Financial Services Product Definition

The FINANCIAL PRODUCT is a highly customizable service that is designed to be used in agreements made between the customer and the financial institution. Financial services products need a much more fluid structure because they often require many modifications over time to reflect the customer's changing needs and demands.

The financial product is either a customized service (or set of services) for a specific customer or may be a predefined service with specific arrangements. In some instances, this FINANCIAL PRODUCT can be pre-established and is used as an offering for many customers, but many times the FINANCIAL PRODUCT is customized for a single customer. The financial product also needs to define what happens if certain conditions arise.

Figure 6.3 shows a data model for a financial services product that has some of the entities from Chapter 3, "Products," in Volume 1 (product category, V1:3.2, and product feature, V1:3.4).

The PRODUCT CATEGORY lists the varying kinds of FINANCIAL PRODUCTs that can be provided. In reviewing the types of FINANCIAL PRODUCTs, there is a common structure around them. Product categories include INVESTMENT VEHICLE, DEPOSIT PRODUCTs, LOAN PRODUCTs, and LEASEs. PRODUCT CATEGORYs may be made up of other PRODUCT CATEGORYs as handled by the PRODUCT CATEGORY ROLLUP entity. The financial services company may use these product categories to report in the areas of profitability, sales, and customer service. Each PRODUCT CATEGORY may have several FINANCIAL PRODUCTs as provided by the PRODUCT CATEGORY CLASSIFICATION.

The FINANCIAL PRODUCT represents a specifically designed financial services offering, such as "A+ Checking" or "Low fee Visa," that has very specific features and functional settings that are offered within the product.

Each product may have a number of PRODUCT FEATUREs and FUNCTIONAL SETTINGs that may be applicable when these products are used in agreements between the customer and financial institution. PRODUCT

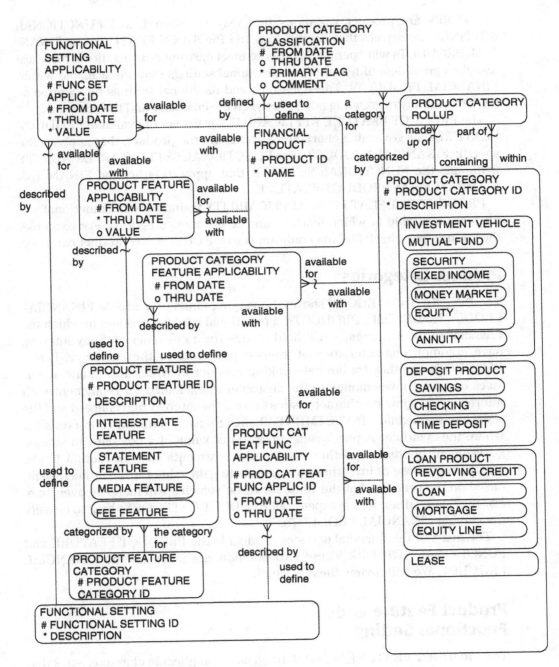

Figure 6.3 Financial services product definition.

FEATUREs are product variations that may be offered, and FUNCTIONAL SETTINGs are drivers that control how the PRODUCT FEATUREs or FINAN-CIAL PRODUCTs will operate. In order to meet customer expectations, there are usually a great deal of features and functional settings that are available within FINANCIAL PRODUCTs. These features and functional settings often serve as the basis for any negotiating points between the customer and the company.

The PRODUCT FEATURE APPLICABILITY is the set of available PRODUCT FEATUREs, or governing characteristics behind the product, that apply to the specific FINANCIAL PRODUCT. The FUNCTIONAL SETTING APPLICABILITY maintains the FUNCTIONAL SETTINGs that apply to either the FINANCIAL PRODUCT or the PRODUCT FEATURE.

PRODUCT CAT FEAT FUNC APPLICABILITY maintains what functional settings are available in which features and/or product categories. For example, the feature "per-check fee" may only apply to the CHECKING product category.

Product Categories

The PRODUCT CATEGORY shows the varying kinds of available FINANCIAL PRODUCTs. DEPOSIT PRODUCTs, a traditional banking product in which the financial services company will hold money for a customer and pay interest, have common characteristics of interest payments to the customer. LOAN PRODUCTs, another traditional banking product in which the financial services company gives money to the customer in exchange for repayment with interest, have common characteristics around the interest rate charged and the repayment schedules. INVESTMENT VEHICLEs have common characteristics where the customer is purchasing a portion of value of a company in stocks, government bonds, or another combined investments such as mutual funds. The main purpose of investment vehicles is to gain value for the money spent, based on the premise that the value for these vehicles will increase over time. For the financial services company, all PRODUCT CATEGORYs help to classify the varying FINANCIAL PRODUCTs.

The heart of the financial services product is the PRODUCT FEATURE and FUNCTIONAL SETTING. These two components make up the FINANCIAL PRODUCT. We will review these in detail.

Product Feature and Functional Setting

The PRODUCT FEATURE is best defined as the applicable characteristics that make up a FINANCIAL PRODUCT and are the fundamental aspects of the FINANCIAL PRODUCT. The FUNCTIONAL SETTING is the driver describing how the PRODUCT FEATURE or FINANCIAL PRODUCT will operate. These govern the overall workings of the product under defined circumstances.

The FUNCTIONAL SETTING affects the PRODUCT FEATURE by including key operational aspects for the PRODUCT FEATURE. It is important to understand that most PRODUCT FEATURES have many functional settings. These represent the parameters that affect how the PRODUCT FEATURE or FINANCIAL PRODUCT works.

Table 6.6 describes specific examples of the relationship between the PRODUCT FEATURE and FUNCTIONAL SETTING. A PRODUCT FEATURE may be "Monthly interest rate," which is further defined via the FUNCTIONAL SETTING of "Apply interest rate at end of month." Another PRODUCT FEATURE of "Statement" may have as a FUNCTIONAL SETTING "Prepare statement every 30 days" or "Prepare statement every 90 days." A second FUNCTIONAL SETTING for "Statement" may be "Mail to the customer." A "Non-sufficient funds fee" will occur under the circumstances of "Apply fee when account balance goes below zero." An "Annual Fee" can occur using the functional setting: "At each renewal anniversary." A "Check fee" feature may have a setting that states that it will occur for "Each check written." Another Feature is shown as "Cash-advance interest rate," which has as a functional setting "Apply rate to cash advance transactions only." "Purchase Interest Rate" has the functional setting of "Apply rate to purchase transactions only."

Financial Product and Functional Setting

Similar to the relationship between PRODUCT FEATURE and FINANCIAL PRODUCT, the FUNCTIONAL SETTING has a relationship to FINANCIAL PRODUCT. In this instance, the FUNCTIONAL SETTING applies at the

Table 6.6 Product Feature and Functional Setting Relationship

PRODUCT FEATURE DESCRIPTION	FUNCTIONAL SETTING DESCRIPTION
Monthly interest rate	Apply interest rate at end of month
Statement	Prepare statement every 30 days
Statement	Prepare statement every 90 days
Statement	Mail to customer
Non-sufficient funds fee	Apply fee when account balance goes below zero
Annual fee	Apply annual fee at each renewal anniversary
Check fee	Apply fee for each check written
Cash-advance interest rate	Apply rate to cash advance transactions only
Purchase interest rate	Apply rate to purchase transactions only

Table 6.7 Financial Product and Functional Setting Relationship

FINANCIAL PRODUCT NAME	FUNCTIONAL SETTING DESCRIPTION
Brokerage A Plus account	Apply fee when brokerage transaction completed
Home owners executive mortgage	Charge points at loan closing
Flexible deposit account	Supply checks on request
A Big Bank reduced-fee credit card	Renews annually

FINANCIAL PRODUCT level instead of at the PRODUCT FEATURE level. The PRODUCT FUNCTIONAL SETTING APPLICABILITY shows which FUNCTIONAL SETTINGs apply to which specific FINANCIAL PRODUCTs as part of the design of the product offering. Table 6.7 shows the relationship between FINANCIAL PRODUCT and FUNCTIONAL SETTING.

Similar to the PRODUCT FEATURE and FUNCTIONAL SETTING relationship, each FINANCIAL PRODUCT is affected by the FUNCTIONAL SETTING through the FUNCTIONAL SETTING APPLICABILITY associative entity. These settings pertain to the product level without regard to any specific feature. In the example given, the FUNCTIONAL SETTING of "Apply fee when brokerage transaction completed" is important to the specific product offering "Brokerage A Plus Account" FINANCIAL PRODUCT. This gives an overall understanding of how the FINANCIAL PRODUCT needs to operate. In the "Home owners executive mortgage," the functional setting may be "Charge points at loan closing." For a "Flexible deposit account" product, "Supply checks on request" is an important functional setting. "Renews annually" is an important functional setting for the "A Big Bank reduced fee credit card" product. This functionality allows the financial services company to customize its product offering by defining how each product works to meet important customer requirements.

Features and Functional Settings for Product Categories

PRODUCT CATEGORYs may also have features and functional settings that relate to the whole category of products; in other words, they relate to all products of a specific category. For instance, SAVINGS type products may have a feature of "statement" with functional settings of "Send every month" or "Send quarterly." This information requirement is handled by the PRODUCT CATEGORY FEATURE APPLICABILITY and PRODUCT CAT FEAT FUNC APPLICABILITY.

A PRODUCT CATEGORY's features may have certain functional settings. The required FUNCTIONAL SETTINGs are established for the PRODUCT CAT-

EGORY FEATURE APPLICABILITY. This information may be used to validate available product features and functional settings. For example, for a product in the category of "deposit product," a "brokerage transaction fee" may not be applicable. This flexible structure allows for the mix and match of PRODUCT FEATUREs and FUNCTIONAL SETTINGs within PRODUCT CATEGORYs and then the ability to use this information as a guide in relating features and settings to specific FINANCIAL PRODUCTs, as determined by the product manager defining each product.

Features and Functional Settings for Products

Once allowable product category features and functions have been established, a FINANCIAL PRODUCT can be set up for the offering to customers. The final, selected functional settings and features for a FINANCIAL PRODUCT are maintained through the PRODUCT FEATURE APPLICABILITY and the FUNCTIONAL SETTING APPLICABILITY. These state what features and functional settings have been applied to create a product offering.

FINANCIAL PRODUCTs, which represent the financial institution's offerings, may be set up in advance for a wide group of potential customers, or they may also be set up on the fly for the needs of a particular customer. For instance, "A Plus Checking" may be a product offering for a bank that may be set up for many individual customers, and its features and functional settings are well understood. A very specific, customized FINANCIAL PRODUCT, "Customized AAA Checking," may be set up for a very wealthy individual, with a set of features and functional settings selected for this product via the PRODUCT FEATURE APPLICABILITY and FUNCTIONAL SETTING APPLICABILITY associative entities.

Example of Predefined Financial Products with Product Features and Functional Settings

Table 6.8 illustrates examples of FINANCIAL PRODUCTs that have been set up in advance to suit broad ranges of customers. Each of the two products shown has the FUNCTIONAL SETTINGS "Renew annually" and "New card every three years." These settings are applicable at the product level and not for specific features.

The features for each product include applicable interest rates, whether checks are supplied, various fees, and credit limits. Each of these features may have one or more functional settings that outline parameters when applying these features.

The product "Low Interest Visa" has two interest rates: One is "Prime +1," which is good for a set period of time, and the other is "Prime +5," which is good for the remaining life of the product. The interest rate feature has a functional setting of "Rate to apply to purchase and cash advances." This product includes a "Credit Limit" of "$5000" with "No charges to exceed limit plus 5%," offers "Checks" to be "Supplied on Request," has an "Annual Fee" of "$20" that is "Applied at anniversary," and has an "Over-the-limit Fee" of "$29" that is "Charged when limit is exceeded." This product is for customers who like to carry a balance on their credit card, but rarely if ever go beyond their credit limit. Customers of this product also use checks for cash advances as well, but they do not pay a different rate for purchases over cash advances.

The second product in the example, "Low-fee Visa," is set for the customer who likes to pay the balance by the end of each month, may carry an occasional balance, and might go over the limit once in a while. In this product, the interest rate is standard at "Prime +9," a "Credit Limit" of "$5000," with an "Annual Fee" of "$0" and an "Over-the-limit Fee" of "$0."

Given the two products, many customers may find one or the other suitable to their needs. In this case, "John Doe" likes product "125," the "Low-interest Visa," because he tends to carry a balance and likes to have a lower rate. He doesn't mind having the occasional fee in order to save on the interest rate. He is very careful about his balance and rarely goes over the limit. On the other hand, "Jane Doe" likes product "240," the "Low-fee Visa," because she usually pays the balance on her account every month. Because she travels frequently, she may occasionally go over her limit and doesn't want the hassle of fees, especially because she pays the invoice in full at the end of the month. Her "Credit limit" also allows for a broader range over the maximum "up to 20%." Occasionally she will carry a balance, but not for too long, so she doesn't mind the higher interest rate.

Financial Products That Are Customized for the Specific Needs of a Customer

Some FINANCIAL PRODUCTs represent a highly customized set of features and functional settings for a specific customer. A question to be answered is why does a financial services company require such customization of its services? The answer lies within the relationship with the customer. Different customers require different levels of service. Let's look at two examples. "John Doe" is an average banking customer with an interest-bearing checking account, a savings account, and a credit card. He requires checks, an ATM/DEBIT card, and a separate credit card. His needs are like many other customers; he needs a checking account to pay invoices, a savings account to keep money aside, and a credit card for travel and/or emergencies.

Table 6.8 Product Features and Functional Settings

FINANCIAL PRODUCT ID	FINANCIAL PRODUCT DESCRIPTION	PRODUCT FEATURE DESCRIPTION	PRODUCT FEATURE APPLICABILITY VALUE	PRODUCT FEATURE APPLICABILITY FROM DATE	PRODUCT FEATURE APPLICABILITY END DATE	FUNCTIONAL SETTING APPLICABILITY
125	Low-interest Visa					Renews annually
						New card every three years
		Interest rate	Prime +1	Account open date	Account open date + three months	Rate to apply to purchase and cash advances
		Interest rate	Prime +5	Account open date + three months	Account close date	Rate to apply to purchase and cash advance
		Checks	Standard	Account open date	Account close date	Supply on request
		Annual fee	$20	Account open date	Account close date	Apply at anniversary
		Credit limit	$5,000	Account open date	Account close date	No charges to exceed limit + 5%
		Over-the-limit fee	$29	Account open date	Account close date	Apply when limit exceeded
240	Low-fee Visa					Renews annually
						New card every three years
		Interest rate	Prime +9	Account open date	Account close date	Rate to apply to purchase and cash advance
		Annual fee	$0	Account open date	Account close date	Apply at anniversary
		Credit limit	$5,000	Account open date	Account close date	No charges to exceed limit + 20%
		Over-the-limit fee	$0	Account open date	Account close date	Apply when limit exceeded

Table 6.9 Standard Financial Product Features and Functional Settings

CUSTOMER NAME	ACCOUNT ID	FINANCIAL PRODUCT	APPLIED PRODUCT FEATURE DESCRIPTION	APPLIED FUNCTIONAL SETTING DESCRIPTION
John Doe	12345	A+ Checking	Statement	Sent every 30 days
			Interest rate	Applied at month-end
			Per-check fee	Fee charged per check
			Minimum balance	Minimum balance required
	22345	Savings Plus Account	Interest rate	Applied at month-end
			Minimum balance	Minimum balance required
	1234-7890	Flexible Pro Credit Card	Interest rate	Charged at end of cycle
			Annual fee	Charge at renewal period
	9999-9874	ATM/debit card Plus	Access Checking/ Savings	Issue card every two years

His product suite might look like many other customers, as shown in Table 6.9. This table shows the standard features and functional settings that are available within for a specific financial product. The selected FINANCIAL PRODUCT, "A+ Checking," could be given to other customers with similar needs, as many different people would benefit from this service.

Many customers require additional customization of their product suite, as their needs are different. Perhaps they want to change some of the features or functional settings, such as what fees are charged and how much. Also, they may want to include different types of financial products and have them inter-related, for example, the ability to transfer funds between savings, checking, and investment accounts.

An alternative look at a customized product suite is shown in Table 6.10. This customization is based on the needs of a small business, "XYZ Company," and the related parties to that business, "Mr. Jones" and "Mr. Smith." As you can see, there is a greater need to customize the products for this customer, as the requirements are quite different from the previous example. While "XYZ Company" needs to have a business checking account, "Mr. Jones" needs a specialized brokerage account linked to his checking account. "Mr. Smith" requires similar accounts, but he needs to have a lease account for the company automobile. In this case, both "Mr. Jones" and "Mr. Smith" benefit from the discounts given to business customers, as they are affiliated with "XYZ Company."

Table 6.10 Customized Product Suite

CUSTOMER NAME	ACCOUNT NUMBER	FINANCIAL PRODUCT DESCRIPTION	PRODUCT FEATURE APPLICABILITY DESCRIPTION	FUNCTIONAL SETTING APPLICABILITY DESCRIPTION
XYZ Company	33345	Customized Business Checking—No Minimum Balance	Statement	Sent every 30 days
			Interest rate	Applied at month-end
			Minimum balance	Minimum balance not required
Mr. Jones	23235	Customized Checking—brokerage 1a	Interest rate	Applied at month-end
			Minimum balance	Minimum balance not required
			Sweep to brokerage	Move any excess to brokerage account
	88990	Customized Brokerage Account 1E	Linked to checking, Invest according to plan	Accept sweep, Purchase XYZ stock on periodic basis
Mr. Smith	34345	Customized Checking—35	Interest rate	Applied at month-end,
			Minimum balance	Minimum balance not required
			Sweep to brokerage	Move any excess to brokerage account
	89000	Customized Brokerage—sweep account	Linked to checking	Accept sweep
			Invest according to plan	Purchase XYZ stock on periodic basis
	99000	Lease—24 month, delayed lease fee	Interest rate	Applied monthly
			Lease fees	Applied at end of term
			Term	24-month term

As you can see from these two examples, the structure within the financial services product model can accommodate both scenarios: a pre-set financial services offering or a customized financial product that is set up for the needs of specific parties. Each required a specific set of PRODUCT FEATUREs and FUNCTIONAL SETTINGs that are applied to make up a FINANCIAL PRODUCT.

Product Category Roll-ups

The final component of the PRODUCT CATEGORY is the capability to roll up the structure for use in reporting. The PRODUCT CATEGORY ROLLUP allows for the relationship between PRODUCT CATEGORYs for this purpose.

From the financial services company's perspective, it is important to understand the effectiveness of the services being offered: How many customers use this service, how profitable are they, and when are changes required? In order to help answer these questions, product information must be aggregated for analysis and comparison. The PRODUCT CATEGORY ROLLUP shows this structure. As Figure 6.11 shows, the "Banking services" has product categories of "Deposit product" and "Loan product." Each PRODUCT CATEGORY has subordinate PRODUCT CATEGORYs, for example "Deposit product" has "Savings," "Checking," and "Time Deposit." "Investment services" have "Investment vehicle" that is further composed of "Mutual fund," "Security," and "Annuity." "Security," has three subordinate PRODUCT CATEGORYs of "Fixed Income," "Money Market," and "Equity."

Table 6.11   Product Category Roll-up

PRODUCT CATEGORY DESCRIPTION	PRODUCT CATEGORY DESCRIPTION	PRODUCT CATEGORY DESCRIPTION	PRODUCT CATEGORY DESCRIPTION
Banking services	Deposit product	Savings	
		Checking	
		Time deposit	
	Loan product	Revolving	
		Simple-interest	
		Mortgage	
Investment services	Investment vehicle	Mutual fund	
		Security	Fixed income
			Money market
			Equity
		Annuity	

Financial Product Regulations and Rules

Now that we have an understanding of a financial services product, we can focus on the regulations and rules that govern the product and its usage. It is important to understand that the financial services industry is highly regulated, both externally by governmental agencies and internally by the organizations' policies and customer agreements. These rules impact how the products function as well as what may or may not be offered. In addition, changes in regulations must be understood for all regulating bodies: federal, state, local, and internal. Other guiding rules may be within the agreement terms made between the customer and the financial institution.

Figure 6.4 shows a data model with FINANCIAL REGULATIONS and associated REGULATION REQUIREMENTs that have FINANCIAL PRODUCT RULEs that impact FINANCIAL PRODUCTs, FINANCIAL PRODUCT CATEGORYs, PRODUCT FEATUREs, and/or FUNCTIONAL SETTINGs. AGREEMENT TERMs that were negotiated with customers may also impose FINANCIAL PRODUCT RULEs that affect the same entities.

As shown in the model, two subtypes of FINANCIAL REGULATIONs exist, GOVERNMENT REGULATION and ORGANIZATION REGULATION. Government regulations are external regulations imposed from varying governmental bodies. These could be at any governmental level, such as the federal, state, and local bodies. Organization regulations are imposed by the financial services company and include policies and procedures defined by that organization and enforced by their own management.

FINANCIAL REGULATIONs may be transcribed and recorded in the **text** attribute and are composed of REGULATION REQUIREMENTs, the understanding of what the enterprise needs to follow. These REGULATION REQUIREMENTs may impact any number of FINANCIAL PRODUCTs, PRODUCT CATEGORYs, PRODUCT FEATUREs, or FUNCTIONAL SETTINGs, hence the FINANCIAL PRODUCT RULE entity that specifies what entities are impacted.

Table 6.12 shows some examples of these FINANCIAL REQUIREMENTs, AGREEMENT TERMs, FINANCIAL PRODUCT RULEs, and their potential impacts. In the example, "Statements cannot be e-mailed to customers" is a government requirement that imposes a rule regarding the "Statement" PRODUCT FEATURE. The FINANCIAL REGULATION "Statements for all savings or investment-oriented products must be sent at least once per year" affects both PRODUCT FEATURE of "Statements" and FUNCTIONAL SETTING of "Statement is to be sent every year." What this implies is that there cannot be a FUNCTIONAL SETTING of "Send no statement," as that would not comply with the regulations. "All fees must be disclosed on account prior to set-up" is a regulation that applies to all "Checking" and "Credit Card" PRODUCT CATEGORYs, regardless of the PRODUCT FEATUREs or FUNCTIONAL SETTINGs.

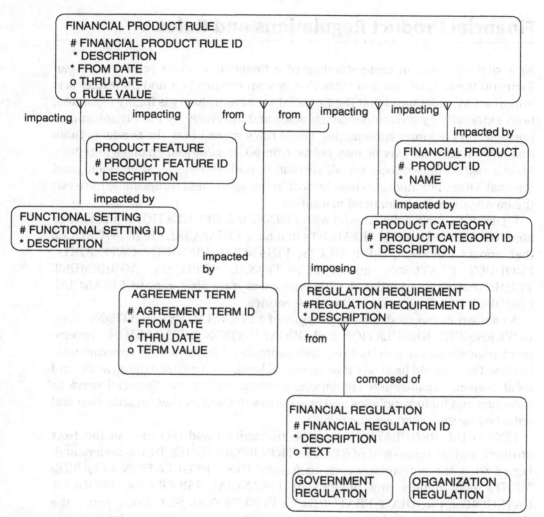

Figure 6.4 Financial product regulations and rules.

The final example, "Waive All ATM Fees," is an agreement term with a specific customer that imposes a rule that applies to a PRODUCT CATEGORY, PRODUCT FEATURE, and a FUNCTIONAL SETTING. This would affect the "ATM Fee" PRODUCT FEATURE and the FUNCTIONAL SETTING of "Fee charged for each ATM transaction." It is important to understand that many "standard" PRODUCT FEATUREs and FUNCTIONAL SETTINGs are affected by rules from the specific agreements.

Notice that these regulations, agreement terms, and rules affect what features and functional settings may be available within different product categories.

Table 6.12 Financial product rules.

REGULATION REQUIREMENT DESCRIPTION	AGREEMENT TERM	FINANCIAL PRODUCT RULE	PRODUCT CATEGORY DESCRIPTION	PRODUCT FEATURE DESCRIPTION	FUNCTIONAL SETTING DESCRIPTION
Statements cannot be e-mailed to customers		Enforce that statements are not e-mailed		Statement	
Statements for all savings or investment-oriented products must be sent at least once per year		Ensure that deposit product statements are sent at least once a year	Deposit product	Statement	Statement is to be sent every year
		Ensure that investment vehicle statements are sent at least once a year	Investment Vehicle		
		Give disclosure statement on fees to customer when setting up checking account	Checking		
All fees for checking and credit card accounts must be disclosed on account prior to set-up		Give disclosure statement on fees to customer when setting up checking account	Credit card		
	Waive all ATM fees		Checking	ATM fee	Fee charged for each ATM transaction

These restrictions, in turn, will dictate what FUNCTIONAL SETTING APPLIC-
ABILITY or PRODUCT FEATURE APPLICABILITY may be applied to FINAN-
CIAL PRODUCTs.

Agreements

The agreement process within financial services companies can be as simple as
a person clicking an "I agree" button on a Web page to accept a standardized
credit card application or as complex as a group of business customers and their
lawyers reviewing each item in as complex financial agreement between a large
corporate and a financial services company. This process of applying for a service involves an agreement. Once accepted by both parties, additional processing will occur in order for the resulting product to be established. Once created,
the customer is then given access to the provided service through a variety of
mechanisms.

Financial Agreements

The AGREEMENT data models in Volume 1 (V1:4.12–4.16) can be used for
financial service organizations. This section will point out a few customizations
to these models for financial service enterprises.

Figure 6.5 shows a subtype of AGREEMENT named FINANCIAL AGREE-
MENT. Typically, the agreement process begins with the application for an
ACCOUNT. This important step outlines the AGREEMENT ITEM and the terms
for an agreement (AGREEMENT TERMs), along with the AGREEMENT STA-
TUS of "applied for." Alternatively, the APPLICATION may be considered a separate entity if there is a substantial amount of additional information that the
enterprise desires to keep about the application (this would be similar to the
application model in Chapter 5, Figure 5.8). Figure 6.5 expands the Volume 1
generic agreement data models by adding the ASSET entity, AGREEMENT
ASSET USAGE entity, the FINANCIAL AGREEMENT subtype, and the relationship to ACCOUNT that potentially results from the AGREEMENT.

Agreement Subtypes and Roles

A key subtype of AGREEMENT in financial service is the FINANCIAL AGREE-
MENT, which is subtyped into LOAN AGREEMENT, INVESTMENT
AGREEMENT, or LEASING AGREEMENT. These are not the only types
of AGREEMENTs made, but they are the most common. These are usually
formed when the PARTY begins the process with an application or a more formal AGREEMENT. This becomes the formal understanding of what the customer is requesting from the company and links all appropriate PARTYs to it in

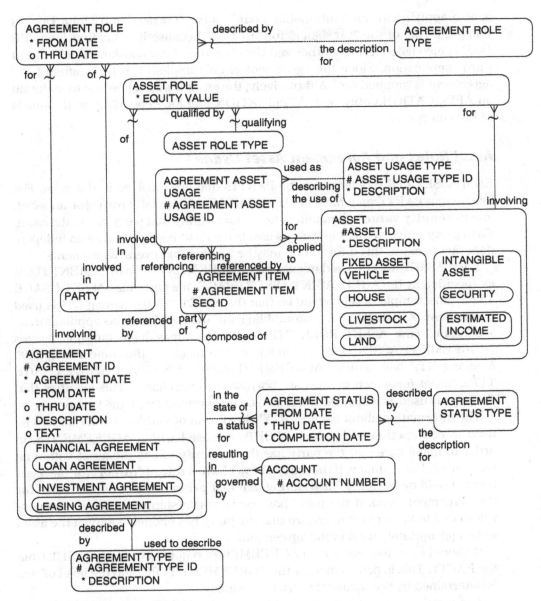

Figure 6.5 Financial agreement.

the AGREEMENT ROLE with a specific AGREEMENT ROLE TYPE played by each party.

An example demonstrates the various roles each party may play in the FINANCIAL AGREEMENT: "John and Jane Doe" are applying for "Checking" and "Credit Card" products in the roles of "Owner" and "Co-Owner." "JR Doe" is also applying for an "Automobile Loan" as the "Owner," and "John Doe" is filling the role of the "Co-signer" for "JR Doe" because it is his first loan. "JR Doe" is also listed as an "Authorized User" on the "John and Jane Doe" "Credit Card" application. Since the agreement is only applied for, the status of the agreement is "applied for." Alternatively, the enterprise may decide to maintain an APPLICATION entity with APPLICATION ROLEs, depending on the needs of the enterprise.

Asset Roles and Agreement Asset Usage

Each ASSET ROLE determines the PARTYs that are involved in the asset. For instance, a PARTY may have an ASSET ROLE of "partially own" for an asset, and the **equity value** will maintain how much equity that party has in the asset. Each party's involvement in various assets needs to be captured as an independent fact because this information may be needed for several agreements.

Each ASSET may be used in either an AGREEMENT or AGREEMENT ITEM as specified by the AGREEMENT ASSET USAGE of a particular ASSET USAGE TYPE. An example of this would be that the ASSET "2000 Mustang GT" is used in the LOAN AGREEMENT "Automobile loan" that "JR Doe" has applied for, as "collateral" (the ASSET ROLE TYPE). An asset may have multiple usages (AGREEMENT ASSET USAGEs) in a loan. For instance, the same asset, "2000 Mustang GT," has another AGREEMENT ASSET USAGE of ASSET USAGE TYPE "asset for which monies are borrowed to purchase." This signifies that the asset is used as collateral and is also being purchased with the loan proceeds.

The information about each PARTY's involvement with an ASSET should be used in conjunction with which ASSETs are used within AGREEMENTS, in order to make sure that the party has the authority to use the asset within an agreement. For instance, if the party doesn't have a role of "owner" for the asset there should be business rules stating that that person cannot use the asset for the agreement. Also, if the party has partial ownership of an asset, business rules need to be in place to ensure that the party has enough equity in the asset to be appropriately used in the agreement.

It should be noted that not all AGREEMENTs require a pledged ASSET from the PARTY. This is determined by the AGREEMENT TYPE, and the level of risk is determined by the financial services company.

The relationship between the PARTY and the ASSET is that a PARTY may have an ASSET ROLE of "owner" for many different ASSETs, which are items of value that can be used in securing an AGREEMENT. These ASSETs may be FIXED ASSETs, such as a car, house, or land, or INTANGIBLE ASSETs, such as a SECURITY or ESTIMATED INCOME.

The most common example of assets used as security is in a LOAN AGREE-MENT, for which a party may pledge an item of value, such as a car or house, as security or collateral on the loan. This is to ensure that the terms of the loan will be met. Should the PARTY fail to live up to the terms of the AGREEMENT, the company would have the right to recover its loss by acquiring the ASSET. It should be noted that only the available equity in the ASSET may be pledged for any ASSET the PARTY owns. No PARTY may pledge an ASSET that he or she does not own, nor may a PARTY pledge an ASSET for more than its available equity. An example of this would be for the "Credit Card" product for "John and Jane Doe," their home equity may be used to secure the card, thus giving them a high credit limit. They can use only the current equity in their home to secure the card.

Agreement Status

Finally, the AGREEMENT is tracked through the AGREEMENT STATUS. Often in processing a FINANCIAL AGREEMENT, a series of steps leads up to its approval. It is still a valid AGREEMENT while in process until it is either accepted or rejected. Should the FINANCIAL AGREEMENT be accepted, it will result in the establishment of an ACCOUNT. Should it be rejected, the agreement process would end, and no resulting account would be opened. Occasionally, an account is opened when the application is received. In this instance, on rejection, the account would be terminated and the service with the customer cancelled.

In our example, "John and Jane Doe" have made an agreement for a "Credit Card" product. During the validation process by the financial services company, it is discovered that they do not meet the criteria for the agreement due to an unacceptable credit rating. The financial services company may offer them another product, thus altering the agreement, or cancel it completely. Should the agreement be canceled, no financial account will be opened.

Delivery

We have covered the changes to the data models for the party, product, and order (agreement) subject data areas. In financial services, there is no specific product shipment as in manufacturing or other industries. There is, however, a product delivery to the customer. Once a service is formalized, the financial services company invokes a delivery mechanism to give the customer access to all required services. Defined by the PRODUCT FEATUREs and FUNCTIONAL SETTINGs of the FINANCIAL PRODUCT, these delivery mechanisms may vary, but they are in force for the life of the service.

Financial Account

In many financial services products, a primary delivery mechanism is the ACCOUNT. It is important to note that not all financial services products have

ACCOUNTs. Some services such as paying invoices for customers or balancing their checking accounts do not have any special accounts, but they may tie to an existing ACCOUNT.

The ACCOUNT should not be confused with the FINANCIAL PRODUCT or AGREEMENT, as previously discussed. As seen earlier, the FINANCIAL PRODUCT reflects how the services requested by the customer will function and work. The AGREEMENT reflects what are the specific services that the financial services company has agreed to deliver to customers under what specific terms. The ACCOUNT monitors all activity or transactions that the customer or the financial services company has performed in relation to the use of the FINANCIAL PRODUCT.

Figure 6.6 provides information about accounts used in the financial service industry. The critical component in this model is the ACCOUNT, a structure established to record all activity for use of a service. The types of ACCOUNTs are determined by its supporting FINANCIAL PRODUCT. For example, a CHECKING ACCOUNT is supported by product within a CHECKING product category. The ACCOUNT is usually based on one main FINANCIAL PRODUCT, such as a particular bank checking product, although it may include one or more FINANCIAL PRODUCTs. This usually occurs over time—an account with "Customized Business Checking" may be updated with "Customized Business Checking—No minimum balance" after a certain point in time. Therefore, one or more FINANCIAL PRODUCTs may be included in the customer's ACCOUNT, which may be for several FINANCIAL PRODUCTs and thus the associative entity, ACCOUNT PRODUCT.

ACCOUNTs have many ACCOUNT TRANSACTIONs. Each ACCOUNT has at least one or more PARTYs involved in different roles or the ACCOUNT ROLE. The ACCOUNT may involve different MEDIA TYPEs, such as plastic cards, paper checks, or computer software. The ACCOUNT and its PARTY ACCOUNT MEDIA may have several statuses, hence the need for the ACCOUNT STATUS and PARTY ACCOUNT MEDIA STATUS. The ACCOUNT may have links to other ACCOUNTs in an ACCOUNT RELATIONSHIP.

Account Product

The type of ACCOUNT is based on the FINANCIAL PRODUCT(s) associated with the ACCOUNT. As from the FINANCIAL PRODUCT discussion, it may change over the life of the ACCOUNT by updating the PRODUCT FEATUREs and/or FUNCTIONAL SETTINGs. Therefore, the ACCOUNT PRODUCT, or the link between the ACCOUNT and the FINANCIAL PRODUCT, has a **from date** and **thru date** to show this migration. For example, "John and Jane Doe" decide to change their "Checking Product." They change from a "standard

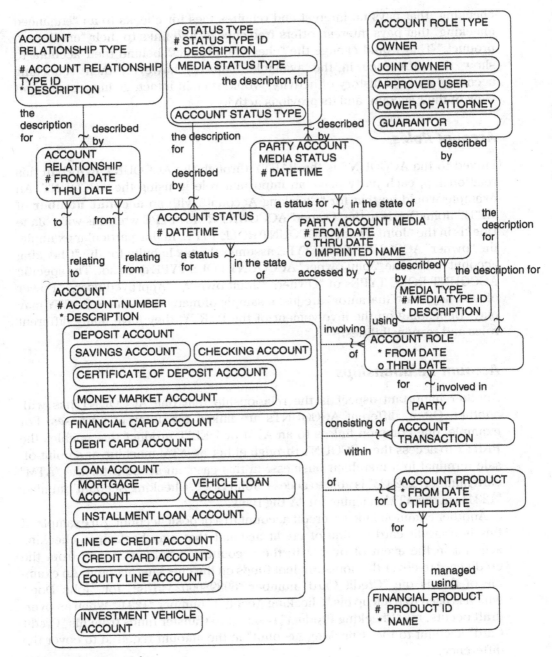

Figure 6.6 Financial account.

checking" that pays no interest and requires fees for checks to an "enhanced checking" that pays interest, offers free checks, and links to their "credit card product." This would change the "checking product" behind their account to show the difference in the available features; however, their "checking account," with its history of activity, would remain intact, giving a consistent view of their account and its previous activity.

Account Roles

Linked to the ACCOUNT is the PARTY through the ACCOUNT ROLE. In this relationship, each party plays an important role in using the ACCOUNT. An example would be that for "Checking Account" with an **account number** of "1234," John Doe is in the "Owner" ACCOUNT ROLE TYPE while his wife, "Jane Doe" is in the "Joint owner" ACCOUNT ROLE TYPE. In this particular example, the "owner" ACCOUNT ROLE TYPE assumes the tax liability for the "Checking account" while the "Joint owner" ACCOUNT ROLE TYPE does not. The specific ACCOUNT ROLE TYPEs of "Owner," "Joint owner," "Approved user," "Power of attorney," or "Guarantor" are just a sample of many roles that a PARTY may play. Depending on the involvement of the PARTY, they have many different roles and responsibilities.

Account Relationships

Another important aspect is the relationship that one ACCOUNT has with another. Often, different ACCOUNTs are linked for different purposes. For example, one common link is to an ATM or DEBIT product that enables the PARTY to access the ACCOUNT through either an ATM machine or a point-of-sale terminal in a merchant business. In this case, an account for the "ATM" card number "232323" is able to access "John Doe" "Checking Account" number "1234" via the ATM machine for "A Big Bank."

Another common link is a credit account to a deposit account. An example of this is a credit card or line of credit account that may back up a checking account in the event of overdraft; the account will borrow money from the credit card to cover the non-sufficient funds on the checking account. An example of this is the "Credit Card" number "898980002345789" for "John Doe," which is used to back up his "Checking Account" number "1234." When an overdraft occurs, his "Checking Product" is set up to transfer funds from his "Credit Card" account to the "Checking Account" in the amount required to cover the difference.

Another important relationship is the linking of an expired account to a current account. This may occur when an account has been closed for some reason, such as lost media or mergers. This enables the tracking of history from one account to another. In this example, "John Doe" had his credit card stolen, then his card is replaced with a new account, "8989789067890." His old account is then closed, but it is linked to the new account in order to maintain a consistent credit profile for him.

Media

Often, access to the account's services is provided on to an ACCOUNT ROLE through PARTY ACCOUNT MEDIA that is of a particular MEDIA TYPE. This currently tends to be a plastic card, such as an ATM or DEBIT card, or paper checks. As the industry grows, this may change over time to other formats, such as software for Internet access. Each party on the account maintains his or her own unique media access to the ACCOUNT through his or her ACCOUNT ROLE. This PARTY ACCOUNT MEDIA allows for each person to gain access to the benefits and service of the account.

For example, "John Doe" has a card with a number "12369" to his "checking account" number "1234," and "Jane Doe" has a card with a number "23969" to the same "checking account." Another example is Visa card number "92369175" for "John Doe," which is embossed with his name on the card while "Jane Doe," with the same number "92369175" for the same Visa "credit card account," has a different card with her name embossed on the card. Should they decide to add their son, "JR Doe," to the "credit card account," a new card would be issued with his name embossed on it.

It is important to track the status for each of the PARTY ACCOUNT MEDIA in the event it should need to be replaced. In this example, should "Jane Doe" lose her card, she would need a new one issued and, depending on why it was lost, may require that a new account be established and all PARTY ACCOUNT MEDIA updated with the appropriate PARTY ACCOUNT MEDIA STATUS. Jane Doe's old card would have a status of "inactive" and her new card would have a status of "active."

Account Status

An ACCOUNT goes through a variety of stages over the course of time. To track this, the ACCOUNT STATUS is generated with a general classification of STATUS TYPE. The subtype ACCOUNT STATUS applies to the ACCOUNT. For example, when "John Doe" first opened his "Checking Account" number "1234," the status for his account was "New" in the first month after opening it. Once the first statement cycle had been completed, the status was updated to "Active" for his account. Should his account need to be evaluated for a particular reason, such as tax considerations, the status would change to "Review," indicating a special activity was underway. If "John Doe" decides to end the agreement and close the account, the status would then change to "Closed," and the account would no longer be available for use.

Account Transaction

Closely related to an ACCOUNT is the ACCOUNT TRANSACTION, which is modeled in Figure 6.7. This entity maintains the transaction activity that the financial institution records when the customer uses the FINANCIAL PRODUCT of the account. The activity may be monetary in nature, such as a DEPOSIT to or WITHDRAWAL from the ACCOUNT, or it may be non-monetary in nature, such as an inquiry or change request. The financial services company providing the product may also generate transaction activity as it processes the ACCOUNT and charges ACCOUNT FEEs or INTEREST or pays INTEREST to the customer.

The ACCOUNT TRANSACTION is generated from the use of the ACCOUNT. These transactions are generally monetary changes to the ACCOUNT. For example, "John Doe" may generate an **account transaction ID** of "13691" when he performs an ACCOUNT TRANSACTION TYPE of DEPOSIT in the **amount** of "$1,000" on "1/2/2000." He may then perform an ACCOUNT TRANSACTION TYPE of WITHDRAWAL in the **amount** of "$100" on "1/4/2000," generating **account transaction ID** of "16912." He may then use his PARTY ACCOUNT MEDIA (see Figure 6.6) of his debit card to generate a "withdrawal" ACCOUNT TRANSACTION TYPE in the **amount** of "$50" on "1/5/2000." Then on "1/9/2000" he may use his debit card in the ATM machine to withdraw "$25" and generate **account transaction ID** of "18211."

ACCOUNT TRANSACTIONs may have ACCOUNT TRANSACTION STATUSes that maintain the status of the transaction such as "posted" or "on hold." ACCOUNT TRANSACTIONs may be related to other ACCOUNT TRANSACTIONs, and the ACCOUNT TRANSACTION RELATIONSHIP provides this capability.

Account Transaction Type

ACCOUNT TRANSACTIONs are subtyped into FINANCIAL TRANSACTIONs and ACCOUNT REQUEST TRANSACTIONs with numerous subtypes within them. For example, "John Doe" has an interest-bearing checking account and is paid the interest due to him during his monthly statement cycle that generates an ACCOUNT TRANSACTION subtype of INTEREST to his **account number** "1234." Specific to securities are SECURITY TRANSACTIONs including BUY TRANSACTION and SELL TRANSACTION. MUTUAL FUND TRANSACTIONs include PURCHASE TRANSACTION, REDEMPTION TRANSACTION, and EXCHANGE TRANSACTION. ACCOUNT TRANSACTIONs may also be non-monetary ACCOUNT REQUEST TRANSACTIONs, such as SPECIAL REQUEST, CHANGE REQUEST, or INQUIRY REQUEST. For example, "Jane Doe" may call the financial services company representatives and ask for information

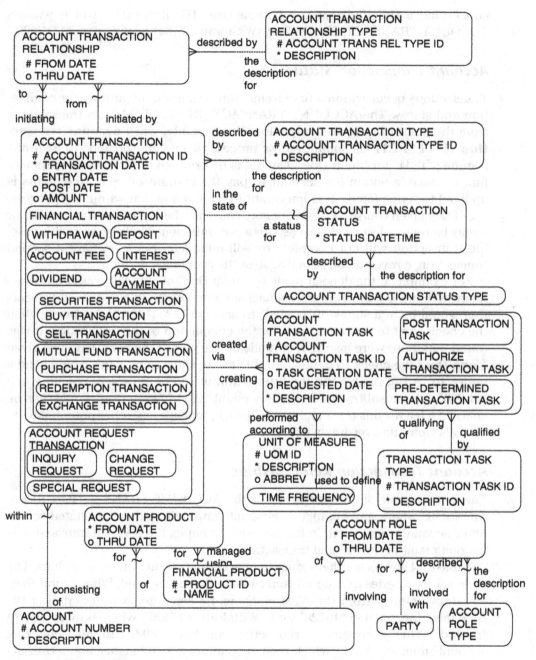

Figure 6.7 Financial account transaction.

concerning a specific **account transaction ID** of "18211," which was an ACCOUNT TRANSACTION TYPE of "Withdrawal" that occurred on "1/9/2000."

Account Transaction Status

Transactions occur within a time frame, thus requiring monitoring for completion and status. The ACCOUNT TRANSACTION STATUS tracks transactions from the point of entry to completion. For example, when **account transaction ID** of "18211" is submitted for process, it may be "posted" to **account number** "1234" for "John Doe." Once it is determined that there are sufficient funds available within his account to pay the amount of "$25," the status is updated to "completed." It is important to understand that within the processing of any given transaction, errors may cause the failure of the transaction, or it may be rejected, such as the case for a non-sufficient funds error. In this case, the transaction will not complete or will complete, but then have a second transaction, a reversal, be issued against the account.

For example, if the deposit made by "John Doe" of "$1,000" was from someone who banked with another financial services company, the deposit transaction would be in a status of "posted" to account "1234" for "John Doe." When the check went to the other bank for the completion of the transaction, it was found that there were insufficient funds on the part of the party who had given "John Doe" the check to deposit. In this event, the issuing bank would send a notice to "A Big Bank," and the transaction would be reversed, resulting in a "$1,000" amount subtracted from his account "1234." "John Doe" would then be charged a fee for this error and would have to manage any other potential withdrawals from the overdrawn account.

Account Transaction Relationships

The last example shows the need for the ACCOUNT TRANSACTION RELATIONSHIP where any number of account transactions may be related to any other account transaction. In the previous example, the reversal transaction is a direct result of the original transaction.

Table 6.14 shows another example of account transaction relationships. The table shows a series of account transactions that are related. When "John Doe" withdraws money from the ATM machine, he generates a transaction at the ATM machine, number "18729" for a "Withdraw" of "$20," which is in a status of "posted." This generates a transaction number "78921" to his "checking account" number "1234," which then encounters a zero balance and a transaction status of "hold" because "Jane Doe" has been paying invoices. A third transaction, number "78902," one to his "credit card," will be generated in order to cover the "$20" overdraft. A fourth transaction, number "78213," a "deposit," to his "checking account" from the "credit card" for "$20," completes

Table 6.14 Transaction Relationships

ACCOUNT TRANSACTION ID	ACCOUNT TRANSACTION TYPE DESCRIPTION	ACCOUNT DESCRIPTION	ENTRY DATE	TRANSACTION AMOUNT	TRANSACTION STATUS DESCRIPTION	RELATED ACCOUNT TRANSACTION ID
18729	ATM withdraw		1/2/2000	$20	Posted	
78921	Withdraw	Checking	1/2/2000	$20	Hold	18729 (generated from this transaction)
78902	Advance	Credit card	1/2/2000	$20	Posted	78921 (generated from this transaction)
78213	Deposit	Checking	1/2/2000	$20	Posted	78902 (generated from this transaction)
78921	Withdraw	Checking	1/3/2000	$20	Posted (change in status as a result of the deposit to checking)	

Table 6.15 Transaction Relationships across Providers

PROVIDER NAME	TRANSACTION NUMBER	TRANSACTION TYPE	TRANSACTION DATE	TRANSACTION AMOUNT	ACCOUNT NUMBER	ACCOUNT DESCRIPTION
A Big Bank	1245	Sweep	1/5/2000	$2,500	21345	Checking
B Broker-age Firm	4431	Deposit	1/5/2000	$2,500	11762	Brokerage

with a status of "posted." The transaction, number "78921," can then gain a "posted" status and is completed on 1/3/2000.

Many different accounts may be involved in account transaction relationships. In a different example shown in Table 6.15, "Jane Smith" has her checking account number "21345" with "A Big Bank," but she maintains a separate brokerage account "11762" with "B Brokerage Firm." She has maintained a minimum balance within her checking account and has periodic "sweep" transactions or transfers to her brokerage accounts, according to a pre-authorized transaction. An account transaction relationship exists between the sweep transaction and the deposit transaction. The sweep transaction withdraws the money from her checking account at "A Big Bank" and the related deposit transaction puts the money into her account number "11762" with "B Brokerage Firm."

Account Transaction Tasks

The previous example illustrates the need for ACCOUNT TRANSACTION TASKs. These functions are used in an automated fashion in order to keep all the functions that the customer requires running smoothly. The common TRANSACTION TASK TYPEs are POST TRANSACTION TASK, which causes the monetary transaction to be credited/debited to a specific account, AUTHORIZE TRANSACTION TASK, which allows for a transaction to occur according to the customer's wishes, and PRE-DETERMINED TRANSACTION TASK, which is a transaction that is set up in advance and specifies a particular point in time when the transaction should occur.

ACCOUNT TRANSACTION TASKs may have a TIME FREQUENCY that specifies an ongoing time frame for which transaction tasks could occur. For example, a customer may request a monthly transfer from one account to another. This is an example of a PRE-DETERMINED TRANSACTION TASK with a TIME FREQUENCY of "monthly."

In continuing the previous example, when Jane's money gets to her account "11762" at "B Brokerage Firm," a series of PRE-DETERMINED TRANSACTION TASKs will occur based on Jane's prior instructions. As shown in Table 6.16, each of these transactions was set up on 1/4/2000 (**task creation date**) and was requested to occur on 1/6/2000 (**requested date**). On the requested date,

Table 6.16 Transaction Task

TRANSACTION TASK ID	TRANSACTION TASK SUBTYPE	ACCOUNT ID	ACCOUNT TRANSACTION TYPE	TRANSACTION AMOUNT	ACCOUNT TRANSACTION TASK CREATION DATE	ACCOUNT TRANSACTION REQUESTED DATE
21639	Pre-determined transaction task	6139	Securities transaction—buy transaction	$500	1/4/2000	1/6/2000
11391	Pre-determined transaction task	3369	Mutual fund transaction—purchase transaction (of stock)	$1,000	1/4/2000	1/6/2000
27993	Pre-determined transaction task	7211	Securities transaction—buy transaction (of bonds)	$500	1/4/2000	1/6/2000
62135	Pre-determined transaction task	92311	Deposit	$500	1/4/2000	1/6/2000

there are four transactions that will occur. First a stock transaction of "buy transaction" will be executed with the amount of "$500." A second transaction of "mutual fund purchase" will be executed with the amount of "$1,000." A third transaction of "bond purchase" will be executed with the amount of "$500." After purchasing her investments, the remainder of her money, "$500," is then a "deposit" to a trust fund managed by the brokerage firm for her children's education. Jane may contact "B Brokerage Firm" and update the set of predetermined transactions as needed. When the time comes to actually run each transaction, the specific ID and date are captured as well as the status of completion. As each transaction successfully completes, Jane's money is systematically invested.

Work Efforts

The financial account and account transactions sections illustrated how the product is delivered to the customer. In order to properly provide customer service on accounts, the financial enterprise may need to complete many ongoing WORK EFFORTs. This section extends the generic work effort models (Volume 1, Chapter 6) to financial services enterprise and includes models for ongoing customer notification and risk analysis.

The first part of this section will cover efforts that include keeping the customer appraised on the status and state of his or her ACCOUNTs, assisting the customer in resolving questions or problems with the use of his or her ACCOUNT, and making the customer aware of potential improvements to the level of service. These efforts have been classified as ACCOUNT NOTIFICATIONs, the activity of informing the customer of the state of the account and the potential of improvement.

After account notification is covered, the next section will provide models to capture the work involved in analyzing risk, for example to help evaluate potential loans.

Account Notification

Within the financial services industry is the account notification process. Built off the WORK EFFORT supertype, this model shows the varying tasks associated with notifications to the customer of the account's status and needs. Within the financial service industry, invoices and statements are periodically prepared and sent to the customer in order to comply with regulatory requirements. In addition to these common tasks, it is also important to contact the customer about potential problems, such as a delinquent loan account, errors found in processing the account transactions, or misuse of the account by another party. In addition to these functions, the marketing efforts of the financial services company would periodically offer additional or improved services to the customers to continually improve the customer relationship. All of these functions are covered within the account notification model.

Notification Task Types

As shown in Figure 6.8, there are several important tasks. The first is the INVOICING TASK, an event that identifies the amount required from the customer to satisfy the agreement. Second, there is the STATEMENT TASK, an event that notifies the customer of the state and activity of his or her account. There is also the MARKETING TASK, an event that notifies the customer of a potential opportunity to improve his or her service. There is the ALERT TASK, an event that notifies the customer of a potential problem or issue with his or her account and its function. Finally, there is the OTHER NOTIFICATION TASK, an event that requires the financial services company to contact the customer for another purpose. All of these are examples of WORK EFFORTs associated with financial services. These normally have a direct relationship to the ACCOUNT and may result in a tangible output, such as an INVOICE or a STATEMENT.

Invoicing and Statement Tasks

As stated, the INVOICING TASK is associated with the standard process of notifying the customer that a payment is due. Based on the PRODUCT FEATUREs and FUNCTIONAL SETTINGs within the FINANCIAL PRODUCT, the INVOICING TASK will be performed according to those guidelines. This is not unlike any other industry, except that often in financial services companies, an accompanying STATEMENT of the account status is usually sent with the INVOICE. While these two items may be sent and processed together, it is clear that they are separate and can be done separately. Some financial institutions will not issue STATEMENTs with the INVOICE, but will process only the INVOICE. The financial institution needs to review each account to see if a payment has been made, compute the balance owed, and post any new obligation to the account.

For example, "Joe Jones" has a "car loan" represented by account number "81912" and owes "$250" each month to the provider of the service, "A Big Bank." Because "A Big Bank" does not send a monthly "statement" about his account, there is a coupon book for "Joe Jones" to use. Once "A Big Bank" receives and "posts" his payment on the first of the month, "A Big Bank" runs the invoicing task on the seventh of the month and sends an invoice to Joe Jones. Joe's payment, which was posted to his account on the first of the month, shows up as paid, and the bank deducts his payment and calculates the new account balance.

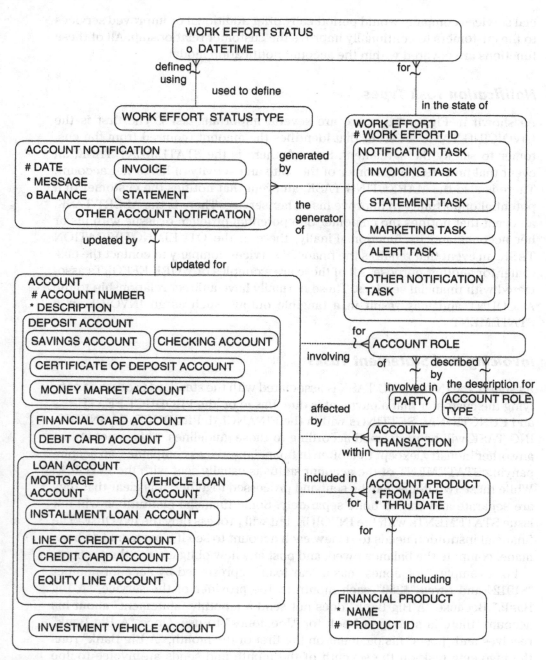

Figure 6.8   Account notification.

The INVOICE entity was modeled in Chapter 7, "Invoicing," in Volume 1 (V1:7.1a). The associated entities related to INVOICE, such as PAYMENT APPLICATION to a PAYMENT, would now relate to INVOICEs and STATEMENTs. Notice that this model in Figure 6.8 enhances the generic data model by including an INVOICE as a subtype of ACCOUNT NOTIFICATION.

STATEMENT TASK is done periodically according to the agreement made with the customer, based on the PRODUCT FEATUREs and FUNCTIONAL SETTINGs contained within the FINANCIAL PRODUCT. The STATEMENT FEATURE (a subtype of PRODUCT FEATURE) and its associated FUNCTIONAL SETTINGs determine the if, when, and how statements are issued. Typically, a statement is issued monthly, but it may be sent quarterly or even annually. Statements usually give a picture of the account's status, showing all transactions that occurred within a period of time, calculated balances, account fees, interest either paid or charged, and any other applicable account transactions.

A common example is a statement prepared for a checking account. It lists all transactions, including the types of transactions: checks paid, fees charged, interest earned, and deposits recorded, and gives balances and totals for the customer to reconcile with his or her records. For example, "John Doe" would receive his monthly statement for his checking account number 1234 showing all the transactions by date. Included would be the account transaction IDs, each transaction amount, and the final computed account balance. The statement may produce a summary of other information as well. Depending on the relationship the customer has with the bank, a statement may include the information associated with multiple accounts.

Marketing Tasks

MARKETING TASK is completed when the sales and/or service departments wish to offer the customer additional services. A common task is a solicitation for a new product the customer does not currently have, such as a credit card or loan product.

For example, "Joe Jones" may have only a "car loan" with "A Big Bank." During the monthly invoicing cycle, it is determined that he does not have a "checking account" with "A Big Bank" but with a competitor. He is sent a letter describing a new product where his "car loan" can be linked with a "checking account" that has a reduced fee structure. When "Joe Jones" receives the information, he is given the opportunity to sign up for the new product by contacting "A Big Bank." In another example, "John and Jane Doe" have their "checking account" with "A Big Bank" as the "preferred checking." Because "JR Doe" is now in college, their extra college expense needs are higher. During their regular statement cycle, it is determined that they could benefit from a low-interest loan that uses their investment equity as collateral. Because they do not wish to liquidate their portfolio, "A Big Bank" offers them a margin loan on their investments to assist with their college needs.

Often, various types of tasks are performed separately, for example, marketing tasks may occur independently of statements tasks. The industry is turning more and more to enhancing its current customer base in order to strengthen its relationship with the customer by offering additional products based on the current relationship. Because of this factor, MARKETING TASKs are often combined with other tasks and generated based upon events that happen within their customers' lives.

Alert Tasks

An ALERT TASK involves telling the customer about a potential problem with his or her account. For example, "A Big Bank" may notify "Jane Doe" that her "Checking account" had a transaction that was "posted" incorrectly and resulted in an error, where the transaction had "posted" more than one time. The bank found the error, corrected it, and now is sending "Jane Doe" information about the potential problem. These proactive tasks let the customer know that the financial services company is monitoring his or her account for problems and correcting any errors. Another, more serious task is in the case of suspected fraud. Should the bank detect that someone was trying to use a customer's account in a fraudulent manner, the bank may call the customer directly or notify the customer by mail. For example, should the "credit card" number for "John and Jane Doe" get stolen, "A Big Bank" may suspect fraud based on when and where transaction activity occurs. Should they identify suspicious behavior on the "credit card account," the fraud department would be notified and the service department would contact "John Doe" to confirm any activity. Based on his response, they may continue the investigation. Other potential activities would be to close the account and open a new account for the customer.

Other Notification Tasks

There are OTHER NOTIFICATION TASKs that a financial services company may perform for the customer, such as a past-due notification, a skip-payment option, a change in service on the account, or any variety of tasks. In this case, each company will need to articulate the required subtypes that fit their needs.

An example of another notification task is if "Joe Jones" did not make his car loan payment within the specified time, the responsible department would contact him about his payment and get the information on when he would send it. Another example is if "A Big Bank" is changing its non-sufficient funds fee, it might include a notification within the statement to customers that own any affected products. Another example would be that because "John Doe" is a responsible customer and pays his credit card invoice every month on time, "A Big Bank" may decide to notify him that his payments will be waived for the months of December and January.

Example of Account Notification Tasks

Table 6.17 summarizes some of the previous transactions.

Analysis Task

A final, specialized task for financial services is the ANALYSIS TASK, as shown in Figure 6.9. This very specific function is found within both insurance and financial services. Figure 6.9 is a different version of the insurance underwriting model (V2:5.6). In either financial services or insurance, the enterprise needs to evaluate potential customers for risk.

Within financial services, it is important to be able to analyze and understand the customer's behavior and his or her ability to execute the activities around his or her account in accordance with the agreements made. If the customer fails to live up to the agreement, say in a lending situation, it could be financially difficult for the financial services company to provide adequate service to other customers. If the customer exceeds the expectation of the financial institution, it may be that the financial institution would wish to encourage the customer to

Table 6.17 Account Notification Tasks

TASK ID	TASK TYPE	DATE ISSUED	ACCOUNT ID	CUSTOMER NAME	MESSAGE DESCRIPTION	BALANCE/ AMOUNT
1234	Invoice	1/15/2000	81912	Joe Jones	Car loan invoice	$250
0123	Statement	1/10/2000	1234	John Doe	Checking statement	$900
89021	Marketing	1/15/2000	81912	Joe Jones	Special checking offer	
87621	Marketing	1/10/2000	1234	Jane Doe	Special college loan	
81290	Alert	1/23/2000	1234	Jane Doe	Transaction posted twice	$50
23461	Alert	1/24/2000	8192	John Doe	Suspected fraud	$200
18921	Other	1/15/2000	81912	Joe Jones	Car loan payment past due	$250
02154	Other	11/1/1999	8192	John Doe	Skip payment for December/ January	$200

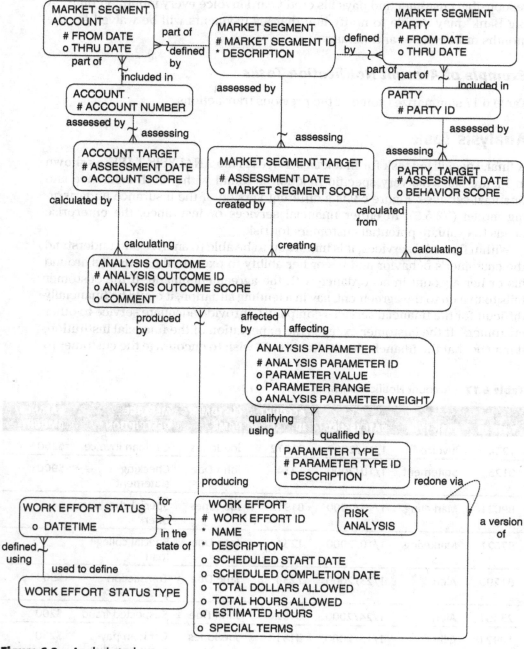

Figure 6.9 Analysis task.

bring other aspects of his or her business under the company's management for improved service and benefit. In either case, the proper analysis of the customer and behavior needs to be understood in order to make sound business decisions.

In this task, the basic idea is to perform some analysis function, such as deriving a credit score for risk assessment or credit worthiness, evaluating a marketing segment for a specific campaign, or assessing the risk for underwriting purposes, either in a loan or insurance. These functions are performed either as a one-time analysis or periodically, such as offering an increased credit limit on a credit card account.

Analysis Task Data Model

Figure 6.9 provides a data model to capture information about risk analysis tasks and outcomes. Financial institutions need to perform RISK ANALYSIS, an event that discovers the viability of the potential loss within a credit exposure. An example would be the assignment of a credit worthiness score for a customer, "Joe Jones." Because he has requested an "Automobile Loan" product, it is necessary to determine if he is capable of fulfilling the agreement to repay the loan. The information that is important for this is the analysis tasks and resulting scores that determine financial decisions such as whether to loan money or increase credit limits. Based on different analytic models, these may be standardized, as in the case of "Joe Jones," or customized, as in the case of a large business looking to set up a commercial loan.

From the WORK EFFORT is the desired ANALYSIS OUTCOME, the result of the understanding of a parameter, such as the effect that the applicant's payment history credit score expressed numerically. The financial institution may also produce scores for a group of ACCOUNTs or PARTYs that fit a profile.

In our example, "Joe Jones" is to be analyzed to determine if he is able to repay the loan. What the credit score represents is the level of risk associated with lending him the amount of money requested. The desired outcome is an empirical measure that will give the loan officer a good idea of whether "Joe Jones" will repay the loan. This is greatly affected by the ANALYSIS PARAMETERs, those influencing factors that require consideration when making the determination. In our example, the credit history, repayment behavior, late payments, missed payments, amount of debt, and level of assets would all be considered when calculating the risk for anyone desiring a loan. Each of these ANALYSIS PARAMETERs would need to be weighed to determine which is the most critical. The analysis rules would determine the result of this understanding. Once identified, the process of determining the score needs to be completed.

The target of the analysis is typically for a PARTY or an ACCOUNT. If it is for an ACCOUNT, the ANALYSIS OUTCOME will yield an ACCOUNT TARGET **account score**. If the analysis is against a party then the ANALYSIS OUTCOME will yield a **behavior score**. In our example, the targeted PARTY is "Joe Jones," who can receive a certain behavior score as a result of an analysis outcome and then may receive another score at a later date. The **assessment date** records when the score was determined. Often a marketing or large-scale project may involve many PARTYs, and therefore each party would have a **behavior score**. As another example, if "John Doe" was requesting an increase to his credit limit on his credit card product, the analysis may focus on the credit card account and how it has been used in the past year.

When a single ACCOUNT is being evaluated, the ACCOUNT TARGET captures the desired result or **account score**. In the preceding example, the credit card account for "John Doe" is evaluated for past performance in payments to assist in determining if a credit limit increase request should be granted. If there is a good payment history, a higher **account score** may be recorded and the customer is more likely to be granted a higher credit limit.

When a single PARTY is being evaluated, the PARTY TARGET stores a **behavior score** for the PARTY. This behavior score could be used to predict the reliability or financial stability of a customer. In the other example, "Joe Jones" is being evaluated for credit worthiness, and the score would be attributed to the PARTY TARGET. It is important to understand that the same parameters may be repeated at different intervals of time, resulting in different scores. For example, if "Joe Jones" is evaluated in June 1999, he may be a higher risk than in June 2000. A contributing factor is that he had just graduated from college in June 1999 and had little time in his job. Being an important factor, it would have significant bearing on the outcome of his score. When reviewed a year later, his risk level may have been lowered if he had continuous employment. The **assessment date** provides the capability of recording scores on several dates.

RISK ANALYSIS may also produce ANALYSIS OUTCOMEs for groups of accounts or parties. A MARKET SEGMENT may be defined by a group of selected accounts with similar characteristics (MARKET SEGMENT ACCOUNT) or a group of selected parties with similar characteristics (MARKET SEGMENT PARTY).

For example, "A Big Bank" wants to evaluate whether it should increase credit limits to customers that are within a particular market segment. It defines a MARKET SEGMENT group based on certain profile aspects, such as no late payments in the past six months, not more than 50 percent of credit limit currently used, debt ratio is less than 30 percent, and net worth exceeds $50,000. The financial institution determines that there are 500,000 customers who fit into the MARKET SEGMENT. A score is applied to the whole market segment based upon ANALYSIS OUTCOMEs for the parameters applicable to the market segment. Based upon the market segment score, they decide to apply a 10 percent credit limit increase for all customers and notify them of the increase.

Table 6.18 Analysis Task—Credit Score

WORK EFFORT DESCRIPTION	ANALYSIS PARAMETER TYPE DESCRIPTION AND PARAMETER VALUE OR RANGE	ANALYSIS PARAMETER WEIGHT	ANALYSIS OUTCOME SCORE	PARTY TARGET BEHAVIOR SCORE	PARTY NAME
Determine automobile loan credit risk	Current income ($50–75,000 per year)	75	100	650	Joe Jones
	Current debt level ($100,000–150,000)	70	50		
	Amount to be borrowed ($75,000)	80	60		
	Time in current job (2 years)	60	240		
	Payment history (good)	70	200		

Example of Risk Analysis Task

Table 6.18 provides an example for Figure 6.9. "Joe Jones" had several analysis parameters reviewed for his credit score, such as "current income," "current debt level," "amount to be borrowed," "time in job," and "payment history." Each of these analysis parameters, with its associated **analysis parameter weight**, were evaluated in each ANALYSIS OUTCOME. Each ANALYSIS OUTCOME resulted in an **outcome analysis score** for each analysis parameter. The scores for the analysis on the party were tallied, and it was determined that the "Joe Jones" **behavior Score** was "650" for this RISK ANALYSIS work effort. Based on rules and regulations of the financial service company, it is determined that his score is sufficient to qualify for the loan, but the minimum period allowed for him to repay is "48 months" with an interest rate of "10 percent." Based on this input, "Joe Jones" decides that he will accept the agreement with "A Big Bank" and get the loan with that bank.

Invoicing, Accounting, and Human Resources

This chapter has covered modifications to the party, product, order, delivery, and work effort models for financial services. The data models for some of the other subject data areas will work quite well in financial services. A good part of the invoicing models can be used for most enterprises with some customization, such as linking the invoice and statement notifications to the payment structures in the invoice chapter (V1:7.8a–7.8b). The accounting and budgeting data models will probably be usable with very few changes. The human resources models should apply as well.

Star Schemas for Financial Services

In the financial services industry, the number of decision support star schema models could be numerous. The intention of this discussion is to highlight the most widely used, effective, and important analysis functions with the financial services industry. It is important to recognize that these are templates and that the individuality of each model rests with the company and group developing it. This section is not intended to be exhaustive, nor will it span all possibilities. The models provided in this section serve to provide the reader with some examples of the types of data that are useful to analyze in financial services.

Analysis Information

The information within this chapter has been at an atomic or transaction oriented level. In developing a solid star schema, it is necessary to understand what business questions need to be answered, what data needs to be analyzed, the significance of the data, and why it must be analyzed. In financial services, the function that requires constant analysis is the use of the account. It is important to analyze this because this gives the company insight into its use, its profitability, and how effectively it meets the customer's needs. Many organization units spend a great deal of time reviewing and using this type of information.

Account analysis will help determine the account activity for various products within the accounts of the customers. This analysis gives insight not only into the account and its effectiveness, but also into the customers and their behaviors. It allows for the measure of many important things: profitability, behavior, cost, and offerings. So many financial service companies have extensively analyzed account activity for these very reasons.

Account Star Schema

The account star schema shown in Figure 6.10 provides an understanding of profitability and activity of accounts and ultimately of customers. Analysis of data from this star schema can help to determine which customers to further pursue, which accounts generate the most revenue, and which accounts deserve more attention, time and money.

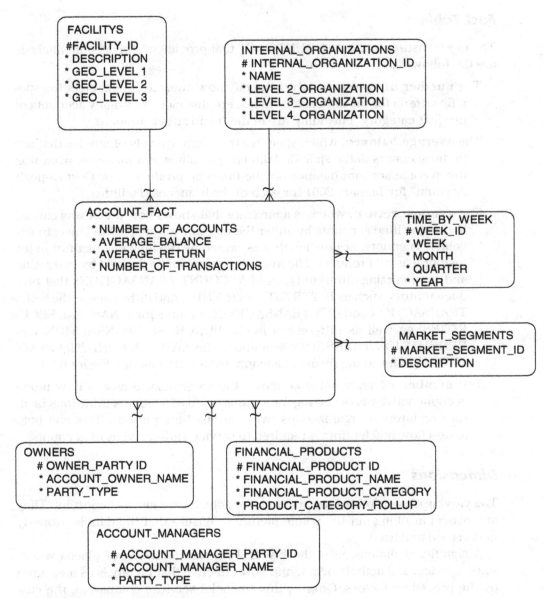

Figure 6.10 Financial account star schema.

Fact Table

The key measures in the ACCOUNT FACT that provide useful account analysis are the following:

The **number of accounts,** which specify how many accounts meet the specific criteria for the dimension values. For instance, how many accounts of product category "checking" are in the "main street" branch?

The **average balance,** which specifies the average levels of monies that are in the accounts in the specified dimension values. For instance, what was the average account balance for the financial product "Low Cost Deposit Account" for January 2001 for each of the branches (facilities)?

The **average return,** which is a measure that shows how much was earned in the specified accounts by either the investor for deposit and investment vehicle accounts, or how much was earned by the financial institution for loan or leasing products. The average return can be derived by extracting and summarizing different types of ACCOUNT TRANSACTIONs that produce returns, such as INTEREST, DIVIDENDS, and difference in the SELL TRANSACTION and BUY TRANSACTION amounts for FINANCIAL SECURITIES, as well as differences in the PURCHASE TRANSACTION and REDEMPTION TRANSACTION amounts for MUTUAL FUND TRANSACTIONS. (Refer to the financial account transaction model, Figure 6.7.)

The **number of transactions** allows the enterprise to assess how much account activity is occurring for various types of accounts in various facilities or internal organizations over various time periods. This can help assess how much effort is required to service various types of accounts.

Dimensions

The varying dimensions of the account star schema are just as important. They are critical in filling out the whole picture to ensure that the data is properly understood and used.

A significant dimension is the FACILITYS, the definition of places where sales, service, and activity occur, and how effective that facility is as measured by the preceding factors. Often within financial services companies, the customer sees the local branch or service location as the point of contact with the company. These are traditionally defined in this way, but they also may represent an automated teller machine in a local supermarket or the telephone center the customer calls to check balances. With the increased use of the Internet, it may be the Web portal that the customer is using.

Each facility may be in a certain geographic area such as in a city, which is in a state, which is in a country. The **geo level 1**, **geo level 2**, and **geo level 3** provide a flexible structure to summarize account activity by geographic regions.

For instance, one could find out the **average_balance** for all accounts by branch (**facility**), by city (**geo_level 1**), by state (**geo_ level 2**), and by country (**geo_level 3**).

While the FACILITYS dimension enables the enterprise to measure account balances and activity by each physical facility associated with the account, the INTERNAL ORGANIZATIONS dimension measures the account balance and activity by departments, divisions, or other internal organizations of the enterprise. For instance, the enterprise may want to know the **number_of_ accounts**, **average_balances,** and **average_returns** for accounts in various types of divisions to assess the performance of those divisions.

The FINANCIAL_PRODUCTS dimension comes from the FINANCIAL PRODUCT and PRODUCT CATEGORY entities. As we discovered in the discussion on FINANCIAL PRODUCT, these FINANCIAL PRODUCTs are categorized into various FINANCIAL PRODUCT CATEGORYs, which could be rolled up into a higher-level PRODUCT CATEGORY ROLLUP. Thus the FINANCIAL_ PRODUCTs dimension provides account analysis such as **average_balance** and **average_return** by **financial_product_name** such as "A+ checking," and/or categorized into a **financial_product_category**, such as "checking" and/or then further categorized into a higher-level product category rollup such as "deposit product."

The OWNERS dimension comes from the ACCOUNT ROLEs of ACCOUNT ROLE TYPE "owner" that was discussed in the ACCOUNT model in Figure 6.6. This dimension allows accounts to be analyzed by the specific owner of the accounts and by the type of party they are, such as the industry they are in or by Standard Industry Classification (SIC) code. The enterprise may want to know the **average_balance** and **average_return** for each account owner and then summarize that information by the industry that each owner is in.

The ACCOUNT_MANAGERS dimension comes from the ACCOUNT ROLEs of ACCOUNT ROLE TYPE "account manager" or possibly "portfolio manager" for MUTUAL FUND products (see Figure 6.6). This allows the enterprise to measure the **average_return** for each account manager or portfolio manager in order to compare the performance of various account managers.

MARKET_SEGMENTS is a demographic categorization of customers or accounts based on certain business criteria such as income level, size of an organization, individual versus organization categorization, types of industry, behavior characteristics, or any combination of these and other factors. Often these market segments are defined by external sources, such as the Census Bureau or marketing organizations. Individual corporations may establish their own segments that make sense for them as well. It allows for the classification of the ACCOUNT_FACTs by these demographic factors in order to determine how much account activity occurs in each segment.

A significant dimension is TIME_BY_WEEK. This star schema provides the TIME_BY_WEEK dimension levels of week, month, quarter, and year to allow the organization to see changes in account measurements each week. The enterprise could measure account information on a daily basis by adding a day level and a key of day id.

Account Transaction Star Schema

The account transaction star schema shown in Figure 6.11 provides additional understanding of behavior of financial accounts. It can help to analyze the nature of customer activity and which customers and facilities require the most effort from a service perspective.

Fact Table

The main facts within the account transaction star schema are **number_of_ transactions** and **total_transaction_amount**. The **number_of_transactions** is a count of the number of transactions that have occurred for the specified dimension values. It tells much about the customer behavior and how the customer uses the services provided by the company. It is an important measure of the effectiveness of each type of activity occurring within accounts and how the company needs to respond to the customer. The **total_transaction_ amount** is the sum of the ACCOUNT_TRANSACTION_FACT amounts for the transactions, as specified by the dimension values. This assists again in measuring the profitability of various facilities, organizations, market segments, and financial products.

Dimensions

The dimensions of the ACCOUNT_TRANSACTION_FACT are very similar to the previous ACCOUNT_FACT table, with the exception of an ACCOUNT_ TRANSACTION_TYPES dimension allowing the enterprise to measure how much activity, in dollars and number of transactions, occurs for each transaction type. As illustrated in the financial account transaction model of Figure 6.7, there are many different types of financial transactions including DEPOSITs, WITHDRAWALS, ACCOUNT FEEs, DIVIDENDs, ACCOUNT PAYMENTs, SECURITIES TRANSACTIONs, such as BUY TRANSACTIONs and SELL TRANSACTIONs, and MUTUAL FUNDS TRANSACTIONs, such as PUR-CHASE TRANSACTIONs, REDEMPTION TRANSACTIONs, and EXCHANGE TRANSACTIONs.

The TIME_BY_DAY dimension is used instead of a TIME_BY_WEEK dimension in order to provide for a lower level of granularity for account transaction information.

Another dimension could also be the ACCOUNT_TRANSACTION_STATUS_ TYPES dimension to analyze account transactions in different states; however,

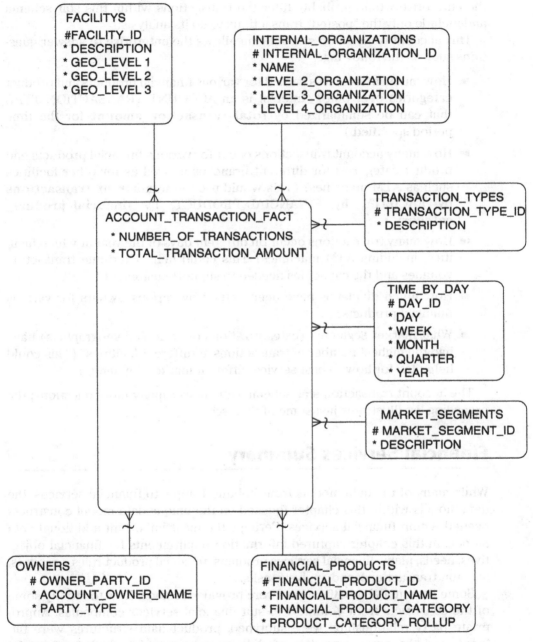

Figure 6.11 Account transaction star schema.

the enterprise would probably filter the transactions within this star schema and include only the "posted" transactions to do its analysis.

This account transaction star schema allows the enterprise to answer questions such as the following:

- How much interest was earned for various financial products and product categories over time? (Interest is an ACCOUNT TRANSACTION TYPE that can be summarized by **total_transaction_amount** for the time period specified.)

- How many account transactions occur for various financial products and product categories for different branches as well as for other facilities such as ATM machines? (This would use the **number_of_transactions** by FACILITY, by FINANCIAL_PRODUCT, by **financial_product_category**.)

- How many transactions occur on different days of the year at which facilities, including ATM machines? This could help determine transaction volumes and the capacities needed to support customers.

- How much dividends have been earned by various owners for various financial products?

- What market segments (categorizations of various demographics) have had the highest number of transactions at different facilities? (This could help plan for how to best service different market segments.)

The account transaction star schema can answer many more questions; the preceding list illustrates just some of the uses.

Financial Services Summary

While many of the data models from Volume 1 apply to financial services, the data models within this chapter focused on the unique data model constructs needed within financial services. Perhaps the most important additional data models in this chapter captured information requirements for financial objectives, needs, plans, financial services products, financial product rules, accounts, account transactions, and analysis tasks.

Some data model modifications were provided to show how to modify some of the constructs from Volume 1 to suit financial services companies. Appropriate party relationships were subtyped, product data structures were tailored, and the agreement data models were subtyped to include financial agreements. Star schemas were provided to analyze accounts and their related account transactions.

Figure 6.12 provides an overall financial services model illustrating the key entities and relationships within this chapter.

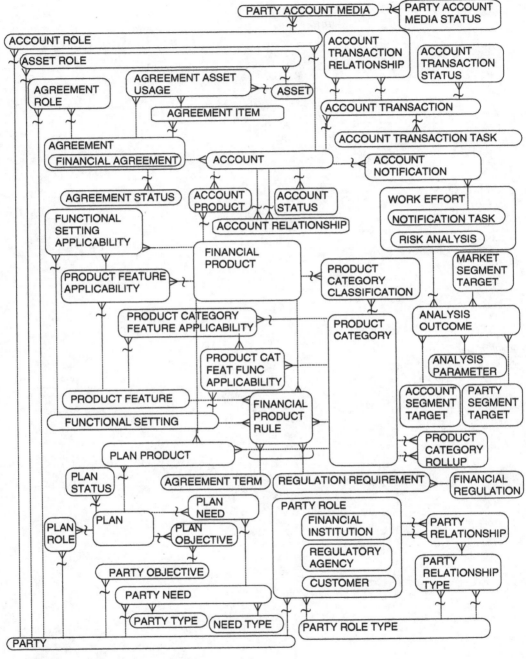

Figure 6.12 Overall financial services model.

CHAPTER 7

Professional Services

Professional services enterprises provide a variety of services through efforts of time and work. These businesses include temporary placement firms, accounting firms, law firms, management consultants, administrative assistance contracting firms, computer consulting firms, office cleaning services, or any other type of organization that bills for its services. Many enterprises that are not exclusively service providers may have need for the models in this chapter because they may provide professional services in conjunction with their other product offerings. For example, firms that provide tangible or intangible goods may provide professional services to support their product offerings. This chapter focuses on the information requirements for enterprises that provide professional services.

Professional services enterprises are concerned with such issues as the following:

- How can we deliver the highest value of service to our clients?
- How can we improve our profit margins and reduce the costs of the professionals that we use?
- How can we increase our revenues and the volume of our services?
- What types of market differentiation can we offer?
- How can we deliver projects on time and within our budgets?

To answer these types of questions, professional services enterprises need to track information about the following:

- The people and organizations they are concerned with, such as their clients, other professional service providers, such as subcontractors or firms to whom the enterprise contracts, the professionals doing the work, partners, suppliers, competitors, associations, and organization units
- The product offerings including their standard services, deliverables-based offerings, and tangible items if they offer them as well
- Engagement information and professional service contracts
- Requirements, proposals/quotes, requests for proposals, and all the information associated with current and future client needs
- Service entry information such as time entries, expense entries, materials usage, and deliverable turnover
- Work effort tracking of projects or engagements of the professional service enterprises
- Invoice and payment tracking of services provided
- Support information such as accounting, budgeting, and human resources management information

Volume 1 addresses many of the needs of a professional services company. For instance, it addresses these topics:

- People and organization structures that can be used within professional services.
- Product structures that a professional services can build on. These product structures need to be capable of handling predefined services, deliverables, and tangible items if the enterprise also provides items.
- Order tracking models that can form the basis for the engagement models needed.
- Requirements, requests, and quotes.
- Agreement models that can form the basis for professional service agreements.
- Work effort models that can be used to track services performed.
- Invoice models that can be used to store professional services invoice information.
- Accounting, budgeting and human resource models to manage finances and people.

Key aspects of professional services that are not addressed in Volume 1 include these:

- Data structures set up specifically for professional services products
- Engagement and engagement item information requirements
- Service entry information including time, materials, and expense entries
- Information and relationships between work efforts, engagements, and service entries

Table 7.1 shows which models can be used directly from Volume 1, which models need to be modified, which Volume 1 models are not used, and which new models are required. This chapter describes the new models as well as generic models that need to be significantly modified to meet the needs of professional service enterprises. (Minor modifications to the generic models from Volume 1 are described in the text.)

People and Organizations in Professional Services

Professional services providers have similar needs to other industries for tracking people and organizations. They need to track information about their professionals, employees, contractors, contacts, other professional service providers, clients, partners, suppliers, competitors, associations, and organization units.

Figure 7.1 shows a data model for PARTY, PARTY ROLEs, and PARTY RELATIONSHIPs within professional services enterprises. Many of the standard roles are included such as EMPLOYEE, CONTACT, SHAREHOLDER, PROSPECT, PARTNER, COMPETITOR, SUPPLIER, ASSOCIATION, ORGANIZATION UNIT, and INTERNAL ORGANIZATION. Some of the standard roles such as FAMILY MEMBER, HOUSEHOLD, REGULATORY AGENCY, DISTRIBUTION CHANNEL, and CUSTOMER are not included. The subtypes PROFESSIONAL, CLIENT, and PROFESSIONAL SERVICES PROVIDER are added as key roles to track within professional services.

The PARTY RELATIONSHIPs—SUPPLIER RELATIONSHIP, ORGANIZATION CONTACT RELATIONSHIP, EMPLOYMENT, PARTNERSHIP, and ORGANIZATION ROLLUP—are standard relationships that can be used for professional service enterprises. CLIENT RELATIONSHIP is used to track one of the most important areas, information about relationships between CLIENTS and INTERNAL ORGANIZATIONS. SUBCONTRACTOR RELATIONSHIP is used to maintain who may be used to subcontract to the professional services enterprise, as well as organizations with which the enterprise may want to subcontract.

Table 7.1 Volume 1 and Volume 2 Data Models for Professional Services

SUBJECT DATA AREA	USE THESE VOLUME 1 MODELS DIRECTLY	MODIFY THESE VOLUME 1 MODELS (AS DESCRIBED IN VOLUME 2)	DO NOT USE THESE VOLUME 1 MODELS	ADD THESE VOLUME 2 MODELS
People and organizations	Party models, V1:2.1–2.14, except V1:2.5. and V1:2.6	Party relationship, V1:2.6 and V1:2.5 (need to add professional services PARTY ROLES and PARTY RELATIONSHIP subtypes as in V2:7.1)		
Product		Product models, V1:3.1, V1:3.2, V1:3.4, V1:3.5, V1:3.7–3.9, Customized professional service products are Professional service products, V2:7.2, and Product components, V2:7.3 (customized version of professional service product associations in V2:7.3)	Product identification, V1 3.3, Inventory item storage, V1:3.6, Product parts, V1:3.10	
Order		Standard order models, V1:4.1–4.8 for supply side processing, Requirements, V1:4.9, (customized with V2:7.4) Requests, V1:4.10, (customized with V2:7.5) Quotes, V1:4.11, (customized with V2:7.6) Agreement models, V1:4.12–4.16 (customized with V2:7.7 and V2:7.8)		Professional service engagements, V2:7.7
Delivery		Shipment models, V1:5.1-5.8 for supply deliveries		Professional service entries, V2:7.9
Work effort		Work effort, V1:6.1-6.12—Expand time entry to cover service entries		Engagements and work efforts, V2:7.10
Invoicing		Invoice models, V1:7.1–7.10		Professional service invoicing, V2:7.11
Accounting	All models, V1:8.1-8.12			
Human resources	All models, V1:9.1–9.14			
Professional service star schema				Professional service time entry star schema V2:7.12

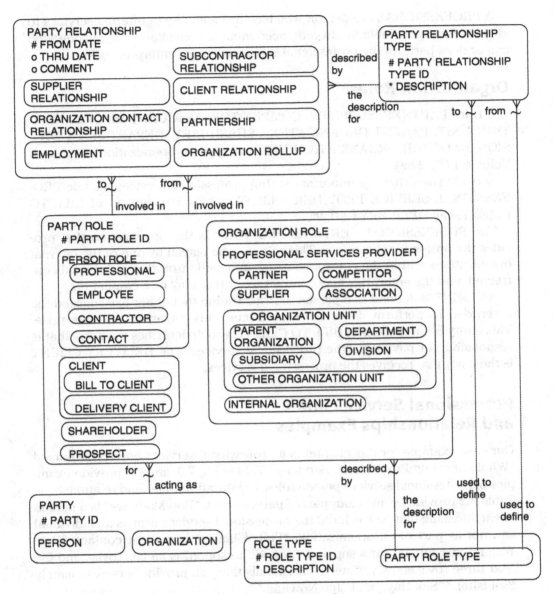

Figure 7.1 Professional services party roles and relationships.

Person Roles

The roles EMPLOYEE, CONTRACTOR, CONTACT, SHAREHOLDER, and PROSPECT are generic person roles that have already been defined in Volume 1 (V1:2.6a). A specific role that is important in professional services is PROFESSIONAL.

A PROFESSIONAL is a person who has the capability of offering services to clients. Examples include lawyers, accountants, consultants, or anyone who can or does perform the professional services that the enterprise offers.

Organization Roles

The roles PARTNER, SUPPLIER, COMPETITOR, ASSOCIATION, ORGANIZATION UNIT, PARENT ORGANIZATION, SUBSIDIARY, DEPARTMENT, DIVISION, or OTHER ORGANIZATION UNIT are generic organization roles from Volume 1 (V1:2.6a).

Specific roles that are important within professional services include PROFESSIONAL SERVICE PROVIDER, CLIENT, which is subtyped of BILL TO CLIENT, and DELIVERY CLIENT.

The PROFESSIONAL SERVICES PROVIDER is the organization that provides the professional services. This role may be played by one of the internal organizations within the enterprise or by an outside firm that may be subcontracted, that the enterprise may contract to, or that may be a competitor.

A CLIENT is defined as a person or organization that either has engaged the enterprise to perform its services or is currently engaging the enterprise. This entity is subtyped into BILL TO CLIENT, which describes the party that is responsible for paying for the professional services. The DELIVERY CLIENT is the party that receives the professional services.

Professional Services Roles and Relationships Examples

Our case example for this chapter is a professional services enterprise named "Whole Shebang Professional Services." Tables 7.2, 7.3, and 7.4 provide examples of professional services person roles, organization roles, and relationships. Table 7.2 provides some examples of person roles. "Rob Mathews" is a person client, meaning that he has hired the professional services firm as an individual and not as part of an organization. "Phil Williams" is a client contact. "Pete Waters" is a contact for a supplier. "Joe Witherspoon" is an employee, and the next three rows show various professionals that can provide services, namely "Sol Isiter," "Sipi Hay." and "Joe Nowitall."

Table 7.3 provides examples of organization roles for a professional service provider. "Whole Shebang Professional Services" is an enterprise that provides all types of professional services including law, accounting, and many types of consulting services. According to Table 7.3, "Whole Shebang Professional Services" is the parent organization behind three divisions, "Whole Shebang Law Offices," "Whole Shebang Accounting," and "Whole Shebang Consulting." "XYZ Accounting Services" is another professional service provider that is not an internal organization and could be a subcontractor of services. Each of these

Table 7.2 Professional Services Person Roles

PERSON ROLE	PERSON NAME
Client (person client)	Rob Mathews
Contact (supplier contact)	Pete Waters
Contact (client contact)	Phil Williams
Employee	Joe Witherspoon
Professional (lawyer)	Sol Isiter
Professional (accountant)	Sipi Hay
Professional (consultant)	Joe Nowitall

also plays the roles of professional service provider and internal organization. "Everything Manufacturing" is an organization client, and "ABC Printing" is a supplier.

Table 7.4 provides additional information about which roles are involved with which relationships. For example, the first two rows show that "Everything Manufacturing" is a client of two internal organizations within the enterprise, "Whole Shebang Law Offices" and "Whole Shebang Accounting." "Phil Williams" is a contact in the manufacturing firm. "Rob Mathews" has a client relationship with "Whole Shebang Professional Services," and "ABC Printing" is

Table 7.3 Professional Services Party Roles

ORGANIZATION ROLE	ORGANIZATION NAME
Professional services provider Internal organization Parent organization	Whole Shebang Professional Services
Professional services provider Internal organization Division	Whole Shebang Law Offices
Professional services provider Internal organization Division	Whole Shebang Accounting
Professional services provider Internal organization Division	Whole Shebang Consulting
Client (organization client)	Everything Manufacturing
Professional services provider	XYZ Accounting Services
Supplier	ABC Printing

Table 7.4 Professional Services Party Relationships

PARTY RELATIONSHIP TYPE	FROM PARTY NAME	TO PARTY NAME
Client relationship	Everything Manufacturing	Whole Shebang Law Offices
Client relationship	Everything Manufacturing	Whole Shebang Accounting
Organization contact relationship (client contact relationship)	Phil Williams	Everything Manufacturing
Client relationship	Rob Mathews	Whole Shebang Professional Services
Supplier relationship	ABC Printing	Whole Shebang Professional Services
Organization contact relationship (supplier contact relationship)	Pete Waters	ABC Manufacturing
Employment	Joe Witherspoon	Whole Shebang Professional Services
Employment	Sol Isiter	Whole Shebang Professional Services
Organization Contact Relationship (contractor)	Sipi Hay	Weknow Accounting Services
Organization Contact Relationship (contractor)	Joe Nowitall	Joe Nowitall, Inc.

a supplier of "Whole Shebang Professional Services." One of its supplier contacts is "Pete Waters." Table 7.4 show that "Joe Witherspoon" is an employee of "Whole Shebang Professional Services." "Sol Isiter," "Sipi Hay," and "Joe Nowitall" are all professionals who have abilities to offer various services. "Sol Isiter" happens to be with "Whole Shebang" while the other two professionals are with other firms. Therefore, "Sol Ister" plays the roles of professional and of employee, while "Sipi Hay" and "Joe Nowitall" have roles as professionals as well as contractors and have an "organization contact relationship" with their respective firms.

Professional Services Products

By definition, professional service organizations focus on selling their services. These organizations may either bill for their time or offer a certain predefined deliverable to their clients. Additionally, these enterprises may sell certain items to complement their services, such as application software.

Professional Services Products Model

Figure 7.2 provides a modified product definition for professional services organizations. This model is a slightly customized version of the generic models in Volume 1, product category (V1:3.2) and product feature (V1:3.4). The

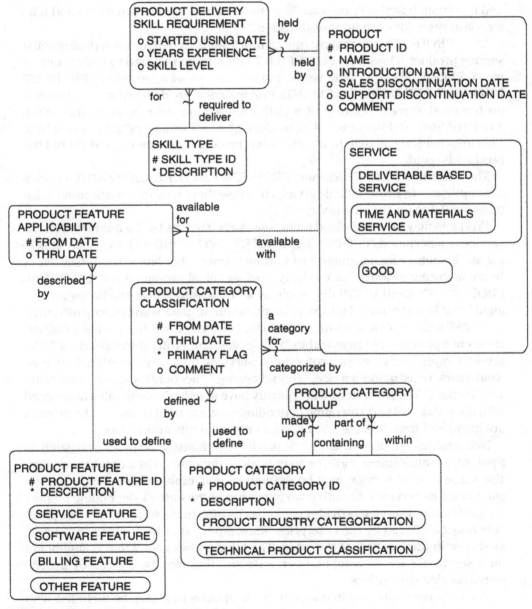

Figure 7.2 Professional services products.

PRODUCT entity is subtyped to include a SERVICE or a GOOD. A SERVICE may be either a DELIVERABLE BASED SERVICE or a TIME AND MATERIALS SERVICE. A deliverable is defined as a predefined work product that will be produced for a client as a result of an engagement or engagement item. A time and materials based service is a standard service offering from the professional services firm that is billed on a time and materials basis. An example of a time and materials based service is an "accounting audit" that a firm offers and bills standard rates for each hour of the audit.

Each PRODUCT may require one or more skills to deliver each professional service product. Therefore, each SKILL TYPE may be required to deliver one or more PRODUCTs and vice versa, hence the associative entity, PRODUCT DELIVERY SKILL REQUIREMENT. For instance, in delivering the standard professional service offering of a data architecture development, the SKILL TYPEs of "data architecture," "data modeling," and "facilitation" may be required. This information will help to identify what professionals are needed should the product be sold.

The PRODUCT FEATURE and PRODUCT FEATURE CATEGORY entities are applicable to professional services because there may be variations and features available on certain services.

Products may be categorized numerous ways, such as by the industry that the service is designated (PRODUCT INDUSTRY CATEGORIZATION), such as selling an "inventory management just-in-time service" that has a categorization of "manufacturing product," or by the type of technical product it is (TECHNICAL PRODUCT CLASSIFICATION), such as a "data warehouse readiness assessment" that has a technical product classification of "data warehousing offering."

Table 7.5 shows examples of products that may exist within a professional services enterprise, in this case within "Whole Shebang Professional Services." The services represent types of professional services that may be offered such as "trademark registration service," "bookkeeping," "accounting audit." and "data architecture." These services will typically have standard billing rates associated with them that will vary over time depending on the market demand. The product pricing model from Volume 1 (V1:3.7) can maintain this information.

Deliverables are predefined work products that are to be produced, such as a patent, a management audit, or an enterprise data model or a database design. The same type of service may be defined as deliverable based services, time and materials services, or both (two instances of the entity), depending on how the professional service provider packages its offerings. Notice that these products may be offered by the enterprise being modeled or by another enterprise, as shown in the last row of the table. The table shows goods that complement their services, such as pamphlets or software, that may be offered by professional service enterprises.

The features show possible variations or options that may be included with the professional service such as offering to register either one trademark or

Table 7.5   Professional Services Products

SERVICE PROVIDER ORGANIZATION	PRODUCT TYPE	PRODUCT NAME	PRODUCT FEATURES
Whole Shebang Law Offices	Time and materials service	Trademark registration service	One mark registration Two mark registration
Whole Shebang Law Offices	Deliverable based service	Providing patent for a product	
Whole Shebang Law Offices	Good	Whole Shebang pamphlet on patents	
Whole Shebang Accounting	Time and materials service	Bookkeeping	Biweekly billing, Monthly billing
Whole Shebang Accounting	Deliverable based service	Accounting audit for medium-sized firm	Legal representation
Whole Shebang Accounting	Good	Whole Shebang accounting software	Source code inclusion
Whole Shebang Consulting	Time and materials service	Data architecture development	
Whole Shebang Consulting	Deliverable based service	Enterprise data model	
Whole Shebang Consulting	Good	Whole Shebang CASE tool	
The Other Consulting Firm	Deliverable based service	Database design review	

two trademarks within the trademark registration service of "Whole Shebang Law Offices" because these may have different charges associated with the offering. That is an example of a SERVICE FEATURE because it is a variation of the type of service that may be provided. The "biweekly" or "monthly" features are examples of features that may be selected as a BILLING FEATURE. The "source code inclusion" is an example of a SOFTWARE FEATURE that may be selected for the "Whole Shebang Accounting Software" product.

Applicability of Other Product Models

The suppliers and manufacturers of products model, V1:3.5, may be used to record which organizations supply which types of services, deliverables, and goods. This may be beneficial in tracking the services offered by other professional service organizations, thus facilitating subcontracting arrangements. This model may also be used for supply-side purchasing.

The inventory item storage model, V1:3.6, will not be included because professional services firms are principally dealing with services and deliverables. It is conceivable that supplies could be stored using these structures; however, in most cases the enterprise will not have the will or means to make this worthwhile.

The product pricing model, V1:3.7, will generally work with a few exceptions. In addition to a **price** attribute on the PRICE COMPONENT there should also be a **rate** attribute to store the standard rates for professional service offerings.

The product costing data model, V1:3.8, is very applicable because it is important to know the costs of services from professionals whether they are with the enterprise or available from other enterprises. Again, it is important to

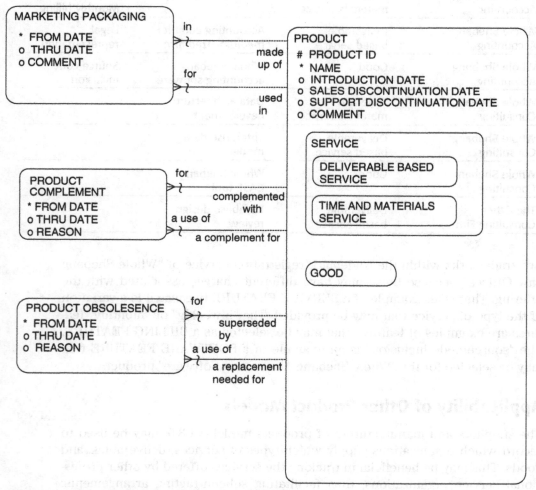

Figure 7.3 Professional services product associations.

identify whether the enterprise will store cost information for each supplier (or professional service firm) for its various types of services. If the enterprise stores only cost information for its own offerings, then the relationship should be from ESTIMATED PRODUCT COST directly to PRODUCT instead of to SUPPLIER PRODUCT.

Professional Service Product Associations

The product association data model, V1:3.9a–3.9b, is applicable in that services may often be made up of other services. There are a number of differences, as illustrated in Figure 7.3. Instead of PRODUCT COMPONENT in Figure 3.9a, the entity MARKETING PACKAGE has been substituted in order to record the bundling of services into a service package. It is highly applicable in that services and deliverables may encompass other deliverables. For instance, a management consulting strategic plan service may consist of a management strategic plan, a management recommendations report, and a series of business models. The "quantity used" and "instructions" attributes have been taken out because these attributes are more significant for tangible assembled items.

The PRODUCT SUBSTITUTE entity is taken out because services generally don't deal with substituting one service or deliverable for another. The PRODUCT OBSOLESCENCE is applicable because services and deliverables may be replaced with other professional service product offerings. The PRODUCT COMPLEMENT is applicable to professional service organizations; for example, a "trademark registration" search service from a law firm may be complementary to a "trademark search" service. While the PRODUCT INCOMPATIBILITY is very applicable to enterprises selling goods, it may not be applicable for professional service enterprises.

Orders

As in most businesses, professional service enterprises also take orders from their clients; however, they are usually referred to as "engagements" because the client engages the services of that firm. Therefore, the structure of the order data models from Volume 1 may be used with some modifications.

The engagement models presented in this section should be used for the sales aspect of the enterprise while the standard order models from Volume 1 may be used on the purchasing side of the enterprise, for instance, in purchasing equipment and/or supplies. The following engagement models may be used to capture information about engagements from the enterprise to clients as well as from other service organizations to the enterprise because subcontracting is a very common practice within professional service firms.

This section is composed of models to capture information about specific engagements as well as overall professional services agreements. The requirements, requests, and quotes data models from Volume 1, V1:4.9–4.11, will be expanded because they are a key information requirement of professional service enterprises. The engagement data models will be based on the order data models from Volume 1 (V1:4.1–4.8) and will store information about commitments to perform time and material tasks or to deliver specific deliverables within project engagements. Sometimes an engagement is referred to as a "statement of work." The agreements data models capture information about the understanding that two or more parties have over time that generally governs the specific engagements.

Professional Services Requirements

In professional services organizations, requisitions, requests, and quotes are integral to the business. The models in Volume 1 are highly applicable; however, the models in this chapter will further expand on these data structures.

In Figure 7.4, the REQUIREMENT entity maintains information about the needs of clients (CLIENT REQUIREMENT) as well as the needs of the professional service enterprise (INTERNAL REQUIREMENT). This gives the organization the flexibility to store requirements from its clients as well as requirements that the enterprise has, such as subcontracting needs that they have given to other organizations.

Each REQUIREMENT may also represent a RESOURCE REQUIREMENT, PROJECT REQUIREMENT, or a PRODUCT REQUIREMENT. A RESOURCE REQUIREMENT represents a need for either the client or the professional services enterprise to hire a professional either on a contract or employee basis. This is also known as a requirement for a temporary or permanent "placement." A PROJECT REQUIREMENT is a deliverables-based requirement to deliver specific outcomes with a work effort, or project. For example, a client may have a requirement for the professional services firm to deliver a sales analysis data warehouse. A PRODUCT REQUIREMENT establishes the need for a specific predefined product that the professional services enterprise may offer. An example is that professional services organization may have a standard offering for a "trademark registration," and in this case the REQUIREMENT would establish a need for this standard PRODUCT.

RESOURCE REQUIREMENTs maintain the NEEDED SKILLs of each SKILL TYPE that the job opening requires. The **years experience** and **skill level** allow the specification of certain levels of required skills. This could be matched against what skills professionals may have (see the human resources model, V1:9.11). PROJECT REQUIREMENTs maintain the NEEDED DELIVERABLEs of DELIVERABLE TYPEs in order to define the desired outcome for the

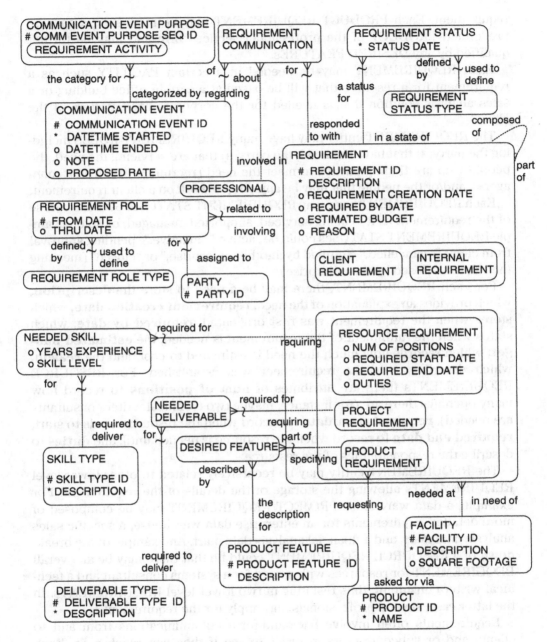

Figure 7.4 Professional services requirements.

requirement. Each PRODUCT REQUIREMENT may be requesting a specific predefined PRODUCT of the professional services firm and may be further qualified by any DESIRED FEATUREs.

Each REQUIREMENT may be needed in a certain FACILITY such as a requirement for a resource that will be based at a certain office building or a sales analysis solution that is needed for the corporate headquarters of the client.

The REQUIREMENT entity may have many REQUIREMENT ROLEs including the party(s) that have the need, the party(s) that are servicing the need, the people who are finding parties to meet the need (recruiters or account managers), and/or the people that may be applying to work on a client requirement.

Each REQUIREMENT has many REQUIREMENT STATUSes over the course of the requirement as it is being serviced, supported, managed, or sold. Example REQUIREMENT STATUSes could be "active," "inactive," "pending approval from client," "cancelled," "fulfilled by another enterprise," or "closed" (meaning the sale was closed by the enterprise).

For each REQUIREMENT, there may be a need to store the **description,** which provides an explanation of the need, **requirement creation date,** which stores when the requirement was first originated, **required by date**, which states when the fulfillment of the requirement is needed, the **estimated budget,** which records how much the need is estimated to cost, and the **reason,** which describes why the requirement was established. For RESOURCE REQUIREMENTs there are attributes of **num of positions** to record how many openings there are (for instance, maybe two technical writer consultants are needed), **required start date** to record when the resource needs to start, **required end date** to record when the resource is needed until, and **duties** to describe the responsibilities of the resource.

The REQUIREMENT entity may be recursively related to other lower-level REQUIREMENTs allowing the storage of the details of the requirement. For example, a data warehouse PROJECT REQUIREMENT may be composed of more detailed requirements for an enterprise data warehouse, a specific sales analysis data mart, and a financial analysis data mart. An example of the breakdown of a RESOURCE REQUIREMENT could be that there may be an overall REQUIREMENT for resources with a need for a systems consultant and a technical writer consultant, thus resulting in two lower-level REQUIREMENTs. In the latter case, several professionals may apply for the requirement.

Requirements often involve back-and-forth communications from and to clients and or subcontractors in order to see if they can reach a fit. Each REQUIREMENT may have several REQUIREMENT COMMUNICATIONs that track activities against the requirement and PROFESSIONALs that may have activities against the requirement. Each REQUIREMENT COMMUNICATION shows which COMMUNICATION EVENTs (that are for the purpose of REQUIREMENT ACTIVITY) are related to REQUIREMENT, and they may be associated with a specific PROFESSIONAL, most likely one who is being considered to help with the fulfillment of the requirement. REQUIREMENT ACTIVITYs that are important to track include "resume submission," "sales meeting," "interview," and "proposal." Depending on the needs of an enterprise, they may track proposals as a separate entity—for example, in the QUOTE entity from Volume 1—or they may track proposals in the REQUIREMENT ACTIVITY entity if there is very little information about their quote.

Table 7.6 provides examples of some of the information that may be contained within the Figure 7.4 requirement data model. "Whole Shebang Law Offices" tracks each requirement and the associated activity. For instance, one of the project requirements is the requirement for a "lawsuit defense" for "Troublesome Distributors," who is in trouble again. The deliverables are the recommendations on how to proceed as well as the resolution of the case. Whole Shebang Law Offices manages the activity associated with this requirement, in this case a meeting with Sol Ister and the prospective client that occurred December 19, 1999, and a proposal on December 27, 1999. Depending on the enterprise and its needs, the proposal may be its own entity and related to the requirement, or as in this case, the details of the proposal are not required and therefore the proposal is regarded as a type of REQUIREMENT COMMUNICATION.

Whole Shebang Accounting has a client with a need for a tax return that represents a standard product offering with standard pricing. The client wants to make sure to get the feature of Whole Shebang's standing behind the return and providing counsel should a tax audit occur. Communications tracking for the requirement consists of a meeting and a verbal commitment to process.

Whole Shebang Consulting records a resource requirement to hire a data modeler on a contract basis. The candidate must have data modeling, facilitation, and database design skills. Notice that each REQUIREMENT COMMUNICATION may or may not have a professional associated with it. The interview activities associated with the data modeling contract show different professionals submitted on different REQUIREMENT COMMUNICATIONs.

The last requirement portrays the client requirement of ABC Consumer, Inc. for a sales analysis system with the deliverables of data conversion programs, sales analysis user interface, end-user reports, and ad hoc reporting capability. This requirement was learned from a sales call from the account manager for ABC Consumer, Inc.

Professional Services Requests and Quotes

A key aspect of the professional services industry is responding to Request for Information (RFI), Requests for Quotes (RFQ), and Requests for Proposals (RFP). The response is usually done via quotes that are part of proposals or statements of work.

Table 7.6 Professional Services Requirement Tracking

REQUIREMENT	NEEDED DELIVERABLES, SKILLS, OR FEATURES	REQUIREMENT ROLE OF SERVICED BY (PROFESSIONAL SERVICES ORGANIZATION)	REQUIREMENT ROLE OF GIVEN BY (PROSPECTIVE CLIENT)	REQUIREMENT ACTIVITY TYPE AND COMMUNICATION EVENT DATE	COMMUNICATION EVENT NOTE	PROFESSIONAL ASSOCIATED
Lawsuit defense (project requirement)	Deliverables: Recommendation on how to proceed, Resolution of case (favorably, it is hoped)	Whole Shebang Law Offices, 3500 Newton St.	Troublesome Distributors, Inc, 2000 Main Street	Meeting with prospective client (December 19, 1999)	Delivered proposal and it seemed that we were the front runner	Sol Isiter
				Proposal of services (December 27, 1999)		
Tax return (product requirement)	Feature— (representation and backup in case of tax audit)	Whole Shebang Accounting, 300 Bore Street	Johnson Unconsolidated Inc, 1200 E. Windsor Avenue	Meeting with prospective client (January 3, 2000)		Sipi Hay

Item	Details	Vendor	Client	Event (date)	Notes	Sipi Hay
Data modeling contract (resource requirement)	Skills needed: Data modeling, Facilitation, Database design	Whole Shebang Consulting, 600 Utah Road	Worldwide Universal Conglomerates, Inc, 100 Hugh Street	Verbal agreement to do return (February 2, 2000)		
				Sales meeting with client (March 4, 2000)		
				Interviewed candidate for contract (March 6, 2000)	Didn't seem to think candidate was sharp	Neal Ditzy
				Interviewed candidate for contract (March 8, 2000)	Liked consultant a great deal	Joe Nowitall
				Verbal agreement over phone to pursue candidate (March 9, 2000)		Joe Nowitall
Develop sales analysis system	Deliverables: Data conversion programs, Sales analysis user interface, End-user reports, Ad hoc reporting capability, Documentation	Whole Shebang Consulting, 600 Utah Road	ABC Consumer Inc, 345 Conser Blvd.	Phone call from account rep (December 5, 2000)		

The models from Volume 1 on requests (V1:4.10) and quotes (V1:4.11) form a solid basis for the data models needed for professional service firms. Figures 7.5 and 7.6 provide slightly customized versions of these models for professional services firms.

Professional Services Requests

Figure 7.5 provides the data model that stores the information requirements that professional services firms need to store incoming and outgoing requests for information, quotes, and proposals. Professional services firms are often asked to bid on their services, and therefore they want to maintain the information on what requests have come in, how they are related to the requirements that they may already be aware of, and what other firms are possibly responding to these requests.

Figure 7.5 is a slightly expanded version of the request model from Volume 1 (see V1:4.10 for more explanations). Each REQUEST may be an RFI (request for information), RFP (request for proposal), or RFQ (request for quote). Each REQUEST has various parties involved through the REQUEST ROLE and various parties that are scheduled to respond to the request (RESPONDING PARTY).

Each of these requests may consist of one or more REQUEST ITEMs. Each REQUEST ITEM represents the recording of each specific item that is being requested. The item may be a request for a REQUIREMENT, NEEDED DELIVERABLE, NEEDED SKILL, DESIRED FEATURE, or PRODUCT.

Because each REQUIREMENT, NEEDED DELIVERABLE, NEEDED SKILL, DESIRED FEATURE, or PRODUCT may be requested more than once (for example, in an RFI and then an RFP) the REQUEST ITEM provides the ability for each of these to be requested in separate items that may occur at separate times.

RFIs, RFPs, or RFQs may be quite lengthy so it may not be practical for the enterprise to record every request item within the request. The professional services firm may want to record REQUEST ITEMs and their related requirement, deliverable, skill, feature, or product because these requests reveal what the client needs.

Table 7.7 provides an example of the information that a professional services firm may store regarding a request for proposal. In Table 7.7, the requirement of ABC Consumer to have a sales analysis system was learned from a phone call and thus recorded. The request to provide a sales analysis system in RFP form was received by the professional services enterprise afterward. The firm understood that seven request items were being asked for, and they were related to some of the requirements and deliverables that were previously known.

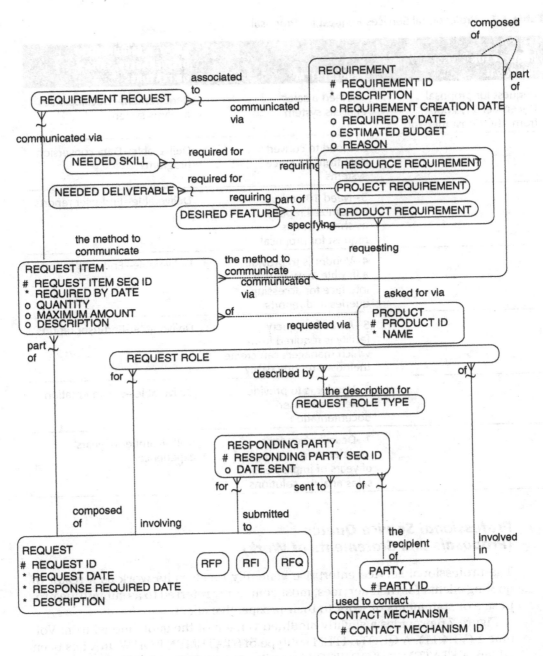

Figure 7.5 Professional services requests.

Table 7.7 Professional Services Request for Proposal

REQUEST FOR PROPOSAL	REQUEST ITEM	RELATED REQUIREMENT, DELIVERABLES, SKILLS, OR FEATURES
Request for proposal December 21, 2000 from ABC Consumer, Inc.	1—Need a sales analysis system	Requirement—Develop sales analysis system
	2—Need to convert data from 3 source systems	Deliverable—Data conversion programs
	3—Need 10 end-user customized reports as shown in this request for proposal	Deliverable—End-user reports
	4—Vendor is to provide a flexible, easy-to-use interface for accessing queries and reports	Deliverable—End-user reports
	5—An ad hoc query facility is required from which managers can create their own reports easily	Deliverable—End-user reports
	6—Vendor is to provide systems and user documentation	Deliverable—documentation
	7—Describe vendor's experience in number of years of implementing sales analysis solutions	Skill—Number of years' experience

Professional Service Quotes (Proposals and Statements of Work)

The professional service enterprise generally receives its work as a result of quoting clients for their services, most commonly referred to as submitting proposals or statements of work to their prospective client.

Figure 7.6 provides a slightly modified version of the quote model from Volume 1 (V1:4.11). A QUOTE ITEM subtype of STATEMENT OF WORK has been added. A STATEMENT OF WORK is similar to a PROPOSAL in that it describes what will be delivered, how, and all the terms associated with the delivery of services. It differs from a PROPOSAL in that the STATEMENT OF WORK usually assumes that the client and professional services firm are in agreement and the statement of work serves to confirm this understanding in writing.

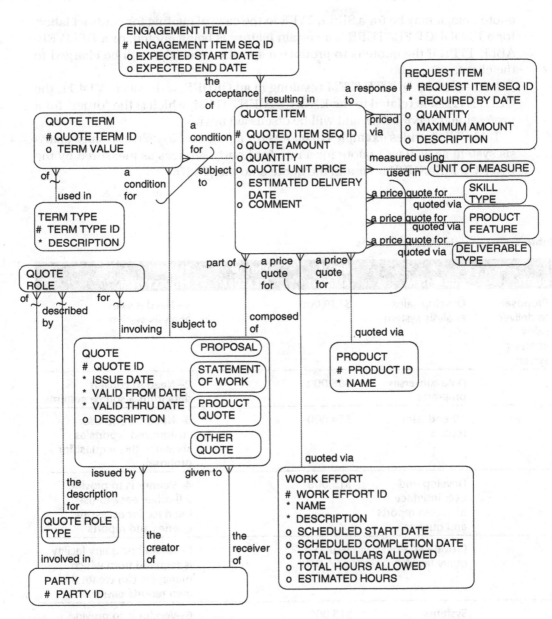

Figure 7.6 Professional services quotes.

QUOTEs are made up of QUOTE ITEMs. In addition to having quotes for PRODUCTs and WORK EFFORTs, some quote items have been added for the professional services model—specifically relationships to SKILL TYPE, PRODUCT FEATURE, and DELIVERABLE TYPE. Depending on the nature of the quote item, it may be for a SKILL TYPE in the case of quoting for contract labor, for a PRODUCT FEATURE if a certain feature is being quoted, or a DELIVERABLE TYPE if the quote is to produce a specific result that will be charged to the client.

Instead of the QUOTE ITEM resulting in an ORDER, as it was in V1:4.11, the QUOTE ITEM is related to the ENGAGEMENT ITEM, which is the "order" for a professional service firm and will be discussed next.

Table 7.7 provides examples of quotes for a proposal to deliver a sales analysis system as well as a quote for a rate for hourly services as measured by the UNIT OF MEASURE hour and the quote amount of $275.

Table 7.7 Example Data for Quotes

QUOTE	QUOTE ITEM	QUOTE AMOUNT	UNIT OF MEASURE	RELATED REQUEST ITEM
Proposal to deliver sales analysis system	Develop sales analysis system	$139,000		1—Need a sales analysis system
	Data conversion programs	$86,000		2—Need to convert data from 3 source systems
	10 end-user reports	$14,000		3—Need 10 end-user customized reports as shown in this request for proposal
	Develop end-user interface to access reports and queries	$15,000		4—Vendor is to provide a flexible, easy-to-use interface for accessing queries and reports
	Provide ad hoc query facility	$9,000		5—An ad hoc query facility is required from which managers can create their own reports easily
	Systems documentation	$15,000		6—Vendor is to provide systems and user documentation
Quote for legal services to provide legal defense counsel	Litigation services	$275	Per hour	

Engagements

Professional services organizations are hired or engaged by their clients to provide particular expertise, provide service offerings (products), hire out resources, or deliver project-oriented work. The "order" or commitment to a client for professional service firms is usually called an engagement. Just as an order may have several items, an engagement may also have several parts or items on it. An engagement may encompass hiring several professionals with different skills, contracting for several deliverables, selling multiple products, or providing a custom job.

Figure 7.7 provides a data model for capturing the information requirements for engagements. It is a modification of the orders and order items model (V1:4.2). The ENGAGEMENT entity stores information about a commitment to contract professional services and/or related products. Each ENGAGEMENT has several ENGAGEMENT ITEMs that each represent a specific contracted service. These contracted services may be either a PROFESSIONAL PLACEMENT (contracting a professional resource), CUSTOM ENGAGEMENT ITEM (a customized work effort for a client), PRODUCT ORDER ITEM (for a predefined standard offering), or OTHER ENGAGEMENT ITEM. The PRODUCT ORDER ITEM is subtyped into STANDARD SERVICE ORDER ITEM to engage in contracting a particular type of service that is offered as a standard product offering, DELIVERABLE ORDER ITEM, to contract to complete a standard DELIVERABLE BASED SERVICE, or GOOD ORDER ITEM, to commit to buying a particular GOOD that is sold by the professional services enterprise. Each ENGAGEMENT ITEM may be fulfilled via the ENGAGEMENT WORK FULFILLMENT entity that is related to a WORK EFFORT.

The roles of the parties, such as the parties placing, receiving, and paying for the engagement, are not shown because the generic model from Volume 1 order roles and contact mechanisms (V1:4.5) may be used as is to handle the needs of the professional services firm.

Types of Engagement Items

The ENGAGEMENT ITEM entity stores each commitment provided within a particular engagement. An ENGAGEMENT ITEM may be either a PROFESSIONAL PLACEMENT, a CUSTOM ENGAGEMENT ITEM, a PRODUCT ORDER ITEM, or an OTHER ENGAGEMENT ITEM. When clients buy professional services, they are either contracting a particular professional whom they have evaluated or they are buying specific products, which may be services, deliverables, or items. A PROFESSIONAL PLACEMENT is a type of item where the client is hiring a particular professional for a certain length of time, and its supertype, ENGAGEMENT ITEM, is therefore related to the PROFESSIONAL entity via the PROFESSIONAL ASSIGNMENT association entity (see Figure 7.9). A CUSTOM ENGAGEMENT ITEM represents a commitment from the professional services

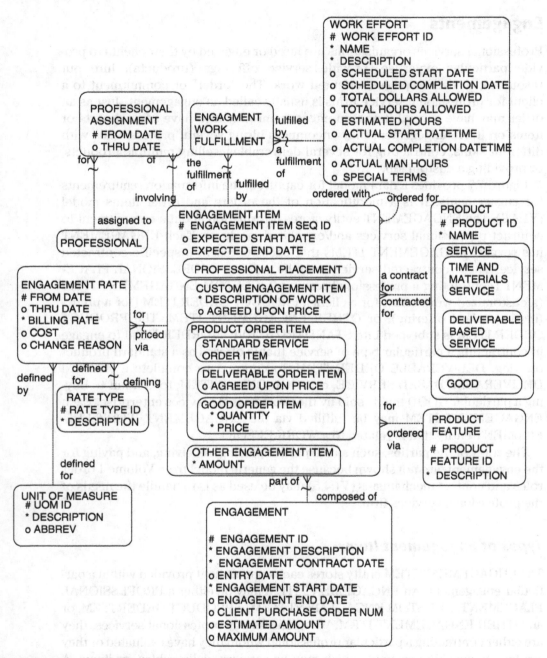

Figure 7.7 Professional services engagement.

enterprise to provide a customized service to the client, such as a contract to build a specific system or to handle a specific accounting engagement. The PRODUCT ORDER ITEM stores a commitment to buy standard items that may be specific services (STANDARD SERVICE ORDER ITEM), deliverables (DELIVERABLE ORDER ITEM), or goods (GOOD ORDER ITEM), and therefore ENGAGEMENT ITEMs may be related to the PRODUCT entity.

Each ENGAGEMENT ITEM may be fulfilled by one or more WORK EFFORTs and vice versa, hence the associative entity ENGAGEMENT WORK FULFILLMENT. This provides for a single ENGAGEMENT ITEM to be fulfilled in several manageable work efforts. For example, there may be an ENGAGEMENT ITEM to build a new Internet order entry system for an international client. The professional services firm may decide to set up multiple projects, one for each country (hence multiple WORK EFFORTs), to fulfill this commitment. Alternatively, there may be many ENGAGEMENT ITEMs related to a single work effort. Perhaps the engagement itemizes the development of the Internet order system, the implementation of it, and the documentation as three separate ENGAGEMENT ITEMs. They may manage the fulfillment of it as a single WORK EFFORT, so therefore there could be many ENGAGMENT ITEMs for a single WORK EFFORT. This structure provides flexibility by allowing the commitments of the engagement to be stated differently than how the project is managed and then linking them together.

WORK EFFORTs are related to the ENGAGEMENT ITEMs supertype to allow flexibility, although this relationship is more important in some items than others. WORK EFFORTs will be very applicable to CUSTOM ENGAGMENT ITEMs to track the work effort associated with delivery. The WORK EFFORT may or may not be applicable to the PROFESSIONAL PLACEMENT because the most important aspect of this is tracking ongoing hours for billing purposes. It may be useful for the professional services firm to understand what the professional is doing and with what type of project(s) he or she is involved. The PRODUCT ORDER ITEMs may or may not have WORK EFFORTs associated with them. For instance, the ordering of a standard GOOD may not have a work effort; however, the implementation of a standard service such as a data architecture review may involve tracking the associated work effort(s).

Engagement Rates

Engagements are a little different than other types of order items in that they are performed over a period of time and the rates are usually subject to change. Therefore the ENGAGEMENT RATE entity provides a mechanism for storing billing rate and the associated costs of the professionals as they may change over time. Even if the rate doesn't change, more than one rate may be associated with an engagement item. For instance, there may be a normal rate and an overtime rate. Various types of rates can be stored in the RATE TYPE entity such as "regular time," "overtime," "time and one half," "weekend hours," and so on. The UNIT OF MEASURE entity allows recording the rate by various measures such as "hourly" or "daily."

Placement versus Deliverables-Based Consulting

One may think that contract placements are quite different from engagements to buy services or deliverables. In the first case, the client is really contracting a specific individual, who may be brokered through an agency. In the second case, the client is engaging certain services or deliverables that the professional services firm is responsible for delivering regardless of the actual professional(s) assigned. One may conclude that the data structures are very different and should not be subtyped.

For example, in professional placement firms there is often a PROFESSIONAL PLACEMENT entity with no overall ENGAGEMENT entity because a placement is usually the only item. In deliverables-based consulting, there are often ENGAGEMENTs with several ENGAGEMENT ITEMS that may encompass many types of services. There could be different data model structures for each of these types of services. The advantage to modeling all of these types of services with a common structure is that a placement firm may easily expand into service and deliverable type engagements, and a service and deliverables type organization may expand into doing placements. The data model in Figure 7.7 accommodates both scenarios and simplifies both the data structures and processes necessary to support these functions. Invoicing functions may be greatly simplified with these structures, allowing the enterprise to bill for both types of services.

Engagement Example

Table 7.8 provides examples of professional service engagements for law, accounting, and consulting. Troublesome Distributors, Inc. has hired Whole Shebang Law Offices to help it defend against a lawsuit. Whole Shebang can record an engagement with three items for three different types of services, "pretrial lawsuit defense," "litigation," and "legal clerical support," each with a different agree-on rate. The rates may be stored in the ENGAGEMENT RATE table, allowing for several rates if the rates change over time or if there are different types of rates—for instance, premium rates for off-hours work.

Johnson Unconsolidated Inc. has hired Whole Shebang Accounting to prepare its corporate tax return. This is a deliverables-based engagement where Whole Shebang is charging a fixed price for a predetermined work product, namely a completed tax return. The second engagement involved hiring Whole Shebang Accounting for accounting services consisting of two items for audit

Table 7.8 Professional Services Engagements

ENGAGEMENT ROLE OF CLIENT	ENGAGEMENT ROLE OF PROFESSIONAL SERVICES ORGANIZATION	ENGAGEMENT	ENGAGEMENT ITEM SUBTYPE	ENGAGEMENT ITEM	RATE	UNIT OF MEASURE
Troublesome Distributors, Inc, 2000 Main Street	Whole Shebang Law Offices, 3500 Newton St.	Lawsuit defense	Service order item	Pretrial lawsuit defense	$180	Hour
			Service order item	Litigation	$200	Hour
			Service order item	Legal clerical support	$50	Hour
Johnson Unconsoli-dated Inc, 1200 E. Windsor Avenue	Whole Shebang Accounting, 300 Bore Street	Tax return	Deliverable order item	Tax return preparation	$3,000	
		Accounting services	Service order item	Auditing	$220	Hour
			Service order item	Bookkeeping	$60	Hour
Worldwide Universal Conglomerates, Inc., 1000 Hugh Street	Whole Shebang Consulting, 600 Utah Road	Data architecture engagement	Deliverable order item	Enterprise data model	$30,000	
			Service order item	Data architecture	$250	Hour
			Professional placement	John Datasmart	$150	Hour
			Good order item	Whole Shebang CASE tool license	$2,000	

services and bookkeeping services, each at different rates. The current rate is shown in the table; however, these rates could change over time.

The last example in the table involves Worldwide Universal Conglomerates, Inc.'s hiring Whole Shebang Consulting to provide a data architecture engagement involving several engagement items. The engagement involves providing a deliverable of an enterprise data model, using Universal Data Models, of course, to bring the price to $30,000. To supplement this deliverable, they have agreed to provide ongoing data architecture services at $250 per hour, which will be part-time reviews. Additionally, Worldwide Universal Conglomerates has contracted John Datasmart as a full-time contractor of Whole Shebang Consulting at $150 per hour. It has also purchased a "Whole Shebang CASE tool license" for $2,000 to help it maintain its data architecture information.

Many of the other data models from Volume 1 can be used for professional services organizations. Most of the order item data models (V1:4.1–4.8.) will apply with a substitution from order to engagement in entity names. The same types of order relationships to parties and contact mechanisms exist (V1:4.3–4.5). The requisition, request, and quote models from Volume 1 (V1:4.9–4.11) are all applicable as illustrated earlier in this chapter.

Professional Services Agreements

You may think we have already covered a type of professional services agreement in the last section, and perhaps technically that is true. The models in this book distinguish between commitments to deliver specific work products versus longer-term governing agreements. This section provides models for ongoing agreements or, in other words, contracts between parties.

Figure 7.8 shows a customized version of the agreement to orders diagram (V1:4.16)and agreement terms (V1:4.14). The subtypes of AGREEMENT now include PROFESSIONAL SERVICES AGREEMENT, which is broken down into CLIENT AGREEMENT and SUBCONTRACTOR AGREEMENT. The CLIENT AGREEMENT entity maintains the overall professional services arrangement between the professional services enterprise and a client. This may include terms for payment, non-disclosure terms, terms related to particular services, and any other terms that are important to establish in the overall relationship between a client and a professional services firm. The SUBCONTRACTOR AGREEMENT stores information about the commitment between the professional services firm and other organizations that subcontract through the enterprise or that subcontract the enterprise to work through them. The agreements pricing model (V1:4.15) will also be applicable for professional service enterprises.

Figure 7.8 shows that the orders to agreements data model (V1:4.16) is very applicable with slight modifications needed. The way most professional service enterprises work is that they set up a professional services agreement with the client and set up engagements that are governed by the agreed pricing and

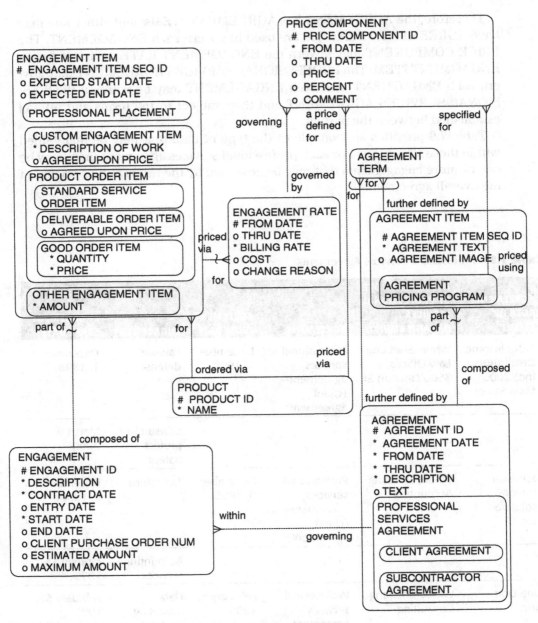

Figure 7.8 Professional service agreement to engagements.

other terms of the overall agreement. Subcontracting arrangements work the same way. There is an overall subcontractor agreement, and then there may be several engagements between the subcontractor and the firm subcontracting the services.

Therefore, the AGREEMENT has AGREEMENT ITEMs, and either one may have AGREEMENT TERMs that are used to govern each ENGAGEMENT. The PRICE COMPONENT may govern the ENGAGEMENT RATE, which is for an ENGAGMENT ITEM. The PROFESSIONAL SERVICES AGREEMENT may govern each ENGAGMENT, and each ENGAGMENT may be within a PROFESSIONAL SERVICES AGREEMENT and then subject to the terms and pricing established between the parties.

Table 7.9 provides an example of the type of data that may be maintained within these structures. For each professional services agreement there may be one or more engagements that may be governed by the terms and/or pricing of the overall agreement.

Table 7.9 Professional Services Agreements

AGREEMENT ROLE OF CLIENT	AGREEMENT ROLE OF PROFESSIONAL SERVICES ORGANIZATION	AGREEMENT	AGREEMENT FROM DATE	ENGAGEMENT	ENGAGEMENT START DATE
Troublesome Distributors, Inc., 2000 Main Street	Whole Shebang Law Offices, 3500 Newton St.	Professional services agreement— (client agreement)	December 1, 1998	Lawsuit defense	December 1, 1998
				Lawsuit to protect patent	March 9, 2000
Johnson Unconsolidated Inc.	Whole Shebang Accounting	Professional services agreement— (client agreement)	December 6, 1998	Tax return	December 6, 1998
				Accounting services	January 15, 1999
Joe Doit, Inc.	Whole Shebang Consulting	Professional services agreement (subcontractor agreement)	February 5, 1999	Data modeling contract	February 5, 1999
				Data warehouse engagement	June 3, 1998

Delivery

Enterprises that provide discrete items usually deliver them via shipments. Professional services enterprises usually deliver their products through time entries. This section will expand the structures in the work effort time tracking model (V1:6.6) to accommodate some of the details within professional services time and expense recording.

Depending on the types of services, these organizations may also have shipments of discrete items. For example, consulting firms may deliver electronic media, such as CD-ROMs, or paper reports to their clients. Accounting firms may deliver tax returns or related software. Law firms may deliver a variety of documentation. The generic shipment models (V1:5.1–5.8) can be used to track these discrete items.

Professional Services Entries

Figure 7.9 expands on the time entry model from the work effort time tracking model in Volume 1 (V1:6.6) and incorporates more details behind the various ways of delivery service. A SERVICE ENTRY provides a mechanism for recording TIME ENTRYs (the recording of time spent on an engagement), EXPENSE ENTRYs (the spending of monies on an engagement), MATERIALS USAGE (the usage of supplies, parts or other materials on the engagement), or DELIVERABLE TURNOVERs (which record the completion and turnover to the client of a deliverable that was committed to in the engagement). The SERVICE ENTRY TYPE allows for other possible types of entries. These SERVICE ENTRYs are important to track activity and progress as well as to be able to bill appropriately. The UNIT OF MEASURE records whether the time is "daily," "hourly," or another unit of measure. Each PROFESSIONAL may be assigned to one or more ENGAGEMENT ITEMs, and each ENGAGEMENT ITEM may have SERVICE ENTRYs that record time, expenses, material usage, and deliverable turnovers.

The TIME ENTRY records the **billing rate** for the professional, which will initially come from the ENGAGEMENT RATE entity; however, it may be overridden here. The TIME ENTRY **cost** represents the amount that the enterprise is paying to the professional. This is valid whether the professional is an employee of the enterprise or is subcontracting because it is important to determine the cost and the profit of the work being done. The time entry allows the rates to be measured by the UNIT OF MEASURE, which may be "hours" or "days" to record the **amount of time,** and this will depend on whether the enterprise bills in hours or days. An alternative database structure could be to record both the **number of hours** and **number of days** as optional attributes in the TIME ENTRY entity.

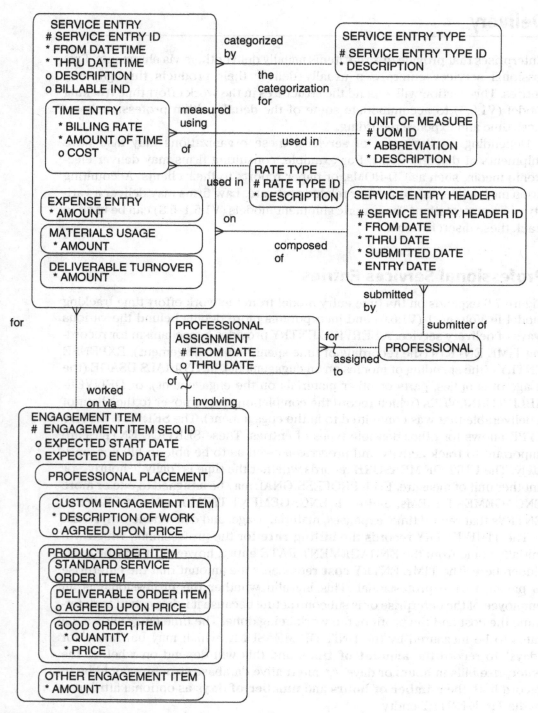

Figure 7.9 Professional services entries.

All of these types of service entries will have an associated **from datetime**, **thru datetime, description** to record the details behind the entry, and a **billable ind** (indicator) to record whether this transaction will be billed to the client.

There may be many service entries on a SERVICE ENTRY HEADER. Another name for this header in the real world may be a time sheet (this is what it is called in Volume 1, V1:6.6; however, the model in this section is providing for more than just time entries). SERVICE ENTRY HEADER is used as the entity name instead of timesheet because the word "timesheet" conveys the name of a mechanism (a piece of paper with time on it) that in the future may not be used. For instance, there may be many ways to enter service entries such as over the Internet or via a workstation. Additionally, there are things on a SERVICE ENTRY HEADER other than time such as materials used or the fact that a deliverable was turned over to a client. The SERVICE ENTRY HEADER is submitted by a PROFESSIONAL.

The model in Figure 7.9 also shows PROFESSIONALs may be on more than one ENGAGEMENT ITEM and vice versa. This many-to-many relationship is resolved by the associative entity PROFESSIONAL ASSIGNMENT. This allows many professionals to be assigned to an engagement item and one professional to be assigned to many engagement items. If service entries are submitted by professionals, why aren't SERVICE ENTRYs related to the PROFESSIONAL ASSIGNMENT? The reason is that the SERVICE ENTRY is already related to the professional via the SERVICE ENTRY HEADER entity.

Table 7.10 describes the type of data associated with SERVICE ENTRYs and SERVICE HEADERs. On January 16, 2000, Sol Isiter submitted a service entry header with three service entries that included two time entries and one expense entry. These service entries covered his time for two different tasks on the lawsuit assignment as well as copying charges incurred. Other SERVICE ENTRY attribute values that are not shown in the table include **amount of time** (in hours or days) and **billing rate** for the time entry and amount for the expense. The next set of service entries submitted as a service header by Sipi Hay included the deliverable turnover of a tax return plus applicable expenses. The last two rows shows that Joe Nowitall had two service entry header submissions, each with a single time entry for his data modeling engagement.

Work Efforts

How do work efforts fit into the model? Should SERVICE ENTRYs be related to ENGAGEMENT ITEMs or to WORK EFFORTs? This question depends on the nature of the professional service provider. Contract-oriented firms will track their professionals and service entries against the engagement item, and deliverable-oriented firms will track service entries against work efforts of their professionals.

Table 7.10 Professional Services Entries

PROFESSIONAL	SERVICE ENTRY HEADER SUBMITTED DATE	SERVICE ENTRY FROM AND THRU DATES	SERVICE ENTRY DESCRIPTION	SERVICE ENTRY TYPE	ENGAGEMENT ITEM
Sol Isiter	January 16, 2000	January 10–12, 2000	Meeting with client to discuss and prepare for case	Time entry	Lawsuit defense
		January 12–14, 2000	Researched similar cases to determine strategy	Time entry	Lawsuit defense
		January 10–14, 2000	Copying charges on similar cases	Expense entry	Lawsuit defense
Sipi Hay	February 6, 2000	January 13–14, 2000	Delivered tax return to client	Deliverable turnover	Tax return
		January 15–15, 2000	Incurred travel expense to visit client	Expense entry	Tax return
Joe Nowitall	January 16, 2000	January 1–16, 2000	Time entry on data model contract	Time entry	Data modeling contract
	February 6, 2000	January 17– February 6, 2000	Time entry on data model contract	Time entry	Data modeling contract

Figure 7.10 provides a model that handles both contract- and deliverable-oriented professional services firms. Generally, placement firms or temporary

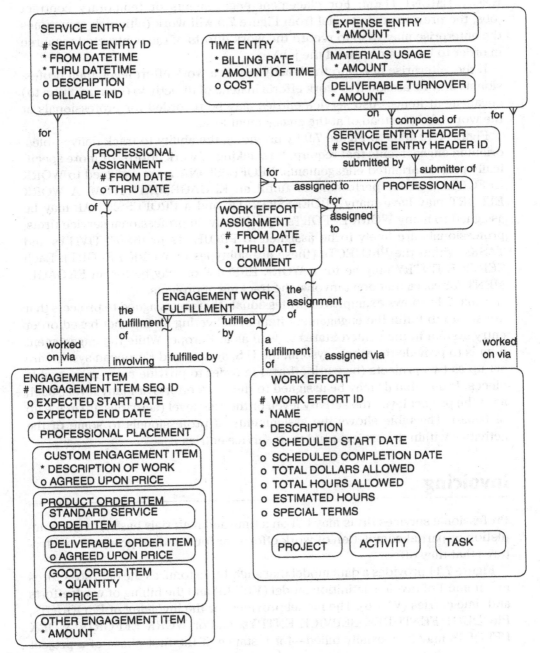

Figure 7.10 Engagements and work efforts.

employment agencies track PROFESSIONALS who are assigned to ENGAGE-MENT ITEMs, and their specific work efforts are not tracked; only their SER-VICE ENTRYs (time and expense entries) are recorded against each ENGAGEMENT ITEM. For placement engagements or temporary contract jobs, the previous data model from Figure 7.9 will work (although sometimes the enterprise may wish to record the work efforts of the contracted resource in order to know more about the job).

If the enterprise needs to track activities at a work effort level, then professionals may be assigned to work efforts instead of directly to (or in addition to) engagement items. Also service entries may be recorded for professionals at the work effort instead of at the engagement level.

Figure 7.10 adds to Figure 7.9 by providing the ability to track deliverables-oriented engagements that require the tracking of work efforts, or more specifically project-oriented engagements. PROFESSIONALs are assigned to WORK EFFORTs that are performed to fulfill an ENGAGEMENT ITEM. A WORK EFFORT may have many PROFESSIONALs, and a PROFESSIONAL may be assigned to many WORK EFFORTs. Specifically, in professional service firms, professionals are likely to be assigned to PROJECTs or the ACTIVITYs and TASKs within the PROJECTs (these are subtypes of WORK EFFORT). Each SERVICE ENTRY may be for a WORK EFFORT or may be for an ENGAGE-MENT for cases that don't involve the tracking of projects.

Table 7.11 shows examples of professionals that are assigned to projects that are set up to fulfill the engagement item of delivering an Internet-based order entry system in the United States as well as in Europe. While the engagement item is to provide the whole system, the U.S. system and European system are set up as two projects (or work efforts) in order to provide more manageable pieces. Professionals may be assigned to the work efforts at many levels, such as at the project level, the activity level, or the task level (activities are made up of tasks). The table shows the assignments of professionals to some of the activities within the projects and their service entries.

Invoicing

Professional services firms may bill on a time and materials basis, for the completion or partial completion of work efforts, or for standard products and features that they offer.

Figure 7.11 provides a data model that slightly customizes the data structures in Volume 1 of invoice definition model (V1:7.1a) and the billing of work efforts and time entries (V1:7.6). The model provides for the invoicing of PRODUCTs, PRODUCT FEATUREs, SERVICE ENTRYs, and/or WORK EFFORTs. WORK EFFORTs may be partially billed—for instance, if the first phase of a project

Table 7.11 Professional Service Entries

ENGAGE-MENT ITEM	WORK EFFORT (PROJECT)	WORK EFFORT (ACTIVITY)	PROFES-SIONAL ASSIGNED	SERVICE ENTRY HEADER SUBMITTED DATE	SERVICE ENTRY FROM AND THRU DATE	AMOUNT OF TIME
Deliver Internet-based order entry system	Deliver U.S.-based order entry system	Require-ments gathering	Joe Comps	February 6, 2000	January 10–16, 2000	39 hours
		Functional analysis			January 17– February 5, 2000	72 hours
		Data modeling	Jerry Damo	January 16, 2000	January 10–16, 2000	86 hours
	Deliver European-based order entry system	Require-ments gathering	Mika Puter	January 20, 2000	January 10–16, 2000	30 hours
					January 19, 2000	

was completed—and therefore the **percentage** field captures how much of the work effort (or project) is being billed. Several SERVICE ENTRYs or WORK EFFORTs may be combined into a single INVOICE ITEM.

Accounting and Human Resources Management

We have covered the changes to the data models for the people and organizations, product, orders, delivery, work efforts, and invoice subject data areas. The data models for accounting and human resources will work quite well in professional services although there may be some minor variations based on the needs of the enterprise.

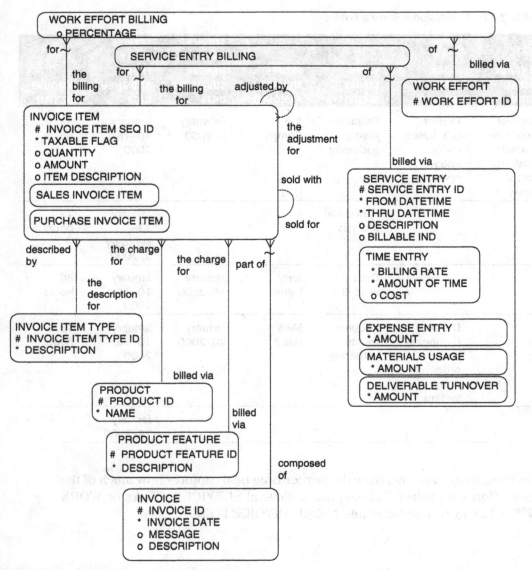

Figure 7.11 Professional service invoicing.

Star Schema for Professional Services

One of the key metrics in professional services is measuring how much time was billed, by whom, for whom, on what project, and when.

Figure 7.12 provides a star schema allowing the analysis of time in order to measure the productivity and profitability of professionals as well as to analyze from where the greatest source of revenues and profits are coming.

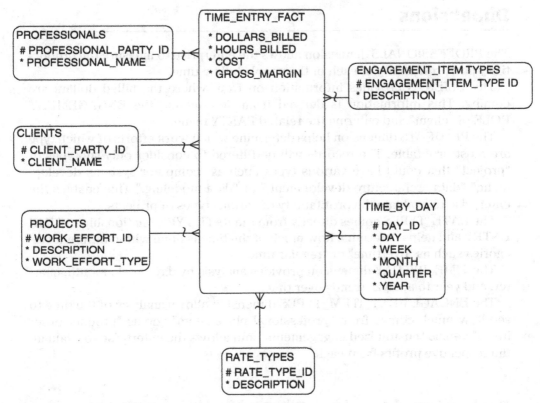

Figure 7.12   Professional service time entry star schema.

Time Entry Fact

The TIME_ENTRY_FACT provides measures that can be derived from data in the subtype TIME ENTRY, a subtype of the SERVICE ENTRY entity. The **dollars_billed** is derived by multiplying the **billing rate** times the **amount of time** attributes of the TIME ENTRY entity. The **hours_billed** is derived by summarizing the **amount of time** and converting any non-hourly unit of measure using the UNIT OF MEASURE relationship to TIME ENTRY as well as the UNIT OF TIME CONVERSION entity (see Figure V1:3.4). The **cost** is the amount that was paid to the professional. The **gross_margin** is the calculation of the TIME ENTRY cost divided by the **dollars_billed**. These measures provide valuable metrics to analyze profitability and revenues of the enterprise.

Dimensions

The PROFESSIONALS dimension allows the enterprise to measure the productivity and profitability of each of the people billing time.

The CLIENTS provides information on from where the billed dollars are coming. This information is derived from determining the ENGAGEMENT ROLE of "client" and entering the related PARTY name.

The PROJECTS dimension helps determine which work efforts of which type are most profitable. The records will be filtered to consider only subtypes of "project" that could have various types such as "computer systems development," "data architecture development," or "data modeling." This enables the enterprise to evaluate the profitability of various types of projects.

The RATE_TYPES comes directly from the RATE TYPE relationship to TIME ENTRY and helps determine how much of the time is done within different categories such as "overtime" or "regular time."

The TIME_BY_DAY dimension provides analysis by day, week, month, quarter, and year to analyze trends over time.

The ENGAGEMENT_ITEM_TYPES dimension allows analysis of the time to see how much comes from "professional placements" versus "product order items" versus "customized engagements" and allows the enterprise to evaluate the respective profits from each.

Professional Services Summary

While many of the data models from Volume 1 apply to professional services, the data models within this chapter focused on the unique data model constructs needed within professional services. The most unique aspect of professional service firms is that their focus is on providing time from their professionals or delivering an intangible effort as opposed to selling a specific tangible item.

Some data model modifications were provided to show how to modify some of the constructs from Volume 1 to suit professional services companies. Appropriate party relationships were subtyped, product data structures were tailored, the requirements were expanded to show the needed deliverables and skills, the order data structures were renamed to engagements, the delivery model was changed to accommodate all types of service entries, such as time entries, expense entries, materials usage, and deliverable turnovers, work efforts were properly related to engagements and service entries, and the invoice models provided flexible structures to bill for service entries, work efforts, and products. The chapter also provided a star schema to analyze hours and dollar amounts.

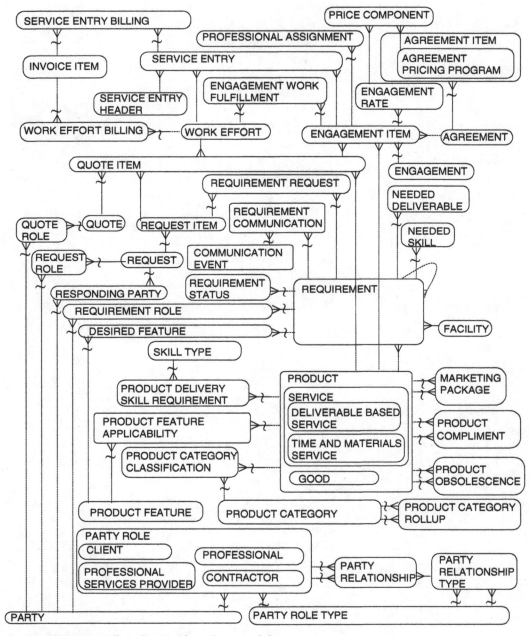

Figure 7.13 Overall professional services model.

Figure 7.13 provides an overall model of the professional service models in this chapter.

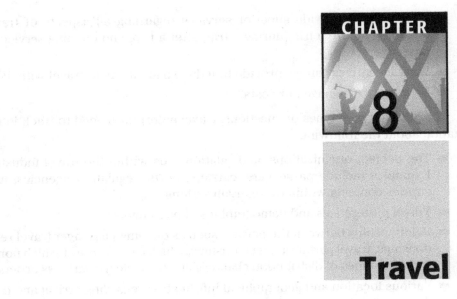

CHAPTER 8

Travel

Travel organizations include travel agencies, airlines, train stations, bus depots, cruise lines, and virtually all enterprises whose goal is to transport individuals from one place to another. Additionally, it includes hotels, car rental agencies, and other enterprises that are involved in accommodating travelers. While there may be other travel-related organizations rendering such services as emergency road service, travel discounts, travel literature, travel accessories, and selling transportation vehicles, this chapter will focus on the information needs associated with the transportation of passengers and accommodation of travelers who need rooms and vehicles. Usually, while these organizations are transporting their passengers, they may also provide other things, such as food, baggage service, entertainment, and other amenities. We will include these and any other aspects of the travel experience as part of the crucial information needs of these travel organizations. While it is common to think of each type of travel organization as having completely different information needs, there are significant common data structures within most travel organizations.

Travel organizations are concerned with issues such as the following:

■ How can we improve our relationships with each traveler?

■ How can we make travel arrangements most convenient?

■ What are the best ways to provide pleasurable travel experiences?

- How can we provide superior services regarding all aspects of travel including before a trip, during a trip, after a trip, and ongoing service to passengers?
- What incentives can we provide to induce passengers to travel with us?
- How can we manage our costs?

To answer these types of questions, travel enterprises need to track information about the following:

- The people, organizations, and relationships within the travel industry. Examples include passengers, carriers, ports, regulatory agencies, and various contacts within these organizations.
- Travel preferences and demographics of passengers.
- Relationships between the parties, such as ongoing passenger travel relationships, travel partnering relationships, which carriers are at which ports, and what types of distribution channels are available for various carriers.
- Various location and geographical information regarding arrival and destination points, routes, service area, target marketing areas, and so on.
- The types of product offerings available from the enterprise being modeled as well as other carriers' offerings.
- The types of agreements that exist between various parties such as corporate agreements and passenger travel contracts.
- Pretravel arrangements, such as reservations, cancellations, and payment.
- Information about the travel experience, such as the various contacts made with the passenger and the service level associated with each aspect of the travel delivery.
- Accumulation of credit on various travel clubs or accounts.
- Other supporting information, such as accounting information to create financial statements and human resource information to track personnel.

Volume 1 provides a starting point to model the needs of travel organizations. For instance, it addresses these issues:

- Data models for parties, roles, and their relationships.
- Product data model constructs that can be used as a starting point for modeling travel product offerings.
- Agreement data model constructs that are the basis for corporate travel agreements.
- Order data structures that could form the basis for reservations. A reservation or a booking could be thought of as an order item. Of course, we will change the terminology while gaining some insight from the Volume 1 data structures.

- Delivery (shipment) data model structures can be used to give us some insight into the delivery of travel-related services. There will be a great degree of modification to these structures because we are very interested in recording information about the complete travel experience. Because we are transporting and accommodating people, there is a lot more information to track about these complex entities than simply delivering a package (packages don't need the same type of care and feeding).

- Travel account information such as accumulated points within promotional travel programs that may be redeemable for free or discounted travel.

- Accounting, budgeting and human resource models to manage finances and people.

Key aspects of travel that are not addressed in Volume 1 include the following:

- The unique aspects of passenger travel and accommodation offerings. Travel organizations don't primarily sell specific instances of products; they sell by availability of their offerings.

- Data structures to handle pretravel arrangements such as reservations, cancellations, and payments (although some of the generic payment structures from Volume 1 are used). Most travel organizations require payment prior to traveling, and that is why the invoicing structures will generally not be used except on the supply-chain side of the enterprise.

- Data structures to accommodate the information needs associated with the travel experience.

- Travel program information, such as award programs in which travelers can accumulate points.

Table 8.1 shows which models can be used directly from Volume 1, which models need to be modified, which models are not used,, and which new models are required. This chapter describes the models from Volume 1 that need significant modifications, plus the new industry models. (Minor modifications are described in the text.)

People and Organizations in Travel

At the heart of the travel business are the passengers and the other people and organizations helping passengers get where they want to go. As with our other chapters, our common data models for people, organizations, roles, and relationships can be used within the travel industry. The only changes needed are to subtype the PARTY ROLE and PARTY RELATIONSHIP entities. Therefore, all the models from Volume 1, Chapter 2 will apply with the exception of V1:2.5 and V1:2.6a, which will be modified to add subtypes for the travel industry. An

Table 8.1 Volume 1 and Volume 2 Data Models for Travel

SUBJECT DATA AREA	USE THESE VOLUME 1 MODELS DIRECTLY	MODIFY THESE VOLUME 1 MODELS (AS DESCRIBED IN VOLUME 2)	DO NOT USE THESE VOLUME 1 MODELS	ADD THESE VOLUME 2 MODELS
People and organizations	Party models, V1:2.1–2.14, Except V1:2.5 and V1:2.6a	Party relationship, V1:2.65 and V1:2.6a (need to add health care PARTY ROLES and PARTY RELATIONSHIP subtypes for travel enterprises)		Travel preferences, V2:8.2
Product	Product models, V1:3.1–3.11			Travel product, V2:8.3
Order		Standard order models, V1:4.1–4.8 for supply side processing, Requisition, request, quote, V1:4.9–4.11, Agreement models, V1:4.12–4.16 (subtype agreements)		Travel reservation V2:8.4, Ticketing, V2:8.5, Travel agreements, V2:8.6, Pricing of agreements and products, V2:8.7
Delivery	Shipment models, V1:5.1–5.8 for supply deliveries			Travel experience, V2:8.8
Work effort	Work effort, V1:6.1–6.11 for internal projects			
Invoicing		Invoice models, V1:7.1–7.10		
Accounting	All models, V1:8.1–8.12			
Human resources	All models, V1:9.1–9.14			
Travel program and travel account				Travel programs and travel accounts, V2:8.9
Travel product data warehouse designs				Passenger transportation offering star schema, V2:8.10, Non-transportation travel product star schema V2:8.11

additional model is shown to reflect a unique and important information requirement within the travel industry—travel preferences.

Figure 8.1 illustrates examples of person roles, organization roles, and party relationships within travel. There are many standard roles as well as roles and relationships specific to travel.

Person Roles

The standard PERSON ROLEs that can be reused in travel are PROSPECT, CONTACT, EMPLOYEE, and DEPENDENT. A travel organization may need to record various prospective travelers, perhaps by researching people who travel via other carriers. If the enterprise markets to organizations, it may decide to alternatively maintain PROSPECT as a subtype of PARTY ROLE. The enterprise may also record contacts within corporate entities, suppliers, or partner accounts. They will need to keep information about their employees, thus the subtype EMPLOYEE. DEPENDENTs are people who are reliant on other people for financial support and are usually within the same family. Spouses and/or children are examples of dependents. Quite often it is important to track the dependents of the passengers to analyze the demographics of families who are traveling.

PERSON ROLEs specific to travel enterprises include INDIVIDUAL CUSTOMER, TRAVELER, INDIVIDUAL PAYER, TRAVEL ACCOUNT MEMBER, TRAVEL STAFF, and OPERATIONS CREW. The individual customer is a person that either travels, pays for travel, or has a travel account. Therefore, the INDIVIDUAL CUSTOMER is subtyped into PASSENGER, INDIVIDUAL PAYER, and TRAVEL ACCOUNT MEMBER. The TRAVELER is an individual who is planning on taking a trip or has taken trips with the enterprise being modeled. The INDIVIDUAL PAYER is a person who is responsible for paying for the travel. The TRAVEL ACCOUNT MEMBER is an individual who has an account with a travel provider. This account could be used to accumulate award points toward free or discounted travel. The TRAVEL STAFF are the people who are coordinating, arranging, and working to provide the travel experience to the passengers. The OPERATIONS CREW are the people who set up the facilities required for travel. For instance, for airline carriers, they may be the people who maintain the aircraft and facilities.

Organization Roles

Standard organization roles include INTERNAL ORGANIZATION, SUPPLIER, HOUSEHOLD, and ORGANIZATION CUSTOMER. Travel organizations will often have many internal organizations, suppliers from which they get their parts or travel amenities, and households that represent groups of people that may travel or have traveled. Travel organizations frequently establish relationships with corporations and other organizations in order to become

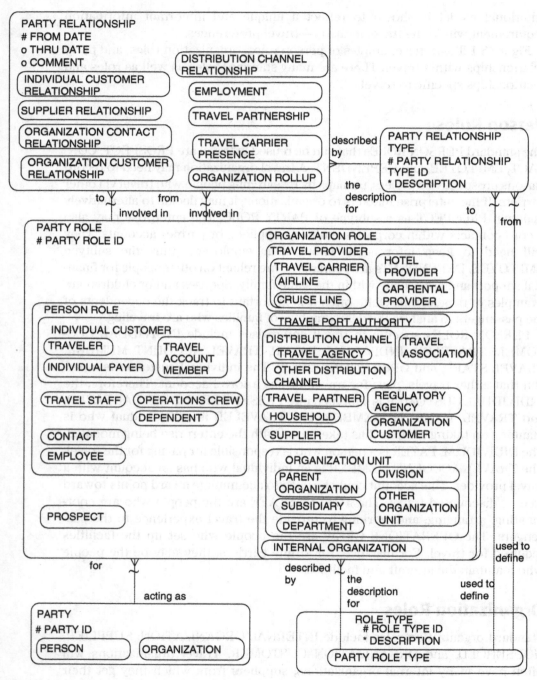

Figure 8.1 Travel party roles and relationships.

their preferred means of travel, and these would be considered organization customers.

Specific organization roles in the travel industry are TRAVEL PROVIDER, TRAVEL PORT AUTHORITY, DISTRIBUTION CHANNEL, TRAVEL PARTNER, TRAVEL ASSOCIATION, and REGULATORY AGENCY. TRAVEL PROVIDERs provide transportation facilities or travel accommodations for travelers. Subtypes of TRAVEL PROVIDER include TRAVEL CARRIERs, HOTEL PROVIDERs, and CAR RENTAL PROVIDERs. TRAVEL CARRIERs represent organizations that provide travel to the passengers. Types of carriers include AIRLINEs and CRUISE LINEs, just to illustrate a couple of examples; however, there are many more such as bus companies, train organizations, and any other type of organization that provides transit to travelers. HOTEL PROVIDERs provide rooms to travelers, and CAR RENTAL PROVIDERs offer vehicles. TRAVEL PORT AUTHORITY represents the organization that manages the travel facilities on which embarkation and disembarkation occurs. DISTRIBUTION CHANNELS are the organizations that sell passenger travel tickets. The most common type of distribution channel for travel is a TRAVEL AGENCY.

Party Relationships

ORGANIZATION CONTACT RELATIONSHIP, EMPLOYMENT, ORGANIZATION STRUCTURE, and SUPPLIER RELATIONSHIP are some of the generic party relationship entities used in the travel business.

Specific PARTY RELATIONSHIPs include INDIVIDUAL CUSTOMER RELATIONSHIP, ORGANIZATION CUSTOMER RELATIONSHIP, DISTRIBUTION CHANNEL RELATIONSHIP, and TRAVEL PARTNERSHIP. INDIVIDUAL CUSTOMER RELATIONSHIP represents the information about the relationship between INDIVIDUAL CUSTOMERs and one or more INTERNAL ORGANIZATIONs. The individual relationship could be for passengers, payers, or travel account members. ORGANIZATION CUSTOMER RELATIONSHIP represents information about the relationship that exists between ORGANIZATION CUSTOMERs and the INTERNAL ORGANIZATIONs of the enterprise. The DISTRIBUTION CHANNEL RELATIONSHIP represents relationships from the enterprise's INTERNAL ORGANIZATION to the various DISTRIBUTION CHANNELs that could apply. TRAVEL PARTNERSHIP represents relationships established between the enterprise's INTERNAL ORGANIZATION and TRAVEL PARTNERS that may work in cooperation with the enterprise in strategic alliances.

As an alternative, more specific data model, detailed relationships can be shown in the data model to record which types of party relationships relate to which types of party roles.

Table 8.2 shows examples of data for travel persons, organizations, roles, and relationships. Our case example for this chapter is a full-service travel enterprise called "Travel Conglomeration, Inc." This enterprise is the parent company for many subsidiary organizations that provide various means of travel. They provide travel arrangements via airlines, boats, trains, and cars. They also provide hotels, rental cars, meals in transit, and many amenities to make the travel experience enjoyable.

Tables 8.2, 8.3, and 8.4 provide examples of person roles, organization roles, and party relationships within this travel enterprise.

Table 8.3 shows that Harry Transit is an individual customer and is a traveler, an individual payer, and a travel account member. Jerry Banner is listed as an individual customer but only a traveler. This means that he does not have a travel account and has not paid for tickets. One reason for this is that he may travel with "Travel Conglomerates" only through his employer, who pays his way. Horace Bruno is an individual customer who does not travel himself, but he pays for other people's tickets. Joe Dreamer is a prospect who has made many travel inquiries, has surfed Travel Conglomerate's Web site, but has never traveled with them. Alice Pleasant is playing the role of a travel staff member, more specifically, a flight attendant.

Some of the roles have subroles. For example, Alice Pleasant is a travel staff member and specifically a flight attendant. Joe Fixit is part of the operations crew, and within that role he plays the role of mechanic.

Table 8.3 illustrates possible roles for organizations within "Travel Conglomerates." Travel Conglomerates has several organizations with different roles—the parent company, an airline carrier, a cruise line, a train company, and a bus company. The model supports storing other travel carriers such as "Everywhere Airlines," a competitive airlines company. Travel Conglomerates also

Table 8.2 Travel Person Roles

PARTY	PERSON ROLE
Harry Transit	Individual customer
Harry Transit	Traveler
Harry Transit	Individual payer
Harry Transit	Travel account member
Jerry Banner	Individual customer
Jerry Banner	Traveler
Horace Bruno	Individual customer
Horace Bruno	Individual payer
Joe Dreamer	Prospect
Alice Pleasant	Travel staff—flight attendant
Joe Fixit	Operations crew—mechanic

Table 8.3 Travel Organization Roles

PARTY	ORGANIZATION ROLE
Travel Conglomerates	Travel provider
Travel Conglomerates Airlines	Travel Carrier—airline
Travel Conglomerates Cruise Lines	Travel Carrier—cruise lines
Travel Conglomerates Train	Travel Carrier—train company
Travel Conglomerates Bus	Travel Carrier—bus company
Everywhere Airlines	Travel Carrier—airline (competitive)
Travel Conglomerates Hotel	Hotel provider
Travel Conglomerates Car Rentals	Car rental provider
Nice'n'fun Travel Agency	Travel agency
Nowhere International Airport	Travel port authority
Discount Travel Club	Travel partner
Travel Info Association	Travel association
Bigger Megalopolis	Organization customer

has a hotel, "Travel Conglomerates Hotel," and a car rental company, "Travel Conglomerates Car Rentals." The data model supports storing distribution channels such as "Nice'n'fun Travel Agency." "Nowhere International Airport" is the organization that runs this airport facility. While an airport is a facility it also has an associated organization about which there is a need to store information. There is a need to store information about travel partners like "Discount Travel Club" with whom "Travel Conglomerates" may have joint marketing arrangements. "Travel Info Association" is an association that travel related companies may join to get up-to-date information on trends within travel. An example of one of the organization customers is "Bigger Megalopolis," a large manufacturer that has a special corporate customer relationship.

Table 8.4 shows examples of typical relationships within the travel industry. The first row shows that "Travel Conglomerates Airlines" is a subsidiary of "Travel Conglomerates." Table 8.2 depicts "Harry Transit" as an individual customer, and Table 8.4 shows that his relationship is with the Cruise lines. "Bigger Megalopolis" has a corporate customer relationship with the entire "Travel Conglomerates" enterprise. "Discount Travel Club" and "Travel Conglomerates" have an ongoing travel partnership relationship. The last row shows that "Travel Conglomerates" has a presence at "Nowhere International Airport." This relationship could be further described with a more detailed type of "major hub" if that best described the relationship.

Table 8.4 Travel Party Relationships

PARTY ROLE 1	PARTY 1	PARTY ROLE 2	PARTY 2	PARTY RELATIONSHIP TYPE
Subsidiary	Travel Conglomerates Airlines	Parent Organization	Travel Conglomerates	Organization roll-up
Individual customer	Harry Transit	Carrier— cruise lines	Travel Conglomerates Cruise Lines	Individual customer relationship
Organization customer	Bigger Megalopolis	Travel provider	Travel Conglomerates	Corporate customer relationship
Travel partner	Discount Travel Club	Travel provider	Travel Conglomerates	Travel partnership
Travel Port— airport	Nowhere International Airport	Travel Carrier— airlines	Travel Conglomerates Airlines	Travel Carrier presence

Travel Preferences

The data model in Figure 8.1 provides most of the modifications necessary to capture the information requirements of the people, organizations, and relationships in the travel industry. There is one more requirement that is important in capturing travel related information—namely, travel preference information.

Figure 8.2 provides a data model suitable for capturing travel preference information. Although this data model is simple, it is very important. In order to serve travelers properly, it is important to capture their preferences and update them as time goes by. In the model, each PARTY may have one or more TRAVEL PREFERENCEs that could be linked to various entities, such as TRAVEL PREFERENCE TYPE, ACCOMMODATION CLASS, TRAVEL PRODUCT, PRODUCT CATEGORY, or FACILITY. This accommodates capturing who has what preferences over time, thus allowing whoever is booking a reservation to request accommodations suitable for the traveler.

PARTY TRAVEL PREFERENCEs may be for individuals or for organizations—for example, corporations that express preferences such as coach seating. The TRAVEL PREFERENCE TYPE allows the specification of traveler desires such as the type of seating, type of meal desired, if non-smoking is needed, the type of bed, type of car, and so on. The ACCOMMODATION CLASS allows the specification of how nice the accommodation is such as "first class," "business class," "coach," or "executive suite (for hotels)." The PRODUCT CATEGORY entity would define the type of travel offering such as "airline flight," "bus ticket," "hotel room," or "car rental" to express what means of travel a

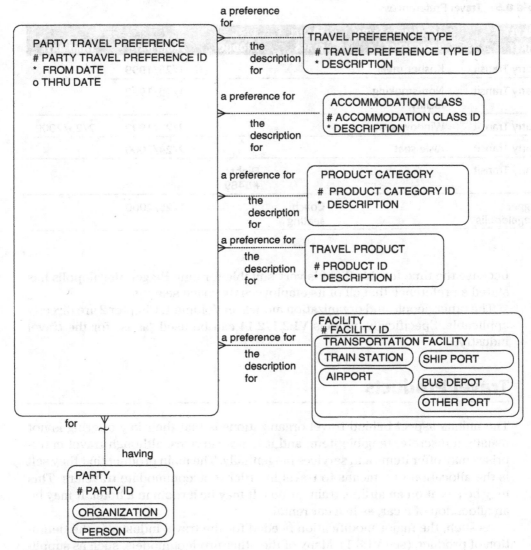

Figure 8.2 Travel preferences.

traveler may prefer. A traveler may have a preference for a specific travel product that leaves from one place to another at a certain time and has a name—for example, flight 5489.

Table 8.5 shows examples of the type of information that would be stored within these data structures. The table shows that Harry Transit has a preference for kosher meals and for non-smoking facilities (this may apply to hotels, rental cars, or any other accommodation). He also had a preference for window seats but then changed that on February 24, 2000 to an aisle seat preference. He specifically likes to travel on Flight 5489 when he has trips that go to LaGuardia

Table 8.5 Travel Preferences

TRAVEL PARTY	ACCOMMODATION PREFERENCE	TRAVEL CLASS	PRODUCT	FROM DATE	THRU DATE
Harry Transit	Kosher meal			1/25/1999	
Harry Transit	Non-smoking facility			1/25/1999	
Harry Transit	Window seat			2/23/1999	2/23/2000
Harry Transit	Aisle seat			2/24/2000	
Harry Transit			Flight #5489		
Bigger Megalopolis		Coach seating		1/25/2000	

because the time for this flight is very suitable for him. Bigger Megalopolis has stated a preference that all of its employees fly coach seating.

The other people and organization models in Volume 1, Chapter 2 are directly applicable. Specifically, models V1:2.1–2.14 can be used "as is" for the travel industry.

Travel Products

The unique aspect behind travel organizations is that their key offering is not usually a discrete, tangible item, and it is not services, although travel enterprises may offer items and services tangentially. The main product that they sell is the allocation of a means to travel in order to accommodate travelers. This may be a seat on an airline, train, or bus. It may be a room in a hotel. It may be an allocation of a car, as in a car rental.

As such, the major modification needed for the travel industry is the definition of product, (see V1:3.1). Many of the other product models, such as suppliers and manufacturers of products (V1:3.2), product pricing (V1:3.7), product costing (V1:3.8), and product associations (V1:3.9a and V1:3.9b), will apply to the travel industry. Inventory item storage (V1:3.6) is not a mainstream information requirement for most travel enterprises although the data structures can be useful to track inventory needed to maintain their facilities.

Product Definition

Figure 8.3 provides a travel product data model that will replace the product definition model from Volume 1 for travel enterprises. The TRAVEL PRODUCT

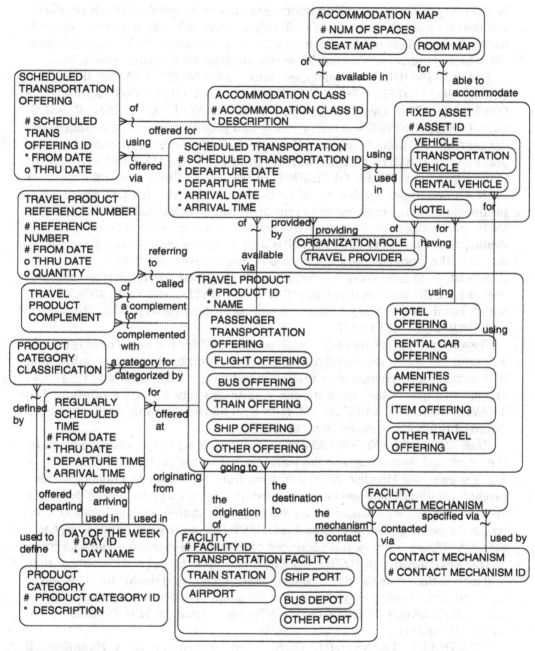

Figure 8.3   Travel products.

is a supertype entity capturing information about all relevant travel products, whether they are the enterprise's offerings, a partner's offerings, or a competitor's offerings. This model will be used in conjunction with Volume 1, Figure 3.5, which records each organization that supplies their various products.

TRAVEL PRODUCT is subtyped into PASSENGER TRANSPORTATION OFFERING, HOTEL OFFERING, RENTAL CAR OFFERING, AMENITIES OFFERING, ITEM OFFERING, and OTHER TRAVEL OFFERING. PASSENGER TRAVEL OFFERINGs are products that provide a means of getting a passenger from one point to another. Subtypes indicate the mode of transportation and include FLIGHT OFFERING, BUS OFFERING, TRAIN OFFERING, SHIP OFFERING, and OTHER OFFERING. HOTEL OFFERING stores the types of hotel accommodations that could be booked. RENTAL CAR OFFERINGs are products that allow passengers to rent their own vehicles. AMENITIES OFFERINGs are products that enhance the travel experience such as meals, videos, drinks, or headsets. ITEM OFFERINGs are tangible items that travel companies may sell like model airplanes, gift shop items, and souvenir items.

As with most industries, products may be classified into more than one category, hence the intersection entity PRODUCT CATEGORY CLASSIFICATION, which resolves the many-to-many relationship between TRAVEL PRODUCT and PRODUCT CATEGORY.

Travel products are identified with **product ID** for the key. There is usually a number by which the travel offering is referenced by the general public, and that number may change over time. For instance, a flight number "1234" may change to flight "9485" even though it is technically the same offering. The TRAVEL PRODUCT REFERENCE NUMBER allows the same product to have different reference numbers over time.

PASSENGER TRANSPORTATION OFFERING is a product that is defined by the origin and destination and the travel times that the product is being offered. For instance, the Monday, 10:30 a.m. train from New York to Philadelphia is a product offering. There are two relationships to FACILITY to denote the origin and destination, which may be an airport, train station, or any location from which the journey starts and ends. Each FACILITY may have multiple CONTACT MECHANISMs such as postal addresses, telephone numbers, or email addresses.

The REGULARLY SCHEDULED TIME provides the normal departure time and arrival time plus the day of the week for arrival and departure. The departure and arrival times may change for the same product; hence, there may be many REGULARLY SCHEDULED TIMEs for a PASSENGER TRANSPORTATION OFFERING.

SCHEDULED TRANSPORTATION is an occurrence of a PASSENGER TRANSPORTATION OFFERING. The Monday 10:30 a.m. train from New York to Philadelphia will be scheduled several times on specific dates. The SCHEDULED TRANSPORTATION has a "departure date," "departure time," "arrival date," and "arrival time" as these could vary slightly from the regularly scheduled times. Each SCHEDULED TRANSPORTATION must be using a TRANS-PORTATION VEHICLE, which is the physical facility that offers the travel. (If the enterprise is interested in tracking all the vehicle(s) that may have been scheduled over time for the same SCHEDULED TRANSPORTATION, then a many-to-many relationship is needed.)

Each TRANSPORTATION VEHICLE has an ACCOMMODATION MAP that specifies how many spaces are available for each class. This entity may specify that the vehicle accommodates 100 seats for ACCOMMODATION CLASS "coach" and 12 seats for ACCOMMODATION CLASS "first class." Similarly, it may specify that a hotel has 50 rooms of ACCOMMODATION CLASS "standard room" and 20 rooms of ACCOMMODATION CLASS "luxury suite."

A SCHEDULED TRANSPORTATION may be offered via several SCHED-ULED TRANSPORTATION OFFERINGs, such as several seats that may be available within certain ACCOMMODATION CLASSES on a SCHEDULED TRANSPORTATION. This entity maintains what is available to be offered on a SCHEDULED TRANSPORTATION. For instance, there may be a quantity of twenty first class seats and two-hundred coach class seats on a particular flight. These numbers could be different from the accommodation seats or rooms within an accommodation map, because travel providers will often make a decision to overbook. The from date and thru date allow the enterprise to track the changes in offerings over time.

Certain products may be for the purposes of complementing other products. For instance, AMENITIES OFFERINGs will often complement certain PAS-SENGER TRANSPORTATION OFFERINGs. HOTEL OFFERINGs may be packaged together with PASSENGER TRANSPORTATION OFFERINGs, such as in a vacation cruise. The TRAVEL PRODUCT COMPLEMENT allows products to be associated with other products in order to handle this requirement.

HOTEL OFFERINGs and RENTAL CAR OFFERINGs have different characteristics than PASSENGER TRAVEL OFFERINGs, and therefore their relationships are different. HOTEL OFFERINGs are associated with specific HOTELs, which are a type of FIXED ASSET. RENTAL CAR OFFERINGs are associated with specific RENTAL VEHICLEs.

The data model also shows which TRAVEL PROVIDER offers which SCHED-ULED TRANSPORTATION as well as which TRAVEL PROVIDER owns which FIXED ASSETs.

Table 8.6 lists a few examples of travel product offerings available within "Travel Conglomerates." One offering, "Flight #5489," is its flight offering between "Denver International Airport" and "La Guardia Airport" from 10:30 a.m. to 4:30 p.m. This offering may be scheduled many times on specific dates with specific vehicles. Table 8.6 shows two instances of SCHEDULED TRANS-PORTATION for this PASSENGER TRAVEL OFFERING. One offering is for October 2, 2000, using the "Ultimate Jet 939 ID# 2545" and one is for October 4, 2000, using the "Ultimate Jet 390 ID# 2398." A similar example is given for a bus

Table 8.6 Passenger Transportation Offerings

TRAVEL OFFERING SUBTYPE	REFERENCE #	ORIGIN ADDRESS	DESTINATION ADDRESS	DEPARTURE TIME	ARRIVAL TIME	SCHEDULED DATE	TRANSPORTATION VEHICLE
Flight offering	Flight #5489	Denver International Airport	La Guardia Airport	10:30 a.m.	4:30 p.m.	10/2/2000	Ultimate Jet 939 ID# 2545
						10/4/2000	Ultimate Jet 390 ID# 2398
Bus offering	Bus trip #4895	Main St. bus terminal	Smith St. bus terminal	4:00 p.m.	7:00 p.m.	11/5/2000	Bus ID #29093
						11/8/2000	Bus ID #29093

Table 8.7   Non-Transportation Travel Products

TRAVEL OFFERING SUBTYPE	DESCRIPTION	HOTEL	RENTAL VEHICLE
Hotel offering	Luxury suite	Budget Hotel	
	Luxury suite	Family Suites Hotel	
Rental Car Offering	Full-sized vehicle		Cadillac vehicle #234
	Mid-sized vehicle		Millenia vehicle #347
	Compact vehicle		Civic vehicle #3499
Amenities Offering	Mixed drink		
	Headset rental		
Item Offering	Souvenir playing cards		
	Model airplane		

offering, bus trip #4895, with the same bus offering having several specific times it is being run.

Table 8.7 shows examples of other travel offerings. These offerings may be from "Travel Conglomerates" or from other organizations. The first two rows show a hotel offering of "luxury suite," which is available in Budget Hotel and Family Suites Hotel. The offerings of "full-sized vehicle," "mid-sized vehicle," and "compact vehicle" are RENTAL CAR OFFERINGs. The specific vehicles "Cadillac Vehicle #234," "Millenia Vehicle #347," and "Civic Vehicle #3499" are examples of RENTAL VEHICLEs that are used to fulfill these offerings. "Mixed drink" and "headset" are examples of AMENITIES OFFERINGs. "Souvenir playing cards" and "model airplane" are examples of ITEM OFFERINGS.

Travel Orders (Reservations)

An order is a commitment to buy particular goods or services. Travel enterprises typically take orders in the form of travel reservations. Similar to the order structure, a reservation may have several items. Each item of the reservation may be for a different passenger or for a different travel offering. They all may have been placed by the same party on the same date, which makes it the same reservation.

Travel enterprises don't view reservations as having items because there is usually only one big denormalized reservation record in their reservation system. Travel reservation systems are a prime example of the need to provide very fast access to information, and therefore they need to keep their information in a very denormalized, quickly accessible structure. However, because our goal is to understand the information requirements, the data models will show the reservation items that are very similar in structure to order items.

The other unique aspect of travel is that payment is usually required up-front at the time or shortly after the reservation is made and before the trip occurs. Therefore, models for ticketing and payments will be included in this section.

Order Models

An order in the travel industry is a reservation. Therefore, the data models presented will use similar structures from Volume 1 and use the term "reservation" instead of "order."

Figure 8.4 is a data model that stores information about travel reservations. RESERVATION stores information about the header record of the travel reservation. There could be many parties associated with a reservation that are recorded in the RESERVATION ROLE that links the various PARTYs and their ROLE TYPEs to the reservation. RESERVATIONs may have many RESERVATION ITEMs that record reservations for the various travelers and products in the reservation. For each item there may be many TRAVELERs on the item, as in the case of many travelers sharing a hotel room, seat, or a car rented to many travelers.

The RESERVATION ITEM may be for a HOTEL OFFERING, CAR RENTAL OFFERING, or a SCHEDULED TRANSPORTATION OFFERING. If it is for a HOTEL OFFERING, then the actual HOTEL is reserved also. If the reservation is for a CAR RENTAL OFFERING, then the address of the CAR RENTAL FACILITY where the car will be picked up must be specified.

Because TRANSPORTATION VEHICLES and HOTELS have ACCOMMODATION MAPs (from Figure 8.3) to show what can be booked, each RESERVATION ITEM may be reserving an ACCOMMODATION SPOT, which would reserve a specific SEAT NUMBER or ROOM NUMBER, which would correspond to a spot that is available within the ACCOMMODATION MAP for that type of accommodation.

The RESERVED TRAVELER handles the case of more than TRAVELER associated with a RESERVATION ITEM. There are situations in which babies or young children may be included in the same reservation item. An example of this is when a "lap child" may be added to an airline reservation and is required to sit in the same seat as the main traveler. Other examples are when more than one traveler reserves a room or rents a car.

While travelers have preferences defined in Figure 8.2 (the travel preferences model), they may override their preferences for the reservation that is stored in the RESERVATION PREFERENCE entity, each of which has a value from the TRAVEL PREFERENCE TYPE. The other preferences from Figure 8.2 don't apply at the time of reservation such as the PRODUCT (because they have already picked it), PRODUCT CATEGORY, ACCOMMODATION CLASS (they

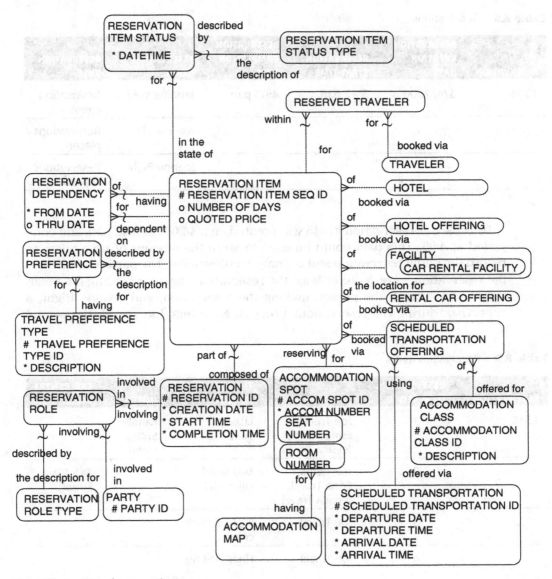

Figure 8.4 Travel reservations.

have already reserved it), and FACILITY (they have already booked something). Each RESERVATION ITEM may have one or more RESERVATION ITEM STATUSes to indicate whether the reservation is "reserved," "booked," "cancelled," and so on.

Tables 8.8 and 8.9 show examples of data that may be stored within this data model. Table 8.8 shows that type of information stored in the reservations header. Table 8.9 shows information stored in the reservations detail.

Table 8.8 Reservations

RESERVATION	RESERVATION CREATION DATE	RESERVATION START TIME	RESERVATION COMPLETION TIME	RESERVATION PARTY	RESERVATION ROLE
1345	3/4/2000	3:42 p.m.	4:03 p.m.	Jennifer Way	Reservation agent
				Joe Travel	Reservations placer
				Joanne Right	Reservations supervisor

In Table 8.8, reservation #1345 was created on 3/4/2000 at 3:42 p.m. and completed at 4:03. This data could be used to store the amount of time taken to record the initial reservation and to analyze efficiencies. The parties involved in the reservation were Jennifer Way, the reservations agent recording the reservation, Joe Travel, the person making the reservation, and Joanne Right, a supervisor during the reservations process. Note that Joe Travel, the person

Table 8.9 Reservation Items

RESERVATION	RESERVATION ITEM SEQ ID	TRAVELER(S)	TRAVEL PRODUCT	HOTEL	CAR RENTAL FACILITY
1345	1	Joe Travel, Edna Travel, Jessica Travel	Luxury suite	Family Suites Hotel	
	2	Joe Travel, Edna Travel, Jessica Travel	Mid-sized car rental		345 Main Street
	3	Joe Travel	Flight #3849, coach		
	4	Joe Travel	Flight #5689, coach		
	5	Edna Travel	Flight #3849, coach		
	6	Edna Travel	Flight #5689, coach		
	7	Jessica Travel	Flight #3849, coach		
	8	Jessica Travel	Flight #5689, coach		

making the reservation, may or may not be involved as a traveler. Which travelers were involved will be recorded at the reservations item level.

Table 8.9 shows examples of reservation items for a specific reservation. The table shows a single reservation for a trip for the "Travel" family, Joe, Edna, and their daughter, Jessica. The first item is to reserve a "Luxury Suite" at the "Family Suites Hotel" that will be shared by the three members of the family. These travelers would each be stored in the RESERVED TRAVELER entity. The second item shows the rental of a car. The third through eighth lines of the table show the airline reservations for each traveler. Each item is related to a SCHEDULED TRANSPORTATION OFFERING, which is defined by two things: the SCHEDULED TRANSPORTATION, a scheduled trip going from one place to another, and an ACCOMMODATION CLASS, for example, "coach." According to the model in Figure 8.3, each SCHEDULED TRANSPORTATION is of a PASSENGER TRANSPORTATION OFFERING, which is called by a TRAVEL PRODUCT REFERENCE NUMBER, in this case flight #3849 and flight #5689.

Ticketing

A unique aspect of the travel industry is that the traveler usually needs to pay in advance for whatever he or she is buying. Of course, the traveler receives proof that he or she has paid and a means to redeem the travel accommodations. This is referred to as a ticket. This may be an airline ticket, a bus ticket, a hotel voucher, or a car rental receipt. Ticketing is more frequently used in scheduled transportation offerings, such as airlines flights, bus trips, cruises, or train rides.

After the reservation is made, a ticket is often issued. This may be issued right after the reservation or sometime after the reservation but before the trip. The ticket may be composed of coupons that correspond to a reservation item. For instance, one may go on a trip from New York to San Francisco and then to Tokyo. This may consist of two coupons, one from New York to San Francisco and one from San Francisco to Tokyo. Both of these coupons may be contained in the same ticket.

Figure 8.5 contains a data model showing the information requirements for ticketing. This is a new model and is not based on any of the models in Volume 1 because ticketing is a unique business process within the travel industry.

For each RESERVATION ITEM there may be one or more COUPONs. For example, a bus reservation from New York to San Francisco may include coupons for each portion of the trip. COUPONs are consolidated into a TICKET, which is used to redeem travel and/or travel accommodations on a trip. There may be SEAT NUMBERs assigned to each COUPON.

The TICKET may inherit many of the properties of the RESERVATION ITEM, such as the TRAVEL PREFERENCE TYPEs, the SCHEDULED TRANSPORTATION OFFERING, the RESERVED TRAVELERS, and so on. The enterprise may

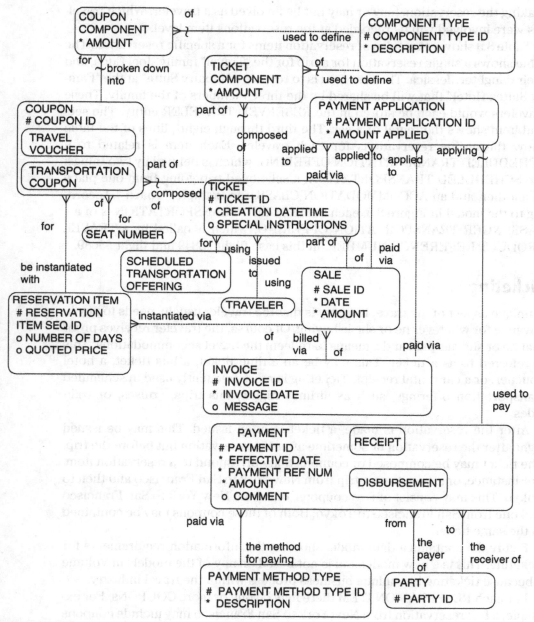

Figure 8.5 Ticketing.

not always have reservations in order to issue a ticket, and therefore the TICKET has relationships to the TRAVELER and SCHEDULED TRANSPORTA-TION OFFERING (which includes the ACCOMMODATION CLASS and the SCHEDULED TRANSPORTATION).

A ticket is usually associated with a specific itinerary for a traveler. TICKETs may be part of the SALE, which may encompass one or more TICKETs as well as other items in the sale (they are not shown here, however); whatever the travel enterprise sells could also be related to the SALE. Each SALE may be paid directly through a PAYMENT APPLICATION or may be billed via an INVOICE that is then paid via a PAYMENT APPLICATION. The entities INVOICE, PAYMENT APPLICATION, PAYMENT, and PAYMENT METHOD are taken from the generic models in Volume 1 (V1:7.8a).

Both a coupon and a ticket may have many components that make up the price. The COUPON COMPONENT and TICKET COMPONENT entities store the price breakup of each of the coupons and tickets, and each is associated with a COMPONENT TYPE. Examples of types of components include various fees, taxes, port charges, and transportation costs.

Table 8.10 portrays an example of coupons and tickets for the previous example's travel reservation. Coupons may be arranged together using any business rules that the travel enterprise decides on. In this case, a travel voucher (i.e. a coupon) was issued for the reservation of the luxury suite. The airline tickets for each person were composed of two flights, providing a round trip ticket, each part of which resulted in the issuance of a coupon. These coupons were packaged together to form a round-trip ticket for each passenger.

Reservation items may or may not even have coupons depending on the nature of the reservation. The reservation for the car rental did not result in

Table 8.10 Ticketing

RESERVATION	RESERVATION ITEM SEQ ID	TRAVELER(S)	PRODUCT	COUPON	TICKET
1345	1	Joe Travel, Edna Travel, Jessica Travel	Luxury suite	1	4585
	2	Joe Travel	Flight #3849, coach	1	666
	3	Joe Travel	Flight #5689, coach	2	666
	4	Edna Travel	Flight #3849, coach	1	667
	5	Edna Travel	Flight #5689, coach	2	667
	6	Jessica Travel	Flight #3849, coach	1	668
	7	Jessica Travel	Flight #5689, coach	2	668

either a coupon or a ticket because the reservation of a car rental is generally paid for at the time of rental.

Agreements

The types of agreements in the travel industry include corporate travel agreements, distribution channel agreements, partnership agreements, and the agreements associated with terms and conditions of a ticket. Much of the agreement models from Volume 1 (see V1:4.12–4.16) can be used to model travel agreements.

Travel Agreements

Figure 8.6 (taken from V1:4.12 and V1:4.14) illustrates the types of agreements that occur in the travel industry. The agreement models from Volume 1, 4.12–4.14 should directly apply, and the AGREEMENT ITEM, AGREEMENT TERM, and AGREEMENT ROLE entities are applicable just as in the generic models from Volume 1.

The only suggested modification is to include the types of agreements that are applicable in the travel industry as subtypes to the AGREEMENT entity. The CORPORATE TRAVEL AGREEMENT is a type of agreement that provides special terms and incentives to corporations in order to promote the use of the travel enterprise's services throughout a corporation. For instance, there may be a corporate agreement between "Travel Conglomerates" and "ABC Corporation" whereby ABC Corporation receives a 10 percent discount on all travel if it attains certain travel volumes.

A DISTRIBUTION CHANNEL AGREEMENT can record terms and conditions (using AGREEMENT TERM) between the various outlets and travel agencies that a travel enterprise uses to sell its products and services. The PARTNER-SHIP AGREEMENT subtype records the terms and conditions associated with various travel enterprises that decide to form strategic alliances in the hope of promoting each other's services. The TRAVELER AGREEMENT entity records the terms and conditions associated with a traveler's ticket. Each ticket issued to a passenger will generally have this agreement attached to it. The data model will store the history and changes to the various terms and conditions associated with different types of travel. The data model also shows some standard constructs such as EMPLOYMENT AGREEMENT and OTHER AGREEMENT.

Pricing of Agreements and Products

Figure 8.7 shows that TRAVEL PRODUCTs and AGREEMENTs may both have PRICE COMPONENTs that will affect the price of the RESERVATION ITEM or TICKET. The model uses generic entities from the "agreement to order" model

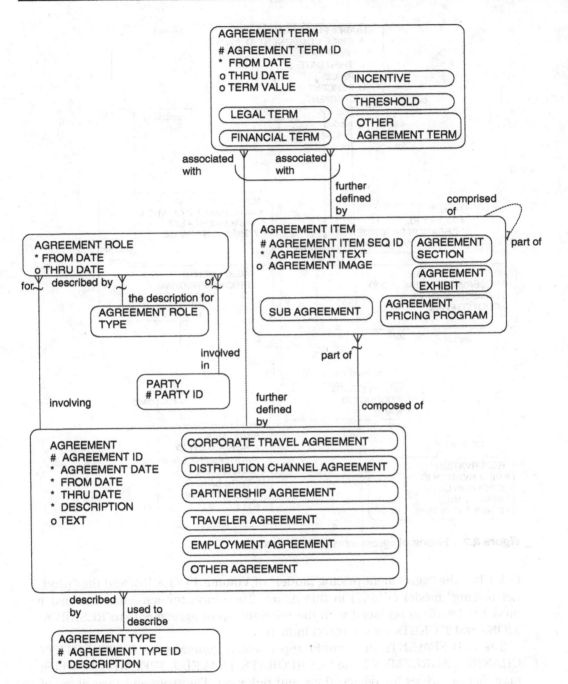

Figure 8.6 Travel agreement.

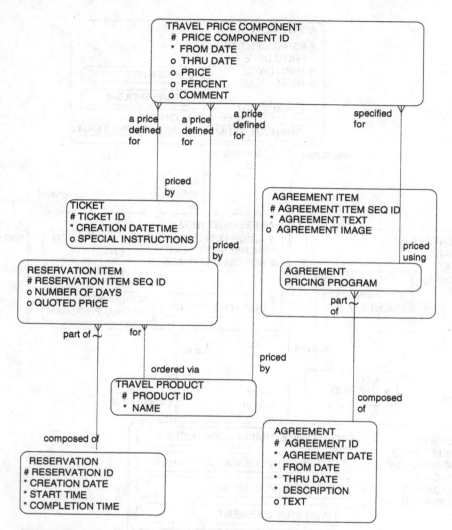

Figure 8.7 Pricing of agreements and products.

(V1:4.16), the "agreement pricing model" of Volume 1 (V1:4.15), and the "product pricing" model (V1:3.7) in this figure. Therefore, the agreement to order model (V1:4.16) is replaced with the relationship of agreements to RESERVATIONs and TICKETs for the travel industry.

The AGREEMENTs that would apply would generally be DISTRIBUTION CHANNEL AGREEMENTs and CORPORATE TRAVEL AGREEMENTs, which may dictate prices for reservations and ticketing. The from and thru dates of the agreements as well as the addendum information would allow the tracking of what terms and conditions were in effect for what periods of time and hence could be traced back to the individual ticket by looking at the date of the ticket.

Delivery (Travel Experience)

The travel enterprise is not about shipping goods or delivering services based on time. Travel enterprises deliver a service that provides for transportation and travel accommodations. The main type of transaction that occurs in the delivery of travel products will be called a "travel experience." In order to find out if and how services were delivered, the data model in this section will store information about the traveler's experiences for his or her flight, bus trip, train ride, cruise, hotel stay, car rental experience, or whatever travel accommodations were provided.

The models in this section are new, although one can make a point that there are some very slight resemblances to the shipment models. At a high level, shipment items are related to order items in order to track what items were delivered as compared to what were ordered. The shipment of a travel enterprise is a "travel experience." Just as shipment items are related to order items, each travel experience may be related to the reservation item to which it is associated.

Shipments are also related to invoices to record that items were shipped and then invoiced. Travel experiences are usually paid for up-front, so each experience may also be related to the "coupon" that serves as the proof of payment for the accommodations.

Figure 8.8 is a data model that records the information requirements of travel experiences and their associated events. Each TRAVEL EXPERIENCE records the experiences and events associated with one and only one TRAVELER. Each TRAVEL EXPERIENCE may be related to a RESERVATION ITEM, TICKET, COUPON, or SALE for that TRAVEL EXPERIENCE. The TRAVEL EXPERI-ENCE may be related to one of the product offerings, which may be a HOTEL, CAR RENTAL OFFERING, or a SCHEDULED TRANSPORTATION OFFERING. Note that the TRAVEL EXPERIENCE may or may not be related to the RESER-VATION ITEM because the traveler may just hop on board or get into the hotel without a reservation. If the reservation is in place, there is no need to record the product offering information because this is available from the RESERVA-TION ITEM. Similarly if the TICKET or COUPON describes the product, then this information would also not need to be recorded again.

Each TRAVEL EXPERIENCE may contain one or more TRAVEL EXPERI-ENCE EVENTs. These events include all "touch" points behind the traveler experience. In other words, the purpose of this information is to record the sta-tuses and people involved at each point in the traveler's journey. Therefore, for each event, the TRAVEL EXPERIENCE EVENT ROLEs and TRAVELER EXPE-RIENCE STATUS are recorded. This will provide an audit trail of everyone that was involved in serving the traveler as well as the status of each event.

Many events could happen within the travel experience. Subtypes include entities that occur within multiple types of travel experiences, whether for

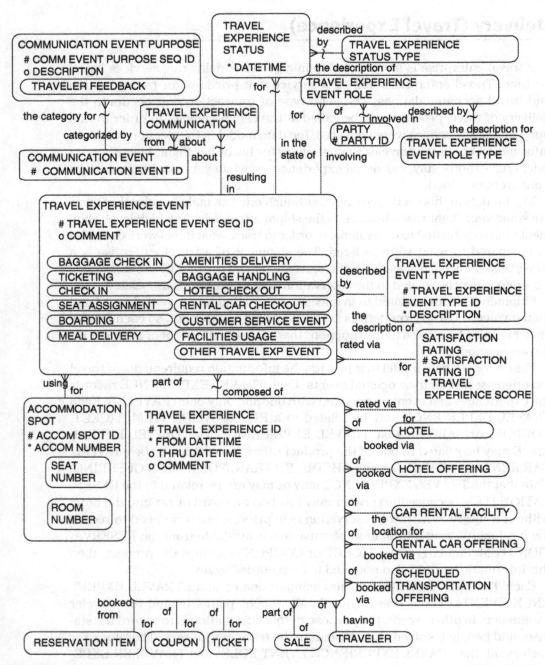

Figure 8.8 Travel experience.

transportation, hotel, or car rental experiences. BAGGAGE HANDLING, TICKETING, CHECK IN, SEAT ASSIGNMENT, BOARDING, MEAL DELIVERY, AMENITIES DELIVERY, and CUSTOMER SERVICE EVENT are all subtypes that could be used for transportation services. CHECK IN, HOTEL CHECKOUT, and BAGGAGE HANDLING are events that occur in hotel service delivery. CHECK IN, RENTAL CAR CHECKOUT, and CUSTOMER SERVICE EVENT are events that occur in renting cars. Many other events could happen, and therefore the OTHER TRAVEL EXP EVENT as well as the TRAVEL EXPERIENCE EVENT TYPE entities imply that there are many more subtypes; the ones shown are representative subtypes.

Each TRAVEL EXPERIENCE EVENT may use a certain ACCOMMODATION SPOT, such as a SEAT NUMBER or ROOM NUMBER. This allows the travel enterprise to record the seat or room that the traveler used, just in case this is helpful for tracking purposes, such as if there was a problem with a specific room.

The data model shows that a COMMUNICATION EVENT may be associated with it that has a COMMUNICATION EVENT PURPOSE of TRAVELER FEEDBACK (see V1:2.12). This allows maintenance of any type of communication such as surveys, complaints, notes, compliments, and so on that are related to travel experience events. Each TRAVEL EXPERIENCE or TRAVEL EXPERIENCE EVENT may have a SATISFACTION RATING to record the level of service for the event. SATISFACTION RATINGs and TRAVELER FEEDBACK are key information items essential to helping travel enterprises improve their service.

Table 8.11 shows data that may be within these data structures. The first row in this table shows that the reservation item for the luxury suite was recorded and linked to travel experience 1234, which involved a few travel experience events. Jerry Townsend answered a call from Joe Travel to confirm late arrival. Peter Houser checked in the travelers, Joe, Edna, and Jessica, and then checked them out a couple of days later. The table also shows some of the events associated with Joe Travel's flight. The event of baggage handling had four status records showing the progression of baggage until the traveler picked it up at the destination airport. The travel experience event comment shows that this was a fragile item. The last rows show that Joe Travel checked in at 3:15 p.m., boarded at 3:30, and was served a meal at 5:00.

This model provides a powerful data model enabling the travel enterprise to know exactly what happened during each travel experience event including the status of each event, who served them, the seat number or room number that was taken, and the traveler's satisfaction with each event if it is known.

Table 8.11 Travel Experience

RESERVATION ITEM SEQ ID	TRAVELER(S)	PRODUCT	TRAVEL EXPERIENCE ID	TRAVEL EXPERIENCE EVENT TYPE	EVENT STATUS	TRAVEL EXPERIENCE EVENT ROLE	TRAVEL EXPERIENCE EVENT COMMENT
1345-1	Joe Travel, Edna Travel, Jessica Travel	Luxury suite	1234	Check in	Called to confirm late arrival, 7:45 p.m.	Jerry Townsend, arrival confirmation	
				Check in	Checked in, 8:30 p.m., 4/5/2000	Peter Houser, front desk clerk	
				Check out	Checked out, 11:00 a.m., 4/7/2000	Peter Houser, front desk clerk	
1345-2	Joe Travel	Flight #3849, coach	2345	Baggage handling	Baggage checked in, 3:00 p.m.	Joe Reginald, arrivals agent	Fragile suitcase
				Baggage handling	Baggage placed on plane, 4:00 p.m.	Harry Sender, baggage handler	
				Baggage handling	Baggage delivered to destination—8PM	George Deliverer—Baggage handler	
				Baggage handling	Baggage checked out at airport, 8:15 p.m.	Linda Checker, baggage check out	
				Check in	Check in on flight, 3:15 p.m.	Ruth Tunder, ticket agent	
				Boarding	Boarded flight—3:30 PM	John Letter—Boarding agent	
				Meal delivery	Meal delivery, 5:00 p.m.	John Giver, flight attendant	

Invoicing

Because most travel enterprises require payment in advance of travel, invoicing is generally not a key information item to track. As shown in Figure 8.5, in some cases the SALE of a TICKET or of another TRAVEL PRODUCT may lead to an INVOICE being sent out to the TRAVELER. If the travel enterprise allows invoicing, the other invoice models and payment models from Volume 1 may be used for invoicing (V1:7.1–7.10).

These models may also be used to track purchase order invoices as well as for travel providers to invoice distribution channels such as travel agencies, or vice versa.

Work Efforts

Travel enterprises that maintain their own vehicles or fixed assets can use the Volume 1 work effort models (V1:6.1–6.13) for repair orders, preventive maintenance, and internal work efforts.

The only modification that could be made is to link work efforts to travel experience events that caused the work effort to happen. Work efforts could be generated as a result of certain travel experiences. If a passenger's bag was damaged, this could lead to a work effort, with subefforts assigned to various parties. This work effort will thus have a relationship to the travel experience event causing the work effort.

Travel Programs and Travel Accounts

Travel accounts provide mechanisms for recording travel activity and provide the traveler with incentives for frequent travel. The travel enterprise may offer many travel programs for which the traveler may become a member and earn points or awards for free or discounted travel.

Figure 8.9 illustrates a data model that shows the main information requirements for travel programs and accounts. Each TRAVEL PROGRAM is set up with certain TRAVEL PROGRAM RULES that are subject to various TRAVEL PROGRAM FACTORs in order to determine how the program operates. Each TRAVEL PROGRAM will usually have many TRAVEL ACCOUNTs, each of which could have one or more PARTYs associated with it. This provides the facility to have more than one TRAVEL ACCOUNT ROLE of "account holder" so that two or more parties can share an account. The TRAVEL ACCOUNT STATUS allows recording various statuses of the TRAVEL ACCOUNT over time. The TRAVEL ACCOUNT ACTIVITY shows the individual transactions that are posted to each TRAVEL ACCOUNT.

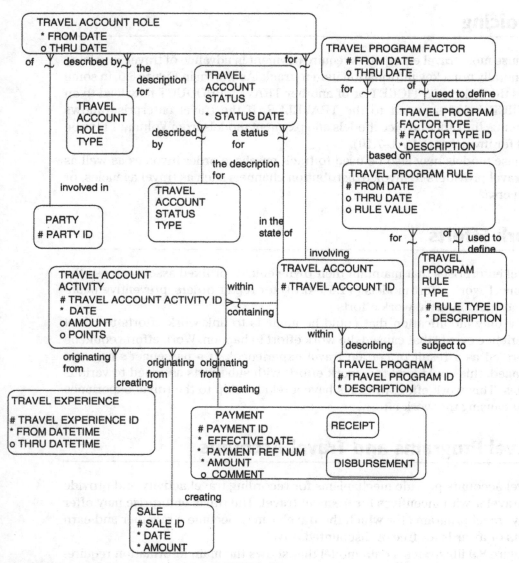

Figure 8.9 Travel programs and travel accounts.

The types of transactions that may lead to, TRAVEL ACCOUNT ACTIVITY include the TRAVEL EXPERIENCE, SALE, or PAYMENT. For instance, a travel experience such as a flight may earn the account member points on the account. A different example would be a SALE, such as credit card transactions, that may earn points on the account. Depending on the travel program of the travel enterprise, there may be other types of transactions that affect the TRAVEL ACCOUNT ACTIVITY, and the modeler may add additional relationships if needed.

Travel Programs, Rules, and Factors

Figure 8.9 provides the data structures required to set up TRAVEL PROGRAMs that are guided by TRAVEL PROGRAM RULEs of TRAVEL PROGRAM RULE TYPEs. These rules, in turn, may be based on many TRAVEL PROGRAM FACTORs, which are each of a TRAVEL PROGRAM FACTOR TYPE. For example, the travel enterprise may set up a TRAVEL PROGRAM called the "Ace Travel Program" that has rules for earning points that can be used to redeem free trips. An example of a TRAVEL PROGRAM RULE TYPE that can be applied to this travel program is "one point earned for each mile on a trip," where the TRAVEL PROGRAM RULE **rule value** may be stored as "1," signifying the number of points earned per mile. There may be many TRAVEL PROGRAM FACTOR TYPEs that apply to this rule, such as "only mileage on paid trips can earn points," which would exclude earning miles on free trips that were paid with travel account mileage points. Another TRAVEL PROGRAM RULE TYPE that is applied to this program may be "25,000 points earns a free round-trip ticket" with the TRAVEL PROGRAM FACTOR TYPEs of "excludes holiday travel" and "excludes international travel."

The TRAVEL ACCOUNT ACTIVITY allows the accumulation of **points** to be used for travel incentives or an **amount**, in case the program allocates dollar amounts that can be used for travel.

This flexible structure allows the enterprise's travel programs, rules, and factors to change over time, without requiring modifications to the data structures. Only the instances of the programs, rules, and factors would need to be changed. The **from date** and **thru date** fields on the TRAVEL PROGRAM RULE and TRAVEL PROGRAM FACTOR allow the enterprise to maintain when each rule and factor is, was, or is going to be in force.

Travel Account Example

Table 8.12 provides an example of data that may be maintained with this data model. One of "Travel Conglomerates" programs is the "Ace Travel Program," which awards points to travelers that may be redeemed for free travel. The

Table 8.12 Travel Account.

TRAVEL PROGRAM	ACCOUNT	ACCOUNT HOLDER	ACCOUNT STATUS	ACCOUNT ACTIVITY	TRAVEL EXPERIENCE ID	CREDIT CARD PAYMENT ID
Ace Travel Program	13874	Joe Travel, Edna Travel	Gold member	1200 points	2345	
				2340 points	3456	
				1450 points		28734

table shows that account 13874 is held by Joe and Edna Travel and that they have achieved "Gold member" status. The table shows three account activity transactions, the first two that are related to specific travel experiences taken and the third that was credited due to a credit card payment ID #28734. Joe and Edna Travel have earned 4,990 points to be used for free travel. The points that are accumulated in the account activity of this account are governed by the travel program's rules that were in force at the time of the travel experience, payment or other transaction affecting the travel account.

Star Schemas for Travel

Transportation offerings may be analyzed differently than other travel products, and thus Figures 8.10 and 8.11 provide examples of star schemas that could be used to track each of these.

Passenger Transportation Offering Star Schema

Figure 8.10 provides a star schema used to analyze how well the travel enterprise is providing passenger transportation services.

Fact Table

The TRANSPORTATION_OFFERING_FACT_TABLE stores measures based on the travel experiences of TRAVEL_PRODUCTs that are in the subtype of PASSENGER_TRANSPORTATION_OFFERING. A number of metrics can be used to determine service levels for these offerings and thus are stored as measures in the fact table. These include the following:

- The number of travel experiences (in order to provide a relative comparison of how many records are being analyzed)
- The sales dollars generated (another relative comparison figure)
- The number of positive comments, such as compliments sent to provider
- The number of negative comments, such as complaints
- The average satisfaction rating that may be determined by surveys
- The number of on-time arrivals (compared with the total number of travel experiences)
- The number of on-time departures (compared with the total number of travel experiences)
- The average number of minutes late for the transportation offering

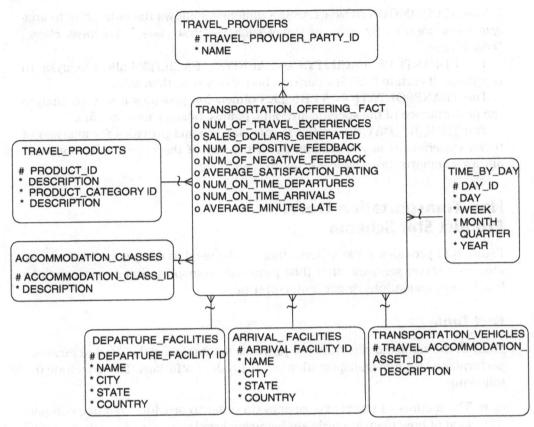

Figure 8.10 Passenger transportation offering star schema.

Dimensions

As shown in the diagram, the preceding measures may be analyzed by TRAVEL_ PROVIDERS, TRAVEL_PRODUCTS, ACCOMMODATION_CLASSES, DEPAR-TURE_FACILITYS, ARRIVAL_FACILITYS, TRANSPORTATION_VEHICLES, or over TIME_BY_DAY.

Because an enterprise may consist of many different travel providers, the dimension TRAVEL_PROVIDERS allows comparisons between these providers. It also provides comparisons of competitive providers if this information is available.

TRAVEL_PRODUCTs that are of subtype PASSENGER TRANSPORTATION OFFERING may be analyzed in this star schema. This may include analysis of various flight, train trip, bus trip, boat trip, or any other offering that transports passengers to and from places.

The ACCOMMODATION_CLASSES dimension allows the enterprise to analyze these metrics by class of travel such as "first class," "business class," "coach," etc.

The DEPARTURE_FACILITYS and ARRIVAL_FACILITYS allow analysis to determine if certain facilities perform better or worse than others.

The TRANSPORTATION_VEHICLES dimension provides a way to analyze the performance of the specific aircrafts, planes, boats, trains, or cars.

The TIME_BY_DAY dimension in this star schema provides for analysis of travel experiences at the granularity of the day of the experiences and then allows summarizations by week, quarter, and year.

Non-Transportation Travel Product Star Schema

Figure 8.11 provides a star schema that can be used to analyze metrics associated with travel services other than passenger transportation service, such as hotel accommodations or car rental offerings.

Fact Table

Many of the same metrics from the previous fact table may be used to measure performance for non-transportation travel product offerings. These include the following:

- The number of travel experiences (in order to provide a relative comparison of how many records are being analyzed)
- The sales dollars generated (another relative comparison figure)
- The number of positive comments, such as compliments sent to provider
- The number of negative comments, such as complaints
- The average satisfaction rating that may be determined by surveys

These are the same as the first five measures of the previous star schema. On-time arrivals, departures, and average minutes late are not measures for these travel products because they do not make sense for hotel and car rental analysis.

Dimensions

As shown in Figure 8.11, the above measures may be analyzed by TRAVEL_PROVIDERS, TRAVEL_PRODUCTS, ACCOMMODATION_CLASSES, TRAVEL_ACCOMMODATION_ASSETS, or over TIME_BY_DAY.

The dimensions TRAVEL_PROVIDERS, TRAVEL_PRODUCTS, ACCOMMODATION_CLASSES, and TIME_BY_DAY apply to non-transportation travel

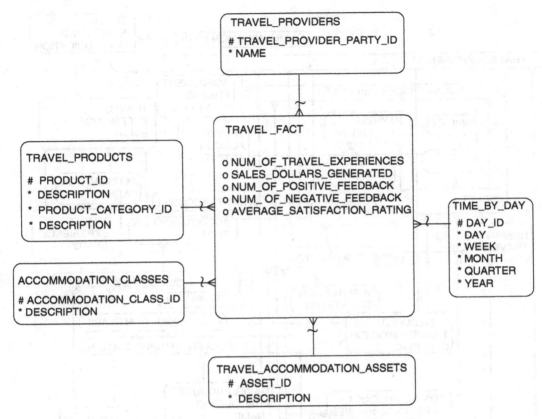

Figure 8.11 Non-transportation travel product star schema.

product offerings, such as hotel and car rental offerings, and have already been described.

The TRAVEL_ACCOMMODATION_ASSETS dimension provides a way to analyze the performance of the specific hotel, car, or facility that is being used for the traveler's accommodations.

Travel Summary

The unique information requirements of travel lie in the nature of their products, reservations, tracking travel experiences, and accumulating account activity within travel accounts for awards redemption. Many of the product model constructs may be used; however, it is necessary to add another level to the product structure to show that products are related to scheduled transportation and then to scheduled transportation offerings, which are then

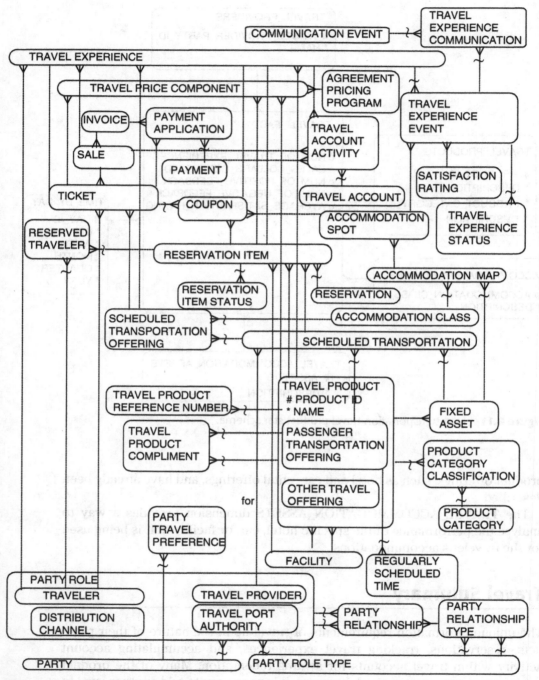

Figure 8.12 Overall travel data model.

reserved or taken. Travel experiences are the method for tracking the delivery of the travel enterprise's services. Travel accounts are set up and activity is recorded to track incentives for frequent travel activity.

Many standard data constructs can be used from Volume 1 including the models for people, organizations, relationships, agreements, orders (for purchase orders), invoicing, accounting, budgeting, and human resources.

Figure 8.12 provides an overall data model for the travel data models within this chapter.

E-Commerce Models

The Internet is having a dramatic effect on business today. As companies' experiences with the Internet mature, their sites move from electronic brochure to distribution channel, support channel, and marketing channel—in short, a direct channel to the customer. In effect, the Web is becoming just another part of business, with its own unique strengths and weaknesses. This chapter focuses on data models that are needed by companies that want to conduct business online. These changes are suitable to businesses that primarily sell directly to customers online as well as other businesses that may use e-commerce to supplement more traditional sales channels.

Companies that provide e-commerce are concerned with such issues as the following:

- How can we build and support a high-quality, innovative, and interactive retail e-commerce presence?
- How can we improve customer service and satisfaction with our offerings?
- How can we maximize revenues and minimize costs?
- How do we build branding and add value for our customers with our Web distribution channel without cannibalizing our existing channels?
- How can we maximize the Web experience of our customers at our site?

To answer these types of questions, enterprises need to track information about the following:

- The people and organizations they are concerned with, namely, distribution channels, customers, visitors, referrers, suppliers, ISPs, employees, and internal organizations
- The new contact mechanisms and combinations of mechanisms that the Internet has brought into existence
- Keeping track of consumers' product and non-product needs
- Needs and subscriptions recorded on Web sites
- Maintaining visitors and information on hits to a Web site
- Maintaining Internet-based orders
- Maintaining Internet-based invoice and billing data
- Maintaining shipments of goods
- Work effort management
- Budgeting and accounting information
- Human resources management

Volume 1 addresses many of the needs of companies looking to implement a retail e-commerce strategy. For instance, it addresses the following:

- People and organizations structures
- Product structures that can be built on to satisfy requirements of displaying and selling products on the Web
- Order data models that can be used for ordering items, activating service, or allowing the purchase of soft products
- Shipment models used to track shipments of products or parts sent out to customers and to allow for downloading of soft products
- Invoice models that can allow for an organization's invoicing needs
- Work effort models
- Accounting, budgeting, and human resource models to manage finances and people

Key aspects of retail e-commerce that are not addressed in Volume 1 include the following:

- New party roles to help track the more complex interactions that can take place on the Web, especially given the more anonymous nature of the Web

- New contact mechanisms and combinations of contact mechanisms that the Internet allows

- Information of user login information and Web site content

- Information about consumer needs as it relates to products, product types, and non-product related needs

- Information about subscriptions recorded on the Web

- Refinements to product structures to allow for information use in a store front or online catalog

- Structures to keep track of visits and visitors for the enterprise's Web sites

- Structures to analyze the data collected by the Web site to assess the effectiveness of the Web site and to find out information about visitors and their interests

Table 9.1 shows which models can be used directly from Volume 1, which models need to be modified, which Volume 1 models are not used, and which new models are required. For the people and organizations area, most of the models from Volume 1 apply; however, we need to add PARTYs, PARTY ROLEs, PARTY RELATIONSHIPs, PARTY NEEDs, and CONTACT MECHA-NISMs suitable to retail e-commerce enterprises. Many of the product models can be used with appropriate modifications to allow for use of PRODUCT OBJECTs and FEATURE OBJECTs in constructing a storefront or online catalog. The most significant data modeling requirement for retail e-commerce is adding new data structures to accommodate information associated with tracking visits and hits to the Web site, tracking consumer needs and access to the site, maintaining Web site content information, maintaining user login preferences information, and maintaining subscriptions. Web star schemas are included for analyzing both visits and more specifically hits. The order, invoicing, billing, accounting, work effort, and human resource models from Volume 1 are generally applicable.

People and Organizations in E-Commerce

Companies that want to have a retail e-commerce presence generally have greater but similar needs for tracking people and organizations as other enterprises. They need to track information about their customers, referrers, visitors, suppliers, ISPs, employees, distribution channels, and organization structures.

Table 9.1 Volume 1 and Volume 2 Data Models for Retail E-Commerce

SUBJECT DATA AREA	USE THESE VOLUME 1 MODELS DIRECTLY	MODIFY THESE VOLUME 1 MODELS (AS DESCRIBED IN VOLUME 2)	DO NOT USE THESE VOLUME 1 MODELS	ADD THESE VOLUME 2 MODELS
People and Organizations	Person, V1:2.1–2.14, except V1:2.3, V1:2.5, V1:2.6, and V1:2.10	Party definition, V1:2.3 (added PARTY subtype of AUTOMATED AGENT as shown in V2:9.1), Party roles and relationships, V1:2.5 and V1:2.6a modified in V1:9.1, Party contact mechanism, V1:2.10 (Modified by adding new subtypes for WEB ADDRESS and IP ADDRESS in Figure V2:9.2)		Web site content and user login, V2:9.3
Product	Product models, V1:3.1–3.11			E-Commerce products and objects, V2:9.4, Party and product needs, V2:9.5
Order		Orders, V1:4.1–4.8, Requisition, request, quote, V1:4.9–4.11, Agreement models, V1:4.12–4.16 (subtype agreements) with slight modifications		Web subscriptions, V2:9.6, Web visits, V2:9.7
Delivery		Shipment models, V1:5.1–5.8, with slight modifications for software downloads		
Work effort		Work effort, V1:6.1–6.13, for internal projects with slight modifications		
Invoicing		Invoice models, V1:7.1–7.10, with slight modifications		
Accounting	All models, V1:8.1–8.12			
Human resources	All models, V1:9.1–9.14			
E-Commerce star schemas				Web server visits star schema, V9:2.8, Server hits star schema, V9:2.9

E-Commerce Parties, Roles, and Relationships

Figure 9.1 shows a data model for PARTY, PARTY ROLEs, and PARTY RELA-TIONSHIPs for enterprises wanting a retail e-commerce presence. The model is taken from the party roles and relationships model from Volume 1 (V1:2.6). The

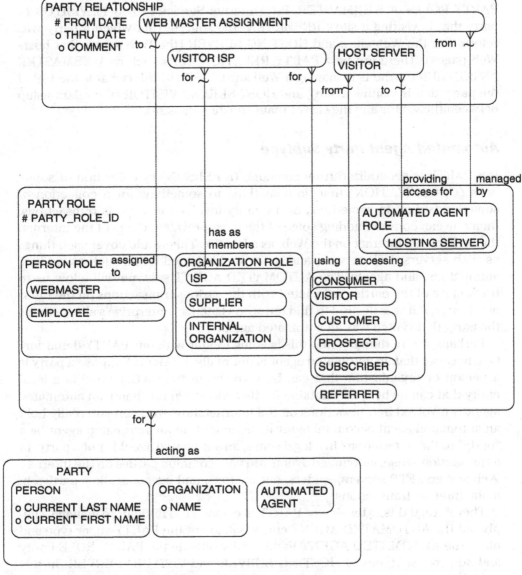

Figure 9.1 Parties, roles, and relationships in e-commerce.

"type" entities of PARTY ROLE TYPE and PARTY RELATIONSHIP TYPE are not shown in this diagram because they have already been provided in each previous chapter. Also, specific relationships are shown to the PARTY RELATIONSHIPs from the PARTY ROLEs to show the nature of these new PARTY RELATIONSHIPs more specifically.

A new PARTY subtype has been added called AUTOMATED AGENT to track the activities of automated entities such as spiders, Web servers, and other automatons that are involved in interacting on the Internet. There are new PARTY ROLEs of WEBMASTER, ISP (Internet Service Provider), VISITOR (a party that is visiting a site), REFERRER (the source from which a party was referred to the Web site), and HOSTING SERVER (the Web server that hosts Web pages). There are new PARTY RELATIONSHIPs such as WEBMASTER ASSIGNMENT (who is managing a Web site), VISITOR ISP (what is the ISP of the party that is visiting a site), and HOST SERVER VISITOR (the relationship between the visitor and the server that is hosting the site).

Automated Agent Party Subtype

If a PARTY is generalized from someone (a PERSON) or collection of someones (ORGANIZATION) that do something to something, or a collection of somethings that do something, or an entity involved in various transactions, then one can consider adding some of the most prevalent doers of the Internet, the servers that interact on the Web, as a PARTY. This would cover such things as Web servers, FTP servers, and more sophisticated doers such as spiders, automatons, and agents. The AUTOMATED AGENT subtype will allow us to track more of the parties associated with the various transactions on the Internet. Hence, if it was desired to find out who visited an enterprise's site, perhaps the party that visited was an automated agent.

Perhaps you're thinking that this is going too far with our PARTY definition. One may say that an automated agent is not really a PARTY. Suppose a party is a person or organization that can be involved in transactions and is a legal entity that can be held accountable for its actions. On one hand, an automated agent is involved in transactions on the Internet; however, can you really hold an automated agent accountable for its actions? Can an automated agent be a "party" to the transaction? In a legal sense, an automated agent is not a party. In a transaction sense, automated agents are very common parties on the Internet. Web servers, FTP servers, spiders, automatons, and agents are key parties in many Internet transactions.

Therefore, if this extension of PARTY is deemed too difficult to manage, simply put the AUTOMATED AGENT entity outside of the PARTY super type and place the AUTOMATED AGENT ROLE entity outside the PARTY ROLE entity and add two subtypes of HOSTING SERVER and VISITING SERVER. In this model the enterprise would have to relate each Web site visit to both the

PARTIES involved and the AUTOMATED AGENTs, even though the visitor could be an AUTOMATED AGENT.

Generic Party Roles from Volume 1

Many of the generic PARTY ROLES are included, such as PERSON ROLEs of WEBMASTER and EMPLOYEE, ORGANIZATION ROLES of SUPPLIER and INTERNAL ORGANIZATION, and other roles such as CUSTOMER and PROSPECT. Many more of the generic subtypes could be included as well.

E-Commerce Party Roles and Relationships

New subtypes include ISP (Internet Service Provider) as an ORGANIZATION ROLE, HOSTING SERVER as an AUTOMATED AGENT ROLE, and REFERRER, VISITOR, and SUBSCRIBER as other roles. An ISP can be important to track, as you may be able to track visitors back to their ISPs. This information can be very useful for targeting marketing and advertising campaigns at certain ISPs of consequence (where most of your visitors may come from). HOSTING SERVER can be used to keep track of what things are on what server, which can be handy if there is a need to have different servers for different parts of the enterprise. A REFERRER is important to track, as this will tell you from which site parties are coming. If the enterprise does Internet marketing campaigns, it can track the effectiveness of these campaigns by tracking what search engines visitors have come from or from what banner ad on what site did the visitor click. A CONSUMER is defined as a party who may be or has been involved in the purchase of the enterprise's services. This could include SUBSCRIBER, VISITOR, CUSTOMER, or PROSPECT (this represents an alternate structure to some of the previous structures where CUSTOMER and PROSPECT were not super typed within PARTY ROLE). A VISITOR is someone who visits a site. They may also be a CUSTOMER, PROSPECT, or some other subtype of CONSUMER. A SUBSCRIBER may be a party who has subscribed to a newsletter, service, or other ongoing request. This is especially useful if the subscription is for a newsletter(s) that the visitor registered for based on his or her interests. This allows the enterprise to target an interested customer base with information and specials tailored to the visitor's interests.

New PARTY RELATIONSHIPs added are WEBMASTER ASSIGNMENT, HOST SERVER VISITOR, and VISITOR ISP. WEBMASTER ASSIGNMENT provides the ability to keep track of which Webmasters maintain which HOSTING Servers. HOST SERVER VISITOR tracks ongoing visitor relationships for each HOSTING SERVER. VISITOR ISP allows tracking of the ISPs that each VISITOR uses. Conjunctively, the HOST SERVER VISITOR and VISITOR ISP would allow the enterprise to track which ISPs typically are using which HOSTING SERVER.

Is There Always a PARTY for a PARTY ROLE?

Throughout each chapter, the model has shown PARTY ROLE as a dependent entity of PARTY, and therefore if there is a PARTY ROLE, there would have to be a PARTY. When a party plays a role of VISITOR on a Web site, though, the enterprise may not know who the PARTY is.

Should the relationship from PARTY ROLE to PARTY be optional then? There is always a PARTY for the visit; the enterprise just may not know the name of party or other identification information. They do know other information for the party. The enterprise may have a great deal of information on the visitor such as what products the visitor has clicked on, what pages he or she visited, and how long he or she has spent where. If the visitor allows "cookies" then he or she can be identified as the same party through many distinct visits.

Therefore, there is information that may be associated with this PARTY, and the enterprise may track the PARTY's information for this particular **party id** *even though the name of party may not be known yet*! Therefore, the PARTY ROLE to PARTY relationship is still mandatory; however, the name attributes on PERSON or ORGANIZATION are optional. Therefore, the **current last name** and **current first name** for PERSON and **name** for ORGANIZATION are now shown as optional attributes for this model.

Example Data for E-Commerce Party Roles and Relationships

Our case example for this chapter is a company named WebSales Inc. Table 9.2 provides examples of roles in the database for this enterprise.

According to Table 9.2, "WebSales Inc.," "WebSales AWIDGET Manufacturing," and "WebSales BWIDGET Manufacturing" are all internal organizations of the enterprise being modeled, namely, "WebSales Inc." The first VISITOR does not have a party name associated with it. Because of the nature of the Web, there will be many instances where a party has visited the site, but the enterprise does not know the name of the party—in this instance, a party ID would still be assigned, and if and when the name becomes known it may be added later. It can be important to keep track of this party and its visits as the party provides valuable information about the nature of the visitors and this party, plus the enterprise might be able to tie this visit or visits to a name later, and thus have a partially built profile of this visitor to the Web site. "John Smith" is a VISITOR and a CUSTOMER. "John Smith" is also a SUBSCRIBER and has subscribed to a monthly newsletter. "Spiderbot" is a VISITOR (in this case it is perhaps a site indexer for a search engine). "Search Engine Inc." is a REFERRER and has referred someone to your site based on the results of some search that the VISITOR did. "Bill Jones" is an EMPLOYEE, a PROSPECT (he has

Table 9.2 Retail E-Commerce Party Roles

PARTY ROLE	PARTY NAME
INTERNAL ORGANIZATION (parent organization)	WebSales, Inc.
INTERNAL ORGANIZATION (subsidiary)	WebSales AWIDGET Manufacturing
INTERNAL ORGANIZATION (subsidiary)	WebSales BWIDGET Manufacturing
VISITOR	
VISITOR	John Smith
CUSTOMER	John Smith
VISITOR	Spiderbot
REFERRER	Search Engine Inc.
EMPLOYEE	Bill Jones
PROSPECT	Bill Jones
WEBMASTER	Bill Jones
SUBSCRIBER	John Smith

visited the Web site and searched for specific products), and he is a WEBMAS-TER (he maintains a Web site).

Table 9.3 provides additional information about which roles are involved within which relationships. It is not enough to simply show the role; it is important to show the various relationships that the same role may play. For

Table 9.3 Retail E-Commerce Party Relationships

PARTY RELATIONSHIP TYPE	FROM PARTY NAME	TO PARTY NAME
Host server visitor	ABC, Inc.	Awidget Web Server
Host server visitor	XYZ, Inc.	Awidget Web Server
Host server visitor	New Business, Inc	Bwidget Web Server
Host server visitor	Just Started, Inc	Bwidget Web Server
Visitor ISP	Really Big ISP	ABC, Inc.
Visitor ISP	Very Large ISP	XYZ, Inc.
Visitor ISP	Teeny Tiny ISP	New Business, Inc
Visitor ISP	Super Small ISP	Just Started, Inc
Webmaster assignment	Bill Jones	Awidget Web Server
Webmaster assignment	Jerry Right	Awidget Web Server
Webmaster assignment	Jerry Right	Bwidget Web Server

example, one may want to establish a party relationship subtype HOST SERVER VISITOR showing visitors on each Web server. This could track the ongoing relationships that visitors to the site have with each AUTOMATED AGENT. One can argue that this may be tracked with the VISIT entity, which will be discussed later in this chapter. It may be important to capture and maintain these key relationships independently of the many visit entries because the enterprise may have learned (perhaps through a phone communication) that a particular party visited the Web site.

The first four rows in Table 9.3 show relationships from "ABC, Inc" and "XYZ, Inc" as visitors of "AWIDGET Web Server," and relationships from "New Business, Inc." and "Just Started, Inc." to "BWIDGET Server." These records can track the relationships of key visitors to the site in order to better manage these Internet relationships.

It can be very useful to track the ISPs of the visitors in order to track which ISPs are most important for a marketing campaign. The next four rows show which ISP each visitor uses. Specifically, "ABC, Inc." uses "REALLY BIG ISP," "XYZ, Inc." uses "VERY LARGE ISP," "New Business Inc." uses "Super Small ISP," and "Just Started, Inc." uses "Teeny Tiny ISP."

From the HOST SERVER VISITOR and VISITOR ISP relationships, the enterprise can deduce which ISPs tend to access which HOST SERVER. From the relationships shown in the table, one can conclude that users from large ISPs access only the "Awidget Web Server." The "Very Large ISP" and "Really Big ISP" tend to access "Awidget Web Server" but not "Bwidget Web Server." The enterprise might consider trying to set up Web links or marketing arrangements with "Really Big ISP" and "Very Large ISP" for both "Awidget Web Server" and "Bwidget Web Server" to see if they can get the customers of these ISPs interested in the "Bwidget Web Server" Web site.

The next three relationships maintain information on who maintains the Web servers. "Bill Jones" is a WEBMASTER for the "Awidget Web Server," but "Jerry Right" is a WEBMASTER for both "Awidget Web Server" and "Bwidget Web Server."

Party Contact Mechanisms in E-Commerce

Figure 9.2 shows an expanded version of the party contact mechanism model from Volume 1 (V1:2.10). Each PARTY may have multiple CONTACT MECHANISMs and vice versa, thus the associative entity, PARTY CONTACT MECHANISM. Each PARTY CONTACT MECHANISM may have many PARTY CONTACT MECHANISM PURPOSEs, such as a WEB ADDRESS being used for the purpose of "technical support for frequently asked questions" as well as "downloading software patches."

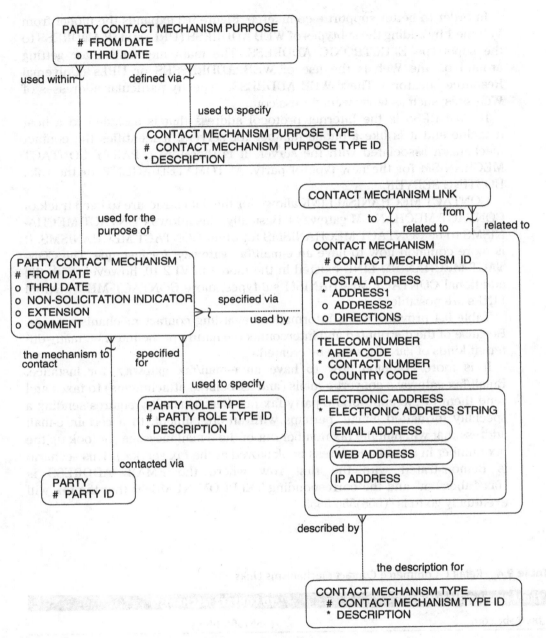

Figure 9.2 Party contact mechanisms for e-commerce.

In order to better support e-commerce, Figure 9.2 expands the model from Volume 1 by adding the subtypes of WEB ADDRESS (URL) and IP ADDRESS to the supertype ELECTRONIC ADDRESS. The main mechanism for getting around on the Web is the use of WEB ADDRESSES or URLs (Universal Resource Locators). These WEB ADDRESSes specify particular addresses of Web sites, such as www.webaddress.com.

IP ADDRESS is the Internet protocol address that is assigned to a host machine and it is like a phone number for servers. It identifies the contact mechanism associated with the server. It is therefore a PARTY CONTACT MECHANISM for the new type of party, AUTOMATED AGENT, or the role, HOSTING SERVER.

CONTACT MECHANISM LINK allows for the data structure to keep track of CONTACT MECHANISM gateways. Basically, this allows CONTACT MECHA-NISMS to be CONTACT MECHANISMS for other CONTACT MECHANISMS. It is more common now to have an e-mail/fax gateway, for instance. The CON-TACT MECHANISM LINK existed in the model in V1:2.10; however, with the additional CONTACT MECHANISM subtypes, more CONTACT MECHANISM LINKs are possible.

Table 9.4 provides some information regarding contact mechanism usage. Because of the distributed and interconnected nature of the Internet, many different kinds of gateways may be created.

It is more common now to have an e-mail/fax gateway, for instance. Email/fax gateways convert e-mails (and associated attachments) to faxes and send them to the appropriate party fax number. It usually requires sending a specially formatted e-mail, perhaps with an attachment, to a certain e-mail address that will pull the fax number out of the e-mail message (or look up the fax number in an online address book stored at the fax service). This scenario is demonstrated with the first row where the EMAIL ADDRESS is "fax@abc.com" and the corresponding TELECOM NUMBER that the fax will eventually go to is "(555)555-5555."

Table 9.4 Retail E-Commerce Contact Mechanisms Links

FROM CONTACT MECHANISM	TO CONTACT MECHANISM
fax@abc.com	(555)555-5555
5555555555@pagerservice.com	(555)555-5555
http://www.pagerservice.com/ 5555555555	(555)555-5555
http://www.ABC_company_homepage.com	http://www.ABC_company_homepage.com/ products.com

Another example of this kind of gateway is an e-mail/pager or URL/pager gateway. By sending an e-mail to a special e-mail address, this service will convert the text of the e-mail to a message for a text pager. A similar service is also available via the Web, where you go to a certain URL, fill out a form with your message, click the submit button, and it will convert your form to a text message and send it to the appropriate pager. These examples are shown in the second and third rows of Table 9.4.

The last row of Table 9.4 provides an example of maintaining information about how WEB ADDRESSes may be related and linked to other WEB ADDRESSes. Web links may be stored in a database when the nature of the links is significant enough to warrant it. Care must be taken to scrutinize which Web links to maintain and not overload the database because there may be a great number of Web links to maintain. For instance, it may be important to store the structure of the Web addresses used in the enterprise's business, in order to maintain which Web links the enterprise is using.

Web Site Content and User Login Information

The Web is often highly dependent on parties logging in to Web sites. Figure 9.3 shows a model for information on WEB SITES and USER LOGINS, that can be used for Web-based applications. The WEB ADDRESS is a type of CONTACT MECHANISM with an **electronic string address** attribute to store the URL, as shown in Figure 9.2. This model shows that each WEB ADDRESS may contain many WEB CONTENTs. This model allows each PARTY to be given one or more USER LOGINs for a WEB ADDRESS for those Web sites that have secured access by USER LOGIN. Each USER LOGIN may be governed by WEB USER PREFERENCEs that control the look and feel of the site for a specific party that has a login account. The LOGIN ACCOUNT HISTORY allows tracking the history of logins and passwords given to access the site.

Web Site Content

Each Web site is the location of one or more WEB CONTENTs, which represent pieces of information that are on the Internet. Enterprises may or may not track this information in a database because the information on the Web is very readily accessible and searchable. It does, however, represent an information requirement of the organization and is therefore maintained in the data model. Each WEB CONTENT may have many WEB CONTENT ROLEs of a WEB CONTENT ROLE TYPE for a PARTY. For instance, the party that created the Web content would be the "author," the party that was responsible for putting the

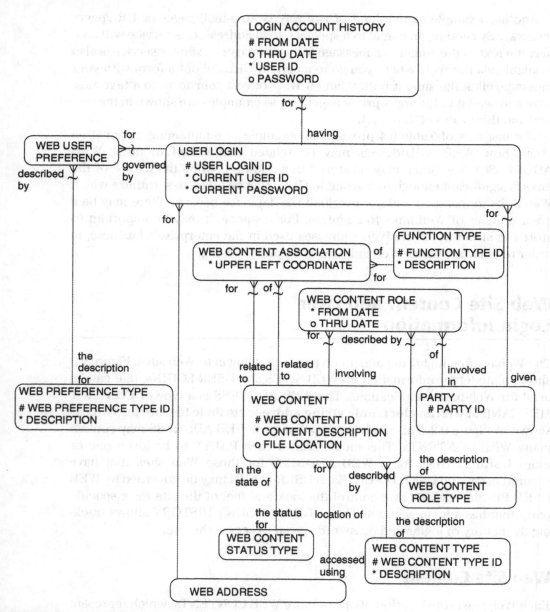

Figure 9.3 Web site content and user login.

content on the Web is usually the "Webmaster,'" and the party that updates the content may be stated as "updater."

Each WEB CONTENT may have a **content description,** which summarizes what is stored and a **file location,** which stores the path name for the actual file that stores the Web content (aserver@C:\web pages\productinfo.html). The WEB CONTENT TYPE is used to categorize the types of Web contents that exist such as "articles," "product descriptions," "company information," and so on. WEB CONTENT STATUS indicates whether the content is currently on the site, pending, or was previously stored on a site.

WEB CONTENT is often related to other WEB CONTENT, and thus the WEB CONTENT ASSOCIATION provides for this requirement. For instance, a textual Web-based product description WEB CONTENT may be related to several WEB CONTENT images, which are used within the product description.

The WEB CONTENT ASSOCIATION **upper left coordinate** provides the ability to store where the Web content object should be placed in context with the WEB CONTENT to which it is associated. For instance, the enterprise may want to drive its Web site updates from a database. The **upper left coordinate** would allow the image to move from one place on an HTML page to another place and be driven by a database entry for simplicity reasons.

The FUNCTION TYPE takes this concept one step further and allows the WEB CONTENT ASSOCIATION functionality to be maintained in the database. For instance, a WEB CONTENT that contains an object and is associated with another WEB CONTENT may act in a certain way, such as a "scrolling list" or a "radio box," which could be possible values of FUNCTION TYPE.

Login Account

Some Web sites require the party to have a USER LOGIN in order to gain access to the site. Once the user has a login, information may be stored about that login account. For example, each USER LOGIN may have many WEB USER PREFERENCEs of WEB PREFERENCE TYPEs in order to provide customized services for each user login. The enterprise may also store a history of the user logins and passwords that can be maintained in a LOGIN ACCOUNT HISTORY.

Table 9.5 provides examples of USER LOGINs and WEB USER PREFERENCEs. The table shows that both "John Smith" and "Richard Smith" have login

Table 9.5   Web Login Account Model

PARTY	WEB SITE	USER LOGIN	WEB USER PREFERENCE
John Smith	www.travel_bookings_made_very_easy.com	Jsmith	Show top 5 best selling cruises
John Smith	www.travel_bookings_made_very_easy.com	Jsmith	Blue Background
Richard Smith	www.travel_bookings_made_very_easy.com	Rsmith	Show travel specials

access to a site called www.travel_bookings_made_very_easy.com. The hosting site has provided for a different look and feel based upon various preferences for their members who have logins. In this case, "John Smith" wants the site to show the top 5 best selling cruises when he logs into the site. "John Smith" also prefers a "Blue Background," so for the areas of the site where the user can customize his or her look and feel, then his background will be blue. "Richard Smith" wants the site to show any travel specials when he logs in.

E-Commerce Products and Objects

E-commerce organizations deal with products and have the same types of product structures as any other enterprise. Therefore, the models in Volume 1 for products (V1:3.1–3.11) are very applicable and can be used. One key need within e-commerce is the need to describe the enterprise's products using various electronic objects such as images, HTML documents, applets, electronic text, and other types of computer-generated objects. Of course, these objects may describe other things about the enterprise aside from their products; for example, they may describe their various internal organizations or the people within the organization. Most of the information described using these objects is usually about the enterprise's products, and thus this data model to track electronic objects will be presented with a focus on describing products in this section.

Figure 9.4 shows a data model to maintain objects that can display product and feature information as part of a storefront. The entities PRODUCT, PRODUCT FEATURE, and PRODUCT FEATURE APPLICABILITY are taken from the generic product feature model (V1:3.4). An OBJECT entity is added to store electronic images, such as ELECTRONIC TEXT, (i.e. an HTML document), IMAGE OBJECTs, which are graphic electronic representations, and OTHER OBJECTs, such as applets, sound files, video clips, and so on.

Each OBJECT may be related to many entities throughout the data model. Figure 9.4 shows a few examples to illustrate how objects may be maintaining electronic information about products, product features, or parties. Thus, OBJECTs may be related to one or more PRODUCTs, PRODUCT FEATUREs, or PARTYs, and OBJECTs are related to the associative entities PRODUCT OBJECT, FEATURE OBJECT, and PARTY OBJECT. By maintaining the object information independently from the Web content, the same object may be stored only once and applied in many different situations.

Each OBJECT may also be used within many contexts. For example, OBJECTS may be used to illustrate products on the Web, to graphically portray the enterprise in a brochure or to download information to a customer's pager. Figure 9.4 shows that each OBJECT may be used within one or more WEB CONTENTs in order to maintain the objects within each part of a Web site. A

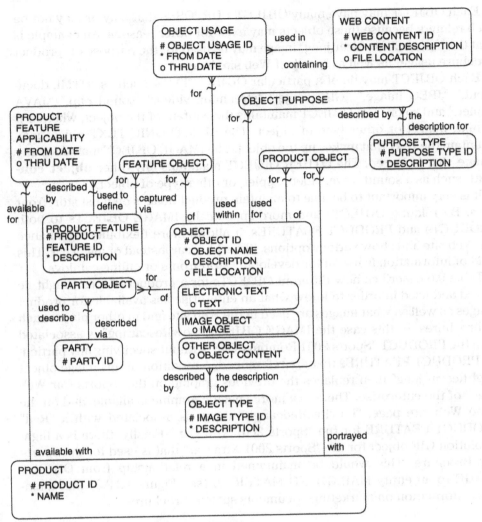

Figure 9.4 E-commerce products and objects.

WEB CONTENT may also contain many OBJECTs. This information provides the enterprise with what objects are used where. This can help identify information about visitors to the Web site and their interests. If the enterprise maintains which WEB CONTENTs are about what OBJECTs, which describe what types of PRODUCTS, PRODUCT FEATUREs, PARTYs and other things, the enterprise can find out the interests of the visitor. For instance, if the enterprise knows that a visitor followed a link to a specific Web page (a WEB CONTENT), and it referenced an object about "red thingamajigs," then the enterprise may be able to deduce that the visitor may have an interest in the product "thingamajigs" with the feature "red."

Each OBJECT may have many OBJECT PURPOSEs that may or may not be Web related, because these objects may exist for other reasons. An example is that the "sports2001redcar.jpeg" image may be used for the purpose of "product brochure usage" as well as "product Web site image."

Each OBJECT may be of a particular OBJECT TYPE, such as "HTML document," "JPEG image," "GIF image," "streaming video," "sound clip," "JAVA applet," and so on. The OBJECT maintains the content of the object, whether it is text, image, or other type of object. The ELECTRONIC TEXT object may maintain the **text** that makes up the object. The IMAGE OBJECT maintains any **image** that is stored. The OTHER OBJECT maintains any other **object content**, such as a sound wave, video, applet, or other type of object.

It is very important to be able to maintain product images on most storefront sites. By relating OBJECTs and more specifically IMAGE OBJECTs to both PRODUCTs and PRODUCT FEATUREs, it allows more flexibility to enhance the Web site and show various options, like a blue car instead of just a car. This kind of information is useful for developing storefronts or online-catalogs.

Table 9.6 describes how different OBJECTs for a product of a car might be stored and used in order to know what an enterprise has available for product images as well as what images are used in the Web site and in other places such as brochures. In this case the IMAGE OBJECT "LowRescar.jpg" is associated with the PRODUCT "Sports 2001 Romonix Car" without specifying any particular PRODUCT FEATUREs that are referenced. A rendition of this image object "highRescar.jpeg" then replaces the previous graphic on the "Sports Car Web Page" of the enterprise. There is a more specific graphic available, and on the same Web site page, "LowResRedcar.gif" image is associated with a "Red" PRODUCT FEATURE for the "Sports 2001 Xtra Car." Finally, there is a high-resolution GIF object for the "Sports 2001 Xtra Car" that is used for the Sports Car Brochure. This would be maintained in a relationship from OBJECT USAGE to an entity MARKETING MATERIAL (see Figure V2:2.3) that maintains information on marketing documents such as brochures.

Orders in E-Commerce

Orders and agreements will be very similar to Volume 1 models (V1:4.1–4.17). They will be merely captured on the Web and stored in a database much the same way that other orders are stored. The Web offers a new way to record and process orders, and it provides the enterprise with additional capabilities to capture much more order-related information. The Web can facilitate the capturing of information on various parties' needs for products because access to this information can be traced electronically through Web visits. Web users can more easily sign up for subscription-based information such as subscribing to discussion groups, subscribing to technical support Web groups, or being put

Table 9.6 E-Commerce Products and Objects

PRODUCT NAME	OBJECT NAME	OBJECT TYPE	OBJECT PURPOSE	OBJECT USAGE	OBJECT USAGE FROM DATE	PRODUCT FEATURE
Sports 2001 Romonix Car	LowRescar.jpeg	Low-resolution JPEG	Web	Related to "Sports car web page" WEB CONTENT	January 5, 2001	
Sports 2001 Romonix Car	HighRescar.jpeg	High-resolution JPEG	Web	Related to "Sports car Web page" WEB CONTENT	March 7, 2001	
Sports 2001 Xtra Car	LowResRedcar.gif	Low-resolution GIF	Web	Related to "Sports car Web page" WEB CONTENT	April 12, 2002	Red
Sports 2001 Xtra Car	HighRescar_1024color.gif	High-resolution GIF	Brochure	Related to "Sports car brochure" MARKETING MATERIAL	May 16, 2001	

on group lists for ongoing product information. Most importantly, the enterprise has the opportunity to capture the information related to Web visits and hits. Specifically, this section will address models to do the following:

- Capture specific needs of parties as they relate to Web visits.

- Capture Web-related subscriptions from visitors. These may be product related, or they may be related to subscribing for certain types of information.

- Capture information about the Web visit. This is perhaps the most important distinction as this information is very unique to the Web.

Party and Product Needs

One of the unique aspects of the Web is its ability to better facilitate capturing needs of the visitor and therefore of prospects and customers. While other models in these volumes have provided for capturing party needs (requirements model, V1:4.9, and the financial service needs model, V2:6.2), these models will be shown with slight modifications because the Web offers additional information about potential needs. Often Web sites allow the capabilities for recording needs and interests of visitors and then providing subscriptions for fulfilling their interests. This section will cover data models to capture needs, and the next section will discuss subscriptions.

Shown in Figure 9.5 are specific PARTY NEEDs of the CONSUMER with the date that the need was identified (**date identified**) and the **description** of the need. Each PARTY NEED may be for a CONSUMER and may be for a PRODUCT or PRODUCT CATEGORY, of a PRODUCT, categorized by a NEED TYPE, and discovered via a SERVER HIT or via a COMMUNICATION EVENT.

The needs are recorded for the PARTY in a PARTY ROLE of CONSUMER. A CONSUMER is defined as a party that may be or has been involved in the purchase of the enterprise's services. As stated before in the "Party Roles and Relationships" section of this chapter, the CONSUMER may be a VISITOR, SUBSCRIBER, CUSTOMER, or PROSPECT, and these are the parties for whom the enterprise generally wants to track needs. Alternatively, the modeler may elect to track related needs to a PARTY as shown in the Chapter 6 (V2:6.2).

The PARTY NEED may be for a PRODUCT TYPE (for instance, there may be a lot of activity on "sports cars") or a PRODUCT (the CONSUMER may click on the image for a specific car).

The needs may be classified by a NEED TYPE, for example, a need for a specific PRODUCT ("a specific car"), for a specific PRODUCT CATEGORY ("interested in sports cars"), or a general need that has not yet been translated to a product ("need for a high-powered engine"). The model allows the enterprise to record the needs of consumers through SERVER HITs, which represent any click on the Web site that may be related to a WEB CONTENT, such as when the consumer clicks on a graphic image, hyperlink to another page, or other object on the site.

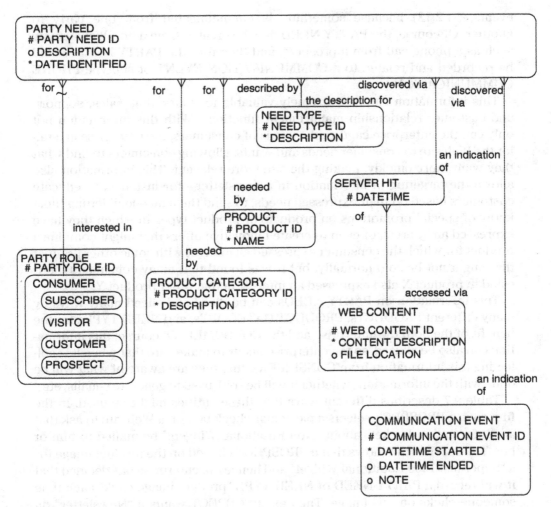

Figure 9.5   Party and product needs.

Each of these SERVER HITs may allow the enterprise to record various PARTY NEEDs. The PARTY NEED instance would have to be based on business rules that the enterprise sets up. For example, when a CONSUMER clicks on a specific product image, a PARTY NEED may be set up for the CONSUMER that has clicked on the image.

The PARTY NEED may be deduced through Web site activity or may be specifically asked for within the Web site. For instance, a specific Web site may have a form in which the CONSUMER can put check marks next to the PRODUCTs, PRODUCTS CATEGORYs, or NEED TYPEs that may be of interest to them. When this type of Web activity occurs, it is considered another type of COMMUNICATION EVENT of subtype WEB SITE COMMUNICATION (see communication events, V1:2.12) because something is communicated from one party to another. Of course, the PARTY NEED may be created from a non-Web activity such as a phone call from a prospect, and therefore the PARTY NEED would be recorded and related to a COMMUNICATION EVENT of subtype PHONE COMMUNICATION.

This information can be extremely valuable for marketing, sales, support, and customer relationship management functions. With this information not only can the enterprise capture the needs of consumers, the enterprise can tailor the Web site to consumer needs and wants, allowing consumers to find what they want more quickly, making the site more relevant. This information also allows the targeting of information in a newsletter—for instance, to educate customers based on their expressed needs, to send them an e-mail letting them know of special promotions on products or product types in which they have expressed an interest, or even to create innovative offers that might combine a product for which the consumer expressed an interest with some other product that might not be sold normally, but it was found that many consumers interested in product X also expressed an interest in that other product Y.

This information on PARTY NEEDs can be diced and sliced many ways by many different PRODUCTs, PRODUCT CATEGORYs, and NEED TYPEs for the benefit of the both the enterprise and the CONSUMER. Of course, this information can also be abused, so the enterprise needs to make sure that when it is collecting this information from CONSUMERs, that they are aware of what will be done with the information (whether it will be sold, used to generate e-mails, etc).

Table 9.7 describes different ways that these entities might be used. In the first row, a PROSPECT selects a particular check box on a Web site to ask that an "Information Packet" about "Non-Rotational Widgets" be mailed to him or her. The second row shows that a PROSPECT clicked on the product image for a "Super fast 1000 Rotational Widget" and hence the enterprise has decided that it will record a PARTY NEED of NEED TYPE "product image click" each time someone clicks on this image. The next PROSPECT wants a "Newsletter" on the PRODUCT CATEGORY "Non-Rotational Widgets." Another PROSPECT calls on the phone to find out when there is a "Special Promotion" on a specific PRODUCT "Blue Rotating Widget." After reviewing the Web site, A CUSTOMER sends an e-mail asking for a "Newsletter" about "Rotational Widgets" as well as "Promotional material" such as a brochure on "Blue Rotating Widgets." Also represented here is a VISTOR that checked a box on the Web site, asking to be sent more information on "Rotational Widgets."

Subscriptions

A subscription is a mechanism that provides for the sending of ongoing information about certain items of interest to the consumer. The information could be about products, product types, or general needs or items of general interest.

Table 9.7 Product Need Entities

PARTY ROLE	NEED TYPE	PRODUCT CATEGORY	PRODUCT	SERVER HIT	COMMUNICATION EVENT	WEB CONTENT
PROSPECT	Information packet requested	Non-rotational widgets			Web site request for information packet	Product sales Web page
PROSPECT	Product image click		Super fast 1000 rota-tional widget	Web Site click on the product image		Super fast 1000 rotational widget Web page
PROSPECT	Newsletter sign up	Non-rotational widgets		Server hit to record check mark for sign up		For more information Web page
PROSPECT	Special promotion request		Blue rotating widget		Phone call communication	
CUSTOMER	Newsletter	Rotational widgets			E-mail	
CUSTOMER	Promotional material request		Blue rotating widgets		E-mail	
VISITOR	Product inform-ation request	Rotational widgets		Server hit–checked box to send more information on rotational widgets		For more information Web page

415

Web users may subscribe to user groups, newsletters, or ongoing product updates and information. The need for subscriptions may be applicable in non-e-commerce situations; however, the Web makes this type of request more practical, and the enterprise may want to maintain this information because the Internet facilitates recording and sending subscription-based information.

The needs model in Figure 9.5 showed only a party's interests, while the subscription model in Figure 9.6 shows SUBSCRIBERs that have formally requested and given permission to receive information and hence have a SUBSCRIPTION concerning PRODUCTs, PRODUCT CATEGORYs, or certain NEED TYPEs. The SUBSCRIPTION may be a NEWSGROUP SUBSCRIPTION (sending the subscriber ongoing newsletters and information), PRODUCT INFORMATION SUBSCRIPTION (sending the subscriber ongoing product information and updates), USER GROUP SUBSCRIPTION (entitling the subscriber to be a member of that user group that exchanges information), or OTHER SUBSCRIPTION, which would account for additional types as maintained in the SUBSCRIPTION TYPE entity. The SUBSCRIPTION may come from an ORDER ITEM (usually for chargeable subscriptions), a COMMUNICATION EVENT (if the communication came from a phone call or other types of communication), or a PARTY NEED if the party was shown to have a need for a subscription.

To track the sending of ongoing information each SUBSCRIPTION may be related to many SUBSCRIPTION FULFILLMENT PIECEs (such as the sending of a piece of information or a newsletter edition) that are part of a SUBSCRIPTION ACTIVITY, such as a comprehensive mailing to all subscribers in a particular SUBSCRIPTION. When the subscriber enters into a subscription, the subscriber will need to leave some form of CONTACT MECHANISM as the means for receiving the subscription.

The ORDER ITEM may store subscriptions that are chargeable and relate them to the selling of a SUBSCRIPTION. Or the enterprise may encourage subscription on a non-chargeable basis, and the subscription may come from a COMMUNICATION EVENT or PARTY NEED. Subscriptions may be used as the basis of marketing campaigns, by targeting information to the users' preferences and interests, and by allowing the subscriber to sign up for information subscriptions in which they are interested. This is known as "opted-in" or permission marketing. This can be a very powerful tool for building customer loyalty, brand, and repeat business, and the Web makes this particularly efficient.

Figure 9.6 shows that the SUBSCRIPTION must be for a SUBSCRIBER that is a PARTY ROLE for a PARTY. On the Web it is possible that the enterprise does not know the name of the PARTY; however, it is still possible to track subscriptions for anonymous PARTYs by assigning the party a party ID and tracking SUBSCRIPTION FULFILLMENT pieces sent to this PARTY's requested CONTACT MECHANISM, for instance an e-mail address.

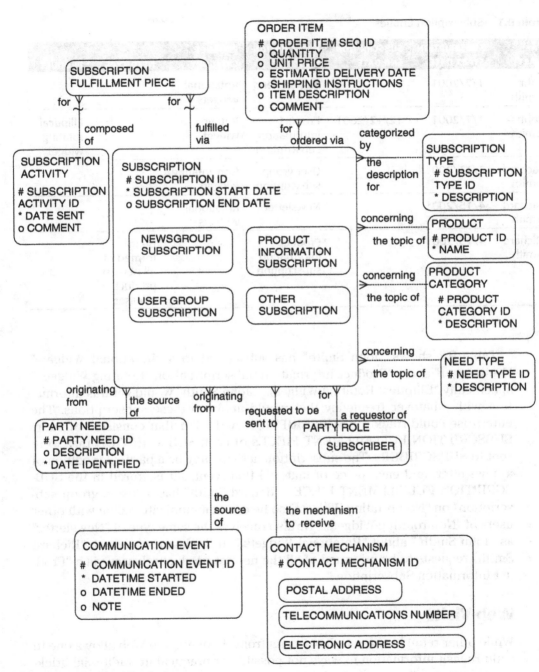

Figure 9.6 Web subscriptions.

Table 9.7 Subscription Entities

PARTY	SUBSCRIPTION START DATE	SUBSCRIPTION END DATE	SUBSCRIPTION TYPE	PRODUCT CATEGORY	NEED TYPE	PRODUCT
John Smith	1/7/2001		Newsletter	Rotational widgets		
John Smith	1/7/2001	12/12/2001	Product information subscription	Rotating widget		Elliptical rotating widget
Richard Smith	3/13/2001		User group subscription	Non-rotating widgets		
Richard Smith	4/15/2001		Newsletter	Rotational widgets		
Richard Smith	4/15/2001		Product information subscription		Be informed of all newest product releases	

Table 9.7 shows "John Smith" has subscribed to a "Rotational Widgets" "Newsletter" and a "Product Information Subscription" on "Rotating Widgets," specifically "Elliptical Rotating Widgets." "John Smith" would get this information with whatever frequency that would apply to these subscriptions. The enterprise could track the SUBSCRIPTION ACTIVITY that consisted of many SUBSCRIPTION FULLFILLMENT PIECEs of each SUBSCRIPTION that were sent to SUBSCRIBERs. The subscription activity may be a particular edition of a newsletter, and each piece of material that went out is stored in the SUBSCRIPTION FULFILLMENT PIECE. "Richard Smith" has a "users group subscription" on "Non-rotating Widgets" so he can communicate online with other users of "Non-rotating Widgets." He also receives the same type of "Newsletter" as "John Smith," about "Rotational Widgets." In the last row record, "Richard Smith" requests to be informed of all the newest product releases via a "Product Information Subscription."

Web Visits

While other retail businesses have visits from shoppers, the Web allows one to capture visit information in ways not possible or practical in traditional brick-and-mortar retail operations. Imagine a large department store. The store is spread over a couple of floors and has dozens of displays and thousands of items. You might have hundreds of people in the store, shopping, buying, browsing, and so on. Now imagine the store trying to track everything that visitors do within the store. It follows them throughout their trip through the store, taking note of what displays they look at, what areas of the store they visited, what items they picked up, what items they put back, and what they bought. As a matter of practicality the store might be able to keep track of how many people stopped at a particular display and maybe how many people came into the store, certainly how many people bought things, how much they bought, and so on. It is impractical, though, to track each shopper throughout his or her entire visit to the store. This is the unique advantage of the Web. Wherever the visitor goes, he or she leaves a trail.

Web Hits and Web Logs

When a visitor goes to the site, his or her browser requests a URL (Universal Resource Locator), or in other words, a Web site address. The Web server then serves up this request. The request might be for a Web page, which will have other requests for things such as graphics within the page, which will lead to more requests to the Web server. Each of these requests is generally referred to as a "hit." The Web server is able to record certain information, usually in a Web log, about each hit as follows:

1. The IP address of the requester (although this might also be an IP address stuck in by a firewall that does Network Address Translation, or NAT, which means that the firewall provides a "public" IP address for the requester behind the firewall that is different from the actual IP address of the requester).

2. The authuser field. This field describes any user ID that the visitor enters during that visit in order to gain access to the page. If a directory on a Web server is protected, the Web server will challenge the user in some fashion (usually user ID and password). The Web server will record the user ID in the access log as long as the user is within the protected area.

3. Usually a date and time field (perhaps with the time zone in it).

4. The request that was made, which usually includes the URL, the HTTP method (like GET, POST, and so on), the protocol (usually HTTP), and the version of the protocol (usually 1.0 or 1.1).

5. The status code, which is the error code that the Web server assigns to the transaction to cover cases from "everything was OK" to "file not found."

6. The number of bytes transferred to the requester.

7. The referring URL (where was the last place the user came from).

8. User agent information, such as what version of what browser was used on what platform. Information on spiders and other agents will show up here as well.

9. Last, cookies, which are arbitrary text strings that the Web server will try to place with the visitors' browser (perhaps on the behalf of an application) to try to keep track of certain special information like tracking sessions, assigning a unique identifier to the visitor, keeping track of information for the user so that when he or she comes back to the site, the site will be able to identify that he or she is the same party, even if the party name or other information about the party is not known.

It should be noted that you might find "-" in some of the fields in the log file. When the Web server can't determine a piece of information for whatever reason, it will put a "-" in that field. If the visitor isn't required to log in, then there will be a "-" in the authuser field, or if the visitor types in the URL, then the referrer field will have a "-" in it, or if the visitor has set the browser so that it will not accept cookies, then the cookies field will have a "-" in it, and so forth. While the log file may show a "-" in some fields, as in Table 9.8, this book represents them as nulls because this represents database instances.

Many tools and utilities are available for analyzing Web server logs, which is good for doing analysis on just the server logs. When you want to use this information in conjunction with other information to build profiles of your visitors to customize content for them or to target your marketing and advertising, then it makes sense to keep track of this information as an integrated part of your business and therefore within an integrated database design. The next section will discuss a data model to do just this.

Web Visits Model

Figure 9.7 shows that a PARTY may be a visitor of many VISITs. A VISIT is a session on a Web site that consists of a collection of SERVER HITs that are related via the information and rules surrounding a VISIT. Useful information about the visit includes the **visit from datetime, visit thru datetime** and the **cookie** string that helps identify the machine that was used for the connection. The VISIT may result in one or more ORDERs.

A VISIT may be composed of one or more SERVER HITs, which has relationships to the USER LOGIN, SERVER HIT STATUS TYPE, the IP ADDRESS of the visitor, the referring URL, the USER AGENT, and the WEB CONTENT to which it is referring. The USER LOGIN stores the authuser field of the Web log as described previously. The SERVER HIT STATUS TYPE may record status information about the hit—for example if a requested file in a server hit was successfully retrieved or if the file was not found. The IP ADDRESS records the address of the machine requesting the server hit. The relationship from SERVER HIT to WEB ADDRESS records the URL of the site that referred the

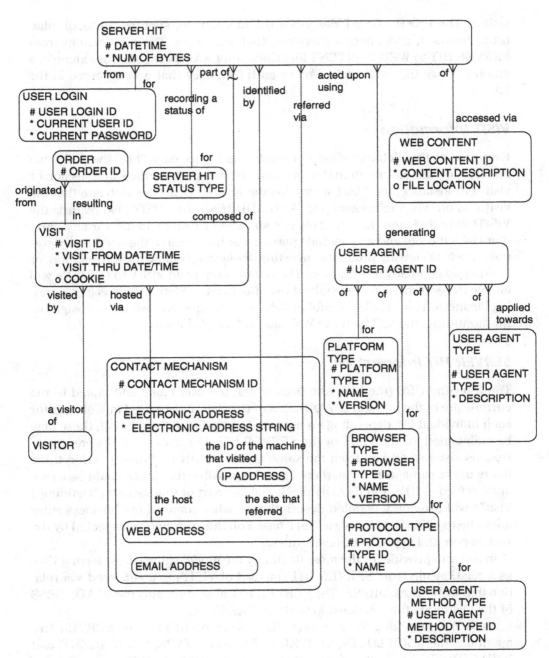

Figure 9.7 Web visits.

visitor. The USER AGENT describes the mechanism, such as protocol, platform, browser, and operating system, that was used. The relationship from SERVER HIT to WEB CONTENT identifies what was accessed—for example, a graphic image that was clicked on or an HTML page that was accessed in the hit.

VISIT Information

Even though the Web logs show some information for each "hit," the VISIT can maintain certain information that is common among hits in the same session or visit. For instance, the VISIT maintains the hosting URL (the Web site that the visitor is on) via a relationship to WEB ADDRESS. The VISIT also records the VISITOR that visited the site. This is a subtype of PARTY ROLE for any party that visits the site and may include parties that have visited the site for any purpose, such as viewing products, investing, looking up employee information, or looking up company information. The relationship from VISIT to ORDERs will enable the enterprise to determine how effective the Web activity is in generating business. This may be helpful in determining effectiveness of campaigns or for monitoring the ability of the Web site to "close" the sale.

SERVER HIT Information

The referring URL (the Web site from which the user came and linked to the current site of the hit) and IP ADDRESS of the visitor are stored in Web logs for each individual hit; depending on how the enterprise defines a visit, these may be maintained for the VISIT or the SERVER HIT. For instance if the enterprise regards visits as all hits from the same USER LOGIN (authuser) within three hours of the same user login, then it may be possible that there could be a separate referring URL and ID ADDRESS. The last part of this section ("Defining a Visit") will provide a detailed description of what some of the business rules might be to effectively derive a VISIT based on the information collected by the Web server and applying business rules.

In order to provide for the most flexibility the model shows the referring URL as a relationship from SERVER HIT (instead of VISIT) to a **referred via** relationship to WEB ADDRESS. The SERVER HIT also maintains the IP ADDRESS of the visitor via the relationship to IP ADDRESS.

Aside from tracking the referring URL and IP ADDRESS, the SERVER HIT maintains the USER LOGIN, SERVER HIT STATUS TYPE, USER AGENT, and WEB CONTENT as well as some attributes in the SERVER HIT.

The SERVER HIT may specify a particular USER LOGIN that has signed in under a login name (this is called the authuser in the Web log). The SERVER HIT may be of a certain status such as "server request successful" or "file not found," which is a value in the SERVER HIT STATUS TYPE (a subtype of STA-TUS TYPE).

The SERVER HIT records the USER AGENT (the type of mechanisms that were used to access the hit). USER AGENT may be of a USER AGENT TYPE, which might be a browser, spider, crawler, and so on. PLATFORM TYPE is what version of what operating system the USER AGENT runs on such as "Windows 98," "Windows 2000," or "Unix." The BROWSER TYPE reveals the name and version of the browser (i.e., Netscape, Internet Explorer, Infobot, etc.). The USER AGENT may specify a PROTOCOL TYPE and USER AGENT METHOD TYPE of the SERVER HIT. An example of a PROTOCOL TYPE would be http, https, ftp, and so on, while the USER AGENT METHOD TYPE might be get, post, and delete.

The SERVER HIT records the particular Web site page or object that was hit. It does this through the relationship from SERVER HIT to the WEB CONTENT, which could point to a specific HTML page, image, or other object that was clicked on in the hit.

SERVER HITs also keep track of the **datetime** stamp of the "hit" or request and the size in bytes (**num of bytes**) of the response.

Defining a Visit

Table 9.8 shows some partial examples of visits. The information here was presumably processed from the actual "Hits" from the Web server to come up with the visit information. These examples demonstrate some of the situations that the enterprise may run into when trying to define via the data what constitutes a visit. Below is a detailed explanation of how this information can be used to define a VISIT.

There are three business rules that need to be implemented to help determine how Table 9.8 is filled in. The first business rule is that a VISITOR is always related to a PARTY; however, the party name and other party information may not be known or recorded. The table refers to the records by their PARTY ID and/or name, so it will be easier to explain the rest of the business rules. Because the nature of the Web is prone to anonymity, in many cases the enterprise will not be able to identify the name of the PARTY to which a VISITOR is related. Because it is required that each VISITOR be associated with a PARTY, some PARTYs will have only **party IDs** and other parties that are able to be identified will have a name (among other information).

A visitor may have set his or her browser to not accept cookies, may never log in to a protected area, and may not buy anything from your site. In this case, the enterprise can track the user through your site only by IP Address, as in the first row of the table. The enterprise knows that someone with the IP Address 10.0.0.1 visited your site 10 minutes before New Year's and left 10 minutes afterward. The

Table 9.8 Party Visits

PARTY ID AND PARTY NAME (OF VISITOR)	USER LOGIN CURRENT USER ID (AUTHUSER IN THE WEB LOGS)	COOKIE	IP ADDRESS	VISIT FROM DATETIME	VISIT THRU DATETIME
39849			10.0.0.1	12/31/1999 23:50:00	1/1/2000 00:10:53
39085		1234567890	10.0.0.1	1/2/2000 08:01:21	1/2/2000 08:43:57
34098		1001001	10.1.1.1	1/1/2000 08:01:45	1/1/2000 08:15:45
48958 John Smith	Jsmith	1001001	10.10.10.10	1/2/2000 08:07:35	1/2/2000 08:12:01
48958 John Smith	Jsmith	1001001	10.9.9.9	1/2/2000 09:31:20	1/2/2000 09:45:17
48958 John Smith		1001001	10.9.9.12	1/3/2000 16:11:59	1/3/2000 16:48:42
69786 Frank Smith			10.0.0.1	1/4/2000 14:23:08	1/4/2000 14:31:22

enterprise might even have a cookie (an ID created by the Web site and attached to the visitor's browser) from the VISITOR, but until the visitor buys something or registers for something, the enterprise may have no idea who the actual party is. The enterprise will still want to keep track of the VISITORs even if the PARTY is anonymous because the PARTY might get identified at some point in the future. Therefore, the enterprise will assign a party ID to the visitor. If the visitor ID is identified later, then the enterprise can change the party ID of the visit to the actual PARTY in order to help build a profile of the PARTY.

An example of this is with the third anonymous record (only a party ID was recorded without knowing that name of the party). Because of the cookie information and the timing of the visit, this visit could be associated with "John Smith." The likely situation here is that "John Smith" visited the site on "1/1/2000," but then registered for something the following day so that he could get into a special area of the site (where you need a user ID and password to enter). However, the party name was not recorded because the IP ADDRESS of the third row was different from the IP address of the fourth row and the same cookie does not necessarily guarantee that it is the same party name. For example, different people may have logged onto a Web site using the same computer.

The second business rule deals with how to define a visit. How does one know when a visit begins and ends? Consider the fourth and fifth rows (the first two "John Smith" rows) of the table. Here we know that "John Smith" came to the site starting at "8:07 a.m." on '1/2/2000.' It looks like "John Smith" was doing something with the site until about "8:12 a.m." that day, and then maybe he went away for a while. Then he came back at "09:31 a.m." Did "John Smith" go to some other site for a while, or did he just get a phone call or get interrupted, then came back to his computer to continue shopping or whatever he was doing on the site? It is normal to pick some sort of inactivity time interval to help define a visit. For instance, the enterprise might pick 30 minutes between clicks for determining a visit (this is a common standard). This inactivity period may vary for different needs, and the enterprise needs to pick something that makes sense for it. If there is a 30-minute video presentation or other Web activity that doesn't require browser measurable user intervention for more than 30 minutes, then 30 minutes won't be a good value for this site. The enterprise might also tie time inactivity with the referring URL to help determine if this is a different visit. In the preceding example, if the "09:31 a.m." visit for "John Smith" has an external referring URL, then "John Smith" left the site at "8:12 a.m." to go to another site.

The third rule also helps to define a visit, but instead of dealing with the visit event, it deals with what attributes are used to define the VISITOR. For purposes of this discussion, we are going to use Authuser, Cookie, and IP ADDRESS to help define the VISITOR of the visit. The **visit from datetime** and **visit thru datetime** are useful here as well. The IP ADDRESS used during a particular visit is a strong identifier of the VISITOR during this particular time frame. Because many ISPs dynamically assign the IP Address to the VISITOR who is dialing in, it isn't enough to track a VISITOR across visits.

Consider the first two rows in Table 9.8. Here, Party ID 39849 seems to have come in on New Year's Eve on IP address "10.0.0.1," and Party ID 39085 came in on "1/2/2000" with the same IP address. Is this the same party? Probably not given that the first party did not accept cookies, but the second party did. People tend not to change their browser settings, but the bottom line is that it is impossible to know. If it was determined later that this was the same party, then the information in the two visits could be consolidated by pointing to the same party.

The "John Smith" records show an even better example of how poor the IP address is for identifying the VISITOR for a visit. Even though the IP addresses for the visits in the fourth and fifth rows are different, it seems that the visitor is the same considering that the visitor has the same authuser (as noted by the relationship to USER LOGIN) and same cookie string that was identified by the server. Cookies are a strong identifier, but not all visitors will accept cookies. Authuser is even better, but again, not everyone will register for a site, and there will be areas on your site where a user ID and password are not required.

Delivery, Work Efforts, Invoicing, Accounting, and Human Resources

We have covered the changes to the data models for the people and organizations, product, and orders subject data areas. The data models for most of the other subject data areas will work quite well in most e-commerce applications.

The only thing worth mentioning for any of these models is that the enterprise may want to add a SHIPMENT METHOD TYPE in the shipment route segments model (V1:5.7) to handle Internet delivery of soft goods like software or information. If someone is buying an information packet from the enterprise that is available in electronic format, then why not let the CUSTOMER download it or get it in e-mail as the fulfillment mechanism for the order? Otherwise, if the enterprise ships out tangible items, the shipment models will work.

The invoicing models should fit for most enterprises with minor customization. The work effort and work order models can be used for Web development and maintenance. The accounting and budgeting data models will probably be usable with very few changes. The human resources models should apply as well.

Web Server Hits Star Schema

Now that this information has been collected from the Web servers, the enterprise needs to be able to analyze it to get the most out of the information possible. Putting this information into star schemas for easier analysis can greatly aid in this effort.

Server Hit Star Schema

Figure 9.8 provides a star schema to analyze Web hits. With this structure, the enterprise will be able to dice and slice the data to find out from where their VISITORs are referred, who is using the Web site and when, what ISPs they come from, what WEB_CONTENT (Web pages, images, or objects) are the most popular, what USER_AGENTS or mechanisms visitors are using to access the site, what type of PRODUCTS the Web server hits refer to, and at what rate is traffic building on the Web site.

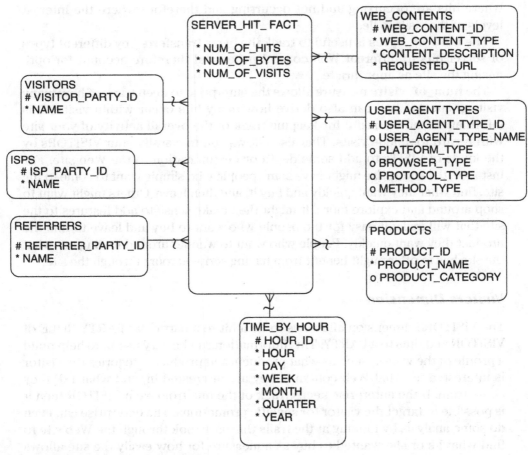

Figure 9.8   Web server hits star schema.

The star schema is based on the number of SERVER HITs and the number of bytes requested by CONSUMER, ISP, REFERRER, WEB CONTENT, USER AGENT, USER LOGIN, and PRODUCT.

Server Hit Fact

The fact table for this schema is SERVER HIT FACT. In this fact table, there are three measures: **num_of_hits,** which is the count of the hits for the selected dimension values, **num_of_bytes**, which is the number of bytes transferred from the hits matching the selected dimension values, and **num_of_visits**, which is the number of Web visits for the selected dimension values.

The **num_of_hits** measure provides valuable information on how many hits occur for various VISTORS, ISPs, REFERRERs, WEB_CONTENTS, PRODUCTS, and **product_categories**. This information may be used to evaluate where hits are occurring and not occurring and therefore where the interest levels of the visitors lie.

The **num_of_bytes** is useful to track the bytes transferred by different types of server hits to different Web content pages and therefore account for optimizing the site as appropriate.

The **num_of_visits** measure allows the enterprise to keep track of how many visits occur and one can also derive how many hits occur within visits. This information can be useful for keeping track of the overall activity of your site with regard to unique visits. This also allows you to classify your VISITORs by the kinds of VISITs to add some depth or customization to the Web site. For instance, the enterprise might have some people who simply want to come to the site, find what they want quickly and buy it, and then leave. Others might want to shop around and explore more. It might then make sense to add features to the site that will make it easy for the people who want to buy and leave to find the product they want quickly. People who want to wander around finding out what the site has to offer might benefit from having scripted tours through the site.

Visitors Dimension

The VISITORS dimension allows us to tie a hit to a particular PARTY ROLE of VISITOR and thus to a PARTY. This information can be very useful to help build a profile of the visitor, such as what products and product categories the visitor is interested in, what Web contents they are interested in, and what ISP they come from. If the enterprise keeps track of the hits from each VISITOR then it is possible to target the visitor for specific promotions. The enterprise can even do some analysis by looking at the trails this user took through the Web site to find what he or she wanted to buy as a measure for how easily the site allows customers to find what they want.

ISPS Dimension

This dimension allows the enterprise to keep track of what hits came from what ISPs. This could be useful in situations where the enterprise wants to put together a marketing campaign to target ISPs. Which ones should the enterprise target?

The enterprise might also want to offload some of the direct traffic to its Web servers if they find that a significant portion of the traffic comes from a certain ISP. One strategy is to make arrangements to have a mirror site for that ISP. This will benefit the VISITORs as well because they should get faster response from the site because the packets won't have as far to go.

The enterprise might also discover that a significant number of purchases happen to come from a particular ISP. The enterprise might be able to use this information to approach the ISP and enter into a partnership with the ISP. For instance, the enterprise could offer a discount to the ISP's customers in order to gain the benefit of being able to market to the ISP's customers.

Referrers Dimension

This dimension is extremely useful for finding out where VISITORs are coming from. This will tell the enterprise what search engines VISITORs are using to find the site. It will also tell what other sites visitors are coming from, which may relate back to a banner or Web site link that the enterprise wants to track. This can be very helpful in determining how successful an Internet marketing campaign has been. Because the referring URL gives the enterprise the keywords that were used in the search, it can also be useful in suggesting other keywords that might be used to help people find the enterprise.

Web Contents Dimension

This dimension lets you know precisely what Web contents, files, or objects have been requested and accessed. There are times when it is helpful to keep track of which Web content is being accessed, such as what pages or images are being accessed in a Web site. By tracking what Web contents are being accessed, the enterprise can determine the popularity of each page and object for different visitors and products over time.

It can be very helpful for determining what pages get the most traffic, what graphics get the most traffic, and so on. This information can be used to help optimize your site, making sure the most heavily visited pages load quickly. It helps the enterprise figure out what parts of the site aren't visited as much, so maybe they need to change the organization of the site to get visitors to go to that part of the site, or maybe they should consider removing that part of the site.

This type of information is also useful to provide to potential advertisers in the hope of attracting them to advertise on specific pages.

User Agent Types Dimension

As technology changes over time and more capabilities are added to browsers, it is useful to keep track of what environments clients VISITORs are using to access the Web site. This will allow the enterprise to optimize the experience for VISITORs by tailoring the site to the abilities of VISITORs' browsers and operating systems. This information will reveal what search agents, spiders, and bots are visiting the site.

Products Dimension

It often may be useful to analyze hits by product and product category. This can give the enterprise an idea of what kind of traffic the products are getting on the Web site. This kind of information can be used to identify what products might need some promotion to increase their traffic. This information can also be used to figure out browse-to-sale rates. Maybe many visitors are looking at the enterprise's products, but they aren't buying because of price or some other reason. There may or may not be a product for a server hit because the hit may not relate to a specific product or product type. Therefore, a blank product instance should be included for the PRODUCTS dimension for occurrences where the product is not applicable. If the hit is related to a product image or product text (or product category image or text), then the product value may be used.

Time by Hour Dimension

This allows the enterprise to assign this hit to a particular date and hour and is useful for looking at which slices of time are most busy. Using this, the enterprise can characterize when the site is the busiest (what hours during the day), what day during the week, what week during the month, what month during the year, and so on. This kind of information is helpful for the operation of the site, so the enterprise knows when it is best to make changes to the site and what time during the year added capacity is needed to handle the extra load.

The level of granularity for this dimension is shown by the hour. If the enterprise desires a lower level of granularity—for instance, if it wants to show hits by the second—then another star schema may be appropriate because this would require a large number of records. The enterprise might want the maximum number of hits in a second as a measure of volume for capacity reasons. The enterprise may also want to measure traffic, week by week, month by month, and so on. For capacity reasons, perhaps only the WEB CONTENTS, USER AGENT TYPES, and TIME dimensions need to be shown in an alternate star schema design that is designed to analyze activity.

Web Visit Star Schema

Figure 9.9 provides a star schema for visits with a fact table of WEB_VISIT_FACT with measures of the following:

- **Num_of_hits.** Provides a count of how many hits occurred for the specified dimension values.

- **Num_of_pages_visited.** Provides a count of how many Web pages were visited during the visit with the specified dimension values.

- **Num_of_products_inquired.** Provides a count of the number of products that were inquired on via a product image or text click.

- **Num_of_products_ordered.** Provides a count for how many products were ordered for the visits with the specified dimension values.

- **Num_of_visits_resulting_in_orders.** Provides a count for how many of the visits of the specified dimension values resulted in sales.

- **Average_visit_time.** Provides a measure of the average time length for visits.

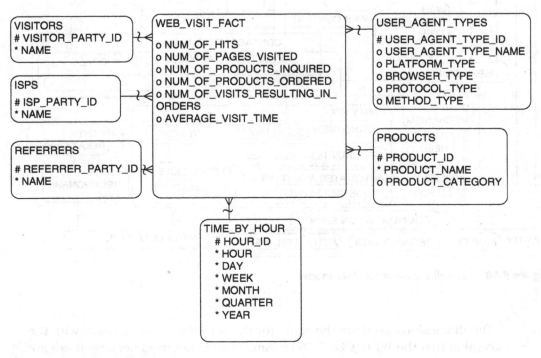

Figure 9.9 Web visits star schema.

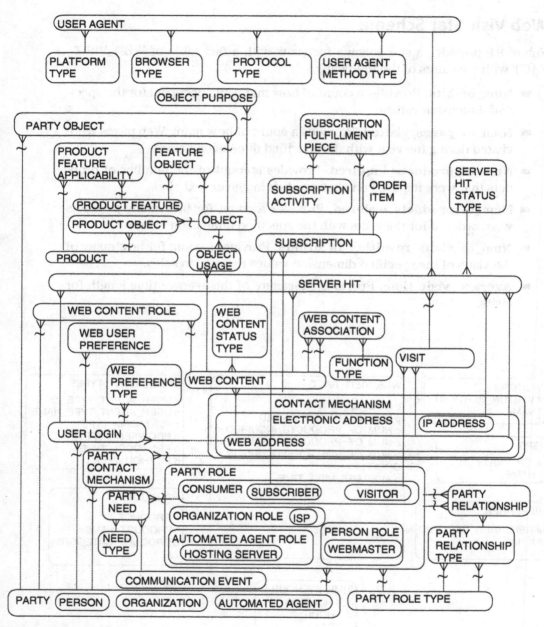

Figure 9.10 Overall e-commerce data model.

The dimensions used are the same for the server hits star schema with the exception that the WEB_CONTENTS dimension is not used because there are often many WEB_CONTENTS references for a VISIT.

E-Commerce Summary

While many of the data models from Volume 1 and Volume 2 are applicable in e-commerce environments, the data models within this chapter focused on the unique data model constructs needed to maintain e-commerce specific information. Perhaps the most important additional data constructs needed are those that capture the information requirements about the VISITOR, WEB CONTENT, USER LOGIN, OBJECT, SUBSCRIPTION, VISIT, and SERVER HIT entities.

Some data model modifications and additional models were provided for enterprises wanting to maintain their e-commerce information more effectively. Appropriate party relationships were subtyped, party contact mechanism subtypes were added, product models were expanded to include objects that may be stored and used on a Web site, party needs as they relate to Web visits were added, Web-based subscriptions were accounted for, a model for Web visits and server hits was added, and two star schemas were provided to analyze hits and visit information.

Figure 9.10 provides an overall e-commerce data model covering the key entities and relationships within this chapter.

CHAPTER

10

Using the Industry Models in the Real World

Now that you have an arsenal of template models at your disposal, the next question is "How can I make the most of these models to really make a difference?" This same question was addressed for the models in Volume 1, and many uses were explained for these models. Additional questions about these industry models are the following:

- How useful are these models for building transaction-oriented systems as well as for building data warehouse applications?

- What if the enterprise needing data models does not neatly fit into one of the chapters of this book? Are these models still relevant?

- How relevant are these models to specific industries? For example, can a property and casualty organization effectively use the insurance models, or does it need a property and casualty data model?

- What if the nature of enterprise needing data models is covered in several of the chapters of this book? How can I use these models?

- Should universal models be set up as specific modules instead of as applications for industries? For instance, many industries involve time and activity tracking that could be set up as a universal data model module.

This chapter addresses these questions.

Using the Models to Build Transaction-Oriented Systems and Data Warehouses

How useful are these models for building transaction-oriented databases as well as for building data warehouse applications?

It is a well-accepted principle that to build an effective transaction-oriented database, the data model is a good place to define the structures. The data models represent a logical perspective and do not assume that the practitioner will implement these models without denormalizing the data for performance reasons. The data model represents the information requirements of the enterprise expressed in a normalized, or non-redundant, format. Certainly, database designers will want to assess performance considerations as well as ease-of-access considerations and translate these structures into a physical database design.

In data warehousing, is it important to understand the nature of the data and relationships when designing decision support databases? Often, practitioners start by using dimensional modeling techniques, and, in fact, this book contains many dimensional (star schema) models to assist in this area. If one jumps into the dimensional models without understanding the nature of the data, though, problems arise.

For instance, if one does not understand the intricacies of the product structures and the nature of product classifications and hierarchies within the enterprise, it may be difficult to properly construct a good data warehouse design. One may assume that a product is classified into a single product category, when there may be a many-to-many relationship between products and product classifications. This type of misunderstanding can often lead to faulty designs as well as faulty understandings of the data presented. For instance, product totals may be miscalculated if they are repeated in several categories.

Another example of a misunderstanding caused by not having a data model may be to create faulty measures within the fact table of a star schema. For example, a shipping star schema with invoice information as measures with the fact table could lead to problems. If the data model shows that there is a many-to-many relationship between shipment items and invoice items and the fact table is at a shipment transaction level, how can the fact table properly maintain the many invoice items that are related to that shipment transaction?

The data models lend perspective and understanding to the nature of the data within the organization. Therefore, it is important to have good data models for building a data warehouse or star schema design as well as for building transaction-oriented databases. Without this knowledge, the enterprise is susceptible to data warehouse design errors, data errors, data transformation errors, excessive time in debugging data warehouse applications due to misunderstandings, and basically not as effective data management and good information.

The approach of using template or universal data models as illustrated in this book can take the edge out of the time-consuming process of data modeling so that practitioners can spend more time using data models as an effective data management tool and less time developing them.

Enterprises in Other Industries

What if the enterprise needing data models does not neatly fit into one of the chapters of this book? Are these models relevant?

While many of the data models are suited for specific industries, the concepts behind these data structures can be widely applied to many industries. Some examples of expanding these data structures for other industries include the following:

- Using the telecommunications network constructs as the basis for developing other facilities' management data models. For example, oil and gas companies need to monitor their facilities and charge by usage of their facilities so there are some similarities to the telecommunications constructs. While the names of entities may change, one can use many of the same constructs and ideas. This approach encourages broader thinking and can be helpful in quality assuring other models.

- Using the manufacturing data models for distributors. Many distributors have similar notions of bill of materials, parts that they assemble (for instance, in creating bundled product packages to sell), and providing substitutability, compatibility, obsolescence, and other product association recursions.

- Travel. Other enterprises may be involved in reservations and ticketing activities such as sports or entertainment event management. These enterprises may use many parts of the reservations and ticketing models.

- Financial services. The model to handle the work tasks to assess risk and to target market segments (V2:6.9) may be used in many industries including insurance firms and venture capital companies.

- Professional services. Many enterprises may be involved in delivering services that complement the goods they sell. They may be in need of the time and deliverable-based data models described in Chapter 7.

- Web. Many organizations promote their products and services on the Web and could use the models contained within this chapter to maintain needs, subscriptions, and Web site visits.

Relevance of Models to Very Specific Industries

How relevant are these models to specific industries? For example, can a property and casualty organization effectively use the insurance models, or does it need a property and casualty data model? Should there be a separate data model for airlines, train enterprises, bus companies, car reservations companies, cruise lines, and other travel enterprises?

On the surface, it may seem that a more specific data model may serve the needs of the organization better because many of the data constructs and data names may be more specific to that particular enterprise. As stated in Chapter 1, there are many reasons that an enterprise might find the broader data model more useful. To summarize these reasons, this model provides a framework that can accommodate a broader vision for that enterprise, more integration across various parts of the enterprise, more stability should changes occur in the enterprise, structures that are easier to modify for that industry because one is working from a broader perspective, and finally, structures that will apply to the specific industry when using these broader models.

Diverse Enterprises Needing Models from Several Chapters

What if the nature of the enterprise needing data models is described in several of the chapters of this book? How can I use the models in this book?

Begin by identifying the common constructs that can be used from Volume 1 and identifying the chapters from Volume 2 that provide reusable constructs. Then it is possible to mix and match and get a jump-start on many generic data model constructs, even if they come from several Volume 1 and Volume 2 chapters.

Should universal models be set up as specific modules instead of as applications for industries? For instance, many industries involve time and activity tracking that could be set up as a Universal Data Model module. The parts bill of materials data constructs may be used for any enterprise that has a need for tracking the composition of parts, equipment, or any other tangible assembly. This could apply to many types of enterprises such as manufacturers, distributors, and repair vendors.

Another approach may be to store modules of reusable data constructs. This book chose to classify these constructs by industry for ease of reference. It would be easy enough to reclassify these constructs into generic constructs that can be used across many industries. The next section provides some guidelines should you choose to reclassify the models in this book.

Setting Up Modularized Data Models for Use Across Industries

This section provides a starting point for renaming and reclassifying these constructs, if you wanted to set up modularized functions that could be used across industries.

Table 10.1 shows some of the models from each of the industry chapters, provides examples of other ways to classify them using the term "modularized construct," and then shows the applicability of these constructs across many applications. The data models may need to be slightly modified to be applicable in other circumstances; however, the overall structure of the data model can be reused. These represent only a sample of some of the applications of these models, and users of this book may find additional applications for many of these data models.

For More Information

We encourage and would appreciate any suggestions, questions, or comments that would help in the further development of Universal Data Models and holistic systems.

For more information, or to contact us for further assistance, please feel free to e-mail us directly at info@univdata.com or visit our Web site at www.universaldatamodels.com. We also encourage you to visit the companion Web site for this book, wiley.com/compbooks/silverston, for the most recent information on both volumes of *The Data Model Resource Book*, the downloadable software, and other universal data models and database designs that are available. For further information on the companion Industry Download products (sold separately), please see "How to Use the Volume 2 Industry Electronic Products" at the end of this volume. This section describes the contents of the Industry Download products and explains how to purchase and use one or more of these industry data model software products.

Table 10.1 Data Model Construct Modules

INDUSTRY	DATA MODEL	MODULARIZED CONSTRUCT	APPLICABILITY
Manufacturing	Parts specification and documentation, V2:2.3, Parts specification roles and status, V2:2.4, Engineering changes models, V2: 2.5	Engineering	Any engineering or design process including manufacturing firms, design firms, systems integrators, computer systems design, architects, and many other engineering functions or design processes within enterprises.
	Bill of materials, V2:2.6, Part substitutions, V2:2.7, Inventory item configurations, V2:2.8	Bill of materials models	Manufacturers, distributors, telecommunication goods companies, or any other firm that has products made up of various parts.
Telecommunications	Product deployment, V2:3.3	Deployed product usage	Any enterprise selling usage of their facilities, public utilities, gas and electric organizations where product usage occurs. Manufacturing firms that need to track usage of their products by the end user.
	Network components, V2:3.5, Network assembly, V2:3.6, Products, circuits and network assemblies, V2:3.7, Products, circuits and network assembly capabilities, V2:3.8	Facilities management	Any enterprise managing facility infrastructures, public utility companies such as electric companies, gas, and oil companies.
	Network components, V2:3.5, network assembly	Geographic location related entities including pathway, geographic point and geographic boundary	Any enterprise managing geographic information such as oil and gas organizations, utilities companies, government organizations, research firms, or manufacturing firms.

Health care	Health care claims payment settlement, V2:4.10	Payment settlement	Any organization that needs to settle payment by going through an evaluation process to determine payments of various amounts. Examples include lawsuit settlements or arbitration settlement.
Insurance	Insurance product rules, V2:5.5	Product rules	Any organization with complex rules associated with how the product operates. Examples include shares of investment properties such as oil wells or financial securities offerings that are governed by regulatory rules.
	Premium schedule, V2:5.13	Renewal billing	Any organization that bills periodically and sets up advanced schedules for billing such as service organizations that bill using fixed monthly amounts, Web hosting companies, credit card companies with ongoing fees, mortgage companies, leasing organizations, and rental management firms.
Financial services	Financial product rule, V2:6.4	Product regulation	Any firm that is subject to the regulations and requirements that are imposed on their offerings. Examples include organizations manufacturing, distributing, or using hazardous materials, such as weapons manufacturers. Variations could also be used for telecommunications companies, financial services companies, or financial securities firms.
	Financial account, V2:6.6 and Financial account transactions, V2:6.7	Accounts and account transaction	Any enterprise that tracks transactions against an account. Examples include organizations that set up billing accounts with payments against the account such as utility firm, wholesaler, or telecommunications firm accounts.

(continues)

Table 10.1 *(continued)*

INDUSTRY	DATA MODEL	MODULARIZED CONSTRUCT	APPLICABILITY
Professional services	All models including professional service offerings, requirements, quotes, requests, engagements, professional service delivery, professional service work efforts, professional service invoicing and service entry analysis, V2:7.1–7.13	Engagement, time, and billing tracking	Any enterprise that tracks and/or bills for projects and/or its time and expenses. Examples include hardware/software companies or any other product or service firm that needs to provide support and/or consulting for their offerings.
Travel	Travel preferences, reservations, ticketing, and experience, V2:8.2, V2:8.4, V2:8.5, V2:8.8	Preferences, reservations, and ticketing	Any enterprise involved in reserving and ticketing customers. Examples include entertainment or sports events bookings.
Web and e-commerce	All web models including product needs, subscriptions, visits, and Internet analysis, V2:9.1–9.10	Internet visits and hits	Any enterprise using the Internet to communicate information about its organization and/or product offerings.
	E-commerce products and objects	Electronic object tracking	Any enterprise maintaining information about their electronic documents, images and other objects.

Entities and Attributes for Manufacturing Models

This appendix defines the attribute domains and lists the entities and attributes from the logical data models and star schema found in Chapter 2, "Manufacturing." This listing includes the entity names, attribute names, primary key indicators, foreign key indicators, and the domain for each attribute.

The domain indicates a standard set of characteristics that can be applied to attributes, including its datatype and length. Table A.1 defines the nature of each domain. When applying the domains to the attributes listed in all the appendices, refer to Table A.1 for recommendations on what datatype and length to use when implementing these models. Of course, the datatype and length of each attribute should be adjusted as appropriate to meet the specific needs of the enterprise.

The domain definitions as they are applied to the attributes in the appendices are used for the SQL code that is contained on the demo CD-ROM at the back of this book as well as in the Industry Downloads (see the section "How to Use the Volume 2 Industry Electronic Products" for more information).

Table A.1 Appendices Domain Definitions

DOMAIN NAME	DATATYPE	SUGGESTED LENGTH	USED FOR
Blob	Blob		Images, graphics, binary information, and any attributes storing electronic object information
Comment	Varchar (variable length character string)	255	Used to store comment attributes that provide for free-form text describing the entity
Currency Amount	Number or money with two decimal places for the cents	9 digits with 2 decimals	Any currency amount that may store monetary figures
Datetime	Date		Used to maintain any date or datetime attribute
Description	Varchar	255	Used for attributes that maintain descriptive information about the entity
Floating point	Float	9 with 4 more decimal points	Used to record information about percentages, calculated fields, variances, statistical attributes, or any attribute needing multiple decimal points
ID	Number	10	A sequential number to establish uniqueness of the entity, to be used for foreign key relationships
Indicator	Character	1	Any flag, indicator, or single character attribute used to indicate the value of an attribute. For example: Yes/No, Male/Female
Long Varchar	Varchar	255	Used to record attributes that generally need a longer string value
Name	Varchar	40	Used to record name information
Numeric	Number		Numbered values without decimal points
Short Varchar	Varchar	40	Used for attributes that generally need a longer string value
Very Long	Varchar	2000	Used for attributes that need a very long string value
Very Short	Varchar	10	Used for attributes that need a very short string value

Entities and Attributes Listing for Manufacturing

Note: The listings for this and other appendices are sorted by entity name, primary key indicator (PK?), foreign key indicator (FK?), and then by column name. Thus, each entity shows the primary key first, then the foreign keys, and then the non-key attributes.

ENTITY NAME	ATTRIBUTE NAME	PK?	FK?	DOMAIN
ACTIVITY USAGE	DEPLOYMENT ID	Yes	Yes	ID
	DEPLOYMENT USAGE ID	Yes	Yes	ID
	UOM ID	No	Yes	ID
	QUANTITY	No	No	Numeric
AGENT	PARTY ID	Yes	Yes	ID
	ROLE TYPE ID	Yes	Yes	ID
ASSOCIATION	PARTY ID	Yes	Yes	ID
	ROLE TYPE ID	Yes	Yes	ID
BILL TO CUSTOMER	PARTY ID	Yes	Yes	ID
	ROLE TYPE ID	Yes	Yes	ID
BILLING FEATURE	PRODUCT FEATURE ID	Yes	Yes	ID
BRAND	PRODUCT FEATURE ID	Yes	Yes	ID
COLOR	PRODUCT FEATURE ID	Yes	Yes	ID
COMPETITOR	PARTY ID	Yes	Yes	ID
	ROLE TYPE ID	Yes	Yes	ID
CONSTRAINT	PART ID	Yes	Yes	ID
	PART SPECIFICATION ID	Yes	Yes	ID
CONTACT	PARTY ID	Yes	Yes	ID
	ROLE TYPE ID	Yes	Yes	ID
CONTAINER	CONTAINER ID	Yes	No	ID
	FACILITY ID	No	Yes	ID
	CONTAINER TYPE ID	No	No	ID
CONTRACTOR	PARTY ID	Yes	Yes	ID
	ROLE TYPE ID	Yes	Yes	ID
CUSTOMER	PARTY ID	Yes	Yes	ID
	ROLE TYPE ID	Yes	Yes	ID
CUSTOMER LOCATION	FACILITY ID	Yes	Yes	ID
CUSTOMER RELATIONSHIP	FROM DATE	Yes	Yes	Datetime
	PARTY ID FROM	Yes	Yes	ID

ENTITY NAME	ATTRIBUTE NAME	PK?	FK?	DOMAIN
	PARTY ID TO	Yes	Yes	ID
	ROLE TYPE ID FROM	Yes	Yes	ID
	ROLE TYPE ID TO	Yes	Yes	ID
DEPARTMENT	PARTY ID	Yes	Yes	ID
	ROLE TYPE ID	Yes	Yes	ID
DEPLOYMENT	DEPLOYMENT ID	Yes	No	ID
	INVENTORY ITEM ID	No	Yes	ID
	PRODUCT ID	No	Yes	ID
	FROM DATE	No	No	Datetime
	THRU DATE	No	No	Datetime
DEPLOYMENT USAGE	DEPLOYMENT ID	Yes	Yes	ID
	DEPLOYMENT USAGE ID	Yes	No	ID
	DEPLOYMENT USAGE TYPE ID	No	Yes	ID
	STANDARD TIME PERIOD ID	No	Yes	ID
	START DATETIME	No	No	Datetime
	THRU DATETIME	No	No	Datetime
	USAGE COMMENT	No	No	Comment
DEPLOYMENT USAGE TYPE	DEPLOYMENT USAGE TYPE ID	Yes	No	ID
DIMENSION	DESCRIPTION	No	No	Description
	PRODUCT FEATURE ID	Yes	Yes	ID
	UOM ID	No	Yes	ID
	NUMBER SPECIFIED	No	No	Numeric
DISTRIBUTION CHANNEL	PARTY ID	Yes	Yes	ID
	ROLE TYPE ID	Yes	Yes	ID
DISTRIBUTION CHANNEL RELATIONSHIP	FROM DATE	Yes	Yes	Datetime
	PARTY ID FROM	Yes	Yes	ID
	PARTY ID TO	Yes	Yes	ID
	ROLE TYPE ID FROM	Yes	Yes	ID

ENTITY NAME	ATTRIBUTE NAME	PK?	FK?	DOMAIN
DISTRIBUTOR	ROLE TYPE ID TO	Yes	Yes	ID
	PARTY ID	Yes	Yes	ID
DIVISION	ROLE TYPE ID	Yes	Yes	ID
	PARTY ID	Yes	Yes	ID
DOCUMENT	ROLE TYPE ID	Yes	Yes	ID
	DOCUMENT ID	Yes	No	ID
	COMMENTS	No	No	Comment
	DATE CREATED	No	No	Datetime
	DOCUMENT LOCATION	No	No	Long varchar
	DOCUMENT TEXT	No	No	Long varchar
	DOCUMENT TYPE ID	No	No	ID
	IMAGE	No	No	Blob
DOCUMENT APPLICABILITY	DOCUMENT ID	Yes	Yes	ID
	DOCUMENT APPLIC SEQ ID	Yes	No	ID
	PART ID	No	Yes	ID
	PRODUCT ID	No	Yes	ID
EMPLOYEE	PARTY ID	Yes	Yes	ID
	ROLE TYPE ID	Yes	Yes	ID
EMPLOYMENT	FROM DATE	Yes	Yes	Datetime
	PARTY ID FROM	Yes	Yes	ID
	PARTY ID TO	Yes	Yes	ID
	ROLE TYPE ID FROM	Yes	Yes	ID
	ROLE TYPE ID TO	Yes	Yes	ID
	TERMINATION REASON ID	No	No	ID
	TERMINATION TYPE ID	No	No	ID
END USER CUSTOMER	PARTY ID	Yes	Yes	ID
ENGINEERING BOM	ROLE TYPE ID	Yes	Yes	ID
	FROM DATE	Yes	Yes	Datetime
	PART ID FOR	Yes	Yes	ID
	PART ID IN	Yes	Yes	ID
ENGINEERING CHANGE	ENGINEERING CHANGE ID	Yes	No	ID
	DESCRIPTION	No	No	Description
ENGINEERING CHANGE IMPACT	ENGINEERING CHANGE ID	Yes	Yes	ID
	FROM DATE	No	Yes	Datetime
	PART ID	No	Yes	ID
	PART ID FOR	No	Yes	ID

ENTITY NAME	ATTRIBUTE NAME	PK?	FK?	DOMAIN
	PART ID IN	No	Yes	ID
	PART SPECIFICATION ID	No	Yes	ID
ENGINEERING CHANGE NOTICE	ENGINEERING CHANGE ID	Yes	Yes	ID
	STATUS TYPE ID	Yes	Yes	ID
ENGINEERING CHANGE PARTY ROLE	ENGINEERING CHANGE ID	Yes	Yes	ID
	PARTY ID	Yes	Yes	ID
	ROLE TYPE ID	Yes	Yes	ID
ENGINEERING CHANGE RELEASE	ENGINEERING CHANGE ID	Yes	Yes	ID
	STATUS TYPE ID	Yes	Yes	ID
ENGINEERING CHANGE REQUEST	ENGINEERING CHANGE ID	Yes	Yes	ID
ENGINEERING CHANGE ROLE TYPE	STATUS TYPE ID	Yes	Yes	ID
	ROLE TYPE ID	Yes	Yes	ID
ENGINEERING CHANGE STATUS	ENGINEERING CHANGE ID	Yes	Yes	ID
	STATUS TYPE ID	Yes	Yes	ID
	EFFECTIVE DATE	No	No	Datetime
ENGINEERING CHANGE STATUS TYPE	STATUS TYPE ID	Yes	Yes	ID
ENGINEERING DOCUMENT	DOCUMENT ID	Yes	Yes	ID
FACILITY	FACILITY ID	Yes	No	ID
	PART OF FACILITY ID	No	Yes	ID
	DESCRIPTION	No	No	Description
	FACILITY NAME	No	No	Name
	FACILITY TYPE ID	No	No	ID
	SQUARE FOOTAGE	No	No	Numeric
FAMILY MEMBER	PARTY ID	Yes	Yes	ID
	ROLE TYPE ID	Yes	Yes	ID
FINISHED GOOD	PART ID	Yes	Yes	ID
FIXED ASSET	FIXED ASSET ID	Yes	No	ID
	FIXED ASSET TYPE ID	No	Yes	ID
	UOM ID	No	Yes	ID
	DATE ACQUIRED	No	No	Datetime
	DATE LAST SERVICED	No	No	Datetime
	DATE NEXT SERVICE	No	No	Datetime
	NAME	No	No	Name
	PARTY ID	No	No	ID

ENTITY NAME	ATTRIBUTE NAME	PK?	FK?	DOMAIN
	PRODUCTION CAPACITY	No	No	Floating point
FIXED ASSET TYPE	ROLE TYPE ID	No	No	ID
	FIXED ASSET TYPE ID	Yes	No	ID
GOOD	DESCRIPTION	No	No	Description
	PRODUCT ID	Yes	Yes	ID
	PART ID	No	Yes	ID
HARDWARE FEATURE	PRODUCT FEATURE ID	Yes	Yes	ID
HOUSEHOLD	PARTY ID	Yes	Yes	ID
	ROLE TYPE ID	Yes	Yes	ID
INTERNAL ORGANIZATION	PARTY ID	Yes	Yes	ID
INVENTORY ITEM	ROLE TYPE ID	Yes	Yes	ID
	INVENTORY ITEM ID	Yes	No	ID
	CONTAINER ID	No	Yes	ID
	FACILITY ID	No	Yes	ID
	PART ID	No	Yes	ID
	PARTY ID	No	Yes	ID
	PRODUCT ID	No	Yes	ID
	LOT ID	No	No	ID
INVENTORY ITEM CONFIGURATION	INVENTORY ITEM ID FOR	Yes	Yes	ID
	INVENTORY ITEM ID IN	Yes	Yes	ID
	FROM DATE	Yes	No	Datetime
	COMMENTS	No	No	Comment
	QUANTITY	No	No	Numeric
	THRU DATE	No	No	Datetime
INVENTORY ITEM STATUS	INVENTORY ITEM ID	Yes	Yes	ID
	STATUS TYPE ID	Yes	Yes	ID
INVENTORY ITEM STATUS TYPE	STATUS TYPE ID	Yes	Yes	ID
MAINTENANCE	WORK EFFORT ID	Yes	Yes	ID
MANUFACTURED PARTS	PART ID	Yes	Yes	ID
	NAME	No	No	Name
	PART TYPE	No	No	Description
MANUFACTURING BOM	FROM DATE	Yes	Yes	Datetime
	PART ID FOR	Yes	Yes	ID
	PART ID IN	Yes	Yes	ID
MANUFACTURING CONFIGURATION	FROM DATE	Yes	Yes	Datetime

ENTITY NAME	ATTRIBUTE NAME	PK?	FK?	DOMAIN
	INVENTORY ITEM ID FOR	Yes	Yes	ID
	INVENTORY ITEM ID IN	Yes	Yes	ID
MARKETING MATERIAL	DOCUMENT ID	Yes	Yes	ID
MARKETING PACKAGE	FROM DATE	Yes	Yes	Datetime
	PRODUCT ID FROM	Yes	Yes	ID
	PRODUCT ID TO	Yes	Yes	ID
	INSTRUCTION	No	No	Long varchar
NON SERIALIZED INVENTORY ITEM	QUANTITY USED	No	No	Numeric
	INVENTORY ITEM ID	Yes	Yes	ID
OPERATING CONDITION	QUANTITY ON HAND	No	No	Numeric
	PART ID	Yes	Yes	ID
	PART SPECIFICATION ID	Yes	Yes	ID
ORDER	ORDER ID	Yes	No	ID
	ENTRY DATE	No	No	Datetime
	ORDER DATE	No	No	Datetime
	VISIT ID	No	No	ID
ORDER ITEM	ORDER ID	Yes	Yes	ID
	ORDER ITEM SEQ ID	Yes	No	ID
	DEPLOYMENT ID	No	Yes	ID
	PRODUCT FEATURE ID	No	Yes	ID
	PRODUCT ID	No	Yes	ID
	BUDGET ID	No	Yes	ID
	BUDGET ITEM SEQ ID	No	Yes	ID
	COMMENTS	No	No	Comment
	ESTIMATED DELIVERY DATE	No	No	Datetime
	ITEM DESCRIPTION	No	No	Description
	QUANTITY	No	No	Numeric
	QUOTE ID	No	No	ID
	QUOTED ITEM SEQ ID	No	No	ID
	SHIPPING INSTRUCTIONS	No	No	Long varchar
	UNIT PRICE	No	No	Currency amount
ORGANIZATION	PARTY ID	Yes	Yes	ID
	NAME	No	No	Name
ORGANIZATION CONTACT RELATIONSHIP	FROM DATE	Yes	Yes	Datetime

ENTITY NAME	ATTRIBUTE NAME	PK?	FK?	DOMAIN
	PARTY ID FROM	Yes	Yes	ID
	PARTY ID TO	Yes	Yes	ID
	ROLE TYPE ID FROM	Yes	Yes	ID
	ROLE TYPE ID TO	Yes	Yes	ID
ORGANIZATION ROLE	PARTY ID	Yes	Yes	ID
	ROLE TYPE ID	Yes	Yes	ID
ORGANIZATION ROLLUP	FROM DATE	Yes	Yes	Datetime
	PARTY ID FROM	Yes	Yes	ID
	PARTY ID TO	Yes	Yes	ID
	ROLE TYPE ID FROM	Yes	Yes	ID
	ROLE TYPE ID TO	Yes	Yes	ID
ORGANIZATION UNIT	PARTY ID	Yes	Yes	ID
	ROLE TYPE ID	Yes	Yes	ID
OTHER DOCUMENT	DOCUMENT ID	Yes	Yes	ID
OTHER FEATURE	PRODUCT FEATURE ID	Yes	Yes	ID
OTHER ORGANIZATION UNIT	PARTY ID	Yes	Yes	ID
	ROLE TYPE ID	Yes	Yes	ID
OTHER PART SPECIFICATION	PART ID	Yes	Yes	ID
	PART SPECIFICATION ID	Yes	Yes	ID
PARENT ORGANIZATION	PARTY ID	Yes	Yes	ID
PART	ROLE TYPE ID	Yes	Yes	ID
	PART ID	Yes	No	ID
	NAME	No	No	Name
PART BOM	PART ID FOR	Yes	Yes	ID
	PART ID IN	Yes	Yes	ID
	FROM DATE	Yes	No	Datetime
	COMMENTS	No	No	Comment
	INSTRUCTIONS	No	No	Long varchar
	PART BOM SEQ ID	No	No	ID
	QUANTITY USED	No	No	Numeric
	THRU DATE	No	No	Datetime
PART BOM SUBSTITUTE	FROM DATE FROM	Yes	Yes	Datetime
	FROM DATE IN TO	Yes	Yes	Datetime
	PART ID FOR FROM	Yes	Yes	ID
	PART ID FOR TO	Yes	Yes	ID

ENTITY NAME	ATTRIBUTE NAME	PK?	FK?	DOMAIN
	PART ID IN FROM	Yes	Yes	ID
	PART ID IN TO	Yes	Yes	ID
	COMMENTS	No	No	Comment
	PREFERENCE	No	No	Very short
	QUANTITY	No	No	Numeric
	THRU DATE	No	No	Datetime
PART REVISION	PART ID FOR	Yes	Yes	ID
	PART ID OF	Yes	Yes	ID
	FROM DATE	Yes	No	Datetime
	REASON	No	No	Long varchar
	THRU DATE	No	No	Datetime
PART SPECIFICATION	PART ID	Yes	Yes	ID
	PART SPECIFICATION ID	Yes	No	ID
	SPECIFICATION TYPE ID	No	Yes	ID
	COMMENTS	No	No	Comment
	DATE DOCUMENTED	No	No	Datetime
	DESCRIPTION	No	No	Description
PART SPECIFICATION ROLE	PART ID	Yes	Yes	ID
	PART SPECIFICATION ID	Yes	Yes	ID
	PARTY ID	Yes	Yes	ID
	ROLE TYPE ID	Yes	Yes	ID
PART SPECIFICATION ROLE TYPE	ROLE TYPE ID	Yes	Yes	ID
PART SPECIFICATION STATUS	PART ID	Yes	Yes	ID
	PART SPECIFICATION ID	Yes	Yes	ID
	STATUS TYPE ID	Yes	Yes	ID
	FROM DATE	Yes	No	Datetime
	THRU DATE	No	No	Datetime
PART SPECIFICATION STATUS TYPE	STATUS TYPE ID	Yes	Yes	ID
PART SUBSTITUTE	PART ID FROM	Yes	Yes	ID
	PART ID TO	Yes	Yes	ID
	FROM DATE	Yes	No	Datetime
	COMMENTS	No	No	Comment
	PREFERENCE	No	No	Long varchar
	QUANTITY	No	No	Numeric
	THRU DATE	No	No	Datetime
PARTNER	PARTY ID	Yes	Yes	ID

ENTITY NAME	ATTRIBUTE NAME	PK?	FK?	DOMAIN
PARTNERSHIP	ROLE TYPE ID	Yes	Yes	ID
	FROM DATE	Yes	Yes	Datetime
	PARTY ID FROM	Yes	Yes	ID
	PARTY ID TO	Yes	Yes	ID
	ROLE TYPE ID FROM	Yes	Yes	ID
	ROLE TYPE ID TO	Yes	Yes	ID
PARTY	PARTY ID	Yes	No	ID
PARTY RELATIONSHIP	PARTY ID FROM	Yes	Yes	ID
	PARTY ID TO	Yes	Yes	ID
	ROLE TYPE ID FROM	Yes	Yes	ID
	ROLE TYPE ID TO	Yes	Yes	ID
	FROM DATE	Yes	No	Datetime
	PARTY RELATIONSHIP TYPE ID	No	Yes	ID
	COMMENTS	No	No	Comment
	PRIORITY TYPE ID	No	No	ID
	STATUS TYPE ID	No	No	ID
	THRU DATE	No	No	Datetime
PARTY RELATIONSHIP TYPE	PARTY RELATIONSHIP TYPE ID	Yes	No	ID
	ROLE TYPE ID VALID FROM	No	Yes	ID
	ROLE TYPE ID VALID TO	No	Yes	ID
	DESCRIPTION	No	No	Description
	NAME	No	No	Name
PARTY ROLE	PARTY ID	Yes	Yes	ID
	ROLE TYPE ID	Yes	Yes	ID
	PARTY ROLE ID	No	No	ID
PARTY ROLE TYPE	ROLE TYPE ID	Yes	Yes	ID
	PART ID	Yes	Yes	ID
PERFORMANCE SPECIFICATION	PART SPECIFICATION ID	Yes	Yes	ID
PERSON	PARTY ID	Yes	Yes	ID
	BIRTH DATE	No	No	Datetime
	COMMENTS	No	No	Comment
	CURRENT FIRST NAME	No	No	Name
	CURRENT LAST NAME	No	No	Name
	CURRENT MIDDLE NAME	No	No	Name
	CURRENT NICKNAME	No	No	Name
	CURRENT PASSPORT EXPIRE DATE	No	No	Datetime
	CURRENT PASSPORT NUMBER	No	No	Numeric
	CURRENT PERSONAL TITLE	No	No	Name
	CURRENT SUFFIX	No	No	Name
	GENDER	No	No	Indicator

ENTITY NAME	ATTRIBUTE NAME	PK?	FK?	DOMAIN
	HEIGHT	No	No	Numeric
	MARTIAL STATUS	No	No	Indicator
	MOTHER'S MADIEN NAME	No	No	Name
	SOCIAL SECURITY NUMBER	No	No	Numeric
	TOTAL YEARS WORK EXPERIENCE	No	No	Numeric
	WEIGHT	No	No	Numeric
PERSON ROLE	PARTY ID	Yes	Yes	ID
	ROLE TYPE ID	Yes	Yes	ID
PLANT	FACILITY ID	Yes	Yes	ID
PLANT LOCATIONS	FACILITY ID	Yes	No	ID
	CITY	No	No	Short varchar
	PLANT NAME	No	No	Name
	STATE	No		Short varchar
PROCESS STEP TYPE	WORK EFFORT TYPE ID	Yes	Yes	ID
PROCESS TYPE	WORK EFFORT TYPE ID	Yes	Yes	ID
PRODUCT	PRODUCT ID	Yes	No	ID
	MANUFACTURER PARTY ID	No	Yes	ID
	PART ID	No	Yes	ID
	UOM ID	No	Yes	ID
	COMMENTS	No	No	Comment
	DESCRIPTION	No	No	Description
	INTRODUCTION DATE	No	No	Datetime
	NAME	No	No	Name
	SALES DISCONTINUATION DATE	No	No	Datetime
	SUPPORT DISCONTINUATION DATE	No	No	Datetime
PRODUCT ASSOCIATION	PRODUCT ID FROM	Yes	Yes	ID
	PRODUCT ID TO	Yes	Yes	ID
	FROM DATE	Yes	No	Datetime
	REASON	No	No	Long varchar
	THRU DATE	No	No	Datetime
PRODUCT DOCUMENT	DOCUMENT ID	Yes	Yes	ID
PRODUCT DRAWING	DOCUMENT ID	Yes	Yes	ID
PRODUCT FEATURE	PRODUCT FEATURE ID	Yes	No	ID
	DESCRIPTION	No	No	Description
	PRODUCT FEATURE CATEGORY ID	No	No	ID

ENTITY NAME	ATTRIBUTE NAME	PK?	FK?	DOMAIN
PRODUCT MODEL	DOCUMENT ID	Yes	Yes	ID
PRODUCT QUALITY	PRODUCT FEATURE ID	Yes	Yes	ID
PRODUCTION RUN	WORK EFFORT ID	Yes	Yes	ID
	QUANTITY PRODUCED	No	No	Numeric
	QUANTITY REJECTED	No	No	Numeric
	QUANTITY TO PRODUCE	No	No	Numeric
PRODUCTION RUN FACT	DAY ID	Yes	Yes	ID
	FACILITY ID	Yes	Yes	ID
	PART ID	Yes	Yes	ID
	PARTY ID	Yes	Yes	ID
	WORK EFFORT TYPE ID	Yes	Yes	ID
	COST	No	No	Currency amount
	COST VARIANCE FROM STANDARD	No	No	Floating point
	DURATION	No	No	Numeric
	DURATION VARIANCE FROM STANDARD	No	No	Floating point
	QUANTITY PRODUCED	No	No	Numeric
	QUANTITY REJECTED	No	No	Numeric
PRODUCTION RUN TYPE	WORK EFFORT TYPE ID	Yes	Yes	ID
	PART ID	No	Yes	ID
PRODUCTION RUN TYPES	WORK EFFORT TYPE ID	Yes	No	ID
	PRODUCTION_RUN_TYPE_DESCRIPTION	No	No	Description
PROSPECT	PARTY ID	Yes	Yes	ID
	ROLE TYPE ID	Yes	Yes	ID
PURCHASE ORDER	ORDER ID	Yes	Yes	ID
	PURCHASE ORDER ID	Yes	No	ID
PURCHASE ORDER ITEM	ORDER ID	Yes	Yes	ID
	ORDER ITEM SEQ ID	Yes	Yes	ID
RAW MATERIAL	PART ID	No	Yes	ID
REGULATORY AGENCY	PARTY ID	Yes	Yes	ID
RESPONSIBLE PARTYS	ROLE TYPE ID	Yes	Yes	ID
	PARTY ID	Yes	No	ID
	FIRST NAME	No	No	Name

ENTITY NAME	ATTRIBUTE NAME	PK?	FK?	DOMAIN
	LAST NAME	No	No	Name
	ORGANIZATION NAME	No	No	Name
ROLE TYPE	ROLE TYPE ID	Yes	No	ID
	DESCRIPTION	No	No	Description
SALES ORDER	ORDER ID	Yes	Yes	ID
SALES ORDER ITEM	ORDER ID	Yes	Yes	ID
	ORDER ITEM SEQ ID	Yes	Yes	ID
	CORRESPONDING PO ID	No	No	ID
SERIALIZED INVENTORY ITEM	INVENTORY ITEM ID	Yes	Yes	ID
	SERIAL NUM	No	No	Description
SERVICE	PRODUCT ID	Yes	Yes	ID
SERVICE CONFIGURATION	FROM DATE	Yes	Yes	Datetime
	INVENTORY ITEM ID FOR	Yes	Yes	ID
	INVENTORY ITEM ID IN	Yes	Yes	ID
SHAREHOLDER	PARTY ID	Yes	Yes	ID
	ROLE TYPE ID	Yes	Yes	ID
SHIP TO CUSTOMER	PARTY ID	Yes	Yes	ID
	ROLE TYPE ID	Yes	Yes	ID
SIZE FEATURE	PRODUCT FEATURE ID	Yes	Yes	ID
SKILL TYPE	SKILL TYPE ID	Yes	No	ID
	DECRIPTION	No	No	Description
SOFTWARE FEATURE	PRODUCT FEATURE ID	Yes	Yes	ID
SPECIFICATION TYPE	SPECIFICATION TYPE ID	Yes	No	ID
	DESCRIPTION	No	No	Description
STANDARD TIME PERIOD	STANDARD TIME PERIOD ID	Yes	No	ID
	FROM DATE	No	No	Datetime
	PERIOD TYPE ID	No	No	ID
	THRU DATE	No	No	Datetime
STATUS TYPE	STATUS TYPE ID	Yes	No	ID
	DESCRIPTION	No	No	Description
SUBASSEMBLY	PART ID	Yes	Yes	ID
SUBSIDIARY	PARTY ID	Yes	Yes	ID
	ROLE TYPE ID	Yes	Yes	ID
SUPPLIER	PARTY ID	Yes	Yes	ID
	ROLE TYPE ID	Yes	Yes	ID
SUPPLIER RELATIONSHIP	FROM DATE	Yes	Yes	Datetime
	PARTY ID FROM	Yes	Yes	ID
	PARTY ID TO	Yes	Yes	ID

ENTITY NAME	ATTRIBUTE NAME	PK?	FK?	DOMAIN
	ROLE TYPE ID FROM	Yes	Yes	ID
	ROLE TYPE ID TO	Yes	Yes	ID
TESTING REQUIREMENT	PART ID	Yes	Yes	ID
	PART SPECIFICATION ID	Yes	No	ID
TIME BY DAY	DAY ID	Yes	No	ID
	DAY	No	No	Very short
	MONTH	No	No	Very short
	QUARTER	No	No	Very short
	WEEK	No	No	Very short
	YEAR	No	No	Very short
TIME PERIOD USAGE	DEPLOYMENT ID	Yes	Yes	ID
	DEPLOYMENT USAGE ID	Yes	Yes	ID
TOLERANCE	PART ID	Yes	Yes	ID
	PART SPECIFICATION ID	Yes	Yes	ID
UNIT OF MEASURE	UOM ID	Yes	No	ID
	ABBREVIATION	No	No	Short varchar
	DESCRIPTION	No	No	Description
VOLUME USAGE	DEPLOYMENT ID	Yes	Yes	ID
	DEPLOYMENT USAGE ID	Yes	Yes	ID
	UOM ID	No	Yes	ID
	QUANTITY	No	No	Numeric
WAREHOUSE	FACILITY ID	Yes	Yes	ID
WORK EFFORT	WORK EFFORT ID	Yes	No	ID
	FACILITY ID	No	Yes	ID
	FIXED ASSET ID	No	Yes	ID
	VERSION OF WORK EFFORT ID	No	Yes	ID
	WORK EFFORT TYPE ID	No	Yes	ID
	ACTUAL COMPLETION DATETIME	No	No	Datetime
	ACTUAL HOURS	No	No	Numeric
	ACTUAL START DATETIME	No	No	Datetime
	DESCRIPTION	No	No	Description
	ESTIMATED HOURS	No	No	Numeric
	NAME	No	No	Name
	SCHEDULED COMPLETION DATE	No	No	Datetime
	SCHEDULED START DATE	No	No	Datetime
	SPECIAL TERMS	No	No	Long varchar
	TOTAL DOLLARS ALLOWED	No	No	Currency amount
	TOTAL HOURS ALLOWED	No	No	Numeric

ENTITY NAME	ATTRIBUTE NAME	PK?	FK?	DOMAIN
WORK EFFORT ASSOCIATION	WORK EFFORT PURPOSE TYPE ID	No	No	ID
	WORK EFFORT ID FROM	Yes	Yes	ID
	WORK EFFORT ID TO	Yes	Yes	ID
WORK EFFORT BREAKDOWN	WORK EFFORT ID FROM	Yes	Yes	ID
	WORK EFFORT ID TO	Yes	Yes	ID
WORK EFFORT CONCURRENCY	WORK EFFORT ID FROM	Yes	Yes	ID
	WORK EFFORT ID TO	Yes	Yes	ID
WORK EFFORT DEPENDENCY	WORK EFFORT ID FROM	Yes	Yes	ID
	WORK EFFORT ID TO	Yes	Yes	ID
WORK EFFORT FIXED ASSET ASSIGNMENT	FIXED ASSET ID	Yes	Yes	ID
	WORK EFFORT ID	Yes	Yes	ID
	ALLOCATED COST	No	No	Currency amount
	COMMENTS	No	No	Comment
	FROM DATE	No	No	Datetime
	STATUS TYPE ID	No	No	ID
	THRU DATE	No	No	Datetime
WORK EFFORT FIXED ASSET STANDARD	FIXED ASSET TYPE ID	Yes	Yes	ID
	WORK EFFORT TYPE ID	Yes	Yes	ID
	ESTIMATED COST	No	No	Currency amount
	ESTIMATED DURATION	No	No	Datetime
	ESTIMATED QUANTITY	No	No	Numeric
WORK EFFORT INVENTORY ASSIGNMENT	INVENTORY ITEM ID	Yes	Yes	ID
	WORK EFFORT ID	Yes	Yes	ID
	QUANTITY	No	No	Numeric
WORK EFFORT PART STANDARD	PART ID	Yes	Yes	ID
	WORK EFFORT TYPE ID	Yes	Yes	ID
	ESTIMATED COST	No	No	Currency amount
	ESTIMATED QUANTITY	No	No	Numeric

ENTITY NAME	ATTRIBUTE NAME	PK?	FK?	DOMAIN
WORK EFFORT PARTY ASSIGNMENT	PARTY ID	Yes	Yes	ID
	ROLE TYPE ID	Yes	Yes	ID
	WORK EFFORT ID	Yes	Yes	ID
	FROM DATE	Yes	No	Datetime
	FACILITY ID	No	Yes	ID
	COMMENTS	No	No	Comment
	THRU DATE	No	No	Datetime
WORK EFFORT PRECEDENCY	WORK EFFORT ID FROM	Yes	Yes	ID
	WORK EFFORT ID TO	Yes	Yes	ID
WORK EFFORT ROLE TYPE	ROLE TYPE ID	Yes	Yes	ID
WORK EFFORT SKILL STANDARD	SKILL TYPE ID	Yes	Yes	ID
	WORK EFFORT TYPE ID	Yes	Yes	ID
	ESTIMATED COST	No	No	Currency amount
	ESTIMATED DURATION	No	No	Numeric
	ESTIMATED NUM PEOPLE	No	No	Numeric
WORK EFFORT STATUS	STATUS TYPE ID	Yes	Yes	ID
	WORK EFFORT ID	Yes	Yes	ID
	DATETIME	No	No	Datetime

ENTITY NAME	ATTRIBUTE NAME	PK?	FK?	DOMAIN
WORK EFFORT STATUS TYPE	STATUS TYPE ID	Yes	Yes	ID
WORK EFFORT TYPE	WORK EFFORT TYPE ID	Yes	No	ID
	FIXED ASSET TYPE ID	No	Yes	ID
	PRODUCT ID	No	Yes	ID
	DELIVERABLE TYPE ID	No	No	ID
	DESCRIPTION	No	No	Description
WORK EFFORT TYPE ASSOCIATION	WORK EFFORT TYPE ID FROM	Yes	Yes	ID
	WORK EFFORT TYPE ID TO	Yes	Yes	ID
WORK EFFORT TYPE BREAKDOWN	WORK EFFORT TYPE ID FROM	Yes	Yes	ID
WORK EFFORT TYPE DEPENDENCY	WORK EFFORT TYPE ID TO	Yes	Yes	ID
	WORK EFFORT TYPE ID FROM	Yes	Yes	ID
WORK REQUIREMENT	WORK EFFORT TYPE ID TO	Yes	Yes	ID
	REQUIREMENT ID	Yes	No	ID
	FIXED ASSET ID	No	Yes	ID
	PRODUCT ID	No	Yes	ID
WORK REQUIREMENT FULFILLMENT	DELIVERABLE ID	No	No	ID
	REQUIREMENT ID	Yes	Yes	ID
	WORK EFFORT ID	Yes	Yes	ID

APPENDIX

B

Entities and Attributes for Telecommunications Models

This appendix lists the entities and attributes from the logical data models and star schema found in Chapter 3, "Telecommunications." This listing includes the entity names, attribute names, primary key indicators, foreign key indicators, and the domain for each attribute.

The domain indicates a standard set of characteristics that can be applied to attributes, including its datatype and length. Table A.1 defines the nature of each domain. When applying the domains to the attributes listed in these appendices, refer to Table A.1 for recommendations on what datatype and length to use when implementing these models. Of course, the datatype and length of each attribute should be adjusted as appropriate to meet the specific needs of the enterprise.

The domain definitions as they are applied to the attributes in the appendices are used for the SQL code that is contained on the demo CD-ROM at the back of this book as well as in the Industry Downloads (see the section "How to Use the Volume 2 Industry Electronic Products" for more information).

Entities and Attributes Listing for Telecommunications Models

ENTITY NAME	ATTRIBUTE NAME	PK?	FK?	DOMAIN
AGREEMENT	AGREEMENT ID	Yes	No	ID
	FROM DATE	No	Yes	Datetime
	PARTY ID FROM	No	Yes	ID
	PARTY ID TO	No	Yes	ID
	PRODUCT ID	No	Yes	ID
	ROLE TYPE ID FROM	No	Yes	ID
	ROLE TYPE ID TO	No	Yes	ID
	AGREEMENT DATE	No	No	Datetime
	AGREEMENT TYPE ID	No	No	ID
	DESCRIPTION	No	No	Description
	TEXT	No	No	Long varchar
AMPLIFIER	THRU DATE	No	No	Datetime
ASSOCIATION	NETWORK COMPONENT ID	Yes	Yes	ID
	PARTY ID	Yes	Yes	ID
	ROLE TYPE ID	Yes	Yes	ID
AVAILABILITY FEATURE	PRODUCT FEATURE ID	Yes	Yes	ID
BILLING AGENT	PARTY ID	Yes	Yes	ID
	ROLE TYPE ID	Yes	Yes	ID
BILLING AGENT ASSIGNMENT	DEPLOYMENT ID	Yes	Yes	ID
	PARTY ID	Yes	Yes	ID
	ROLE TYPE ID	Yes	Yes	ID
	FROM DATE	No	No	Datetime
	THRU DATE	No	No	Datetime
BILLING AGENT RELATIONSHIP	FROM DATE	Yes	Yes	Datetime
	PARTY ID FROM	Yes	Yes	ID
	PARTY ID TO	Yes	Yes	ID
	ROLE TYPE ID FROM	Yes	Yes	ID
	ROLE TYPE ID TO	Yes	Yes	ID
BILLING FEATURE	PRODUCT FEATURE ID	Yes	Yes	ID
CABLE WIRING	NETWORK COMPONENT ID	Yes	Yes	ID
CALL DETAIL	DEPLOYMENT ID	Yes	Yes	ID
	DEPLOYMENT USAGE ID	Yes	Yes	ID
	CONTACT MECHANISM CALLED FROM	No	No	Short varchar

ENTITY NAME	ATTRIBUTE NAME	PK?	FK?	DOMAIN
	CONTACT MECHANISM CALLED TO	No	No	Short varchar
CAPABILITY TYPE	CAPABILITY TYPE ID	Yes	No	ID
	DESCRIPTION	No	No	Description
CENTRAL OFFICE	FACILITY ID	Yes	Yes	ID
CHANNEL SUBSCRIPTION	PRODUCT ID	Yes	Yes	ID
CIRCUIT	CIRCUIT ID	Yes	No	ID
	CIRCUIT TYPE ID	No	Yes	ID
CIRCUIT PRESENCE	CIRCUIT ID	Yes	Yes	ID
	NETWORK ASSEMBLY ID	Yes	Yes	ID
	FROM DATE	Yes	No	Datetime
	THRU DATE	No	No	Datetime
CIRCUIT TYPE	CIRCUIT TYPE ID	Yes	No	ID
	DESCRIPTION	No	No	Description
CIRCUIT TYPE CAPABILITY	CAPABILITY TYPE ID	Yes	Yes	ID
	CIRCUIT TYPE ID	Yes	Yes	ID
	VALUE	No	No	Numeric
COMMUNICATION APPEARANCE	NETWORK COMPONENT ID	Yes	Yes	ID
COMMUNICATION ID ASSIGNMENT	COMMUNICATION ID	Yes	Yes	ID
	NETWORK COMPONENT ID	Yes	Yes	ID
	FROM DATE	No	No	Datetime
	THRU DATE	No	No	Datetime
COMMUNICATION IDENTIFIER	COMMUNICATION ID	Yes	No	ID
COMPETITOR	CONTACT MECHANISM ID	No	Yes	ID
	PARTY ID	Yes	Yes	ID
	ROLE TYPE ID	Yes	Yes	ID
CONNECTION COMPONENT	NETWORK COMPONENT ID	Yes	Yes	ID
CONNECTION COMPONENT TYPE	GEOGRAPHIC LOCATION ID	No	Yes	ID
	NETWORK COMPONENT TYPE ID	Yes	Yes	ID
CONNECTIVITY FEATURE	PRODUCT ID	Yes	Yes	ID

ENTITY NAME	ATTRIBUTE NAME	PK?	FK?	DOMAIN
CONNECTIVITY SERVICE	PRODUCT ID	Yes	Yes	ID
CONTACT	PARTY ID	Yes	Yes	ID
	ROLE TYPE ID	Yes	Yes	ID
CONTACT MECHANISM	CONTACT MECHANISM ID	Yes	No	ID
	CONTACT MECHANISM TYPE ID	No	No	ID
CONTRACTOR	PARTY ID	Yes	Yes	ID
	ROLE TYPE ID	Yes	Yes	ID
CREDIT CARD OFFERING	PRODUCT ID	Yes	Yes	ID
CUSTOMER LOCATION	FACILITY ID	Yes	Yes	ID
CUSTOMERS	CUSTOMER PARTY ID	Yes	No	ID
	CUSTOMER TYPE	No	No	Description
	NAME	No	No	Name
DEDICATED LINE	PRODUCT ID	Yes	Yes	ID
DEPARTMENT	PARTY ID	Yes	Yes	ID
	ROLE TYPE ID	Yes	Yes	ID
DEPLOYMENT	DEPLOYMENT ID	Yes	No	ID
	INVENTORY ITEM ID	No	Yes	ID
	PRODUCT ID	No	Yes	ID
	FROM DATE	No	No	Datetime
	THRU DATE	No	No	Datetime
DEPLOYMENT FEATURE	DEPLOYMENT ID	Yes	Yes	ID
	PRODUCT FEATURE ID	Yes	Yes	ID
	FROM DATE	No	No	Datetime
	THRU DATE	No	No	Datetime
DEPLOYMENT IMPLEMENTATION	DEPLOYMENT ID	Yes	Yes	ID
	DEPLOYMENT IMPLEMENTATION ID	Yes	No	ID
	CIRCUIT ID	No	Yes	ID
	COMMUNICATION ID	No	Yes	ID
	NETWORK ASSEMBLY ID	No	Yes	ID
	NETWORK COMPONENT ID	No	Yes	ID
	FROM DATE	No	No	Datetime
	THRU DATE	No	No	Datetime
DEPLOYMENT ROLE	DEPLOYMENT ID	Yes	Yes	ID
	PARTY ID	Yes	Yes	ID
	ROLE TYPE ID	Yes	Yes	ID

ENTITY NAME	ATTRIBUTE NAME	PK?	FK?	DOMAIN
DEPLOYMENT ROLE TYPE	ROLE TYPE ID	Yes	Yes	ID
DEPLOYMENT USAGE	DEPLOYMENT ID	Yes	Yes	ID
	DEPLOYMENT USAGE ID	Yes	No	ID
	DEPLOYMENT USAGE TYPE ID	No	Yes	ID
	STANDARD TIME PERIOD ID	No	Yes	ID
	START DATETIME	No	No	Datetime
	THRU DATETIME	No	No	Datetime
	USAGE COMMENT	No	No	Comment
DEPLOYMENT USAGE BILLING	DEPLOYMENT ID	Yes	Yes	ID
	DEPLOYMENT USAGE ID	Yes	Yes	ID
	INVOICE ID	Yes	Yes	ID
	INVOICE ITEM SEQ ID	Yes	Yes	ID
	CUSTOMER PARTY ID	Yes	Yes	ID
DEPLOYMENT USAGE FACT	DEPLOYMENT USAGE TYPE ID	Yes	Yes	ID
	FACILITY ID	Yes	Yes	ID
	HOUR ID ENDED	Yes	Yes	ID
	HOUR ID STARTED	Yes	Yes	ID
	PRODUCT ID	Yes	Yes	ID
	UOM ID	Yes	Yes	ID
	BILLED AMOUNT	No	No	Currency amount
	QUANTITY	No	No	Numeric
DEPLOYMENT USAGE TYPE	DEPLOYMENT USAGE TYPE ID	Yes	No	ID
	DESCRIPTION	No	No	Description
DEPLOYMENT USAGE TYPES	DEPLOYMENT USAGE TYPE ID	Yes	No	ID
	DESCRIPTION	No	No	Description
DEVICE	NETWORK COMPONENT ID	Yes	Yes	ID
	GEOGRAPHIC LOCATION ID	No	Yes	ID
DEVICE TYPE	NETWORK COMPONENT TYPE ID	Yes	Yes	ID
DISTRIBUTION CHANNEL	PARTY ID	Yes	Yes	ID
	ROLE TYPE ID	Yes	Yes	ID
DISTRIBUTION CHANNEL RELATIONSHIP	FROM DATE	Yes	Yes	Datetime
	PARTY ID FROM	Yes	Yes	ID
	PARTY ID TO	Yes	Yes	ID
	ROLE TYPE ID FROM	Yes	Yes	ID

ENTITY NAME	ATTRIBUTE NAME	PK?	FK?	DOMAIN
DIVISION	ROLE TYPE ID TO	Yes	Yes	ID
	PARTY ID	Yes	Yes	ID
	ROLE TYPE ID	Yes	Yes	ID
ELECTRONIC ADDRESS	CONTACT MECHANISM ID	Yes	Yes	ID
	ELECTRONIC ADDRESS STRING	No	No	Description
ELECTRONIC ADDRESS ID	COMMUNICATION ID	Yes	No	ID
EMPLOYEE	ELECTRONIC ADDRESS STRING	No	No	Description
	PARTY ID	Yes	Yes	ID
	ROLE TYPE ID	Yes	Yes	ID
EMPLOYMENT	FROM DATE	Yes	Yes	Datetime
	PARTY ID FROM	Yes	Yes	ID
	PARTY ID TO	Yes	Yes	ID
	ROLE TYPE ID FROM	Yes	Yes	ID
	ROLE TYPE ID TO	Yes	Yes	ID
	TERMINATION REASON ID	No	No	ID
	TERMINATION TYPE ID	No	No	ID
FACILITY	FACILITY ID	Yes	No	ID
	PART OF FACILITY ID	No	Yes	ID
	DESCRIPTION	No	No	Description
	FACILITY NAME	No	No	Name
	FACILITY TYPE ID	No	No	ID
	SQUARE FOOTAGE	No	No	Numeric
FACILITY DEPLOYMENT	DEPLOYMENT ID	Yes	Yes	ID
	FACILITY ID	Yes	Yes	ID
	PARTY ID	Yes	Yes	ID
FACILITYS	FACILITY ID	Yes	No	ID
	FACILITY NAME	No	No	Name
	GEO LEVEL 1	No	No	Description
	GEO LEVEL 2	No	No	Description
	GEO LEVEL 3	No	No	Description
FAMILY MEMBER	PARTY ID	Yes	Yes	ID
	ROLE TYPE ID	Yes	Yes	ID
FEATURE INTERACTION DEPENDENCY	PRODUCT FEATURE ID FACTOR IN	Yes	Yes	ID
FEATURE INTERACTION INCOMPATIBILITY	PRODUCT FEATURE ID OF	Yes	Yes	ID
	PRODUCT FEATURE ID FACTOR IN	Yes	Yes	ID

ENTITY NAME	ATTRIBUTE NAME	PK?	FK?	DOMAIN
	PRODUCT FEATURE ID OF	Yes	Yes	ID
FIBER WIRING	NETWORK COMPONENT ID	Yes	Yes	ID
FILTER	NETWORK COMPONENT ID	Yes	Yes	ID
FREQUENCY SHIFTER	NETWORK COMPONENT ID	Yes	Yes	ID
GEOGRAPHIC BOUNDARY	GEOGRAPHIC LOCATION ID	Yes	Yes	ID
	ABBREVIATION	No	No	Short varchar
	GEO BOUNDARY TYPE ID	No	No	ID
	GEO CODE	No	No	Short varchar
GEOGRAPHIC LOCATION	NAME	No	No	Name
	GEOGRAPHIC LOCATION ID	Yes	Yes	ID
	DESCRIPTION	No	No	Description
GEOGRAPHIC POINT	GEOGRAPHIC LOCATION ID	Yes	Yes	ID
GOOD	PRODUCT ID	Yes	Yes	ID
	PART ID	No	No	ID
HOUSEHOLD	PARTY ID	Yes	Yes	ID
	ROLE TYPE ID	Yes	Yes	ID
INSTALLATION AND REPAIR SERVICE	PRODUCT ID	Yes	Yes	ID
INTERNAL ORGANIZATION	PARTY ID	Yes	Yes	ID
INTERNET ACCESS	ROLE TYPE ID	Yes	Yes	ID
INVENTORY ITEM	PRODUCT ID	Yes	No	ID
	INVENTORY ITEM ID	Yes	No	ID
	FACILITY ID	No	Yes	ID
	PARTY ID	No	Yes	ID
	PRODUCT ID	No	Yes	ID
	CONTAINER ID	No	No	ID
	LOT ID	No	No	ID
	PART ID	No	No	ID
INVOICE	INVOICE ID	Yes	No	ID
	BILLED FROM PARTY ID	No	Yes	ID
	BILLED TO PARTY ID	No	Yes	ID
	PARTY ID	No	Yes	ID
	ROLE TYPE ID	No	Yes	ID
	SENT FROM CONTACT MECH ID	No	Yes	ID
	SENT TO CONTACT MECH ID	No	Yes	ID
	BILLING ACCOUNT ID	No	No	ID

ENTITY NAME	ATTRIBUTE NAME	PK?	FK?	DOMAIN
	DESCRIPTION	No	No	Description
	INVOICE DATE	No	No	Datetime
	MESSAGE	No	No	Long varchar
INVOICE ITEM	INVOICE ID	Yes	Yes	ID
	INVOICE ITEM SEQ ID	Yes	No	ID
	ADJUSTED BY INVOICE ID	No	Yes	ID
	ADJUSTED BY INVOICE ITEM SEQ ID	No	Yes	ID
	INVENTORY ITEM ID	No	Yes	ID
	PRODUCT FEATURE ID	No	Yes	ID
	PRODUCT ID	No	Yes	ID
	SOLD WITH INVOICE ID	No	Yes	ID
	SOLD WITH INVOICE ITEM SEQ ID	No	Yes	ID
	UOM ID	No	Yes	ID
	AMOUNT	No	No	Currency amount
	INVOICE ITEM TYPE ID	No	No	ID
	ITEM DESCRIPTION	No	No	Description
	QUANTITY	No	No	Numeric
	TAXABLE FLAG	No	No	Indicator
LISTING	LISTING ID	Yes	No	ID
	PRODUCT ID	No	Yes	ID
	TEXT	No	No	Long varchar
LISTING OFFERING	PRODUCT ID	Yes	Yes	ID
LOADING COIL	NETWORK COMPONENT ID	Yes	Yes	ID
LOCAL CONNECTIVITY	PRODUCT ID	Yes	Yes	ID
LONG DISTANCE CONNECTIVITY	PRODUCT ID	Yes	Yes	ID
MARKETING PACKAGE	FROM DATE	Yes	Yes	Datetime
	PRODUCT ID FROM	Yes	Yes	ID
	PRODUCT ID TO	Yes	Yes	ID
	INSTRUCTION	No	No	Long varchar
	QUANTITY USED	No	No	Numeric
MICROWAVE COMPONENT	NETWORK COMPONENT ID	Yes	Yes	ID
NETWORK ASSEMBLY	NETWORK ASSEMBLY ID	Yes	No	ID
NETWORK ASSEMBLY	NETWORK ASSEMBLY TYPE ID	No	Yes	ID
NETWORK ASSEMBLY STRUCTURE	NETWORK ASSEMBLY ID MADE OF	Yes	Yes	ID

ENTITY NAME	ATTRIBUTE NAME	PK?	FK?	DOMAIN
	NETWORK ASSEMBLY ID PART OF	Yes	Yes	ID
	FROM DATE	Yes	No	Datetime
	THRU DATE	No	No	Datetime
NETWORK ASSEMBLY TYPE	NETWORK ASSEMBLY TYPE ID	Yes	No	ID
	DESCRIPTION	No	No	Description
NETWORK ASSEMBLY TYPE CAPABILITY	CAPABILITY TYPE ID	Yes	Yes	ID
	NETWORK ASSEMBLY TYPE ID	Yes	Yes	ID
	VALUE	No	No	Numeric
NETWORK COMPONENT	NETWORK COMPONENT ID	Yes	No	ID
	FACILITY ID	No	Yes	ID
	NETWORK COMPONENT TYPE ID	No	Yes	ID
	SERIAL NUM	No	No	Description
NETWORK COMPONENT ASSEMBLY	NETWORK ASSEMBLY ID	Yes	Yes	ID
	NETWORK COMPONENT ID	Yes	Yes	ID
	FROM DATE	Yes	No	Datetime
	THRU DATE	No	No	Datetime
NETWORK COMPONENT TYPE	NETWORK COMPONENT TYPE ID	Yes	No	ID
	DESCRIPTION	No	No	Description
NETWORK CONFIGURATION SETTING	NETWORK ASSEMBLY ID	Yes	Yes	ID
	NETWORK COMPONENT ID	Yes	Yes	ID
	FROM DATE	Yes	No	Datetime
	THRU DATE	No	No	Datetime
	NETWORK COMPONENT TYPE ID	Yes	No	ID
	NETWORK SETTING ID	Yes	Yes	ID
	VALUE	No	No	Numeric
NETWORK SERVER	NETWORK COMPONENT ID	Yes	Yes	ID
	GEOGRAPHIC LOCATION ID	No	Yes	ID
NETWORK SERVER TYPE	NETWORK COMPONENT TYPE ID	Yes	Yes	ID
NETWORK SETTING TYPE	NETWORK SETTING ID	Yes	No	ID
	DESCRIPTION	No	No	Description
NETWORK SUPPORT STRUCTURE	NETWORK COMPONENT ID	Yes	Yes	ID
NON SERIALIZED INVENTORY ITEM	GEOGRAPHIC LOCATION ID	No	Yes	ID
	INVENTORY ITEM ID	Yes	Yes	ID
	QUANTITY ON HAND	No	No	Numeric
ONE TIME CHARGE	PRICE COMPONENT ID	Yes	Yes	ID

ENTITY NAME	ATTRIBUTE NAME	PK?	FK?	DOMAIN
OPTIONAL FEATURE	FROM DATE	Yes	Yes	Datetime
	PRODUCT FEATURE ID	Yes	Yes	ID
	PRODUCT ID	Yes	Yes	ID
ORDER	ORDER ID	Yes	No	ID
	ENTRY DATE	No	No	Datetime
	ORDER DATE	No	No	Datetime
ORDER	VISIT ID	No	No	ID
ORDER ITEM	ORDER ID	Yes	Yes	ID
	ORDER ITEM SEQ ID	Yes	No	ID
	DEPLOYMENT ID	No	Yes	ID
	PRODUCT FEATURE ID	No	Yes	ID
	PRODUCT ID	No	Yes	ID
	BUDGET ID	No	No	ID
	BUDGET ITEM SEQ ID	No	No	ID
	COMMENTS	No	No	Comment
	ESTIMATED DELIVERY DATE	No	No	Datetime
	ITEM DESCRIPTION	No	No	Description
	QUANTITY	No	No	Numeric
	QUOTE ID	No	No	ID
	QUOTED ITEM SEQ ID	No	No	ID
	SHIPPING INSTRUCTIONS	No	No	Long varchar
	SUBSCRIPTION ID	No	No	ID
	UNIT PRICE	No	No	Currency amount
ORGANIZATION	PARTY ID	Yes	Yes	ID
	NAME	No	No	Name
ORGANIZATION CONTACT RELATIONSHIP	FROM DATE	Yes	Yes	Datetime
	PARTY ID FROM	Yes	Yes	ID
	PARTY ID TO	Yes	Yes	ID
	ROLE TYPE ID FROM	Yes	Yes	ID
	ROLE TYPE ID TO	Yes	Yes	ID
ORGANIZATION CUSTOMER	PARTY ID	Yes	Yes	ID
ORGANIZATION CUSTOMER RELATIONSHIP	ROLE TYPE ID	Yes	Yes	ID
	FROM DATE	Yes	Yes	Datetime
	PARTY ID FROM	Yes	Yes	ID
	PARTY ID TO	Yes	Yes	ID

ENTITY NAME	ATTRIBUTE NAME	PK?	FK?	DOMAIN
	ROLE TYPE ID FROM	Yes	Yes	ID
	ROLE TYPE ID TO	Yes	Yes	ID
ORGANIZATION ROLE	PARTY ID	Yes	Yes	ID
	ROLE TYPE ID	Yes	Yes	ID
ORGANIZATION ROLLUP	FROM DATE	Yes	Yes	Datetime
ORGANIZATION ROLLUP	PARTY ID FROM	Yes	Yes	ID
	PARTY ID TO	Yes	Yes	ID
	ROLE TYPE ID FROM	Yes	Yes	ID
	ROLE TYPE ID TO	Yes	Yes	ID
ORGANIZATION UNIT	PARTY ID	Yes	Yes	ID
	ROLE TYPE ID	Yes	Yes	ID
OTHER ORGANIZATION UNIT	PARTY ID	Yes	Yes	ID
OTHER PRODUCT FEATURE	ROLE TYPE ID	Yes	Yes	ID
	PRODUCT FEATURE ID	Yes	Yes	ID
OTHER TELE-COMMUNICATIONS SERVICE	PRODUCT ID	Yes	Yes	ID
PARENT ORGANIZATION	PARTY ID	Yes	Yes	ID
PARTNER	ROLE TYPE ID	Yes	Yes	ID
	PARTY ID	Yes	Yes	ID
PARTNERSHIP	ROLE TYPE ID	Yes	Yes	ID
	FROM DATE	Yes	Yes	Datetime
	PARTY ID FROM	Yes	Yes	ID
	PARTY ID TO	Yes	Yes	ID
	ROLE TYPE ID FROM	Yes	Yes	ID
	ROLE TYPE ID TO	Yes	Yes	ID
PARTY	PARTY ID	Yes	No	ID
PARTY FACILITY	FACILITY ID	Yes	Yes	ID
	PARTY ID	Yes	Yes	ID
PARTY RELATIONSHIP	PARTY ID FROM	Yes	Yes	ID
	PARTY ID TO	Yes	Yes	ID
	ROLE TYPE ID FROM	Yes	Yes	ID
	ROLE TYPE ID TO	Yes	Yes	ID
	FROM DATE	Yes	No	Datetime
	PARTY RELATIONSHIP TYPE ID	No	Yes	ID
	COMMENTS	No	No	Comment

ENTITY NAME	ATTRIBUTE NAME	PK?	FK?	DOMAIN
	PRIORITY TYPE ID	No	No	ID
	STATUS TYPE ID	No	No	ID
	THRU DATE	No	No	Datetime
PARTY RELATIONSHIP TYPE	PARTY RELATIONSHIP TYPE ID	Yes	No	ID
	ROLE TYPE ID VALID FROM	No	Yes	ID
	ROLE TYPE ID VALID TO	No	Yes	ID
	DESCRIPTION	No	No	Description
	NAME	No	No	Name
PARTY ROLE	PARTY ID	Yes	Yes	ID
	ROLE TYPE ID	Yes	Yes	ID
	PARTY ROLE ID	No	No	ID
PARTY ROLE TYPE	ROLE TYPE ID	Yes	Yes	ID
PATHWAY	GEOGRAPHIC LOCATION ID	Yes	Yes	ID
PERFORMANCE CHARACTERISTIC	PRODUCT FEATURE ID	Yes	Yes	ID
	UOM ID	No	Yes	ID
	NUMBER SPECIFIED	No	No	Numeric
PERSON	PARTY ID	Yes	Yes	ID
	BIRTH DATE	No	No	Datetime
	COMMENTS	No	No	Comment
	CURRENT FIRST NAME	No	No	Name
	CURRENT LAST NAME	No	No	Name
	CURRENT MIDDLE NAME	No	No	Name
	CURRENT NICKNAME	No	No	Name
	CURRENT PASSPORT EXPIRE DATE	No	No	Datetime
	CURRENT PASSPORT NUMBER	No	No	Numeric
	CURRENT PERSONAL TITLE	No	No	Name
	CURRENT SUFFIX	No	No	Name
	GENDER	No	No	Indicator
	HEIGHT	No	No	Numeric
	MARTIAL STATUS	No	No	Indicator
	MOTHER'S MADIEN NAME	No	No	Name
	SOCIAL SECURITY NUMBER	No	No	Numeric
	TOTAL YEARS WORK EXPERIENCE	No	No	Numeric
	WEIGHT	No	No	Numeric
PERSON ROLE	PARTY ID	Yes	Yes	ID
	ROLE TYPE ID	Yes	Yes	ID
POSTAL ADDRESS	CONTACT MECHANISM ID	Yes	Yes	ID
	ADDRESS1	No	No	Description
	ADDRESS2	No	No	Description

ENTITY NAME	ATTRIBUTE NAME	PK?	FK?	DOMAIN
	DIRECTIONS	No	No	Long varchar
PRICE COMPONENT	PRICE COMPONENT ID	Yes	No	ID
	GEOGRAPHIC LOCATION ID	No	Yes	ID
	PARTY ID	No	Yes	ID
	PRODUCT FEATURE ID	No	Yes	ID
	PRODUCT ID	No	Yes	ID
	AGREEMENT ID	No	No	ID
	AGREEMENT ITEM SEQ ID	No	No	ID
	COMMENTS	No	No	Comment
	FROM DATE	No	No	Datetime
	ORDER VALUE ID	No	No	ID
	PARTY TYPE ID	No	No	ID
	PERCENT	No	No	Floating point
	PRICE	No	No	Currency amount
	PRODUCT CATEGORY ID	No	No	ID
	QUANTITY BREAK ID	No	No	ID
	RATE TYPE ID	No	No	ID
	SALE TYPE ID	No	No	ID
	THRU DATE	No	No	Datetime
	UOM ID	No	No	ID
PRODUCT	PRODUCT ID	Yes	No	ID
	MANUFACTURER PARTY ID	No	Yes	ID
	UOM ID	No	Yes	ID
	COMMENTS	No	No	Comment
	DESCRIPTION	No	No	Description
	INTRODUCTION DATE	No	No	Datetime
	NAME	No	No	Name
	PART ID	No	No	ID
	SALES DISCONTINUATION DATE	No	No	Datetime
	SUPPORT DISCONTINUATION DATE	No	No	Datetime
PRODUCT ASSOCIATION TYPE	PRODUCT ASSOCIATION TYPE ID	Yes	No	ID
PRODUCT CAPABILITY	DESCRIPTION	No	No	Description
	CAPABILITY TYPE ID	Yes	Yes	ID
	PRODUCT ID	Yes	Yes	ID
PRODUCT COMPLEMENT	VALUE	No	No	Numeric
	FROM DATE	Yes	Yes	Datetime

ENTITY NAME	ATTRIBUTE NAME	PK?	FK?	DOMAIN
	PRODUCT ID FROM	Yes	Yes	ID
	PRODUCT ID TO	Yes	Yes	ID
	REASON	No	No	Long varchar
PRODUCT DEPENDENCY	FROM DATE	Yes	Yes	Datetime
	PRODUCT ID FROM	Yes	Yes	ID
	PRODUCT ID TO	Yes	Yes	ID
PRODUCT FEATURE	PRODUCT FEATURE ID	Yes	No	ID
	DESCRIPTION	No	No	Description
	PRODUCT FEATURE CATEGORY ID	No	No	ID
PRODUCT FEATURE APPLICABILITY	PRODUCT FEATURE ID	Yes	Yes	ID
	PRODUCT ID	Yes	Yes	ID
	FROM DATE	Yes	No	Datetime
	THRU DATE	No	No	Datetime
PRODUCT FEATURE INTERACTION	PRODUCT FEATURE ID FACTOR IN	Yes	Yes	ID
	PRODUCT FEATURE ID OF	Yes	Yes	ID
	PRODUCT ID	No	Yes	ID
PRODUCT INCOMPATIBILITY	FROM DATE	Yes	Yes	Datetime
	PRODUCT ID FROM	Yes	Yes	ID
	PRODUCT ID TO	Yes	Yes	ID
	REASON	No	No	Long varchar
PRODUCT OBSOLESCENCE	FROM DATE	Yes	Yes	Datetime
	PRODUCT ID FROM	Yes	Yes	ID
	PRODUCT ID TO	Yes	Yes	ID
	REASON	No	No	Long varchar
	SUPERCESSION DATE	No	No	Datetime
PRODUCT SUBSTITUTE	FROM DATE	Yes	Yes	Datetime
	PRODUCT ID FROM	Yes	Yes	ID
	PRODUCT ID TO	Yes	Yes	ID
	COMMENTS	No	No	Comment
	QUANTITY	No	No	Numeric
PRODUCTS	PRODUCT ID	Yes	No	ID
	PRODUCT CATEGORY	No	No	Description
	PRODUCT NAME	No	No	Name

ENTITY NAME	ATTRIBUTE NAME	PK?	FK?	DOMAIN
PROSPECT	PARTY ID	Yes	Yes	ID
	ROLE TYPE ID	Yes	Yes	ID
PURCHASE ORDER	ORDER ID	Yes	No	ID
	PURCHASE ORDER ID	Yes	No	ID
PURCHASE ORDER ITEM	ORDER ID	Yes	Yes	ID
	ORDER ITEM SEQ ID	Yes	No	ID
	PART ID	No	No	ID
RECURRING CHARGE	PRICE COMPONENT ID	Yes	Yes	ID
	UOM ID	No	No	ID
REGULATORY AGENCY	PARTY ID	Yes	Yes	ID
	ROLE TYPE ID	Yes	Yes	ID
REQUIRED FEATURE	FROM DATE	Yes	Yes	Datetime
	PRODUCT FEATURE ID	Yes	Yes	ID
	PRODUCT ID	Yes	Yes	ID
RESIDENTIAL CUSTOMER	PARTY ID	Yes	Yes	ID
RESIDENTIAL CUSTOMER RELATIONSHIP	ROLE TYPE ID	Yes	Yes	ID
	FROM DATE	Yes	Yes	Datetime
	PARTY ID FROM	Yes	Yes	ID
	PARTY ID TO	Yes	Yes	ID
	ROLE TYPE ID FROM	Yes	Yes	ID
	ROLE TYPE ID TO	Yes	Yes	ID
ROLE TYPE	ROLE TYPE ID	Yes	No	ID
	DESCRIPTION	No	No	Description
ROUTER	NETWORK COMPONENT ID	Yes	Yes	ID
SELECTABLE FEATURE	FROM DATE	Yes	Yes	Datetime
	PRODUCT FEATURE ID	Yes	Yes	ID
	PRODUCT ID	Yes	Yes	ID
SERIALIZED INVENTORY ITEM	INVENTORY ITEM ID	Yes	Yes	ID
	SERIAL NUM	No	No	Description
SERVICE	PRODUCT ID	Yes	Yes	ID
SERVICE AGREEMENT OFFERING	PRODUCT ID	Yes	Yes	ID
SERVICE ORDER	ORDER ID	Yes	Yes	ID
SERVICE ORDER ITEM	ORDER ID	Yes	Yes	ID
	ORDER ITEM SEQ ID	Yes	Yes	ID
	COMMUNICATION ID	No	Yes	ID
SHAREHOLDER	PARTY ID	Yes	Yes	ID

ENTITY NAME	ATTRIBUTE NAME	PK?	FK?	DOMAIN
STANDARD FEATURE	ROLE TYPE ID	Yes	Yes	ID
	FROM DATE	Yes	Yes	Datetime
	PRODUCT FEATURE ID	Yes	Yes	ID
	PRODUCT ID	Yes	No	ID
STANDARD TIME PERIOD	STANDARD TIME PERIOD ID	Yes	No	ID
	FROM DATE	No	No	Datetime
	PERIOD TYPE ID	No	No	ID
	THRU DATE	No	No	Datetime
SUBSIDIARY	PARTY ID	Yes	Yes	ID
	ROLE TYPE ID	Yes	Yes	ID
SUPPLIER	PARTY ID	Yes	Yes	ID
	ROLE TYPE ID	Yes	Yes	ID
SUPPLIER RELATIONSHIP	FROM DATE	Yes	Yes	Datetime
	PARTY ID FROM	Yes	Yes	ID
	PARTY ID TO	Yes	Yes	ID
	ROLE TYPE ID FROM	Yes	Yes	ID
	ROLE TYPE ID TO	Yes	Yes	ID
SUPPORT STRUCTURE TYPE	NETWORK COMPONENT TYPE ID	Yes	Yes	ID
SWITCH	NETWORK COMPONENT ID	Yes	Yes	ID
TELECOM NUMBER ID	COMMUNICATION ID	Yes	Yes	ID
	AREA CODE	No	No	Numeric
	CONTACT NUMBER	No	No	Numeric
	COUNTRY CODE	No	No	Numeric
TELECOM PRODUCT ASSOCIATION	PRODUCT ID FROM	Yes	Yes	ID
	PRODUCT ID TO	Yes	Yes	ID
	FROM DATE	Yes	No	Datetime
	NETWORK ASSEMBLY TYPE ID	No	Yes	ID
	NETWORK COMPONENT TYPE ID	No	Yes	ID
	PRODUCT ASSOCIATION TYPE ID	No	Yes	ID
	REASON	No	No	Long varchar
	THRU DATE	No	No	Datetime
TELECOMMUNICATIONS ACCESSORY	PRODUCT ID	Yes	Yes	ID
TELECOMMUNICATIONS CARRIER	PARTY ID	Yes	Yes	ID
	ROLE TYPE ID	Yes	Yes	ID

ENTITY NAME	ATTRIBUTE NAME	PK?	FK?	DOMAIN
TELECOMMUNICATIONS CARRIER RELATIONSHIP	FROM DATE	Yes	Yes	Datetime
	PARTY ID FROM	Yes	Yes	ID
	PARTY ID TO	Yes	Yes	ID
	ROLE TYPE ID FROM	Yes	Yes	ID
	ROLE TYPE ID TO	Yes	Yes	ID
TELECOMMUNICATIONS DEVICE	PRODUCT ID	Yes	Yes	ID
TELECOMMUNICATIONS NUMBER	CONTACT MECHANISM ID	Yes	No	ID
	AREA CODE	No	No	Numeric
	CONTACT NUMBER	No	No	Short varchar
TELECOMMUNICATIONS SYSTEM	CONTRY CODE	No	No	Numeric
	PRODUCT ID	Yes	Yes	ID
TIME BY HOUR	HOUR ID	Yes	No	ID
	DAY	No	No	Very short
	HOUR	No	No	Very short
	MONTH	No	No	Very short
	QUARTER	No	No	Very short
	WEEK	No	No	Very short
	YEAR	No	No	Very short
TIME PERIOD USAGE	DEPLOYMENT ID	Yes	Yes	ID
	DEPLOYMENT USAGE ID	Yes	Yes	ID
UNIT OF MEASURE	UOM ID	Yes	No	ID
	ABBREVIATION	No	No	Short varchar
	DESCRIPTION	No	No	Description
UNIT OF MEASURES	UOM ID	Yes	No	ID
	ABBREVIATION	No	No	Short varchar
	DESCRIPTION	No	No	Description
UTILIZATION CHARGE	PRICE COMPONENT ID	Yes	Yes	ID
	UOM ID	Yes	Yes	ID
UTILIZATION CHARGE	QUANTITY	No	Yes	Numeric
VOLUME USAGE	DEPLOYMENT ID	Yes	Yes	ID
	DEPLOYMENT USAGE ID	Yes	Yes	ID
	UOM ID	No	Yes	ID
	QUANTITY	No	No	Numeric
WIRELESS CONNECTIVITY	PRODUCT ID	Yes	Yes	ID

Entities and Attributes for Health Care Models

This appendix lists the entities and attributes from the logical data models and star schema found in Chapter 4, "Health Care." This listing includes the entity names, attribute names, primary key indicators, foreign key indicators, and the domain for each attribute.

The domain indicates a standard set of characteristics that can be applied to attributes, including its datatype and length. Table A.1 defines the nature of each domain. When applying the domains to the attributes listed in these appendices, refer to Table A.1 for recommendations on what datatype and length to use when implementing these models. Of course, the datatype and length of each attribute should be adjusted as appropriate to meet the specific needs of the enterprise.

The domain definitions as they are applied to the attributes in the appendices are used for the SQL code that is contained on the demo CD-ROM at the back of this book as well as in the Industry Downloads (see the section "How to Use the Volume 2 Industry Electronic Products" for more information).

Entities and Attributes Listing for Health Care Models

ENTITY NAME	ATTRIBUTE NAME	PK?	FK?	DOMAIN
AGREEMENT	AGREEMENT ID	Yes	No	ID
	AGREEMENT TYPE ID	No	Yes	ID
	FROM DATE	No	No	Datetime
	PARTY ID FROM	No	Yes	ID
	PARTY ID TO	No	Yes	ID
	ROLE TYPE ID FROM	No	Yes	ID
	ROLE TYPE ID TO	No	Yes	ID
	AGREEMENT DATE	No	No	Datetime
	DESCRIPTION	No	No	Description
	PRODUCT ID	No	No	ID
	TEXT	No	No	Long varchar
	THRU DATE	No	No	Datetime
AGREEMENT EXHIBIT	AGREEMENT ID	Yes	Yes	ID
	AGREEMENT ITEM SEQ ID	Yes	Yes	ID
AGREEMENT ITEM	AGREEMENT ID	Yes	Yes	ID
	AGREEMENT ITEM SEQ ID	Yes	No	ID
	PART OF AGREEMENT ID	No	Yes	ID
	PART OF AGREEMENT ITEM SEQ ID	No	Yes	ID
	AGREEMENT IMAGE	No	No	Blob
	AGREEMENT TEXT	No	No	Long varchar
AGREEMENT PRICING PROGRAM	AGREEMENT ID	Yes	Yes	ID
	AGREEMENT ITEM SEQ ID	Yes	Yes	ID
AGREEMENT ROLE	AGREEMENT ID	Yes	Yes	ID
	PARTY ID	Yes	Yes	ID
	ROLE TYPE ID	Yes	Yes	ID
AGREEMENT ROLE TYPE	ROLE TYPE ID	Yes	Yes	ID
AGREEMENT SECTION	AGREEMENT ID	Yes	Yes	ID
	AGREEMENT ITEM SEQ ID	Yes	Yes	ID
AGREEMENT TYPE	AGREEMENT TYPE ID	Yes	No	ID
	DESCRIPTION	No	No	Description
ALTERNATIVE MED CATEGORY	HEALTH CARE DISCIPLINE ID	Yes	Yes	ID
AMOUNT TYPE	AMOUNT TYPE ID	Yes	No	ID
	DESCRIPTION	No	No	Description
CATEGORY OFFERING	HEALTH CARE DISCIPLINE ID	Yes	Yes	ID

ENTITY NAME	ATTRIBUTE NAME	PK?	FK?	DOMAIN
	HEALTH CARE OFFERING ID	Yes	No	ID
CERTIFICATION	PARTY ID	Yes	Yes	ID
	QUAL TYPE ID	Yes	Yes	ID
CERTIFICATION REQUIREMENT	CERTIFICATION TYPE ID	Yes	Yes	ID
	HEALTH CARE OFFERING ID	Yes	Yes	ID
CERTIFICATION STATUS	HEALTH CARE DELIVERY ID	Yes	Yes	ID
	STATUS TYPE ID	Yes	Yes	ID
	STATUS DATE	Yes	No	Datetime
CERTIFICATION STATUS TYPE	STATUS TYPE ID	Yes	Yes	ID
CERTIFICATION TYPE	CERTIFICATION TYPE ID	Yes	No	ID
	DESCRIPTION	No	No	Description
CLAIM	CLAIM ID	Yes	No	ID
	AGREEMENT ID	No	Yes	ID
	CLAIM SUBMISSION DATE	No	No	Datetime
	CLAIM TYPE ID	No	No	ID
CLAIM ITEM	CLAIM ID	Yes	Yes	ID
	CLAIM ITEM SEQ ID	Yes	No	ID
	CLAIM SERVICE CODE	No	Yes	ID
	UOM ID	No	Yes	ID
	CLAIM AMOUNT	No	No	Currency amount
	DAMAGE TYPE ID	No	No	ID
	INCIDENT ID	No	No	ID
	INSURED ASSET ID	No	No	ID
	QUANTITY	No	No	Numeric
CLAIM ITEM DIAGNOSIS CODE	CLAIM ID	Yes	Yes	ID
	CLAIM ITEM SEQ ID	Yes	Yes	ID
	DIAGNOSIS TYPE ID	Yes	Yes	ID
CLAIM PAYMENT AMOUNT	CLAIM SETTLEMENT AMOUNT ID	Yes	Yes	ID
CLAIM RESUBMISSION	CLAIM SETTLEMENT ID	Yes	Yes	ID
	CLAIM ID FOR	Yes	Yes	ID
CLAIM ROLE	CLAIM ID WITH	Yes	Yes	ID
	CLAIM ID	Yes	Yes	ID

ENTITY NAME	ATTRIBUTE NAME	PK?	FK?	DOMAIN
	PARTY ID	Yes	Yes	ID
	ROLE TYPE ID	Yes	Yes	ID
CLAIM ROLE TYPE	ROLE TYPE ID	Yes	Yes	ID
CLAIM SERVICE CODE	CLAIM SERVICE CODE	Yes	No	ID
	ABBREVIATION	No	No	Short varchar
	DESCRIPTION	No	No	Description
CLAIM SETTLEMENT	CLAIM SETTLEMENT ID	Yes	No	ID
	CLAIM ID	No	Yes	ID
	CLAIM ITEM SEQ ID	No	Yes	ID
	DATE SETTLED	No	No	Datetime
CLAIM SETTLEMENT AMOUNT	CLAIM SETTLEMENT ID	Yes	Yes	ID
	CLAIM SETTLEMENT AMOUNT ID	Yes	No	ID
	AMOUNT TYPE ID	No	Yes	ID
	EXPLANATION OF BENEFIT TYPE ID	No	Yes	ID
	PAYMENT ID	No	Yes	ID
	AMOUNT	No	No	Currency amount
	EXPLANATION	No	No	Long varchar
CLAIM STATUS	CLAIM ID	Yes	Yes	ID
	STATUS TYPE ID	Yes	Yes	ID
	DATETIME	No	No	Datetime
CLAIM STATUS TYPE	STATUS TYPE ID	Yes	No	ID
CLINIC	FACILITY ID	Yes	Yes	ID
CONTACT	PARTY ID	Yes	Yes	ID
	ROLE TYPE ID	Yes	Yes	ID
CONTACT MECHANISM	CONTACT MECHANISM ID	Yes	No	ID
	CONTACT MECHANISM TYPE ID	No	Yes	ID
COVERED INDIVIDUAL	AGREEMENT ID	Yes	Yes	ID
	PARTY ID	Yes	Yes	ID
	ROLE TYPE ID	Yes	Yes	ID
CPT CODE	CLAIM SERVICE CODE	Yes	Yes	ID
DEDUCTIBLE AMOUNT	CLAIM SETTLEMENT AMOUNT ID	Yes	Yes	ID
	CLAIM SETTLEMENT ID	Yes	Yes	ID
DEGREE	PARTY ID	Yes	Yes	ID
	QUAL TYPE ID	Yes	Yes	ID
DELIVERY OUTCOME	HEALTH CARE DELIVERY ID	Yes	Yes	ID
	DELIVERY OUTCOME ID	Yes	No	ID
	OUTCOME TYPE ID	No	Yes	ID
	OUTCOME EXPLANATION	No	No	Long varchar
DENTAL CATEGORY	HEALTH CARE DISCIPLINE ID	Yes	Yes	ID
DENTAL CLAIM	CLAIM ID	Yes	Yes	ID
DEPARTMENT	PARTY ID	Yes	Yes	ID
	ROLE TYPE ID	Yes	Yes	ID
DIAGNOSIS	DIAGNOSIS ID	Yes	No	ID
	DIAGNOSIS TYPE ID	No	Yes	ID
	HEALTH CARE EPISODE ID	No	Yes	ID
	DIAGNOSIS DATE	No	No	Datetime
DIAGNOSIS TREATMENT	DIAGNOSIS ID	Yes	Yes	ID
	HEALTH CARE DELIVERY ID	Yes	Yes	ID
DIAGNOSIS TYPE	DIAGNOSIS TYPE ID	Yes	No	ID
	ABBREVIATION	No	No	Short varchar
	DESCRIPTION	No	No	Description
DIAGNOSIS TYPES	DIAGNOSIS TYPE ID	Yes	No	ID
	DESCRIPTION	No	No	Description
DISALLOWED AMOUNT	CLAIM SETTLEMENT AMOUNT ID	Yes	Yes	ID
	CLAIM SETTLEMENT ID	Yes	Yes	ID
DIVISION	PARTY ID	Yes	Yes	ID
	ROLE TYPE ID	Yes	Yes	ID
DME DELIVERY	HEALTH CARE DELIVERY ID	Yes	Yes	ID
DRG	DRG ID	Yes	No	ID
	NAME	No	No	Name
DRG CLASSIFICATION	DIAGNOSIS TYPE ID	Yes	Yes	ID
	DRG ID	Yes	Yes	ID
DRUG ADMINISTRATION	CLAIM SERVICE CODE	Yes	Yes	ID
	HEALTH CARE DELIVERY ID	Yes	Yes	ID
DURABLE MEDICAL EQUIP OFFERING	HEALTH CARE OFFERING ID	Yes	Yes	ID
ELECTRONIC ADDRESS	CONTACT MECHANISM ID	Yes	Yes	ID
	ELECTRONIC ADDRESS STRING	No	No	Description
EMPLOYEE	PARTY ID	Yes	Yes	ID
	ROLE TYPE ID	Yes	Yes	ID
EMPLOYER	PARTY ID	Yes	Yes	ID

ENTITY NAME	ATTRIBUTE NAME	PK?	FK?	DOMAIN
EMPLOYMENT	ROLE TYPE ID	Yes	Yes	ID
	FROM DATE	Yes	Yes	Datetime
	PARTY ID FROM	Yes	Yes	ID
	PARTY ID TO	Yes	Yes	ID
	ROLE TYPE ID FROM	Yes	Yes	ID
	ROLE TYPE ID TO	Yes	Yes	ID
	TERMINATION REASON ID	No	No	ID
	TERMINATION TYPE ID	No	No	ID
EMPLOYMENT AGREEMENT	AGREEMENT ID	Yes	Yes	ID
EPISODE OUTCOME	HEALTH CARE EPISODE ID	Yes	Yes	ID
	EPISODE OUTCOME ID	Yes	No	ID
	OUTCOME TYPE ID	No	Yes	ID
	OUTCOME EXPLANATION	No	No	Long varchar
EPISODE TYPE	EPISODE TYPE ID	Yes	No	ID
	DESCRIPTION	No	No	Description
EPISODE TYPES	EPISODE TYPE ID	Yes	No	ID
	DESCRIPTION	No	No	Description
EXAMINATION	HEALTH CARE DELIVERY ID	Yes	Yes	ID
EXPLANATION OF BENEFIT TYPE	EXPLANATION OF BENEFIT TYPE ID	Yes	No	ID
	DESCRIPTION	No	No	Description
FACILITY	FACILITY ID	Yes	No	ID
	FACILITY TYPE ID	No	Yes	ID
	PART OF FACILITY ID	No	Yes	ID
	DESCRIPTION	No	No	Description
	FACILITY NAME	No	No	Name
	SQUARE FOOTAGE	No	No	Numeric
FACILITY ROLE TYPE	ROLE TYPE ID	Yes	Yes	ID
FACILITY TYPE	FACILITY TYPE ID	Yes	No	ID
	DESCRIPTION	No	No	Description
FAMILY DEPENDENCY	FROM DATE	Yes	Yes	Datetime
	PARTY ID FROM	Yes	Yes	ID
	PARTY ID TO	Yes	Yes	ID
	ROLE TYPE ID FROM	Yes	Yes	ID
	ROLE TYPE ID TO	Yes	Yes	ID
FLOOR	FACILITY ID	Yes	Yes	ID
GEOGRAPHIC BOUNDARY	GEOGRAPHIC LOCATION ID	Yes	No	ID
	ABBREVIATION	No	No	Short varchar
	GEO BOUNDARY TYPE ID	No	No	ID

ENTITY NAME	ATTRIBUTE NAME	PK?	FK?	DOMAIN
	GEO CODE	No	No	Short varchar
GROUP	NAME	No	No	Name
	PARTY ID	Yes	Yes	ID
	ROLE TYPE ID	Yes	Yes	ID
GROUP INSURANCE POLICY	AGREEMENT ID	Yes	Yes	ID
	PARTY ID	No	Yes	ID
	ROLE TYPE ID	No	Yes	ID
HCPCS CODE	CLAIM SERVICE CODE	Yes	Yes	ID
HEALTH CARE AID OFFERING	HEALTH CARE OFFERING ID	Yes	Yes	ID
HEALTH CARE CATEGORY	HEALTH CARE DISCIPLINE ID	Yes	No	ID
	DESCRIPTION	No	No	Description
HEALTH CARE CLAIM	CLAIM ID	Yes	Yes	ID
HEALTH CARE DELIVERY	HEALTH CARE DELIVERY ID	Yes	No	ID
	HEALTH CARE EPISODE ID	No	Yes	ID
	HEALTH CARE OFFERING ID	No	Yes	ID
	HEALTH CARE VISIT ID	No	Yes	ID
	DELIVERY NOTES	No	No	Long varchar
HEALTH CARE DELIVERY ASSOCIATION	FROM DATE	No	No	Datetime
	THRU DATE	No	No	Datetime
	HEALTH CARE DELIVERY ID FROM	Yes	Yes	ID
HEALTH CARE DELIVERY BILLING	HEALTH CARE DELIVERY ID TO	Yes	Yes	ID
	HEALTH CARE DELIVERY ID	Yes	Yes	ID
	INVOICE ID	Yes	Yes	ID
	INVOICE ITEM SEQ ID	Yes	Yes	ID
HEALTH CARE DELIVERY CLAIM SUBMISSION	CLAIM ID	Yes	Yes	ID
	CLAIM ITEM SEQ ID	Yes	Yes	ID
	HEALTH CARE DELIVERY ID	Yes	Yes	ID
HEALTH CARE DELIVERY ROLE	HEALTH CARE DELIVERY ID	Yes	Yes	ID
	PARTY ID	Yes	Yes	ID
	ROLE TYPE ID	Yes	Yes	ID

ENTITY NAME	ATTRIBUTE NAME	PK?	FK?	DOMAIN
HEALTH CARE DELIVERY ROLE	FROM DATE	Yes	No	Datetime
	THRU DATE	No	No	Datetime
HEALTH CARE DELIVERY ROLE TYPE	ROLE TYPE ID	Yes	Yes	ID
HEALTH CARE EPISODE	HEALTH CARE EPISODE ID	Yes	No	ID
	EPISODE TYPE ID	No	Yes	ID
	INCIDENT ID	No	Yes	ID
	PARTY ID	No	Yes	ID
	ROLE TYPE ID	No	Yes	ID
	DESCRIPTION	No	No	Description
	EPISODE CREATE DATE	No	No	Datetime
HEALTH CARE EPISODE FACT	DIAGNOSIS TYPE ID	Yes	Yes	ID
	EPISODE TYPE ID	Yes	Yes	ID
	INCIDENT TYPE ID	Yes	Yes	ID
	OUTCOME TYPE ID	Yes	Yes	ID
	PATIENT TYPE ID	Yes	Yes	ID
	PRACTITIONER PARTY ID	Yes	Yes	ID
	PROVIDER PARTY ID	Yes	Yes	ID
	WEEK ID	Yes	Yes	ID
	AVG TIME LENGTH OF EPISODE	No	No	Numeric
	NUM EPISODES	No	No	Number
	NUM HEALTH CARE DELIVERIES	No	No	Numeric
	NUM HEALTH CARE VISITS	No	No	Numeric
	TOTAL CHARGES	No	No	Currency amount
HEALTH CARE GOOD OFFERING	HEALTH CARE OFFERING ID	Yes	Yes	ID
HEALTH CARE OFFERING	HEALTH CARE OFFERING ID	Yes	No	ID
	NAME	No	No	Name
HEALTH CARE OFFERING COMPOSITION	HEALTH CARE OFFERING ID	Yes	Yes	ID
	CONSISTING OF HEALTH CARE OFFERING ID FOR	Yes	Yes	ID
HEALTH CARE POLICY	AGREEMENT ID	Yes	Yes	ID
HEALTH CARE PRACTICE	PARTY ID	Yes	Yes	ID
	ROLE TYPE ID	Yes	Yes	ID

ENTITY NAME	ATTRIBUTE NAME	PK?	FK?	DOMAIN
HEALTH CARE PROVIDER ORGANIZATION	PARTY ID	Yes	Yes	ID
	ROLE TYPE ID	Yes	Yes	ID
	INDIV HC PRACTITIONER FROM	Yes	Yes	ID
HEALTH CARE REFERRAL	INDIV HC PRACTITIONER TO	Yes	Yes	ID
	PARTY ID	Yes	Yes	ID
	PARTY ID FROM	Yes	Yes	ID
	PARTY ID TO	Yes	Yes	ID
	ROLE TYPE ID	Yes	Yes	ID
	REFERRAL ID	No	No	ID
	DIAGNOSIS ID	Yes	Yes	ID
	HEALTH CARE EPISODE ID	No	Yes	ID
	COMMENTS	No	No	Comment
	DATE	No	No	Datetime
HEALTH CARE SERVICE OFFERING	HEALTH CARE OFFERING ID	Yes	Yes	ID
HEALTH CARE VISIT	HEALTH CARE VISIT ID	Yes	No	ID
	CONTACT MECHANISM ID	No	Yes	ID
	FACILITY ID	No	Yes	ID
	PARTY ID	No	Yes	ID
	ROLE TYPE ID	No	Yes	ID
	FROM DATE	No	No	Datetime
	THRU DATE	No	No	Datetime
HEALTH CARE VISIT ROLE	HEALTH CARE VISIT ID	Yes	Yes	ID
	PARTY ID	Yes	Yes	ID
	ROLE TYPE ID	Yes	Yes	ID
HEALTH CARE VISIT ROLE TYPE	ROLE TYPE ID	Yes	Yes	ID
HEALTH CARE VISIT STATUS	HEALTH CARE VISIT ID	Yes	Yes	ID
	STATUS TYPE ID	Yes	No	ID
	STATUS DATE	No	No	Datetime
HEALTH CARE VISIT STATUS TYPE	STATUS TYPE ID	Yes	Yes	ID
HOME CARE CLAIM	CLAIM ID	Yes	Yes	ID
HOSPITAL	FACILITY ID	Yes	Yes	ID
HOSPITAL CATEGORY	HEALTH CARE DISCIPLINE ID	Yes	Yes	ID
HOUSEHOLD	PARTY ID	Yes	Yes	ID
	ROLE TYPE ID	Yes	Yes	ID

ENTITY NAME	ATTRIBUTE NAME	PK?	FK?	DOMAIN
HOUSEHOLD MEMBERSHIP	FROM DATE	Yes	Yes	Datetime
	PARTY ID FROM	Yes	Yes	ID
	PARTY ID TO	Yes	Yes	ID
	ROLE TYPE ID FROM	Yes	Yes	ID
	ROLE TYPE ID TO	Yes	Yes	ID
ICD9 CODE	DIAGNOSIS TYPE ID	Yes	Yes	ID
INCIDENT	INCIDENT ID	Yes	No	ID
	INCIDENT TYPE ID	No	Yes	ID
	DESCRIPTION	No	No	Description
	EMPL RELATED IND	No	No	Indicator
	INCIDENT DATE	No	No	Datetime
INCIDENT TYPE	INCIDENT TYPE ID	Yes	No	ID
	DESCRIPTION	No	No	Description
INCIDENT TYPES	INCIDENT TYPE ID	Yes	No	ID
	DESCRIPTION	No	No	Description
INDIVIDUAL HEALTH CARE PRACTITIONER	PARTY ID	Yes	Yes	ID
	ROLE TYPE ID	Yes	Yes	ID
INDIVIDUAL HEALTH CARE PRACTITIONERS	PRACTITIONER PARTY ID	Yes	No	ID
	FIRST NAME	No	No	Name
	LAST NAME	No	No	Name
INDIVIDUAL	AGREEMENT ID	Yes	Yes	ID
INSURANCE POLICY	PARTY ID	No	Yes	ID
	ROLE TYPE ID	No	Yes	ID
INSTITUTION	PARTY ID	Yes	Yes	ID
	ROLE TYPE ID	Yes	Yes	ID
INSTITUTIONAL CLAIM	CLAIM ID	Yes	Yes	ID
INSURANCE POLICY	AGREEMENT ID	Yes	Yes	ID
	PARTY ID	Yes	Yes	ID
	ROLE TYPE ID	No	Yes	ID
	POLICY NUMBER	No	No	Number
INSURANCE PROVIDER	PARTY ID	Yes	Yes	ID
INSURANCE RECEIPT	ROLE TYPE ID	Yes	Yes	ID
	PAYMENT ID	Yes	Yes	ID
INSURED CONTRACT HOLDER	PARTY ID	Yes	Yes	ID
	ROLE TYPE ID	Yes	Yes	ID
INSURED DEPENDENT	PARTY ID	Yes	Yes	ID

ENTITY NAME	ATTRIBUTE NAME	PK?	FK?	DOMAIN
	ROLE TYPE ID	Yes	Yes	ID
	AGREEMENT ID	No	Yes	ID
	ENROLLMENT ID	No	No	ID
	GROUP PARTY ID	No	No	ID
	GROUP ROLE TYPE ID	No	No	ID
	INSURED PARTY ID	No	No	ID
	INSURED ROLE TYPE ID	No	No	ID
INSURED INDIVIDUAL	PARTY ID	Yes	Yes	ID
	ROLE TYPE ID	Yes	Yes	ID
	PARTY ID	Yes	Yes	ID
INSURED ORGANIZATION	ROLE TYPE ID	Yes	Yes	ID
	PARTY ID	Yes	Yes	ID
INSURED PARTY	ROLE TYPE ID	Yes	Yes	ID
	PARTY ID	Yes	Yes	ID
INTERNAL ORGANIZATION	ROLE TYPE ID	Yes	Yes	ID
	PARTY ID	Yes	No	ID
INVENTORY ITEM	INVENTORY ITEM ID	Yes	No	ID
	FACILITY ID	No	Yes	ID
	PARTY ID	No	Yes	ID
	PRODUCT ID	No	Yes	ID
	CONTAINER ID	No	No	ID
	LOT ID	No	No	ID
	PART ID	No	No	ID
INVOICE	INVOICE ID	Yes	No	ID
	BILLED FROM PARTY ID	No	Yes	ID
	BILLED TO PARTY ID	No	Yes	ID
	SENT FROM CONTACT MECH ID	No	Yes	ID
	SENT TO CONTACT MECH ID	No	Yes	ID
	BILLING ACCOUNT ID	No	No	ID
	DESCRIPTION	No	No	Description
	INVOICE DATE	No	No	Datetime
	MESSAGE	No	No	Long varchar
	PARTY ID	No	No	ID
	ROLE TYPE ID	No	No	ID
INVOICE ITEM	INVOICE ID	Yes	Yes	ID
	INVOICE ITEM SEQ ID	Yes	No	ID
	ADJUSTED BY INVOICE ID	No	Yes	ID
	ADJUSTED BY INVOICE ITEM SEQ ID	No	Yes	ID
	SOLD WITH INVOICE ID	No	Yes	ID
	SOLD WITH INVOICE ITEM SEQ ID	No	Yes	ID

ENTITY NAME	ATTRIBUTE NAME	PK?	FK?	DOMAIN
	UOM ID	No	Yes	ID
	AMOUNT	No	No	Currency amount
	INVENTORY ITEM ID	No	No	ID
	INVOICE ITEM TYPE ID	No	No	ID
	ITEM DESCRIPTION	No	No	Description
	PRODUCT FEATURE ID	No	No	ID
	PRODUCT ID	No	No	ID
	QUANTITY	No	No	Numeric
	TAXABLE FLAG	No	No	Indicator
INVOICE RESUBMISSION	INVOICE ID FOR	Yes	Yes	ID
INVOICE STATUS	INVOICE ID WITH	Yes	Yes	ID
	INVOICE ID	Yes	Yes	ID
	STATUS TYPE ID	Yes	Yes	ID
	STATUS DATE	Yes	No	Datetime
INVOICE STATUS TYPE	STATUS TYPE ID	Yes	No	ID
	DESCRIPTION	No	No	Description
LICENSE	LICENSE ID	Yes	No	ID
	GEOGRAPHIC LOCATION ID	No	Yes	ID
	HC PROVIDER PARTY ID	No	Yes	ID
	HC PROVIDER ROLE TYPE ID	No	Yes	ID
	INDIV HC PARTY ID	No	Yes	ID
	INDIV HC ROLE TYPE ID	No	Yes	ID
	LICENSE TYPE ID	No	Yes	ID
	DATE ISSUED	No	No	Datetime
	LICENSE DESCRIPTION	No	No	Description
	LICENSE NUMBER	No	No	Numeric
	VALID THRU	No	No	Datetime
LICENSE TYPE	LICENSE TYPE ID	Yes	No	ID
	DESCRIPTION	No	No	Description
MAIN AGREEMENT	AGREEMENT ID	Yes	Yes	ID
	AGREEMENT ITEM SEQ ID	Yes	Yes	ID
MEDICAL BUILDING	FACILITY ID	Yes	Yes	ID
MEDICAL CLAIM	CLAIM ID	Yes	Yes	ID
MEDICAL CONDITION	MEDICAL CONDITION TYPE ID	Yes	Yes	ID
	PARTY ID	Yes	Yes	ID
	ROLE TYPE ID	Yes	Yes	ID
	MEDICAL CONDITION ID	Yes	No	ID
	COMMENTS	No	No	Comment
	FROM DATE	No	No	Datetime

ENTITY NAME	ATTRIBUTE NAME	PK?	FK?	DOMAIN
MEDICAL CONDITION TYPE	THRU DATE	No	No	Datetime
	MEDICAL CONDITION TYPE ID	Yes	No	ID
MEDICAL OFFICE	DESCRIPTION	No	No	Description
	FACILITY ID	Yes	Yes	ID
NETWORK	PARTY ID	Yes	Yes	ID
	ROLE TYPE ID	Yes	Yes	ID
NEUTRACEUTICAL OFFERING	HEALTH CARE OFFERING ID	Yes	Yes	ID
ORGANIZATION	PARTY ID	Yes	Yes	ID
	NAME	No	No	Name
ORGANIZATION CONTACT RELATIONSHIP	FROM DATE	Yes	Yes	Datetime
	PARTY ID FROM	Yes	Yes	ID
	PARTY ID TO	Yes	Yes	ID
	ROLE TYPE ID FROM	Yes	Yes	ID
	ROLE TYPE ID TO	Yes	Yes	ID
ORGANIZATION ROLE	PARTY ID	Yes	Yes	ID
	ROLE TYPE ID	Yes	Yes	ID
ORGANIZATION ROLLUP	FROM DATE	Yes	Yes	Datetime
	PARTY ID FROM	Yes	Yes	ID
	PARTY ID TO	Yes	Yes	ID
	ROLE TYPE ID FROM	Yes	Yes	ID
	ROLE TYPE ID TO	Yes	Yes	ID
ORGANIZATION UNIT	PARTY ID	Yes	Yes	ID
	ROLE TYPE ID	Yes	Yes	ID
OTHER AGREEMENT	AGREEMENT ID	Yes	Yes	ID
OTHER HEALTH CARE CATEGORY	HEALTH CARE DISCIPLINE ID	Yes	Yes	ID
OTHER HEALTH CARE FACILITY	FACILITY ID	Yes	Yes	ID
OTHER HEALTH CARE PROVIDER ORG	PARTY ID	Yes	Yes	ID
OTHER HEALTH GOOD OFFERING	ROLE TYPE ID	Yes	Yes	ID
	HEALTH CARE OFFERING ID	Yes	Yes	ID
OTHER HEALTH SERVICE OFFERING	HEALTH CARE OFFERING ID	Yes	Yes	ID
OTHER PAYMENT	PAYMENT ID	Yes	Yes	ID
OUTCOME TYPE	OUTCOME TYPE ID	Yes	No	ID
	DESCRIPTION	No	No	Description

ENTITY NAME	ATTRIBUTE NAME	PK?	FK?	DOMAIN
OUTCOME TYPES	OUTCOME TYPE ID	Yes	No	ID
	DESCRIPTION	No	No	Description
PARTNERSHIP	FROM DATE	Yes	Yes	Datetime
	PARTY ID FROM	Yes	Yes	ID
	PARTY ID TO	Yes	Yes	ID
	ROLE TYPE ID FROM	Yes	Yes	ID
	ROLE TYPE ID TO	Yes	Yes	ID
PARTY	PARTY ID	Yes	No	ID
PARTY CONTACT MECHANISM	CONTACT MECHANISM ID	Yes	Yes	ID
	PARTY ID	Yes	Yes	ID
	FROM DATE	Yes	No	Datetime
	ROLE TYPE ID	No	Yes	ID
	COMMENTS	No	No	Comment
	EXTENSION	No	No	Very short
	NON-SOLICITATION INDICATOR	No	No	Indicator
	THRU DATE	No	No	Datetime
PARTY FACILITY	FACILITY ID	Yes	Yes	ID
	PARTY ID	Yes	Yes	ID
	ROLE TYPE ID	No	Yes	ID
PARTY QUALIFICATION	PARTY ID	Yes	Yes	ID
	QUAL TYPE ID	Yes	Yes	ID
	FROM DATE	No	No	Datetime
	THRU DATE	No	No	Datetime
PARTY RELATIONSHIP	PARTY ID FROM	Yes	Yes	ID
	PARTY ID TO	Yes	Yes	ID
	ROLE TYPE ID FROM	Yes	Yes	ID
	ROLE TYPE ID TO	Yes	Yes	ID
	FROM DATE	Yes	No	Datetime
	PARTY RELATIONSHIP TYPE ID	No	Yes	ID
	COMMENTS	No	No	Comment
	PRIORITY TYPE ID	No	No	ID
	STATUS TYPE ID	No	No	ID
	THRU DATE	No	No	Datetime
PARTY RELATIONSHIP TYPE	PARTY RELATIONSHIP TYPE ID	Yes	No	ID
	ROLE TYPE ID VALID FROM	No	Yes	ID
	ROLE TYPE ID VALID TO	No	Yes	ID
	DESCRIPTION	No	No	Description
PARTY ROLE	NAME	No	No	Name
	PARTY ID	Yes	Yes	ID
	ROLE TYPE ID	Yes	Yes	ID

ENTITY NAME	ATTRIBUTE NAME	PK?	FK?	DOMAIN
PARTY ROLE TYPE	PARTY ROLE ID	No	No	ID
	ROLE TYPE ID	Yes	Yes	ID
PARTY SKILL	PARTY ID	Yes	Yes	ID
	SKILL TYPE ID	Yes	Yes	ID
	RATING	No	No	Numeric
	SKILL LEVEL	No	No	Numeric
	STARTED USING DATE	No	No	Datetime
	YEARS EXPERIENCE	No	No	Numeric
PATIENT	PARTY ID	Yes	Yes	ID
	ROLE TYPE ID	Yes	Yes	ID
PATIENT PRACTIONER RELATIONSHIP	FROM DATE	Yes	Yes	Datetime
	PARTY ID FROM	Yes	Yes	ID
	PARTY ID TO	Yes	Yes	ID
	ROLE TYPE ID FROM	Yes	Yes	ID
	ROLE TYPE ID TO	Yes	Yes	ID
PATIENT PROVIDER AGREEMENT	AGREEMENT ID	Yes	Yes	ID
PATIENT PROVIDER RELATIONSHIP	FROM DATE	Yes	Yes	Datetime
	PARTY ID FROM	Yes	Yes	ID
	PARTY ID TO	Yes	Yes	ID
	ROLE TYPE ID FROM	Yes	Yes	ID
	ROLE TYPE ID TO	Yes	Yes	ID
PATIENT RECEIPT	PAYMENT ID	Yes	Yes	ID
PATIENT TYPES	PATIENT TYPE ID	Yes	No	ID
	DESCRIPTION	No	No	Description
PAYMENT	PAYMENT ID	Yes	No	ID
	FROM PARTY ID	No	Yes	ID
	PAYMENT METHOD TYPE ID	No	Yes	ID
	PAYMENT TYPE ID	No	Yes	ID
	TO PARTY ID	No	Yes	ID
	AMOUNT	No	No	Currency amount
	COMMENTS	No	No	Comment
	EFFECTIVE DATE	No	No	Datetime
	PAYMENT REF NUM	No	No	Description
PAYMENT APPLICATION	PAYMENT ID	Yes	Yes	ID
	PAYMENT APPLICATION ID	Yes	No	ID
	INVOICE ID	No	Yes	ID
	INVOICE ITEM SEQ ID	No	Yes	ID

ENTITY NAME	ATTRIBUTE NAME	PK?	FK?	DOMAIN
	AMOUNT APPLIED	No	No	Currency amount
	BILLING ACCOUNT ID	No	No	ID
PAYMENT METHOD TYPE	PAYMENT METHOD TYPE ID	Yes	No	ID
	DESCRIPTION	No	No	Description
PAYMENT TYPE	PAYMENT TYPE ID	Yes	No	ID
	DESCRIPTION	No	No	Description
PAYOR	PARTY ID	Yes	Yes	ID
	ROLE TYPE ID	Yes	Yes	ID
PERSON	PARTY ID	Yes	Yes	ID
	BIRTH DATE	No	No	Datetime
	COMMENTS	No	No	Comment
	CURRENT FIRST NAME	No	No	Name
	CURRENT LAST NAME	No	No	Name
	CURRENT MIDDLE NAME	No	No	Name
	CURRENT NICKNAME	No	No	Name
	CURRENT PASSPORT EXPIRE DATE	No	No	Datetime
	CURRENT PASSPORT NUMBER	No	No	Numeric
	CURRENT PERSONAL TITLE	No	No	Name
	CURRENT SUFFIX	No	No	Name
	GENDER	No	No	Indicator
	HEIGHT	No	No	Numeric
	MARTIAL STATUS	No	No	Indicator
	MOTHER'S MADIEN NAME	No	No	Name
	SOCIAL SECURITY NUMBER	No	No	Numeric
	TOTAL YEARS WORK EXPERIENCE	No	No	Numeric
	WEIGHT	No	No	Numeric
PERSON ROLE	PARTY ID	Yes	Yes	ID
	ROLE TYPE ID	Yes	Yes	ID
PHARMACEUTICAL OFFERING	HEALTH CARE OFFERING ID	Yes	Yes	ID
PHYSICAL CHARACTERISTIC	PARTY ID	Yes	Yes	ID
	PHYSICAL CHAR TYPE ID	Yes	Yes	ID
	ROLE TYPE ID	Yes	Yes	ID
	FROM DATE	No	No	Datetime
	THRU DATE	No	No	Datetime
	VALUE	No	No	Numeric

ENTITY NAME	ATTRIBUTE NAME	PK?	FK?	DOMAIN
PHYSICAL CHARACTERISTIC TYPE	PHYSICAL CHAR TYPE ID	Yes	No	ID
	DESCRIPTION	No	No	Description
PHYSICIAN CATEGORY	HEALTH CARE DISCIPLINE ID	Yes	Yes	ID
POSTAL ADDRESS	CONTACT MECHANISM ID	Yes	Yes	ID
	ADDRESS1	No	No	Description
	ADDRESS2	No	No	Description
	DIRECTIONS	No	No	Long varchar
PRACTICE AFFILIATION	FROM DATE	Yes	Yes	Datetime
	PARTY ID FROM	Yes	Yes	ID
	PARTY ID TO	Yes	Yes	ID
	ROLE TYPE ID FROM	Yes	Yes	ID
	ROLE TYPE ID TO	Yes	Yes	ID
PRACTITIONER DIAGNOSIS	DIAGNOSIS ID	Yes	Yes	ID
	PARTY ID	Yes	Yes	ID
	ROLE TYPE ID	Yes	Yes	ID
PRACTITIONER REFERRING RELATIONSHIP	FROM DATE	Yes	Yes	Datetime
	PARTY ID FROM	Yes	Yes	ID
	PARTY ID TO	Yes	Yes	ID
	ROLE TYPE ID FROM	Yes	Yes	ID
	ROLE TYPE ID TO	No	Yes	ID
	DIAGNOSIS TYPE ID	No	Yes	ID
	EPISODE TYPE ID	No	Yes	ID
	INDIV HC PRACTITIONER FROM	No	Yes	ID
	INDIV HC PRACTITIONER TO	No	Yes	ID
	PARTY ID	No	Yes	ID
	ROLE TYPE ID	No	Yes	ID
PROCEDURE OFFERING	HEALTH CARE OFFERING ID	Yes	Yes	ID
PROCEDURE DELIVERY	HEALTH CARE DELIVERY ID	Yes	Yes	ID
PROVIDER NETWORK	FROM DATE	Yes	Yes	Datetime
	PARTY ID FROM	Yes	Yes	ID
	PARTY ID TO	Yes	Yes	ID
	ROLE TYPE ID FROM	Yes	Yes	ID
	ROLE TYPE ID TO	Yes	Yes	ID

ENTITY NAME	ATTRIBUTE NAME	PK?	FK?	DOMAIN
PROVIDER NETWORK AGREEMENT	AGREEMENT ID	Yes	Yes	ID
PROVIDER OFFERING	HEALTH CARE OFFERING ID	Yes	Yes	ID
	PARTY ID	Yes	Yes	ID
	ROLE TYPE ID	Yes	Yes	ID
	FROM DATE	No	No	Datetime
	THRU DATE	No	No	Datetime
PROVIDER ORGANIZATIONS	PROVIDER PARTY ID	Yes	No	ID
	ORGANIZATION NAME	No	No	Name
PURCHASE AGREEMENT	AGREEMENT ID	Yes	No	ID
QUALIFICATION TYPE	QUAL TYPE ID	Yes	No	ID
	DESCRIPTION	No	No	Description
REGULATORY AGENCY	PARTY ID	Yes	Yes	ID
REVENUE CODE	ROLE TYPE ID	Yes	Yes	ID
	CLAIM SERVICE CODE	Yes	Yes	ID
ROLE TYPE	ROLE TYPE ID	Yes	No	ID
	DESCRIPTION	No	No	Description
ROOM	FACILITY ID	Yes	Yes	ID
SHIPMENT	SHIPMENT ID	Yes	No	ID
	DESTINATION CONTACT MECH ID	No	Yes	ID
	INQUIRY CONTACT MECH ID	No	Yes	ID
	RECEIVER PARTY ID	No	Yes	ID
	RECEIVING TELECOMM CONTACT MECH ID	No	Yes	ID
	SENDER PARTY ID	No	Yes	ID
	SOURCE CONTACT MECH ID	No	Yes	ID
	ACTUAL SHIP COST	No	No	Currency amount
	ESTIMATED ARRIVAL DATE	No	No	Datetime
	ESTIMATED READY DATE	No	No	Datetime
	ESTIMATED SHIP COST	No	No	Currency amount
	ESTIMATED SHIP DATE	No	No	Datetime
	HANDLING INSTRUCTIONS	No	No	Long varchar
	LAST UPDATED	No	No	Datetime
	LATEST CANCEL DATE	No	No	Datetime
SHIPMENT ITEM	SHIPMENT ID	Yes	Yes	ID
	SHIPMENT ITEM SEQ ID	Yes	No	ID

ENTITY NAME	ATTRIBUTE NAME	PK?	FK?	DOMAIN
	PRODUCT ID	Yes	Yes	ID
	QUANTITY	No	No	Numeric
	SHIPMENTS CONTENT DESCRIPTION	No	No	Description
SHIPMENT ITEM BILLING	INVOICE ID	Yes	Yes	ID
	INVOICE ITEM SEQ ID	Yes	Yes	ID
	SHIPMENT ID	Yes	Yes	ID
	SHIPMENT ITEM SEQ ID	Yes	Yes	ID
SKILL TYPE	SKILL TYPE ID	Yes	No	ID
	DECRIPTION	No	No	Description
STATUS TYPE	STATUS TYPE ID	Yes	No	ID
	DESCRIPTION	No	No	Description
SUB AGREEMENT	AGREEMENT ID	Yes	Yes	ID
	AGREEMENT ITEM SEQ ID	Yes	Yes	ID
SUBSIDIARY	PARTY ID	Yes	Yes	ID
SUPPLIER	ROLE TYPE ID	Yes	Yes	ID
	PARTY ID	Yes	Yes	ID
	ROLE TYPE ID	Yes	Yes	ID
SUPPLIER DISBURSEMENT	PAYMENT ID	Yes	Yes	ID
SUPPLIER RELATIONSHIP	FROM DATE	Yes	Yes	Datetime
	PARTY ID FROM	Yes	Yes	ID
	PARTY ID TO	Yes	Yes	ID
	ROLE TYPE ID FROM	Yes	Yes	ID
	ROLE TYPE ID TO	Yes	Yes	ID
SUPPLY ADMINISTRATION	HEALTH CARE DELIVERY ID	Yes	Yes	ID
SUPPLY OFFERING	HEALTH CARE OFFERING ID	Yes	Yes	ID
SYMPTOM	SYMPTOM ID	Yes	No	ID
	HEALTH CARE EPISODE ID	No	Yes	ID
	SYMPTOM TYPE ID	No	Yes	ID
	DESCRIPTION	No	No	Description
SYMPTOM TYPE	SYMPTOM TYPE ID	Yes	No	ID
	DESCRIPTION	No	No	Description
TELECOMMUNICATIONS NUMBER	CONTACT MECHANISM ID	Yes	Yes	ID
	AREA CODE	No	No	Numeric
	CONTACT NUMBER	No	No	Short varchar
	CONTRY CODE	No	No	Numeric

ENTITY NAME	ATTRIBUTE NAME	PK?	FK?	DOMAIN
THIRD PARTY ADMINISTRATOR	PARTY ID	Yes	Yes	ID
	ROLE TYPE ID	Yes	Yes	ID
TIME BY WEEK	WEEK ID	Yes	No	ID
	MONTH	No	No	Very short
	QUARTER	No	No	Very short
	WEEK	No	No	Very short
	YEAR	No	No	Very short
UNIT OF MEASURE	UOM ID	Yes	No	ID
	ABBREVIATION	No	No	Short varchar

ENTITY NAME	ATTRIBUTE NAME	PK?	FK?	DOMAIN
USUAL AND CUSTOMARY AMOUNT	DESCRIPTION	No	No	Description
	CLAIM SETTLEMENT AMOUNT ID	Yes	Yes	ID
VISION CATEGORY	CLAIM SETTLEMENT ID	Yes	Yes	ID
	HEALTH CARE DISCIPLINE ID	Yes	Yes	ID
VISIT REASON	HEALTH CARE VISIT ID	Yes	Yes	ID
	VISIT REASON ID	Yes	No	ID
	HEALTH CARE EPISODE ID	No	Yes	ID
VISIT REASON	SYMPTOM ID	No	Yes	ID
	DESCRIPTION	No	No	Description

Entities and Attributes for Insurance Models

This appendix lists the entities and attributes from the models and star schema found in Chapter 5, "Insurance." This listing includes the entity names, attribute names, primary key indicators, foreign key indicators, and the domain for each attribute.

The domain indicates a standard set of characteristics that can be applied to attributes, including its datatype and length. Table A.1 defines the nature of each domain. When applying the domains to the attributes listed in these appendices, refer to Table A.1 for recommendations on what datatype and length to use when implementing these models. Of course, the datatype and length of each attribute should be adjusted as appropriate to meet the specific needs of the enterprise.

The domain definitions as they are applied to the attributes in the appendices are used for the SQL code that is contained on the demo CD-ROM at the back of this book as well as in the Industry Downloads (see the section "How to Use the Volume 2 Industry Electronic Products" for more information).

Entities and Attributes Listing for Insurance Models

ENTITY NAME	ATTRIBUTE NAME	PK?	FK?	DOMAIN
ACCIDENT	INCIDENT ID	Yes	Yes	ID
ACCIDENT INSURANCE	PRODUCT CATEGORY ID	Yes	Yes	ID
ACTUARIAL ANALYSIS	ACTUARIAL ANALYSIS ID	Yes	No	ID
	AGREEMENT ID	No	Yes	ID
	AGREEMENT ITEM SEQ ID	No	Yes	ID
	ANALYSIS PARAMETER ID	No	Yes	ID
	COVERAGE LEVEL ID	No	Yes	ID
	COVERAGE TYPE ID	No	Yes	ID
	POLICY ITEM PREMIUM SEQ ID	No	Yes	ID
	PRODUCT FEATURE ID	No	Yes	ID
	PRODUCT ID	No	Yes	ID
	WORK EFFORT ID	No	Yes	ID
	ACTUARIAL SCORE	No	No	Numeric
	COMMENTS	No	No	Comment
ADJUDICATION FACTOR	ADJUDICATION RULE ID	Yes	Yes	ID
	ADJUDICATION FACTOR ID	Yes	No	ID
	ADJUDICATION FACTOR TYPE ID	No	Yes	ID
	ADJUDICATION FACTOR DESCRIPTION	No	No	Description
ADJUDICATION FACTOR TYPE	ADJUDICATION FACTOR TYPE ID	Yes	No	ID
	FACTOR TYPE DESCRIPTION	No	No	Description
ADJUDICATION RULE	ADJUDICATION RULE ID	Yes	No	ID
	ADJUDICATION RULE TYPE ID	No	Yes	ID
	CLAIM SETTLEMENT ID	No	Yes	ID
	RULE DESCRIPTION	No	No	Description
ADJUDICATION RULE TYPE	ADJUDICATION RULE TYPE ID	Yes	No	ID
	FACTOR DESCRIPTION	No	No	Description
ADJUSTMENT TYPE	ADJUSTMENT TYPE ID	Yes	No	ID
	ADJUSTMENT PERCENT	No	No	Floating point
	DESCRIPTION	No	No	Description
AGREEMENT	AGREEMENT ID	Yes	No	ID
	AGREEMENT TYPE ID	No	Yes	ID
	FROM DATE	No	Yes	Datetime
	PARTY ID FROM	No	Yes	ID

ENTITY NAME	ATTRIBUTE NAME	PK?	FK?	DOMAIN
	PARTY ID TO	No	Yes	ID
	ROLE TYPE ID FROM	No	Yes	ID
	ROLE TYPE ID TO	No	Yes	ID
	AGREEMENT DATE	No	No	Datetime
	DESCRIPTION	No	No	Description
	PRODUCT ID	No	No	ID
	TEXT	No	No	Long varchar
AGREEMENT EXHIBIT	THRU DATE	No	No	Datetime
	AGREEMENT ID	Yes	Yes	ID
	AGREEMENT ITEM SEQ ID	Yes	Yes	ID
AGREEMENT ITEM	AGREEMENT ID	Yes	Yes	ID
	AGREEMENT ITEM SEQ ID	Yes	No	ID
	PART OF AGREEMENT ID	No	Yes	ID
	PART OF AGREEMENT ITEM SEQ ID	No	Yes	ID
	AGREEMENT IMAGE	No	No	Blob
	AGREEMENT TEXT	No	No	Long varchar
AGREEMENT ROLE	AGREEMENT ID	Yes	Yes	ID
	PARTY ID	Yes	Yes	ID
	ROLE TYPE ID	Yes	Yes	ID
AGREEMENT ROLE TYPE	ROLE TYPE ID	Yes	Yes	ID
AGREEMENT SECTION	AGREEMENT ID	Yes	Yes	ID
	AGREEMENT ITEM SEQ ID	Yes	Yes	ID
AGREEMENT TYPE	AGREEMENT TYPE ID	Yes	No	ID
	DESCRIPTION	No	No	Description
AMOUNT TYPE	AMOUNT TYPE ID	Yes	No	ID
	DESCRIPTION	No	No	Description
ANALYSIS PARAMETER	ANALYSIS PARAMETER ID	Yes	No	ID
	PARAMETER TYPE ID	No	Yes	ID
	ANALYSIS PARAMETER WEIGHT	No	No	Floating point
	PARAMETER RANGE	No	No	Numeric
	PARAMETER VALUE	No	No	Numeric
APPLICATION	APPLICATION ID	Yes	No	ID
	INSURED ASSET ID	No	Yes	ID
	DESCRIPTION	No	No	Description
APPLICATION ITEM	APPLICATION ID	Yes	Yes	ID

ENTITY NAME	ATTRIBUTE NAME	PK?	FK?	DOMAIN
APPLICATION ITEM	APPLICATION ITEM SEQ ID	Yes	No	ID
	COVERAGE LEVEL ID	No	Yes	ID
	COVERAGE TYPE ID	No	Yes	ID
	PRODUCT FEATURE ID	No	Yes	ID
	PRODUCT ID	No	Yes	ID
	DESCRIPTION	No	No	Description
APPLICATION ROLE	APPLICATION ID	Yes	Yes	ID
	PARTY ID	Yes	Yes	ID
	ROLE TYPE ID	Yes	Yes	ID
APPLICATION ROLE TYPE	ROLE TYPE ID	Yes	Yes	ID
APPLICATION STATUS	APPLICATION ID	Yes	Yes	ID
	STATUS TYPE ID	Yes	Yes	ID
	STATUS DATE	No	No	Datetime
APPLICATION STATUS TYPE	STATUS TYPE ID	Yes	Yes	ID
APPRAISAL	APPRAISAL ID	Yes	No	ID
	CLAIM SETTLEMENT ID	No	Yes	ID
	PARTY ID	No	Yes	ID
	ROLE TYPE ID	No	Yes	ID
	APPRAISAL DATE	No	No	Datetime
	APPRAISAL RESULT	No	No	Long varchar
BENEFICIARY	PARTY ID	Yes	Yes	ID
	ROLE TYPE ID	Yes	Yes	ID
CARE PROVIDER SELECTION	INSURED IND PARTY ID	Yes	Yes	ID
	INSURED IND ROLE TYPE ID	Yes	Yes	ID
	CARE PROVIDER SELECTION ID	Yes	No	ID
	ENROLLMENT ID	No	Yes	ID
	GROUP PARTY ID	No	Yes	ID
	GROUP ROLE TYPE ID	No	Yes	ID
	INDIV HC PRACT PARTY ID	No	Yes	ID
	INDIV HC PRACT ROLE TYPE ID	No	Yes	ID
	INSURED PARTY ID	No	Yes	ID
	INSURED ROLE TYPE ID	No	Yes	ID
	FROM DATE	No	No	Datetime
	THRU DATE	No	No	Datetime
CASUALTY INSURANCE	PRODUCT CATEGORY ID	Yes	Yes	ID
CASUALTY INSURANCE POLICY	AGREEMENT ID	Yes	Yes	ID

ENTITY NAME	ATTRIBUTE NAME	PK?	FK?	DOMAIN
CASUALTY POLICY ITEM	AGREEMENT ID	Yes	Yes	ID
	AGREEMENT ITEM SEQ ID	Yes	Yes	ID
	INSURED ASSET ID	No	Yes	ID
CLAIM	CLAIM ID	Yes	No	ID
	AGREEMENT ID	No	Yes	ID
	CLAIM TYPE ID	No	Yes	ID
	CLAIM SUBMISSION DATE	No	No	Datetime
CLAIM FACT	COVERAGE LEVEL ID	Yes	Yes	ID
	COVERAGE TYPE ID	Yes	Yes	ID
	DAY ID	Yes	Yes	ID
	GEOGRAPHIC LOCATION ID	Yes	Yes	ID
	INSURED ASSET ID	Yes	Yes	ID
	PARTY TYPE ID	Yes	Yes	ID
	PRODUCT CATEGORY ID	Yes	Yes	ID
	PRODUCT ID	Yes	Yes	ID
	RISK LEVEL TYPE ID	Yes	Yes	ID
	CLAIM ITEM REQUESTED AMOUNT	No	No	Currency amount
	CLAIM PAYMENT AMOUNT	No	No	Currency amount
	ESTIMATED COST	No	No	Currency amount
CLAIM ITEM	CLAIM ID	Yes	Yes	ID
	CLAIM ITEM SEQ ID	Yes	No	ID
	DAMAGE TYPE ID	No	Yes	ID
	INCIDENT ID	No	Yes	ID
	INSURED ASSET ID	No	Yes	ID
	UOM ID	No	Yes	ID
	CLAIM AMOUNT	No	No	Currency amount
	CLAIM SERVICE CODE	No	No	ID
	QUANTITY	No	No	Numeric
CLAIM ITEM DOCUMENT	CLAIM ID	Yes	Yes	ID
	CLAIM ITEM SEQ ID	Yes	Yes	ID
	DOCUMENT ID	Yes	Yes	ID
CLAIM PAYMENT AMOUNT	CLAIM SETTLEMENT AMOUNT ID	Yes	Yes	ID
CLAIM RESUBMISSION	CLAIM ID FOR	Yes	Yes	ID
	CLAIM ID WITH	Yes	Yes	ID

ENTITY NAME	ATTRIBUTE NAME	PK?	FK?	DOMAIN
CLAIM ROLE	CLAIM ID	Yes	Yes	ID
	PARTY ID	Yes	Yes	ID
	ROLE TYPE ID	Yes	Yes	ID
CLAIM ROLE TYPE	ROLE TYPE ID	Yes	Yes	ID
CLAIM SETTLEMENT	CLAIM SETTLEMENT ID	Yes	No	ID
	CLAIM ID	No	Yes	ID
	CLAIM ITEM SEQ ID	No	Yes	ID
	DATE SETTLED	No	No	Datetime
CLAIM SETTLEMENT AMOUNT	CLAIM SETTLEMENT ID	Yes	Yes	ID
	CLAIM SETTLEMENT AMOUNT ID	Yes	No	ID
	AMOUNT TYPE ID	No	Yes	ID
	EXPLANATION OF BENEFIT TYPE ID	No	Yes	ID
	PAYMENT ID	No	Yes	ID
	AMOUNT	No	No	Currency amount
	EXPLANATION	No	No	Long varchar
CLAIM STATUS	CLAIM ID	Yes	Yes	ID
	STATUS TYPE ID	Yes	Yes	ID
	DATETIME	No	No	Datetime
CLAIM STATUS TYPE	STATUS TYPE ID	Yes	No	ID
CLAIM TYPE	CLAIM TYPE ID	Yes	No	ID
	DESCRIPTION	No	No	Description
CLAIMS ADJUSTOR	PARTY ID	Yes	Yes	ID
	ROLE TYPE ID	Yes	Yes	ID
COINSURANCE	COVERAGE LEVEL ID	Yes	Yes	ID
	PERCENTAGE	No	No	Floating point
CONTACT	PARTY ID	Yes	Yes	ID
	ROLE TYPE ID	Yes	Yes	ID
COPAY	COVERAGE LEVEL ID	Yes	Yes	ID
	AMOUNT	No	No	Currency amount
COVERAGE AMOUNT	COVERAGE LEVEL ID	Yes	Yes	ID
	COVERAGE AMOUNT	No	No	Currency amount
COVERAGE AVAILABILITY	COVERAGE LEVEL ID	Yes	Yes	ID
	COVERAGE TYPE ID	Yes	Yes	ID
	PRODUCT ID	Yes	Yes	ID
	FROM DATE	Yes	No	Datetime

ENTITY NAME	ATTRIBUTE NAME	PK?	FK?	DOMAIN
	THRU DATE	No	No	Datetime
COVERAGE CATEGORY	COVERAGE CATEGORY ID	Yes	No	ID
	DESCRIPTION	No	No	Description
COVERAGE DEPENDENCY	COVERAGE INTERACTION ID	Yes	Yes	ID
COVERAGE INCOMPATIBILITY	COVERAGE INTERACTION ID	Yes	Yes	ID
COVERAGE INTERACTION	COVERAGE INTERACTION ID	Yes	No	ID
	COVERAGE LEVEL ID FROM	No	Yes	ID
	COVERAGE LEVEL ID TO	No	Yes	ID
	COVERAGE TYPE ID FROM	No	Yes	ID
	COVERAGE TYPE ID TO	No	Yes	ID
	FROM DATE FROM	No	Yes	Datetime
	FROM DATE TO	No	Yes	Datetime
	PRODUCT ID FROM	No	Yes	ID
	PRODUCT ID TO	No	Yes	ID
COVERAGE LEVEL	COVERAGE LEVEL ID	Yes	No	ID
	COVERAGE LEVEL BASIS ID	No	Yes	ID
	COVERAGE LEVEL TYPE ID	No	Yes	ID
COVERAGE LEVEL BASIS	COVERAGE LEVEL BASIS ID	Yes	No	ID
	DESCRIPTION	No	No	Description
COVERAGE LEVEL TYPE	COVERAGE LEVEL TYPE ID	Yes	No	ID
	DESCRIPTION	No	No	Description
COVERAGE LEVELS	COVERAGE LEVEL ID	Yes	No	ID
	DESCRIPTION BASIS	No	No	Description
	COVERAGE LEVEL	No	No	Description
COVERAGE RANGE	COVERAGE LEVEL ID	Yes	Yes	ID
	COVERAGE LIMIT FROM	No	No	Currency amount
	COVERAGE LIMIT THRU	No	No	Currency amount
COVERAGE TYPE	COVERAGE TYPE ID	Yes	No	ID
	COVERAGE CATEGORY ID	No	Yes	ID
	DESCRIPTION	No	No	Description
COVERAGE TYPE COMPOSITION	COVERAGE TYPE ID FROM	Yes	Yes	ID
	COVERAGE TYPE ID OF	Yes	Yes	ID
COVERAGE TYPES	COVERAGE TYPE ID	Yes	No	ID
	COVERAGE CATEGORY	No	No	Description

ENTITY NAME	ATTRIBUTE NAME	PK?	FK?	DOMAIN
	DESCRIPTION	No	No	Description
DAMAGE TYPE	DAMAGE TYPE ID	Yes	No	ID
DEDUCTIBILITY	DESCRIPTION	No	No	Description
	COVERAGE LEVEL ID	Yes	Yes	ID
	DEDUCTIBLE AMOUNT	No	No	Currency amount
DEDUCTIBLE AMOUNT	CLAIM SETTLEMENT AMOUNT ID	Yes	Yes	ID
DENTAL CLAIM	CLAIM SETTLEMENT ID	Yes	Yes	ID
	CLAIM ID	Yes	Yes	ID
DEPARTMENT	PARTY ID	Yes	Yes	ID
	ROLE TYPE ID	Yes	Yes	ID
DEPENDENT	PARTY ID	Yes	Yes	ID
	ROLE TYPE ID	Yes	Yes	ID
DISABILITY CLAIM	CLAIM ID	Yes	Yes	ID
DISABILITY INSURANCE	PRODUCT CATEGORY ID	Yes	Yes	ID
DISABILITY INSURANCE POLICY	AGREEMENT ID	Yes	Yes	ID
DISABILITY POLICY ITEM	AGREEMENT ID	Yes	Yes	ID
	AGREEMENT ITEM SEQ ID	Yes	Yes	ID
DISALLOWED AMOUNT	CLAIM SETTLEMENT AMOUNT ID	Yes	Yes	ID
	CLAIM SETTLEMENT ID	Yes	Yes	ID
DISCOUNT PREMIUM ADJUSTMENT	POLICY PREMIUM ADJUSTMENT ID	Yes	Yes	ID
DISTRIBUTION CHANNEL	PARTY ID	Yes	Yes	ID
	ROLE TYPE ID	Yes	Yes	ID
DISTRIBUTION CHANNEL RELATIONSHIP	FROM DATE	Yes	Yes	Datetime
	PARTY ID FROM	Yes	Yes	ID
	PARTY ID TO	Yes	Yes	ID
	ROLE TYPE ID FROM	Yes	Yes	ID
	ROLE TYPE ID TO	Yes	Yes	ID
DIVISION	PARTY ID	Yes	Yes	ID
	ROLE TYPE ID	Yes	Yes	ID
DOCUMENT	DOCUMENT ID	Yes	No	ID
	DOCUMENT TYPE ID	No	Yes	ID
	COMMENTS	No	No	Comment
	DATE CREATED	No	No	Datetime

ENTITY NAME	ATTRIBUTE NAME	PK?	FK?	DOMAIN
	DOCUMENT LOCATION	No	No	Long varchar
	DOCUMENT TEXT	No	No	Long varchar
	IMAGE	No	No	Blob
DOCUMENT TYPE	DOCUMENT TYPE ID	Yes	No	ID
	DESCRIPTION	No	No	Description
EMPLOYEE	PARTY ID	Yes	Yes	ID
	ROLE TYPE ID	Yes	Yes	ID
EMPLOYER	PARTY ID	Yes	Yes	ID
	ROLE TYPE ID	Yes	Yes	ID
EMPLOYMENT	FROM DATE	Yes	Yes	Datetime
	PARTY ID FROM	Yes	Yes	ID
	PARTY ID TO	Yes	Yes	ID
	ROLE TYPE ID FROM	Yes	Yes	ID
	ROLE TYPE ID TO	Yes	Yes	ID
	TERMINATION REASON ID	No	No	ID
	TERMINATION TYPE ID	No	No	ID
EMPLOYMENT AGREEMENT	AGREEMENT ID	Yes	Yes	ID
ENROLLMENT	GROUP PARTY ID	Yes	Yes	ID
	GROUP ROLE TYPE ID	Yes	Yes	ID
	INSURED PARTY ID	Yes	Yes	ID
	INSURED ROLE TYPE ID	Yes	Yes	ID
	ENROLLMENT ID	Yes	No	ID
ENROLLMENT ELECTION	ENROLLMENT ID	Yes	Yes	ID
	GROUP PARTY ID	Yes	Yes	ID
	GROUP ROLE TYPE ID	Yes	Yes	ID
	INSURED PARTY ID	Yes	Yes	ID
	INSURED ROLE TYPE ID	Yes	Yes	ID
	ENROLLMENT ELECTION ID	No	Yes	ID
	COVERAGE LEVEL ID	No	Yes	ID
	COVERAGE TYPE ID	No	Yes	ID
EXPLANATION OF BENEFIT TYPE	EXPLANATION OF BENEFIT TYPE ID	Yes	No	ID
	DESCRIPTION	No	No	Description
FACTOR RATE	INSURANCE RATE ID	Yes	Yes	ID
GEOGRAPHIC BOUNDARY	GEOGRAPHIC LOCATION ID	Yes	No	ID
	ABBREVIATION	No	No	Short varchar

ENTITY NAME	ATTRIBUTE NAME	PK?	FK?	DOMAIN
	GEO BOUNDARY TYPE ID	No	No	ID
	GEO CODE	No	No	Short varchar
GEOGRAPHIC BOUNDARYS	NAME	No	No	Name
	GEOGRAPHIC LOCATION ID	Yes	No	Number
	ABBREVIATION	No	No	Short varchar
	GEO BOUNDARY TYPE ID	No	No	ID
	GEO CODE	No	No	Short varchar
	NAME	No	No	Name
GROUP	PARTY ID	Yes	Yes	ID
	ROLE TYPE ID	Yes	Yes	ID
GROUP DISABILITY INSURANCE	PRODUCT CATEGORY ID	Yes	Yes	ID
GROUP HEALTH INSURANCE	PRODUCT CATEGORY ID	Yes	Yes	ID
GROUP INSURANCE POLICY	AGREEMENT ID	Yes	Yes	ID
	PARTY ID	No	Yes	ID
	ROLE TYPE ID	No	Yes	ID
HEALTH CARE CLAIM	CLAIM ID	Yes	Yes	ID
HEALTH CARE DELIVERY	HEALTH CARE DELIVERY ID	Yes	No	ID
	DELIVERY NOTES	No	No	Long varchar
	FROM DATE	No	No	Datetime
	HEALTH CARE EPISODE ID	No	No	ID
	HEALTH CARE OFFERING ID	No	No	ID
	HEALTH CARE VISIT ID	No	No	ID
	THRU DATE	No	No	Datetime
HEALTH CARE DELIVERY CLAIM SUBMISSION	CLAIM ID	Yes	Yes	ID
	CLAIM ITEM SEQ ID	Yes	Yes	ID
	HEALTH CARE DELIVERY ID	Yes	Yes	ID
HEALTH CARE NETWORK AGREEMENT	AGREEMENT ID	Yes	Yes	ID
HEALTH CARE POLICY	AGREEMENT ID	Yes	Yes	ID

ENTITY NAME	ATTRIBUTE NAME	PK?	FK?	DOMAIN
HEALTH CARE POLICY ITEM	AGREEMENT ID	Yes	Yes	ID
	AGREEMENT ITEM SEQ ID	Yes	Yes	ID
HEALTH INSURANCE	PRODUCT CATEGORY ID	Yes	Yes	ID
HOME OWNERS INSURANCE	PRODUCT CATEGORY ID	Yes	Yes	ID
HOUSE CLAIM	CLAIM ID	Yes	Yes	ID
HOUSEHOLD	PARTY ID	Yes	Yes	ID
	ROLE TYPE ID	Yes	Yes	ID
ILLNESS	INCIDENT ID	Yes	Yes	ID
INCIDENT	INCIDENT ID	Yes	No	ID
	INCIDENT TYPE ID	No	Yes	ID
	DESCRIPTION	No	No	Description
	EMPL RELATED IND	No	No	Indicator
	INCIDENT DATE	No	No	Datetime
INCIDENT CLAIM ITEM	CLAIM ID	Yes	Yes	ID
	CLAIM ITEM SEQ ID	Yes	Yes	ID
	INCIDENT ID	Yes	Yes	ID
INCIDENT PROPERTY DAMAGE	DAMAGE TYPE ID	Yes	Yes	ID
	INCIDENT ID	Yes	Yes	ID
	INSURED ASSET ID	Yes	Yes	ID
	DAMAGE DESCRIPTION	No	No	Description
INCIDENT ROLE	INCIDENT ID	Yes	Yes	ID
	PARTY ID	Yes	Yes	ID
	ROLE TYPE ID	Yes	Yes	ID
INCIDENT ROLE TYPE	ROLE TYPE ID	Yes	Yes	ID
INCIDENT TYPE	INCIDENT TYPE ID	Yes	No	ID
	DESCRIPTION	No	No	Description
INDIVIDUAL DISABILITY INSURANCE	PRODUCT CATEGORY ID	Yes	Yes	ID
INDIVIDUAL HEALTH CARE PRACTITIONER	PARTY ID	Yes	Yes	ID
	ROLE TYPE ID	Yes	Yes	ID
INDIVIDUAL HEALTH INSURANCE	PRODUCT CATEGORY ID	Yes	Yes	ID
INDIVIDUAL INSURANCE POLICY	AGREEMENT ID	Yes	Yes	ID
	PARTY ID	No	Yes	ID
	ROLE TYPE ID	No	Yes	ID
INDIVIDUAL OR GROUP	PRODUCT CATEGORY ID	Yes	Yes	ID

ENTITY NAME	ATTRIBUTE NAME	PK?	FK?	DOMAIN
INDUSTRY TARGET CATEGORIZATION	PRODUCT CATEGORY ID	Yes	Yes	ID
INSTITUTIONAL CLAIM	CLAIM ID	Yes	Yes	ID
INSURANCE ADMINISTRATOR	PARTY ID	Yes	Yes	ID
	ROLE TYPE ID	Yes	Yes	ID
INSURANCE AGENCY	PARTY ID	Yes	Yes	ID
	ROLE TYPE ID	Yes	Yes	ID
INSURANCE AGENT	PARTY ID	Yes	Yes	ID
	ROLE TYPE ID	Yes	Yes	ID
INSURANCE AGENT TO PROVIDER RELATIONSHIP	FROM DATE	Yes	Yes	Datetime
	PARTY ID FROM	Yes	Yes	ID
	PARTY ID TO	Yes	Yes	ID
	ROLE TYPE ID FROM	Yes	Yes	ID
	ROLE TYPE ID TO	Yes	Yes	ID
INSURANCE FACTOR	INSURANCE FACTOR ID	Yes	No	ID
	DESCRIPTION	No	No	Description
	FACTOR VALUE	No	No	Numeric
INSURANCE PARTNER	PARTY ID	Yes	Yes	ID
	ROLE TYPE ID	Yes	Yes	ID
INSURANCE POLICY	AGREEMENT ID	Yes	Yes	ID
	PARTY ID	No	Yes	ID
	ROLE TYPE ID	No	Yes	ID
	POLICY NUMBER	No	No	Number
INSURANCE PRODUCT	PRODUCT ID	Yes	No	ID
	COMMENTS	No	No	Comment
	INTRODUCTION DATE	No	No	Datetime
	NAME	No	No	Name
	SALES DISCONTINUATION DATE	No	No	Datetime
	SUPPORT DISCONTINUATION DATE	No	No	Datetime
INSURANCE PRODUCTS	PRODUCT ID	Yes	No	ID
INSURANCE PROVIDER	NAME	No	No	Name
	PARTY ID	Yes	Yes	ID
INSURANCE RATE	ROLE TYPE ID	Yes	Yes	ID
	INSURANCE RATE ID	Yes	No	ID
	COVERAGE LEVEL ID	No	Yes	ID
	COVERAGE TYPE ID	No	Yes	ID

ENTITY NAME	ATTRIBUTE NAME	PK?	FK?	DOMAIN
	GEOGRAPHIC LOCATION ID	No	Yes	ID
	INSURED ASSET TYPE ID	No	Yes	ID
	PARTY TYPE ID	No	Yes	ID
	PERIOD TYPE ID	No	Yes	ID
	PRODUCT FEATURE ID	No	Yes	ID
	PRODUCT ID	No	Yes	ID
	RISK LEVEL TYPE ID	No	Yes	ID
	FROM DATE	No	No	Datetime
	RATE AMOUNT	No	No	Currency amount
	THRU DATE	No	No	Datetime
INSURANCE RATE ANALYSIS SOURCE	ACTUARIAL ANALYSIS ID	Yes	Yes	ID
	INSURANCE RATE ANALYSIS SEQ ID	Yes	No	ID
	INSURANCE FACTOR ID	No	Yes	ID
	INSURANCE RATE ID	No	Yes	ID
INSURANCE RATE FACTOR	INSURANCE FACTOR ID	Yes	Yes	ID
	INSURANCE RATE ID	Yes	Yes	ID
INSURANCE SUPPORT STAFF	PARTY ID	Yes	Yes	ID
	ROLE TYPE ID	Yes	Yes	ID
INSURANCE TYPE CATEGORIZATION	PRODUCT CATEGORY ID	Yes	Yes	ID
INSURED ASSET	INSURED ASSET ID	Yes	No	ID
	BOOK VALUE	No	No	Currency amount
	DESCRIPTION	No	No	Description
INSURED ASSET TYPE	INSURED ASSET TYPE ID	Yes	No	ID
	DESCRIPTION	No	No	Description
INSURED ASSETS	INSURED ASSET ID	Yes	Yes	ID
	BOOK VALUE	No	No	Currency amount
	DESCRIPTION	No	No	Description
INSURED CONTRACT HOLDER	PARTY ID	Yes	Yes	ID
INSURED DEPENDENT	ROLE TYPE ID	Yes	Yes	ID
	PARTY ID	Yes	Yes	ID
	AGREEMENT ID	No	Yes	ID
	ENROLLMENT ID	No	Yes	ID
	GROUP PARTY ID	No	Yes	ID

ENTITY NAME	ATTRIBUTE NAME	PK?	FK?	DOMAIN
	GROUP ROLE TYPE ID	No	Yes	ID
	INSURED PARTY ID	No	Yes	ID
	INSURED ROLE TYPE ID	No	Yes	ID
INSURED HOUSE	INSURED ASSET ID	Yes	Yes	ID
	ASSET ID	Yes	No	ID
	FIXED ASSET ID	Yes	No	ID
INSURED INDIVIDUAL	PARTY ID	Yes	Yes	ID
	ROLE TYPE ID	Yes	Yes	ID
INSURED ORGANIZATION	PARTY ID	Yes	Yes	ID
	ROLE TYPE ID	Yes	Yes	ID
INSURED PARTY	PARTY ID	Yes	Yes	ID
	ROLE TYPE ID	Yes	Yes	ID
INSURED PARTY TO AGENT RELATIONSHIP	FROM DATE	Yes	Yes	Datetime
	PARTY ID FROM	Yes	Yes	ID
	PARTY ID TO	Yes	Yes	ID
	ROLE TYPE ID FROM	Yes	Yes	ID
	ROLE TYPE ID TO	Yes	Yes	ID
INSURED PARTY TO INS PROV RELATIONSHIP	FROM DATE	Yes	Yes	Datetime
	PARTY ID FROM	Yes	Yes	ID
	PARTY ID TO	Yes	Yes	ID
	ROLE TYPE ID FROM	Yes	Yes	ID
	ROLE TYPE ID TO	Yes	Yes	ID
INSURED TARGET	ACTUARIAL ANALYSIS ID	Yes	Yes	ID
	INSURED ASSET TYPE ID	Yes	Yes	ID
INSURED VEHICLE	INSURED ASSET ID	Yes	Yes	ID
	ASSET ID	Yes	No	ID
	FIXED ASSET ID	Yes	No	ID
INTERNAL ORGANIZATION	PARTY ID	Yes	Yes	ID
	ROLE TYPE ID	Yes	Yes	ID
INVOICE ITEM	INVOICE ID	Yes	No	ID
	INVOICE ITEM SEQ ID	Yes	No	ID
	ADJUSTED BY INVOICE ID	No	Yes	ID
	ADJUSTED BY INVOICE ITEM SEQ ID	No	Yes	ID
	PRODUCT FEATURE ID	No	Yes	ID
	SOLD WITH INVOICE ID	No	Yes	ID

ENTITY NAME	ATTRIBUTE NAME	PK?	FK?	DOMAIN
	SOLD WITH INVOICE ITEM SEQ ID	No	Yes	ID
	UOM ID	No	Yes	ID
	AMOUNT	No	No	Currency amount
	INVENTORY ITEM ID	No	No	ID
	INVOICE ITEM TYPE ID	No	No	ID
	ITEM DESCRIPTION	No	No	Description
	PRODUCT ID	No	No	ID
	QUANTITY	No	No	Numeric
	TAXABLE FLAG	No	No	Indicator
LIFE INSURANCE	PRODUCT CATEGORY ID	Yes	Yes	ID
LIFE INSURANCE CLAIM	CLAIM ID	Yes	Yes	ID
LIFE INSURANCE POLICY	AGREEMENT ID	Yes	Yes	ID
LIFE POLICY ITEM	AGREEMENT ID	Yes	Yes	ID
	AGREEMENT ITEM SEQ ID	Yes	Yes	ID
MEDICAL CLAIM	CLAIM ID	Yes	Yes	ID
MOTOR VEHICLE ACCIDENT	DRIVING INCIDENT ID	Yes	Yes	ID
MOTOR VEHICLE INCIDENT	INCIDENT ID	Yes	Yes	ID
	INCIDENT ID	Yes	Yes	ID
MOTOR VEHICLE TICKET	DRIVING INCIDENT ID	Yes	No	ID
	DRIVING INCIDENT ID	Yes	Yes	ID
	INCIDENT ID	Yes	Yes	ID
NATURAL DISASTER INSURANCE	PRODUCT CATEGORY ID	Yes	Yes	ID
OPTIONAL COVERAGE	COVERAGE LEVEL ID	Yes	Yes	ID
	COVERAGE TYPE ID	Yes	Yes	ID
	FROM DATE	Yes	Yes	Datetime
	PRODUCT ID	Yes	Yes	ID
ORGANIZATION	PARTY ID	Yes	Yes	ID
	NAME	No	No	Name
ORGANIZATION CONTACT RELATIONSHIP	FROM DATE	Yes	Yes	Datetime
	PARTY ID FROM	Yes	Yes	ID
	PARTY ID TO	Yes	Yes	ID
	ROLE TYPE ID FROM	Yes	Yes	ID
	ROLE TYPE ID TO	Yes	Yes	ID
ORGANIZATION ROLE	PARTY ID	Yes	Yes	ID

ENTITY NAME	ATTRIBUTE NAME	PK?	FK?	DOMAIN
	ROLE TYPE ID	Yes	Yes	ID
ORGANIZATION ROLLUP	FROM DATE	Yes	Yes	Datetime
	PARTY ID FROM	Yes	Yes	ID
	PARTY ID TO	Yes	Yes	ID
	ROLE TYPE ID FROM	Yes	Yes	ID
	ROLE TYPE ID TO	Yes	Yes	ID
ORGANIZATION UNIT	PARTY ID	Yes	Yes	ID
	ROLE TYPE ID	Yes	Yes	ID
OTHER AGREEMENT	AGREEMENT ID	Yes	Yes	ID
OTHER COVERAGE LEVEL	COVERAGE LEVEL ID	Yes	Yes	ID
OTHER INSURANCE	PRODUCT CATEGORY ID	Yes	Yes	ID
OTHER INSURANCE	AGREEMENT ID	Yes	Yes	ID
OTHER POLICY ITEM	AGREEMENT ID	Yes	Yes	ID
	AGREEMENT ITEM SEQ ID	Yes	Yes	ID
OTHER PROPERTY INSURANCE	PRODUCT CATEGORY ID	Yes	Yes	ID
OTHER STAFF	PARTY ID	Yes	Yes	ID
	ROLE TYPE ID	Yes	Yes	ID
PARAMETER TYPE	PARAMETER TYPE ID	Yes	No	ID
	DESCRIPTION	No	No	Description
PARTNERSHIP	FROM DATE	Yes	Yes	Datetime
	PARTY ID FROM	Yes	Yes	ID
	PARTY ID TO	Yes	Yes	ID
	ROLE TYPE ID FROM	Yes	Yes	ID
	ROLE TYPE ID TO	Yes	Yes	ID
PARTNERSHIP AGREEMENT	AGREEMENT ID	Yes	Yes	ID
PARTY	PARTY ID	Yes	No	ID
PARTY RELATIONSHIP	PARTY ID FROM	Yes	Yes	ID
	PARTY ID TO	Yes	Yes	ID
	ROLE TYPE ID FROM	Yes	Yes	ID
	ROLE TYPE ID TO	Yes	Yes	ID
	FROM DATE	Yes	No	Datetime
	PARTY RELATIONSHIP TYPE ID	No	Yes	ID
	COMMENTS	No	No	Comment
	PRIORITY TYPE ID	No	No	ID
	STATUS TYPE ID	No	No	ID
	THRU DATE	No	No	Datetime

ENTITY NAME	ATTRIBUTE NAME	PK?	FK?	DOMAIN
PARTY RELATIONSHIP TYPE	PARTY RELATIONSHIP TYPE ID	Yes	No	ID
	ROLE TYPE ID VALID FROM	No	Yes	ID
	ROLE TYPE ID VALID TO	No	Yes	ID
	DESCRIPTION	No	No	Description
	NAME	No	No	Name
PARTY ROLE	PARTY ID	Yes	Yes	ID
	ROLE TYPE ID	Yes	Yes	ID
	PARTY ROLE ID	No	No	ID
PARTY ROLE TYPE	ROLE TYPE ID	Yes	Yes	ID
PARTY TYPE	PARTY TYPE ID	Yes	No	ID
	DESCRIPTION	No	No	Description
PARTY TYPES	PARTY TYPE ID	Yes	No	ID
	DESCRIPTION	No	No	Description
PAYMENT	PAYMENT ID	Yes	No	ID
	FROM PARTY ID	No	Yes	ID
	PAYMENT METHOD TYPE ID	No	Yes	ID
	PAYMENT TYPE ID	No	Yes	ID
	TO PARTY ID	No	Yes	ID
	AMOUNT	No	No	Currency amount
	COMMENTS	No	No	Comment
	EFFECTIVE DATE	No	No	Datetime
	PAYMENT REF NUM	No	No	Description
PAYMENT METHOD TYPE	PAYMENT METHOD TYPE ID	Yes	No	ID
	DESCRIPTION	No	No	Description
PAYMENT TYPE	PAYMENT TYPE ID	Yes	No	ID
	DESCRIPTION	No	No	Description
PAYOR	PARTY ID	Yes	Yes	ID
	ROLE TYPE ID	Yes	Yes	ID
PERIOD TYPE	PERIOD TYPE ID	Yes	No	ID
	DESCRIPTION	No	Yes	Description
PERSON	PARTY ID	Yes	No	ID
	BIRTH DATE	No	No	Datetime
	COMMENTS	No	No	Comment
	CURRENT FIRST NAME	No	No	Name
	CURRENT LAST NAME	No	No	Name
	CURRENT MIDDLE NAME	No	No	Name
	CURRENT NICKNAME	No	No	Name
	CURRENT PASSPORT EXPIRE DATE	No	No	Datetime

ENTITY NAME	ATTRIBUTE NAME	PK?	FK?	DOMAIN
	CURRENT PASSPORT NUMBER	No	No	Numeric
	CURRENT PERSONAL TITLE	No	No	Name
	CURRENT SUFFIX	No	No	Name
	GENDER	No	No	Indicator
	HEIGHT	No	No	Numeric
	MARTIAL STATUS	No	No	Indicator
	MOTHER'S MADIEN NAME	No	No	Name
	SOCIAL SECURITY NUMBER	No	No	Numeric
	TOTAL YEARS WORK EXPERIENCE	No	No	Numeric
	WEIGHT	No	No	Numeric
PERSON ROLE	PARTY ID	Yes	Yes	ID
	ROLE TYPE ID	Yes	Yes	ID
POLICY ITEM	AGREEMENT ID	Yes	Yes	ID
	AGREEMENT ITEM SEQ ID	Yes	Yes	ID
	COVERAGE LEVEL ID	No	Yes	ID
	COVERAGE TYPE ID	No	Yes	ID
	PRODUCT FEATURE ID	No	Yes	ID
	QUOTE ID	No	Yes	ID
	QUOTED ITEM SEQ ID	No	Yes	ID
POLICY ITEM PREMIUM	AGREEMENT ID	Yes	Yes	ID
	AGREEMENT ITEM SEQ ID	Yes	Yes	ID
	POLICY ITEM PREMIUM SEQ ID	Yes	Yes	ID
	INSURANCE RATE ID	No	Yes	ID
	PREMIUM AMOUNT	No	No	Currency amount
POLICY ITEM PREMIUM BILLING	AGREEMENT ID	Yes	Yes	ID
	AGREEMENT ITEM SEQ ID	Yes	Yes	ID
	INVOICE ID	Yes	Yes	ID
	INVOICE ITEM SEQ ID	Yes	Yes	ID
	POLICY ITEM PREMIUM SEQ ID	Yes	Yes	ID
POLICY PREMIUM ADJUSTMENT	POLICY PREMIUM ADJUSTMENT ID	Yes	No	ID
	ADJUSTMENT TYPE ID	No	Yes	ID
	AGREEMENT ID	No	Yes	ID
	AGREEMENT ITEM SEQ ID	No	Yes	ID
	POLICY ITEM PREMIUM SEQ ID	No	Yes	ID
	PREMIUM SCHEDULE ID	No	Yes	ID
	PERCENTAGE	No	No	Floating point
PREMIUM SCHEDULE	PREMIUM SCHEDULE ID	Yes	No	ID

ENTITY NAME	ATTRIBUTE NAME	PK?	FK?	DOMAIN
	AGREEMENT ID	No	Yes	ID
	PERIOD TYPE ID	No	Yes	ID
	DUE DATE	No	No	Datetime
	INSURED FROM DATE	No	No	Datetime
	INSURED THRU DATE	No	No	Datetime
	PREMIUM AMOUNT	No	No	Currency amount
	VALID FROM DATE	No	No	Datetime
	VALID THRU DATE	No	No	Datetime
PRODUCT CATEGORY	PRODUCT CATEGORY ID	Yes	No	ID
	DESCRIPTION	No	No	Description
PRODUCT CATEGORY CLASSIFICATION	PRODUCT CATEGORY ID	Yes	Yes	ID
	PRODUCT ID	Yes	Yes	ID
	FROM DATE	Yes	No	Datetime
	COMMENTS	No	No	Comment
	PRIMARY FLAG	No	No	Indicator
	THRU DATE	No	No	Datetime
PRODUCT CATEGORY ROLLUP	PARTY TYPE ID MADE UP OF	Yes	Yes	ID
	PARTY TYPE ID PART OF	Yes	Yes	ID
PRODUCT CATEGORYS	PRODUCT CATEGORY ID	Yes	No	ID
	DESCRIPTION	No	No	Description
PRODUCT FEATURE	PRODUCT FEATURE ID	Yes	Yes	ID
	PRODUCT FEATURE CATEGORY ID	No	Yes	ID
	DESCRIPTION	No	No	Description
PRODUCT FEATURE CATEGORY	PRODUCT FEATURE CATEGORY ID	Yes	No	ID
	DESCRIPTION	No	No	Description
PRODUCT FEATURE COVERAGE	PRODUCT FEATURE ID	Yes	Yes	ID
	PRODUCT ID	Yes	Yes	ID
	PROD FTR SEQ ID	Yes	No	ID
	COVERAGE TYPE ID	No	Yes	ID
	FROM DATE	No	No	Datetime
	THRU DATE	No	No	Datetime
PRODUCT RULE	RULE TYPE ID	Yes	Yes	ID
	PRODUCT RULE ID	Yes	No	ID
	COVERAGE LEVEL ID	No	Yes	ID
	COVERAGE TYPE ID	No	Yes	ID
	INSURED ASSET TYPE ID	No	Yes	ID

ENTITY NAME	ATTRIBUTE NAME	PK?	FK?	DOMAIN
	INT ORG PARTY ID	No	Yes	ID
	INT ORG ROLE TYPE ID	No	Yes	ID
	PRODUCT FEATURE ID	No	Yes	ID
	PRODUCT ID	No	Yes	ID
	REG AGENCY PARTY ID	No	Yes	ID
	REG AGENCY ROLE TYPE ID	No	Yes	ID
	DESCRIPTION	No	No	Description
	FROM DATE	No	No	Datetime
	RULE VALUE	No	No	Numeric
	THRU DATE	No	No	Datetime
PROPERTY CLAIM	CLAIM ID	Yes	Yes	ID
PROPERTY DAMAGE	INCIDENT ID	Yes	Yes	ID
PROPERTY INSURANCE	PRODUCT CATEGORY ID	Yes	Yes	ID
PROPERTY INSURANCE POLICY	AGREEMENT ID	Yes	Yes	ID
PROPERTY LOSS	INCIDENT ID	Yes	Yes	ID
PROPERTY POLICY ITEM	AGREEMENT ID	Yes	Yes	ID
	AGREEMENT ITEM SEQ ID	Yes	Yes	ID
	INSURED ASSET ID	No	Yes	ID
PROPERTY THEFT	INCIDENT ID	Yes	Yes	ID
PROSPECT	PARTY ID	Yes	Yes	ID
	ROLE TYPE ID	Yes	Yes	ID
QUOTE	QUOTE ID	Yes	No	ID
	CREATOR OF PARTY ID	No	Yes	ID
	RECEIVER OF PARTY ID	No	Yes	ID
	DESCRIPTION	No	No	Description
	ISSUE DATE	No	No	Datetime
	VALID FROM DATE	No	No	Datetime
	VALID THRU DATE	No	No	Datetime
QUOTE ITEM	QUOTE ID	Yes	Yes	ID
	QUOTED ITEM SEQ ID	Yes	No	ID
	APPLICATION ID	No	Yes	ID
	APPLICATION ITEM SEQ ID	No	Yes	ID
	COVERAGE LEVEL ID	No	Yes	ID
	COVERAGE TYPE ID	No	Yes	ID
	INSURED ASSET ID	No	Yes	ID
	PRODUCT FEATURE ID	No	Yes	ID
	PRODUCT ID	No	Yes	ID
	UOM ID	No	Yes	ID
	WORK EFFORT ID	No	Yes	ID

ENTITY NAME	ATTRIBUTE NAME	PK?	FK?	DOMAIN
	COMMENTS	No	No	Comment
	ESTIMATED DELIVERY DATE	No	No	Datetime
	ESTIMATED POLICY DATE	No	No	Datetime
	ESTIMATED PREMIUM AMOUNT	No	No	Currency amount
	QUANTITY	No	No	Numeric
	QUOTE UNIT PRICE	No	No	Currency amount
	REQUEST ID	No	No	ID
	REQUEST ITEM SEQ ID	No	No	ID
QUOTE ROLE	PARTY ID	Yes	Yes	ID
	QUOTE ID	Yes	Yes	ID
	ROLE TYPE ID	Yes	Yes	ID
QUOTE ROLE TYPE	ROLE TYPE ID	Yes	Yes	ID
QUOTE TERM	TERM TYPE ID	Yes	Yes	ID
	QUOTE TERM ID	Yes	No	ID
	QUOTE ID	Yes	Yes	ID
	QUOTED ITEM SEQ ID	No	Yes	ID
	TERM VALUE	No	No	Numeric
REGULATORY AGENCY	PARTY ID	Yes	Yes	ID
	ROLE TYPE ID	Yes	Yes	ID
REMITTANCE NOTICE	REMITTANCE NOTICE ID	Yes	No	ID
	REMITTANCE NOTICE SENT DATE	No	No	Datetime
REMITTANCE NOTICE PARTY	PARTY ID	Yes	Yes	ID
	REMITTANCE NOTICE ID	Yes	Yes	ID
	PAYMENT ID	No	Yes	ID
REQUIRED COVERAGE	COVERAGE LEVEL ID	Yes	Yes	ID
	COVERAGE TYPE ID	Yes	Yes	ID
	FROM DATE	Yes	Yes	Datetime
	PRODUCT ID	Yes	Yes	ID
RISK ANALYSIS	WORK EFFORT ID	Yes	Yes	ID
RISK LEVEL TYPE	RISK LEVEL TYPE ID	Yes	No	ID
	DESCRIPTION	No	No	Description
RISK LEVEL TYPES	RISK LEVEL TYPE ID	Yes	No	ID
	DESCRIPTION	No	No	Description
RISK RATE	INSURANCE RATE ID	Yes	Yes	ID
ROLE TYPE	ROLE TYPE ID	Yes	No	ID
	DESCRIPTION	No	No	Description
RULE TYPE	RULE TYPE ID	Yes	No	ID
	DESCRIPTION	No	No	Description

ENTITY NAME	ATTRIBUTE NAME	PK?	FK?	DOMAIN
SELECTABLE COVERAGE	COVERAGE LEVEL ID	Yes	Yes	ID
	COVERAGE TYPE ID	Yes	Yes	ID
	FROM DATE	Yes	Yes	Datetime
	PRODUCT ID	Yes	Yes	ID
SETTLEMENT ROLE	CLAIM SETTLEMENT ID	Yes	Yes	ID
	PARTY ID	Yes	Yes	ID
SETTLEMENT ROLE TYPE	PARTY ID	Yes	Yes	ID
SPECIALTY INSURANCE	PRODUCT CATEGORY ID	Yes	Yes	ID
STANDARD COVERAGE	COVERAGE LEVEL ID	Yes	Yes	ID
	COVERAGE TYPE ID	Yes	Yes	ID
	FROM DATE	Yes	Yes	Datetime
	PRODUCT ID	Yes	Yes	ID
STATUS TYPE	STATUS TYPE ID	Yes	No	ID
	DESCRIPTION	No	No	Description
SUB AGREEMENT	AGREEMENT ID	Yes	Yes	ID
	AGREEMENT ITEM SEQ ID	Yes	Yes	ID
SUBSIDIARY	PARTY ID	Yes	Yes	ID
	ROLE TYPE ID	Yes	Yes	ID
SUPPLIER	PARTY ID	Yes	Yes	ID
	ROLE TYPE ID	Yes	Yes	ID
SUPPLIER AGREEMENT	AGREEMENT ID	Yes	Yes	ID
SUPPLIER RELATIONSHIP	FROM DATE	Yes	Yes	Datetime
	PARTY ID FROM	Yes	Yes	ID
	PARTY ID TO	Yes	Yes	ID
	ROLE TYPE ID FROM	Yes	Yes	ID
	ROLE TYPE ID TO	Yes	Yes	ID
SURCHARGE PREMIUM ADJUSTMENT	POLICY PREMIUM ADJUSTMENT ID	Yes	Yes	ID
SUSPECT	PARTY ID	Yes	Yes	ID
	ROLE TYPE ID	Yes	Yes	ID
TERM LIFE INSURANCE	PRODUCT CATEGORY ID	Yes	Yes	ID
TERM TYPE	TERM TYPE ID	Yes	No	ID
	DESCRIPTION	No	No	Description
TIME BY DAY	DAY ID	Yes	No	ID
	DAY	No	No	Very short
	MONTH	No	No	Very short
	QUARTER	No	No	Very short
	WEEK	No	No	Very short
	YEAR	No	No	Very short
TRUSTEE	PARTY ID	Yes	Yes	ID
	ROLE TYPE ID	Yes	Yes	ID
UNIT OF MEASURE	UOM ID	Yes	No	ID
	ABBREVIATION	No	No	Short varchar
	DESCRIPTION	No	No	Description
UNIVERSAL LIFE INSURANCE	PRODUCT CATEGORY ID	Yes	Yes	ID
USUAL AND CUSTOMARY AMOUNT	CLAIM SETTLEMENT AMOUNT ID	Yes	Yes	ID
VEHICLE CLAIM	CLAIM SETTLEMENT ID	Yes	Yes	ID
	CLAIM ID	Yes	Yes	ID
VEHICLE INSURANCE	PRODUCT CATEGORY ID	Yes	Yes	ID
VESSEL INSURANCE	PRODUCT CATEGORY ID	Yes	Yes	ID
WHOLE LIFE INSURANCE	PRODUCT CATEGORY ID	Yes	Yes	ID
WORK EFFORT	WORK EFFORT ID	Yes	No	ID
	VERSION OF WORK EFFORT ID	No	Yes	ID
	ACTUAL COMPLETION DATETIME	No	No	Datetime
	ACTUAL HOURS	No	No	Numeric
	ACTUAL START DATETIME	No	No	Datetime
	ASSET ID	No	No	ID
	DESCRIPTION	No	No	Description
	ESTIMATED HOURS	No	No	Numeric
	FACILITY ID	No	No	ID
	FIXED ASSET ID	No	No	ID
	NAME	No	No	Name
	SCHEDULED COMPLETION DATE	No	No	Datetime
	SCHEDULED START DATE	No	No	Datetime
	SPECIAL TERMS	No	No	Long varchar
	TOTAL DOLLARS ALLOWED	No	No	Currency amount
	TOTAL HOURS ALLOWED	No	No	Numeric
	WORK EFFORT PURPOSE TYPE ID	No	No	ID
	WORK EFFORT TYPE ID	No	No	ID

Entities and Attributes for Financial Services Models

This appendix lists the entities and attributes from the models and star schemas found in Chapter 6, "Financial Services." This listing includes the entity names, attribute names, primary key indicators, foreign key indicators, and the domain for each attribute.

The domain indicates a standard set of characteristics that can be applied to attributes, including its datatype and length. Table A.1 defines the nature of each domain. When applying the domains to the attributes listed in these appendices, refer to Table A.1 for recommendations on what datatype and length to use when implementing these models. Of course, the datatype and length of each attribute should be adjusted as appropriate to meet the specific needs of the enterprise.

The domain definitions as they are applied to the attributes in the appendices are used for the SQL code that is contained on the demo CD-ROM at the back of this book as well as in the Industry Downloads (see the section "How to Use the Volume 2 Industry Electronic Products" for more information).

Entities and Attributes Listing for Financial Services Models

ENTITY NAME	ATTRIBUTE NAME	PK?	FK?	DOMAIN
ACCESS FEATURE	PRODUCT FEATURE ID	Yes	Yes	ID
ACCOUNT	ACCOUNT NUMBER	Yes	No	Numeric
	AGREEMENT ID	No	Yes	ID
ACCOUNT FACT	ACCOUNT MANAGER PARTY ID	Yes	Yes	ID
	FACILITY ID	Yes	Yes	ID
	FINANCIAL PRODUCT ID	Yes	Yes	ID
	INTERNAL ORGANIZATION ID	Yes	Yes	ID
	MARKET SEGMENT ID	Yes	Yes	ID
	OWNER PARTY ID	Yes	Yes	ID
	PARTY ID	Yes	Yes	ID
	WEEK ID	Yes	Yes	ID
	AVERAGE BALANCE	No	No	Currency amount
	AVERAGE RETURN	No	No	Floating point
	NUMBER OF ACCOUNTS	No	No	Numeric
	NUMBER OF TRANSACTIONS	No	No	Numeric
ACCOUNT FEE	ACCOUNT NUMBER	Yes	Yes	Numeric
	ACCOUNT TRANSACTION ID	Yes	Yes	ID
ACCOUNT MANAGER	ACCOUNT MANAGER PARTY ID	Yes	No	ID
	ACCOUNT MANAGER NAME	No	No	Name
	PARTY TYPE	No	No	Name
ACCOUNT NOTIFICATION	ACCOUNT NUMBER	Yes	Yes	Numeric
	DATE	Yes	No	Datetime
	WORK EFFORT ID	No	Yes	ID
	BALANCE	No	No	Currency amount
	MESSAGE	No	No	Long varchar
ACCOUNT PAYMENT	ACCOUNT NUMBER	Yes	Yes	Numeric
	ACCOUNT TRANSACTION ID	Yes	Yes	ID
ACCOUNT PRODUCT	ACCOUNT NUMBER	Yes	Yes	Numeric
	PRODUCT ID	Yes	Yes	ID
	FROM DATE	No	No	Datetime
	THRU DATE	No	No	Datetime
ACCOUNT RELATIONSHIP	ACCOUNT NUMBER FROM	Yes	Yes	Numeric
	ACCOUNT NUMBER TO	Yes	Yes	Numeric

ENTITY NAME	ATTRIBUTE NAME	PK?	FK?	DOMAIN
	ACCOUNT RELATIONSHIP TYPE ID	Yes	Yes	ID
	FROM DATE	Yes	No	Datetime
	THRU DATE	No	No	Datetime
ACCOUNT RELATIONSHIP TYPE	ACCOUNT RELATIONSHIP TYPE ID	Yes	No	ID
ACCOUNT REQUEST TRANSACTION	DESCRIPTION	No	No	Description
	ACCOUNT NUMBER	Yes	Yes	Numeric
ACCOUNT ROLE	ACCOUNT TRANSACTION ID	Yes	Yes	ID
	ACCOUNT NUMBER	Yes	Yes	Numeric
	PARTY ID	Yes	Yes	ID
	ROLE TYPE ID	Yes	Yes	ID
	FROM DATE	No	No	Datetime
	THRU DATE	No	No	Datetime
ACCOUNT ROLE TYPE	ROLE TYPE ID	Yes	Yes	ID
ACCOUNT STATUS	ACCOUNT NUMBER	Yes	Yes	Numeric
	STATUS TYPE ID	Yes	Yes	ID
	DATETIME	Yes	No	Datetime
ACCOUNT STATUS TYPE	STATUS TYPE ID	Yes	Yes	ID
ACCOUNT TARGET	ACCOUNT NUMBER	Yes	Yes	Numeric
	ACCOUNT SCORE	No	No	Numeric
ACCOUNT TRANSACTION	ACCOUNT NUMBER	Yes	Yes	Numeric
	ACCOUNT TRANSACTION ID	Yes	No	ID
	ACCOUNT TRANSACTION TYPE ID	No	Yes	ID
	AMOUNT	No	No	Currency amount
ACCOUNT TRANSACTION FACT	ENTRY DATE	No	No	Datetime
	POST DATE	No	No	Datetime
	TRANSACTION DATE	No	No	Datetime
	DAY ID	Yes	Yes	ID
	FACILITY ID	Yes	Yes	ID
	FINANCIAL PRODUCT ID	Yes	Yes	ID
	INTERNAL ORGANIZATION ID	Yes	Yes	ID
	MARKET SEGMENT ID	Yes	Yes	ID
	OWNER PARTY ID	Yes	Yes	ID

ENTITY NAME	ATTRIBUTE NAME	PK?	FK?	DOMAIN
	PARTY ID	Yes	Yes	ID
	TRANSACTION TYPE ID	Yes	Yes	ID
	NUMBER OF TRANSACTIONS	No	No	Numeric
	TOTAL TRANSACTION AMOUNT	No	No	Currency amount
ACCOUNT TRANSACTION RELATIONSHIP	ACCOUNT NUMBER	Yes	Yes	Numeric
	ACCOUNT TRANSACTION ID FROM	Yes	Yes	ID
	ACCOUNT TRANSACTION ID TO	Yes	Yes	ID
	ACCOUNT TRANS REL TYPE ID	No	Yes	ID
ACCOUNT TRANSACTION RELATIONSHIP TYPE	ACCOUNT TRANS REL TYPE ID	Yes	No	ID
	DESCRIPTION	No	No	Description
ACCOUNT TRANSACTION STATUS	ACCOUNT NUMBER	Yes	Yes	Numeric
	ACCOUNT TRANSACTION ID	Yes	Yes	ID
	STATUS TYPE ID	Yes	Yes	ID
	STATUS DATETIME	No	No	Datetime
ACCOUNT TRANSACTION TASK	TRANSACTION TASK ID	Yes	Yes	ID
	ACCOUNT NUMBER	No	Yes	Numeric
	ACCOUNT TRANSACTION ID	No	Yes	ID
	UOM ID	No	Yes	ID
	DESCRIPTION	No	No	Description
	REQUESTED DATE	No	No	Datetime
	TASK CREATION DATE	No	No	Datetime
ACCOUNT TRANSACTION TASK TYPE	TRANSACTION TASK ID	Yes	No	ID
	DESCRIPTION	No	No	Description
ACCOUNT TRANSACTION TYPE	ACCOUNT TRANSACTION TYPE ID	Yes	No	ID
	DESCRIPTION	No	No	Description
ACCOUNT TRANSACTION TYPES	TRANSACTION TYPE ID	Yes	Yes	ID
	DESCRIPTION	No	No	Description
AGREEMENT	AGREEMENT ID	Yes	No	ID
	AGREEMENT TYPE ID	No	Yes	ID
	FROM DATE	No	Yes	Datetime
	PARTY ID FROM	No	Yes	ID

ENTITY NAME	ATTRIBUTE NAME	PK?	FK?	DOMAIN
	PARTY ID TO	No	Yes	ID
	ROLE TYPE ID FROM	No	Yes	ID
	ROLE TYPE ID TO	No	Yes	ID
	AGREEMENT DATE	No	No	Datetime
	DESCRIPTION	No	No	Description
	PRODUCT ID	No	No	ID
AGREEMENT	TEXT	No	No	Long varchar
	THRU DATE	No	No	Datetime
AGREEMENT ASSET USAGE	ASSET ID	Yes	Yes	ID
	AGREEMENT ASSET USAGE ID	Yes	No	ID
	AGREEMENT ID	No	Yes	ID
	AGREEMENT ITEM SEQ ID	No	Yes	ID
	ASSET USAGE TYPE ID	No	Yes	ID
AGREEMENT ITEM	AGREEMENT ID	Yes	Yes	ID
	AGREEMENT ITEM SEQ ID	Yes	No	ID
	PART OF AGREEMENT ID	No	Yes	ID
	PART OF AGREEMENT ITEM SEQ ID	No	Yes	ID
	AGREEMENT IMAGE	No	No	Blob
	AGREEMENT TEXT	No	No	Long varchar
AGREEMENT ROLE	AGREEMENT ID	Yes	Yes	ID
	PARTY ID	Yes	Yes	ID
	ROLE TYPE ID	Yes	Yes	ID
AGREEMENT ROLE TYPE	ROLE TYPE ID	Yes	Yes	ID
AGREEMENT STATUS	AGREEMENT ID	Yes	Yes	ID
	STATUS TYPE ID	Yes	Yes	ID
	COMPLETION DATE	No	No	Datetime
	FROM DATE	No	No	Datetime
	THRU DATE	No	No	Datetime
AGREEMENT STATUS TYPE	STATUS TYPE ID	Yes	Yes	ID
AGREEMENT TERM	AGREEMENT TERM ID	Yes	No	ID
	TERM TYPE ID	Yes	No	ID
	AGREEMENT ID	No	Yes	ID
	AGREEMENT ITEM SEQ ID	No	Yes	ID
	FROM DATE	No	No	Datetime
	TERM VALUE	No	No	Numeric
	THRU DATE	No	No	Datetime
AGREEMENT TYPE	AGREEMENT TYPE ID	Yes	No	ID

ENTITY NAME	ATTRIBUTE NAME	PK?	FK?	DOMAIN
	DESCRIPTION	No	No	Description
ALERT TASK	WORK EFFORT ID	Yes	Yes	ID
ANALYSIS OUTCOME	WORK EFFORT ID	Yes	Yes	ID
	ANALYSIS OUTCOME ID	Yes	No	ID
	ACCOUNT NUMBER	No	Yes	Numeric
	ANALYSIS PARAMETER ID	No	Yes	ID
	MARKET SEGMENT ID	No	Yes	ID
	PARTY ID	No	Yes	ID
	ANALYSIS OUTCOME SCORE	No	No	Numeric
	COMMENTS	No	No	Comment
ANALYSIS PARAMETER	ANALYSIS PARAMETER ID	Yes	No	ID
	PARAMETER TYPE ID	No	Yes	ID
	ANALYSIS PARAMETER WEIGHT	No	No	Floating point
	PARAMETER RANGE	No	No	Numeric
	PARAMETER VALUE	No	No	Numeric
ANNUITY	PRODUCT CATEGORY ID	Yes	Yes	ID
APPROVED USER	ROLE TYPE ID	Yes	Yes	ID
ASSET	ASSET ID	Yes	No	ID
	DESCRIPTION	No	No	Description
ASSET ROLE	ASSET ID	Yes	Yes	ID
	PARTY ID	Yes	Yes	ID
	ROLE TYPE ID	Yes	Yes	ID
	EQUITY VALUE	No	No	Numeric
ASSET ROLE TYPE	ROLE TYPE ID	Yes	Yes	ID
ASSET USAGE TYPE	ASSET USAGE TYPE ID	Yes	No	ID
	DESCRIPTION	No	No	Description
AUTHORIZE TRANSACTION TASK	TRANSACTION TASK ID	Yes	Yes	ID
BILLING TASK	WORK EFFORT ID	Yes	Yes	ID
BUY TRANSACTION	ACCOUNT NUMBER	Yes	Yes	Numeric
	ACCOUNT TRANSACTION ID	Yes	No	ID
CERTIFICATE OF DEPOSIT ACCOUNT	ACCOUNT NUMBER	Yes	Yes	Numeric
CHANGE REQUEST	ACCOUNT NUMBER	Yes	Yes	Numeric
	ACCOUNT TRANSACTION ID	Yes	Yes	ID
CHECKING	PRODUCT CATEGORY ID	Yes	Yes	ID
CHECKING ACCOUNT	ACCOUNT NUMBER	Yes	Yes	Numeric
COMPETITOR	PARTY ID	Yes	Yes	ID
	ROLE TYPE ID	Yes	Yes	ID
CONTACT	PARTY ID	Yes	Yes	ID
	ROLE TYPE ID	Yes	Yes	ID

ENTITY NAME	ATTRIBUTE NAME	PK?	FK?	DOMAIN
CONTRACTOR	PARTY ID	Yes	Yes	ID
	ROLE TYPE ID	Yes	Yes	ID
CONTROLLING SYNDICATOR	PARTY ID	Yes	Yes	ID
CREDIT CARD ACCOUNT	ROLE TYPE ID	Yes	Yes	ID
	ACCOUNT NUMBER	Yes	Yes	Numeric
CUSTOMER	PARTY ID	Yes	Yes	ID
	ROLE TYPE ID	Yes	Yes	ID
CUSTOMER RELATIONSHIP	FROM DATE	Yes	Yes	Datetime
	PARTY ID FROM	Yes	Yes	ID
	PARTY ID TO	Yes	Yes	ID
	ROLE TYPE ID FROM	Yes	Yes	ID
	ROLE TYPE ID TO	Yes	Yes	ID
DEBIT CARD ACCOUNT	ACCOUNT NUMBER	Yes	Yes	Numeric
DEPARTMENT	PARTY ID	Yes	Yes	ID
	ROLE TYPE ID	Yes	Yes	ID
DEPOSIT	ACCOUNT NUMBER	Yes	Yes	Numeric
	ACCOUNT TRANSACTION ID	Yes	Yes	ID
	FINANCIAL ACCOUNT TRANS ID	Yes	No	ID
DEPOSIT ACCOUNT	ACCOUNT NUMBER	Yes	Yes	Numeric
DEPOSIT PRODUCT	PRODUCT CATEGORY ID	Yes	Yes	ID
DIVIDEND	ACCOUNT NUMBER	Yes	Yes	Numeric
	ACCOUNT TRANSACTION ID	Yes	Yes	ID
DIVISION	PARTY ID	Yes	Yes	ID
	ROLE TYPE ID	Yes	Yes	ID
EMPLOYEE	PARTY ID	Yes	Yes	ID
	ROLE TYPE ID	Yes	Yes	ID
EMPLOYMENT	FROM DATE	Yes	Yes	Datetime
	PARTY ID FROM	Yes	Yes	ID
	PARTY ID TO	Yes	Yes	ID
	ROLE TYPE ID FROM	Yes	Yes	ID
	ROLE TYPE ID TO	Yes	Yes	ID
	TERMINATION REASON ID	No	No	ID
	TERMINATION TYPE ID	No	No	ID
EQUITY	ASSET ID	Yes	Yes	ID
	PRODUCT CATEGORY ID	Yes	Yes	ID
EQUITY LINE	PRODUCT CATEGORY ID	Yes	Yes	ID
EQUITY LINE ACCOUNT	ACCOUNT NUMBER	Yes	Yes	Numeric

ENTITY NAME	ATTRIBUTE NAME	PK?	FK?	DOMAIN
FINANCIAL TRANSACTION	ACCOUNT NUMBER	Yes	Yes	Numeric
	ACCOUNT TRANSACTION ID	Yes	Yes	ID
FIXED ASSET	ASSET ID	Yes	No	ID
	FIXED ASSET ID	Yes	No	ID
	UOM ID	No	Yes	ID
	DATE ACQUIRED	No	No	Datetime
	DATE LAST SERVICED	No	No	Datetime
	DATE NEXT SERVICE	No	No	Datetime
	FIXED ASSET TYPE ID	No	No	ID
	NAME	No	No	Name
	PARTY ID	No	No	ID
	PRODUCTION CAPACITY	No	No	Floating point
FIXED INCOME ·	ROLE TYPE ID	No	No	ID
	ASSET ID	Yes	Yes	ID
	PRODUCT CATEGORY ID	Yes	No	ID
FUNCTIONAL SETTING	FUNCTIONAL SETTING ID	Yes	No	ID
	DESCRIPTION	No	No	Description
FUNCTIONAL SETTING APPLICABILITY	FUNCTIONAL SETTING ID	Yes	Yes	ID
	FUNC SET APPLIC ID	Yes	No	ID
	PRODUCT FEATURE ID	No	Yes	ID
	PRODUCT ID	No	No	ID
	FROM DATE	No	No	Datetime
	THRU DATE	No	No	Datetime
	VALUE	No	No	Numeric
GOVERNMENT REGULATION	FINANCIAL REGULATION ID	Yes	Yes	ID
GUARANTOR	ROLE TYPE ID	Yes	Yes	ID
HOUSE	ASSET ID	Yes	Yes	ID
	FIXED ASSET ID	Yes	Yes	ID
HOUSEHOLD	PARTY ID	Yes	Yes	ID
	ROLE TYPE ID	Yes	Yes	ID
INFORMAL RELATIONSHIP	FROM DATE	Yes	Yes	Datetime
	PARTY ID FROM	Yes	Yes	ID
	PARTY ID TO	Yes	Yes	ID
	ROLE TYPE ID FROM	Yes	Yes	ID
	ROLE TYPE ID TO	Yes	Yes	ID
INQUIRY REQUEST	ACCOUNT NUMBER	Yes	Yes	Numeric
	ACCOUNT TRANSACTION ID	Yes	Yes	ID

ENTITY NAME	ATTRIBUTE NAME	PK?	FK?	DOMAIN
ESTIMATED INCOME	ASSET ID	Yes	Yes	ID
EXCHANGE TRANSACTION	ACCOUNT NUMBER	Yes	Yes	Numeric
	ACCOUNT TRANSACTION ID	Yes	Yes	ID
FACILITYS	FACILITY ID	Yes	No	ID
	FACILITY NAME	No	No	Name
	GEO LEVEL 1	No	No	Description
	GEO LEVEL 2	No	No	Description
	GEO LEVEL 3	No	No	Description
FEE FEATURE	PRODUCT FEATURE ID	Yes	Yes	ID
FINANCIAL AGREEMENT	AGREEMENT ID	Yes	Yes	ID
FINANCIAL CARD ACCOUNT	ACCOUNT NUMBER	Yes	Yes	Numeric
FINANCIAL INSTITUTION	PARTY ID	Yes	Yes	ID
	ROLE TYPE ID	Yes	Yes	ID
FINANCIAL PRODUCT	PRODUCT ID	Yes	No	ID
	NAME	No	No	Name
FINANCIAL PRODUCT RULE	FINANCIAL PRODUCT RULE ID	Yes	No	ID
	AGREEMENT TERM ID	No	Yes	ID
	FUNCTIONAL SETTING ID	No	Yes	ID
	PRODUCT CATEGORY ID	No	Yes	ID
	PRODUCT FEATURE ID	No	Yes	ID
	PRODUCT ID	No	Yes	ID
	REGULATION REQUIREMENT ID	No	Yes	ID
	TERM TYPE ID	No	Yes	ID
	DESCRIPTION	No	No	Description
	FROM DATE	No	No	Datetime
	RULE VALUE	No	No	Numeric
	THRU DATE	No	No	Datetime
FINANCIAL PRODUCTS	FINANCIAL PRODUCT ID	Yes	No	ID
	FINANCIAL PRODUCT CATEGORY	No	No	Description
	FINANCIAL PRODUCT NAME	No	No	Name
	PRODUCT CATEGORY ROLLUP	No	No	Description
FINANCIAL REGULATION	FINANCIAL REGULATION ID	Yes	No	ID
	DESCRIPTION	No	No	Description
	TEXT	No	No	Long varchar

ENTITY NAME	ATTRIBUTE NAME	PK?	FK?	DOMAIN
INSTALLMENT LOAN ACCOUNT	ACCOUNT NUMBER	Yes	Yes	Numeric
INTANGIBLE ASSET	ASSET ID	Yes	Yes	ID
INTEREST	ACCOUNT NUMBER	Yes	Yes	Numeric
	ACCOUNT TRANSACTION ID	Yes	Yes	ID
INTEREST RATE FEATURE	PRODUCT FEATURE ID	Yes	Yes	ID
INTERNAL ORGANIZATION	PARTY ID	Yes	Yes	ID
	ROLE TYPE ID	Yes	Yes	ID
INTERNAL ORGANIZATIONS	INTERNAL ORGANIZATION ID	Yes	No	ID
	PARTY ID	Yes	No	ID
	LEVEL 2 ORGANIZATION	No	No	Description
	LEVEL 3 ORGANIZATION	No	No	Description
	LEVEL 4 ORGANIZATION	No	No	Description
	NAME	No	No	Name
INVESTMENT AGREEMENT	AGREEMENT ID	Yes	Yes	ID
INVESTMENT OBJECTIVE	FROM DATE	Yes	Yes	Datetime
	PARTY ID	Yes	Yes	ID
INVESTMENT VEHICLE	PRODUCT CATEGORY ID	Yes	Yes	ID
INVESTMENT VEHICLE ACCOUNT	ACCOUNT NUMBER	Yes	Yes	Numeric
INVESTOR	PARTY ID	Yes	Yes	ID
	ROLE TYPE ID	Yes	Yes	ID
INVOICE	ACCOUNT NUMBER	Yes	Yes	Numeric
	DATE	Yes	Yes	Datetime
	INVOICE ID	Yes	No	ID
	BILLED FROM PARTY ID	No	Yes	ID
	BILLED TO PARTY ID	No	Yes	ID
	BILLING ACCOUNT ID	No	Yes	ID
	DESCRIPTION	No	No	Description
	MESSAGE	No	No	Long varchar
	SENT FROM CONTACT MECH ID	No	No	ID
	SENT TO CONTACT MECH ID	No	No	ID
JOINT OWNER	PARTY ID	Yes	Yes	ID
	ROLE TYPE ID	Yes	Yes	ID
	ASSET ID	Yes	Yes	ID
LAND	FIXED ASSET ID	Yes	Yes	ID

ENTITY NAME	ATTRIBUTE NAME	PK?	FK?	DOMAIN
LEASE	PRODUCT CATEGORY ID	Yes	Yes	ID
LEASING AGREEMENT	AGREEMENT ID	Yes	Yes	ID
LENDING OBJECTIVE	FROM DATE	Yes	Yes	Datetime
	PARTY ID	Yes	Yes	ID
LINE OF CREDIT ACCOUNT	ACCOUNT NUMBER	Yes	Yes	Numeric
LIVESTOCK	ASSET ID	Yes	Yes	ID
	FIXED ASSET ID	Yes	Yes	ID
LOAN	PRODUCT CATEGORY ID	Yes	Yes	ID
LOAN ACCOUNT	ACCOUNT NUMBER	Yes	Yes	Numeric
LOAN AGREEMENT	AGREEMENT ID	Yes	Yes	ID
LOAN CUSTOMER	PARTY ID	Yes	Yes	ID
	ROLE TYPE ID	Yes	Yes	ID
LOAN PRODUCT	PRODUCT CATEGORY ID	Yes	Yes	ID
MARKET SEGMENT	MARKET SEGMENT ID	Yes	No	ID
	DESCRIPTION	No	No	Description
MARKET SEGMENT ACCOUNT	ACCOUNT NUMBER	Yes	Yes	Numeric
	MARKET SEGMENT ID	Yes	Yes	ID
	FROM DATE	Yes	No	Datetime
	THRU DATE	No	No	Datetime
MARKET SEGMENT PARTY	MARKET SEGMENT ID	Yes	Yes	ID
	PARTY ID	Yes	Yes	ID
	FROM DATE	Yes	No	Datetime
	THRU DATE	No	No	Datetime
MARKET SEGMENT TARGET	MARKET SEGMENT ID	Yes	Yes	ID
	MARKET SEGMENT SCORE	No	No	Numeric
MARKET SEGMENTS	MARKET SEGMENT ID	Yes	No	ID
	DESCRIPTION	No	No	Description
MARKETING TASK	WORK EFFORT ID	Yes	Yes	ID
MEDIA STATUS TYPE	STATUS TYPE ID	Yes	Yes	ID
MEDIA TYPE	MEDIA TYPE ID	Yes	No	ID
	DESCRIPTION	No	No	Description
MONEY MARKET	ASSET ID	Yes	Yes	ID
	PRODUCT CATEGORY ID	Yes	Yes	ID
MONEY MARKET ACCOUNT	ACCOUNT NUMBER	Yes	Yes	Numeric
MORTGAGE	PRODUCT CATEGORY ID	Yes	Yes	ID
MORTGAGE ACCOUNT	ACCOUNT NUMBER	Yes	Yes	Numeric

ENTITY NAME	ATTRIBUTE NAME	PK?	FK?	DOMAIN
MUTUAL FUND	PRODUCT CATEGORY ID	Yes	Yes	ID
MUTUAL FUND TRANSACTION	ACCOUNT NUMBER	Yes	Yes	Numeric
	ACCOUNT TRANSACTION ID	Yes	Yes	ID
NEED TYPE	NEED TYPE ID	Yes	No	ID
	DESCRIPTION	No	No	Description
NOTIFICATION TASK	WORK EFFORT ID	Yes	Yes	ID
OBJECTIVE TYPE	OBJECTIVE TYPE ID	Yes	No	ID
	DESCRIPTION	No	No	Description
ORGANIZATION	PARTY ID	Yes	Yes	ID
	NAME	No	No	Name
ORGANIZATION CONTACT RELATIONSHIP	FROM DATE	Yes	Yes	Datetime
	PARTY ID FROM	Yes	Yes	ID
	PARTY ID TO	Yes	Yes	ID
	ROLE TYPE ID FROM	Yes	Yes	ID
	ROLE TYPE ID TO	Yes	Yes	ID
ORGANIZATION REGULATION	FINANCIAL REGULATION ID	Yes	Yes	ID
ORGANIZATION ROLE	PARTY ID	Yes	Yes	ID
	ROLE TYPE ID	Yes	Yes	ID
ORGANIZATION UNIT	PARTY ID	Yes	Yes	ID
	ROLE TYPE ID	Yes	Yes	ID
OTHER ACCOUNT NOTIFICATION	ACCOUNT NUMBER	Yes	Yes	Numeric
	DATE	Yes	Yes	Datetime
OTHER NOTIFICATION TASK	WORK EFFORT ID	Yes	Yes	ID
OTHER ORGANIZATION UNIT	PARTY ID	Yes	Yes	ID
OWNER	ROLE TYPE ID	Yes	Yes	ID
OWNERS	ROLE TYPE ID	Yes	Yes	ID
	OWNER PARTY ID	Yes	No	ID
	ACCOUNT OWNER NAME	No	No	Name
	PARTY TYPE	No	No	Short varchar
PARAMETER TYPE	PARAMETER TYPE ID	Yes	No	ID
	DESCRIPTION	No	No	Description
PARENT ORGANIZATION	PARTY ID	Yes	Yes	ID
	ROLE TYPE ID	Yes	Yes	ID

ENTITY NAME	ATTRIBUTE NAME	PK?	FK?	DOMAIN
PARTICIPATING SYNDICATOR	PARTY ID	Yes	Yes	ID
PARTNER	ROLE TYPE ID	Yes	Yes	ID
	PARTY ID	Yes	Yes	ID
	ROLE TYPE ID	Yes	Yes	ID
PARTY	PARTY ID	Yes	No	ID
PARTY ACCOUNT MEDIA	ACCOUNT NUMBER	Yes	Yes	Numeric
	PARTY ID	Yes	Yes	ID
	ROLE TYPE ID	Yes	Yes	ID
	FROM DATE	Yes	No	Datetime
	MEDIA TYPE ID	No	Yes	ID
	IMPRINTED NAME	No	No	Name
	THRU DATE	No	No	Datetime
PARTY ACCOUNT MEDIA STATUS	ACCOUNT NUMBER	Yes	Yes	Numeric
	DATETIME	Yes	Yes	Datetime
	PARTY ID	Yes	Yes	ID
	ROLE TYPE ID	Yes	Yes	ID
	STATUS TYPE ID	Yes	Yes	ID
PARTY NEED	PARTY ID	Yes	Yes	ID
	PARTY NEED ID	Yes	No	ID
	NEED TYPE ID	No	Yes	ID
	PARTY TYPE ID	No	Yes	ID
	PLAN ID	No	Yes	ID
	PRODUCT CATEGORY ID	No	Yes	ID
	PRODUCT ID	No	Yes	ID
	COMMUNICATION EVENT ID	No	No	ID
	DATE TIME	No	No	Datetime
	DESCRIPTION	No	No	Description
	VISIT ID	No	No	ID
PARTY OBJECTIVE	PARTY ID	Yes	Yes	ID
	FROM DATE	Yes	No	Datetime
	OBJECTIVE TYPE ID	No	Yes	ID
	AMOUNT	No	No	Numeric
	DESCRIPTION	No	No	Description
	GOAL DATE	No	No	Datetime
	THRU DATE	No	No	Datetime
PARTY RELATIONSHIP	PARTY ID FROM	Yes	Yes	ID
	PARTY ID TO	Yes	Yes	ID
	ROLE TYPE ID FROM	Yes	Yes	ID
	ROLE TYPE ID TO	Yes	Yes	ID

ENTITY NAME	ATTRIBUTE NAME	PK?	FK?	DOMAIN
	FROM DATE	Yes	No	Datetime
	PARTY RELATIONSHIP TYPE ID	No	Yes	ID
	STATUS TYPE ID	No	Yes	ID
	COMMENTS	No	No	Comment
	PRIORITY TYPE ID	No	No	ID
	THRU DATE	No	No	Datetime
PARTY RELATIONSHIP STATUS TYPE	STATUS TYPE ID	Yes	Yes	ID
PARTY RELATIONSHIP TYPE	PARTY RELATIONSHIP TYPE ID	Yes	No	ID
	ROLE TYPE ID VALID FROM	No	Yes	ID
	ROLE TYPE ID VALID TO	No	Yes	ID
	DESCRIPTION	No	No	Description
	NAME	No	No	Name
PARTY ROLE	PARTY ID	Yes	Yes	ID
	ROLE TYPE ID	Yes	Yes	ID
	PARTY ROLE ID	No	No	ID
PARTY ROLE TYPE	ROLE TYPE ID	Yes	Yes	ID
PARTY TARGET	PARTY ID	Yes	Yes	ID
	BEHAVIOR SCORE	No	No	Numeric
PARTY TYPE	PARTY TYPE ID	Yes	No	ID
	DESCRIPTION	No	No	Description
PERSON	PARTY ID	Yes	Yes	ID
	BIRTH DATE	No	No	Datetime
	COMMENTS	No	No	Comment
	CURRENT FIRST NAME	No	No	Name
	CURRENT LAST NAME	No	No	Name
	CURRENT MIDDLE NAME	No	No	Name
	CURRENT NICKNAME	No	No	Name
	CURRENT PASSPORT EXPIRE DATE	No	No	Datetime
	CURRENT PASSPORT NUMBER	No	No	Numeric
	CURRENT PERSONAL TITLE	No	No	Name
	CURRENT SUFFIX	No	No	Name
	GENDER	No	No	Indicator
	HEIGHT	No	No	Numeric
	MARTIAL STATUS	No	No	Indicator
	MOTHER'S MAIDEN NAME	No	No	Name
	SOCIAL SECURITY NUMBER	No	No	Numeric
	TOTAL YEARS WORK EXPERIENCE	No	No	Numeric
	WEIGHT	No	No	Numeric
PERSON ROLE	PARTY ID	Yes	Yes	ID

ENTITY NAME	ATTRIBUTE NAME	PK?	FK?	DOMAIN
PLAN	ROLE TYPE ID	Yes	Yes	ID
	PLAN ID	Yes	No	ID
	PLAN TYPE ID	No	Yes	ID
	DESCRIPTION	No	No	Description
	FROM DATE	No	No	Datetime
	THRU DATE	No	No	Datetime
PLAN NEED	PARTY ID	Yes	Yes	ID
	PARTY NEED ID	Yes	Yes	ID
	PLAN ID	Yes	Yes	ID
	SCORE	No	No	Numeric
PLAN OBJECTIVE	FROM DATE	Yes	Yes	Datetime
	PARTY ID	Yes	Yes	ID
	PLAN ID	Yes	Yes	ID
	SCORE	No	No	Numeric
PLAN PRODUCT	PLAN ID	Yes	Yes	ID
	PRODUCT CATEGORY ID	No	Yes	ID
	PRODUCT ID	No	Yes	ID
	FROM DATE	No	No	Datetime
	THRU DATE	No	No	Datetime
PLAN ROLE	PARTY ID	Yes	Yes	ID
	PLAN ID	Yes	Yes	ID
	ROLE TYPE ID	Yes	Yes	ID
	THRU DATE	No	No	Datetime
PLAN ROLE TYPE	ROLE TYPE ID	Yes	Yes	ID
PLAN STATUS	PLAN ID	Yes	Yes	ID
	STATUS TYPE ID	No	No	Datetime
	DATE	No	No	Datetime
PLAN STATUS TYPE	STATUS TYPE ID	Yes	Yes	ID
PLAN TYPE	PLAN TYPE ID	Yes	No	ID
	DESCRIPTION	No	No	Description
POST TRANSACTION TASK	TRANSACTION TASK ID	Yes	Yes	ID
POWER OF ATTORNEY	ROLE TYPE ID	Yes	Yes	ID
PRE-DETERMINED TRANSACTION TASK	TRANSACTION TASK ID	Yes	Yes	ID
PRODUCT CATEGORY	PRODUCT CATEGORY ID	Yes	No	ID
	DESCRIPTION	No	No	Description
PRODUCT CATEGORY CLASSIFICATION	PRODUCT CATEGORY ID	Yes	Yes	ID
	PRODUCT ID	Yes	Yes	ID
	FROM DATE	Yes	No	Datetime
	COMMENTS	No	No	Comment

ENTITY NAME	ATTRIBUTE NAME	PK?	FK?	DOMAIN
	PRIMARY FLAG	No	No	Indicator
	THRU DATE	No	No	Datetime
PRODUCT CATEGORY FEAT FUNC APPLICABILITY	FUNCTIONAL SETTING ID	Yes	Yes	ID
	PRODUCT CATEGORY ID	Yes	Yes	ID
	PRODUCT FEATURE ID	No	Yes	ID
PRODUCT CATEGORY FEATURE APPLICABILITY	PRODUCT CATEGORY ID	Yes	Yes	ID
	PRODUCT FEATURE ID	Yes	Yes	ID
	FROM DATE	No	No	Datetime
	THRU DATE	No	No	Datetime
PRODUCT CATEGORY ROLLUP	PARTY TYPE ID MADE UP OF	Yes	Yes	ID
	PARTY TYPE ID PART OF	Yes	Yes	ID
PRODUCT FEATURE	PRODUCT FEATURE ID	Yes	No	ID
	PRODUCT FEATURE CATEGORY ID	No	Yes	ID
	DESCRIPTION	No	No	Description
PRODUCT FEATURE APPLICABILITY	PRODUCT FEATURE ID	Yes	Yes	ID
	PRODUCT ID	Yes	Yes	ID
	FROM DATE	No	No	Datetime
	THRU DATE	No	No	Datetime
	VALUE	No	No	Numeric
PRODUCT FEATURE CATEGORY	PRODUCT FEATURE CATEGORY ID	Yes	No	ID
	DESCRIPTION	No	No	Description
PROSPECT	PARTY ID	Yes	Yes	ID
	ROLE TYPE ID	Yes	Yes	ID
	FROM DATE	Yes	Yes	Datetime
PROSPECT RELATIONSHIP	PARTY ID FROM	Yes	Yes	ID
	PARTY ID TO	Yes	Yes	ID
	ROLE TYPE ID FROM	Yes	Yes	ID
	ROLE TYPE ID TO	Yes	Yes	ID
PURCHASE TRANSACTION	ACCOUNT NUMBER	Yes	Yes	Numeric
	ACCOUNT TRANSACTION ID	Yes	Yes	ID
REDEMPTION TRANSACTION	ACCOUNT NUMBER	Yes	Yes	Numeric
	ACCOUNT TRANSACTION ID	Yes	Yes	ID

ENTITY NAME	ATTRIBUTE NAME	PK?	FK?	DOMAIN
REGULATION REQUIREMENT	REGULATION REQUIREMENT ID	Yes	No	ID
	AGREEMENT ID	No	Yes	ID
	FINANCIAL REGULATION ID	No	Yes	ID
	DESCRIPTION	No	No	Description
REGULATORY AGENCY	PARTY ID	Yes	Yes	ID
	ROLE TYPE ID	Yes	Yes	ID
REVOLVING CREDIT	PRODUCT CATEGORY ID	Yes	Yes	ID
RISK ANALYSIS	WORK EFFORT ID	Yes	Yes	ID
ROLE TYPE	ROLE TYPE ID	Yes	No	ID
	DESCRIPTION	No	No	Description
SAVINGS	PRODUCT CATEGORY ID	Yes	Yes	ID
SAVINGS ACCOUNT	ACCOUNT NUMBER	Yes	Yes	Numeric
SECURITIES TRANSACTION	ACCOUNT NUMBER	Yes	Yes	Numeric
	ACCOUNT TRANSACTION ID	Yes	Yes	ID
SECURITY	ASSET ID	Yes	Yes	ID
	PRODUCT CATEGORY ID	Yes	Yes	ID
SELL TRANSACTION	ACCOUNT NUMBER	Yes	Yes	Numeric
	ACCOUNT TRANSACTION ID	Yes	Yes	ID
SHAREHOLDER	PARTY ID	Yes	Yes	ID
	ROLE TYPE ID	Yes	Yes	ID
SHAREHOLDER RELATIONSHIP	FROM DATE	Yes	Yes	Datetime
	PARTY ID FROM	Yes	Yes	ID
	PARTY ID TO	Yes	Yes	ID
	ROLE TYPE ID FROM	Yes	Yes	ID
	ROLE TYPE ID TO	Yes	Yes	ID
SPECIAL REQUEST	ACCOUNT NUMBER	Yes	Yes	Numeric
	ACCOUNT TRANSACTION ID	Yes	Yes	ID
STATEMENT	ACCOUNT NUMBER	Yes	Yes	Numeric
	DATE	Yes	Yes	Datetime
STATEMENT FEATURE	PRODUCT FEATURE ID	Yes	Yes	ID
STATEMENT TASK	WORK EFFORT ID	Yes	Yes	ID
STATUS TYPE	STATUS TYPE ID	Yes	No	ID
	DESCRIPTION	No	No	Description
SUBSIDIARY	PARTY ID	Yes	Yes	ID
	ROLE TYPE ID	Yes	Yes	ID
SUPPLIER	PARTY ID	Yes	Yes	ID
	ROLE TYPE ID	Yes	Yes	ID

ENTITY NAME	ATTRIBUTE NAME	PK?	FK?	DOMAIN
SUPPLIER RELATIONSHIP	FROM DATE	Yes	Yes	Datetime
	PARTY ID FROM	Yes	Yes	ID
	PARTY ID TO	Yes	Yes	ID
	ROLE TYPE ID FROM	Yes	Yes	ID
	ROLE TYPE ID TO	Yes	Yes	ID
SYNDICATOR RELATIONSHIP	FROM DATE	Yes	Yes	Datetime
	PARTY ID FROM	Yes	Yes	ID
	PARTY ID TO	Yes	Yes	ID
	ROLE TYPE ID FROM	Yes	Yes	ID
	ROLE TYPE ID TO	Yes	Yes	ID
TIME BY DAY	DAY ID	Yes	No	ID
	DAY	No	No	Very short
	MONTH	No	No	Very short
	QUARTER	No	No	Very short
	WEEK	No	No	Very short
	YEAR	No	No	Very short
TIME BY WEEK	WEEK ID	Yes	No	ID
	MONTH	No	No	Very short
	QUARTER	No	No	Very short
	WEEK	No	No	Very short
	YEAR	No	No	Very short
TIME DEPOSIT	PRODUCT CATEGORY ID	Yes	Yes	ID
TIME FREQUENCY	UOM ID	Yes	Yes	ID
TRANSACTION STATUS TYPE	STATUS TYPE ID	Yes	Yes	ID
UNIT OF MEASURE	UOM ID	Yes	No	ID
	ABBREVIATION	No	No	Short varchar
	DESCRIPTION	No	No	Description
VEHICLE	ASSET ID	Yes	Yes	ID
	FIXED ASSET ID	Yes	Yes	ID
VEHICLE LOAN ACCOUNT	ACCOUNT NUMBER	Yes	Yes	Numeric
WITHDRAWAL	ACCOUNT NUMBER	Yes	Yes	Numeric
	ACCOUNT TRANSACTION ID	Yes	Yes	ID

ENTITY NAME	ATTRIBUTE NAME	PK?	FK?	DOMAIN
	FINANCIAL ACCOUNT TRANS ID	Yes	No	ID
	PAYMENT ID	No	No	ID
WORK EFFORT	WORK EFFORT ID	Yes	No	ID
	ASSET ID	No	Yes	ID
	FIXED ASSET ID	No	Yes	ID
	VERSION OF WORK EFFORT ID	No	Yes	ID
	ACTUAL COMPLETION DATETIME	No	No	Datetime
	ACTUAL HOURS	No	No	Numeric
	ACTUAL START DATETIME	No	No	Datetime
	DESCRIPTION	No	No	Description
	ESTIMATED HOURS	No	No	Numeric
	FACILITY ID	No	No	ID
	NAME	No	No	Name
	SCHEDULED COMPLETION DATE	No	No	Datetime
	SCHEDULED START DATE	No	No	Datetime
	SPECIAL TERMS	No	No	Long varchar
	TOTAL DOLLARS ALLOWED	No	No	Currency amount
	TOTAL HOURS ALLOWED	No	No	Numeric
	WORK EFFORT PURPOSE TYPE ID	No	No	ID
	WORK EFFORT TYPE ID	No	No	ID
WORK EFFORT STATUS	STATUS TYPE ID	Yes	Yes	ID
	WORK EFFORT ID	Yes	Yes	ID
	DATETIME	No	No	Datetime
WORK EFFORT STATUS TYPE	STATUS TYPE ID	Yes	Yes	ID
WORKER	PARTY ID	Yes	Yes	ID
	ROLE TYPE ID	Yes	Yes	ID

Entities and Attributes for Professional Services Models

This appendix lists the entities and attributes from the logical data models and star schemas found in Chapter 7, "Professional Services." This listing includes the entity names, attribute names, primary key indicators, foreign key indicators, and the domain for each attribute.

The domain indicates a standard set of characteristics that can be applied to attributes, including its datatype and length. Table A.1 defines the nature of each domain. When applying the domains to the attributes listed in these appendices, refer to Table A.1 for recommendations on what datatype and length to use when implementing these models. Of course, the datatype and length of each attribute should be adjusted as appropriate to meet the specific needs of the enterprise.

The domain definitions as they are applied to the attributes in the appendices are used for the SQL code that is containedon the demo CD-ROM at the back of this book as well as in the Industry Downloads (see the section "How to Use the Volume 2 Industry Electronic Products" for more information).

Entities and Attributes Listing for Professional Services Models

ENTITY NAME	ATTRIBUTE NAME	PK?	FK?	DOMAIN
ACTIVITY	WORK EFFORT ID	Yes	Yes	ID
AGREEMENT	AGREEMENT ID	Yes	No	ID
	FROM DATE	No	Yes	Datetime
	PARTY ID FROM	No	Yes	ID
	PARTY ID TO	No	Yes	ID
	ROLE TYPE ID FROM	No	Yes	ID
	ROLE TYPE ID TO	No	Yes	ID
	AGREEMENT DATE	No	No	Datetime
	AGREEMENT TYPE ID	No	No	ID
	DESCRIPTION	No	No	Description
	PRODUCT ID	No	No	ID
	TEXT	No	No	Long varchar
	THRU DATE	No	No	Datetime
AGREEMENT ITEM	AGREEMENT ID	Yes	Yes	ID
	AGREEMENT ITEM SEQ ID	Yes	No	ID
	PART OF AGREEMENT ID	No	Yes	ID
	PART OF AGREEMENT ITEM SEQ ID	No	Yes	ID
	AGREEMENT IMAGE	No	No	Blob
	AGREEMENT TEXT	No	No	Long varchar
AGREEMENT PRICING PROGRAM	AGREEMENT ID	Yes	Yes	ID
AGREEMENT TERM	AGREEMENT ITEM SEQ ID	Yes	Yes	ID
	TERM TYPE ID	Yes	Yes	ID
	AGREEMENT TERM ID	Yes	No	ID
	AGREEMENT ID	No	Yes	ID
	AGREEMENT ITEM SEQ ID	No	Yes	ID
	FROM DATE	No	No	Datetime
	TERM VALUE	No	No	Numeric
	THRU DATE	No	No	Datetime
ASSOCIATION	PARTY ID	Yes	Yes	ID
	ROLE TYPE ID	Yes	Yes	ID
BILL TO CLIENT	PARTY ID	Yes	Yes	ID
	ROLE TYPE ID	Yes	Yes	ID
BILLING FEATURE	PRODUCT FEATURE ID	Yes	Yes	ID
CLIENT	PARTY ID	Yes	Yes	ID
	ROLE TYPE ID	Yes	Yes	ID
CLIENT RELATIONSHIP	FROM DATE	Yes	Yes	Datetime

ENTITY NAME	ATTRIBUTE NAME	PK?	FK?	DOMAIN
	PARTY ID FROM	Yes	Yes	ID
	PARTY ID TO	Yes	Yes	ID
	ROLE TYPE ID FROM	Yes	Yes	ID
	ROLE TYPE ID TO	Yes	Yes	ID
CLIENT REQUIREMENT	REQUIREMENT ID	Yes	Yes	ID
CLIENTS	CLIENT PARTY ID	Yes	No	ID
	CLIENT NAME	No	No	ID
COMMUNICATION EVENT	COMMUNICATION EVENT ID	Yes	No	ID
	FROM DATE	No	Yes	Datetime
	PARTY ID FROM	No	Yes	ID
	PARTY ID TO	No	Yes	ID
	ROLE TYPE ID FROM	No	Yes	ID
	ROLE TYPE ID TO	No	Yes	ID
	CASE ID	No	No	ID
	CONTACT MECHANISM TYPE ID	No	No	ID
	DATETIME ENDED	No	No	Datetime
	DATETIME STARTED	No	No	Datetime
	NOTE	No	No	Comment
	STATUS TYPE ID	No	No	ID
COMMUNICATION EVENT PURPOSE	COMMUNICATION EVENT ID	Yes	Yes	ID
	COMMUNICATION EVENT PRP TYP ID	Yes	No	ID
	DESCRIPTION	No	No	Description
COMPETITOR	PARTY ID	Yes	Yes	ID
	ROLE TYPE ID	Yes	Yes	ID
CONTACT	PARTY ID	Yes	Yes	ID
	ROLE TYPE ID	Yes	Yes	ID
CONTACT MECHANISM	CONTACT MECHANISM ID	Yes	No	ID
	CONTACT MECHANISM TYPE ID	No	No	ID
CONTRACTOR	PARTY ID	Yes	Yes	ID
	ROLE TYPE ID	Yes	Yes	ID
CUSTOM ENGAGEMENT ITEM	ENGAGEMENT ID	Yes	Yes	ID
	ENGAGEMENT ITEM SEQ ID	Yes	Yes	ID

ENTITY NAME	ATTRIBUTE NAME	PK?	FK?	DOMAIN
	AGREEMENT ID	No	Yes	ID
	CLIENT PURCHASE ORDER NUMBER	No	No	Numeric
	ENGAGEMENT CONTRACT DATE	No	No	Datetime
	ENGAGEMENT DATE	No	No	Datetime
	ENGAGEMENT DESCRIPTION	No	No	Description
	ENGAGEMENT END DATE	No	No	Datetime
	ENGAGEMENT START DATE	No	No	Datetime
	ESTIMATED AMOUNT	No	No	Currency amount
	MAXIMUM AMOUNT	No	No	Currency amount
ENGAGEMENT ITEM	ENGAGEMENT ID	Yes	Yes	ID
	ENGAGEMENT ITEM SEQ ID	Yes	No	ID
	PRODUCT FEATURE ID	No	Yes	ID
	PRODUCT ID	No	Yes	ID
	QUOTE ID	No	Yes	ID
	QUOTED ITEM SEQ ID	No	Yes	ID
	EXPECTED END DATE	No	No	Datetime
	EXPECTED START DATE	No	No	Datetime
ENGAGEMENT ITEM TYPES	ENGAGEMENT ITEM TYPE ID	Yes	No	ID
	DESCRIPTION	No	No	Description
ENGAGEMENT RATE	ENGAGEMENT ID	Yes	Yes	ID
	ENGAGEMENT ITEM SEQ ID	Yes	Yes	ID
	RATE TYPE ID	Yes	Yes	ID
	FROM DATE	Yes	No	Datetime
	UOM ID	No	Yes	ID
	BILLING RATE	No	No	Currency amount
	CHANGE REASON	No	No	Long varchar
	COST	No	No	Currency amount
	THRU DATE	No	No	Datetime
ENGAGEMENT WORK FULFILLMENT	ENGAGEMENT ID	Yes	Yes	ID
	ENGAGEMENT ITEM SEQ ID	Yes	Yes	ID
	WORK EFFORT ID	Yes	Yes	ID
EXPENSE ENTRY	SERVICE ENTRY ID	Yes	Yes	ID
	AMOUNT	No	No	Currency amount
FACILITY	FACILITY ID	Yes	No	ID

ENTITY NAME	ATTRIBUTE NAME	PK?	FK?	DOMAIN
CUSTOM ENGAGEMENT ITEM	AGREED UPON PRICE	No	No	Currency amount
	DESCRIPTION OF WORK	No	No	Description
DELIVERABLE	DELIVERABLE ID	Yes	No	ID
	DELIVERABLE TYPE ID	No	Yes	ID
	DESCRIPTION	No	No	Description
	NAME	No	No	Name
DELIVERABLE BASED SERVICE	PRODUCT ID	Yes	Yes	ID
DELIVERABLE ORDER ITEM	ENGAGEMENT ID	Yes	Yes	ID
	ENGAGEMENT ITEM SEQ ID	Yes	Yes	ID
	ORDER ID	Yes	Yes	ID
	ORDER ITEM SEQ ID	Yes	Yes	ID
	AGREED UPON PRICE	No	No	Currency amount
DELIVERABLE TURNOVER	SERVICE ENTRY ID	Yes	Yes	ID
	AMOUNT	No	No	Currency amount
DELIVERABLE TYPE	DELIVERABLE TYPE ID	Yes	No	ID
	DESCRIPTION	No	No	Description
DELIVERY CLIENT	PARTY ID	Yes	Yes	ID
	ROLE TYPE ID	Yes	Yes	ID
DEPARTMENT	PARTY ID	Yes	Yes	ID
	ROLE TYPE ID	Yes	Yes	ID
DESIRED FEATURE	REQUIREMENT ID	Yes	Yes	ID
	DESIRED FEATURE ID	Yes	No	ID
	PRODUCT FEATURE ID	No	Yes	ID
	OPTIONAL IND	No	No	Indicator
DIVISION	PARTY ID	Yes	Yes	ID
	ROLE TYPE ID	Yes	Yes	ID
EMPLOYEE	PARTY ID	Yes	Yes	ID
	ROLE TYPE ID	Yes	Yes	ID
EMPLOYMENT	FROM DATE	Yes	Yes	Datetime
	PARTY ID FROM	Yes	Yes	ID
	PARTY ID TO	Yes	Yes	ID
	ROLE TYPE ID FROM	Yes	Yes	ID
	ROLE TYPE ID TO	Yes	Yes	ID
	TERMINATION REASON ID	No	No	ID
	TERMINATION TYPE ID	No	No	ID
ENGAGEMENT	ENGAGEMENT ID	Yes	No	ID

ENTITY NAME	ATTRIBUTE NAME	PK?	FK?	DOMAIN
	PART OF FACILITY ID	No	Yes	ID
	DESCRIPTION	No	No	Description
	FACILITY NAME	No	No	Name
	FACILITY TYPE ID	No	No	ID
	SQUARE FOOTAGE	No	No	Numeric
GOOD	PRODUCT ID	Yes	Yes	ID
	PART ID	No	No	ID
GOOD ORDER ITEM	ENGAGEMENT ID	Yes	Yes	ID
	ENGAGEMENT ITEM SEQ ID	Yes	Yes	ID
	ORDER ID	Yes	Yes	ID
	ORDER ITEM SEQ ID	Yes	Yes	ID
	PRODUCT FEATURE ID	No	Yes	ID
	PRICE	No	No	Currency amount
	QUANTITY	No	No	Numeric
INTERNAL ORGANIZATION	PARTY ID	Yes	Yes	ID
INTERNAL REQUIREMENT	ROLE TYPE ID	Yes	Yes	ID
	REQUIREMENT ID	Yes	Yes	ID
INVOICE	INVOICE ID	Yes	No	ID
	BILLED FROM PARTY ID	No	Yes	ID
	BILLED TO PARTY ID	No	Yes	ID
	SENT FROM CONTACT MECH ID	No	Yes	ID
	SENT TO CONTACT MECH ID	No	Yes	ID
	BILLING ACCOUNT ID	No	Yes	ID
	DESCRIPTION	No	No	Description
	INVOICE DATE	No	No	Datetime
	MESSAGE	No	No	Long varchar
	PARTY ID	No	No	ID
	ROLE TYPE ID	No	No	ID
INVOICE ITEM	INVOICE ID	Yes	Yes	ID
	INVOICE ITEM SEQ ID	Yes	No	ID
	ADJUSTED BY INVOICE ID	No	Yes	ID
	ADJUSTED BY INVOICE ITEM SEQ ID	No	Yes	ID
	INVOICE ITEM TYPE ID	No	Yes	ID
	PRODUCT FEATURE ID	No	Yes	ID
	PRODUCT ID	No	Yes	ID
	SOLD WITH INVOICE ID	No	Yes	ID

ENTITY NAME	ATTRIBUTE NAME	PK?	FK?	DOMAIN
	SOLD WITH INVOICE ITEM SEQ ID	No	Yes	ID
	UOM ID	No	Yes	ID
	AMOUNT	No	No	Currency amount
	INVENTORY ITEM ID	No	No	ID
	ITEM DESCRIPTION	No	No	Description
	QUANTITY	No	No	Numeric
	TAXABLE FLAG	No	No	Indicator
INVOICE ITEM TYPE	INVOICE ITEM TYPE ID	Yes	No	ID
	DESCRIPTION	No	No	Description
MARKETING PACKAGE	FROM DATE	Yes	Yes	Datetime
	PRODUCT ID FROM	Yes	Yes	ID
	PRODUCT ID TO	Yes	Yes	ID
	INSTRUCTION	No	No	Long varchar
	QUANTITY USED	No	No	Numeric
MATERIALS USAGE	SERVICE ENTRY ID	Yes	Yes	ID
	AMOUNT	No	No	Currency amount
NEEDED DELIVERABLE	DELIVERABLE TYPE ID	Yes	Yes	ID
	REQUIREMENT ID	Yes	Yes	ID
NEEDED SKILL	REQUIREMENT ID	Yes	Yes	ID
	SKILL TYPE ID	Yes	Yes	ID
	SKILL LEVEL	No	No	Numeric
	YEARS EXPERIENCE	No	No	Numeric
ORGANIZATION CONTACT RELATIONSHIP	FROM DATE	Yes	Yes	Datetime
	PARTY ID FROM	Yes	Yes	ID
	PARTY ID TO	Yes	Yes	ID
	ROLE TYPE ID FROM	Yes	Yes	ID
	ROLE TYPE ID TO	Yes	Yes	ID
ORGANIZATION ROLE	PARTY ID	Yes	Yes	ID
	ROLE TYPE ID	Yes	Yes	ID
ORGANIZATION ROLLUP	FROM DATE	Yes	Yes	Datetime
	PARTY ID FROM	Yes	Yes	ID
	PARTY ID TO	Yes	Yes	ID
	ROLE TYPE ID FROM	Yes	Yes	ID
	ROLE TYPE ID TO	Yes	Yes	ID
ORGANIZATION UNIT	PARTY ID	Yes	Yes	ID

ENTITY NAME	ATTRIBUTE NAME	PK?	FK?	DOMAIN
	ROLE TYPE ID	Yes	Yes	ID
OTHER ENGAGEMENT ITEM	ENGAGEMENT ID	Yes	Yes	ID
	ENGAGEMENT ITEM SEQ ID	Yes	Yes	ID
	AMAOUNT	No	No	Currency amount
OTHER FEATURE	PRODUCT FEATURE ID	Yes	Yes	ID
OTHER ORGANIZATION UNIT	PARTY ID	Yes	Yes	ID
PARENT ORGANIZATION	ROLE TYPE ID	Yes	Yes	ID
	PARTY ID	Yes	Yes	ID
PARTNER	ROLE TYPE ID	Yes	Yes	ID
	PARTY ID	Yes	Yes	ID
	ROLE TYPE ID	Yes	Yes	ID
PARTNERSHIP	FROM DATE	Yes	Yes	Datetime
	PARTY ID FROM	Yes	Yes	ID
	PARTY ID TO	Yes	Yes	ID
	ROLE TYPE ID FROM	Yes	Yes	ID
	ROLE TYPE ID TO	Yes	Yes	ID
PARTY	PARTY ID	Yes	No	ID
PARTY RELATIONSHIP	PARTY ID FROM	Yes	Yes	ID
	PARTY ID TO	Yes	Yes	ID
	ROLE TYPE ID FROM	Yes	Yes	ID
	ROLE TYPE ID TO	Yes	Yes	ID
	FROM DATE	Yes	No	Datetime
	PARTY RELATIONSHIP TYPE ID	No	Yes	ID
	COMMENTS	No	No	Comment
	PRIORITY TYPE ID	No	No	ID
	STATUS TYPE ID	No	No	ID
	THRU DATE	No	No	Datetime
PARTY RELATIONSHIP TYPE	PARTY RELATIONSHIP TYPE ID	Yes	No	ID
	ROLE TYPE ID VALID FROM	No	Yes	ID
	ROLE TYPE ID VALID TO	No	Yes	ID
	DESCRIPTION	No	No	Description
	NAME	No	No	Name
PARTY ROLE	PARTY ID	Yes	Yes	ID
	ROLE TYPE ID	Yes	Yes	ID
	PARTY ROLE ID	No	No	ID
PARTY ROLE TYPE	ROLE TYPE ID	Yes	Yes	ID
PERSON ROLE	PARTY ID	Yes	Yes	ID

ENTITY NAME	ATTRIBUTE NAME	PK?	FK?	DOMAIN
	ROLE TYPE ID	Yes	Yes	ID
PRICE COMPONENT	PRICE COMPONENT ID	Yes	No	ID
	AGREEMENT ID	No	Yes	ID
	AGREEMENT ITEM SEQ ID	No	Yes	ID
	ENGAGEMENT ID	No	Yes	ID
	ENGAGEMENT ITEM SEQ ID	No	Yes	ID
	FROM DATE	No	Yes	Datetime
	PRODUCT CATEGORY ID	No	Yes	ID
	PRODUCT FEATURE ID	No	Yes	ID
	PRODUCT ID	No	Yes	ID
	RATE TYPE ID	No	Yes	ID
	COMMENTS	No	No	Comment
	GEOGRAPHIC LOCATION ID	No	No	ID
	ORDER VALUE ID	No	No	ID
	PARTY ID	No	No	ID
	PARTY TYPE ID	No	No	ID
	PERCENT	No	No	Floating point
	PRICE	No	No	Currency amount
	QUANTITY BREAK ID	No	No	ID
	SALE TYPE ID	No	No	ID
	THRU DATE	No	No	Datetime
	UOM ID	No	No	ID
PRODUCT	PRODUCT ID	Yes	No	ID
	UOM ID	No	Yes	ID
	COMMENTS	No	No	Comment
	DESCRIPTION	No	No	Description
	INTRODUCTION DATE	No	No	Datetime
	MANUFACTURER PARTY ID	No	No	ID
	NAME	No	No	Name
	PART ID	No	No	ID
	SALES DISCONTINUATION DATE	No	No	Datetime
	SUPPORT DISCONTINUATION DATE	No	No	Datetime
PRODUCT ASSOCIATION	PRODUCT ID FROM	Yes	Yes	ID
	PRODUCT ID TO	Yes	Yes	ID
	FROM DATE	Yes	No	Datetime
	REASON	No	No	Long varchar
	THRU DATE	No	No	Datetime

ENTITY NAME	ATTRIBUTE NAME	PK?	FK?	DOMAIN
PRODUCT ORDER ITEM	ENGAGEMENT ID	Yes	Yes	ID
	ENGAGEMENT ITEM SEQ ID	Yes	Yes	ID
	ORDER ID	Yes	No	ID
	ORDER ITEM SEQ ID	Yes	No	ID
	PRODUCT ID	No	Yes	ID
PRODUCT REQUIREMENT	REQUIREMENT ID	Yes	Yes	ID
	PRODUCT ID	No	Yes	ID
PROFESSIONAL	PARTY ID	Yes	Yes	ID
	ROLE TYPE ID	Yes	Yes	ID
PROFESSIONAL ASSIGNMENT	ENGAGEMENT ID	Yes	Yes	ID
	ENGAGEMENT ITEM SEQ ID	Yes	Yes	ID
	PARTY ID	Yes	Yes	ID
	ROLE TYPE ID	Yes	Yes	ID
	FROM DATE	Yes	No	Datetime
	THRU DATE	No	No	Datetime
PROFESSIONAL PLACEMENT	ENGAGEMENT ID	No	No	ID
	ENGAGEMENT ITEM SEQ ID	Yes	Yes	ID
PROFESSIONAL SERVICES PROVIDER	PARTY ID	Yes	Yes	ID
	ROLE TYPE ID	Yes	Yes	ID
PROFESSIONALS	PROFESSIONAL PARTY ID	Yes	No	ID
	PROFESSIONAL NAME	No	No	Name
PROGRAM	WORK EFFORT ID	Yes	Yes	ID
PROJECT REQUIREMENT	REQUIREMENT ID	Yes	Yes	ID
PROJECTS	WORK EFFORT ID	Yes	No	ID
	DESCRIPTION	No	No	Description
	WORK EFFORT TYPE	No	No	Description
PROSPECT	PARTY ID	Yes	Yes	ID
	ROLE TYPE ID	Yes	Yes	ID
PURCHASE INVOICE ITEM	INVOICE ID	Yes	Yes	ID
	INVOICE ITEM SEQ ID	Yes	Yes	ID
QUOTE	QUOTE ID	Yes	No	ID
	CREATOR OF PARTY ID	No	Yes	ID
	RECEIVER OF PARTY ID	No	Yes	ID
	DESCRIPTION	No	No	Description
	ISSUE DATE	No	No	Datetime

ENTITY NAME	ATTRIBUTE NAME	PK?	FK?	DOMAIN
PRODUCT CATEGORY	PRODUCT CATEGORY ID	Yes	No	ID
	DESCRIPTION	No	No	Description
PRODUCT CATEGORY CLASSIFICATION	PRODUCT CATEGORY ID	Yes	Yes	ID
	PRODUCT ID	Yes	Yes	ID
	FROM DATE	Yes	No	Datetime
	COMMENTS	No	No	Comment
	PRIMARY FLAG	No	No	Indicator
	THRU DATE	No	No	Datetime
PRODUCT CATEGORY ROLLUP	PARTY TYPE ID MADE UP OF	Yes	Yes	ID
	PARTY TYPE ID PART OF	Yes	Yes	ID
PRODUCT COMPLEMENT	FROM DATE	Yes	Yes	Datetime
	PRODUCT ID FROM	Yes	Yes	ID
	PRODUCT ID TO	Yes	Yes	ID
	REASON	No	No	Long varchar
PRODUCT DELIVERY SKILL REQUIREMENT	PRODUCT ID	Yes	Yes	ID
	SKILL TYPE ID	Yes	Yes	ID
	SKILL LEVEL	No	No	Short varchar
	STARTED USING DATE	No	No	Datetime
	YEARS EXPERIENCE	No	No	Numeric
PRODUCT FEATURE	PRODUCT FEATURE ID	Yes	No	ID
	DESCRIPTION	No	No	Description
	PRODUCT FEATURE CATEGORY ID	No	No	ID
PRODUCT FEATURE APPLICABILITY	PRODUCT FEATURE ID	Yes	Yes	ID
	PRODUCT ID	Yes	Yes	ID
	FROM DATE	Yes	No	Datetime
	THRU DATE	No	No	Datetime
PRODUCT INDUSTRY CATEGORIZATION	PRODUCT CATEGORY ID	Yes	Yes	ID
PRODUCT OBSOLESCENCE	FROM DATE	Yes	Yes	Datetime
	PRODUCT ID FROM	Yes	Yes	ID
	PRODUCT ID TO	Yes	Yes	ID
	REASON	No	No	Long varchar
	SUPERCESSION DATE	No	No	Datetime

ENTITY NAME	ATTRIBUTE NAME	PK?	FK?	DOMAIN
	VALID FROM DATE	No	No	Datetime
	VALID THRU DATE	No	No	Datetime
QUOTE ITEM	QUOTE ID	Yes	Yes	ID
	QUOTED ITEM SEQ ID	Yes	No	ID
	DELIVERABLE TYPE ID	No	Yes	ID
	PRODUCT FEATURE ID	No	Yes	ID
	PRODUCT ID	No	Yes	ID
	REQUEST ID	No	Yes	ID
	REQUEST ITEM SEQ ID	No	Yes	ID
	SKILL TYPE ID	No	Yes	ID
	UOM ID	No	Yes	ID
	WORK EFFORT ID	No	Yes	ID
	COMMENTS	No	No	Comment
	ESTIMATED DELIVERY DATE	No	No	Datetime
	QUANTITY	No	No	Numeric
	QUOTE UNIT PRICE	No	No	Currency amount
QUOTE ROLE	PARTY ID	Yes	Yes	ID
	QUOTE ID	Yes	Yes	ID
	ROLE TYPE ID	Yes	Yes	ID
QUOTE ROLE TYPE	ROLE TYPE ID	Yes	Yes	ID
QUOTE TERM	TERM TYPE ID	Yes	Yes	ID
	QUOTE TERM ID	Yes	No	ID
	QUOTE ID	No	Yes	ID
	QUOTED ITEM SEQ ID	No	Yes	ID
	TERM VALUE	No	No	Numeric
RATE TYPE	RATE TYPE ID	Yes	No	ID
	DESCRIPTION	No	No	Description
RATE TYPES	RATE TYPE ID	Yes	No	ID
	DESCRIPTION	No	No	Description
REQUEST	REQUEST ID	Yes	No	ID
	DESCRIPTION	No	No	Description
	REQUEST DATE	No	No	Datetime
	RESPONSE REQUIRED DATE	No	No	Datetime
REQUEST ITEM	REQUEST ID	Yes	Yes	ID
	REQUEST ITEM SEQ ID	Yes	No	ID
	DESCRIPTION	No	No	Description
	MAXIMUM AMOUNT	No	No	Currency amount
	QUANTITY	No	No	Numeric
	REQUIRED BY DATE	No	No	Datetime
REQUEST ROLE	PARTY ID	Yes	Yes	ID

ENTITY NAME	ATTRIBUTE NAME	PK?	FK?	DOMAIN
	REQUEST ID	Yes	Yes	ID
	ROLE TYPE ID	Yes	Yes	ID
REQUEST ROLE TYPE	ROLE TYPE ID	Yes	No	ID
REQUIREMENT	REQUIREMENT ID	Yes	No	ID
	FACILITY ID	No	Yes	ID
	PART OF REQUIREMENT ID	No	Yes	ID
	DESCRIPTION	No	No	Description
	ESTIMATED BUDGET	No	No	Currency amount
	QUANTITY	No	No	Numeric
	REASON	No	No	Long varchar
	REQUIRED BY DATE	No	No	Datetime
	REQUIREMENT CREATION DATE	No	No	Datetime
	REQUIREMENT TYPE ID	No	No	ID
REQUIREMENT ACTIVITY	COMMUNICATION EVENT ID	Yes	Yes	ID
	COMMUNICATION EVENT PRP TYP ID	Yes	Yes	ID
REQUIREMENT COMMUNICATION	COMMUNICATION EVENT ID	Yes	Yes	ID
	REQUIREMENT ID	Yes	Yes	ID
	PARTY ID	No	Yes	ID
	ROLE TYPE ID	No	Yes	ID
REQUIREMENT REQUEST	REQUEST ID	Yes	Yes	ID
	REQUEST ITEM SEQ ID	Yes	Yes	ID
	REQUIREMENT ID	Yes	Yes	ID
REQUIREMENT ROLE	PARTY ID	Yes	Yes	ID
	REQUIREMENT ID	Yes	Yes	ID
	ROLE TYPE ID	Yes	Yes	ID
	FROM DATE	Yes	No	Datetime
	THRU DATE	No	No	Datetime
REQUIREMENT ROLE TYPE	ROLE TYPE ID	Yes	Yes	ID
REQUIREMENT STATUS	REQUIREMENT ID	Yes	Yes	ID
	STATUS TYPE ID	Yes	Yes	ID
	STATUS DATE	No	No	Datetime
REQUIREMENT STATUS TYPE	STATUS TYPE ID	Yes	No	ID
RESOURCE REQUIREMENT	REQUIREMENT ID	Yes	Yes	ID

ENTITY NAME	ATTRIBUTE NAME	PK?	FK?	DOMAIN
	DUTIES	No	No	Long varchar
	NUM OF POSITIONS	No	No	Numeric
	REQUIRED END DATE	No	No	Datetime
	REQUIRED START DATE	No	No	Datetime
RESPONDING PARTY	PARTY ID	Yes	Yes	ID
	REQUEST ID	Yes	Yes	ID
	RESPONDING PARTY SEQ ID	Yes	No	ID
	CONTACT MECHANISM ID	No	Yes	ID
	DATE SENT	No	No	Datetime
RFI	REQUEST ID	Yes	Yes	ID
RFP	REQUEST ID	Yes	Yes	ID
RFQ	REQUEST ID	Yes	Yes	ID
ROLE TYPE	ROLE TYPE ID	Yes	No	ID
	DESCRIPTION	No	No	Description
SALES INVOICE ITEM	INVOICE ID	Yes	Yes	ID
	INVOICE ITEM SEQ ID	Yes	Yes	ID
SERVICE	PRODUCT ID	Yes	No	ID
SERVICE ENTRY	SERVICE ENTRY ID	No	No	ID
	ENGAGEMENT ID	No	Yes	ID
	ENGAGEMENT ITEM SEQ ID	No	Yes	ID
	SERVICE ENTRY HEADER ID	No	Yes	ID
	SERVICE ENTRY TYPE ID	No	Yes	ID
	WORK EFFORT ID	No	Yes	ID
	BILLABLE IND	No	No	Indicator
	DESCRIPTION	No	No	Description
	FROM DATE	No	No	Datetime
	THRU DATE	No	No	Datetime
SERVICE ENTRY BILLING	INVOICE ID	Yes	Yes	ID
	INVOICE ITEM SEQ ID	Yes	Yes	ID
	SERVICE ENTRY ID	Yes	No	ID
SERVICE ENTRY HEADER	SERVICE ENTRY HEADER ID	Yes	No	ID
	PARTY ID	No	Yes	ID
	ROLE TYPE ID	No	Yes	ID
	ENTRY DATE	No	No	Datetime
	FROM DATE	No	No	Datetime
	SUBMITTED DATE	No	No	Datetime
	THRU DATE	No	No	Datetime
SERVICE ENTRY TYPE	SERVICE ENTRY TYPE ID	Yes	No	ID
	DESCRIPTION	No	No	Description

ENTITY NAME	ATTRIBUTE NAME	PK?	FK?	DOMAIN
SERVICE FEATURE	PRODUCT FEATURE ID	Yes	Yes	ID
SHAREHOLDER	PARTY ID	Yes	Yes	ID
	ROLE TYPE ID	Yes	Yes	ID
SKILL TYPE	SKILL TYPE ID	Yes	No	ID
	DESCRIPTION	No	No	Description
SOFTWARE FEATURE	PRODUCT FEATURE ID	Yes	Yes	ID
STANDARD SERVICE ORDER ITEM	ENGAGEMENT ID	Yes	Yes	ID
	ENGAGEMENT ITEM SEQ ID	Yes	Yes	ID
	ORDER ID	Yes	Yes	ID
	ORDER ITEM SEQ ID	Yes	Yes	ID
SUBCONTRACTOR RELATIONSHIP	FROM DATE	Yes	Yes	Datetime
	PARTY ID FROM	Yes	Yes	ID
	PARTY ID TO	Yes	Yes	ID
	ROLE TYPE ID FROM	Yes	Yes	ID
	ROLE TYPE ID TO	Yes	Yes	ID
SUBSIDIARY	PARTY ID	Yes	Yes	ID
	ROLE TYPE ID	Yes	Yes	ID
SUPPLIER	PARTY ID	Yes	Yes	ID
	ROLE TYPE ID	Yes	Yes	ID
SUPPLIER RELATIONSHIP	FROM DATE	Yes	Yes	Datetime
	PARTY ID FROM	Yes	Yes	ID
	PARTY ID TO	Yes	Yes	ID
	ROLE TYPE ID FROM	Yes	Yes	ID
	ROLE TYPE ID TO	Yes	Yes	ID
TASK	WORK EFFORT ID	Yes	Yes	ID
TECHNICAL PRODUCT CLASSIFICATION	PRODUCT CATEGORY ID	Yes	Yes	ID
TERM TYPE	TERM TYPE ID	Yes	No	ID
	DESCRIPTION	No	No	Description
TIME AND MATERIALS SERVICE	PRODUCT ID	Yes	Yes	ID
TIME BY DAY	DAY ID	Yes	No	ID
	DAY	No	No	Very short
	MONTH	No	No	Very short
	QUARTER	No	No	Very short
	WEEK	No	No	Very short
	YEAR	No	No	Very short
TIME ENTRY	SERVICE ENTRY ID	Yes	Yes	ID
	RATE TYPE ID	No	Yes	ID

ENTITY NAME	ATTRIBUTE NAME	PK?	FK?	DOMAIN
	UOM ID	No	Yes	ID
	WORK EFFORT ID	No	Yes	ID
	AMOUNT OF TIME	No	No	Numeric
	BILLING RATE	No	No	Currency amount
	COMMENTS	No	No	Comment
	COST	No	No	Currency amount
	FROM DATETIME	No	No	Datetime
	HOURS	No	No	Numeric
	PARTY ID	No	No	ID
	ROLE TYPE ID	No	No	ID
	THRU DATETIME	No	No	Datetime
TIME ENTRY FACT	CLIENT PARTY ID	Yes	Yes	ID
	DAY ID	Yes	Yes	ID
	ENGAGEMENT ITEM TYPE ID	Yes	Yes	ID
	PROFESSIONAL PARTY ID	Yes	Yes	ID
	RATE TYPE ID	Yes	Yes	ID
	WORK EFFORT ID	Yes	Yes	ID
	COST	No	No	Currency amount
	DOLLARS BILLED	No	No	Currency amount
	GROSS MARGIN	No	No	Floating point
	HOURS BILLED	No	No	Numeric
UNIT OF MEASURE	UOM ID	Yes	No	ID
	ABBREVIATION	No	No	Short varchar
	DESCRIPTION	No	No	Description
WORK EFFORT	WORK EFFORT ID	Yes	No	ID
	FACILITY ID	No	Yes	ID
	VERSION OF WORK EFFORT ID	No	Yes	ID

ENTITY NAME	ATTRIBUTE NAME	PK?	FK?	DOMAIN
	ACTUAL COMPLETION DATETIME	No	No	Datetime
	ACTUAL HOURS	No	No	Numeric
	ACTUAL START DATETIME	No	No	Datetime
	ASSET ID	No	No	ID
	DESCRIPTION	No	No	Description
	ESTIMATED HOURS	No	No	Numeric
	FIXED ASSET ID	No	No	ID
	NAME	No	No	Name
	SCHEDULED COMPLETION DATE	No	No	Datetime
	SCHEDULED START DATE	No	No	Datetime
	SPECIAL TERMS	No	No	Long varchar
	TOTAL DOLLARS ALLOWED	No	No	Currency amount
	TOTAL HOURS ALLOWED	No	No	Numeric
	WORK EFFORT PURPOSE TYPE ID	No	No	ID
	WORK EFFORT TYPE ID	No	No	ID
WORK EFFORT ASSIGNMENT	PARTY ID	Yes	Yes	ID
	ROLE TYPE ID	Yes	Yes	ID
	WORK EFFORT ID	Yes	Yes	ID
	FROM DATE	Yes	No	Datetime
	COMMENTS	No	No	Comment
	THRU DATE	No	No	Datetime
WORK EFFORT BILLING	INVOICE ID	Yes	Yes	ID
	INVOICE ITEM SEQ ID	Yes	Yes	ID
	WORK EFFORT ID	Yes	Yes	ID
	PERCENTAGE	No	No	Floating point

Entities and Attributes for Travel Models

This appendix lists the entities and attributes from the models and star schemas found in Chapter 8, "Travel." This listing includes the entity names, attribute names, primary key indicators, foreign key indicators, and the domain for each attribute.

The domain indicates a standard set of characteristics that can be applied to attributes, including its datatype and length. Table A.1 defines the nature of each domain. When applying the domains to the attributes listed in these appendices, refer to Table A.1 for recommendations on what datatype and length to use when implementing these models. Of course, the datatype and length of each attribute should be adjusted as appropriate to meet the specific needs of the enterprise.

The domain definitions as they are applied to the attributes in the appendices are used for the SQL code that is contained on the demo CD-ROM at the back of this book as well as in the Industry Downloads (see the section "How to Use the Volume 2 Industry Electronic Products" for more information).

Entities and Attributes Listing for Travel Models

ENTITY NAME	ATTRIBUTE NAME	PK?	FK?	DOMAIN
ACCOMMODATION CLASS	ACCOMMODATION CLASS ID	Yes	No	ID
	DESCRIPTION	No	No	Description
ACCOMMODATION CLASSES	ACCOMMODATION CLASS ID	Yes	No	ID
	DESCRIPTION	No	No	Description
ACCOMMODATION MAP	ACCOMMODATION CLASS ID	Yes	Yes	ID
	FIXED ASSET ID	Yes	Yes	ID
	NUMBER OF SPACES	Yes	No	Numeric
ACCOMMODATION SPOT	ACCOMMODATION SPOT ID	Yes	No	ID
	ACCOMMODATION CLASS ID	No	Yes	ID
	FIXED ASSET ID	No	Yes	ID
	NUMBER OF SPACES	No	Yes	Numeric
	ACCOM NUMBER	No	No	Numeric
AGREEMENT	AGREEMENT ID	Yes	No	ID
	AGREEMENT TYPE ID	No	Yes	ID
	FROM DATE	No	Yes	Datetime
	PARTY ID FROM	No	Yes	ID
	PARTY ID TO	No	Yes	ID
	ROLE TYPE ID FROM	No	Yes	ID
	ROLE TYPE ID TO	No	Yes	ID
	AGREEMENT DATE	No	No	Datetime
	DESCRIPTION	No	No	Description
	PRODUCT ID	No	No	ID
	TEXT	No	No	Long varchar
	THRU DATE	No	No	Datetime
AGREEMENT EXHIBIT	AGREEMENT ID	Yes	Yes	ID
	AGREEMENT ITEM SEQ ID	Yes	Yes	ID
AGREEMENT ITEM	AGREEMENT ID	Yes	Yes	ID
	AGREEMENT ITEM SEQ ID	Yes	No	ID
	PART OF AGREEMENT ID	No	Yes	ID
	PART OF AGREEMENT ITEM SEQ ID	No	Yes	ID
	AGREEMENT IMAGE	No	No	Blob
	AGREEMENT TEXT	No	No	Long varchar
AGREEMENT PRICING PROGRAM	AGREEMENT ID	Yes	Yes	ID

ENTITY NAME	ATTRIBUTE NAME	PK?	FK?	DOMAIN
	AGREEMENT ITEM SEQ ID	Yes	Yes	ID
AGREEMENT ROLE	AGREEMENT ID	Yes	Yes	ID
	PARTY ID	Yes	Yes	ID
	ROLE TYPE ID	Yes	Yes	ID
AGREEMENT ROLE TYPE	ROLE TYPE ID	Yes	Yes	ID
AGREEMENT SECTION	AGREEMENT ID	Yes	Yes	ID
	AGREEMENT ITEM SEQ ID	Yes	Yes	ID
AGREEMENT TERM	AGREEMENT TERM ID	Yes	No	ID
	TERM TYPE ID	No	Yes	ID
	AGREEMENT ID	No	Yes	ID
	AGREEMENT ITEM SEQ ID	No	Yes	ID
	FROM DATE	No	No	Datetime
	TERM VALUE	No	No	Numeric
	THRU DATE	No	No	Datetime
AGREEMENT TYPE	AGREEMENT TYPE ID	Yes	No	ID
	DESCRIPTION	No	No	Description
AIRLINE	PARTY ID	Yes	Yes	ID
	ROLE TYPE ID	Yes	Yes	ID
AIRPORT	FACILITY ID	Yes	Yes	ID
AMENITIES DELIVERY SEQ ID	TRAVEL EXPERIENCE EVENT	Yes	Yes	ID
AMENITIES OFFERING	TRAVEL EXPERIENCE ID	Yes	Yes	ID
	PRODUCT ID	Yes	Yes	ID
ARRIVAL FACILITYS	ARRIVAL FACILITY ID	Yes	No	ID
	CITY	No	No	Short varchar
	COUNTRY	No	No	Short varchar
	NAME	No	No	Name
	STATE	No	No	Short varchar
BAGGAGE CHECK IN	TRAVEL EXPERIENCE EVENT SEQ ID	Yes	Yes	ID
	TRAVEL EXPERIENCE ID	Yes	Yes	ID
BAGGAGE HANDLING	TRAVEL EXPERIENCE EVENT SEQ ID	Yes	Yes	ID
	TRAVEL EXPERIENCE ID	Yes	Yes	ID

ENTITY NAME	ATTRIBUTE NAME	PK?	FK?	DOMAIN
BOARDING	TRAVEL EXPERIENCE EVENT SEQ ID	Yes	Yes	ID
	TRAVEL EXPERIENCE ID	Yes	Yes	ID
BUS DEPOT	FACILITY ID	Yes	Yes	ID
BUS OFFERING	PRODUCT ID	Yes	Yes	ID
CAR RENTAL FACILITY	FACILITY ID	Yes	Yes	ID
CAR RENTAL PROVIDER	PARTY ID	Yes	Yes	ID
	ROLE TYPE ID	Yes	Yes	ID
CHECK IN	TRAVEL EXPERIENCE EVENT SEQ ID	Yes	Yes	ID
	TRAVEL EXPERIENCE ID	Yes	Yes	ID
COMMUNICATION EVENT	COMMUNICATION EVENT ID	Yes	No	ID
	FROM DATE	No	Yes	Datetime
	PARTY ID FROM	No	Yes	ID
	PARTY ID TO	No	Yes	ID
	ROLE TYPE ID FROM	No	Yes	ID
	ROLE TYPE ID TO	No	Yes	ID
	CASE ID	No	No	ID
	CONTACT MECHANISM TYPE ID	No	No	ID
	DATETIME ENDED	No	No	Datetime
	DATETIME STARTED	No	No	Datetime
	NOTE	No	No	Comment
	STATUS TYPE ID	No	No	ID
COMMUNICATION EVENT PURPOSE	COMMUNICATION EVENT ID	Yes	Yes	ID
	COMMUNICATION EVENT PRP TYP ID	Yes	No	ID
	DESCRIPTION	No	No	Description
COMPONENT TYPE	COMPONENT TYPE ID	Yes	No	ID
	DESCRIPTION	No	No	Description
CONTACT	PARTY ID	Yes	Yes	ID
	ROLE TYPE ID	Yes	Yes	ID
CONTACT MECHANISM	CONTACT MECHANISM ID	Yes	No	ID
	CONTACT MECHANISM TYPE ID	No	No	ID
CORPORATE TRAVEL AGREEMENT	AGREEMENT ID	Yes	Yes	ID
COUPON	TICKET ID	Yes	Yes	ID
	COUPON ID	Yes	No	ID
	ACCOMMODATION SPOT ID	No	Yes	ID
	RESERVATION ID	No	Yes	ID

ENTITY NAME	ATTRIBUTE NAME	PK?	FK?	DOMAIN
COUPON	RESERVATION ITEM SEQ ID	No	Yes	ID
COMPONENT	COMPONENT TYPE ID	Yes	Yes	ID
	COUPON ID	Yes	Yes	ID
	TICKET ID	Yes	Yes	ID
	AMOUNT	No	No	Currency amount
CRUISE LINE	PARTY ID	Yes	Yes	ID
	ROLE TYPE ID	Yes	Yes	ID
CUSTOMER	TRAVEL EXPERIENCE EVENT SEQ ID	Yes	Yes	ID
SERVICE EVENT	TRAVEL EXPERIENCE ID	Yes	Yes	ID
DAY OF THE WEEK	DAY ID	Yes	No	ID
	DAY NAME	No	No	Name
DEPARTMENT	PARTY ID	Yes	Yes	ID
	ROLE TYPE ID	Yes	Yes	ID
DEPARTURE FACILITYS	DEPARTURE FACILITY ID	Yes	No	ID
	CITY	No	No	Short varchar
	COUNTRY	No	No	Short varchar
	NAME	No	No	Name
	STATE	No	No	Short varchar
DEPENDENT	PARTY ID	Yes	Yes	ID
	ROLE TYPE ID	Yes	Yes	ID
DISBURSEMENT	PAYMENT ID	Yes	Yes	ID
DISTRIBUTION CHANNEL	PARTY ID	Yes	Yes	ID
DISTRIBUTION CHANNEL AGREEMENT	ROLE TYPE ID	Yes	Yes	ID
	AGREEMENT ID	Yes	Yes	ID
DISTRIBUTION CHANNEL RELATIONSHIP	FROM DATE	Yes	Yes	Datetime
	PARTY ID FROM	Yes	Yes	ID
	PARTY ID TO	Yes	Yes	ID
	ROLE TYPE ID FROM	Yes	Yes	ID
	ROLE TYPE ID TO	Yes	Yes	ID
DIVISION	PARTY ID	Yes	Yes	ID
	ROLE TYPE ID	Yes	Yes	ID

ENTITY NAME	ATTRIBUTE NAME	PK?	FK?	DOMAIN
EMPLOYEE	PARTY ID	Yes	Yes	ID
	ROLE TYPE ID	Yes	Yes	ID
EMPLOYMENT	FROM DATE	Yes	Yes	Datetime
	PARTY ID FROM	Yes	Yes	ID
	PARTY ID TO	Yes	Yes	ID
	ROLE TYPE ID FROM	Yes	Yes	ID
	ROLE TYPE ID TO	Yes	Yes	ID
	TERMINATION REASON ID	No	No	ID
	TERMINATION TYPE ID	No	No	ID
EMPLOYMENT AGREEMENT	AGREEMENT ID	Yes	Yes	ID
FACILITIES USAGE	TRAVEL EXPERIENCE EVENT SEQ ID	Yes	Yes	ID
	TRAVEL EXPERIENCE ID	Yes	Yes	ID
FACILITY	FACILITY ID	Yes	No	ID
	PART OF FACILITY ID	No	Yes	ID
	DESCRIPTION	No	No	Description
	FACILITY NAME	No	No	Name
	FACILITY TYPE ID	No	No	ID
	SQUARE FOOTAGE	No	No	Numeric
FACILITY CONTACT MECHANISM	CONTACT MECHANISM ID	Yes	Yes	ID
	FACILITY ID	Yes	Yes	ID
FINANCIAL TERM	AGREEMENT TERM ID	Yes	Yes	ID
	TERM TYPE ID	Yes	Yes	ID
FIXED ASSET	FIXED ASSET ID	Yes	No	ID
	PARTY ID	No	Yes	ID
	ROLE TYPE ID	No	Yes	ID
	DATE ACQUIRED	No	No	Datetime
	DATE LAST SERVICED	No	No	Datetime
	DATE NEXT SERVICE	No	No	Datetime
	FIXED ASSET TYPE ID	No	No	ID
	NAME	No	No	Name
	PRODUCTION CAPACITY	No	No	Floating point
	UOM ID	No	No	ID
FLIGHT OFFERING	PRODUCT ID	Yes	Yes	ID
HOTEL	FIXED ASSET ID	Yes	Yes	ID
	PRODUCT ID	No	Yes	ID
HOTEL CHECK OUT	TRAVEL EXPERIENCE EVENT SEQ ID	Yes	Yes	ID
	TRAVEL EXPERIENCE ID	Yes	Yes	ID

ENTITY NAME	ATTRIBUTE NAME	PK?	FK?	DOMAIN
HOTEL OFFERING	PRODUCT ID	Yes	Yes	ID
HOTEL PROVIDER	PARTY ID	Yes	Yes	ID
	ROLE TYPE ID	Yes	Yes	ID
HOUSEHOLD	PARTY ID	Yes	Yes	ID
	ROLE TYPE ID	Yes	Yes	ID
INCENTIVE	AGREEMENT TERM ID	Yes	Yes	ID
	TERM TYPE ID	Yes	Yes	ID
INDIVIDUAL CUSTOMER	PARTY ID	Yes	Yes	ID
INDIVIDUAL CUSTOMER RELATIONSHIP	ROLE TYPE ID	Yes	Yes	ID
	FROM DATE	Yes	Yes	Datetime
	PARTY ID FROM	Yes	Yes	ID
	PARTY ID TO	Yes	Yes	ID
	ROLE TYPE ID FROM	Yes	Yes	ID
	ROLE TYPE ID TO	Yes	Yes	ID
INDIVIDUAL PAYER	PARTY ID	Yes	Yes	ID
	ROLE TYPE ID	Yes	Yes	ID
INTERNAL ORGANIZATION	PARTY ID	Yes	Yes	ID
	ROLE TYPE ID	Yes	Yes	ID
INVOICE	INVOICE ID	Yes	No	ID
	BILLED FROM PARTY ID	No	Yes	ID
	BILLED TO PARTY ID	No	Yes	ID
	SENT FROM CONTACT MECH ID	No	Yes	ID
	SENT TO CONTACT MECH ID	No	Yes	ID
	BILLING ACCOUNT ID	No	No	ID
	DESCRIPTION	No	No	Description
	INVOICE DATE	No	No	Datetime
	MESSAGE	No	No	Long varchar
	PARTY ID	No	No	ID
ITEM OFFERING	ROLE TYPE ID	No	No	ID
	PRODUCT ID	Yes	Yes	ID
LEGAL TERM	AGREEMENT TERM ID	Yes	Yes	ID
	TERM TYPE ID	Yes	Yes	ID
MEAL DELIVERY	TRAVEL EXPERIENCE EVENT SEQ ID	Yes	Yes	ID
	TRAVEL EXPERIENCE ID	Yes	Yes	ID
OPERATIONS CREW	PARTY ID	Yes	Yes	ID
	ROLE TYPE ID	Yes	Yes	ID
ORGANIZATION	PARTY ID	Yes	Yes	ID

ENTITY NAME	ATTRIBUTE NAME	PK?	FK?	DOMAIN
ORGANIZATION CONTACT RELATIONSHIP	NAME	No	No	Name
	FROM DATE	Yes	Yes	Datetime
	PARTY ID FROM	Yes	Yes	ID
	PARTY ID TO	Yes	Yes	ID
	ROLE TYPE ID FROM	Yes	Yes	ID
	ROLE TYPE ID TO	Yes	Yes	ID
ORGANIZATION CUSTOMER	PARTY ID	Yes	Yes	ID
	ROLE TYPE ID	Yes	Yes	ID
ORGANIZATION CUSTOMER RELATIONSHIP	FROM DATE	Yes	Yes	Datetime
	PARTY ID FROM	Yes	Yes	ID
	PARTY ID TO	Yes	Yes	ID
	ROLE TYPE ID FROM	Yes	Yes	ID
	ROLE TYPE ID TO	Yes	Yes	ID
ORGANIZATION ROLE	PARTY ID	Yes	Yes	ID
	ROLE TYPE ID	Yes	Yes	ID
ORGANIZATION ROLLUP	FROM DATE	Yes	Yes	Datetime
	PARTY ID FROM	Yes	Yes	ID
	PARTY ID TO	Yes	Yes	ID
	ROLE TYPE ID FROM	Yes	Yes	ID
	ROLE TYPE ID TO	Yes	Yes	ID
ORGANIZATION UNIT	PARTY ID	Yes	Yes	ID
	ROLE TYPE ID	Yes	Yes	ID
OTHER AGREEMENT	AGREEMENT ID	Yes	Yes	ID
OTHER AGREEMENT TERM	AGREEMENT TERM ID	Yes	Yes	ID
	TERM TYPE ID	Yes	Yes	ID
OTHER DISTRIBUTION CHANNEL	PARTY ID	Yes	Yes	ID
	ROLE TYPE ID	Yes	Yes	ID
OTHER OFFERING	PRODUCT ID	Yes	Yes	ID
OTHER ORGANIZATION UNIT	PARTY ID	Yes	Yes	ID
	ROLE TYPE ID	Yes	Yes	ID
OTHER PORT	FACILITY ID	Yes	Yes	ID

ENTITY NAME	ATTRIBUTE NAME	PK?	FK?	DOMAIN
OTHER TRAVEL EXPERIENCE EVENT	TRAVEL EXPERIENCE EVENT SEQ ID	Yes	Yes	ID
	TRAVEL EXPERIENCE ID	Yes	Yes	ID
OTHER TRAVEL OFFERING	PRODUCT ID	Yes	Yes	ID
PARENT ORGANIZATION	PARTY ID	Yes	Yes	ID
	ROLE TYPE ID	Yes	Yes	ID
PARTNERSHIP AGREEMENT	AGREEMENT ID	Yes	Yes	ID
PARTY	PARTY ID	Yes	No	ID
PARTY RELATIONSHIP	PARTY ID FROM	Yes	Yes	ID
	PARTY ID TO	Yes	Yes	ID
	ROLE TYPE ID FROM	Yes	Yes	ID
	ROLE TYPE ID TO	Yes	Yes	ID
	FROM DATE	Yes	No	Datetime
	PARTY RELATIONSHIP TYPE ID	No	Yes	ID
	COMMENTS	No	No	Comment
	PRIORITY TYPE ID	No	No	ID
	STATUS TYPE ID	No	No	ID
	THRU DATE	No	No	Datetime
PARTY RELATIONSHIP TYPE	PARTY RELATIONSHIP TYPE ID	Yes	No	ID
	ROLE TYPE ID VALID FROM	No	Yes	ID
	ROLE TYPE ID VALID TO	No	No	ID
	DESCRIPTION	No	No	Description
	NAME	No	No	Name
PARTY ROLE	PARTY ID	Yes	Yes	ID
	ROLE TYPE ID	Yes	Yes	ID
PARTY ROLE TYPE	PARTY ROLE ID	No	Yes	ID
	ROLE TYPE ID	Yes	Yes	ID
PARTY TRAVEL PREFERENCE	PARTY ID	Yes	Yes	ID
	PARTY TRAVEL PREFERENCE ID	Yes	No	ID
	ACCOMMODATION CLASS ID	No	Yes	ID
	FACILITY ID	No	Yes	ID
	PRODUCT CATEGORY ID	No	Yes	ID
	PRODUCT ID	No	Yes	ID
	TRAVEL PREFERENCE TYPE ID	No	Yes	ID
	FROM DATE	No	No	Datetime
	THRU DATE	No	No	Datetime

ENTITY NAME	ATTRIBUTE NAME	PK?	FK?	DOMAIN
PASSENGER TRANSPORTATION OFFERING	PRODUCT ID	Yes	Yes	ID
	FACILITY ID GOING TO	No	Yes	ID
	FACILITY ID ORIGINATING FROM	No	Yes	ID
PAYMENT	PAYMENT ID	Yes	No	ID
	FROM PARTY ID	No	Yes	ID
	PAYMENT METHOD TYPE ID	No	Yes	ID
	TO PARTY ID	No	Yes	ID
	AMOUNT	No	No	Currency amount
	COMMENTS	No	No	Comment
	EFFECTIVE DATE	No	No	Datetime
	PAYMENT REF NUM	No	No	Description
	PAYMENT TYPE ID	No	No	ID
PAYMENT APPLICATION	PAYMENT ID	Yes	Yes	ID
	PAYMENT APPLICATION ID	Yes	No	ID
	INVOICE ID	No	Yes	ID
	SALE ID	No	Yes	ID
	TICKET ID	No	Yes	ID
	AMOUNT APPLIED	No	No	Currency amount
PAYMENT METHOD TYPE	PAYMENT METHOD TYPE ID	Yes	No	ID
	DESCRIPTION	No	No	Description
PERSON	PARTY ID	Yes	Yes	ID
	BIRTH DATE	No	No	Datetime
	COMMENTS	No	No	Comment
	CURRENT FIRST NAME	No	No	Name
	CURRENT LAST NAME	No	No	Name
	CURRENT MIDDLE NAME	No	No	Name
	CURRENT NICKNAME	No	No	Name
	CURRENT PASSPORT EXPIRE DATE	No	No	Datetime
	CURRENT PASSPORT NUMBER	No	No	Numeric
	CURRENT PERSONAL TITLE	No	No	Name
	CURRENT SUFFIX	No	No	Name
	GENDER	No	No	Indicator
	HEIGHT	No	No	Numeric
	MARTIAL STATUS	No	No	Indicator
	MOTHER'S MADIEN NAME	No	No	Name

ENTITY NAME	ATTRIBUTE NAME	PK?	FK?	DOMAIN
	SOCIAL SECURITY NUMBER	No	No	Numeric
	TOTAL YEARS WORK EXPERIENCE	No	No	Numeric
	WEIGHT	No	No	Numeric
PERSON ROLE	PARTY ID	Yes	Yes	ID
	ROLE TYPE ID	Yes	Yes	ID
POSTAL ADDRESS	CONTACT MECHANISM ID	Yes	Yes	ID
	ADDRESS1	No	No	Description
	ADDRESS2	No	No	Description
	DIRECTIONS	No	No	Long varchar
PRODUCT CATEGORY	PRODUCT CATEGORY ID	Yes	No	ID
	DESCRIPTION	No	No	Description
PRODUCT CATEGORY CLASSIFICATION	PRODUCT CATEGORY ID	Yes	Yes	ID
	PRODUCT ID	Yes	Yes	ID
	FROM DATE	Yes	No	Datetime
	COMMENTS	No	No	Comment
	PRIMARY FLAG	No	No	Indicator
	THRU DATE	No	No	Datetime
PROSPECT	PARTY ID	Yes	Yes	ID
	ROLE TYPE ID	Yes	Yes	ID
RECEIPT	PAYMENT ID	Yes	Yes	ID
	ACCOUNT NUMBER	No	No	Numeric
	ACCOUNT TRANSACTION ID	No	No	ID
REGULARLY SCHEDULED TIME	FINANCIAL ACCOUNT TRANS ID	No	No	ID
	FROM DATE	Yes	No	Datetime
	DAY ID OFFERED ARRIVING	No	Yes	ID
	DAY ID OFFERED DEPARTING	No	Yes	ID
	PRODUCT ID	No	Yes	ID
	ARRIVAL TIME	No	No	Datetime
	DEPARTURE TIME	No	No	Datetime
	THRU DATE	No	No	Datetime
REGULATORY AGENCY	PARTY ID	Yes	Yes	ID
	ROLE TYPE ID	Yes	Yes	ID
RENTAL CAR CHECKOUT	TRAVEL EXPERIENCE EVENT SEQ ID	Yes	Yes	ID
	TRAVEL EXPERIENCE ID	Yes	Yes	ID ·
RENTAL CAR OFFERING	PRODUCT ID	Yes	Yes	ID

ENTITY NAME	ATTRIBUTE NAME	PK?	FK?	DOMAIN
RENTAL VEHICLE	FIXED ASSET ID	Yes	Yes	ID
	PRODUCT ID	No	Yes	ID
RESERVATION	RESERVATION ID	Yes	No	ID
	COMPLETION TIME	No	No	Datetime
	CREATION DATE	No	No	Datetime
	START TIME	No	No	Datetime
	RESERVATION ID	Yes	Yes	ID
RESERVATION DEPENDENCY	RESERVATION ITEM SEQ ID FOR	Yes	Yes	ID
	RESERVATION ITEM SEQ ID OF	Yes	Yes	ID
	FROM DATE	No	No	Datetime
	THRU DATE	No	No	Datetime
RESERVATION ITEM	RESERVATION ID	Yes	Yes	ID
	RESERVATION ITEM SEQ ID	Yes	No	ID
	ACCOMMODATION CLASS ID	No	Yes	ID
	ACCOMMODATION SPOT ID	No	Yes	ID
	FACILITY ID	No	Yes	ID
	HOTEL FIXED ASSET ID	No	Yes	ID
	HOTEL PRODUCT ID	No	Yes	ID
	PRODUCT ID	No	Yes	ID
	RENTAL CAR PRODUCT ID	No	Yes	ID
	SALE ID	No	Yes	ID
	SCHED TRANS PRODUCT ID	No	Yes	ID
	SCHEDULED TRANS OFFERING ID	No	Yes	ID
	SCHEDULED TRANSPORTATION ID	No	Yes	ID
	VEHICLE FIXED ASSET ID	No	Yes	ID
	NUMBER OF DAYS	No	No	Numeric
	QUOTED PRICE	No	No	Currency amount
RESERVATION ITEM STATUS	RESERVATION ID	Yes	Yes	ID
	RESERVATION ITEM SEQ ID	Yes	Yes	ID
	STATUS TYPE ID	Yes	Yes	ID
	DATE TIME	No	No	Datetime
RESERVATION ITEM STATUS TYPE	STATUS TYPE ID	Yes	Yes	ID
RESERVATION PREFERENCE	RESERVATION ID	Yes	Yes	ID
	RESERVATION ITEM SEQ ID	Yes	Yes	ID
	TRAVEL PREFERENCE TYPE ID	Yes	Yes	ID
RESERVATION ROLE	RESERVATION ID	Yes	Yes	ID
RESERVED TRAVELER	PARTY ID	Yes	Yes	ID

ENTITY NAME	ATTRIBUTE NAME	PK?	FK?	DOMAIN
	RESERVATION ID	Yes	Yes	ID
	RESERVATION ITEM SEQ ID	Yes	Yes	ID
	ROLE TYPE ID	Yes	Yes	ID
ROLE TYPE	ROLE TYPE ID	Yes	No	ID
	DESCRIPTION	No	No	Description
ROOM MAP	ACCOMMODATION CLASS ID	Yes	Yes	ID
	FIXED ASSET ID	Yes	Yes	ID
	NUMBER OF SPACES	Yes	Yes	Numeric
ROOM NUMBER	ACCOMMODATION SPOT ID	Yes	Yes	ID
SALE	SALE ID	Yes	No	ID
	INVOICE ID	No	Yes	ID
	AMOUNT	No	No	Currency amount
SATISFACTION RATING	DATE	No	No	Datetime
	SATISFACTION RATING ID	Yes	No	ID
	TRAVEL EXPERIENCE SCORE	No	No	Numeric
SCHEDULED TRANSPORTATION	FIXED ASSET ID	Yes	Yes	ID
	PRODUCT ID	Yes	Yes	ID
	SCHEDULED TRANSPORTATION ID	Yes	No	ID
	PARTY ID	No	Yes	ID
	ROLE TYPE ID	No	Yes	ID
	ARRIVAL DATE	No	No	Datetime
	ARRIVAL TIME	No	No	Datetime
	DEPARTURE DATE	No	No	Datetime
	DEPARTURE TIME	No	No	Datetime
SCHEDULED TRANSPORTATION OFFERING	ACCOMMODATION CLASS ID	Yes	Yes	ID
	FIXED ASSET ID	Yes	Yes	ID
	PRODUCT ID	Yes	Yes	ID
	SCHEDULED TRANSPORTATION ID	Yes	Yes	ID
	SCHEDULED TRANS OFFERING ID	Yes	No	ID
	FROM DATE	No	No	Datetime
	QUANTITY	No	No	Numeric
	THRU DATE	No	No	Datetime
SEAT ASSIGNMENT	TRAVEL EXPERIENCE EVENT SEQ ID	Yes	Yes	ID
	TRAVEL EXPERIENCE ID	Yes	Yes	ID
SEAT MAP	ACCOMMODATION CLASS ID	Yes	Yes	ID

ENTITY NAME	ATTRIBUTE NAME	PK?	FK?	DOMAIN
	FIXED ASSET ID	Yes	Yes	ID
SEAT NUMBER	NUMBER OF SPACES	Yes	Yes	Numeric
SHIP OFFERING	ACCOMMODATION SPOT ID	Yes	Yes	ID
SHIP PORT	PRODUCT ID	Yes	Yes	ID
STATUS TYPE	FACILITY ID	Yes	Yes	ID
	STATUS TYPE ID	Yes	No	ID
	DESCRIPTION	No	No	Description
SUB AGREEMENT	AGREEMENT ID	Yes	Yes	ID
	AGREEMENT ITEM SEQ ID	Yes	Yes	ID
SUBSIDIARY	PARTY ID	Yes	Yes	ID
	ROLE TYPE ID	Yes	Yes	ID
SUPPLIER	PARTY ID	Yes	Yes	ID
	ROLE TYPE ID	Yes	Yes	ID
SUPPLIER RELATIONSHIP	FROM DATE	Yes	Yes	Datetime
	PARTY ID FROM	Yes	Yes	ID
	PARTY ID TO	Yes	Yes	ID
	ROLE TYPE ID FROM	Yes	Yes	ID
	ROLE TYPE ID TO	Yes	Yes	ID
THRESHOLD	AGREEMENT TERM ID	Yes	Yes	ID
	TERM TYPE ID	Yes	Yes	ID
TICKET	TICKET ID	Yes	No	ID
	ACCOMMODATION CLASS ID	No	Yes	ID
	FIXED ASSET ID	No	Yes	ID
	PARTY ID	No	Yes	ID
	PRODUCT ID	No	Yes	ID
	ROLE TYPE ID	No	Yes	ID
	SALE ID	No	Yes	ID
	SCHEDULED TRANS OFFERING ID	No	Yes	ID
	SCHEDULED TRANSPORTATION ID	No	Yes	ID
	CREATION DATE	No	No	Datetime
	SPECIAL INSTRUCTIONS	No	No	Long varchar
TICKET COMPONENT	COMPONENT TYPE ID	Yes	Yes	ID
	TICKET ID	Yes	Yes	ID
	AMOUNT	No	No	Currency amount
TICKETING	TRAVEL EXPERIENCE EVENT SEQ ID	Yes	Yes	ID
	TRAVEL EXPERIENCE ID	Yes	Yes	ID
TIME BY DAY	DAY ID	Yes	No	ID
	DAY	No	No	Very short
	MONTH	No	No	Very short

ENTITY NAME	ATTRIBUTE NAME	PK?	FK?	DOMAIN
	QUARTER	No	No	Very short
	WEEK	No	No	Very short
	YEAR	No	No	Very short
TRAIN OFFERING	PRODUCT ID	Yes	Yes	ID
TRAIN STATION	FACILITY ID	Yes	Yes	ID
TRANSPORTATION COUPON	COUPON ID	Yes	Yes	ID
	TICKET ID	Yes	Yes	ID
TRANSPORTATION FACILITY	FACILITY ID	Yes	Yes	ID
TRANSPORTATION OFFERING FACT	ACCOMMODATION CLASS ID	Yes	Yes	ID
	ARRIVAL FACILITY ID	Yes	Yes	ID
	DAY ID	Yes	Yes	ID
	DEPARTURE FACILITY ID	Yes	Yes	ID
	PRODUCT ID	Yes	Yes	ID
	TRAVEL ACCOMMODATION ASSET ID	Yes	Yes	ID
	TRAVEL PROVIDER PARTY ID	Yes	Yes	ID
	AVERAGE MINUTES LATE	No	No	Numeric
	AVERAGE SATISFACTION RATING	No	No	Numeric
	NUMBER OF NEGATIVE FEEDBACK	No	No	Numeric
	NUMBER OF ON TIME ARRIVALS	No	No	Numeric
	NUMBER OF ON TIME DEPARTURES	No	No	Numeric
	NUMBER OF POSITIVE FEEDBACK	No	No	Numeric
	NUMBER OF TRAVEL EXPERIENCES	No	No	Numeric
	SALES DOLLARS GENERATED	No	No	Currency amount
TRANSPORTATION VEHICLE	FIXED ASSET ID	Yes	Yes	ID
TRANSPORTATION VEHICLES	TRAVEL ACCOMMODATION ASSET ID	Yes	No	ID
	DESCRIPTION	No	No	Description
TRAVEL ACCOMMODATION ASSETS	TRAVEL ACCOMMODATION ASSET ID	Yes	No	ID
TRAVEL ACCOUNT	DESCRIPTION	No	No	Description
	TRAVEL ACCOUNT ID	Yes	No	ID
	TRAVEL PROGRAM ID	No	Yes	ID

ENTITY NAME	ATTRIBUTE NAME	PK?	FK?	DOMAIN
TRAVEL ACCOUNT ACTIVITY	TRAVEL ACCOUNT ID	Yes	Yes	ID
	TRAVEL ACCOUNT ACTIVITY ID	Yes	No	ID
	PAYMENT ID	No	Yes	ID
	SALE ID	No	Yes	ID
	TRAVEL EXPERIENCE ID	No	Yes	ID
	AMOUNT	No	No	Currency amount
	DATE	No	No	Datetime
	POINTS	No	No	Numeric
TRAVEL ACCOUNT MEMBER	PARTY ID	Yes	Yes	ID
	ROLE TYPE ID	Yes	Yes	ID
TRAVEL ACCOUNT ROLE	PARTY ID	Yes	Yes	ID
	ROLE TYPE ID	Yes	Yes	ID
	TRAVEL ACCOUNT ID	No	Yes	ID
	FROM DATE	No	No	Datetime
	THRU DATE	No	No	Datetime
TRAVEL ACCOUNT ROLE TYPE	ROLE TYPE ID	Yes	Yes	ID
TRAVEL ACCOUNT STATUS	STATUS TYPE ID	Yes	Yes	ID
	TRAVEL ACCOUNT ID	Yes	Yes	ID
	STATUS DATE	No	No	Datetime
TRAVEL ACCOUNT STATUS TYPE	STATUS TYPE ID	Yes	Yes	ID
TRAVEL AGENCY	PARTY ID	Yes	Yes	ID
	ROLE TYPE ID	Yes	Yes	ID
TRAVEL ASSOCIATION	PARTY ID	Yes	Yes	ID
	ROLE TYPE ID	Yes	Yes	ID
TRAVEL CARRIER	PARTY ID	Yes	Yes	ID
	ROLE TYPE ID	Yes	Yes	ID
TRAVEL CARRIER PRESENCE	FROM DATE	Yes	Yes	Datetime
	PARTY ID FROM	Yes	Yes	ID
	PARTY ID TO	No	Yes	ID
	ROLE TYPE ID FROM	No	Yes	ID
	ROLE TYPE ID TO	No	Yes	ID
TRAVEL EXPERIENCE	TRAVEL EXPERIENCE ID	Yes	No	ID
	ACCOMMODATION CLASS ID	No	Yes	ID
	CAR RENTAL FACILITY ID	No	Yes	ID
	COUPON ID	No	Yes	ID
	HOTEL FIXED ASSET ID	No	Yes	ID
	HOTEL PRODUCT ID	No	Yes	ID
	RENTAL CAR PRODUCT ID	No	Yes	ID
	RESERVATION ID	No	Yes	ID
	RESERVATION ITEM SEQ ID	No	Yes	ID
	SALE ID	No	Yes	ID
	SATISFACTION RATING ID	No	Yes	ID
	SCHED TRANS PRODUCT ID	No	Yes	ID
	SCHEDULED TRANS OFFERING ID	No	Yes	ID
	SCHEDULED TRANSPORTATION ID	No	Yes	ID
	TICKET ID	No	Yes	ID
	TRAVELER PARTY ID	No	Yes	ID
	TRAVELER ROLE TYPE ID	No	Yes	ID
	VEHICLE FIXED ASSET ID	No	Yes	ID
	COMMENTS	No	No	Comment
	FROM DATE	No	No	Datetime
	THRU DATE	No	No	Datetime
TRAVEL EXPERIENCE COMMUNICATION	COMMUNICATION EVENT ID	Yes	Yes	ID
	TRAVEL EXPERIENCE EVENT SEQ ID	Yes	Yes	ID
TRAVEL EXPERIENCE EVENT	TRAVEL EXPERIENCE ID	Yes	Yes	ID
	TRAVEL EXPERIENCE EVENT SEQ ID	Yes	Yes	ID
	ACCOMMODATION SPOT ID	No	Yes	ID
	SATISFACTION RATING ID	No	Yes	ID
	TRAVEL EXPERIENCE EVENT TYPE ID	No	Yes	ID
	COMMENTS	No	No	Comment
TRAVEL EXPERIENCE EVENT ROLE	PARTY ID	Yes	Yes	ID
	ROLE TYPE ID	Yes	Yes	ID
	TRAVEL EXPERIENCE EVENT SEQ ID	Yes	Yes	ID
	TRAVEL EXPERIENCE ID	Yes	Yes	ID
TRAVEL EXPERIENCE EVENT ROLE TYPE	ROLE TYPE ID	Yes	No	ID
TRAVEL EXPERIENCE EVENT TYPE	TRAVEL EXPERIENCE EVENT TYPE ID	Yes	No	ID
	DESCRIPTION	No	No	Description

ENTITY NAME	ATTRIBUTE NAME	PK?	FK?	DOMAIN
TRAVEL EXPERIENCE STATUS	STATUS TYPE ID	Yes	Yes	ID
	TRAVEL EXPERIENCE EVENT SEQ ID	Yes	Yes	ID
	TRAVEL EXPERIENCE ID	Yes	Yes	ID
	DATE TIME	No	No	Datetime
TRAVEL EXPERIENCE STATUS TYPE	STATUS TYPE ID	Yes	Yes	ID
TRAVEL FACT	ACCOMMODATION CLASS ID	Yes	Yes	ID
	DAY ID	Yes	Yes	ID
	PRODUCT ID	Yes	Yes	ID
	TRAVEL ACCOMMODATION ASSET ID	Yes	Yes	ID
	TRAVEL PROVIDER PARTY ID	Yes	Yes	ID
	AVERAGE SATISFACTION RATING	No	No	Numeric
	NUMBER OF NEGATIVE FEEDBACK	No	No	Numeric
	NUMBER OF POSITIVE FEEDBACK	No	No	Numeric
	NUMBER OF TRAVEL EXPERIENCES	No	No	Numeric
	SALES DOLLARS GENERATED	No	No	Currency amount
TRAVEL PARTNER	PARTY ID	Yes	Yes	ID
	ROLE TYPE ID	Yes	Yes	ID
TRAVEL PARTNERSHIP	FROM DATE	Yes	Yes	Datetime
	PARTY ID FROM	Yes	Yes	ID
	PARTY ID TO	Yes	Yes	ID
	ROLE TYPE ID FROM	Yes	Yes	ID
	ROLE TYPE ID TO	Yes	Yes	ID
TRAVEL PORT AUTHORITY	PARTY ID	Yes	Yes	ID
	ROLE TYPE ID	Yes	Yes	ID
TRAVEL PREFERENCE TYPE	TRAVEL PREFERENCE TYPE ID	Yes	No	ID
	DESCRIPTION	No	No	Description
TRAVEL PRICE COMPONENT	PRICING COMPONENT ID	Yes	No	ID
	AGREEMENT ID	No	Yes	ID
	AGREEMENT ITEM SEQ ID	No	Yes	ID
	PRODUCT ID	No	Yes	ID
	RESERVATION ID	No	Yes	ID
	RESERVATION ITEM SEQ ID	No	Yes	ID
	TICKET ID	No	Yes	ID
	COMMENTS	No	No	Comment
	FROM DATE	No	No	Datetime
	GEOGRAPHIC BOUNDARY ID	No	No	ID
	ORDER VALUE ID	No	No	ID
	PARTY ID	No	No	ID
	PARTY TYPE ID	No	No	ID
	PERCENT	No	No	Floating point
	PRICE	No	No	Currency amount
	PRODUCT CATEGORY ID	No	No	ID
	PRODUCT FEATURE ID	No	No	ID
	QUANTITY BREAK ID	No	No	ID
	SALE TYPE ID	No	No	ID
	THRU DATE	No	No	Datetime
	UOM ID	No	No	ID
TRAVEL PRODUCT	PRODUCT ID	Yes	No	ID
	NAME	No	No	Description
TRAVEL PRODUCT COMPLEMENT	TRAVEL PRODUCT ID FOR	Yes	Yes	ID
	TRAVEL PRODUCT ID OF	Yes	Yes	ID
TRAVEL PRODUCT REFERENCE NUMBER	PRODUCT ID	Yes	Yes	ID
	FROM DATE	Yes	No	Datetime
	REFERENCE NUMBER	Yes	No	Numeric
	THRU DATE	No	No	Datetime
TRAVEL PRODUCTS	PRODUCT ID	Yes	No	ID
	NAME	No	No	Description
TRAVEL PROGRAM	TRAVEL PROGRAM ID	Yes	No	ID
	DESCRIPTION	No	No	Description
TRAVEL PROGRAM FACTOR	FROM DATE	Yes	Yes	Datetime
	TRAVEL PROGRAM FACTOR TYPE ID	Yes	Yes	ID
	TRAVEL PROGRAM ID	Yes	Yes	ID
	TRAVEL PROGRAM RULE TYPE ID	Yes	Yes	ID
	THRU DATE	No	No	Datetime
TRAVEL PROGRAM FACTOR TYPE	TRAVEL PROGRAM FACTOR TYPE ID	Yes	Yes	ID
	DESCRIPTION	No	No	Description
TRAVEL PROGRAM RULE	TRAVEL PROGRAM ID	Yes	Yes	ID

ENTITY NAME	ATTRIBUTE NAME	PK?	FK?	DOMAIN
	TRAVEL PROGRAM RULE TYPE ID	Yes	Yes	ID
	FROM DATE	Yes	No	Datetime
	RULE VALUE	No	No	Numeric
	THRU DATE	No	No	Datetime
TRAVEL PROGRAM RULE TYPE	TRAVEL PROGRAM RULE TYPE ID	Yes	No	ID
	DESCRIPTION	No	No	Description
TRAVEL PROVIDER	PARTY ID	Yes	Yes	ID
	ROLE TYPE ID	Yes	Yes	ID
TRAVEL PROVIDERS	TRAVEL PROVIDER PARTY ID	Yes	No	ID
	NAME	No	No	Name
TRAVEL STAFF	PARTY ID	Yes	Yes	ID

ENTITY NAME	ATTRIBUTE NAME	PK?	FK?	DOMAIN
	ROLE TYPE ID	Yes	Yes	ID
TRAVEL VOUCHER	COUPON ID	Yes	Yes	ID
	TICKET ID	Yes	Yes	ID
TRAVELER	PARTY ID	Yes	Yes	ID
	ROLE TYPE ID	Yes	Yes	ID
TRAVELER AGREEMENT	AGREEMENT ID	Yes	Yes	ID
TRAVELER FEEDBACK	COMMUNICATION EVENT ID	Yes	Yes	ID
	COMMUNICATION EVENT PRP TYP ID	Yes	Yes	ID
VEHICLE	FIXED ASSET ID	Yes	Yes	ID

Entities and Attributes for E-Commerce Models

This appendix lists the entities and attributes from the models and star schemas found in Chapter 9, "E-Commerce." This listing includes the entity names, attribute names, primary key indicators, foreign key indicators, and the domain for each attribute.

The domain indicates a standard set of characteristics that can be applied to attributes, including its datatype and length. Table A.1 defines the nature of each domain. When applying the domains to the attributes listed in these appendices, refer to Table A.1 for recommendations on what datatype and length to use when implementing these models. Of course, the datatype and length of each attribute should be adjusted as appropriate to meet the specific needs of the enterprise.

The domain definitions as they are applied to the attributes in the appendices are used for the SQL code that is contained on the demo CD-ROM at the back of this book as well as in the Industry Downloads (see the section "How to Use the Volume 2 Industry Electronic Products" for more information).

Entities and Attributes Listing for E-Commerce Models

ENTITY NAME	ATTRIBUTE NAME	PK?	FK?	DOMAIN
AUTOMATED AGENT	PARTY ID	Yes	Yes	ID
AUTOMATED AGENT ROLE	PARTY ID	Yes	Yes	ID
	ROLE TYPE ID	Yes	Yes	ID
BROWSER TYPE	BROWSER TYPE ID	Yes	No	ID
	NAME	No	No	Name
	VERSION	No	No	Very short
COMMUNICATION EVENT	COMMUNICATION EVENT ID	Yes	No	ID
	CONTACT MECHANISM TYPE ID	No	Yes	ID
	FROM DATE	No	Yes	Datetime
	PARTY ID FROM	No	Yes	ID
	PARTY ID TO	No	Yes	ID
	ROLE TYPE ID FROM	No	Yes	ID
	ROLE TYPE ID TO	No	Yes	ID
	CASE ID	No	No	ID
	DATETIME ENDED	No	No	Datetime
	DATETIME STARTED	No	No	Datetime
	NOTE	No	No	Comment
	STATUS TYPE ID	No	No	ID
CONSUMER	PARTY ID	Yes	Yes	ID
	ROLE TYPE ID	Yes	Yes	ID
CONTACT MECHANISM	CONTACT MECHANISM ID	Yes	No	ID
	CONTACT MECHANISM TYPE ID	No	Yes	ID
CONTACT MECHANISM LINK	CONTACT MECHANISM TYPE ID	No	Yes	ID
	CONTACT MECHANISM ID	Yes	Yes	ID
	CONTACT MECHANISM ID FROM	Yes	Yes	ID
CONTACT MECHANISM PURPOSE TYPE	CONTACT MECHANISM PURPOSE	Yes	No	ID
	TYPE ID	No	No	ID
	DESCRIPTION	No	No	Description
CONTACT MECHANISM TYPE	CONTACT MECHANISM TYPE ID	Yes	No	ID
	DESCRIPTION	No	No	Description
CUSTOMER	PARTY ID	Yes	Yes	ID
	ROLE TYPE ID	Yes	Yes	ID

ENTITY NAME	ATTRIBUTE NAME	PK?	FK?	DOMAIN
ELECTRONIC ADDRESS	CONTACT MECHANISM ID	Yes	Yes	ID
	ELECTRONIC ADDRESS STRING	No	No	Description
ELECTRONIC TEXT	OBJECT ID	Yes	Yes	ID
	TEXT	No	No	Long varchar
EMAIL ADDRESS	CONTACT MECHANISM ID	Yes	Yes	ID
EMPLOYEE	PARTY ID	Yes	Yes	ID
	ROLE TYPE ID	Yes	Yes	ID
FEATURE OBJECT	OBJECT ID	Yes	Yes	ID
	PRODUCT FEATURE ID	Yes	Yes	ID
FUNCTION TYPE	FUNCTION TYPE ID	Yes	No	ID
	DESCRIPTION	No	No	Description
HOST SERVER VISITOR	FROM DATE	Yes	Yes	Datetime
	PARTY ID FROM	Yes	Yes	ID
	PARTY ID TO	Yes	Yes	ID
	ROLE TYPE ID FROM	Yes	Yes	ID
	ROLE TYPE ID TO	Yes	Yes	ID
HOSTING SERVER	PARTY ID	Yes	Yes	ID
	ROLE TYPE ID	Yes	Yes	ID
IMAGE OBJECT	OBJECT ID	Yes	Yes	ID
	IMAGE	No	No	Blob
INTERNAL ORGANIZATION	PARTY ID	Yes	Yes	ID
IP ADDRESS	ROLE TYPE ID	Yes	Yes	ID
ISP	CONTACT MECHANISM ID	Yes	Yes	ID
	PARTY ID	Yes	Yes	ID
	ROLE TYPE ID	Yes	Yes	ID
ISPS	ISP PARTY ID	Yes	No	ID
	NAME	No	No	Name
LOGIN ACCOUNT HISTORY	PARTY ID	Yes	Yes	ID
	USER LOGIN ID	Yes	Yes	ID
	FROM DATE	Yes	No	Datetime
	PASSWORD	No	No	Very short
	THRU DATE	No	No	Datetime
	USER ID	No	No	Short varchar
NEED TYPE	NEED TYPE ID	Yes	No	ID

ENTITY NAME	ATTRIBUTE NAME	PK?	FK?	DOMAIN
NEWSGROUP SUBSCRIPTION	DESCRIPTION	No	No	Description
	SUBSCRIPTION ID	Yes	Yes	ID
OBJECT	OBJECT ID	Yes	No	ID
	IMAGE TYPE ID	No	Yes	ID
	DESCRIPTION	No	No	Description
	FILE LOCATION	No	No	Description
	OBJECT NAME	No	No	Name
OBJECT PURPOSE	OBJECT ID	Yes	Yes	ID
	PURPOSE TYPE ID	Yes	Yes	ID
OBJECT TYPE	IMAGE TYPE ID	Yes	No	ID
	DESCRIPTION	No	No	Description
ORDER	ORDER ID	Yes	No	ID
	VISIT ID	No	Yes	ID
	ENTRY DATE	No	No	Datetime
	ORDER DATE	No	No	Datetime
ORDER ITEM	ORDER ID	Yes	Yes	ID
	ORDER ITEM SEQ ID	Yes	No	ID
	PRODUCT FEATURE ID	No	Yes	ID
	PRODUCT ID	No	Yes	ID
	SUBSCRIPTION ID	No	Yes	ID
	BUDGET ID	No	No	ID
	BUDGET ITEM SEQ ID	No	No	ID
	COMMENTS	No	No	Comment
	DEPLOYMENT ID	No	No	ID
	ESTIMATED DELIVERY DATE	No	No	Datetime
	ITEM DESCRIPTION	No	No	Description
	QUANTITY	No	No	Numeric
	QUOTE ID	No	No	ID
	QUOTED ITEM SEQ ID	No	No	ID
	SHIPPING INSTRUCTIONS	No	No	Long varchar
	UNIT PRICE	No	No	Currency amount
ORGANIZATION	PARTY ID	Yes	Yes	ID
	NAME	No	No	Name
ORGANIZATION ROLE	PARTY ID	Yes	Yes	ID
	ROLE TYPE ID	Yes	Yes	ID
OTHER OBJECT	OBJECT ID	Yes	Yes	ID
	OBJECT CONTENT	No	No	Blob
OTHER SUBSCRIPTION	SUBSCRIPTION ID	Yes	Yes	ID

ENTITY NAME	ATTRIBUTE NAME	PK?	FK?	DOMAIN
PARTY	PARTY ID	Yes	No	ID
PARTY CONTACT MECHANISM	CONTACT MECHANISM ID	Yes	Yes	ID
	PARTY ID	Yes	Yes	ID
	FROM DATE	Yes	No	Datetime
	ROLE TYPE ID	No	Yes	ID
	COMMENTS	No	No	Comment
	EXTENSION	No	No	Very short
	NON-SOLICITATION INDICATOR	No	No	Indicator
	THRU DATE	No	No	Datetime
PARTY CONTACT MECHANISM PURPOSE	CONTACT MECHANISM ID	Yes	Yes	ID
	CONTACT MECHANISM PURPOSE TYPE ID	Yes	Yes	ID
	FROM DATE	Yes	Yes	Datetime
	PARTY ID	Yes	Yes	ID
	THRU DATE	No	No	Datetime
PARTY NEED	PARTY ID	Yes	Yes	ID
	ROLE TYPE ID	Yes	Yes	ID
	PARTY NEED ID	Yes	No	ID
	COMMUNICATION EVENT ID	No	Yes	ID
	DATE TIME	No	Yes	Datetime
	NEED TYPE ID	No	Yes	ID
	PRODUCT CATEGORY ID	No	Yes	ID
	VISIT ID	No	Yes	ID
	DESCRIPTION	No	No	Description
	PARTY TYPE ID	No	No	ID
	PRODUCT ID	No	No	ID
PARTY OBJECT	OBJECT ID	Yes	Yes	ID
	PARTY ID	Yes	Yes	ID
PARTY RELATIONSHIP	PARTY ID FROM	Yes	Yes	ID
	PARTY ID TO	Yes	Yes	ID
	ROLE TYPE ID FROM	Yes	Yes	ID
	ROLE TYPE ID TO	Yes	Yes	ID
	FROM DATE	Yes	No	Datetime
	COMMENTS	No	No	Comment
	PARTY RELATIONSHIP TYPE ID	No	No	ID
	PRIORITY TYPE ID	No	No	ID
	STATUS TYPE ID	No	No	ID
	THRU DATE	No	No	Datetime

ENTITY NAME	ATTRIBUTE NAME	PK?	FK?	DOMAIN
PARTY ROLE	PARTY ID	Yes	Yes	ID
	ROLE TYPE ID	Yes	Yes	ID
	PARTY ROLE ID	No	No	ID
PARTY ROLE TYPE	ROLE TYPE ID	Yes	Yes	ID
PERSON	PARTY ID	Yes	Yes	ID
	BIRTH DATE	No	No	Datetime
	COMMENTS	No	No	Comment
	CURRENT FIRST NAME	No	No	Name
	CURRENT LAST NAME	No	No	Name
	CURRENT MIDDLE NAME	No	No	Name
	CURRENT NICKNAME	No	No	Name
	CURRENT PASSPORT EXPIRE DATE	No	No	Datetime
	CURRENT PASSPORT NUMBER	No	No	Numeric
	CURRENT PERSONAL TITLE	No	No	Name
	CURRENT SUFFIX	No	No	Name
	GENDER	No	No	Indicator
	HEIGHT	No	No	Numeric
	MARTIAL STATUS	No	No	Indicator
	MOTHER'S MADIEN NAME	No	No	Name
	SOCIAL SECURITY NUMBER	No	No	Numeric
	TOTAL YEARS WORK EXPERIENCE	No	No	Numeric
	WEIGHT	No	No	Numeric
PERSON ROLE	PARTY ID	Yes	Yes	ID
	ROLE TYPE ID	Yes	Yes	ID
PLATFORM TYPE	PLATFORM TYPE ID	Yes	No	ID
	NAME	No	No	Name
	VERSION	No	No	Very short
POSTAL ADDRESS	CONTACT MECHANISM ID	Yes	Yes	ID
	ADDRESS1	No	No	Description
	ADDRESS2	No	No	Description
	DIRECTIONS	No	No	Long varchar
PRODUCT	PRODUCT ID	Yes	No	ID
	MANUFACTURER PARTY ID	No	Yes	ID
	COMMENTS	No	No	Comment
	DESCRIPTION	No	No	Description
	INTRODUCTION DATE	No	No	Datetime
	NAME	No	No	Name
	PART ID	No	No	ID
	SALES DISCONTINUATION DATE	No	No	Datetime

ENTITY NAME	ATTRIBUTE NAME	PK?	FK?	DOMAIN
	SUPPORT DISCONTINUATION DATE	No	No	Datetime
	UOM ID	No	No	ID
PRODUCT CATEGORY	PRODUCT CATEGORY ID	Yes	No	ID
	DESCRIPTION	No	No	Description
PRODUCT FEATURE	PRODUCT FEATURE ID	Yes	No	ID
	DESCRIPTION	No	No	Description
	PRODUCT FEATURE CATEGORY ID	No	No	ID
PRODUCT FEATURE APPLICABILITY	PRODUCT FEATURE ID	Yes	Yes	ID
	PRODUCT ID	Yes	Yes	ID
	FROM DATE	Yes	No	Datetime
	THRU DATE	No	No	Datetime
PRODUCT INFORMATION SUBSCRIPTION	SUBSCRIPTION ID	Yes	Yes	ID
PRODUCT OBJECT	PRODUCT ID	Yes	Yes	ID
	OBJECT ID	No	Yes	ID
PRODUCTS	PRODUCT ID	Yes	No	ID
	PRODUCT CATEGORY	No	No	Description
	PRODUCT NAME	No	No	Name
PROSPECT	PARTY ID	Yes	Yes	ID
	ROLE TYPE ID	Yes	Yes	ID
PROTOCOL TYPE	PROTOCOL TYPE ID	Yes	No	ID
	NAME	No	No	Name
PURPOSE TYPE	PURPOSE TYPE ID	Yes	No	ID
	DESCRIPTION	No	No	Description
REFERRER	PARTY ID	Yes	Yes	ID
	ROLE TYPE ID	Yes	Yes	ID
REFERRERS	REFERRER PARTY ID	Yes	Yes	ID
	NAME	No	No	Name
ROLE TYPE	ROLE TYPE ID	Yes	No	ID
	DESCRIPTION	No	No	Description
SERVER HIT	VISIT ID	Yes	Yes	ID
	DATE TIME	Yes	No	Datetime
	ID BY IP CONTACT MECHANISM ID	No	Yes	ID
	PARTY ID	No	Yes	ID
	REF BY WEB CONTACT MECHANISM ID	No	Yes	ID
	STATUS TYPE ID	No	Yes	ID

ENTITY NAME	ATTRIBUTE NAME	PK?	FK?	DOMAIN
SUBSCRIPTION TYPE	SUBSCRIPTION TYPE ID	Yes	No	ID
	DESCRIPTION	No	No	Description
SUPPLIER	PARTY ID	Yes	Yes	ID
	ROLE TYPE ID	Yes	Yes	ID
TELECOMMUNICATIONS NUMBER	CONTACT MECHANISM ID	Yes	Yes	ID
	AREA CODE	No	No	Numeric
	CONTACT NUMBER	No	No	Short varchar
	CONTRY CODE	No	No	Numeric
TIME BY HOUR	HOUR ID	Yes	No	ID
	DAY	No	No	Very short
	HOUR	No	No	Very short
	MONTH	No	No	Very short
	QUARTER	No	No	Very short
	WEEK	No	No	Very short
	YEAR	No	No	Very short
USER AGENT	USER AGENT ID	Yes	No	ID
	BROWSER TYPE ID	No	Yes	ID
	PLATFORM TYPE ID	No	Yes	ID
	PROTOCOL TYPE ID	No	Yes	ID
	USER AGENT METHOD TYPE ID	No	Yes	ID
	USER AGENT TYPE ID	No	Yes	ID
USER AGENT METHOD TYPE	USER AGENT METHOD TYPE ID	Yes	No	ID
	DESCRIPTION	No	No	Description
USER AGENT TYPE	USER AGENT TYPE ID	Yes	No	ID
	DESCRIPTION	No	No	Description
USER AGENT TYPES	USER AGENT TYPE	Yes	No	Description
	BROWSER TYPE	No	No	Description
	METHOD TYPE	No	No	Description
	PLATFORM TYPE	No	No	Description
	PROTOCOL TYPE	No	No	Description
	USER AGENT TYPE NAME	No	No	Name
USER GROUP SUBSCRIPTION	SUBSCRIPTION ID	Yes	Yes	ID
USER LOGIN	PARTY ID	Yes	Yes	ID
	USER LOGIN ID	Yes	No	ID
	CONTACT MECHANISM ID	No	Yes	ID
	CURRENT PASSWORD	No	No	Very short
	CURRENT USER ID	No	No	Short varchar

ENTITY NAME	ATTRIBUTE NAME	PK?	FK?	DOMAIN
	USER AGENT ID	No	Yes	ID
	USER LOGIN ID	No	Yes	ID
	WEB CONTENT ID	No	Yes	ID
	NUM OF BYTES	No	No	Numeric
SERVER HIT FACT	HOUR ID	Yes	Yes	ID
	ISP PARTY ID	Yes	Yes	ID
	PRODUCT ID	Yes	Yes	ID
	REFERRER PARTY ID	Yes	Yes	ID
	USER AGENT TYPE ID	Yes	Yes	ID
	VISITOR PARTY ID	Yes	Yes	ID
	WEB CONTENT ID	Yes	Yes	ID
	NUMBER OF BYTES	No	No	Numeric
	NUMBER OF HITS	No	No	Numeric
	NUMBER OF VISITS	No	No	Numeric
SERVER HIT STATUS TYPE	STATUS TYPE ID	Yes	Yes	ID
STATUS TYPE	STATUS TYPE ID	Yes	No	ID
	DESCRIPTION	No	No	Description
SUBSCRIBER	PARTY ID	Yes	Yes	ID
	ROLE TYPE ID	Yes	Yes	ID
	SUBSCRIPTION ID	Yes	No	ID
SUBSCRIPTION	COMMUNICATION EVENT ID	No	Yes	ID
	CONTACT MECHANISM ID	No	Yes	ID
	NEED TYPE ID	No	Yes	ID
	ORIGINATED FROM ROLE TYPE ID	No	Yes	ID
	ORIGINATING FROM PARTY ID	No	Yes	ID
	PARTY ID	No	Yes	ID
	PARTY NEED ID	No	Yes	ID
	PRODUCT CATEGORY ID	No	Yes	ID
	PRODUCT ID	No	Yes	ID
	ROLE TYPE ID	No	Yes	ID
	SUBSCRIPTION TYPE ID	No	Yes	ID
	SUBSCRIPTION END DATE	No	No	Datetime
	SUBSCRIPTION START DATE	No	No	Datetime
SUBSCRIPTION ACTIVITY	SUBSCRIPTION ACTIVITY ID	Yes	No	ID
	COMMENTS	No	No	Comment
	DATE SENT	No	No	Datetime
SUBSCRIPTION FULFILLMENT PIECE	SUBSCRIPTION ACTIVITY ID	Yes	Yes	ID
	SUBSCRIPTION ID	Yes	Yes	ID

ENTITY NAME	ATTRIBUTE NAME	PK?	FK?	DOMAIN
VISIT	VISIT ID	Yes	No	ID
	CONTACT MECHANISM ID	No	Yes	ID
	PARTY ID	No	Yes	ID
	ROLE TYPE ID	No	Yes	ID
	COOKIE	No	No	Short varchar
	VISIT FROM DATE/TIME	No	No	Datetime
	VISIT THRU DATE/TIME	No	No	Datetime
VISITOR	PARTY ID	Yes	Yes	ID
	ROLE TYPE ID	Yes	Yes	ID
VISITOR ISP	FROM DATE	Yes	Yes	Datetime
	PARTY ID FROM	Yes	Yes	ID
	PARTY ID TO	Yes	Yes	ID
	ROLE TYPE ID FROM	Yes	Yes	ID
VISITORS	VISITOR PARTY ID	Yes	No	ID
	NAME	No	No	Name
WEB ADDRESS	CONTACT MECHANISM ID	Yes	Yes	ID
WEB CONTENT	WEB CONTENT ID	No	No	ID
	STATUS TYPE ID	No	Yes	ID
	WEB CONTENT TYPE ID	No	Yes	ID
	CONTENT DESCRIPTION	No	No	Description
	FILE LOCATION	No	No	Short varchar
WEB CONTENT ASSOCIATION	WEB CONTENT ID FOR	Yes	Yes	ID
	WEB CONTENT ID OF	Yes	Yes	ID
	CONTACT MECHANISM ID	No	Yes	ID
	FUNCTION TYPE ID	No	Yes	ID
	UPPER LEFT COORDINATE	No	No	Numeric
WEB CONTENT OBJECT USAGE	OBJECT ID	Yes	Yes	ID
	WEB CONTENT ID	Yes	Yes	ID
	FROM DATE	Yes	Yes	Datetime
	THRU DATE	No	No	Datetime
WEB CONTENT ROLE	PARTY ID	Yes	Yes	ID
	ROLE TYPE ID	Yes	Yes	ID
	WEB CONTENT ID	Yes	Yes	ID
	FROM DATE	No	No	Datetime
	THRU DATE	No	No	Datetime
WEB CONTENT ROLE TYPE	ROLE TYPE ID	Yes	Yes	ID

ENTITY NAME	ATTRIBUTE NAME	PK?	FK?	DOMAIN
WEB CONTENT STATUS TYPE	STATUS TYPE ID	Yes	Yes	ID
WEB CONTENT TYPE	WEB CONTENT TYPE ID	Yes	No	ID
	DESCRIPTION	No	No	Description
WEB CONTENTS	WEB CONTENT ID	Yes	No	ID
	CONTENT DESCRIPTION	No	No	Description
	REQUESTED URL	No	No	Short varchar
	WEB CONTENT TYPE	No	No	Description
WEB MASTER	PARTY ID	Yes	Yes	ID
	ROLE TYPE ID	Yes	Yes	ID
WEB MASTER ASSIGNMENT	FROM DATE	Yes	Yes	Datetime
	PARTY ID FROM	Yes	Yes	ID
	PARTY ID TO	Yes	Yes	ID
	ROLE TYPE ID FROM	Yes	Yes	ID
	ROLE TYPE ID TO	Yes	Yes	ID
WEB PREFERENCE TYPE	WEB PREFERENCE TYPE ID	Yes	No	ID
	DESCRIPTION	No	No	Description
WEB USER PREFERENCE	PARTY ID	Yes	Yes	ID
	USER LOGIN ID	Yes	Yes	ID
	WEB PREFERENCE TYPE ID	Yes	Yes	ID
WEB VISIT FACT	HOUR ID	Yes	Yes	ID
	ISP PARTY ID	Yes	Yes	ID
	PRODUCT ID	Yes	Yes	ID
	REFERRER PARTY ID	Yes	Yes	ID
	USER AGENT TYPE ID	Yes	Yes	ID
	VISITOR PARTY ID	Yes	Yes	ID
	AVERAGE VISIT TIME	No	No	Numeric
	NUMBER OF HITS	No	No	Numeric
	NUMBER OF PAGES VISITED	No	No	Numeric
	NUMBER OF PRODUCTS INQUIRED	No	No	Numeric
	NUMBER OF PRODUCTS ORDERED	No	No	Numeric
	NUMBER OF VISITS RESULTING IN ORDERS	No	No	Numeric

List of Entities and Their Associated Figures

The following appendix shows all entities from Volumes 1 and 2 and where the entity appears in the volumes. Figures starting with "v1" correspond to Figures in the first volume, and "v2" to the second volume.

Other Reusable Data Model and Data Warehouse Design Resources

Hopefully, it is evident that reusing data models and data warehouse designs is extremely valuable. There are many other sources for reusable data model and data warehouse design constructs. In order to design systems more quickly and with higher quality, it only makes sense to use whatever sources of models are available—for example, models from vendors, models available on Web sites, models available within application packages, models available within the enterprise itself, models available from people's past experiences, and models available from other publications. The following publications, while not exhaustive, provide some practical sources for reusable data models and data warehouse designs.

Reusable Data Model Resources

Barker, Richard. *CASE*Method™ Entity Relationship Modeling*. Addison-Wesley. 1989 (Note: this book focuses mostly on CASE*Method and data modeling conventions; however, it contains some useful data model constructs and ideas.)

Fowler, Martin. *Analysis Patterns: Reusable Object Models*. Addison-Wesley. 1997. (Note: Though this book is an object-oriented patterns book, many of these patterns apply to data modeling.)

Hay, David C. *Data Model Patterns: Conventions of Thought*. Dorset House. 1996.

Reingruber, Michael C., and William W. Gregory. *The Data Modeling Handbook: A Best-Practice Approach to Building Quality Data Models.*

Silverston, Len. *"Is Your Organization Too Unique to Use Universal Data Models?"* Data Management Review 8:8. September 1998.

Simsion, Graeme C. Revised and updated by Graham C. Witt & Graeme C. Simsion. *Data Modeling Essentials*. Coriolis. 2000.

Reusable Data Warehouse Design Resources

Adamson, Christopher, and Michael Venerable. *Data Warehouse Design Solutions*. John Wiley & Sons. 1998

Connely, McNeill, and Mosimann. *The Multi-Dimensional Manager, 24 Ways to Impact Your Bottom Line in 90 Days*. Cognos. 1997

Kimball, Ralph. *The Data Warehouse Toolkit: Practical Techniques for Building Dimensional Data Warehouses*. John Wiley & Sons. 2000.

How to Use the Volume 2 Industry Electronic Products

The data models in this book are available in an electronic format and can be licensed and downloaded via the Web site, http://silverston.wiley.com. Each industry model contains electronic versions of the diagrams, SQL scripts to implement the models on various database platforms, and reports listing the entities, tables, attributes, columns, subject data areas, relationships, and other model information for that industry. The electronic components for each industry product include the diagrams, SQL, and reports for the entities, attributes, and relationships that are listed in that industry's chapter and associated appendix. For instance, the manufacturing electronic product includes all the diagrams from Chapter 2, all the SQL code to implement the entities and attributes in Appendix A, and numerous reports listing and cross-referencing the database objects for the manufacturing industry models in this book.

The CD-ROM in the back of this book contains demo files to illustrate what you can expect from the Volume 2 industry models. The CD-ROM contains a directory, **\v2 demo,** which includes a sample diagram, SQL code, and reports for a single data model from Volume 2 (V2:4.7 Health care delivery) to illustrate the type of content you can expect in the electronic Industry Download products. Of course, the industry electronic products will include the diagrams, SQL code, and reports for the entire industry as described by the related chapter in this book and its corresponding appendix.

The full contents of the Volume 2 downloads may be purchased from the Web site, http://silverston.wiley.com, or by contacting John Wiley and Sons via phone at (800) 225-5945.

Contents of the Industry Electronic Products

The Volume 2 electronic downloadable products, as well as the Volume 2 demo, includes SQL scripts to implement the models, reports describing the models, and electronic versions of the data model diagrams. SQL scripts are included that can be run in Oracle and SQL Server. Generic ODBC scripts are also included for use with other relational database management systems. These SQL scripts may be used either to build a database or to reverse-engineer the models into a CASE tool for further analysis and modifications.

The reports show a great deal of information and cross-referencing on the subject data areas, entities, corresponding figures for entities, attributes, tables, and columns. Electronic versions of the data model diagrams are included in Visio format and JPEG format. The JPEG files allow you to view all the models electronically, using either a browser or any program that can open JPEGs. The Visio files allow you to modify the data model diagrams for your own purposes, if you own Visio 2000 software.

Within each of the root directories are five more directories: three directories for each of database platforms, one for reports (**\reports**), and one for the diagrams (**\data model diagrams**). This structure is the same on the demo as well as the installation of the full products.

Each of the three database-named directories contains SQL scripts for each supported database. SQL scripts for Oracle are found in the **\oracle** directory, Microsoft SQL Server in the **\sql server** directory, and generic OBDC scripts are in the **\odbc** directory.

Within each of the subdirectories can be found files that contain the actual SQL code needed to build the described models. The files with a **.tab** extension can be used to build all the tables and referential integrity constraints for the model. The files with an **.ind** extension contain the SQL code to build all the indexes. The files with a **.drp** extension contain the SQL code to drop the tables that have been built. The SQL Server and ODBC directories contain additional **.tab** scripts that allow tables to be built without referential integrity constraints (these have a "nori" before the filename extension—for example "sqlservermfg-nori.tab").

Each electronic industry product contains the electronic SQL scripts, diagrams, and reports for the corresponding chapter and appendix within this book. For instance, the **manufacturing** electronic product contains the electronic diagrams for the models in Chapter 2, and reports and SQL scripts to implement the manufacturing models that are described in Appendix A. Similarly, the **telecommunications** electronic product contains the electronic diagrams, reports, and SQL scripts to build the models described in Chapter 3 and Appendix B. Thus each chapter and corresponding appendix of this book have a corresponding industry electronic product, each sold separately.

These industry electronic products provide a very easy mechanism for physically instantiating the models in this book, customization of the SQL scripts, customization of the diagrams (you will need software that allows modifications to Visio 2000 or jpeg formats), loading the models into your CASE tool, or viewing reports about the models. All SQL scripts have been thoroughly tested for Oracle 7.3 platforms and Microsoft SQL Server 7.0; and generic ODBC scripts are provided that can be easily modified for other database platforms. Database vendors generally support upward compatibility of SQL scripts.

Using the Scripts

Using the scripts provided in the industry electronic products is quite simple. Scripts can be used immediately if no changes need to be made, or they can be copied to a working directory on a hard drive or file server so they can be edited before execution. In either case, the scripts are ASCII files that can be loaded and executed from the standard SQL interface for the database selected (e.g., SQL*Plus for Oracle, Sql Server Query Analyzer for Microsoft SQL Server, and so on). Be sure to execute the files (to build tables) before the **.ind** file (which builds indexes).

Most modeling tools have a reverse-engineering feature, which allows the extraction of objects from the database into the CASE tool. So once the models have been built in the target database, tools such as Oracle Designer/2000, ERwin, or StarDesignor can be used to reverse-engineer the database objects for further analysis or reengineering. Many popular CASE tools even have the ability to reverse-engineer directly from the SQL scripts.

How to Use the Industry Electronic Products in Conjunction with the *Data Model Resource CD-ROM, Volume 1*

Each of the industry model scripts may be used in conjunction with the Volume 1 CD-ROM scripts. The industry model scripts contain all the SQL to implement the industry models of this book, which contain relationships to the applicable Volume 1 tables. Each of the industry electronic products corresponds to the entities and attributes of a particular chapter and appendix in this book. These industry models can be used together with the generic Volume 1 data model scripts, enabling a flexible means of selecting the desired models and SQL scripts for your organization.

The CD-ROM in the back of this book provides a sample of Volume 1 electric product, found in the directory **\v1 demo**. The sample consists of the SQL scripts, reports, and a diagram for the V1:2.6a model, "Common Party Relationships." The full product includes the SQL scripts, reports, and electronic diagrams for the whole book.

The electronic products were designed to provide modular, mix-and-match capabilities, allowing the modeler to add the desired industry components to the generic Volume 1 data model constructs. These industry database scripts provide relationships to Volume 1 table names, using many of the same table names (when appropriate), primary keys, and the same foreign key constraints as the Volume 1 models, thus making it easier for the modeler to merge the generic Volume 1 models and industry models. The modeler may decide to implement the generic Volume 1 models and enhance them with one or more industry model(s) to provide additional and enhanced constructs. Alternatively, the modeler can start with an industry model then enhance the industry with additional constructs from the Volume 1 electronic product.

The decisions of which models to use and how to integrate them is subjective in nature and will vary based on the needs of your organization. For example, the modeler implementing the health care electronic product may decide to use the HEALTH CARE OFFERING constructs, the PRODUCT constructs from the Volume 1 electronic product, or a combination of both. The modeler may also decide to use the SQL constructs for PATIENT and then enhance them with the additional "party" constructs from the Volume 1 CD-ROM. Additionally, the modeler may decide to enhance the models with components from other industries, such as including the PARTY NEED constructs from the Financial industry product and/or constructs from the E-Commerce industry product.

Many CASE tools provide the ability to merge models by reverse-engineering them in the tools under separate applications or subject data areas and then consolidating them into a single model. Alternatively, the modeler may decide to manually review the models and decide which entities to include, which relationships are appropriate for his enterprise, and the most appropriate ways to link the data models and database constructs.

Platform-Specific and Other Information on the Electronic Products

Please refer to the readme.htm file on the accompanying CD-ROM for notes on specific platforms and additional comments about the Volume 2 downloads and the Volume 1 electronic product. Also refer to the companion Web site http://silverston.wiley.com for additional information and/or updates regarding the electronic products.

Index

Page references followed by italic *t* indicate material in tables.

The **Data Model Resource Book**

Revised Edition

Volume 1
A Library of Universal Data Models for All Enterprises

by LEN SILVERSTON
Foreword by GRAEME SIMSION

This book arms you with a powerful set of data models and data warehouse designs that you can use to jumpstart your database development projects. You get proven models for common business functions—and you'll save countless hours and thousands of dollars in database development costs.

ISBN 0-471-38023-7

Paper

560 pages

- Fully updated and revised to include many new and expanded data models

- Customize enterprise and logical data models that meet the specific needs of your organization

- Convert logical data models to data warehouses and data marts

- Develop physical data designs and evaluate design options based on the universal data models

- Integrate databases and data warehouses across the enterprise

- Validate your organization's existing data models

CD-ROM sold separately

- Provides the SQL code you'll need to implement the models described in the book or to reverse-engineer them into your CASE tool

- View a free demonstration of Volume 1 data models on the Volume 2 CD-ROM

WILEY
Publishers Since 1807

Wiley Computer Publishing   Timely. Practical. Reliable.